MARKETING EFFECTIVENESS

MARKETING EFFECTIVENESS

INSIGHTS FROM ACCOUNTING AND FINANCE

STANLEY J. SHAPIRO

SIMON FRASER UNIVERSITY

V. H. KIRPALANI

CONCORDIA UNIVERSITY

ALLYN AND BACON, INC.
BOSTON   LONDON   SYDNEY   TORONTO

Library of Congress Cataloging in Publication Data
Main entry under title:

Marketing effectiveness, insights from accounting and
  finance.

  Bibliography: p.
  Includes index.
  1. Marketing management—Addresses, essays, lectures.
I. Shapiro, Stanley J. II. Kirpalani, V. H. (Vishnu H.),
date
HF5415.13.M345   1984   658.8   83–11930
ISBN 0–205–07994–6

Printed in the United States of America

10 9 8 7 6 5 4 3 2 1   88 87 86 85 84

To Prakash, Tara, and Arjun

To Roberta

Contents

List of Exercises

Preface

Some time has now passed since we first decided to explore the interface between accounting/finance and marketing. Our intention from the beginning was to offer an exciting course in this generally neglected area and to develop a pedagogical package that others who shared our interest could also use. These twin tasks have proven far more difficult to achieve than we originally anticipated. However, five efforts at teaching a "money and marketing" course have taught us much. The purpose of this preface is to place "on the record" the results of what has turned out to be an academic voyage of exploration.

Those enrolled in the initial money and marketing course, offered at McGill University in the winter of 1976, were first assigned a series of required readings and then evaluated on their mastery of the technique or approach presented therein. The students clearly demonstrated their ability first to memorize and then to play back the various steps in the application of each technique. But we remained uncertain as to their ability to apply that technique! What appeared necessary was a series of specially designed exercises or problems that could be used to determine whether or not students had mastered the assigned material.

Exercises geared to articles were first introduced in the winter of 1978. They proved very effective in helping students to gain a real mastery of relevant tools and techniques. Consequently, such exercises have become an increasingly important part of the money and marketing course. Twenty problems drawn from the pool of exercises found in this volume were assigned during the spring 1981 semester.

The meticulousness with which students must read the articles in order to solve the problems has proven to have another entirely unexpected benefit. A significant number of articles have been found to have either serious conceptual weaknesses or, much more frequently, irritating and sometimes important arithmetic errors. Students who discover such shortcomings in published material become far more discriminating readers of other literature and far less trusting of the printed word.

The preparation of appropriate exercises proved to be a difficult task. What constitutes ambiguous wording is only revealed after one finds two or three different interpretations of a problem. Another difficulty involves designing exercises that are structurally similar to the approach found in an article but that nevertheless require thought as well as number crunching. Finally, one all too often finds an apparently attractive "how to" article whose illustration and/or formula is deficient in some respect which makes actual use of the technique impossible.

The above-mentioned pedagogical problems greatly complicated preparation of the teaching package. Of all the approaches that could be used, which format would best facilitate student mastery of the marketing effectiveness potential of accounting and finance? Years of classroom experimentation eventually revealed that the most appropriate pedagogical approach is one that stresses, almost exclusively, "how to" and "hands on" experience.

The editorial focus on a practical problem-solving format has been achieved at some cost. Some articles that we found intrinsically interesting literature have not been included because we considered them to be prerequisite reading, too specialized in content, methodological rather than applied, lacking in general application or operational significance, or concerned with topics more appropriately studied in other marketing courses.

In Parts II through VIII readers will find twenty-six articles, each of which describes how a technique based in accounting or finance can assist in the more effective allocation of marketing effort. These articles have been grouped somewhat arbitrarily under a variety of headings. For example, certain selections appearing under the designations "decision making" and "control" might have been presented in relation to an equally relevant marketing mix component. Another approach would have involved classifying literature in terms of the technique primarily employed, with separate sections for break-even analysis, return-on-investment, and the like.

Far more important than the organizing typology, however, is the fact that each article has been selected as one of the very best of its kind. Each article found in Parts II through VIII spells out, in detail sufficient for student mastery, how a given approach or combination of approaches can be employed. These are, first and foremost, "how to" articles. Each selection is followed by two problems designed to indicate whether the reader has mastered the approach being advocated in that article. A solution to each problem is to be found in the accompanying Instructor's Guide.

The articles finally selected for inclusion are not the only ones for which we prepared problems testing the reader's actual degree of mastery—these are articles that have demonstrated particular pedagogical value in extensive classroom testing. Since balance and breadth of coverage were also essential, the mix of articles represents a cross-section of both techniques and areas of application.

Not all the selections in this volume are "how to" articles for which exercises have been prepared. The introduction to Part I contains a review of relevant analytical techniques. The five articles in Part I then focus on very important conceptual issues that the authors believe deserve relatively lengthy treatment in any money and marketing course. Included in this category are a discussion of the full costing versus contribution margin controversy, a note of caution regarding the use by marketers of the ROI approach, a review of weaknesses in existing physical distribution costing systems, an introduction to inflation accounting and its relevance to marketing, and the presentation of sample reporting formats. The single article in Part IX explores the very real organizational barriers to achieving the desired degree of cooperation between accounting/finance and marketing.

In addition to becoming familiar with the relevant literature and having an opportunity to apply the various techniques and approaches that make each selection important, those who work their way through the volume will receive two other auxiliary, but by no means minor, benefits. First, readers will develop their skill in utilizing numerate, profit-and-loss-based analysis to solve marketing problems, a skill all too many marketers lack. Second, readers will put themselves in a better position to be alert to and appreciative of subsequent publications in this same area.

We believe that, relatively speaking, what accounting and finance could contribute to marketing has been neglected. This volume is an attempt to correct matters by bringing together a mix of highly relevant material in a format that will encourage student mastery and subsequent professional use. If the volume contributes, even modestly, to improving marketing's interface with accounting and finance, we will consider the net present value of the time, effort, and energy invested therein to be more than adequate.

The task of acknowledgment is complicated by the fact that this volume was a decade in the making. What has finally emerged differs greatly from what was originally planned, and a great many individuals contributed to this pedagogical metamorphosis. Academics are, generally speaking, poor keepers of records, and we are not the exceptions to this rule. The project was discussed over the years with a substantial number of colleagues. Five successive student classes have served as our product-in-use sample. Since our listing of these colleagues and former students would be incomplete, it is best that all those in the "consulted" and "test marketed" segments remain the intellectual equivalent of unknown soldiers. But just as homage is regularly offered to unknown soldiers, we offer our thanks to the unsung heroes of this venture.

A number of professors, however, made contributions of such a magnitude that they must not go unacknowledged. In the early 1960s, Wroe Alderson frequently reminded Shapiro of the need to bridge the gap between marketers and financial types. That author's other personal guru, David D. Monieson of Queen's University, has also repeatedly stressed the managerial importance of the marriage of money and marketing. Direct contact with such academic pioneers in this interface area as Jacob Schiff, Frank Mossman, Harold Fox, and the late Charles Sevin was more limited. However, both the authors and their readers owe these seminal thinkers a real debt of gratitude.

Two colleagues in accounting at McGill University, Haim Falk and Larry Gordon, were most helpful in ever so gently indicating where earlier approaches were invalid and earlier drafts inadequate. The "invisible college" of those interested in the interface of money and marketing eventually put us into what proved to be remarkably fruitful written contact with R. M. S. Wilson of the University of Sheffield. Professor Wilson most graciously furnished the results of his own research, writing, and editorial efforts in our shared area of concern. Additional international input of great value was obtained from G. L. Harrison of McQuarie University, New South Wales, Australia, and D. B. Taylor of the University of Waikato, Hamilton, New Zealand. Finally, a meaningful dialogue on the marriage of money and marketing has been conducted over the years with Paul Anderson of Virginia Polytechnic Institute, Robert Lusch of the University of Oklahoma, and Roger Kerin of Southern Methodist University. We are most grateful for the inspiration and the assistance received from all of these colleagues.

A number of extremely able young researchers participated both in the evaluation of articles and in the preparation of exercises. First and foremost in this category is the indispensable Marie-Jose Errunza. Mrs. Errunza initially helped immeasurably in the compilation of an annotated bibliography that was published by the American Marketing Association in 1979. She then proceeded to prepare a substantial number of article-based exercises, many of which appear in this volume. Considerable assistance in screening articles and in preparing exercises was also provided by Mee Ling Kaun, shortly after Ms. Kaun received her MBA degree from McGill University. Three remarkably able Simon Fraser students—Jon Koppang, Philippe Van Buuren, and Tor Melsom—subsequently became very much involved both in the final selection of materials and in a concerted effort to eliminate all remaining ambiguities in the wording of exercises and the preparation of sample solutions.

Clerical assistance at McGill University was provided by two long-time keyboard colleagues, Olga Borawecki and Wendy Laidecker. The sorely overworked secretaries of the S.F.U. Department of Business Administration and of Concordia University subsequently furnished much-needed office support. During the late 1970s, the McGill University Educational Development Fund and the McGill Faculty of Management served as "in house" research funding agencies. The related tasks of first keeping track of all the many pieces to this editorial puzzle and then putting that puzzle together in a form suitable for publication were carried out with great professionalism by Shaheen Lalji, ably assisted by Karim Lalji.

We are also grateful for the willingness of the many publishers and authors, identified by name elsewhere in this volume, who gave us permission to reprint the thirty-one selections. A few authors even made a point of calling previously published errors in calculation to our attention.

Finally, we must acknowledge the patience shown and the forbearance demonstrated by our wives, Roberta and Prakash, as this volume painfully evolved over an entire decade. The return on that investment of patience and forbearance may appear, after discounting and with due regard for risk, entirely inadequate. Be that as it may, a dedication of the volume to our spouses is all we have to offer at this time.

S.J.S.
V.H.K.

PART I

A Marketer's Review
of Relevant Techniques
and Related Readings

The sections that follow review a compendium of techniques from accounting and finance applicable to marketing management concerns. This review is intended as a refresher rather than as a substitute for the initial introduction to such topics presented in texts on introductory accounting, finance, and managerial economics. Readers who find this review inadequate or incomplete are urged to examine more detailed treatments; however, those with a firm grasp of the approaches discussed should still find the section deserving of attention, since each technique has been presented in a manner designed to facilitate subsequent marketing applications.

Break-Even Analysis; Full and Direct Costing

Break-even analysis is essentially a means of integrating the costs, revenues, and output of an organization so as to illustrate the probable effects of alternative levels of output on profit. The technique is a speedy and comparatively simple one to employ, and under certain circumstances it provides reasonably accurate insights as to expected profitability. Knowledge of the break-even point may also reveal the degree of risk associated with alternative courses of action. For decision-making purposes, reasonable accuracy is often sufficient as a clear indication of the more profitable decision. The technique can also quite easily be made more sophisticated by the incorporation of probabilistic measures of risk and by the discounting of both future revenues and projected expenses. This section describes the nature and underlying assumptions of break-even analysis and highlights differences between what might somewhat simplistically be called the accountant's and the economist's approach to the use of this tool.

The Accountant's Break-Even Chart

The customary accountant's break-even chart is based on the assumption that costs are either completely fixed or completely variable. Similarly, price is fixed; it is dependent neither on output nor on the quantity being sold. The illustration shown in Figure 1 can be considered a representation of the accountant's break-even chart. Such a chart is a static representation in that it illustrates the relationships between costs and revenues at a given time. A quantitative example of this approach is presented in the discussion of a profit planning equation on page 6.

Since selling price and average variable cost are assumed constant over the relevant

3

FIGURE 1

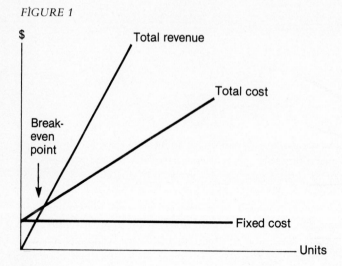

volume range, the total revenue and cost lines in Figure 1 are linear. This, in turn, implies that the profit area will continue to widen as volume increases to full capacity. Despite its popularity, the accountant's break-even approach is widely faulted by academics and consultants for assuming static revenue-output and cost-output relationships and for not taking into account either change or risk. The approach has been further criticized for neglecting the dependence of profits on numerous other factors, including production processes, the effectiveness of promotional efforts, and the composition of demand.

The Economist's Break-Even Chart

The economist's approach to break-even analysis accepts the aforementioned criticisms as valid and, consequently, utilizes a greatly modified break-even chart. In the economist's chart, as found in Figure 2, note the curvilinear total revenue and cost lines and the existence of a maximum profit point which could be at a level considerably below full capacity. Note also that a fixed plant and a static technology are still assumed. The economist's curvilinear representation incorporates the concepts of marginal utility, a downward sloping demand curve under conditions of imperfect competition, and the law of diminishing returns. Also reflected is the argument that, as output approaches full capacity, marginal cost rises because of resource bottlenecks and the extra wear and tear on machinery (Wyles, 1963).

The economist's approach to break-even analysis, however, is not always operationally superior to that of the accountant. The latter approach remains a useful financial tool for firms in oligopolistic industries, where prices are often "sticky"; plants are generally large, with considerable excess capacity; and variable

FIGURE 2

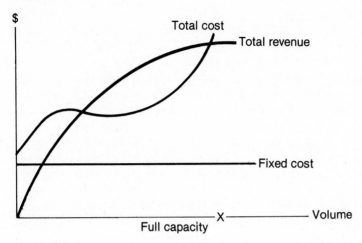

costs are relatively constant while accounting for a relatively low proportion of the final selling price. Examples of such industries are petroleum refining, steel manufacturing, and the production of industrial chemicals. The accountant's approach could also be employed in many monopolistically competitive consumer goods industries in which primary emphasis is placed on the use of nonprice forms of marketing effort. Empirical studies have shown that variable costs are indeed linear for several different enterprises over pertinent ranges of output (Dean, 1949).

Relevant Concepts of Cost

Both break-even approaches assume a constant product mix during a given period, because any change in this mix would alter revenues, costs, product contribution, and, consequently, the corporate break-even level (Bell, 1969). However, an important difference exists between the way accountants and economists interpret costs. Economists generally regard cost as the level of compensation paid to owners of factors who supply these resources to the firm. The cost of any factor is equal to what that factor could command in its most profitable use. In short, cost to the economists means opportunity cost. In contrast, the accountant views cost as an outward flow of assets associated with business transactions. Expenditures and, in particular, depreciation and inventory values are usually expressed in terms of dollars based on original or past costs. The economist would prefer to express these accounting values in replacement terms and allow for the principle of opportunity cost. An economist would also include dividends paid to stockholders as a cost of producing income. Each approach has its merits, but the two remain conceptually very different.

Direct Costing versus Absorption Costing

The differences between a direct costing and an absorption or full costing approach to break-even analysis must also be considered. The more customary approach incorporates a form of direct costing. Variable costs are presented as volume-dependent and fixed costs as time-dependent. There is only one break-even point, and all fixed costs for a given time period must be recouped from current revenue, as such costs are not inventoriable. Differences between production and sales quantities are reflected in inventory, which is valued at variable cost.

Under absorption costing, fixed manufacturing cost is spread over the entire output. Contribution margin per unit grows with an increase in production volume. If inventories increase because production exceeds sales, then absorption costing will show a higher net income than direct costing, since under absorption costing some fixed manufacturing costs have been carried into inventory (Solomons, 1968). Proponents of absorption costing maintain that inventories should carry a fixed cost component, because both fixed and variable cost are incurred to produce goods. Corporate accounting systems can accommodate either a direct costing or an absorption costing approach. However, direct costing is more consistent with the contribution-based approach to decision making required for effective marketing planning and control (Kirpalani and Shapiro, 1973).

The Profit Planning Equation.   When expressed in algebraic rather than geometric terms, either approach to break-even analysis can be used as a relatively simplified approach to profit planning. The following has been proposed as a profit planning equation that specifically incorporates marketing expenses (adapted from Kotler, 1972):

$$Z = [(P - k) - c]Q - F - M$$

where Z = total profit; P = list price; k = allowances such as freight allowances, commission, discounts, etc.; c = production and marketing variable costs such as labor costs, delivery costs, and customer credit costs; Q = number of units sold; F = fixed nonmarketing costs such as general overhead, rent, and electricity; M = discretionary marketing costs such as advertising expenses; $[(P - k) - c]$ = contribution margin per unit, or list price minus allowances and minus variable costs; and $[(P - k) - c]Q$ = total contribution margin. At the break-even quantity, $Z = 0$, so

$$Q_{\text{Break-even}} = \frac{F + M}{[(P - k) - c]}$$

If F = \$100, M = \$50, P = \$10, k = \$1, and c = \$4, then

$$Q_{\text{Break-even}} = \frac{\$100 + \$50}{\$[(10 - 1) - 4]} = \frac{\$150}{\$5} = 30 \text{ units}$$

If the break-even level of dollar sales is required, one can multiply the 30 units by the price of $10 to obtain $300; or, alternatively, one can arrive at this figure directly by using the contribution margin percentage per unit in the equation. The contribution margin per unit is $[(P - k) - c]$, or $\$[(10 - 1) - 4] = \$5$, which in percentage terms is 0.5% of the price.

$$\text{Break-even \$ sales} = \frac{F + M}{\text{contribution margin percentage}}$$

$$= \frac{\$100 + \$50}{0.5} = \frac{\$150}{0.5} = \$300$$

Operational Information

There are essentially two methods of obtaining the information required for constructing a break-even chart. The first is judgmental, in that the user classifies costs as fixed or variable by answering the question of whether the cost in question would increase if output were to increase. Inevitably, borderline cases will emerge as semivariable in nature. One will also find costs going up in step fashion, such as when salespeople are paid a bonus of a fixed amount after they reach a certain quota, or when additional warehouse space is rented after sales exceed a certain volume. The break-even chart can be adapted, as depicted in Figure 3, to incorporate these adjustments.

As an alternative to judgment, one could employ a statistical or historical approach

FIGURE 3

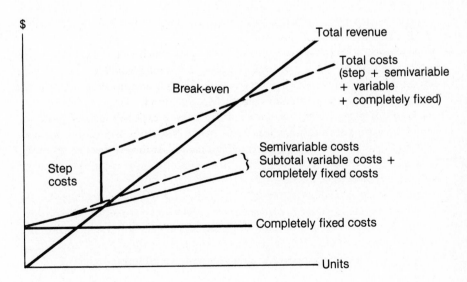

in estimating costs. In the simplest instance, a trend line is generated by the method of "least squares" to estimate costs at different levels of output. Alternatively, more sophisticated techniques involving dollar adjustments of various costs could be used. Two or more total revenue lines could even be generated, given different marketing assumptions and different probabilities of marketing success.

Limitations of Break-Even Analysis

The static profit-output relationship, the approach that underlies the notion of break-even analysis, contains the basis for most of the criticisms leveled against the technique. Actual profits are dependent on such factors as changes in technology, competitive behavior, the quality of management, and many other variables that cannot be recognized by a break-even technique which displays oversimplified cost and revenue functions and assumes static given relationships to output. A few of the main limitations of break-even analysis are clear from what has been stated earlier. Others are made more explicit below (Haynes, 1969).

1. *Break-even charts usually are not corrected for changes in factor prices.* Past data should in fact be adjusted for such changes in wages, the prices of raw materials, and other factor inputs.
2. *The analysis usually assumes a single given price over a substantial range of volume.* However, it is possible to overcome this difficulty by sketching multiple total revenue lines, each based on a different estimated price.
3. *The analysis usually is based on accounting data and suffers from the limitations of such data.* For example, the neglect of the opportunity cost criterion, the use of arbitrary depreciation estimates based on book value, inappropriate allocations of overhead costs—all reduce the technique's effectiveness unless the necessary adjustments, such as a contribution approach to marketing segment profitability, are employed.
4. *The valuation of inventory carried over from one period to the next presents a costing problem normally glossed over in break-even analysis.* However, it is possible to make adjustments that will render inventory a neutral factor in consideration of profits associated with current levels of output.
5. *The cost and revenue functions usually employed in break-even analysis sometimes incorrectly incorporate other costs which may not be associated exclusively with output in that time period.* Some corporate taxes and maintenance expenses, for example, may not be entirely the result of current output. Again, it is possible to make adjustments to correct for such factors.
6. *Another limitation that has to be overcome is the measure of output to be used on the break-even chart when output consists of more than one product.* Consider, for example, a line of television sets of varying screen sizes. It is generally easier to measure output using sales dollars, a procedure that weights the various products according to sales value, rather than to determine the relative costs of production. Con-

ceptually, however, this dollar sales procedure suffers from the fact that a change in relative prices automatically shifts the importance of the various products even though there may have been no corresponding adjustment in relative costs.

7. *Marketing costs are conceptually difficult to handle in break-even analysis.* Marketing costs are not a result of output changes; rather, to a significant extent, they cause such output changes. Moreover, the relationship between marketing costs and output both varies over time and depends to some degree on the product life cycle. Such factors reduce the accuracy of linear projections of past marketing-sales relationships.

Benefits of Break-Even Analysis

Despite the preceding list of its limitations, break-even analysis remains useful under certain circumstances. This type of analysis is simple to employ and easily understood. The importance of any technique's being readily comprehended by the firm's executives must never be forgotten. The question really becomes one of what degree of analytical simplification is justified under a given set of circumstances. One need not use a scalpel when a meat axe will do. Those organizations experiencing rapid changes in their main cost components, in product and sales mix, and in technology will profit little from break-even analysis. In most firms, however, break-even analysis will prove useful to managers familiar with its limitations and simplifications. Management depends heavily on analytical tools that cut through the complexity of reality and focus attention on the fundamental relationships. Break-even analysis is obviously such a tool.

Moreover, it is evident that many managers take great interest in the break-even point as revealed by break-even analysis. Their reasoning seems to be that given the uncertainty of the marketplace, it is almost impossible to determine the exact amount that will be sold. It is far more possible, such executives would maintain, to determine whether future volume will exceed a projected break-even point which could include a specified return on investment. If the probability of exceeding this break-even volume is extremely high, the manager may be willing to proceed without very much additional information as to actual sales. Although such thinking can be faulted as unlikely to maximize profits, it is entirely consistent with the concept of the corporation as a "satisficing" entity.

ROI and Capital Budgeting

Return on investment and capital budgeting concepts can be utilized in almost every area of marketing expenditure. Investments are made in market development through the level of marketing effort directed toward new products, customer generation, promotion, sales training, marketing channels, and numerous other marketing activities. All of these investments require the allocation of capital to marketing projects with benefits expected to be realized only in the future and therefore necessarily involving risk. Consequently, such investments should be evaluated in terms of the magnitude and timing of expected future cash flows relative to (1) initial and subsequent costs of the marketing project, (2) the time value of money, and (3) the incremental risk added to the enterprise as a whole through the impact of the proposed activity on the marketing function. This is done through the use of the ROI and related capital budgeting concepts described below in some detail.

Return on Investment as a Concept

The application of ROI enables the user to compare current performance with either a historical average or a standard return. Moreover, ROI measures help management decision makers in their efforts to determine more nearly optimum marketing investment policies.

Capital budgeting has probably become the most technically advanced area of financial management. Such budgeting includes discounted cash flow methods which recognize the time value of money. The basic concept is that of return on investment on a time-adjusted basis. Return on investment is a far better measure of the profitability of an existing or future investment than are such guides as earnings per share or earnings on sales. In its simplest form, ROI is computed by the formula

$$\text{ROI} = \frac{\text{earnings}}{\text{investment}} = \frac{\text{earnings}}{\text{sales}} \times \frac{\text{sales}}{\text{investment}}$$

This use of the three factors—earnings, sales, and investment—has the virtue of yielding measures both of earnings on sales, or profit margin, and the rate at which capital turns over in a given year. Earnings as a percentage of sales reflects degree of success in maintaining satisfactory control of costs; the rate at which capital turns over is a guide to whether the firm's capital is being employed efficiently. The definitions of the terms *return* and *investment* must be mutually consistent. If marketing investments, in the sense of marketing expenditures incurred now which will yield benefits over time, are actually treated as pre-tax expenses, then for ROI calculations the return should also be measured in terms of pre-tax profits. Alternatively, both the return and the investment could be treated on a post-tax basis.

The factors underlying earnings and turnover can be illustrated by what is known as the Du Pont chart, reproduced in Figure 4. E. I. Du Pont de Nemours and Company believes that an enterprise can best judge the effectiveness of its efforts in ROI terms.

Capital Budgeting Techniques

ROI analysis and present value comparisons are intended to answer two questions. The first relates to whether an investment ought to be made, the second to how that investment ranks with others according to some common measure. Capital budgeting involves a current investment in which the benefits, expressed in cash

FIGURE 4. Relationship of factors affecting return on investment

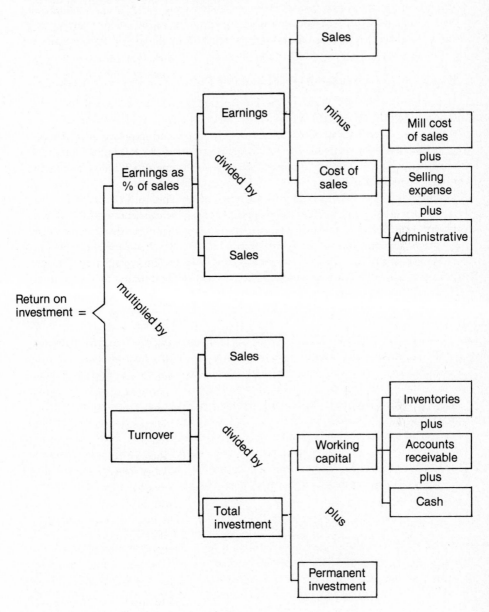

flows, are received sometime in the future. Approaches to capital budgeting in general use for marketing management purposes include the payback method, the average rate of return method, the discounted or net present value method, and the internal rate of return method. Although these four methods differ in complexity and in approach, they require the same estimates of future revenue and expenses.

Simplified Approaches—Average Rate of Return and Payback Methods

A simple example will illustrate the information needed for a capital budgeting decision. Assume an investment of $1,000, with an expected life of five years and straight-line depreciation of $200 a year. The project is expected to have cash earnings of $400 per year and—minus depreciation—a taxable stream of $200 a year. If income is taxed at the 50 percent rate, taxes amount to $100 a year. The net profit, or additional book income after taxes and depreciation, is $100; the cash flow includes the $100 of profit plus depreciation of $200, or $300 in total.

The average rate of return is an accounting concept which represents the average annual net profit after taxes on the average investment. In the example provided above, the average annual net profit after taxes is $100; the average investment—assuming straight-line depreciation—is $1,000/2 or $500. The average rate of return, therefore, is $100/$500 or 20 percent. The payback method determines the number of years required to recover the initial cash investment. It is the ratio of the initial fixed investment to the annual cash inflow. The payback period, therefore, is $1,000/$300 or 3.33 years.

The virtue of both the above methods lies in their simplicity. The principal shortcomings of the average rate of return follow from its being calculated on accounting income rather than on cash flows. Also, the time value of money is ignored; benefits in the first and last year are valued similarly. The payback method similarly ignores the time value of money. Moreover, it cannot be regarded as a time measure of profitability, since it does not consider cash flows after the payback period. Two projects with the same payback period are considered equivalent, even though only one may yield cash flows in subsequent years. The payback method continues in use because it provides limited insight into the risk and liquidity of a project. A short payback period supposedly implies lesser risk because of the earlier resolution of uncertainty.

More Sophisticated Methods—IRR and NPV

The two more sophisticated approaches to ROI analysis, the internal rate of return and net present value methods, both allow for the time value of money (Henrici, 1968). Table 1 shows how a capital investment of $1,000 with an annual cash flow of $300 will yield an internal rate of return of about 16 percent. This is the discount rate that equates the present value of the cash outlay (investment) with the cash inflows. Solving for the internal rate of return usually involves a trial and error interpolation procedure using present value tables.

TABLE 1

End of year	Outlay	Inflow	16% discount rate	Present worth of inflows
0	$1,000			
1		$300	.8621	$259
2		300	.7431	223
3		300	.6407	192
4		300	.5523	165
5		300	.4761	142
TOTAL	$1,000		3.2743	$981

Deciding whether the investment is an acceptable one involves comparing the actual internal rate with a required rate of return, known also as the cutoff level. With competing proposals, the one with the most favorable internal rate of return would be ranked highest.

Net present value analysis, on the other hand, starts with a required rate of return and then discounts all proposed cash flows back to a net present value using this rate. As shown in Table 2, the net present value using a 15 percent discount rate is positive at $6; if 15 percent were the firm's agreed-upon discount rate, then this proposal would be considered an acceptable investment.

TABLE 2

End of year	Outlay	Inflow	15% discount rate	Present worth of inflows
0	$1,000			
1		$300	.8696	$ 261
2		300	.7561	227
3		300	.6575	197
4		300	.5718	172
5		300	.4972	149
TOTAL	$1,000		3.3522	$1,006

As the above results are expressed in absolute rather than relative magnitudes, it is necessary to compute a profitability index, sometimes termed a present value index, to rank different projects in terms of their relative desirability. This is very simply done by using the following formula:

$$PVI = \frac{\text{present value of cash inflows}}{\text{present value of cash outflows}} = \frac{\$1,006}{\$1,000} = 1.006$$

The two discounted cash flow methods occasionally give contradictory results. Why is this the case? The internal rate of return implies that cash inflows can be reinvested in other projects at that same internal rate of return. The net present value method assumes that any subsequent reinvestment will be at the somewhat lower required or minimum rate of return. The net present value method is generally preferred, since it seems inappropriate to use the same implied reinvestment rate for all proposals (Hirshleifer, 1958).

Projecting cash flows requires reliable revenue and cost estimates for each year of the market life of the product associated with the proposed investment. Any forecast of a product's annual unit sales depends on its specific marketing strategy; the projected market environment; the forecast of total market demand, given the above strategy and environment; and, finally, the product's expected share of this demand. The projection of cash flows also requires statements about the confidence that may be placed in the above forecasts. Similarly, estimates with confidence levels are required for manufacturing costs, marketing costs, and the expected investment in facilities needed at various levels of output under different marketing strategies.

When confidence levels are generated, one is explicitly considering an uncertain future. The most sophisticated method of dealing with such uncertainties is via risk analysis involving the use of probability distribution statistics and computer simulation (Hertz, 1968). Methods for taking risk into account include adjustment of the required rate of return, calculation of the certainty equivalent of cash flows,

FIGURE 5

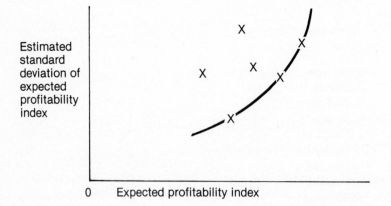

direct analysis of the probability distribution of possible outcomes under varying assumptions as to expected cash flows over time, and direct incorporation of the utility preferences of marketing management into the investment decision.

When two marketing strategies both qualify on the basis of their resulting profitability indices, one must choose between them by assessing the risk and return associated with each strategy. It can be assumed that the firm will rationally seek to maximize the profitability index for any given level of risk; and that, alternatively, for a given profitability index it will try to minimize the total risk involved. Figure 5 illustrates the situation for a feasible set of new product proposals in a given market environment.

For each level of risk, the boundary line defines the firm's most efficient combination of profitability index and risk. A combination is not efficient if there is another combination with either a higher profitability index and a lower or equivalent standard deviation or, alternatively, an equivalent profitability index and a lower standard deviation. Marketing management should therefore choose proposals close to this boundary line. The selection of the most desirable combination of investments will depend on the utility preferences of management with respect to profit and risk (Van Horne, 1968).

Limitations of ROI as a Control Tool

Considerable difference of opinion presently exists concerning the use of ROI as a control or evaluation of performance tool rather than as a decision criterion in the allocation of corporate resources. The ROI method of control is generally recognized as having a number of positive attributes.

1. It is a single comprehensive measure and a common denominator, so that comparisons can be made directly among divisions within the company, with outside companies, or with alternative investment opportunities.
2. It measures how well division managers have used their resource allocations, thereby providing a means for detailed post-auditing of capital investment proposals.
3. Since managers are evaluated on their ability to optimize ROI, they will be motivated to do so.

It has been argued, however, that a number of technical defects tend to lower the value of ROI controls when common assets are used in different divisions that may have varying ROI targets. Difficulties also arise out of the accounting methods used to measure ROI. In addition, other problems cited include difficulties in setting an equitable annual ROI objective when new products are being introduced and in assigning responsibility for deviation from ROI objectives in a world of many uncontrollable elements. Finally, there is some criticism of the motivational defects and other drawbacks associated with the fact that optimization of divisional ROI, especially when transfer prices are involved, may not lead to optimization of company

ROI. To deal with such shortcomings, Dearden proposes various remedies centering around the controlling of profits separately and apart from the control of the amount of fixed assets (1969).

Weston, in answer to Dearden, maintains that the ROI system must be seen as a process. Managers should not be evaluated on the basis of the size of the ROI the division earns. Instead, performance evaluation should be related to the potential for the division. The ROI system must be combined with a review process by top management which focuses on the difference between the actual performance of a division and the projections that have been made. Weston argues that, when so employed, the ROI approach remains a very useful performance evaluation and control device (1972).

Contribution Margin, Cost Allocation, and Control

The contribution margin approach stresses the difference between what the firm obtains for a given product or from a given market segment and the incremental costs incurred in gaining that revenue. These incremental costs are volume dependent, as opposed to fixed costs, which are not incremental but rather time dependent. A contribution-based, decision-oriented accounting information system facilitates the evaluation of possible courses of action. Table 3 illustrates a relatively sophisticated proposed format for disclosing territorial contribution. Especially noteworthy are the allowances made for the user cost of fixed assets and the cost of capital (Stanton and Buskirk, 1969).

Advocates of the contribution margin approach maintain that efforts to allocate or prorate common costs are confusing and misleading. Often there is no way in which common costs can be objectively assigned (Solomons, 1968). The end result of any such allocation, they argue, is simply a reflection of how a certain manager would like costs to vary. Also, behavioral disagreements and the politics of expense allocations often prevent management from correctly analyzing the cost impact of proposed courses of action.

Advocates of full costing, on the other hand, believe that all costs which bear a relationship to the units in question should be assigned to these units for purposes of measuring their profitability. They further believe that each unit must bear its share of the firm's overhead cost of doing business as well as its own direct costs (Kirpalani and Shapiro, 1973).

However, even those who support full costing agree that it cannot be used to evaluate alternatives. Further analysis is required, because any indirect costs that have been allocated may not be affected by the proposed course of action. For example, discontinuing service in an unprofitable territory does not eliminate all the costs associated with that territory—fixed costs that have been allocated may remain unchanged even if the territory is eliminated.

TABLE 3. *Budgeted operation—Territory A*

	Amount	Type of cost
Revenues	$1,200.00	
Less: Variable costs		
Current value of expired direct variable services performed by segment	200.00	Variable
Standard cost of services provided to segment by other parts of firm	120.00	Variable
Cost of capital (10%) × current value of average working capital used	80.00	Semivariable, as part of work capital may be fixed
Segment contribution margin	800.00	
Less: Direct out-of-pocket fixed costs incurred by or for segment	280.00	Fixed
Segment controllable margin	520.00	
Less: Specific long-run costs		
User cost in current value of direct fixed assets of segment based on estimated decline at the closed period	150.00	Obsolescence portion fixed, user portion variable
Cost of capital (10%) × current value of average direct fixed capital	160.00	Fixed
Net segment margin	$ 210.00	

Source: "Report of the Committee on Cost and Profitability Analyses for Marketing," *The Accounting Review*, Supplement to 47 (1972), p. 592.

Cost Allocation

Marketing costs include all the expenses incurred to obtain the order from the customer, to effect distribution of the goods to the customer, and finally to collect what is due the firm. In addition, the expenditures involved in the determination of customer wants, the delineation of market opportunities, and the development of new products should also be considered marketing costs.

The first step in marketing or distribution cost analysis involves assigning expenditures to the marketing functions for which such costs were incurred. The entire marketing effort is divided into component functions such as advertising, direct selling, storage, transportation, and credit. Each of these major functions can, in turn, be broken down into further divisions, until many costs can be identified and segregated directly when incurred. Costs that cannot be apportioned directly to a single function can be allocated between functions either on the basis of relative benefits received by performing the function or on the basis of the services provided and the activities performed.

Comparison of the actual costs incurred in performing a function with the costs that should have been incurred provides an initial measure of marketing efficiency. Comparison for marketing control purposes is facilitated when costs are classified by marketing functions rather than simply by the nature of the expense, such as rent and wages. However, cost allocation and analysis by marketing function performed is not sufficiently detailed to provide adequate control.

To obtain the more specific information needed for effective marketing cost control, a combination of direct and indirect methods can be used to allocate the cost of the various marketing functions to any of a number of reporting units, including the product, the type of customer, the channel of distribution, and the territory and the organizational division (Mossman and Worrell, 1966). The problem of selecting the appropriate basis of allocation is not always a simple one; it is most satisfactorily solved when attacked on a firm-by-firm basis. Table 4 indicates how functional expenses are assigned to different marketing outlets using a basis of allocation selected by management. The profit and loss statement by marketing outlet found in Table 5 suggests that only one of the firm's three types of outlets is making any significant contribution to corporate profitability.

TABLE 4. *Basis for allocating functional expenses to channels*

Channel type	Selling No. of sales calls in period	Advertising No. of advertise-ments	Packing and delivery No. of orders placed in period	Billing and collecting No. of orders placed in period
Hardware	200	50	50	50
Garden supply	65	20	21	21
Department stores	10	30	9	9
	275	100	80	80
Functional expense / No. of units	$\dfrac{\$5,500}{275} = \$20$	$\dfrac{\$3,100}{100} = \$31$	$\dfrac{\$4,800}{80} = \$60$	$\dfrac{\$2,400}{80} = \$30$

TABLE 5. *Profit and loss statements for channels*

	Hard-ware	Garden supply	Dept. stores	Whole company
Sales	$30,000	$10,000	$20,000	$60,000
Cost of goods sold	19,500	6,500	13,000	39,000
Gross margin	$10,500	$ 3,500	$ 7,000	$21,000
Expenses				
Selling ($20 per call)	4,000	1,300	200	5,500
Advertising				
($31 per advertisement)	1,550	620	930	3,100
Packing and delivery				
($60 per order)	3,000	1,260	540	4,800
Billing ($30 per order)	1,500	630	270	2,400
Total expenses	$10,050	$ 3,810	$ 1,940	$15,800
Net profit (or loss)	$ 450	$ (310)	$ 5,060	$ 5,200

Standard Costing

Planning and control require that standard costs be used for budgeting and performance measurement. When this sort of analysis is correlated with the study of market
potential and actual sales, it reveals misdirected sales efforts and costs which are not
justified by results. Expected standard future costs should be used for decision making
that relates to the future. To do this not only requires the best possible estimate of
variable and program costs; opportunity costs must also be included for the use of
scarce segment or corporate resources.

The chief argument against using standard costs in marketing hinges on the
difficulty of determining them exactly. The argument can probably never be
accepted or rejected in general terms; each firm must make its own decision as to the
feasibility of standard costs. The chief argument in favor of standard costs is the need
for a basis of comparison between the actual and the expected. Another strong
point is the manner in which such standards can be used to arrive at those costs actually
related to the sales revenue of the period. In contrast, many of the actual marketing
and administrative expenditures incurred in a particular period have no relation to
sales booked during that same period.

The reported contribution margin of the segment as indicated in Table 6 measures
actual performance against the budgeted figures set forth in Table 3. An imputed
charge for the use of working capital is made, since presumably such capital could
be profitably assigned to alternative uses if it became available. Deducting the cost
of services provided to the segment by other parts of the firm has the additional

TABLE 6. *Performance report—Territory A*

	Actual	Budget	Difference
Revenues	$1,200.00	$1,200.00	
Less: Variable costs			
Current value of expired direct variable services performed by the segment	220.00	200.00	(20.00)
Standard cost of services provided to the segment by other parts of the firm	110.00	120.00	(10.00)
Cost of capital (10%) × current value of average working capital used	85.00	80.00	(5.00)
Segment contribution margin	785.00	800.00	(15.00)
Less: Direct out-of-pocket fixed costs			
incurred by or for segment	300.00	280.00	(20.00)
Segment-controllable margin	485.00	520.00	(35.00)
Less: Specific long-run costs			
User cost in current value of direct fixed assets of segment based on estimated decline during period	145.00	150.00	(5.00)
Cost of capital (10%) × current value of average direct fixed capital	170.00	160.00	(10.00)
Net segment margin	$170.00	210.00	(40.00)

Source: Adapted from "Report of the Committee on Cost and Profitability Analyses for Marketing," *The Accounting Review*, Supplement to 47 (1972), p. 593.

benefit of allowing an adjustment for differing levels of responsibility. For example, assume that credit and collection policies are controlled at the corporate level. A change in the level and age of receivables resulting from new company policies can be distinguished from changes arising in the normal course of locally controllable operations. Increases due to the former should not be attached to the segment, while those due to the latter are properly deductible.

The two remaining levels of segment contribution require the deduction of costs that are generally unavoidable in the short run. However, discretionary out-of-pocket fixed costs are budgeted on a periodic basis, and hence their effect on profits is somewhat more controllable than that of the remaining charges. Information as to segment-controllable margin therefore becomes important for evaluating segment performance. Further, deduction of long-run costs is made to arrive at the net segment margin. These costs are imputed rather than out of pocket.

They are made to charge the segment for assets and capital that it preempts other segments from using. Such a deduction is necessary in order to measure the segment's economic impact on corporate performance.

Effective marketing control procedures require cost accounting systems that properly associate expenses and income with lines of authority and marketing responsibilities. All control systems involve the four elements of standard determination, performance measurement, causal analysis, and corrective action. The standards consist of planned achievement levels for different variables at stated points in the year. For example, sales quotas and sales expense budgets become standards within the plan against which periodic results are checked.

Financial Variance Analysis

Variance analysis is a useful financial tool for determining the cause of performance deviations. This technique should not be confused with the analysis of variance, a statistical methodology for analyzing the sources contributing to the variation in a set of numbers. Variance analysis is a special accounting technique that reveals the relative contribution of different factors to a reported deviation in performance (Beam, 1973). When actual dollar sales for a product line are different from targeted sales, the variance could be due to price differences, volume fluctuations, or changes in the product mix. To find out the contribution of each possible source of the total variance, it is necessary to examine, one at a time, the deviations from standard figures as given in the plan for each variable while holding all others constant. Such a procedure focuses on the individual elements that make up total planned sales. This form of analysis also permits each variation from plan to be measured in terms of its effect on profit.

For example, if planned sales were $3,600 made up of 300 units at $12 each but actual sales turned out to be $3,000 through sales of 300 units at $10 each, then the variance is caused entirely by a price decline. If, however, actual sales were 250 units at $12 each, then there is no price variance. The total variance would be due to a volume decline. In the case of a multiproduct line, one can have, in addition, a mix variance reflecting itself in a changed overall actual average price. Table 7 presents a reporting format that reveals the impact in a specific case of variations in price, in volume, in the product mix, and in specific product line expenses.

Variance analysis is often also applied to profit deviations to determine the extent to which these variations are due to price, volume, or mix. The price variance is the difference between actual sales at actual prices and actual sales at standard prices. Actual sales at standard price less standard variable costs discloses the actual, as opposed to the planned, standard profit contribution for the reporting period. Any difference between this amount and the planned amount of standard profit contribution is explained by volume and mix variances.

The volume variance is revealed by multiplying the difference between actual sales and planned sales by the planned percentage of standard profit contribution.

TABLE 7. The A.B.C. Company variance analysis necktie product line earnings, 1974

1974	Gross sales		Standard profit contribution on gross sales				Specific product line expenses		Product line earnings	
	Variance ($000's)	Actual ($000's)	Variance (%)	Actual (%)	Variance ($000's)	Actual ($000's)	Variance ($000's)	Programmed ($000's)	Variance ($000's)	Actual ($000's)
Jan.	100	1,240	(2.0)	35.3	13	438	(2)	70	11	368
Feb.	10	1,394	1.1	37.1	(12)	517	—	19	(12)	498
March	(10)	883	0.5	37.5	1	331	(8)	76	(7)	255
1st quarter	100	3,517	(0.1)	36.6	2	1,286	(10)	165	(8)	1,121

Summary of variance from profit plan

	Standard profit contribution ($000's)			Specific product line expenses ($000's)				
Actual product line earnings ($000's)	Price	Volume	Mix	Advertising	Markdowns	Cost of returns	Catalog	Planned product line earnings ($000's)
1,121	0	(15)	17	(6)	4	(7)	(1)	1,129
		17 − 15 = 2		4 − (6 + 7 + 1) = −10				1,121 − 1,129 = −8

Source: Adapted from Sanford R. Simon, *Managing Marketing Profitability* (New York: American Management Association, Inc., 1969), pp. 186–187.

The mix variance is the difference between the percentage of profit contribution actually received and the planned percentage of standard profit contribution multiplied by the actual sales volume at standard prices. This last variance is the result of selling a different mix than planned of the products within a product line when such items make varying standard profit contributions (Simon, 1969). (Although the above is a standard method, differences of opinion exist as to the preferred way of calculating variances for multiproduct firms [Chumachenko, 1968].)

Output budgeting is another recent approach which attempts to relate all cost items to sector objectives so that it is clear which resources are being devoted toward each end and with what results (Wills, 1972). Traditional accounting methods have tended to concentrate on the departments or functional areas within the firm doing the spending rather than the ends to which these expenditures are directed. This orientation has been dictated by the requirement of meeting specific objectives in terms of profit contribution or minimum cost operation. A view that is increasingly being accepted, however, is that the true objectives of the firm should be stated not in terms of performance criteria for functions, but rather in terms of "missions" —such as entertainment or thirst satisfaction—which cut across functional areas. For example, a mission goal could be a given share of the entertainment market.

The setting of budgets using a mission orientation requires the adoption of radically different methods. Under existing procedures, functions are allocated a budget that is historically or arbitrarily defined. Function managers are then exhorted to perform as effectively as they can within the budget. A mission-oriented approach requires the determination of the necessary level of input from each function to achieve mission goals. In the same way that mission costs are clearly identified, it is necessary to have an indication of the benefits that each mission produced. Output budgeting presents the decision maker with a means of evaluating alternatives in terms of cost-effectiveness.

Discounts, Allowances, Credit, and Ratio Analysis

What factors determine the wisdom of varying the cash discount? Changing that discount will affect the speed at which receivables are paid and thus necessitate an adjustment in the amount of investment in receivables. Consider, for example, a firm with annual credit sales of $1.2 million and an average collection period of two months even though the firm's terms are net 45 days. Such a firm turns its receivables over six times a year, and its average receivables balance is $200,000.

Assume now that this firm introduces a 2 percent discount for payment within ten days, that 50 percent of its customers would take advantage of this cash discount, and that the average collection period would be reduced to one month. The cost of the cash discount becomes 2% × 0.50 × $1.2 million or $12,000. Receivables now turn over twelve times a year, however, and the average receivables balance becomes $100,000. If the average cost of a unit is 90 percent of its sales price, the actual reduction of investment in receivables is $90,000. If the firm's required return on investment is 20 percent, a $90,000 reduction in receivables reduces costs by $18,000. Since this saving is substantially greater than the $12,000 cost of the proposed cash discount, the firm should offer such a discount.

The desirability of lengthening the period for which credit is extended also depends on the additional costs and revenues involved. Unfortunately, estimating both the additional volume of sales that could be generated and the additional profit associated with these incremental sales is not an easy task. In such calculations, the firm's required return on investment must be treated as a charge against the additional investment in receivables associated with increased sales. The expected increase in the average collection period or, conversely, the inevitable slowdown in the rate at which receivables will turn over must also be estimated, along with any net change in bad debts.

Marketing management could also be reviewing plans to increase its annual sales by $12,000 through selling to a market segment that seems likely to have a bad debt ratio of 5 percent. Let us assume the firm's product costs are 90 percent of selling price and its receivables turn over six times a year. On incremental sales of $12,000, the firm would gross $1,200. Since bad debts will amount to $540 (5% × $12,000 × 90%), the firm will net $1,200 − $540 or $660. The incremental investment in receivables necessitated by the new policy is $12,000/6 or $2,000. The return on this incremental investment, therefore, is $660/$2,000 = 33%. However, 33 percent is a conservative estimate of return, since 10 percent of the accounts receivable figure represents earnings rather than the cost of goods sold. This being the case, the actual return is $660/$1,800 = 37%. This figure must, of course, be adjusted for any net changes in the overall level of bad debts as well as for any expected increase in the average collection period, or, conversely, any slowdown in the rate at which receivables turn over (Block, 1974). Once the necessary calculations have been made for this and alternative courses of action, the firm can ascertain whether selling to the proposed market segment represents the most efficient use of funds.

Credit Terms and Conditions

It has been argued that, for a firm with excess capacity evaluating a doubtful credit-lengthening policy, the appropriate bad debt consideration is not the selling price or even the average cost of manufacture, but rather the incremental costs of production (Kaplan, 1967). However, this line of reasoning can be misleading, since the difference between the average and the incremental costs of units lost through bad debts has to be apportioned over the remainder of the output. Such apportionment would raise the average costs on the balance of output and, correspondingly, the investment in receivables and inventory, while simultaneously diminishing the earnings margin.

Assume that a firm has annual sales of $1,000,000 made up of 500 units at

$2,000 each. The earnings margin is 20 percent; the average cost of a unit is $1,600, but the incremental cost is $1,200. Inventory consists of 50 units carried at an average cost of $1,600 each. Inventory investment therefore is $80,000, and the firm also has an investment in accounts receivable of $80,000. Assume further that the firm is considering a credit-lengthening policy expected to increase bad debts by 10 units. These units represent $16,000 at average cost but only $12,000 at incremental cost. If the firm based its decision on the incremental costs of anticipated bad debts, then the difference of $4,000 between the average and the incremental cost would have to be apportioned over the balance of output. In effect, the total value of output at average cost would rise from $800,000 by that $4,000 or 0.5 percent. Correspondingly, the investment in inventory and receivables would also rise by 0.5 percent. The earnings margin would simultaneously diminish from $200,000 by $4,000 or 2 percent.

The preceding illustration is a simplified presentation which abstracts from the effects of taxes, increased investment in receivables, and other financial ramifications of credit lengthening. However, the fact remains that considering bad debt units at only the incremental cost of production is misleading. The difference between these incremental costs and the average costs of the same units has to be borne by other accounts, to the detriment of the firm's earnings.

Ratio Analysis

In its control endeavors marketing management is often interested in relative financial figures as well as absolute ones. Financial ratios and the calculation of percentages permit the comparison of results between areas and over time. They are thus very useful in pinpointing areas of activity that may require managerial attention.

Financial ratios can be divided into four types: liquidity, debt, coverage, and profitability. These different types of ratios are all described in the major financial texts (Van Horne, 1980). Reference will be made here only to liquidity ratios and to certain marketing performance ratios. Corporate, debt, and coverage ratios are concerned with the long-term liquidity of the firm and its capital structure—topics not of immediate concern to marketing managers. The return on investment ratio, on the other hand, has already been discussed in considerable detail.

Liquidity Ratios

Liquidity ratios of immediate interest to marketing managers include the liquidity of receivables, the aging of accounts payable, and the liquidity of inventories. Receivables are only liquid insofar as they can be collected in a reasonable period of time. The basic ratio for analyzing receivables is the average collection period:

$$\frac{\text{receivables} \times \text{days in year}}{\text{annual credit sales}}$$

For example, if receivables are $25 and annual credit sales are $100, the average collection period would be slightly over 91 days:

$$\frac{\$25 \times 365 \text{ days}}{\$100}$$

If the terms of sale offered by a firm are 2/10 net 60, the ratio of 91 days indicates that a sizeable proportion of receivables are beyond the final due date of 60 days.

Another way of viewing the above ratio is to look at the receivables turnover calculated as

$$\frac{\text{annual credit sales}}{\text{receivables}} \quad \text{or} \quad \frac{\$100}{\$25} = 4$$

Further insight into receivables is obtained through an aging of accounts. This procedure involves tabulating the proportion of outstanding receivables by the month in which the billing took place. Receivables shown on the books are only as good as the likelihood that they will be collected. Thus the existence of receivables from months long past suggests a likely bad debt. Note also that the bad debts/credit sales ratio indicates the risk of selling on credit.

The liquidity of inventories is another useful measure. The inventory turnover ratio indicates the rapidity with which the inventory is converted into sales. The ratio is calculated by dividing cost of goods sold by average inventory. In general, a high rate of inventory turnover indicates efficient inventory management. However, it could also be a sign of inadequate inventory, and could consequently underlie a pattern of frequent stockouts. Marketing management must consider whether profitability could actually be raised by carrying a larger or more complete inventory. Conversely, too low an inventory turnover ratio indicates a slow-moving or possible obsolescent inventory.

Marketing Performance Ratios

Ratios and percentages commonly used in efforts to evaluate and to control marketing performance include the following:

1. Expense to sale ratios (such as advertising expense to sales, cost per sales call, cost per sales prospect).
2. Gross profit to sales ratios.
3. Percentage of goods sold on deals.
4. Percentage of returned merchandise.
5. Ratio of order backlog to current sales.
6. Sales concentration indices (such as percentage of sales from top 20 percent of customers).
7. Number of months' inventory with distributors or industrial customers.
8. Bad debts ratio.

FIGURE 6

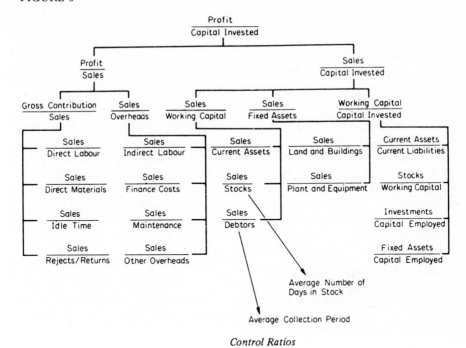

Control Ratios

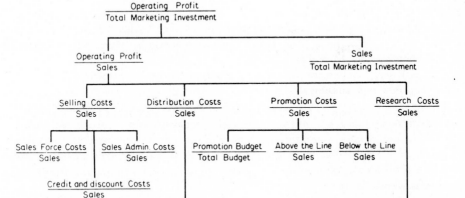

Marketing Control Ratios

Source: R. M. S. Wilson, *Management Controls in Marketing* (London; William Heinemann Ltd, 1973), p. 102. © R. M. S. Wilson 1973. Reprinted by permission of William Heinemann Limited.

Each ratio is useful both at one point in time and over time. Cross-sectional comparisons indicate which marketing segments, products, and territories are performing poorly. Comparisons over time reveal trends in performance within the same reporting unit. In either case, further analysis may reveal the basic causes of poor performance and suggest possible corrective actions. Figure 6 depicts a large number of useful control ratios, some general in nature and others more specific to marketing.

Their merits notwithstanding, ratios and percentages have two important limitations. First, they are averages that do not indicate the distribution and range of the absolute figures. Also, a change in a ratio can be caused by a change in numerator, a change in denominator, or a change in both. Consequently, percentage and ratio analyses are of more use in identifying problem areas than in finding solutions to these problems.

Competitive Bidding

All sophisticated competitive bidding models have to take into account three variables: the size of the bid, the expected profit if the bid is accepted, and the probability that the bid will be accepted. The basic objective of these probabilistic bidding models is to find the optimum combination of probability of acceptance and of profit if so accepted. The elementary competitive bidding model assumes that the bidder has only one known competitor and no capacity constraints (Morse, 1975). In fact, a bidder usually has several known or unknown competitors and may have capacity limitations. Fortunately, the optimizing model for competitive bidding can be extended to cover such situations. The reader will find a detailed illustration of how this is done spelled out in the article by Morse which appears as reading number 13 in this collection.

In practice, many firms aspire to a target return on investment and apply a markup designed to achieve this return to some measure of their costs (Brooks, 1978). Table 8 outlines the difference between the expected present value approach now in intellectual favor and the more operational markup approach. Any costs or difficulties of gathering information notwithstanding, the expected present value approach to competitive bidding is of great value. It makes explicit all the factors which should be considered in a markup approach to maximize the firm's net present worth.

What if the company fails in a bidding situation in which follow-up contracts are likely and the firm winning the initial contract is also favored to win any subsequent contracts?

In such a case, a lower price may be paid on an initial contract if the probability is high that a follow-up contract can be won at a higher level of profitability. The problem then becomes one of determining which combination of initial bid and follow-up bid would generate an expected rate of return equal to the firm's target.

TABLE 8. *Competitive bidding in theory and practice*

Decide whether or not to prepare a bid and incur bid preparation costs.

↓ YES   NO ↓

Decide whether or not to incur full search costs.   Stop.

↓ YES   NO ↓

EPVC approach	Markup approach
Calculate all net incremental costs in EPV terms. Include all explicit and implicit costs (including opportunity costs) now and in the future which are expected to be incurred as a result of this contract. Deduct in EPV terms all future revenues and opportunity revenues such as goodwill and costs avoided as a result of obtaining this contract.	Calculate all explict costs associated with this contract. Add allocated overhead charges and bid preparation costs to arrive at your "standard" cost base.
↓	↓
Estimate the probabilities of success at each of several possible bid prices.	Apply standard markup percentage to this cost base to arrive at your standard bid price for this contract.
↓	↓
Calculate the EPVC for each of these bid prices and identify the bid price which maximizes EPVC.	(i) Bid at this standard price if doing so in the past has kept your capacity utilization and profitability at preferred levels and if there are no extraordinary incremental costs or benefits associated with this contract.
↓	(ii) Bid below this standard price if capacity utilization and profitability are both lower than desired and/or if there are extraordinary incremental net benefits expected in the future as a result of this contract.
(i) Bid at "maximum EPVC" price if this type of decision is taken frequently and if there are no aesthetic, political or other non-monetary considerations involved.	(iii) Bid above this standard price if capacity utilization is higher and profitability lower than is desired and/or if there are extraordinary incremental costs expected in the future as a result of this contract.
(ii) Bid below the "maximum EPVC" price if indicated by the certainty equivalent criterion or by aesthetic or political considerations.	↓
(iii) Bid above the "maximum EPVC" price if indicated by the certainty equivalent criterion or by aesthetic or political considerations.	(i) If successful this time, no change necessary unless receiving too many jobs for your limited capacity, in which case raise the standard markup for your next bid (and investigate plant expansion).
↓	(ii) If unsuccessful this time, no change necessary unless receiving too few jobs with subsequent underutilization of your plant, in which case reduce the standard markup for your next bid (and investigate plant contraction).
(i) If successful this time, no change necessary unless successful so often that probabilities appear to be understated. If so, raise success probabilities for your next bid (and investigate plant expansion).	
(ii) If unsuccessful this time, no change necessary unless unsuccessful so often that probabilities appear to be overstated. If so, reduce success probabilities for your next bid (and investigate plant contraction).	

Source: Evan Douglas, "The Theory of Competitive Bidding and Its Lesson for the Practical Maximization of Net Present Worth," *The Montreal Business Report* (second quarter, 1980), p. 62.

Probabilities, Risk, and Payoff

Any long-term investment involves considerable uncertainty because of both the length of time involved and the inherent risk. The investment may eventually turn out well and yield a large yearly cash inflow. It may, on the other hand, prove disappointing and yield only moderate cash flows. A good example of this is an investment in an oil well, which may turn out well or poorly. The success of other investments may depend on the impossible-to-predict actions of competitors.

How should such uncertainties be handled? Faced with such difficulties, the company could insist on a higher rate of return. For example, instead of applying a target ROI rate of 10 percent after taxes, the company might use a rate of 15 percent for especially risky ventures. Because of the uncertainties inherent in all capable budgeting decisions, one can expect relatively larger ROI rates, considerably in excess of prevailing interest rates. Another approach may be taken when probabilities can be assigned to the possible outcomes of an investment. Decisions can then be based on the average or "expected value" of the outcomes. The following example will both clarify the point and introduce the concept of expected monetary value.

TABLE 9

Outcome	Probability	Prob. × outcome (EMV)
Success (50,000)	0.5	$25,000
Moderate success (20,000)	0.3	6,000
Failure (0)	0.2	0
Average expected value		$31,000
Cash flows: $31,000 × 5.650[a]		$175,150
Investment		200,000
Net present value		−$ 24,850

[a] Present value of $1 per year, 10 years at 12%.

The Exeter Company is considering an investment in an oil well. The well will cost $200,000. There is a 50 percent chance that the well will be successful and yield cash flows of $50,000 each year for ten years. There is a 30 percent chance that it will be a moderate success and return cash flows of $20,000 a year for ten years. There is a 20 percent chance that the well will fail and return zero cash flows for the next ten years. The company desires a 12 percent return on its investments. What is the net present value of the oil well investment? (Ignore income taxes.)

If the oil well is a success, the actual present value will turn out to be $82,500 or

[($50,000 × 5.650) − $200,000]. On the basis of the available information, however, the company should reject this investment. The use of an expected value does not mean that the actual result will be a negative net present value of $24,850; it means, rather, that if the company made a series of similar investments with these probabilities, the average net present value over the long run would be − $24,850.

An approach using expected values and probabilities is applicable to many investment decisions. It is a technique for dealing with the uncertainties that usually exist in capital budgeting. Of course, the wrong decision can still be made. The wrong outcomes may have been assumed, or inaccurate probabilities may have been assigned, but such risks exist in most business decisions. This possibility of error again illustrates that accounting information does not assure success and is no substitute for management skill.

The Measurement of Business Risk

In choosing between two proposals with the same expected value, one must look at the dispersion of the probability distributions. The conventional measure of dispersion is the standard deviation, which for a single period's possible outcome is

$$\alpha = \sqrt{\sum_{x=1}^{n} (A_{xt} - \bar{A}_t)^2 P_{xt}}$$

where A_{xt} is a cash flow for the xth probability of occurrence of that cash flow and $\bar{A}_t$ is the expected value of cash flows in period t. Since two proposals are very likely to have different cash flows and probabilities, one proposal will most likely have a higher standard deviation, indicating a greater dispersion of possible outcomes.

A measure of relative dispersion that is often used is the coefficient of variation. This is simply the standard deviation of the probability distribution over its expected value. Proposal 1 with an expected value of $10,000 may have a standard deviation of $2,000 and thus a coefficient of variation of 0.20. Proposal 2's comparative figures could be $12,000, $3,000, and 0.25, respectively. Thus the coefficient of variation serves as a relative measure of the degree of business risk.

The measurement of risk can get more involved when one studies cash flows from an investment over time. For most investment proposals the cash flow in one future period depends in part on the cash flows in previous periods. If an investment proposal turns bad in the early years, the probability is high that cash flows in later years also will be lower than originally expected. The consequence of cash flows being correlated over time is that the standard deviation of the probability distribution of possible net present values or possible rates of return is larger than it would be under the assumption of independent cash flows. To obtain a realistic assessment of the consequences of dependence over time, one could use conditional probabilities, but such a procedure is difficult to implement.

The study of risk has no boundaries. More complex methods than those discussed above include a simulation approach. More complex situations include those with multiple investment projects which are to some degree correlated. One can also become involved in a situation that necessitates a sequence of investment decisions over time, an analytical problem that can be handled by a decision tree approach. The scope of this book limits the extent to which we can explore the fascinating subject of risk. For more information on this topic, the interested reader is referred to any of the major financial management texts.

References

Beam, Thomas J. (November 1973). "Mix Variance in Gross Profit Analysis." *Management Accounting*, pp. 38–40.

Bell, Albert L. (February 1969). "Break-Even Charts vs. Marginal Graphs." *Management Accounting*, pp. 32–35.

Block, Dr. Stanley (May 1974). "Accounts Receivable as an Investment." *Credit and Financial Management*, pp. 32–35.

Brooks, Douglas G. (January 1978). "Bidding for the Sake of Follow-on Contracts." *Journal of Marketing*, Vol. 42, pp. 35–38.

Chumachenko, Nikolai G. (October 1968). "Once Again the Volume–Mix–Price/Cost Variance Analysis." *The Accounting Review*, pp. 753–762.

Dean, Joel (May 1949). "Cost Structures of Enterprises and Break-Even Techniques." *American Economic Review*, pp. 150–160.

Dearden, John (May-June 1969). "The Case Against ROI Control." *Harvard Business Review*, Vol. 47, pp. 124–135.

Douglas, Evan J. (1980). *Managerial Economics*. (Englewood Cliffs, New Jersey: Prentice-Hall).

Haynes, William Warren (1969). *Managerial Economics*. (Austin, Texas: Business Publications Inc. and Georgetown, Ontario: Irwin-Dorsey Ltd.), pp. 218–220.

Herson, Richard, J. L., and Ronald S. Hertz (March-April 1968). "Direct Costing in Pricing: A Critical Appraisal." *Management Series*, pp. 35–44.

Henrici, Stanley B. (May-June 1968). "Eyeing the ROI." *Harvard Business Review*, pp. 88–97.

Hertz, David B. (January-February 1968). "Investment Policies That Pay Off." *Harvard Business Review*, pp. 96–108.

Hirshleifer, J. (August 1958). "On the Theory of Optimal Investment Decision." *Journal of Political Economy*, Vol. 66, pp. 329–352.

Kaplan, Robert M. (March-April 1967). "Credit Risks and Opportunities." *Harvard Business Review*, pp. 83–88.

Kirpalani, V. H., and S. J. Shapiro (1979). *Marketing Effectiveness: Insights from Accounting and Finance—An Annotated Bibliography 1960–1977*, Bibliography Series #33 (Chicago, Illinois: American Marketing Association).

Kirpalani, V. H., and S. J. Shapiro (July 1973). "Financial Dimensions of Marketing Management." *Journal of Marketing*, pp. 40–42.

Kotler, Philip (1972). Adapted from *Marketing Management*, 2nd ed. (Englewood Cliffs, New Jersey: Prentice-Hall, Inc.).

Lorie, James H., and Leonard J. Savage (October 1955). "Three Problems in Rationing Capital." *Journal of Business*, Vol. 28, pp. 229–239.

Morse, Wayne J. (April 1975). "Probabilistic Bidding Models: A Synthesis." *Business Horizons*, Vol. 18, pp. 67–74.

Mossman, Frank H., and Malcolm J. Worrell, Jr. (Autumn 1966). "Analytical Methods of Measuring Marketing Profitability: A Matrix Approach." *Business Topics*, pp. 25–45.

Phyrr, Peter A. (1973). *Zero-Base Budgeting* (New York: John Wiley and Sons, Inc.).

Simon, Sanford R. (1969). *Managing Marketing Profitability* (New York: American Management Association, Inc.).

Solomons, David (July 1968). "Breakeven Analysis Under Absorption Costing." *The Accounting Review*, pp. 447–452.

Stanton, William J., and Richard H. Buskirk (1969). *Management of the Sales Force*, 3rd ed. (Homewood, Illinois: Richard D. Irwin, Inc.), pp. 595–613.

Van Horne, James C. (1980). *Financial Management and Policy*, 5th ed. (Englewood Cliffs, New Jersey: Prentice-Hall, Inc.).

Weston, Fred J. (August 1972). "ROI Planning and Control." *Business Horizons*, Vol. 15, pp. 25–42.

Wills, Gordon, Christopher Martin, and Walter David (1972). *Output Budgeting in Marketing*, Management Decision Monograph (UK: University of Bradford, Management Centre).

Wyles, R. J. D. (1963). *Price, Cost and Output* (New York: Frederick A. Prague), pp. 51–52.

The Allocation Controversy in Marketing Cost Analysis

1

John J. Wheatley

Controversy about the question of cost allocation in marketing or distribution cost analysis, as it is often called, has gone on for several decades. A review of more than two dozen currently available introductory marketing texts reveals the persistent nature of the debate.[1]

It seems worthwhile to try to resolve the issue. Businessmen who received their academic training prior to 1950, and who are now in management positions, are very likely to be *misinformed* on the matter or, at the very least, *confused* about it unless they have kept abreast of new developments in the field of managerial accounting. This unsatisfactory situation could, unfortunately, be perpetuated for another 15 or 20 years. Many of the post-1950 graduates, and even those students now in our colleges and universities who have had to depend on introductory accounting and marketing courses for information and guidance on this topic, find themselves in the same predicament.

I. "Net Profit" and "Contribution Margin"

The two methods of dealing with the cost allocation problem are usually identified as the "net profit" and the "contribution margin" approaches. The former requires the assignment of all costs (both direct and indirect) incurred by the segment[2] of the business being analyzed; the latter calls for only the assignment of those costs which are directly attributable to the segment or activity being studied.

The net profit, or full-cost, approach to marketing cost analysis essentially involves development of a traditional financial profit and loss statement for a segment; the net profit (or loss) is determined by matching the revenues generated by the segment and the costs associated with it along with an equitable and reasonably allocated share of the overhead costs of the business.

Reprinted from the *University of Washington Business Review*, Volume 30, Number 4 (Summer 1971), pp. 61–70, with the permission of the Journal of Contemporary Business, University of Washington.

[1] The dispute is not restricted to elementary books in the field, either. See, for example, J. A. Howard, *Marketing Management* (Homewood, Illinois: R. D. Irwin, Inc., 1963), p. 183. And, for an opposing viewpoint, W. Alderson and P. E. Green, *Planning and Problem Solving in Marketing* (Homewood, Illinois: R. D. Irwin, Inc., 1964), p. 559.

[2] A segment has been defined as "any line of activity or subdivision of the business for which separate determination of costs and sales is wanted. Examples might be: division, products, customers, plants, order sizes, territories, and channels of distribution." Charles T. Horngren, *Cost Accounting: A Managerial Emphasis* (Englewood Cliffs, N.J.: Prentice-Hall, Inc., 1962), p. 348.

Beckman and Davidson are typical of those who favor the net profit approach to marketing cost analysis. Using a functional cost approach to the analysis of a metal products distributor or wholesaler, they point out:

> Practically all of the costs are joint costs.
> The problem is to find the best way to allocate such joint or indirect costs to each product line under consideration.... The procedure is (1) to select a realistic measure of the variability of each functional cost among categories, (2) to determine what proportion of the total cost of each function should be charged to each category, and (3) to make the necessary calculations to allocate a specific amount of cost to each category....
> The main point is that the analysis shows which product lines contribute a profit and which do not.[3]

The contribution margin approach also calls for a determination of the revenues attributable to a segment, but, instead of a full cost allocation, only those costs directly incurred by the segment are subtracted from earnings. The residual figure is not called profit but instead is referred to as a contribution to overhead and profit.[4] The resulting document is, consequently, unlike a typical financial income statement.

Matthews *et al.*, among others, espouse the contribution margin approach:

> Their first step is generally to determine the gross margin and allocable expenses associated with each segment of the business whose effectiveness is to be measured. The remaining nonallocated expenses can be treated as overhead, with a "contribution to overhead and profit" then figured for each segment.[5]

Using the contribution margin approach, profitability by segment may also be determined by distinguishing between fixed and variable direct costs. The advantage of this "variable cost contribution margin" method is the clear separation of variable from fixed costs, in addition to the separation of direct and indirect costs. This refinement may be important in some situations, such as when direct fixed costs are a large proportion of total direct costs; but it is, unfortunately, a point that is frequently ignored by marketing writers. Assigning only variable direct costs to a segment provides what might be called the *gross contribution* to overhead and profit. Taking into account nonvariable direct costs, in addition, results in a determination of the *net contribution* by a segment.

While most marketing writers appear to feel that there are significant differences between the two approaches and tend to favor one over the other, a few, while admitting these differences and acknowledging the usefulness of marketing cost analysis, do not indicate a preference or the circumstances under which one method or the other should be employed.[6]

Actually, both approaches do have a place in marketing cost analysis work.

---

[3] T. N. Beckman and W. R. Davidson, *Marketing* (New York: Ronald Press Company, 1967), p. 803.
[4] J. B. Matthews, *et al., Marketing* (New York: McGraw-Hill Book Co., 1964), p. 526.
[5] Ibid.
[6] See, for example, W. J. Stanton, *Fundamentals of Marketing* (New York: McGraw-Hill Book Co., 1967), p. 674.

However, it is not an either/or proposition, nor is it a matter of indifference as to which approach is used in a particular set of circumstances.

While the controversy between the proponents of the net profit approach and those favoring the contribution margin method appears to hinge on the question of cost allocation, closer examination reveals that the assumptions about the nature of the term "cost" and the general accounting orientation flowing from this distinction are at the heart of the dispute. Moreover, there seems to be a lack of awareness among some marketing writers of the existence of these assumptions, in part, at least, because many of them are implicit rather than explicit.

II. Importance of Marketing Cost Analysis

It is worth making an attempt to resolve the controversy about the allocation of costs not only to clear up the confusion and misunderstanding about the subject, but because there is widespread agreement about the importance and potential usefulness of marketing cost analysis for management purposes.

The emphasis in the last 15 or 20 years on the marketing concept has done much to heighten the importance of marketing cost analysis, primarily as a result of the increased responsibilities assigned to marketing managers. The extent to which this is true is revealed in the original statement by the General Electric Company in 1952 of the new role of marketing in that company:

> Thus marketing, through its studies and research, will establish for the engineer, the designer, and the manufacturing man, what the customer wants in a given product; what price he is willing to pay; and where and when it will be wanted. Marketing would have authority in product planning, product scheduling, and inventory control, as well as in the sales, distribution, and serving of the product.[7]

Marketing cost analysis also creates opportunities for marketing management personnel at every level in a company because it is capable of bringing about increases in operating efficiency. More concretely, it represents an opportunity to increase profits and improve a firm's competitive position. Marketing costs are typically substantial for most enterprises, and cost analysis may even be necessary to merely maintain a favorable industry position in a competitive business environment. One prominent accountant has gone so far as to say that "the most important single aspect of intelligent attention-directing and problem-solving is the knowledge of cost behavior patterns and influences."[8]

III. The Source and Nature of Cost Information

Managing involves several distinguishable activities: developing plans, establishing and maintaining control of operations, and making and executing decisions. All of

---

[7] *Annual Report of the General Electric Company for the Year 1952*, p. 21.
[8] Charles T. Horngren, *Accounting for Management Control* (Englewood Cliffs, New Jersey: Prentice-Hall, Inc., 1970), p. 233.

these activities require information if they are to be done well, and one of the essential kinds of information needed concerns the behavior of costs. Virtually all such cost information comes from the accounting records of an organization. This fact is at least partially responsible for some of the difficulties encountered in utilizing marketing cost analysis.

The *accounting information*, upon which marketing cost analysis depends, *is used for a variety of other purposes* besides marketing cost analysis. These various uses are not mutually exclusive, but they are, however, reasonably distinct from one another. The first use to which cost information is put has to do with the stewardship function of top management. It is mainly financial in character and of importance primarily to stockholders and taxing authorities; it is also, essentially, backward-looking. The question of what has happened during a period of time with reference to the matter of earnings or losses and of where the firm stands financially as of a given date is of limited usefulness for management purposes. The second use for accounting information about the behavior of costs is more clearly managerial in nature; it is to determine where the firm's problem areas lie. The third use of cost information, while it is of vestigial interest for financial accounting purposes, is even more obviously managerially oriented; it is to determine what future decisions management should make in light of its goals and the alternatives open to it.

Unfortunately, not all accountants, and, consequently, marketing textbook authors following their lead, understand or appreciate either the distinction about the different purposes for which cost information may be gathered, or, more importantly, that *different kinds of cost information are needed for each of these purposes.* The concept of "cost," like that of "price," is an ambiguous and nebulous one that depends for its definition on the use to which it is put. In financial accounting, of course, cost is not usually ambiguous; it is the measurement of an expenditure or payment made for a benefit received.[9] However, in a managerial setting, "what is cost depends upon what sacrifices are really produced by a particular business decision."[10]

The traditional financial accounting approach to the determination of cost is governed by rules and conventions that are quite rigidly defined. These rules are intended to permit users of such information to learn what the profits or losses have been for a firm over a stated period of time—they also allow comparisons between different time periods or among different firms.

The task of the marketing manager, on the other hand, is to determine what concept of cost is most useful for a particular task and what adjustments to conventional accounting data might need to be made. Flexibility in defining cost for financial purposes is justifiably quite limited; for managerial purposes it is not only

[9] H. A. Finney and H. E. Miller, *Principles of Accounting* (New York: Prentice-Hall, Inc., 1953), p. 398.
[10] Joel Dean, *Managerial Economics* (New York: Prentice-Hall, Inc., 1951), p. 271.

appropriate but also necessary. Decisions that a marketing manager must make regarding his firm's future operations are, for example, based on *estimates of future costs* and revenues rather than on current or historical costs or revenues which are useful only as a guide for estimating what is likely to be experienced in the future. Opportunity costs, another concept of cost useful for decision-making purposes, never show up in conventional accounting records at all.

IV. Reasons for Exclusive Adherence to the Net Profit Approach

One of the reasons for the utilization of the net profit or financial approach to marketing cost analysis, and its concomitant emphasis on acquisition or book costs in situations where it is inappropriate, is historical. Cost data are, and always have been, gathered mainly for financial purposes. This financial orientation has undoubtedly contributed both to the utilization of the available cost information in unmodified form and to greater stress being placed on profits rather than on problem identification and/or problem solving. Long before any discussions appeared in either the accounting or marketing literature on appropriate concepts of cost for purposes other than financial reporting, businessmen and academicians were concerned with the topic of cost analysis. And, it is not surprising that they should have attempted to deal with managerial issues with whatever information, techniques, and theory were available at the time.[11]

Another, and perhaps even more important, reason for the misunderstanding about the basic nature of the term cost is that the distinction referred to above, while not new, is of relatively recent origin in the accounting literature.

It is only within the last 20 years, in fact, that accountants have begun to deal with the utilization of accounting information for other than primarily financial purposes on anything approaching a systematic basis.[12] The emergence of a genuinely managerial orientation among accountants was undoubtedly precipitated, or at least facilitated, by the simultaneous growth of interest among economists in applying economic theory to the task of operating a business enterprise.[13] However, these developments very probably came along too late to be integrated into the major accounting works dealing with marketing cost analyses now in print and upon which many marketing textbook authors have placed such heavy reliance.[14] The two accounting books emphasize the usefulness of the net profit approach

---

[11] See, for example, J. W. Millard, "Analysis of Wholesale Distribution Costs" (Paper read at the A.M.A. Marketing Executives' Conference, Chicago, March 1928).

[12] The first textbook in accounting to take a managerial approach was R. H. Robnett, T. M. Hill and J. A. Beckett, *Accounting: A Management Approach* (Chicago, Illinois: R. D. Irwin, Inc., 1951).

[13] The first major book in this area was Joel Dean, *op. cit.*

[14] The two volumes are J. B. Heckert and R. B. Miner, *Distribution Costs* (New York: Ronald Press Co., 1953) and D. R. Longman and M. Schiff, *Practical Distribution Cost Analysis* (Homewood, Illinois: R. D. Irwin, Inc., 1955).

to cost analysis rather than the contribution margin method.[15] While they deal with management problems, these books have, essentially, a traditional financial accounting flavor, and they may be said to represent an extension of financial accounting concepts and techniques to the task of marketing cost analysis.

V. Significance of a Financial Accounting Orientation

The significance of the failure on the part of financially oriented accountants to take into account the ambiguity inherent in the term cost may be illustrated by examination of the effect of this assumption in the case of an analysis of a firm's product line or mix. The financial approach does, as its advocates claim, place great emphasis upon profits. As a corollary, the proposition that every product should stand on its own feet and carry its share of the load is widely accepted by proponents of the net profit approach to marketing cost analysis. Beckett points out that among those who prefer to determine net profits by segments:

> there is merit in computing a net profit . . . because in the long run, each . . . must produce profits computed on some reasonable and realistic basis.[16]

In other words, each segment should be viewed as a kind of profit center within the firm.

This stress on the determination of profits rather than on planning, exercising control, or making and executing operating decisions leads to some serious difficulties. One of the most important of these is a tendency to ignore some significant aspects of the basic nature of demand.

The demand for a particular product in a multiproduct offering should, more often than not, be viewed as being interrelated with the demand for all of the products in the line. One product frequently helps to sell another, and the absence of a product may cause the sale of another product to decline. In other words, the whole product line may often be greater than the sum of its parts in terms of sales and profits. Businessmen and retailers, in particular, have long recognized this as a basis for the selection of a product mix. As Bliss has pointed out:

> [A] concern with total receipts is always present in the thinking of a merchant who handles a variety of goods. The demand for any single item of the several goods in stock is never isolated in the eyes of the decision maker.[17]

---

[15] In fairness to Heckert and Miner it should be noted that they do observe that "each approach has its own area of usefulness, in most cases clearly indicated by the nature of the decision management must make."[a] Some marketing writers have apparently either overlooked or ignored this observation.

[a] Heckert, op. cit., p. 31.

[16] J. A. Beckett, "The Art and Science of Distribution Costing," National Association of Cost Accountants Bulletin, Section I, XXXII, No. 8 (April 1951), p. 901. Additional evidence for this statement may also be found in National Association of Cost Accountants Bulletin, No. 9, Sec. 4 (New York: May 1951), XXXII, p. 931 and M. Melman, "Marketing Cost Analysis, Development and Current Practices," Accounting Review (January 1963), p. 121.

[17] C. P. Bliss, "Non-price Competition at the Department Store Level," Journal of Marketing, XVII (April 1953), p. 359.

When revenues are influenced by the existence of interrelated or interdependent demand it is invalid to talk about the profitability of individual segments of a business, such as products or the production of specific products. The idea that each product "must produce profits computed on some reasonable and realistic basis" is simply wrong. In a multiproduct firm, each product is capable of contributing to the sales and profits of all the other products in the line. Therefore, generally speaking *the basic unit for profit analysis ought not to be the product, but the firm*—the firm, in fact, should be viewed as an entity, or system, which exercises control over a pool of resources and whose task it is to develop strategies and tactics to achieve goals such as profits.

Profits for a firm, it should be remembered, are maximized at any point in time when the difference between *total costs* and *total revenues* is greatest. It is usually impossible to say what the profit picture would be like at some future date if one or more products were to be deleted from a product line, short of an experiment or a decision to actually drop the products. The reason for this is that buyer behavior cannot be assumed to be unaffected by such an action on the vendor's part, because purchasers regard the seller's offer as encompassing more than a physical entity. The purchaser buys a mix of things, and his patronage depends on his buying motives. Essentially, he is seeking satisfaction, and satisfaction is derived not only from the physical product itself, but also from a host of other elements of the transaction, such as available assortments, information, credit, and convenience. The latter consideration can, for instance, be very important to both industrial buyers and individual consumers. Suppose for a moment that a retail food store decided, on the basis of a product profit analysis, to discontinue handling sugar, butter, eggs, coffee, bread, and milk because they were unprofitable. In spite of the fact that the retailer might still carry several thousand food products, all of which were judged to be profitable, he would certainly run the risk of becoming unprofitable *as a business enterprise* because many of his customers would be unwilling to experience the inconvenience of going elsewhere for these frequently purchased items.

VI. The Proper Use of Marketing Cost Analysis

Marketing costs may be studied for a variety of management purposes and in a number of areas.[18] Costs may, for example, be examined for purposes of achieving control over marketing operations. This has been one of the major objectives in studying the behavior of costs in manufacturing plants. Marketing cost analysis for control purposes requires determination of cost standards for a particular marketing activity and feedback, in the form of cost data, on the question of how well or badly these standards are being adhered to in practice. Marketing costs can also be

---

[18] Costs may have to be determined for purposes other than management or financial reporting; for example, for legal purposes. Under such circumstances, costs are usually determined by whatever set of rules must be applied for the particular occasion. These rules may be different from either financial or managerial accounting practices.

investigated with planning in mind; budgeting future marketing operations would be an instance of this sort. New ways of using budgets have emerged in recent years. For example, flexible budgets have been developed which are designed to anticipate costs at different or changing levels of sales activity instead of at a single or static level. Finally, costs may be studied for decision-making or problem-solving purposes in day-to-day operating matters.

Scatter diagrams are frequently used in examining cost behavior. However, when a number of factors affect costs simultaneously, other more sophisticated techniques, such as multiple correlation analysis, may have to be used to depict the relationship.[19]

Cost analysis is appropriate in all of the areas of marketing in which management is able to exercise its influence: in pricing, advertising, selling, product planning, and location or channel matters.[20]

The nature of a particular marketing cost analysis is governed in part by the area of application or the segment chosen for study, but also by the purpose of the analysis and the level in the organization for which the analysis is being prepared.

The last point is one that is generally ignored and consequently accounts for another, and quite substantial, part of the difficulty in understanding and using marketing cost analysis.

Top management—e.g., the board of directors—of a firm faced with a decision on whether or not to build a new plant in order to produce more of a product presently in the firm's product line requires a different kind of analysis than does the sales manager of the same firm pondering the question of how best to utilize his sales force in order to move the company's current output of that product to market profitably. The board of directors needs to know if the product in question is currently profitable or is likely to be so in the future. The problem that faces it is essentially financial in character, and its time horizon is different from that of lower-level operating executives, such as sales managers. The board is faced with making a decision that involves the possibility of making commitments for additional resources at some future date. The matter of whether or not top management's desired rate-of-return-on-investment is being achieved, or is likely to be achieved, is of paramount importance. Under such circumstances, an appropriate marketing cost analysis would typically require a full allocation of costs. Long-run decisions of this sort, of course, also call for the application of the discounted-cash-flow method of analysis. This takes into account the time-value of money, and, frequently, a sensitivity analysis designed to show the impact of different parameter estimates upon the forecasted outcome. The board of directors is unlikely to authorize a new venture if indications are that it is likely to be unprofitable. The distinction between

---

[19] See, for example, John S. Chiu and Don T. DeCoster, "Multiple Product Costing by Multiple Correlation Analysis," *The Accounting Review*, Vol. XLI (October 1966), pp. 673–680.

[20] A detailed list of applications in each of these areas may be found in Heckert and Miner, *op. cit.*, p. 24, and B. R. Canfield, *Sales Administration* (Englewood Cliffs, N.J.: Prentice-Hall, Inc., 1961), pp. 606–610.

the net profit and the contribution margin approaches actually disappears in this situation because all costs can be viewed as variable in the long run.

The sales manager, at a lower level in the administrative structure of the firm, is faced with a different, short-run decision—the issue of the best way to utilize the resources presently committed to achieving the firm's goals. Minimizing losses may be an acceptable level of performance for the sales manager.

If all costs, including indirect costs, are allocated to the product by the sales manager, he is in danger of being misled. Arbitrary allocations of fixed indirect costs of, say, production facilities not being used to capacity may have the effect of making a large-volume, low-margin product appear unprofitable. The importance of joint or common costs and differences in costs that are not related to differences in volume are also sometimes hidden because the determination of profits by products usually involves the use of at least some allocation bases that are arbitrary. The reliability and usefulness to the sales manager of cost data determined in this manner depends, of course, on the extent and magnitude of these arbitrarily allocated joint costs.

The contribution margin approach, on the other hand, calls attention to the magnitude of common or joint costs and minimizes the possibility of action leading to the elimination of a product earning something in excess of its out-of-pocket costs. The net profit approach in this kind of situation is obviously inappropriate. When, in the short run, alternative courses of action are being compared, fixed or sunk costs are, for instance, irrelevant. These types of decisions call for the use of what accountants now refer to as the *relevant cost* approach.

For the sales manager it is a question of making an estimate of the probable future costs and revenues associated with each of the alternative courses of action open to him and choosing the one with the greatest expected payoff or the least loss. Costs that do not change should not be considered. In other words, the sales manager's primary concern is one of relative rather than absolute profitability.

Attention to the purpose and level in an organization for which a marketing cost analysis is made is also important for control purposes. Cost and revenue budgets for a sales manager and information about costs incurred and revenues generated by the sales force should not contain elements that are beyond the control or influence of the executive in charge. Responsibility and authority should be co-extensive. A manager has to be able to do something about costs and revenues if he is to be held responsible for results. Profits under the control of an executive are, as Dean has pointed out, "usually quite different from net profits ... since the latter get the impact of allocated overheads."[21]

Additional examples of the importance both of the purpose of a particular marketing cost analysis and of the administrative level for which it is prepared can be found in every area of marketing.

---

[21] Joel Dean, *op. cit.*, p. 41.

VII. Conclusions

We may conclude by recognizing that marketing cost analysis need not be avoided because of the controversy surrounding its use. By itself, it does not usually provide enough information upon which to take action, but it is an important and valuable managerial tool with which marketing managers should be familiar because of the many opportunities that exist to use it profitably. In fact, because there are so many opportunities to use marketing cost analysis, it is not surprising to find that there is an element of art as well as science involved in its application.

The perpetuation of the cost allocation controversy is due, first, to a failure on the part of some marketing writers to recognize the ambiguous nature of the term cost and, second, to the existence of a strong tendency on their part to take, albeit unwittingly, a basically financial accounting orientation toward marketing cost analysis. A managerial accounting orientation on the part of all marketers would help to resolve the controversy, along with recognition of the fact that cost information is useful for a variety of different purposes and that what constitutes an appropriate definition of the term cost depends on the purpose for which the information is gathered.

Successful utilization of marketing cost analysis requires analysts and managers alike to understand that the cost allocation issue is not an either/or question *or* a "six-of-one and a half-dozen of the other" proposition.

Effective marketing cost analysis requires, first, attention to the purpose or nature of the decision or plan to be made or the control process being established, and, second, consideration of the level in the organization for which the analysis is being prepared. Conventional financial accounting data on costs and revenues are useful in some circumstances for internal decision-making purposes but, more often than not, cost data must be modified and a different cost concept utilized for managerial purposes. It is not enough for such information to be accurate—it must also be relevant.

Finally, the importance of cost analysis techniques should not obscure the point that it is the behavioral consequences of marketing cost analysis that really matters. It is the *effect* of using either the net profit or contribution margin approach on management behavior that counts; and, the application of one approach or the other to the cost allocation problem does have the potential to affect the response of managers in particular planning, control, or decision-making situations.

Advertising Theory and the Capital Budgeting Model

2

Lawrence X. Tarpey

Advertising is perhaps one of the most important policy instruments the decision maker can use to encourage demand for his firm's products and to maintain its competitive position in the market. Broadly construed, advertising consists of those activities by which visual or oral messages are addressed to selected areas of the public for the purpose of informing and influencing them to buy products or services, or to be inclined favorably towards the sponsor of a message. As contrasted with publicity or propaganda, advertising messages are identified with the advertiser. Rarely will a company resort to a single means of sales effort, and so advertising is usually used in conjunction with personal selling and sales promotion.

For the purposes of this analysis two classes of advertising have significance—product advertising, which seeks to build the reputation of a specific seller's goods or brands and to promote their sale to dealers or ultimate consumers, and institutional advertising, which seeks to build consumer attitudes or dealer good-will to promote patronage, loyalty, and favor to the seller or brand. Generally, product advertising is brand advertising and represents direct action in nature while institutional advertising represents indirect action.[1] The differential characteristic is the immediacy of response.

Despite the differing response, from the firm's standpoint every advertising outlay is treated as a business expense.[2] Revenues expended for both types of demand creation activity are usually highly discretionary in nature and find their source in current revenues.[3] The advertising appropriation is often mechanically tied to short-run sales forecasts where the planning horizon varies in time from a month up to a year. Thus, the advertising budget is concerned with the short run and with current assets and expenses.

[1] Neil Borden and M. V. Marshall, *Advertising Management* (rev. ed.; Homewood, Ill.: Richard D. Irwin, 1959), p. 3. The authors make the point that product advertising can be indirect action also where the objective is to develop primary demand. However, this type of advertising does not exclusively benefit one company.

[2] Adolph Matz, O. J. Curry, and G. W. Frank, *Cost Accounting* (3rd ed.; Cincinnati: South Western Publishing Co., 1962), pp. 23–25. Accountants refer to general advertising outlays as period costs or revenue expenses.

[3] F. Shull, "The Advertising Appropriation in the Rubber Industry: A Study in Decision Making" (unpublished Ph.D. dissertation, Graduate School, Michigan State University, 1956), p. 234. Shull found that executives considered it bad business practice and refused to borrow, even on short-term credit, to pay for advertising.

Advertising as an Investment

Because certain advertising outlays are not intended to generate an immediate sales response, their benefits accrue to the firm over an extended period of time. This time lag, if it extends beyond the current accounting period, has the effect of making these expenditures investment outlays rather than expense items. In other words, it is possible to regard a particular advertising outlay as a capital good which depreciates over time.

Accounting Practice

In accounting practice, advertising that is prepaid is considered a *current* asset. The rationale is based on tradition and the assumption that the investment in these assets will be realized within the operating cycle of a business, or one year, whichever is longer. All assets not classified as current are considered to be noncurrent. Logically, advertising with long-term benefits should be classed as noncurrent assets, although traditional accounting practice has not treated them as such.

Economics of the Firm

Economic theory would seem to dictate that long-term advertising outlays be viewed as capital investments rather than as current business expenses. The definition of capital expenditures given by most authorities in the literature treats as crucial the length of time involved in the payback of the outlay. De Chazeau says, "Capital expenditures are cash outlays which take several years to produce an equivalent return of cash." Joel Dean speaks of capital in terms of a rate of turnover into cash of the commitment and considers that the time involved to return the initial cash outlay is the important criterion for determining whether an item belongs on the capital budget. Bierman and Smidt point out that the advertising program that is designed to improve a firm's image should be considered an investment because it is hoped that benefits will continue long after the money has been spent.[4] While economists (and accountants) probably consider the minimum time involved to be one year, the important point is that there is a substantial time lapse from the time of the initial outlay until all benefits are realized.

What Research Shows

Economists have attempted to deal theoretically with the question of treating delayed advertising response as a capital investment. Benjamin, Jolly, and Maitland have attempted to construct mathematical models and to run experiments that would predict and measure response to advertising over time. They found that advertising response rises exponentially over time to its maximum, then decays exponentially

---

[4] M. G. De Chazeau, *The Regularization of Business Investment* (Princeton, N.J.: National Bureau of Economic Research, 1954), p. 37; Joel Dean, *Managerial Economics* (Englewood Cliffs, N.J.: Prentice-Hall, Inc., 1951); J. R. Meyer and Edwin Kuh, *The Investment Decision: An Empirical Study* (Cambridge, Mass.: Harvard University Press, 1957), p. 6; and Harold Bierman and S. Smidt, *The Capital Budgeting Decision* (New York: The Macmillan Co., 1960), p. 3.

to some "steady state" value. Jastrum has attempted a purely theoretical treatment of distributed lags in the effect of advertising expenditures on a firm's revenue, but his research has not been tested empirically.[5] Kuehn, in a very complete and complicated marketing model that treats advertising as an investment, established the rule: "Those products should be advertised that will result in a return on capital invested equal to or greater than the returns from other possible investments, such as new equipment or research." Vidale and Wolfe develop a similar model in which advertising is viewed as a form of investment, and the method of analysis proceeds to find that rate of discount which will equate cost and total advertising response, defined as the rate of return on investment for the product. Another analysis of test market results, using a Markov process model, has resulted in a more accurate determination of the payout period in which the initial advertising investment is recouped.[6] Telser has developed a mode of analysis for measuring the economic return of promotion expenditures when the advertising outlay is viewed as a capital investment made for the purpose of purchasing an asset.[7]

While these attempts at analysis are encouraging, the unsatisfactory results are equally discouraging. So far none of the researchers or model builders have approached the problem directly. Very little thought has been given to applying a genuine capital budgeting model to the situation. Understanding any business problem must precede its solution; because a model constitutes a well-defined or analytical statement of the problem it is reasonable and logical to use this approach to advertising expenditures. This approach can help to describe the problem so that all of the variables, assumptions, limiting conditions, and so forth are made explicit and are therefore more readily understood.

Developing and Using a Model

Some important new developments in statistical decision theory suggest the possibility of extending formal analysis of uncertainty to business problems that now lack analytical frameworks. Bayesian statistics applies to decision problems in which the outcome of a decision is uncertain and in which some judgment can be made regarding the preference for one outcome over another. The advertising investment decision can certainly be viewed as one that is made in the presence of uncertainty.

To date no research has attempted to fit any of these existing statistical decision

---

[5] B. Benjamin, W. P. Jolly, and J. Maitland, "Operational Research and Advertising: Theories of Response," *Operational Research Quarterly*, II (December, 1960), 205–218. Others have tried to explain the investment aspects of advertising from the standpoint of macroeconomics. One of the best discussions can be found in E. A. Lever, *Advertising and Economic Theory* (New York: Oxford University Press, 1947), Chap. 7. See also R. W. Jastrum, "A Treatment of Distributed Lags in the Theory of Advertising Expenditure," *Journal of Marketing*, XX (July, 1955), pp. 36–46.

[6] The preceding models are from A. A. Kuehn, "A Model for Budgeting Advertising," in *Mathematical Models and Methods in Marketing*, Y. Bass and others (Homewood, Ill.: Richard D. Irwin, 1961), pp. 108, 315–52, and 361.

[7] Lester G. Telser, "Advertising and Cigarettes," *Journal of Political Economy*, LXX (October, 1962), pp. 471–99.

theory models to this particular problem. Perhaps the closest example to be found in the literature is Frank Bass' article, "Marketing Research Expenditures—A Decision Model" (*Journal of Business*, January, 1963). Here Bass develops a decision model that enables the businessman to utilize all the available information pertinent to the decision and to summarize it in probability assignments and conditional profit estimates. This study attempts to develop a formal analysis that provides a decision rule for each possible outcome of proposed marketing research studies. However, this marketing research expenditure model might easily be adapted to include advertising expenditures.

Many difficulties inhere in the problem of constructing a model as a frame of reference in which this general problem of advertising investments can be treated. The purpose here is not to reach a final solution to the problem but to define and to refine most of the basic questions that the decision maker must face and resolve if advertising outlays are ever going to be placed in the capital budget.

Capital budgeting can be defined as a systematic procedure designed to help management select those capital expenditure projects that will tend to increase the present net worth of the stockholders. This involves collecting information about possible capital expenditure projects, estimating the profitability of each project, and rejecting those that are unprofitable.

What the Model Assumes

As a plan or framework to guide the choices of business executives, the traditional capital budgeting model makes two important assumptions: (1) that future data (for example, cash flows) are known with some degree of certainty; and (2) that the decision maker desires a set of rules to enable him to make profit-maximizing decisions. It is important to know whether these two assumptions are valid before proceeding to apply a rather orthodox model to the unorthodox problem of advertising investments.

Certainty of Data

In practice, the problem of estimating the decision parameters of any economic model is difficult; but in the case of long-term promotional expenditures the task is almost impossible. Two important facts required for any capital budgeting model are the cost of capital and cash proceeds. Traditionally the firm secures funds to support its advertising and other sales promotion campaigns by means of internal capital rationing, but this procedure may be poor economics if the cost of those retained earnings is greater than the expected rate of return on the promotional project.[8] To reject a long-term promotional project simply because the cash position at the time does not justify the expenditure may also be poor economics. The rate

---

[8] The rate of cost of retained earnings is considered an opportunity cost concept—the rate of return that could be earned by investing those funds in their next best use, whether inside or outside the firm; or the rate of return the stockholder could receive if the earnings instead were paid in dividends.

of return on the promotional project may justify its inclusion in the planned capital expenditures, even though external financing is necessary to supplement the capital budget.

Cash flows resulting from advertising expenditures are usually more difficult to measure than those resulting from outlays on plant and equipment. Advertisements, for example, are costs that produce sales and revenue. Thus their economic justification is not independent of the outlay itself because an accurate estimate of cash flows from any advertisement necessarily involves a sales forecast; but sales are partly a result of the thing being measured—in this case, advertising. In economic terms, this means that the marginal revenue productivity of an advertisement is not a simple function of its dollar cost.

The high degree of uncertainty of dollar returns from promotional expenditures further complicates the decision. Advertising dollars are usually appropriated and budgeted on the basis of certain assumptions about competitive behavior, business conditions, and so forth. Unfortunately, many of the economic variables that can affect the promotional elasticity of a product cannot be effectively controlled by the advertising manager, and the resulting uncertainty adds an element of risk to advertising investments.

Maximization of Profit

While economic theorists have found that the goal of profit maximization has the practical characteristics of rationality and measurability, the hierarchy of goals in a business may or may not include it. In fact, marketing managers tend to view the effects of their promotional decisions in terms of their impact on sales rather than profits. Consequently, advertising expenditures (depending on the type of advertising) are normally justified in the light of such considerations as increases in market share, units sold, tonnage shipped, readership, and so forth. To convert into profit any of these incremental sales benefits that flow from specific promotional outlays is a formidable task indeed, involving not only the problem of determining which sales benefits are the direct result of the expenditure, but also of converting them into a net cash flow that can be plugged into a present value or a yield formula. Unless this identification and conversion process is undertaken, the economic worth of that promotional outlay cannot be accurately measured or, more important, precisely compared with alternative choices.

Questions the Model Must Answer

Ideally, for a capital budgeting model to be useful in making decisions about advertisement investments, it must provide the businessman with the means for answering three fundamental questions:

1. How much money will be needed for all investments including these long-lived promotions in the subsequent budget period?

2. How much money will be available, from what sources and at what cost?

3. How should the available money be allocated among alternatives?

The first of these complex questions is a capital demand problem; the second is a supply problem; and the last is a rationing problem.

The Demand Question

If long-term advertising expenditures are to be treated as capital budget items, the firm must include them in its survey of anticipated needs for capital. These capital investment, or search, surveys are often phrased in terms of need, as: How much new capital will be needed in order to accomplish a specific marketing task such as increasing per capita sales in a specified geographic area? Thus, in terms of promotional outlays, need and demand become approximately the same. The intensity of demand for promotional capital must be measured not by its earnings, but by the marketing tasks assigned to it. However, as pointed out earlier, meaningful economic analysis will require the decision maker to translate these tasks into some sort of dollar earnings flow.

Measuring Investment Worth.   Most of the writers who have investigated the problems of treating advertising as a capital outlay have restricted their discussions to the decision of how to measure investment worth. All of them have avoided the question of converting sales results into net cash flows attributable to the advertisement, although this figure is vital for measuring the worth of any investment.

A review of the literature on capital budgeting will show some of the important ways of measuring and ranking investments:

1. Rate of return
2. Present value method
3. The payback period
4. Proceeds per dollar of outlay
5. The payback reciprocal
6. Return on book investment (accountant's method)
7. Capitalized earning rate (engineer's method).

Unfortunately, certain authorities disagree as to which method is theoretically correct. Dean advocates the rate of return or yield method, Bierman and Smidt argue for the present value method, and Spencer and Siegelman claim that the payout reciprocal is a good rule-of-thumb method for approximating the theoretically correct measure of an investment's worth, pointing out that businessmen have used it successfully for many years.[9]

---

[9] Dean, *Managerial Economics*, p. 10; Bierman and Smidt, *The Capital Budgeting Decision*; and Milton H. Spencer and Louis Siegelman, *Managerial Economics* (Homewood, Ill.: Richard D. Irwin, 1959), pp. 389–90. See also: Trefftzs and Dilbeck of the University of Southern California recently surveyed over 100 firms on the West Coast regarding their capital budgeting practices. They found that most of the firms had an established review procedure but lacked uniform formulas for calculating returns on investment. See "Some Current Practices in Capital Budgeting" (Los Angeles, Calif.: University of Southern California, 1964).

Measuring the economic worth of an investment requires certain information, no matter which method is employed. One must know (1) the size of the expenditure and how it is to be spent over time (that is, in a single time period or over successive time periods); (2) the size and time distribution of the cash inflows resulting from the investment; and (3) the cost of capital that the firm is using to finance the project in question. For example, under the present value method, if the rate of discount, equating the present value of outlays with the present value of cash earnings over the life of the project, is less than the cost of capital, the project should be rejected. With advertising investments any of the above measurement techniques can be used only if the required data are available. Generally, they are not.

Dependency.   Advertising investment outlays, unlike many other capital expenditures, are seldom independent investments. The sales promoting ability of an advertising dollar is a function of other types of expenditures, such as sales training programs, which complement the advertising program. The expected benefits from advertising expenditures affect cash flows of other investments in the following way. The purchase of new plant or equipment may be made to depend in a very large part on the firm's forecast of future sales, which in turn are largely a function of promotional effort made in behalf of the commodities in question.[10] A firm's selling efforts can prove to be of little or no value unless backed up by an adequate sales force and inventories. In this instance advertising and personal selling not only complement each other but are mutually interdependent.

Another aspect of dependency relates to the need for promotion or selling effort in launching new products or maintaining demand for old ones. Product decisions are not usually made independently of the marketing department, because the revenues needed to provide the firm with a return on its production facilities are derived from the sale of the product. Thus, production and promotion expenses tend to be so interdependent as to be of a joint nature.

The Supply Question

Most firms have two general sources of funds: internal and external. The internal funds are generated by current operations and appear on the accounting records as noncash expenditures (for example, depreciation) and as retained earnings. Outside capital is derived from the sale of bonds, notes, mortgages, assets, or equity stock. Working capital is generally not considered part of the capitalization of the firm.

Traditionally, current operating revenues are the source of advertising funds. However, if advertising expenditures of a certain type are to be placed in the capital budget, then the decision maker must now consider external sources of funds as well as internal; otherwise, certain advertising projects with a high rate of return

---

[10] Stepping up the total volume of advertising in the maturity phase of a product's life cycle can have the effect of sustaining market growth at the expense of a more rapid fall in later sales. In this way it is possible for advertising to contribute to overestimating production capacity and thus lead to unused facilities at a later time.

may not be undertaken because the firm does not have the necessary liquid assets to finance them. When the firm thus ignores external sources of capital, it runs the risk of rejecting some very profitable investment opportunities.

The Rationing Question

The capital rationing problem is one of matching supply against demand. Here the decision maker is forced to rank investments according to a standard of profitability or urgency and to eliminate those which cannot meet the minimum standard for acceptance. Clearly, to compare the purchase of a new piece of machinery with the purchase of a promotional campaign to improve a brand's image is to compare unlike objects; a common denominator, profitability, is needed. But measurements of the dollar and cents benefits that will accrue to the firm from the promotional outlay are at best difficult and risky. The need for better measurement techniques is obvious. Development of decision theory using probability techniques is a hopeful breakthrough in this area.

Related Problems

Another difficulty that arises when a company attempts to treat certain advertising outlays as capital budget items is in the area of income tax structure. It is not unreasonable to assume that the IRS would consider these outlays on an accounting base with other types of investments, and would require the firm to develop an acceptable depreciation formula for advertisement investments.

Also, when calculating the worth of an advertising investment, the decision maker must estimate the promotional elasticity of the intended expenditure in relation to its effects on the firm's production costs. Market saturation levels, product life cycle, competitive advertising, and distributors' reactions are some other factors that need to be estimated. By placing long-term advertising projects in the capital budget, the firm takes some authority and responsibility for these decisions out of the hands of the marketing department, while still relying on that department for information. Although these possibilities do not exhaust all of the difficulties that might face the firm as a consequence of treating some promotional outlays as investments, they do illustrate the range and types of problems to be anticipated.

The idea of placing certain types of promotional items in the capital budget is revolutionary, if not completely alien to many business executives. At this juncture it is merely an idea and not a recommendation. Before seriously suggesting that such a plan be implemented or attempted certain steps must be taken.

First, both middle and top management need to be made aware of these new ideas and then must be prepared to think them through honestly and critically. Practically speaking, this means that management at all levels must be willing to abandon traditional methods of financing and managing its promotional programs, if necessary. In other words, conventional wisdom must give way to creative innovation if the economic promise of such innovation—discounted by some risk factor—exceeds the dollar return from the old ways of doing things.

Second, much more research is needed in this general problem area. The primary purpose of this article is to explore the questions of whether long-term promotional outlays can be fitted into a capital budgeting framework; its effect should have been to raise some important questions in the readers' minds. To find answers to many of these questions will require studious research. For example, treating certain types of advertising expenditures as capital items will probably involve some organizational changes; budget proposals for the advertising program will normally originate in the advertising department. The character, extent, and impact of these changes can only be conjectured until serious research yields some definite findings.

This general problem of advertising investments is, in fact, constructed of many smaller problems. Before any of them can be resolved each must be properly identified and defined. The task is a serious challenge which must be taken up not only by the academic researcher but by the intelligent business executive as well.

Managing Distribution Costs for Better Profit Performance

3

Douglas M. Lambert   Howard M. Armitage

In recent years economic uncertainty and inflation have combined to seriously erode the real profit performance of most businesses. Consequently, it has become necessary for the top-management team to investigate alternative avenues of revenue generation and cost reduction. Many firms have discovered that few areas offer the potential for profit improvement that can be found in the distribution function. In many companies where distribution has not been managed as an integrated system, successful implementation of the integrated physical distribution concept can lead to significant improvements in the bottom line.[1] The foundation of the integrated physical distribution management concept is total-cost analysis, which is required if the potential savings are to be realized. However, many opportunities are being missed, and many less-than-optimal decisions are being made, because of the lack of (1) an accurate cost data base, and (2) an information system to measure the total corporate impact of changes in the distribution area.

This article indicates the impact of inadequate distribution-cost information on corporate profitability and illustrates how these deficiencies can be overcome. A description of the systems approach to management of distribution activities is followed by an examination of the type of costs and the system necessary for successful implementation of the integrated physical distribution management concept.

For many years, physical distribution was viewed as a fragmented and often uncoordinated set of activities. Decisions in traffic, for example, were made in isolation of their effects on warehousing and inventory levels. Efforts to improve customer service were accomplished at the expense of inventory-carrying costs, and channel decisions were made without knowing their effect on total corporate profitability. However, the notion that a firm's total distribution costs could be reduced, customer service improved, and interdepartmental conflicts substantially lessened

---

[1] For a good review of the integrated physical distribution concept and for the economic benefits resulting from institutional coordination, see James L. Heskett, "Sweeping Changes in Distribution," *Harvard Business Review*, March-April 1973, pp. 123–132.

by coordinating distribution activities has emerged as an important concept. This concept has become known as "integrated physical distribution management" and, because of its tremendous potential for cost savings, has quickly become one of the hottest topics in business.

Total-cost analysis is the key to managing the physical distribution function. Exhibit 1 illustrates the elements of total logistical costs; the arrows indicate the trade-offs that must be evaluated when estimating customer-service levels, purchasing policies, transportation policies, warehousing, and setting inventory levels. At any given customer-service level, management should minimize total logistical cost rather than attempt to minimize the cost of each component. This is critical because attempts to reduce individual costs are often accomplished at the expense of increased total cost. For example, storing all finished-goods inventory in a small number of distribution centers helps minimize warehousing costs but leads to an increase in freight expense. Similarly, savings resulting from large-order purchases may be entirely offset by greater inventory-carrying costs. In a nutshell, reductions in one set of costs invariably increase the costs of other logistical components. Effective management and real cost savings can be accomplished only by viewing distribution as an integrated system and minimizing its total cost.

Analyzing total costs in lieu of the traditional emphasis on individual component performance leads to the ability to make cost trade-off decisions. For example, profits can be enhanced if the increase in inventory-carrying costs and field warehousing costs is less than the savings obtained from the lower associated freight costs. Similarly, increased customer-service levels should be justified by comparing the additional profit contribution to the additional costs of providing such service levels.

The total-cost concept, with its emphasis on trade-off analysis, has provided practitioners with a very useful framework to help guide the management of distribution activities. However, while the concept has been widely accepted, its full potential has yet to be reached. Increasingly, it is becoming clear that the cost analysis essential for implementation of the integrated physical distribution management concept has not been successfully carried out in industry. If trade-offs that lead to profit improvements are to be made, it is imperative that management be able to account for the costs associated with each component and to know how changes in such components affect total cost and profits.

Case Studies

As the cost of distribution continues to rise, this requirement becomes increasingly critical. Depending on the nature of the company, estimates of distribution costs ranging from 15% to 50% of total sales are not uncommon. However, these are at best only educated guesses since they are usually based on costs incorrectly computed by management. From a corporate standpoint, the continued inability to track and manage distribution costs means missed opportunities and expensive mistakes. The following four case examples will serve to highlight these issues.

Case 1—The Effect of Freight Averages on Customer/Product Profitability
Freight costs are a major expense in most companies, yet few attempt to track their actual freight costs by customer. Those that do, tend to rely on the use of national freight averages. These averages, however, do not indicate the actual costs of moving each product to its destination; thus customer profitability is wrong.

EXHIBIT 1. Cost trade-offs required in the logistics system

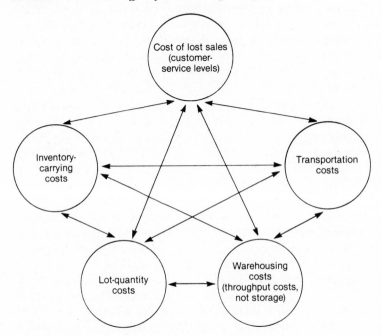

Note: Total costs = Inventory carrying costs + Lot quantity costs + Warehousing costs + Transportation costs + Costs of lost sales. The arrows indicate the interactions between sets of costs. Trade-offs are made between the various cost areas with the objective of minimizing total costs.

Source: Adapted from Douglas M. Lambert and Bernard J. LaLonde, "Inventory Carrying Cost," *Management Accounting,* August 1976, p. 33.

   To illustrate, Company A used a national average freight rate calculated by taking the total corporate transportation bill as a percentage of total sales revenue. To determine product profitability, the same cost (4% of sales) was applied to products moving by common carrier from Chicago to New York and from Chicago to Los Angeles as that used on deliveries in the Chicago area, where the company's own vehicles made the deliveries.

The fallacy of this approach is threefold: First, management was unable to determine the profitability of individual products or customers; the averaging process hid the fact that delivery to distant customers may be highly unprofitable, thereby reducing the overall corporate rate of return. Second, using the same percentage rate for all products ignores the impact of product characteristics, such as weight and cube, on freight rates and, consequently, on product and customer profitability. Finally, a trade-off analysis between the cost of the current system and that of an alternative system, where carload shipments go first to a regional warehouse on the West Coast and then on to the customers in that market, is made more difficult if actual customer delivery costs are not known. The result of simplifying the allocation of freight costs in this company led to lower overall profit performance.

Case 2—Inability to Distinguish Between Fixed and Variable Costs

Company B utilized a product-reporting statement that deducted manufacturing, distribution, and marketing costs from sales to arrive at a gross profit for each product. The profit statement was used for making decisions about the acceptability of product performance, the assignment of marketing support, and the deletion of products. The allocation of distribution costs to each product was carried out on an X, Y, Z basis, in which the X products are allocated a certain amount of distribution cost, the Y products twice as much as X, and the Z products three times as much as X. These allocations contained costs such as warehouse labor, supplies, and freight expense, which varied with activity, and costs such as corporate allocations, depreciation, and administration costs of the corporate fleet, that remained fixed irrespective of activity levels.

Several of the company's products, including one that was among its top 10 in terms of sales performance, were showing negative profits and hence were candidates for being discontinued. An analysis revealed, however, that a large proportion of the total distribution cost (as well as some manufacturing cost) was fixed and would not be saved if the products were eliminated. In fact, discontinuing these products would cause total corporate profitability to be much worse than before, since all revenues related to these products would disappear but all of the costs would not. The only costs saved would be the variable ones. The fixed costs (which in this case were substantial) would be incurred irrespective of product additions or deletions. In fact, if the products were discontinued, the existing fixed costs would be redistributed to the remaining products, leading to the very real possibility that even more products would appear to be unprofitable.

Furthermore, the X, Y, Z classification method was found to be subject to wide swings in accuracy. Category Z products often took less time to store, pick from warehouse stock, and ship than did Category X products, even though they were being allocated three times the distribution cost. In effect, because of the distribution costing system, the company had inaccurate information about product profitability and hence total performance suffered.

Case 3—The Pitfalls of Allocation

Most distribution costing systems are in their infancy and rely heavily on allocations to determine the performance of segments such as products, customers, territories, divisions, or functions. Company C provides an example of such allocations that led to erroneous decision making and loss of corporate dollars. The firm is a multidivision corporation that manufactured and sold high-margin pharmaceuticals as well as a number of lower margin packaged-goods products. The company maintained a number of field warehouse locations managed by corporate staff. These climate-controlled facilities were designed for the pharmaceutical business and required security and housekeeping practices that far exceeded those necessary for normal packaged goods. To fully use the facilities, however, the company encouraged nonpharmaceutical divisions to store their products in these distribution centers.

Although the costs of operating the warehouses were largely fixed, corporate policy was to allocate costs to user divisions on the basis of the square footage occupied. Due to the pharmaceutical warehousing requirements, this charge was relatively high. The corporate divisions were managed on a decentralized profit-center basis, and one division's distribution executive realized that he could obtain similar services at lower cost to his division by using a public warehouse. For this reason, he withdrew his products from the corporate facilities and began to use public warehouses. Although the volume of product handled and stored in the corporate distribution center decreased significantly, relatively little savings were realized in terms of the distribution center's total costs. This was because of the high proportion of fixed costs. Consequently, the company allocated approximately the same cost over fewer users, which made it even more attractive for the other user divisions to change to public warehouses to obtain lower rates. The result was higher, not lower, *total* company warehousing costs. The corporate warehousing costs were primarily fixed and would not change significantly, whether the space was occupied or not. When the nonpharmaceutical divisions moved to public warehouses, the company continued to incur the same expenses for its own warehouses, as well as the additional public warehousing charges. In effect, the distribution costing system motivated divisional distribution managers to act in a manner that was not in the best interests of the company, and total costs escalated.

Case 4—Control Deficiencies

Control of costs and motivation of key personnel are critical in every business activity. Distribution is no exception. However, the control concepts so successfully utilized by other functional areas have not been widely adopted for distribution activities. In some cases the argument has been advanced that distribution is different from other disciplines and cannot be evaluated with the same tools. In most cases, however, the application has never been attempted. A particular case in point is the application of the flexible-budgeting concept.

Company D maintained an annual budget for its branch warehousing costs. These costs consisted of variable and fixed expenses. Each month, the budget was divided by 12 and compared to the actual costs of that month. Differences from the budget were recorded as variances on which management took action. However, the sales of Company D were seasonal and some months were far more active than others. During peak periods, the variances were virtually always unfavorable, while during slow months, the variances were favorable. Productivity ratios, on the other hand, gave different results. During peak periods productivity calculations were high, and during slower periods these ratios dropped. In such a situation, neither cost control nor employee motivation is being adequately addressed.

Dividing the budget by 12 and comparing it to actual costs means that management is trying to compare costs at two different levels of operation—the planned budget and the actual budget. However, the costs should be the same only if actual activity is equal to 1/12 of the planned activity. A far more acceptable approach is to recognize that a proportion of the costs are variable and should go up or down with the level of output. Flexing the budget to reflect what the incurred costs ought to have been at the operating level allows a true measure of efficiency and productivity and provides more meaningful evaluations of individual performance.

These examples are by no means unique. A recent survey of 300 North American firms revealed that the individual cost components, such as inventory-carrying costs; transportation costs by channel, product, or customer; order-processing costs; warehousing costs; and production lot-quantity costs necessary to implement distribution cost trade-off analyses were generally unavailable.[2] In fact, not a single firm reported

EXHIBIT 2. *Controlling distribution activities*

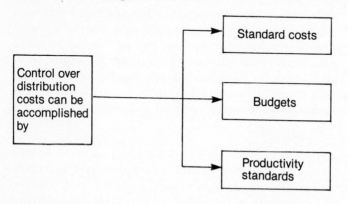

[2] D. M. Lambert and J. T. Mentzer, "Is Integrated Physical Distribution Management a Reality?" *Journal of Business Logistics*, vol. 2, no. 1, 1980, pp. 18–27.

the availability of all the cost components. This lack of adequate data makes analysis extremely difficult and leads to the conclusion that the distribution costing system does not readily lend itself to effective distribution management, if such effectiveness can be defined as the ability to make the right operational and strategic choices. The next section discusses how many of these problems can be overcome.

Controlling Distribution Costs

Abnormal levels of costs can only be detected and controlled if we know what they ought to be for various levels of activities. As shown in Exhibit 2, distribution performance can be monitored by using standard costs, budgets, and/or productivity standards. These tools can be used alone or in combination with each other.

Standard Costs

Control of costs through predetermined standards and flexible budgets is the most comprehensive type of control system available. In essence, this method represents a frontal assault on distribution costs because it attempts to determine what the costs should be under certain operating conditions. Standards can be and have been set for such warehouse operations as stock picking, loading, receiving, replenishing, storing, and packing merchandise. In addition, they have been successfully utilized in order processing, transportation, and even clerical functions.

However, the use of standards has not been widespread. In part, this is due to the widespread belief that distribution costs are inherently quite different from costs found in other areas of the business. While there may be some merit to this argument, distribution activities are, by nature, repetitive operations, and as such lend themselves to control by standards. A more compelling reason why standard costs have not achieved widespread acceptance is that few attempts have been made to install such systems. This phenomenon is directly attributable to the fact that only recently has the importance of distribution cost control been recognized. This is unfortunate because the management accountants and industrial engineers of most firms have a wealth of experience in installing standard costs in the production area, which with some effort could be expanded into distribution.

A standard tells management the expected cost of performing selected activities and allows for comparisons to determine whether operating inefficiencies have occurred. For example, Exhibit 3 illustrates a type of report that is useful at the operating level. In addition, the costs of distribution activities can be aggregated by department, division, function, or total; compared to their standard; and included as part of a regular weekly or monthly performance report.

One such level of aggregation that would be of interest to a company president is shown in Exhibit 4. This report allows the president to see at a glance why targeted net income has not been reached. On one hand, there is a difference due to ineffectiveness that simply indicates the net income that the company has lost

EXHIBIT 3. Weekly pick-operation summary

Items picked during week	12,500
Hours accumulated on picking activities	290
Standard hours allowed for picks performed	250
Variation in hours (variance)	40
Standard cost per labor hour	$ 7
Variation in cost due to inefficiency	$ 280★

★Cost was $280 over budget because of 40 picking hours in excess of standard hours allowed.

because of its inability to meet its budgeted level of sales. On the other hand, there is also an inefficiency factor. This factor indicates that at the level of sales actually achieved, the income should have been $32,800. The difference between $32,800 and the actual income of $25,200 is the variation due to inefficiency.

Budgets

Conceptually, there is little doubt regarding the general superiority of standard costs for control. However, there will be times when the use of standards is inappropriate. This is particularly true in situations that have essentially nonrepetitive tasks and for which work–unit measurements are difficult to establish. In these situations control can still be achieved through budgetary practices. However, the extent to which the budget is successful depends on whether individual cost behavior patterns can be predicted, and whether the budget can be flexed to reflect changes in operating conditions.

Most distribution budgets are static; that is, they are a plan developed for a budgeted level of output. If actual activity happens to be the same as budgeted, a realistic comparison of costs can be made, and control will be effective. However, seldom is this the case. Seasonal patterns or internal factors will invariably lead to different levels of activity. The efficiency at these various levels can be determined only if the reporting system can compare the actual costs with what they should have been at the operating level achieved. In a warehousing example, for instance, the estimated or budgeted level of activity may be 1,000 line items per month. The actual level of activity, however, may be only 750. Comparing the budgeted costs of 1,000 line items against the actual costs at 750 leads to the spurious conclusion that the operation has been efficient since items such as overtime, temporary help, packing, postage, and order processing all will be less than budget. A flexible budget, on the other hand, indicates what the costs should have been at the 750–line–order level of activity, and a true dollar measure of efficiency results.

Clearly, the key to successful implementation of a flexible budget lies in the analysis of cost behavior patterns. To date, little of this analysis has been carried

EXHIBIT 4. *Segment analysis (could be products, customers, geographical, divisions, total, etc.)*

	Budget	Variance due to ineffectiveness	Standard allowed for output level achieved	Explanation of variation from budget	
				Variance due to inefficiency	Actual results
Net sales	$200,000	$40,000	$160,000	—	$160,000
Cost of goods sold (variable manufacturing cost)	120,000	24,000	96,000	—	96,000
Manufacturing contribution	80,000	16,000	64,000	—	64,000
Marketing and physical-distribution costs (variable with segment)	24,000	4,800	19,200	7,600	26,800
Segment contribution margin	56,000	11,200	44,800	7,600	37,200
Assignable nonvariable costs (fixed costs directly attributable to segment)	12,000	—	12,000	—	12,000
Segment controllable margin	$ 44,000	$11,200	$ 32,800	$7,600	$ 25,200

Assumption: Actual sales revenue decreased as a result of lower volume. The average price per unit sold remained the same. (If the average price per unit changes, then an additional variance—the marketing variance—can be computed.)

Difference in income = $18,800 ($44,000 − $25,200)

Explained by:

Ineffectiveness (inability to reach target-sales objective) $11,200

Inefficiency at operating level of $160,000 7,600

$18,800

out in a distribution context. Once again, the expertise of the management accountant and industrial engineer can be invaluable in applying such tools as the high/low method, scatter-diagram techniques, and regression analysis to delineate those costs that vary from those that do not. All of these techniques utilize previous cost data to determine a variable rate per unit of activity and a total fixed-cost component. Once this is accomplished, the flexible budget for control becomes a reality; although it should be pointed out that, unlike a standard, the techniques are based on past cost behavior patterns that undoubtedly contain a number of inefficiencies. The predicted measure of cost, therefore, may not be a measure of what the activity should cost, but an estimate of what it will cost based on the results of a previous period.

Productivity Standards

Distribution costs also can be controlled by the use of productivity ratios. These ratios take the form of

$$\text{productivity} = \frac{\text{measure of output}}{\text{measure of input}}$$

$$P = \frac{MO}{MI}$$

For example, the relationship between orders shipped and labor hours might be expressed as

$$\frac{\text{number of orders shipped this period}}{\text{number of labor hours worked this period}}$$

or

$$\frac{OS}{H}$$

Although the use of productivity measures has found widespread acceptance in the distribution function, these measures are subject to three common deficiencies:

1. The actual productivity measure calculated is seldom compared to a productivity standard. For instance, the previous example indicates the ratio of the number of orders shipped to labor hours this period, but does not indicate what that relationship *ought* to be.
2. The fixed and variable elements are seldom delineated, so that a productivity measure may go up or down solely due to activity. This results in a measure of utilization, not of efficiency.
3. Productivity measures are expressed in terms of physical units and are seldom translated into the dollar effect of efficient or inefficient operations.

Despite these limitations, productivity measures are useful indicators, particularly in the absence of standard costs and flexible budgets. Not only do they provide operating guidelines; they are also easily understood by employees and management alike. Nevertheless, it is not easy to calculate the dollar magnitude of changes in productivity measures, and thus it is difficult to gauge the savings that can be generated through more efficient operations.

Sound Distribution Decisions

While substantial savings can be generated when management is able to compare its actual costs against a set of predetermined standards or budgets, even greater opportunities for profit improvement exist in the area of decision making. However, the ability to choose between such issues as hiring an additional transport or enlarging the company's fleet; increasing deliveries or increasing inventories; consolidating warehouses or expanding field facilities; and adding or deleting territories, products, or customers requires a knowledge of how well existing segments are currently performing and what revenues and costs will change with alternative choices. This implies two ingredients: (1) a system that can aggregate data in such a way that routine information on profitability of individual customers, product lines, territories, or channels can be obtained; and (2) a system in which data have been analyzed by fixed and variable components so that incremental costs and revenues of various strategies can be developed. There is a great deal of work being done in this information-processing area that lends itself to the type of data-reporting schemes suggested. For example, one promising data-base system is a central storage system where source documents are fed into a data base in coded form.[3] Inputs can be coded according to function, subfunction, territory, product, revenue or expense, channel, or a host of other possibilities. When combined with the computer, the system is capable of filing large amounts of data and allows rapid aggregation and retrieval of various modules of information for decision analysis. With this information, management is in a position to evaluate the profitability of various segments. In addition, the data base permits the user to stimulate trade-off situations and determine the effect of proposed system and strategic changes on total cost.

Conclusion

The integrated physical distribution management concept was first introduced almost two decades ago. Today, many of the obstacles confronting full implementation of the concept appear to have been removed. However, because of the lack of an adequate data base and information system, much of the critical cost analysis essential to implement the concept has not been carried out; hence the savings and profit improvement promised have not been fully realized.

---

[3] F. H. Mossman, W. J. E. Crissy, and P. M. Fischer, *Financial Dimensions of Marketing Management* (New York, John Wiley & Sons, 1978).

Corporations have spared little expense in developing, maintaining, and improving the reporting systems in the area of production and finance. Further improvements to these systems, however, seem to offer only marginal returns. On the other hand, investments in productivity improvements in distribution are currently estimated to return their annual investment 18 times.[4] Surely, it is time to give some concerted effort to the distribution costing system and to cash in on these returns.

---

[4] A. T. Kearney, *Measuring Productivity in Physical Distribution* (Chicago, National Council of Physical Distribution Management, 1978).

The Impact of Inflation Accounting on Marketing Decisions

4

Frederick E. Webster, Jr.   James A. Largay III   Clyde P. Stickney

Inflation has become a persistent and increasingly important fact of economic life in the United States in recent years. The Consumer Price Index (CPI) compiled by the U.S. Bureau of Labor Statistics increased approximately 25% in the five-year period from 1967 to 1972, roughly 5% per year. From 1972 to 1977, the CPI increased by almost 50%, an average annual rate approaching 10%. The annual rate of inflation in 1978 was more than 9% (Bureau of Economic Statistics, Inc. 1979) and is reported to have been approximately 13% in 1979. Press reports for the first quarter of 1980 suggest that inflation was running in excess of an annual rate of 18%. Significant price inflation, once regarded as a minor economic problem that appeared from time to time in an overheated economy, now appears to be a chronic phenomenon that must be accounted for in economic and financial decision making.

The Financial Accounting Standards Board, the accounting rule-making body, issued a pronouncement in September 1979 requiring supplemental disclosures of the effects of inflation on the financial statements of most large publicly held firms beginning with the 1979 annual reports (FASB 1979). Those 1979 annual reports leave little doubt that these changes in financial reporting requirements will have a direct impact on the managerial assessment of specific products, markets, and businesses as well as on marketing decisions relating to pricing, service, promotion, and distribution. To give just one example, in the 1979 Annual Report of the General Electric Company (1980), Reginald H. Jones, Chairman of the Board and Chief Executive Officer, noted:

> Severe inflation distorts the financial reporting of business, giving the illusion of soaring profits when, in fact, real profits—profits stripped of their inflationary increments—have failed to keep pace with the rising costs of replacing buildings, machinery and equipment, maintaining inventories, and supporting research and development.

A management made cognizant of the impact of inflation on reported sales and income figures undoubtedly will begin to evaluate decisions relating to products, customer selection, pricing, service, credit and accounts receivable, promotion, distribution, and inventory policies in the new light shed by these inflation-adjusted figures. The purpose of our article is to show, through the use of examples, how

Reprinted with permission from the *Journal of Marketing*, vol. 44 (Fall 1980), pp. 9–17, published by the American Marketing Association.

inflation-adjusted accounting is likely to influence marketing decision making. We suggest that the major impact will probably be a heightened emphasis on measures of asset utilization. Marketing managers are likely to find their performance being evaluated by measures of return-on-assets-employed (including inventories and accounts receivable as well as plant and equipment) by product, customer, sales territory, and market segment, rather than the more traditional measures of sales volume, market share, and profit margin contribution.[1] Though these changes will not occur overnight, and it may be too early to measure the full impact of the new FASB requirements (which are still regarded as "experimental"), the potential significance of their impact can already be seen.

The Problem of Historical Costs

Conventional financial statements report all activities in terms of the nominal number of dollars expended at the time assets were acquired, or "acquisition cost." Thus, a piece of equipment purchased for $10,000 in 1975 would be carried at $10,000 on the balance sheet in 1980, minus accumulated depreciation calculated on the $10,000 base. Likewise, inventories and the cost of goods sold would be stated in terms of the prices paid for those goods.

Historical cost accounting fails to recognize two important, but different, effects of inflation. First, no recognition is given to the fact that the dollar does not represent a constant, or stable, measuring unit over time. The purchasing power of the 1975 dollar, as measured perhaps by the CPI, is not the same as the purchasing power of the 1980 dollar. Yet accountants add historical cost amounts for inventories and other assets as though the measuring units were the same. Such procedures are just as illogical as adding the number of dollars in a U.S. bank account to the number of pounds in a London bank account to obtain total cash. The measuring units are just not the same.

The second deficiency of historical cost accounting is that, prior to sale, no recognition is given to changes in the prices of the specific assets held by a firm.[2] Whereas the concern with the stability of the measuring unit is with changes in the *general* purchasing power of the dollar, the concern in this second case is with changes in the *specific* prices of particular assets. In a period of rising prices, traditional accounting practice tends to overstate the profitability of most enterprises by understating the current cost of replacing inventory items sold and plant and equipment

---

[1] The assumption that asset utilization will become more important in the evaluation of marketing managers' performance is supported by interviews with more than 20 CEO's and other members of top management conducted in 1979 and 1980 by the senior author, in connection with a research project supported by the Amos Tuck School of Business Administration, Dartmouth College, and the Marketing Science Institute. Although that research is not the basis for this article, it does support an important assumption made here—viz., that these new financial reporting requirements will significantly alter managerial accounting practice and the way top management views products, customers, sales territories, and market segments.

[2] Some minor exceptions arise in the case of "lower-of-cost-or-market" adjustments to inventories and marketable equity securities.

used. The Commerce Department has estimated that the result has been an over-statement of corporate profits by 30 to 40%, an amount that could equal $50 billion or more in the United States annually (*Business Week* 1979).

The Required Supplemental Disclosures

Developing an understanding of the disclosures required under Statement 33, the new pronouncement of the Financial Accounting Standards Board, is perhaps done most easily with an example.[3] Table 1 lists the data used in the illustration. A firm begins its first year of operations, 1980, with $400 in cash and contributed capital. On January 1, 1980, the CPI is assumed to be 200. The firm immediately acquires two widgets for $100 each and a piece of equipment for $100. During the first six months of 1980, general price inflation is 5%. Thus, the CPI increases from 200 to 210. On July 1, 1980, one widget is sold for $240 and the widget is replaced at the new higher replacement cost of $115. Other expenses paid on July 1, 1980, total $100. During the second six months of 1980, general price inflation is 10% (the CPI increases from 210 to 231).

Financial statements prepared according to several inflation accounting methods are illustrated in Table 2.

Historical Cost/Nominal Dollar Accounting

Column 1 of Table 2 shows the results for 1980 as they would be reported in the conventional financial statements. Sales is stated at the nominal dollars received

TABLE 1. Data for inflation accounting illustration

Balance sheet as of Jan. 1, 1980
Cash: $400
Contributed capital: $400

	January 1, 1980	June 30, 1980	December 31, 1980
CPI	200 (5% increase)	210 (10% increase)	231
Cost of one widget	$100	$115	$140
Cost of equipment	$100	$110	$120
Transactions	1. Buy 2 widgets at $100 each, $200	1. Sell 1 widget for $240; replace widget at $115	Close books and prepare statements
	2. Purchase equipment (5 yr. life) for $100	2. Pay other expenses of $100	

[3] Readers wishing to pursue these accounting issues and techniques in more depth are referred to: Vancil (1976); Sterling (1975); Stickney (1977); and Largay and Livingstone (1976).

TABLE 2. Illustration of financial statements reflecting inflation accounting (minimum required disclosures are shown in boldface type)

	(1) Historical cost nominal dollars	(2) Historical cost constant dollars	(3) Current cost nominal dollars	(4) Current cost constant	(4) Current cost dollars
Income statement					
Sales	240	264.0	240		264.0
Cost of goods sold	100	115.5[a]	115	126.5[m]	
Depreciation	20	23.1[b]	22[h]	24.2[n]	
Other expenses	100	110.0[c]	100	110.0	
	220	248.6	237		260.7
Operating income	20	**15.4**	**3**		3.3
Realized holding gains:					
Goods sold	—	—	**15**[i]		**11.0**[o]
Depre. assets used	—	—	**2**[j]		**1.1**[p]
Unrealized holding gains:					
Inventory	—	—	**65**[k]		**38.0**[q]
Depre. assets	—	—	**16**[l]		**3.6**[r]
Purchasing power loss	—	**(18.0)**[d]	—		**(18.0)**
Net income	20	**(2.6)**	101		39.0
Balance sheet					
Cash	125	125.0	125		125
Inventory	215	242.0[e]	**280**		280
Equipment	100	115.5[f]	120	120	
Acc. depre.	(20)	(23.1)	(24)	(24)	
Total assets	80 / 420	92.4 / 459.4	96 / 501	96	501
Contributed capital	400	462.0[g]	400		462
Retained earnings	20	(2.6)	101		39
Total equity	420	459.4	501		501

[a] 100 × (231/200) = 115.5
[b] 100 × (231/200) = 115.5; 115.5/5 = 23.1
[c] 100 × (231/210) = 110
[d] [100 × (10/200) × (231/210)] + 125 × (21/210) = 5.50 + 12.50 = 18
[e] 100 × (231/200) + 115 × (231/210) = 242
[f] 100 × (231/200) = 115.5; 115.5/5 = 23.1
[g] 400 × (231/200) = 462
[h] 110/5 = 22
[i] 115 − 100 = 15
[j] 22 − 20 = 2
[k] 280 − 215 = 65
[l] 96 − 80 = 16
[m] 115 × (231/210) = 126.5
[n] 22 × (231/210) = 24.2
[o] 126.5 − 115.5 = 11
[p] 24.2 − 23.1 = 1.1
[q] 280 − 242 = 38
[r] 96 − 92.4 = 3.6

when the widget was sold. Cost of goods sold, inventory, depreciation, and equipment are reported at the nominal dollars expended when the inventory and equipment were acquired. The reported net income of $20 fails to reflect either changes in the general purchasing power of the dollar or changes in the specific prices of the inventory and equipment.

Historical Cost/Constant Dollar Accounting

Column 2 of Table 2 shows income statement and balance sheet amounts restated to dollars of constant general purchasing power. Historical cost valuations are still used. However, historical cost amounts are restated to dollars of constant purchasing power at the end of 1980. For example, the purchasing power received when the inventory item was sold for $240 on July 1, 1980, is equivalent to receiving $264 of December 31, 1980, purchasing power. Likewise, the sacrifice in purchasing power when the widget was purchased for $100 on January 1, 1980, is equivalent to sacrificing $115.50 in purchasing power on December 31, 1980. Thus, an equivalent measuring unit underlies the amounts in column 2. (Note that these restated amounts do not represent the current replacement cost of the specific assets. The specific prices of these assets could have changed in an entirely different direction and pattern than prices in general.)

One new element in column 2 is the *purchasing power gain or loss on monetary items*. A firm that holds cash or claims to cash during a period of inflation loses general purchasing power. A firm that borrows from others during inflation gains general purchasing power. The purchasing power gain or loss is a measure of the increase or decrease in general purchasing power during a period due to being in a net lending position (purchasing power loss) or net borrowing position (purchasing power gain). In the illustration, the firm held $100 of cash during the first six months of the year while the general purchasing power of the dollar decreased 5%. It therefore lost $5 of general purchasing power. This represents a loss of $5.50 measured in dollars of December 31, 1980, purchasing power. The firm also held $125 during the last six months of the year. With 10% inflation during this six-month period, an additional loss in purchasing power of $12.50 is realized. The arithmetic is shown in note d to Table 2. The purchasing power gain or loss on net monetary items is not reported in the conventional financial statements. It is a unique element in the income statement under constant dollar accounting.

Current Cost/Nominal Dollar Accounting

Whereas column 2 restates historical cost amounts for changes in the general price level, column 3 reports amounts in terms of the current replacement cost of specific assets.[4] Matched against sales are the current cost of replacing the widget sold and

---

[4] Controversy persists within the accounting profession as to the appropriate concept of replacement cost. Some argue that the current cost of replacing the specific assets held by the firm is most relevant. For example, the replacement

the services of equipment used.[5] Hence neither revenues nor current costs are measured in end-of-year constant dollars, but in dollars of various vintages within the current year. Operating income (sales minus expenses measured at current replacement cost) reports the firm's ability to maintain its operating capacity. If sales revenue is not large enough to replace goods or services used up, the firm will have to cut back its level of operations unless outside financing is secured.

Current cost income statements also include a new element—*realized and unrealized holding gains and losses.* A holding gain or loss arises from holding an asset while its replacement cost increases. The widget purchased on January 1, 1980, for $100 was held during the first six months of the year while its replacement cost increased to $115. When the widget is sold on this date, the firm realizes a holding gain of $15 ($= \$115 - \$100$). Likewise, a holding gain of $40 ($= \$140 - \$100$) would be reported on the other widget acquired on January 1, 1980, and a holding gain of $25 ($= \$140 - \$115$) would be reported on the widget acquired on July 1, 1980. The latter two holding gains would be characterized as "unrealized" ($\$65 = \$40 + \$25$) because the widgets have not yet been sold.

Whether holding gains constitute an increase in the value of a firm is a subject of considerable controversy. Proponents argue that firms that purchase assets early in anticipation of increases in replacement costs are better off than firms that delay purchases and must pay the higher replacement costs. Opponents argue that firms cannot use such holding gains as the basis for dividend payments without impairing the ability to replace those assets used or sold.

The balance sheet on a current cost basis reports assets at their current replacement cost at year end.

Current Cost/Constant Dollar Accounting

Observe that although column 3 reports amounts in terms of current replacement cost, the current cost amounts are measured in terms of dollars of varying general purchasing power. Sales and expenses are measured in terms of dollars of midyear purchasing power. The amounts shown for various assets are measured in terms of dollars of end-of-the-year purchasing power. Column 4 presents all amounts in column 3 restated to an end-of-year constant dollar basis.

Perhaps the most interesting disclosures in column 4 are the holding gains. Because the reported amounts indicate the extent to which changes in prices of a firm's specific assets exceeded the change in the general price level, they are referred to

---

cost of a 30-year-old steel mill is the current cost of acquiring or constructing a steel mill with identical physical and operating characteristics. Others argue that the current cost of replacing existing assets with assets serving the same function is more appropriate. For example, the replacement cost of a 30-year-old steel mill that produces 100,000 tons of steel per year is the current cost of acquiring a new steel mill with the same output, or productive capacity. The current cost of the new steel mill would be adjusted downward to reflect the used condition of the asset owned but would not be adjusted to reflect the technological superiority of the new steel mill.

[5] Note that the use of a LIFO rather than a FIFO cost-flow assumption for inventories in historical cost accounting generates a cost of goods sold which typically approximates the current cost of units sold (also see footnote 7). To a lesser extent, the use of accelerated rather than straight-line depreciation in historical cost accounting provides an analogous result in the case of depreciation expense.

as *real holding gains.* Also shown in column 4 is the purchasing power loss on net monetary items.

Required Supplemental Disclosures

The FASB does not require the supplemental disclosure of all the information in columns 2, 3, and 4 at the present time. The Board encourages experimentation, recognizing the need for an educational effort to inform statement users of the usefulness of the information. The minimum disclosures required are shown in boldface in Table 2. For companies having fiscal years ending on or after December 25, 1979, the boldface information from column 2 must be disclosed; firms may delay presenting the boldface information in columns 3 and 4 for one year. In addition, a summary of selected historical, constant dollar, and current cost information for the most recent five years must be disclosed but the first year of current cost data need not be reported for fiscal years ending prior to December 25, 1980.

New Criteria of Marketing Effectiveness

These specific developments in accounting standards are occurring against a background of more general management concern about the financial impact of marketing decisions. With the prime lending rate reaching 20% in the spring of 1980 and most firms paying 1 to 2% over that for their short-term borrowing to finance current operations (especially inventories and accounts receivable), small changes in profit margins become especially meaningful. The slow growth that characterizes many consumer and industrial markets has caused distributors and end users to stretch out their payments for goods received, putting further pressures on the marketer's financial situation. Longer term prospects for market growth are clouded by substantial demographic shifts, including a slower rate of population growth and a significant increase in the average age of the population.

As corporate managements attempt to cope with and plan for the combined forces of inflation, tight money supply, high interest rates, and low rates of growth in the economy in general and in specific markets, they will need new criteria to evaluate marketing performance. Commonly used measures such as gross margin, return on sales, and changes in market share all have a shortcoming—they do not take into account the financial resources committed to a particular product, customer, sales territory, or market segment. This shortcoming can be corrected by using such measures of performance as return on investment, return on equity, and return on assets employed.

At the same time, management must be prepared to incorporate the new inflation-adjusted accounting information into these additional measures of performance. Costs must be redefined to take into account changes in prices of plant, equipment, raw materials, working capital, and the labor that have gone into inventories of finished goods and work in process. The effect will almost always be to reduce profit estimates below levels indicated by traditional accounting methods. Attractiveness of particular products, customers, sales territories, market segments, and even total businesses may be changed accordingly. The amount of the profit decrease will depend, in general terms, on the amount of capital (plant, equipment, and working capital) committed to a particular marketing unit (product, customer, territory, etc.) and specific price changes of factors such as raw materials and energy used by that marketing unit. Marketing units that look like real "winners" on the basis of traditional accounting methods and measures such as gross margin and return on sales can quickly become "losers" when inflation-adjusted costs and capital requirements are considered.

Measuring Marketing Performance

Marketing projects and activities, and marketing line managers such as field sales managers, sales promotion managers, product managers, and market managers, are characteristically evaluated by measures of sales volume, market share, and gross margin contribution. In the words of one chief executive officer interviewed a short time ago, "We have said to the marketing people, you get the sales volume and the contribution margin and we'll worry about how to finance it." When top management complains about marketing and sales managers' lack of "a profit orientation," they usually are asking for more concern for contribution margin (defined as revenue minus cost of goods sold and marketing expenses), more control over direct marketing expenses ("increased productivity"), and less concern with gross sales volume per se. Only in the recent past has top management gone the next step and expressed concern with the total level of asset commitment to specific products and markets.

Though the concern for profit versus sales seems very straightforward in the abstract, it is a major management issue in practice. Marketing people are in fact under severe pressure to produce *sales volume*, to meet *sales quotas*, and to capture and hold *market share*. These are the typical measures of operating performance used to evaluate marketing people. A manager is usually given a budget to work with at the beginning of the operating period (after a process of budget planning and review that results in allocation of marketing dollars to territories, products, and markets), and is then charged with responsibility for maximizing the sales volume, and perhaps contribution dollars, within that budget constraint.

In recent years, guided by the logic of the product portfolio approach[6] and by better understanding of the financial aspects of business strategy, top managements and corporate planners have begun to use estimates of return on investment, in its various forms, to evaluate marketing projects and activities and to allocate financial

---

[6] These approaches are described and evaluated by Abell and Hammond (1979).

resources among them. These more sophisticated measures of marketing performance treat products, customers, market segments, and sales territories as competing uses of scarce financial resources. Each requires a certain commitment of plant and equipment, working capital, and marketing expenditures. When these resource commitments are factored into the calculation of profitability, simple measures of sales volume and profit margin contribution are evaluated in a new light. The emphasis is shifted to the rate of profit per dollar invested in each marketing activity. Top management is called upon to make subjective judgments and to assess tradeoffs between business growth requiring additional investment for future profitability and positive cash flow from limited investments in the short term.

Inflation accounting adds yet another dimension to the increasingly sophisticated assessment of the financial implications of marketing decisions. The performance of marketing managers in the future is certain to be increasingly evaluated in terms of asset utilization by measures of return on assets employed for product, market segment, sales territory, and other marketing control units, adjusted to reflect the current level of general or specific prices.

Implications for Marketing Management

Virtually all areas of marketing decision making—market segmentation, product strategy, pricing strategy, distribution, salesforce management, advertising, and sales promotion—will be influenced by the new inflation accounting data. In general, the greatest impact will be in those products and markets requiring heavy capital investments in fixed assets and working capital. In particular, old plant will imply high replacement cost (*and* high depreciation). High current inventory costs will increase the measure of capital required when LIFO (last-in, first-out) is used and will decrease operating income under FIFO (first-in, first-out).[7]

Inflation accounting will produce evidence of the need for larger and probably more frequent increases in selling prices than would be indicated by traditional accounting methods. With operating income as the key measure of profit, maintaining the desired level of profitability will require increases in selling prices, to the extent permitted by competitive pressures, to offset the higher current costs reflected under inflation accounting.

As return on assets becomes a more significant measure of marketing performance, marketing managers will feel the pressure to improve their performance by increasing the ratio of operating income to sales as well as by increasing the ratio of sales to assets, the "asset turnover" ratio. The reason is seen in the simple relationship:

---

[7] In a period of rising prices, LIFO leads to a lower inventory cost on the balance sheet than FIFO but will generate a cost of goods sold figure in the income statement which closely approximates current replacement cost. In contrast, FIFO results in balance sheet values for inventory that are close to current cost but cost of goods sold amounts that reflect older (and lower) costs.

$$\text{return on assets} = \frac{\text{operating income}}{\text{assets}} = \frac{\text{operating income}}{\text{sales}} \times \frac{\text{sales}}{\text{assets}}$$

Note that inflation accounting is likely to exert a "double whammy" on return-on-asset (or return-on-investment) calculations. First, maintaining present selling prices in the face of higher current cost depreciation and cost of goods sold will reduce operating income (which excludes holding gains), the numerator. Second, the growing replacement cost of assets increases the denominator. The results are sharp declines in measured return on investment.

Illustration of How Inflation-Adjusted Accounting Data Can Influence the Evaluation of Performance of Marketing Units

To indicate how the relative desirability of marketing units can be changed by the new accounting information, we analyze three hypothetical marketing units. The illustrations focus on the potentially dramatic differences between historical cost and current cost accounting data. We believe that most firms will discard constant dollar information in favor of current cost data. The rates of general inflation used in constant dollar accounting provide insights into interest rates and into the implications of net monetary positions. Yet they rarely measure the effect of changing prices on a particular marketing decision, marketing unit, or business firm. We now turn to the numerical illustrations presented in Table 3.

Comments on the Performance Measurements

The examples show how the move to new measures of performance such as return on assets can change the performance ranking. Consider first the historical data alone. Marketing unit C has top ranking under the more traditional gross margin/sales ratio with a whopping 50%! Yet because of its relative capital intensity, it drops to third when return on assets is computed. Marketing unit B is preferred on the basis of historical return on assets.

Notice how the use of current cost data can affect the traditional gross margin/sales ratios. Unit B comes out well at 25%, although it drops below unit A when the operating income/sales ratio is computed. In terms of current cost return on assets, unit A comes out best, even though the current cost data have reduced its return on assets from 20 to 4.29%.

Purchasing Power Gain or Loss on Monetary Items

We believe that the most useful piece of information generated by constant dollar accounting is the purchasing power gain or loss on monetary items. It provides a rough measure of the direct effect of inflation on the value of net monetary items

TABLE 3. Comparison of current cost and historical cost information in performance evaluation of marketing units

	Marketing Unit A		Marketing Unit B		Marketing Unit C	
	Hist. cost	Current cost	Hist. cost	Current cost	Hist. cost	Current cost
Sales	$8,000,000	$8,000,000	$5,000,000	$5,000,000	$3,000,000	$3,000,000
Cost of goods sold:						
Variable costs	$4,000,000	$4,500,000	$2,000,000	$2,250,000	$1,000,000	$1,100,000
Depreciation of plant and equipment	1,000,000	1,750,000	1,000,000	1,500,000	500,000	1,410,000
	$5,000,000	6,250,000	$3,000,000	$3,750,000	$1,500,000	$2,510,000
Gross margin	$3,000,000	$1,750,000	$2,000,000	$1,250,000	$1,500,000	$ 490,000
Marketing expenses	1,000,000	1,000,000	1,000,000	1,000,000	500,000	500,000
Operating income	$2,000,000	$ 750,000	$1,000,000	$ 250,000	$1,000,000	($ 10,000)
Gross margin/sales	37.5%	21.88%	40%	25%	50%	13.33%
Operating income/sales	25%	9.38%	20%	5%	33.33%	Loss
Capital requirements (investment in assets)	$10,000,000	$17,500,000	$4,000,000	$6,000,000	$5,000,000	$18,000,000
Return on assets (= Operating income/capital requirements)	20%	4.29%	25%	4.17%	16.67%	Loss
Identifiable net monetary assets (liabilities)	$400,000		0		($200,000)	
General inflation rate	10%		10%		10%	
Purchasing power gain (loss) on monetary items	($40,000)		—		$20,000	

owned or owed by firms. In Table 3, marketing unit A requires a net monetary asset position of $400,000 which will be responsible for a $40,000 loss in purchasing power during a year of 10% inflation. If this $40,000 purchasing power loss is used to reduce A's operating income, its current cost return on assets falls to 4.06% [= ($750,000 − $40,000)/$17,500,000], below that of unit B.

Furthermore, the purchasing power gain on monetary items accruing to marketing unit C converts its current cost loss situation to one of marginal profitability.

Managerial Reaction to Conflicting Performance Measurements

Although alternative measures of performance often provide conflicting signals, the problem is exacerbated by the current cost information. The outputs of historical cost accounting systems are based on completed transactions and are generally verifiable. In contrast, current cost information is a subjective answer to a "what if" question. *If* plant, equipment, merchandise displays and so forth are replaced soon, what will their cost be? What is reasonable depreciation on their estimated current cost? And so forth.

The marketing manager who faces performance evaluation with current cost information must be cognizant of several factors.

1. Current cost estimates are not unique and are subject to assumptions about timing of resource replacements and whether specific assets *or* productive capacity is to be replaced.
2. If management has no plans to replace assets in the short term, estimated replacement costs may be irrelevant.
3. For a going concern with contemplated resource replacements during a period of rising prices, current cost estimates are much better indicators of the economic value of resources than their historical costs.
4. Return on assets measurements which incorporate current cost data provide management with a good sense of the ability of a given marketing unit to support the capital committed to it over the intermediate to long term.
5. Constant dollar information is not likely to be particularly relevant in marketing decisions *unless* a particular marketing unit regularly requires a substantial net monetary asset or liability position. In such cases, management should consider calculating the purchasing power gain or loss on monetary items.

Significant discussion (some would say "controversy") is continuing in the accounting profession about the desirability of various methods for estimating current replacement costs, changes in prices, and so on. Concern has been expressed that inflation-adjusted figures, because they involve more "subjectivity" than historical costs, can be more easily manipulated by the managers whose performance is being evaluated. Though this is clearly a legitimate concern, it must be recognized as a separate issue relating to behavioral implications of accounting data and procedures, not the central concern in thinking about the impact of inflation. To a significant degree, of course, all measures of cost and asset commitment are based on subjective judgment and negotiated understandings among all parties influenced by these estimates. Some managers are better than others in using accounting data, of whatever kind, to their own advantage. Our modest objective has been to help marketing managers understand how inflation-adjusted data will differ from those based on historical cost. We are confident that those managers who have read this article will hold a significant advantage in the new business environment over those who have not!

Summary

We have outlined alternative approaches to accounting for the effects of inflation and have sketched the wide range of ramifications for the marketing decision maker. The following conclusions summarize the major points.

1. Persistent inflation causes firm profits to be overstated by traditional, generally accepted accounting principles.
2. Large publicly held firms are now being required to disclose a combination of constant dollar and current replacement cost adjustments to historical cost accounting data.
3. Corporate managements are likely to make increased use of inflation-adjusted financial data in their decision making as these data become the generally accepted measures of performance used by investors and stockholders in evaluating management.
4. Marketing managers will be evaluated by a more complex set of measurements with emphasis on those relating to asset utilization.
5. Virtually all areas of marketing decision making will be influenced, but the most affected are likely to be pricing and distribution.

To respond to these pressures positively, marketing managers will need a better understanding of accounting and financial management than that of their predecessors. The characteristic marketing manager's emphasis in analysis and action on sales volume, gross margin, and market share must be replaced by a more general management focus on bottom-line profitability and return on investment. Top management will think increasingly in terms of total resource allocation across products and markets, assessing the total product portfolio in terms of complex tradeoffs between business growth opportunities in markets requiring additional investment for future profitability versus cash generation now in markets with limited or negative investment. Heightened awareness of the impact of inflation on measures of corporate financial performance will undoubtedly sharpen management concern for this dilemma. Marketing management must adopt new attitudes, what might be called "a general management orientation," as well as make use of the sophisticated measurements, analytical techniques, and strategic planning approaches that are available to help cope with the new pressures and complexities.

References

Abell, Derek F., and John S. Hammond (1979), *Strategic Market Planning*, Englewood Cliffs, New Jersey: Prentice-Hall, Inc.

Bureau of Economic Statistics, Inc. (1979), *Handbook of Basic Economic Statistics*, 33 (July), 99–103.

Business Week (1979), "Inflation Accounting" (October 15), 68.

Financial Accounting Standards Board (1979), "Financial Reporting and Changing Prices," *Statement of Financial Accounting Standards No. 33* (September).

General Electric Company (1980), "1979 Annual Report," Annual Report Issue of *The General Electric Investor*, 5.

Largay III, James A., and J. Leslie Livingstone (1976), *Accounting for Changing Prices*, New York: Wiley/Hamilton.

Sterling, Robert R. (1975), "Relevant Financial Reporting in an Age of Price Changes." *Journal of Accountancy* (February), 42–51.

Stickney, Clyde P. (1977), "Adjustments for Changing Prices," in *Handbook of Modern Accounting*, 2nd edition, Sidney Davidson and Roman L. Weil, eds., New York: McGraw-Hill.

Vancil, Richard F. (1976), "Inflation Accounting—The Great Controversy," *Harvard Business Review* (March–April).

Marketing Achievement Reporting: A Profitability Approach

5

William F. Christopher

"What is a business success?" Is it profitability? ROI? Profitability measures are important, but they are only part of the scorekeeping in business. And the profitability measures we commonly use have two big limitations:

(1) Present profitability results very significantly from past decisions and actions. In important ways, A. P. Sloan is still earning present-day General Motors profits. Our scorekeeping must report the effect of *present* actions.
(2) Profit data, as calculated by generally accepted accounting principles, does not reflect inflation and other dollar value changes on a current basis, so it is grossly inadequate as a measure of real economic profit on which the firm's survival and its future depend.

To answer our question "What is success?" we cannot look only at profitability. We have to look further to what the business does now and what it intends to do in the *future*. In many companies the successful solution to the profit problem has almost always begun with identifying very clearly just what it is that we can build our success on. Most often this question has been answered in terms of:

(a) How we will apply our:
   People skills,
   Capital, raw material, and energy resources,
   Technology,
   Market position.
(b) To offer superior value to selected markets and target clients.
(c) Within environmental constraints:
   Political,
   Social,
   Ecological,
   Economic.
(d) And focusing primarily on areas of change.

Growth is an important form of change, and the one on which industry has particularly concentrated for performance improvement. But success can be built

Reprinted by permission of the publisher from *Industrial Marketing Management*, vol. 6, pp. 149–162. Copyright 1977 by Elsevier North Holland, Inc.

FIGURE 1

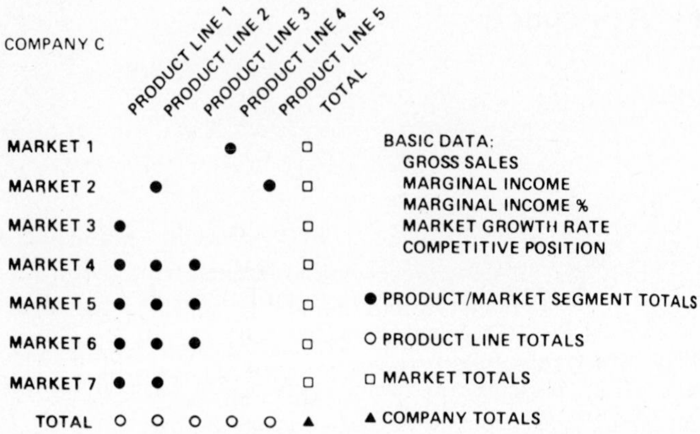

COMPANY C

	PRODUCT LINE 1	PRODUCT LINE 2	PRODUCT LINE 3	PRODUCT LINE 4	PRODUCT LINE 5	TOTAL	
MARKET 1				●		□	BASIC DATA: GROSS SALES
MARKET 2	●			●		□	MARGINAL INCOME MARGINAL INCOME %
MARKET 3	●					□	MARKET GROWTH RATE COMPETITIVE POSITION
MARKET 4	●	●	●			□	
MARKET 5	●	●	●			□	● PRODUCT/MARKET SEGMENT TOTALS
MARKET 6	●	●	●			□	O PRODUCT LINE TOTALS
MARKET 7	●	●				□	□ MARKET TOTALS
TOTAL	O	O	O	O	O	▲	▲ COMPANY TOTALS

also on other forms of change—technological, social, environmental, political. Success can come from making it *different* (in response to changing needs), as well as from making it *more* (in response to aggregate demand). For the timid, change is frightening. For the satisfied, change is threatening. But for the confident, change is opportunity. Sales and marketing has to be a profession for the confident.

Our answer to the question "What is business success?" can be found, in specific terms, by answering six important strategy questions.

What are (or should be) our outputs?
Who are (or should be) our clients?
What does (or will) the client buy?
What is (or can be) our "superior client value"?
What will we concentrate on to build company success?
What therefore should be our major objectives?

Sometimes in developing our answers to these questions I have used the corporate strategy matrix recommended by Igor Ansoff.[1] Figure 1 shows this matrix as developed by the management group of a South American company.

Each of the solid circles represents a product-market segment. Totals of the rows are market totals. Totals of the columns are product line totals. At the lower right are the company totals. For each of the product-market segments, and for the totals as appropriate, basic operating data was assembled: gross sales, marginal income, marginal income rate, market growth rate, and competitive position. From this information and from its operating experience, this company decided that its client

---

[1] Igor Ansoff, *Corporate Strategy*, McGraw-Hill Book Company, 1965.

values were primarily in terms of marketing strengths and organized its operations by markets served. Each market row became a P&L business.

Company D, Figure 2, a job-shop manufacturer of components, defined its business into three product groups. There was very little overlap in clients and market segments served. For product groups 1 and 2, superior customer values were defined and each of these was organized as a profit-center business. For product group 3, income performance was poor and no superior customer value was identified on which success could be built. This business was sold or divested.

Another company, Company F, defined its very complex customer/product line mix into five strategic businesses partly by product line and partly by market served. These product-market strategic businesses are illustrated in Figure 3.

In all three companies, for each of the businesses as defined, the "superior customer value" was identified on which the company could build its business success. And resources were concentrated on those particular businesses and business segments where growth or change was greatest. Success, however, could not be only in terms of products, markets, and competition. There also had to be an awareness of and an accommodation with the other environments impacting the business.

Survival and future success depends on environmental relationships as importantly as on current profitability. Figure 4 shows the diverse environments that comprise today's business environment. There is the company environment operating within the commercial environment of suppliers, clients, and competitors. But the world today is far more than this.

FIGURE 2

COMPANY D	PRODUCT GROUP 1	PRODUCT GROUP 2	PRODUCT GROUP 3	TOTAL
INDUSTRY 1	●			□
INDUSTRY 2	●			□
INDUSTRY 3	●			□
INDUSTRY 4	●			□
INDUSTRY 5	●	●		□
INDUSTRY 6		●		□
INDUSTRY 7		●		□
INDUSTRY 8		●		□
INDUSTRY 9			●	□
TOTAL	○	○	○	▲

FIGURE 3

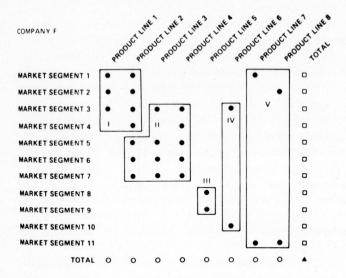

There are also the economic, the technical, the ecological, the social, and the political environments with their regional, national, and international aspects. All of these environments interact with all others to continually change the world of business. In these changes and in these relationships there are opportunities as well as constraints, so we must develop an anticipatory awareness of environmental change and by our actions accommodate the enterprise to this change.

This thinking process can be summarized in a briefly stated but very thoughtfully developed business plan. One successful format for such a plan is shown in Figure 5. Note that this is a short, 3-page summary, not a 50- or 200-page document. But in this very short written plan is very clearly stated just what the ball game is; just what business success means. This summary plan provides the control panel for piloting the business to the achievement of its objectives. It provides the starting point for our better scorekeeping.

In stating objectives in the business plan, the key performance areas as defined originally by Peter Drucker are very useful. They are:

- Market standing
- Innovation
- Productivity
- Physical and financial resources
- Profitability

FIGURE 4

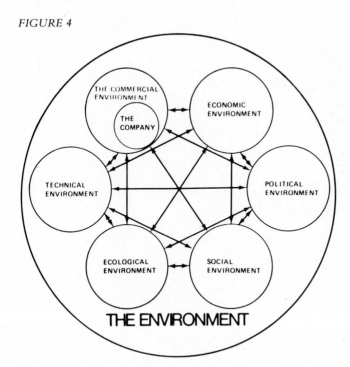

- Motivation and organization development
- Public responsibility

Marked with bullets are those key performance areas where marketing has an important responsibility—note that all of the key performance areas are marked with bullets.

Objectives in these key performance areas are stated in the business plan and become the integrating focus for the objectives of sub-units and individuals. The importance of objectives is not only "what they are" but also "how they were developed." The following principles help immensely in arriving at good objectives, and in achieving them:

INDIVIDUAL OBJECTIVES

(1) Set by subordinate with approval by manager
(2) Few in number rather than many
(3) Change or modify as conditions change
(4) Use as one of the bases for reward

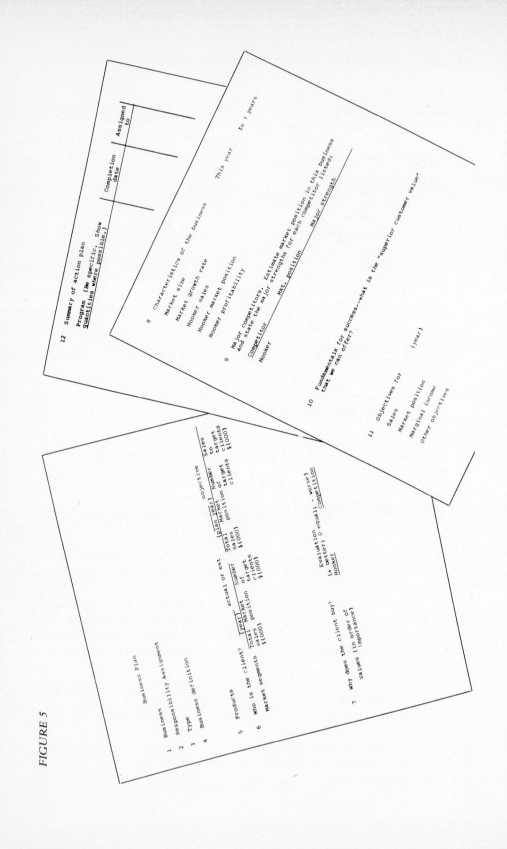

FIGURE 5

(5) Are measurable, with automatic feedback
Use numbers
Set target dates
Express in end result terms
(6) Review frequently between manager and subordinate

GROUP OBJECTIVES

(1) Set by dialog among the group
(2) Few in number rather than many
(3) Change or modify as conditions change
(4) Use as a major basis for recognition
(5) Are measurable, with automatic feedback to all members of the group
Use numbers
Set target dates
Express in end result terms
(6) Review frequently through dialog among the group

Better scorekeeping for sales and marketing then becomes a matter of measuring: (a) performance toward the achievement of goals set in this way, and (b) on a day to day basis the achievement of the action plan programs that have been agreed on as necessary to the achievement of these goals. A few important principles should be mentioned:

(1) Data parallels action. Employees and work groups receive feedback on the results of their effort immediately or very shortly after the work is done.
(2) Feedback is informative and in relation to goal achievement rather than evaluative of personal performance.
(3) Feedback goes to the individual or work group doing the job. It may or may not go to the manager.
(4) If the report does go to the manager, the manager's use of the report is to support and assist the individual or work group in goal achievement.
(5) Feedback relates to goal achievement. It is not an expository summary of activity.
(6) Reports deal only with significant measurements, not with all the details.
(7) At higher levels, feedback is in the form of aggregated data related to group or unit goals.
(8) At the highest (corporate) level, no transaction or sub-unit aggregated data is required but rather overall summaries of trends toward achievement of major goals.

It can be recognized from the above that improved scorekeeping for sales and marketing rests solidly on three disciplines, each supported by established theory:

THEORY

(1) Systems Theory

(2) Motivation Theory
(3) Economic Theory

DISCIPLINE

(1) Cybernetics
(2) Behavioral Science
(3) Managerial Economics

These three disciplines combine to provide knowledge and motivation to employees, supervisors, managers, and executives that help them achieve their objectives. And this is done with a much smaller flow of data between organizational levels than is now customarily found in reporting systems. It enables each individual and each group to concentrate on what matters, with each group successfully achieving its objectives, supporting rather than contending with other groups. Too many score-keeping systems today encourage much too much interference and not nearly enough support.

Profit Responsibility

What about the key performance area of profitability? who is responsible for profit? how can profitability be measured so that appropriate actions will be taken? what scorekeeping will provide the measurements?

First, who is responsible for profit? Is Marketing responsible? Sales volume and pricing are key elements in profitability. Or is Manufacturing responsible? Production costs, too, are a key determinant of profit. Is Purchasing also responsible? We cannot have good production costs without reasonable input costs for raw materials and energy. Labor relations and motivation are also reflected in costs. New products and product improvements by R&D may be a major factor. Is the financial department responsible? They assemble all of the numbers and provide interpretation and guidance. Asking the question: "Who is responsible for profits?" is like asking whether the mother or the father is responsible for raising the child. Is the center, or tackle, or quarterback, or line backer responsible for winning the ball game? The best answer is that all are responsible, together. And this answer to profit responsibility is fundamental to the assumptions that underlie the managerial economics approach that is most helpful in making a business profitable. Here are the assumptions:

- Profitability is a function of the total business unit, not of individual products or product groups.
- Common costs, fixed costs, and other time-oriented overheads will not be allocated to individual products or product groups, but rather will be assigned to the organizational units which incur them.
- The interacting elements that contribute to profitability will be the points of

action for profit improvement. Actions will be in the form of control (cost reduction) and creativity (output increase).

- Evaluation of what is important will be based on the company's purpose, or mission—its definition of where and how it will build its success.

This is not a new set of assumptions. For many years it has been known to work successfully in business operations. But in recent years many companies have chosen to operate from a different set of assumptions for which there is little empirical evidence of merit. But in spite of this lack of evidence, many businesses have chosen a full costing system which assigns fixed costs to individual products and assumes that by these calculations, if individual products are made profitable, the company will be profitable. This is an operational mode of the totum-quantum theory which states that the total is the sum of its parts. And in this case the parts are assumed to be individual products, and all costs are assumed to relate to products. This theory and this set of assumptions has failed many times; it has not been seen to succeed. Its alleged successes impute to other, unrecognized sources. But the totum-quantum assumptions remain popular because they sound so logical that we seldom take the trouble to notice that they don't work. Instead what does work is the systems theory concept that profit is a function of the total business unit, that there are many interrelationships within the business and between the business and its environment, and it is these interrelationships and connectivities that must be managed if we are to make a profit. These can be very simply organized for any business unit in a very practical income model. To construct this model we first restate the Income Statement in marginal income accounts. Table 1 is an income statement for a company with a profit problem, shown in the conventional format, and then recast into marginal income accounts.

We can now prepare the income model, as shown in Figure 6.

Looking at this model we can dialog its interactions, and connectivities, to help us determine whether and how improvements can be made. There are three and only three possibilities:

(1) Sales can be increased;
(2) Fixed costs can be reduced;
(3) Marginal income rate can be increased by:
    (a) Reducing variable cost,
    (b) Increasing price,
    (c) Improving mix.

Marketing and sales have major responsibilities for all of these possible actions:

(1) Responsibility for sales volume;
(2) Responsibility for those fixed costs associated with marketing, sales, and distribution;

TABLE 1. *Marginal income accounts*

Company P Conventional income statement ($ add 000)			Company P Income statement by marginal income accounts ($ add 000)		
Net sales		$7,745	Net sales		$7,745
Customers		7,565	Variable costs		4,953
Transfer		180	Marginal income		2,792
Cost of goods sold		7,257	Marginal income %		36.05
Gross profit		488	Fixed costs		3,419
SGA expense		1,115	Manufacturing	2,304	
Selling	455		Distribution	350	
Distribution	350		Selling	455	
Development	95		Development	95	
Administration	215		Administration	215	
Operating income		(627)	Breakeven (fixed costs		
Other income/expense		7	divided by MI%)		9,484
Pretax income		(620)	Sales above (below)		
			breakeven		(1,739)
			Operating income (sales above or below break-even × MI%)		(627)
			Other income/expense		7
			Pretax income		(620)

(3) Responsibility for variable costs associated with sales: commissions, returns, allowances, incentives, freight;
(4) Responsibility for pricing and for "selling the price";
(5) Responsibility for mix—and in most businesses there are many, many opportunities for profit improvement here, in:
Product mix,
Customer mix,
Market segment mix,
Geographic mix,
Domestic/international mix,
Distribution channel mix,
Order size mix,
... and combinations of the above.

For Company P, which had had a consistent record of losses, the solution was to increase marginal income rate by concentrating on a different mix of products to be sold to a different mix of customers. This led to organization and program

FIGURE 6

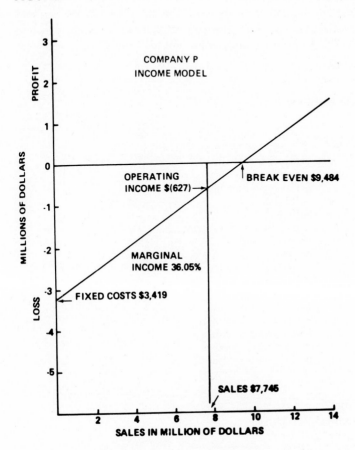

changes in development, production, and sales, with new objectives for each. The scorekeeping related to these new objectives. Three months later our scorekeeping told us we were "on course" even though the company was still losing money. By a year later, this business was profitable, and it has been highly profitable over subsequent years. Our better scorekeeping started with putting ourselves into a better ball game.

Let's look in some detail at a better scorekeeping system for the key performance area of profitability—a scorekeeping system that can help all decision makers to make good decisions, at the right time.

Profitability objectives for sales and marketing will typically be defined in terms of sales volume, marginal income, fixed costs, breakeven, and operating income. But the objectives and the scorekeeping feedback will differ at different levels.

Let's look at profitability scorekeeping in a typical large company structure comprised of a corporate headquarters, divisions and subsidiary companies, and business units within the divisions and companies. Within business units, sales and marketing individuals and operating supervision will be directly concerned with

TABLE 2. *Reporting feedback on profitability; level one*

Individuals and first line supervision	
Sales volume	Transactions, by client
	Dollar totals monthly:
	By client
	By territory
	By district or region
Marginal income rate	By transaction
	Monthly:
	By product
	By client
	By territory
Fixed costs	By expenditure
	Accounts totals, monthly
Breakeven	Business unit, monthly
Operating income	Business unit, monthly
Income model	Business unit, monthly

TABLE 3. *Reporting feedback on profitability; level two*

Business unit management Monthly	
Sales volume	Dollar totals:
	By product group
	By market
	By target client
	Total for business unit
Marginal income rate	By product line
	Total, business unit
Fixed costs	By organizational unit
Breakeven	Business unit
Operating income	Business unit
Income model	Business unit

profitability goals and feedback by transactions and for individual clients, but they will also be informed as to the business unit's total income model, as shown in Table 2.

At the business unit management level, data is aggregated monthly to relate to business unit objectives, as shown in Table 3.

At the company level, data is aggregated to relate to company objectives, as shown in Table 4.

At the corporate level, reporting feedback also relates to corporate objectives, as shown in Table 5.

TABLE 4. Reporting feedback on profitability; level three

Company headquarters Monthly	
Sales volume	Business units
	Total company
Marginal income rate	Business units
	Total company
Fixed costs	Major aggregates
	Total company
Breakeven	Business units
	Total company
Operating income	Business units
	Total company
Income model	Business units
	Total company

TABLE 5. Reporting feedback on profitability; level four

Corporate headquarters Monthly	
Sales volume	Company totals
	Corporate total
Marginal income rate	—
Fixed costs	—
Breakeven	—
Operating income	Company totals
	Corporate totals

TABLE 6. *Reporting feedback on market position*

	Market share	Unit sales	New products
1. Individuals and first line supervision	Target clients Other clients	Transactions, by client Product totals monthly: By territory By district	Sales, by client
2. Business unit management	Product lines Market segments Target clients	Product totals monthly: By product group By market	Dollar sales Unit sales Target client sales
3. Company management	Product line	Product totals by product group	Dollar sales

Market Position

Now let's look at another key performance area—Market Position. Again, the scorekeeping will be different for each organizational level and will provide the feedback needed at each level for accomplishing objectives at that level. This means transaction and client data at the individual level, and appropriate aggregates at higher levels. For the key performance area of Market Position, the reporting feedback in one company looks like the data given in Table 6.

Business success is achieved where the client is, more than in our plants. External returns from the market are more appropriate measures than internal returns on investment. Success is more in manufacturing satisfied, repeat customers than in manufacturing products. And the most important of these are our target clients in each market area. Figure 7 shows one example of feedback reporting on target client sales at the business unit level. Figure 8 shows the monthly feedback at the district and individual salesman levels. Here individual target client names are shown. The salesmen, in addition, receive individual transaction data on a current basis.

Figure 9 shows another example of target client monthly feedback to salesmen and district managers. Here can be seen each month's sales and year-to-date sales, always looked at in relation to the objective. This kind of summary report, maintained over several years, helps us to think in terms of trends, direction, and goal achievement. At the salesman level, customer sales planning provides target client data on potential, and other situational intelligence that helps us to provide "superior customer value" in achieving sales objectives. Each transaction improves both the client's income model and ours.

Figure 10 illustrates the kind of feedback reporting system that I recommend. There is voluminous feedback from the work itself at the transaction level, but only a reasonable and a needed amount for each individual to achieve his objectives. At each higher level, aggregates are reported as needed to achieve objectives at that level. Flows between levels are moderate. Work group efforts are coordinated

FIGURE 7

DIVISION INDUSTRIAL
CLIENTES ESPECIALES
VENTAS NETAS (000)

RESUMEN
MES   ZONA

Clientes		Mes. Act. 1,976	Mes Act. 1,975	Var. %	Acumul. 1,976	Acumul. 1,975	Var. %	Target para. 1,976
District 1	37	1,868.0	676.6	176	6,133.8	2,533.8	142	24,100.0
Clientes KTA	7	1,491.7	373.4	299	4,915.6	1,660.7	196	20,100.0
Otros	30	376.3	303.2	24	1,218.0	873.1	40	4,000.0
District 2	48	1,531.2	821.6	86	4,250.0	1,980.2	114	19,180.0
Clientes KTA	9	960.7	394.2	144	1,885.2	1,070.5	76	13,700.0
Otros	39	570.5	427.4	33	2,364.8	909.7	159	5,480.0
District 3	13	1,234.9	188.3	556	2,929.0	1,972.8	48	8,530.0
Clientes KTA	3	1,179.6	145.3	712	2,696.1	1,776.7	52	7,030.0
Otros	10	55.3	43.0	28	232.9	196.1	19	1,500.0
District 4	30	983.6	198.7	395	1,738.6	1,008.7	72	15,795.0
Clientes KTA	5	589.6	32.8	NS	673.4	533.1	26	11,700.0
Otros	25	394.0	165.9	137	1,065.2	475.6	124	4,095.0
District 5	8	114.6	54.6	109	276.6	101.7	174	1,800.0
Clientes KTA	3	103.0	35.3	191	255.9	57.4	346	1,500.0
Otros	5	11.6	19.3	(40)	20.7	44.3	(53)	300.0
District 6	7	76.9	97.9	(22)	200.8	127.3	58	1,073.0
Clientes KTA	3	69.6	12.7	448	188.1	12.7	NS	873.0
Otros	4	7.3	85.2	(92)	12.7	114.6	(89)	200.0
TOTAL	143	5,809.2	2,037.7	185	15,528.8	7,724.5	100	70,478.0
	30	4,394.2	993.7	342	10,614.3	5,111.1	108	54,903.0
	113	1,415.0	1,044.0	36	4,914.3	2,613.4	88	15,575.0

through dialog and are linked also through dialog to other groups. All is focused on achieving objectives. It is less a scorekeeping system to help managers evaluate subordinates, and more a cybernetic feedback system to help each person and unit succeed in accomplishing desired results. Evaluation becomes simple as we focus more on successful achievement.

One other, very important perspective is feedback. Feedback in this system is more than just specific numbers. Each measure is seen in relation to trend and changes in trends. It is direction—trends and changes in trends—that matters. So each monthly figure is viewed—not as a variance from budget—but as one more measure of a trend. The management job then is not to explain the variance or to conform reported results to a budget, but to *influence the trend in ways that enable*

FIGURE 8

DIVISION INDUSTRIAL
CLIENTES ESPECIALES
VENTAS NETAS (000)

RESUMEN
MES   Marzo   ZONA   No.1

Clientes	Mes. Act. 1,976	Mes. Act. 1,975	Var. %	Acumul. 1,976	Acumul. 1,975	Var. %	Target para. 1,976
Clientes KTA	1,491.7	373.4	299	4,915.6	1,660.7	196	20,100.0
KTA 1	447.0	(120.3)	—	1,888.7	(108.8)	—	6,800.0
KTA 2	263.6	196.0	34	682.6	665.0	2.0	4,500.0
KTA 3	164.9	110.4	49	797.1	343.8	131	2,000.0
KTA 4	107.6	122.1	(12)	598.2	506.9	18	2,500.0
KTA 5	—	—	—	118.3	(13.4)	—	1,300.0
KTA 6	504.3	65.2	673	687.3	267.2	157	2,000.0
KTA 7	4.3	—	—	143.4	—	—	1,000.0
Otros	376.3	303.2	24	1,218.0	873.1	40	4,000.0
Cliente	—	—	—	23.1	—	—	
Cliente	8.3	18.8	(56)	8.3	40.0	(80)	
Cliente	—	—	—	—	114.8	—	
Cliente	13.1	—	—	21.0	—	—	
Cliente	69.2	—	—	122.3	66.7	83	
Cliente	—	41.6	—	17.5	42.4	(59)	
Cliente	—	—	—	—	—	—	
Cliente	6.3	59.0	(90)	56.6	133.4	(50)	
Cliente	—	13.4	—	76.4	54.6	39	
Cliente	5.2	—	—	40.0	—	—	
Cliente	—	12.7	—	1.9	12.7	(85)	
Cliente	—	—	—	—	—	—	
Cliente	0.5	—	—	1.0	—	—	
Cliente	—	—	—	—	36.3	—	
Cliente	—	—	—	—	—	—	

us to reach our goals. The measurement of trend for each data series must be carefully chosen. Measures used successfully include:

- 4-week moving average,
- 12-month moving total,
- Box-Jenkins.

Figure 11 is one example of a trend chart, in this case showing that we are on course toward achieving a very ambitious business unit sales objective.

I cannot give you all the details of a better scorekeeping system for sales and

FIGURE 9

TERRITORY _____

ACCOUNTS & PROSPECTS (M – MONTH) (Y – YEAR TO DATE)		1975 ACTUAL SALES	1976 SALES GOAL	JAN	FEB	MAR	APR	MAY
TOTAL TERRITORY	M							
	Y							
TOTAL TARGET ACCOUNTS	M							
	Y							
KTA 1	M							
	Y							
KTA 2	M							
	Y							
KTA 3	M							
	Y							
KTA 4	M							
	Y							
KTA 5	M							
	Y							

FIGURE 10

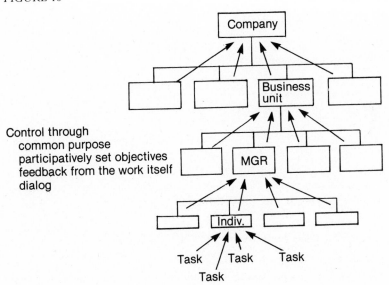

Control through
   common purpose
   participatively set objectives
   feedback from the work itself
   dialog

marketing that is conceptually different from what most of us are accustomed to. Performancewise, this system offers an important advantage. It works. It applies cybernetic feedback, motivation, and managerial economics to help individuals and groups succeed.

FIGURE 11

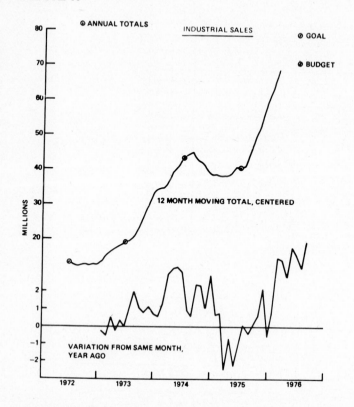

I hope I have provided enough of the concept, and enough of the details, so that those interested in applying this scorekeeping approach—which I call "Achievement Reporting"—can do so. To encourage others in this direction, I will conclude with an example of how the methods I am recommending to you changed a struggling company into a highly successful, profitable enterprise.

Concluding Example

Satisfactory profitability for this company, which we will call Company S, would be in the range of $3 million. Results over several years, up to the time of our rebuilding and better scorekeeping program, were as shown in Table 7.

In July 1975, the management group of this company studied its situation, and determined where and how it could build its success.

(1) Overall company objectives were developed in the framework of the seven key performance areas listed earlier.

TABLE 7. Profitability at Company S

Year	Net income ($ thousands)
1969	$1,020
1970	855
1971	1,176
1972	1,413
1973	2,244
1974	1,716
June, 1975 (6 months annualized)	(1,572)

(2) The total business was defined into six business segments. This was the most difficult and time-consuming part of the program, and required conceptual thinking more than analytical.

(3) Income statements by marginal income accounts were prepared for each of the business segments, and for the total company, using the format shown in Figure 12. Statements were prepared from January 1975, so that current trends of key measures could be identified.

(4) "Superior customer values" were identified for each of the business segments.

(5) Business plans for each of the business segments were developed using a format similar to that shown earlier, Figure 5.

(6) Sales personnel identified target accounts, developed situational data for each, and set sales objectives.

(7) In each business segment, the management group dialoged their business plan and their monthly income models and developed specific objectives for:
Market position
   Total sales
   Target client sales
Profitability
   Marginal income rate
   Fixed costs
Other key performance area objectives as appropriate

(8) A better scorekeeping, feedback system was established:
  (a) Salesmen and supervisors received:
     Transaction data, by account
     Monthly summaries by account with emphasis on the target accounts, using reports similar to those shown in Figure 7 and Figure 8.
  (b) Business managers received:
     Monthly income model

FIGURE 12. Income statement by marginal income accounts

	Av. Mo. 1974	Av. Mo. 1975	Av. Mo. 1976 B	1976 JAN	FEB	MAR	APR	MAY	JUN	JUL	AUG	SEPT	OCT	NOV	DEC
1. GROSS SALES															
2. VARIABLE COSTS															
a) RAW MATERIALS															
b) ENERGY															
c) ROYALTIES															
d) COMMISSIONS															
e) FREIGHT															
f) RETURNS & ALLOW.															
g) OTHER															
3. MARGINAL INCOME															
4. MI %															
5. FIXED COSTS															
a) MFG.															
1) PEOPLE															
2) DEPRECIATION															
3) OTHER															
b) SALES															
c) ADM.															
d) OTHER															
6. BREAK—EVEN															
7. SALES ABOVE (BELOW) BE															
8. OPERATING INCOME															
9. OTHER INCOME & EXPENSE															
a) INTEREST INCOME															
b) INTEREST EXPENSE															
c) OTHER INCOME															
d) OTHER EXPENSE															
10. INCOME BEFORE TAX															
11. INCOME TAX															
12. NET INCOME															

Target client sales reports

Reports on achievement of the business plan action plans

(9) Business managers and the company president together dialog monthly results and trends in:

Marginal income rate

Fixed costs

Breakeven

Sales volume

Target client sales

Key action plans

(10) Decisions are made as necessary to keep the company and each business segment "on track" toward the achievement of its objectives. The scorekeeping feedback not only indicates when and where decisions are needed; it also provides the information needed for making the decision.

This program involved many individuals in a very responsible way in their business segment and their company success. Both motivation and operating results improved. By year end, 1975, the company had achieved breakeven operations, and this year the company will have the highest income in its history, and for the

FIGURE 13

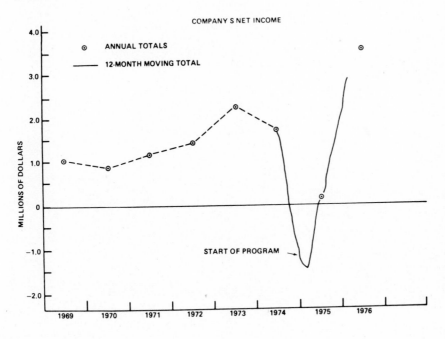

first time, well above "satisfactory." Figure 13 shows the income trend chart for this company.

This is only one of many examples I have seen and worked with that demonstrates the effectiveness of the feedback system of scorekeeping. It combines general systems theory, behavioral science, and managerial economics into a new style of management and feedback control reporting that can define and achieve success in the complex environment we work in today. It works where other, older methods now seem to be inadequate, or even failing. If you are having difficulty with your present scorekeeping methods I suggest you stop "adding to" and "improving." Instead, think through very clearly "what is success." Then use achievement reporting to get there.

Recommendations for
Further Reading

Arnstein, William E. "What Didn't We Earn Last Month?" *Management Review*, 62 (October 1973), 25–33.

Direct costing is a widely accepted method of determining how much each item contributes to covering overhead and the generation of a profit. However, the usual monthly direct cost statement only tells us what we earned. No insight is provided into the question "What didn't we earn last month?" For this to be known, a firm must set attainable objectives for its month-to-month operations. There must also be ideal standards from which to measure deviations on a monthly, quarterly or semiannual basis. A number of different reasons for the occurrence of such deviations are reviewed and an illustration provided of the profits that might be lost through each such deviation. The reporting format directs attention to the areas that provide the greatest potential for profit improvement.

Baumol, William J., and Charles H. Sevin. "Marketing Costs and Mathematical Programming," *Harvard Business Review*, 35 (September–October 1957), 52–60.

Marketing management seldom realizes how much of its marketing effort brings in only very small returns, since there is little in the way of a systematic attempt to evaluate specific portions of this effort. However, the use of distribution cost analysis and mathematical programming combined can result in substantially reduced marketing costs, increased marketing efficiency, and greater profits. Treatment of costs, steps in the analysis, and the link with mathematical and/or somewhat simpler linear programming are outlined. A few inexpensive computations that will help to improve distribution cost analyses are suggested in an appendix.

Böer, Germain B. *Direct Cost and Contribution Accounting: An Integrated Managerial Accounting System*. New York: Wiley-Interscience, 1974, 246 pp.

Direct cost information can be used in planning and controlling costs in any organization's production, marketing and administrative functions. This book emphasizes the role of direct cost and contribution data in an integrated management accounting system and explores the many techniques that utilize such data.

Three chapters are of special relevance to marketers. How a direct cost system provides relevant information for evaluating product, salespeople, and territory performance is the subject of Chapter Seven. Such a system is shown to identify deviations from profit targets by organization segment and by product segment; it also pinpoints the dollar deviations caused by price, cost, volume, and mix changes.

Chapter Ten focuses on situations in which direct cost information can lead to better pricing decisions. Lastly, one finds in Chapter Eleven discussions of pricing for standard products versus custom products, of intracompany pricing versus pricing to outside customers, and of the desirability of an overall pricing plan.

Goodman, Sam R. *Techniques of Profitability Analysis.* New York: John Wiley & Sons, Inc., 1970, 219 pp.

The author considers this volume to be "primarily aimed at the business executive who is interested in understanding the ramifications of finance in the functional areas of marketing, manufacturing and administration." In some respects, the book is a summary statement of and elaboration on Goodman's previously published articles. Topics to which one or more chapters are devoted include the nature of the marketing controller concept and the desirability of establishing such a position; the case for using relevant rather than either absorption or direct costing in evaluating marketing alternatives; how the operating statement can be made useful at all levels of responsibility; the profitability implications of the product life cycle; the use of return on investment in a myriad of areas, including acquisitions, new product development, product pricing, and segmental analysis; and, a profitability-oriented approach to sales analysis and incentive plan development.

Herson, Richard J. L., and Ronald S. Hertz, "Direct Costing in Pricing: A Critical Reappraisal," *Management Services*, 5 (March-April 1968), 130–135.

Contrary to popular thinking, a policy of using "direct" or variable costs as a basis for pricing may have very harmful consequences. For example, a direct costing pricing policy does not establish a minimum profit margin useful in comparisons of profitability by product. By omitting fixed or capacity costs, direct costs may result in some products being underpriced and others overpriced. This in turn could create shifts in demand and a less profitable product mix. Direct costing also makes unrealistic assumptions as to the accuracy with which such factors as demand weaknesses, costs, and product mixes can be estimated. Other conceptual weaknesses include: (1) the tendency of costs fixed in the short run to become variable over time or at higher levels of production; and (2) the hidden arbitrariness that often underlies direct costing. Though direct costing can provide useful supplementary information, primary reliance upon a full cost pricing discipline is more appropriate.

Jaedicke, Robert K., and Alexander A. Robichek. "Cost-Volume-Profit Analysis Under Conditions of Uncertainty," *Accounting Review*, 39 (October 1964), 917–926.

The sales volume required to attain a given level of profits and the most profitable combination of products to produce and sell are examples of decision areas where cost-volume-profit analysis could prove extremely useful. Traditionally, such analysis does not include adjustments for risk and/or uncertainty. In any given instance, this factor may severely limit the technique's usefulness. Illustrations of how a risk analysis might be carried out and probabilities arrived at are to be found in this article. How the statement of probabilities with respect to various levels of profits and losses could aid a decision maker is also discussed in some detail.

Milligan, Bruce L. "Contributing Margin in Decision-Making," *Management Accounting*, 51 (October 1969), 33–38.

The concept of contribution margin, defined as net sales minus direct costs, is a simple but nevertheless exceedingly useful one. General applications include calculating actual or proposed break-even points and margins of safety under various sets of assumptions regarding prices and target net income. Essentially similar applications are useful in controlling and evaluating profit contribution by salespeople and by grade of product and in making appropriate pricing decisions. A number of applications in operations decision making are also illustrated, with examples taken from paper manufacturing but with obvious relevance to many other types of production.

Moore, Carl L. "An Extension of Break-Even Analysis," *Management Accounting*, 50 (May 1969), 55–58.

Conventional break-even analysis can easily be adapted for use in estimating the sales that will be required to yield the derived net inflow of funds or net working capital required from operations. If depreciation is the only nonoperating source of funds, then a modified break-even equation need not be employed. However, other charges and credits affect the flow of funds, and the break-even approach advanced can allow for all these possibilities. It also facilitates improved communication within the organization and lends itself to computer simulations of the impact of different values and different variables.

Ray, David. "Distribution Costing: The Current State of the Art," *International Journal of Physical Distribution*, 6 (No. 2, 1975), Monograph, 36 pp.

The apparent failure of firms to evolve a satisfactory costing scheme for their physical distribution (PD) systems is revealed as now giving way before a sustained attempt to rationalize PD costs. An attempt is made to evaluate past and current literature on distribution costing systems. Further, it is found that conventional accounting methods do not provide for adequate differentiation of physical distribution costs. The distinctive nature of the different accounting schemes in use and their informational requirements are discussed. Both the shortfalls in a financial accounting approach to physical distribution, and the complex, ambiguous relationship between PD and the formal company financial statement are examined. A total distribution viewpoint and a profit analysis method are recommended, especially when this can be done within the framework of a missions approach.

"Report by the Committee on Cost and Profitability Analyses for Marketing," *Accounting Review*, supplement to Vol. 47 (June 1972), 574–615.

This special report by a committee of the American Accounting Association begins by first reviewing and then evaluating current methods of accounting for marketing activities. Specific improvements that would improve the usefulness of accounting data in allocating marketing effort and evaluating marketing performance are then recommended. A total cost systems approach for planning and efficiently controlling distribution costs is also presented. Use of a contribution approach and a common modular data base to measure both the past and the expected future performance of various marketing segments (customers, territories, products, channels and salespeople) is advocated. The informational outputs required for segmental analysis are identified and the use of variance analysis is illustrated in some detail. The report is the source document upon which committee members drew in numerous subsequent publications.

Sevin, Charles H. *Marketing Productivity Analysis.* New York: McGraw-Hill Book Company, 1965, 137 pp.

In its author's own words, this monograph reveals "How any business firm can increase its sales volume or its net profits very substantially, and more than once, by obtaining and using (1) marketing-cost and profitability information and (2) marketing experimentation information to do a better job of allocating its marketing efforts to the various segments of the business." Optimizing and maximizing are rejected as objectives in resource allocation because of the seeming impossibility of achieving such objectives. Detailed discussions are found of cost and profitability studies in the manufacturing, wholesaling and retailing segments and of the procedures available for increasing the productivity of products, customers and territories. The treatment of distribution costing draws heavily on the author's previously published work. However, new ground is covered in the closing sections which stress the need for experimentation in marketing, the improvements in productivity that could follow from a systematic program of experimentation, and some of the problems involved in establishing such a program.

Shank, John K., and Neil C. Churchill. "Variance Analysis: A Management Oriented Approach," *Accounting Review*, 52 (October 1977), 950–957.

An approach to teaching variance analysis to students that could well be employed with line managers is presented. All variances are organized in terms of their impact on the reported net profit of the unit, and a multilevel approach to analysis is employed. To illustrate the approach, a profit variance of $45 is first broken down into sales, revenue and cost components. At the next level, the relative contribution to this variance of changes in the level of sales activity and of price/cost changes is determined. Still further requirements will reveal the impact of differences in expected versus actual sales, in projected as opposed to actual sales mixes, and in attained rather than budgeted prices. The basic procedure involves holding everything except one factor constant and then calculating the separate impact of that factor's being at a level other than planned. The analytical process would end when the additional level of complexity introduced through continued analysis no longer appeared justified by the new insights provided.

PART II

Decision Making

Marketing Research Expenditures: A Decision Model

6

Frank M. Bass

Recent developments in statistical decision theory suggest the possibility of extending formal analysis of uncertainty to classes of problems for which no analytical framework has previously existed. The so-called Bayesian statistics has application in decision problems in which there is uncertainty about the outcome of a decision and in which some statement can be made regarding the preference for one outcome relative to another.[1] The application area that is the concern of this paper is marketing research.

The need for marketing research as an implement of decision-making arises essentially because of uncertainty. Presumably, the purpose of marketing research in such cases is to reduce the uncertainty. If this is true, the risk reduction associated with reduced uncertainty, and hence the marketing research, has some value. This paper deals with the following questions:

1. How does one place a value on marketing research?
2. How does one decide in a particular instance whether or not to conduct a marketing research study?
3. How does one choose among alternative marketing research projects?

A Brief Outline

The model employed here is one developed by Robert Schlaifer and Howard Raiffa for dealing with decision problems under uncertainty.[2] If one must choose between two decisions when the outcome or result of each decision is known in advance, the choice is obvious. In most business decisions the outcome or result of the decision may be measured in dollars. The decision rule is then: "Choose the act with the highest profit or lowest cost." When there is uncertainty regarding

[1] For a discussion of the framework of Bayesian analysis and a comparison with "classical" statistics see Jack Hirshleifer, "The Bayesian Approach to Statistical Decision: An Exposition," *Journal of Business*, XXXIV (October 1961), 471–89.

[2] For a detailed, but simple, discussion of the basic model and an application in production control see Robert Schlaifer, *Probability and Statistics for Business Decisions* (New York: McGraw-Hill Book Co., 1959), chaps. xxii, xxxiii, and xxxiv. For a more general summary of the method of analysis see Howard Raiffa and Robert Schlaifer, *Applied Statistical Decision Theory* (Boston: Division of Research, Graduate School of Business Administration, Harvard University), chap. i. Also see Harry V. Roberts, "The New Business Statistics," *Journal of Business*, XXXIII (January 1960), 21–30.

the outcome of a particular decision, but when the decision-maker can specify the *possible* outcomes, it is intuitively appealing to assign probability measures reflecting the degree of uncertainty. The model discussed here involves the assignment of probabilities subjectively by the decision-maker to the possible, but unknown, "states of nature." Each state has a given consequence for the firm that may be measured in dollars or some other appropriate index. In deciding between two acts each of which has a set of states, consequences, and probabilities, the choice would go to the act having the greatest expected value, or weighted average of the index of consequences.

Use of Expected Value as a Decision Criterion

In deciding between two acts. expected monetary value will ordinarily be an acceptable decision criterion if the best consequence is not too great or the worst consequence too bad. For example, it might be wise to avoid an act that has bankruptcy as a possible consequence even though this act has a higher expected profit than another act. Conversely, in choosing between $1,500 certain and an act which has 1/1000 probability of yielding $1,000,000 and 999/1000 probability of yielding $0, some people would choose the latter in spite of the higher expected value of the former. However, where expected monetary value fails as a useful decision criterion, it is possible, provided the decision-maker will agree to a few simple conditions and provide some information about his preference for given sums of money and certain gambles, to convert monetary consequences into an index the weighted average of which will serve as a decision criterion that will be acceptable to the decision-maker if he is consistent.[3] Throughout the remainder of this paper it is assumed that the monetary consequences are within a range such that the decision-maker is willing to choose among acts on the basis of their expected monetary values.

Subjective Probability

The following comments are directed to those who object to the assignment of subjective probabilities:

a) Many, if not most, business decisions are once-and-only decisions and consequently no objective (i.e., relative frequency) statistics are available. Hence insistence upon objective probability measures precludes rigorous analysis of the most common and the most important class of business problems.
b) Use of subjective probabilities permits the incorporation into the decision model in a formal way of the many non-objective variables business executives usually take into account in making decisions informally. The end result of "experience,"

---

[3] For a brief, informal discussion of utility theory see Schlaifer, *op. cit.*, chap. ii. For an axiomatic treatment of utility theory see R. D. Luce and H. Raiffa, *Games and Decisions* (New York: John Wiley & Sons, 1957), chap. ii.

"knowledge of the market," etc., is summarized in the subjective probabilities assigned by the decision-maker himself.

c) The purpose of the analysis in which subjective probabilities are employed is to permit the decision-maker to arrive at a decision that is consistent with his explicitly stated beliefs about the "state of nature" and values assigned to consequences, not "truth," whatever that is.

The technique for assigning subjective probabilities is simple. The decision-maker chooses a probability, p, for each possible event in such a way that he would be *indifferent* to the right to receive a prize *if that event occurs* and the *right to a lottery* drawing for the prize in which he holds $p \times$ (number of tickets in the lottery) tickets. If he prefers to take the prize *if the event occurs* rather than a lottery drawing for the prize in which he holds pN tickets, the probability assignment, p, to the event is too small. If he prefers the lottery to the prize if the event occurs, the probability assignment to the event is too high. Thus the probability assignment, a number between 0 and 1, to each possible outcome of the decision reflects the *degree of belief* that that outcome will occur.

Suppose a decision-maker is considering the following gamble: He is to draw from an urn containing only red and black balls. If a red ball is drawn he will win a certain sum of money, but if a black ball is drawn he will lose a certain sum of money. This is analogous to a business decision in which it is possible to either make a profit of a fixed amount or incur a loss of a fixed amount. Just as the decision-maker facing a business situation does not know which of the two possible results will occur, the decision-maker in the urn gamble does not know whether a red or a black ball will be drawn from the urn. Perhaps even more importantly, he does not even know the number of red and black balls in the urn and thus cannot determine the relative frequency probability of either of the two events. It is not necessarily true, however, that he has *no* information upon which to base his decision. He may be permitted to give the urn a casual inspection or even to run his fingers through the balls. Similarly, the businessman will have *some* information at his disposal in the decision problem he faces. Thus if one insists upon a relative frequency interpretation of probability, by implication, the casual information available to the decision-maker is denied validity in a precise analysis of the decision choice.

To obtain the decision-maker's subjective probability assignments to the two possible events in the urn problem, we give him a choice of having the drawing made from the urn described above or from a second urn. Suppose the second urn contains ninety red and ten black balls. Then if the decision-maker prefers to have the drawing made from the second urn rather than the first, we know that a probability assignment of .9 to the event, "a red ball is drawn," is too high. We then keep reducing the ratio of red to black balls in the second urn until we find the ratio for which the decision-maker is indifferent as to whether the drawing is made from the first or the second urn. If, when the second urn contains forty red and sixty black balls, the decision-maker does not care whether the drawing is made from the first or from the second urn, we conclude that the decision-maker's subjective probability assignments for "red" and "black" are .4 and .6 respectively. These probabilities reflect the decision-maker's willingness to act and summarize all of the "information" he has at his command. In a business situation subjective probabilities for each of the possible events may be derived in an entirely analogous fashion.

The Model

The example of the basic decision model to be developed in this paper involves the question of whether or not to do marketing research before introducing a new product. Let us suppose that the company has developed a new product and has conducted some preliminary consumer studies and that the decision-maker appraises the situation (Table 1).

Here he is only willing to consider three possible states of nature as being significant for consideration.[4] The discounted (present value) future profits which will result from each of the three market share results and the corresponding probabilities are shown in Table 1. If a decision must be made now between introducing the new product and not introducing it, the new product would be introduced, since the expected value of this act is $.7 \times \$10$ million $+ .1 \times \$1$ million $+ .2 \times -\$5$ million $= \$6.1$ million as against an expected value of $1 \times \$0 = \$0$ for not introducing the new brand.

Expected Value of "Perfect" Information

The real question here is whether or not it is worthwhile to collect some additional marketing research information before making the final decision. Remembering that we are using the expected-value decision criterion, it will perhaps seem natural to make this decision on the basis of a comparison of the expected value of the

TABLE 1. *Possible market shares, profits, and probability assessments for a new product*

Market shares (possible states of nature)	Discounted profits (consequences)	Probabilities
θ_1 = capture 10 per cent of market	$10,000,000	.7
θ_2 = capture 3 per cent of market	$ 1,000,000	.1
θ_3 = capture 0 per cent of market	$-\$ 5,000,000$	.2

[4] It would be entirely possible to refine this to the point of considering θ (market share) as varying continuously from 0 to 1. The example here has been purposely simplified. A more realistic continuous case is considered later.

optimal act *before the research*, $6.1 million in this case, and the expected value of the optimal act *after the research* less the cost of the research.

At this point it may be useful to calculate the greatest conceivable increase in expected value that "perfect" information might provide. To do this we define "expected profit under certainty" as the expected profit we would realize if we were to take the best action for the state of nature that actually materializes. Although the decision we are considering is unique, expected profit under certainty does provide a useful yardstick. In this case, if θ_1 or θ_2 prevails the optimal act will be to introduce the new product with payoffs of $10 million and $1 million, respectively, while if θ_3 is the true state of nature, the optimal act will be not to introduce the new product for a payoff of $0. Although we are not using probabilities in a relative frequency sense, it is helpful, and always permissible, to think of them in that way in interpreting expected profit under certainty. Thus, if the same decision problem were faced many times, each time knowing the true state of nature in advance, we would make a profit of $10 million 7/10 of the time, a profit of $1 million 1/10 of the time, and a profit of $0 2/10 of the time. Therefore, expected profit under certainty is $7/10 \times \$10$ million $+ 1/10 \times \$1$ million $+ 2/10 \times \$0 = \$7.1$ million. The difference between expected profit under certainty and expected profit under the optimal act, $7.1 million $-$ $6.1 million, is called the "expected value of perfect information." Thus we know immediately that the value of the marketing research cannot possibly exceed $1 million, and if the cost of the proposed research exceeds this amount we know that the risk reduction is not worth the cost.

Specific Research Proposals

The next question to be decided is whether or not specific research proposals are worth their cost, having already ruled out proposals in which the cost exceeds $1 million. Under consideration, let us assume, are two potential marketing research activities, a test marketing operation and a consumer panel test. The cost of the test marketing research plan is $100,000, while the consumer panel study will cost $10,000.

Test Marketing

At this point we will require additional probability assignments from the decision-maker. Specifically, we will require the assignment of probabilities to each of the relevant outcomes of the research investigation conditional upon a given state of nature being the true state.[5] For example, in Table 2 the decision-maker has indicated

---

[5] Alternatively we could ask for unconditional probability assignments for the outcomes of the test market and for conditional probability assignments for the possible states of nature given a particular outcome of the test market. The choice between these two methods of arriving at *joint* probabilities should be made on the basis of utilizing most effectively the decision-maker's experience and knowledge. Also, just as it is possible to consider the state of nature as varying continuously from 0 to 1, it is also possible to consider the possible outcomes of the test marketing as varying continuously. These refinements, while adding to the complexities of calculation, do not alter the basic nature of the analysis.

TABLE 2. *Conditional probabilities of possible outcomes of test market*

| | Outcomes | | | |
| | Sell 10 per cent of market or more in test (Z_1) | Sell 5–10 per cent of market in test (Z_2) | Sell less than 5 per cent in test (Z_3) | Total |
States				
Market share = 10 per cent–θ_1	.6	.3	.1	1.0
Market share = 3 per cent–θ_2	.3	.6	.1	1.0
Market share = 0 per cent–θ_3	.1	.1	.8	1.0

that three possible outcomes of the test market are relevant: $Z_1 =$ selling 10 per cent of the market or more in the test; $Z_2 =$ selling 5 to 10 per cent of the test market; $Z_3 =$ selling less than 5 per cent of the test market. Designating "probability of Z_1 given θ_1 is the true state of nature" by $P(Z_1|\theta_1)$, we see that the decision-maker has assigned a probability of .6 to $P(Z_1|\theta_1)$, whereas the probability assigned to "selling" 5 to 10 per cent of the test market given θ_1 is the true state, $P(Z_2|\theta_1)$, is .3.

Posterior Analysis

Now suppose we ask: What is the expected profit of introducing the new product if we have observed some specific outcome of the test market, say Z_3, and what is the expected profit of not introducing the new product if we have observed this same outcome? In other words, we are placing ourselves in a position of having observed Z_3 and asking what we would do in this circumstance. If, having observed Z_3, the expected profit of a_1 (the decision to introduce the new product) is greater than the expected profit of a_2 (the decision not to introduce the new product), we will, of course, introduce the new product. Otherwise, we will not.

In order to carry out this "posterior" analysis we will need the probabilities of θ_1, θ_2, and θ_3 being true conditional upon having observed Z_3. Therefore we will need $P(\theta_1|Z_3)$, $P(\theta_2|Z_3)$, and $P(\theta_3|Z_3)$. We already have enough data to calculate these probabilities since they were implicitly determined when the decision-maker explicitly assigned unconditional probabilities to θ_1, θ_2, and θ_3 and conditional probabilities to Z_1, Z_2, and Z_3. If we are told that Z_3 is true, it is intuitively clear that we should alter our probability assignment for θ_1 in order to take into account this information. Thus

$$P(\theta_1|Z_3) = \frac{\text{probability that } \theta_1 \text{ and } Z_3 \text{ are both true}}{\text{probability that } Z_3 \text{ is true}}.$$

Similarly,

$$P(Z_i|\theta_j) = \frac{\text{probability that } \theta_j \text{ and } Z_i \text{ are both true}}{\text{probability that } \theta_j \text{ is true}}.$$

In Tables 1 and 2 the decision-maker has already assigned probabilities $P(\theta_j)$, $j = 1$, 2, 3, and $P(Z_i|\theta_j)$, $i, j = 1$, 2, 3. Using the latest equation above, then, we may compute the probability that θ_j and Z_i are both true $= P(Z_i|\theta_j)P(\theta_j)$, since this follows, algebraically, from the equation. These computations are shown in Table 3. Notice that the sum of the row values equals the previously assigned unconditional probabilities $P(\theta_j)$, $j = 1$, 2, 3. Similarly, the sum of the column values represents the unconditional probabilities $P(Z_i)$, $i = 1$, 2, 3. Thus, in Table 3 we have all the data necessary to compute $P(\theta_j|Z_i)$, $i, j = 1$, 2, 3. For example, $P(\theta_1|Z_3) = .07/.24 = .292$; $P(\theta_2|Z_3) = .01/.24 = .041$; $P(\theta_3|Z_3) = .16/.24 = .666$. Therefore, the expected profit for a_1, the decision to introduce the new brand, if we test-market the product and if we find that we sell less than 5 per cent of the market in the

TABLE 3. Joint probabilities of states and test outcomes

States	Test outcomes Z_1	Z_2	Z_3	$P(\theta_j)$
θ_1	.42	.21	.07	.7
θ_2	.03	.06	.01	.1
θ_3	.02	.02	.16	.2
$P(Z_i)$	.47	.29	.24	1.00

test (observe Z_3), is $.283 \times \$10$ million $+ .041 \times \$1$ million $+ .666 \times -\$5$ million $= -\$459$ million, while under the same circumstances the expected profit for a_2, the decision not to introduce the new product, is obviously \$0. Hence, if we should observe Z_3 in the test we would choose a_2 and expect to make \$0. The reader can show that if Z_2 is observed the expected profit for a_1 is \$7.09 million, while if Z_i is observed the expected profit for a_1 is \$8.794 million. Thus, if either Z_1 or Z_2 is observed the choice of decision will be a_1. Notice that the posterior analysis specifies a decision rule for each outcome of the test.

Preposterior Analysis

Having determined the expected profit of the optimal decision, a_1 or a_2, conditional upon each of the three outcomes of the test market, we are now in a position to calculate the unconditional expected profit of the decision to test-market the new product and to compare it with the expected profit of the decision to act without the benefit of the test-market information. Figure 1 summarizes the analysis.

FIGURE 1. *Analysis of proposal to test-market new product*

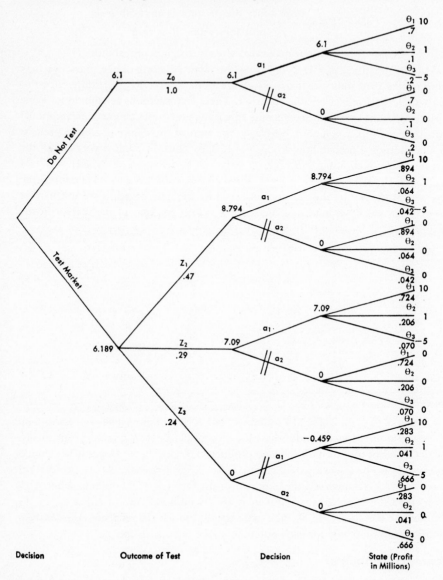

Decision   Outcome of Test   Decision   State (Profit
                                                                                            in Millions)

To find the expected profit of the decision to test-market the new brand, neglecting the cost of the test, the conditional expected profits of the optimal act, a_1 or a_2, are multiplied by their respective probabilities of being operative and summed. Thus, the probability of Z_1 resulting in the test, $P(Z_1)$, is .47, while $P(Z_2) = .29$, and $P(Z_3) = .24$. The expected profits conditional upon Z_1, Z_2, and Z_3, respectively, are \$8.794 million, \$7.09 million, and \$0. Hence the expected profit of the decision to test-market the new product is .47 × \$8.794 million + .29 × \$7.09 million + .24 × \$0 = \$6.189 million.

Starting from the left we see in the decision tree in Figure 1 that if we take the branch of the tree labeled "Do not test," we look forward to an expected profit of \$6.1 million. This figure was previously derived from the probabilities and conditional profits in Table 1. If we decide not to obtain test-market information, the optimal act is a_1 since a_1 leads to an expected profit of \$6.1 million while a_2 leads to an expected profit of \$0. The branch of the tree labeled "Test market" leads to an expected profit of \$6.189 million. Therefore in choosing between the branch "Do not test" and the branch "Test market," we should choose to obtain the test-market information as long as the cost of this information does not exceed \$89,000. If the cost of test-market information exceeds \$89,000, the decision to buy the information is not consistent with the rule: "Choose the act with the greatest expected profit."

If we choose the "Test market" branch of the decision tree, three results of the test-market experiment are possible: Z_1, Z_2, or Z_3. If Z_1 or Z_2 is the result of the test-market experiment, a_1 is the optimal act since in either case the expected profit associated with a_1 conditional upon either Z_1 or Z_2 is greater than the expected profit associated with a_2. However, if Z_3 is the measurement in the test market, a_2 will yield a higher expected profit than a_1.

We see clearly in the decision tree the action choice we should make at each stage. We always choose the branch with the greatest expected profit. In this case we should reject the test-marketing plan since the information will cost \$100,000.

A Brief Overview

The Bayesian approach to decisions under uncertainty utilizes the expected-value decision rule. It recognizes that the outcome of a decision depends upon which of the several possible "states of nature" is the true state of nature. Probability assignments are then made for each possible state of nature in such a way that they reflect the decision-maker's willingness to act. Thus, having adopted the expected-value decision criterion, the decision choice depends upon the probability assignments. When it is possible, as in the case of marketing research, to collect additional information before acting, the decision-maker looks ahead to the possible outcomes of the research and asks himself how he would revise the original probability assignments conditional upon each of these results turning up on the research. This is valuable in itself in that it forces the decision-maker to evaluate the research design and to consider the relevance of the possible results to the decision problem. In all too many instances marketing-research studies have no real application to the basic decision under review. Suppose, for example, that a choice between act 1 and act 2 is being considered and suppose further that a marketing-research investigation can have three possible results. If the decision-maker says that he would always choose act 1 regardless of which of these results occurs in the research, the marketing research is without value as far as the basic decision is concerned. The research has value only when the research results can affect the decision. Bayesian analysis provides a formal system for evaluating research in advance.

Consumer Panel

To determine the value of the consumer panel information, we must proceed in the same fashion as we did with the test marketing. First, the decision-maker assigns probabilities to Z_i, $i = 1, 2 \ldots, n$, conditional on θ_j, $j = 1, 2, 3$, being the true state of nature. Let us suppose that we ask panel members to compare the new product with their present brand in certain basic characteristics. Suppose further:

$Z_1 = 25$ per cent or more of the panel report the new product to be superior to their present brand in two or more basic characteristics.

$Z_2 = 10$–25 per cent of the panel report the new product to be superior to their present brand in two or more characteristics.

$Z_3 =$ less than 10 per cent of the panel report the new product to be superior to their present brand in two or more characteristics.

Obviously there are many different ways to tabulate the possible outcomes of the consumer panel data and hence there are many possible ways to specify the Z_i's. Selection of the experimental observations is a matter of judgment. In general, this should be done in such a way that one would be willing to change the prior

TABLE 4. *Conditional probabilities of possible outcomes of consumer panel*

	Outcomes		
States	25 per cent or more superior (Z_1)	10–25 per cent superior (Z_2)	Less than 10 per cent superior (Z_3)
Market share = 10 per cent–θ_1	.8	.1	.1
Market share = 3 per cent–θ_2	.3	.4	.3
Market share = 0 per cent–θ_3	.1	.1	.8

FIGURE 2. *Analysis of proposal for consumer panel research*

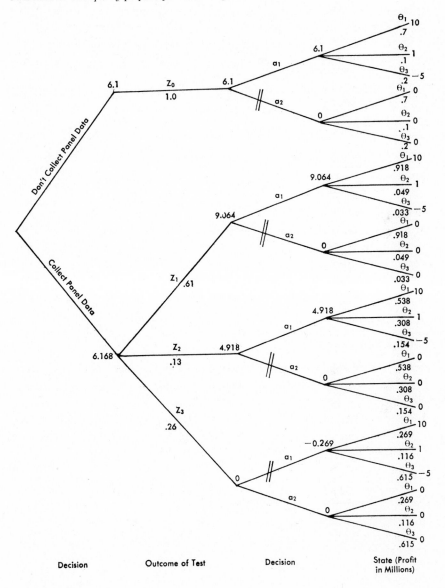

probability assignments if a particular result of the experiment turns up. The general criterion is: "Of all the possible outcomes of the test, which ones will make me change my mind about my original probability assignments?" Thus the posterior probability, $P(\theta_j | Z_i)$, will, in general, be substantially different from $P(\theta_j)$.

Table 4 shows the conditional probability assignments to Z_1, Z_2, and Z_3, while Table 5 shows the joint distribution.

Figure 2 reveals that the consumer panel data is worth up to $68,000. Since the cost of the panel data is only $10,000, the panel information is well worth its cost.

TABLE 5. *Joint probabilities of states and panel outcomes*

| States | Panel outcomes | | | |
	Z_1	Z_2	Z_3	$P(\theta_j)$
θ_1	.56	.07	.07	.7
θ_2	.03	.04	.03	.1
θ_3	.02	.02	.16	.2
$P(Z_i)$	.61	.13	.26	1.00

Perfect Predictor

Suppose we are examining the value of information in a situation where the market share, p, of the new product can be any number within certain limits, p_L and p_M. In other words we know market share cannot exceed p_M and cannot be less than p_L, but may be any number between these limits. For example, suppose we know that the market share will not be less than .12 nor more than .40. Let us assume further that profit varies in a linear fashion with p, market share.

Linear Profit Function

As an example suppose that discounted future profit depends on market share in such a way that

$$\text{profit of the new product} = -\$700{,}000 + \$10{,}000{,}000(p - p_L).$$

If $p_L = .12$, then p_B, the break-even market share, is .19. This is illustrated in Figure 3. Thus maximum profit is $2.1 million when market share is .40. Now if the decision-maker assigns a probability distribution to p, where $p_L \leqslant p \leqslant p_M$, the expected profit for the decision to introduce the new brand is

$$-\$700{,}000 + \$10{,}000{,}000[\text{expected value of } (p - p_L)].$$

FIGURE 3. *Profit conditional on market share*

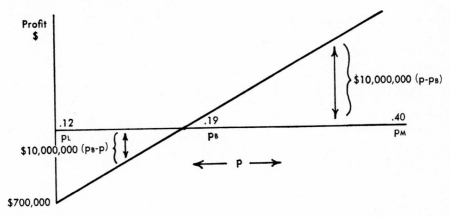

Thus to obtain the expected profit for the decision to introduce the new product we need only to replace p by its expected value. Therefore, if the probability distribution assigned by the decision-maker is such that the expected value of p is greater than p_B, the decision-maker will introduce the new product; otherwise he will not.

"Equally Likely Distribution"

Now let us suppose that the decision-maker feels that knowing the outcome of the test-marketing operation is equivalent to knowing p. In other words, the test market is a perfect predictor of p. In this case, the expected value of the market information is the same as the expected value of perfect information.

Let us determine the value of the test-market information when the decision-maker feels that every value of p between .12 and .40 is equally likely. We consider this distribution only for its simplicity, not because it would necessarily be realistic! In this case the expected value of p is $.12 + 1/2 (.40 - .12) = .26$. Since this is greater than p_B, if the decision-maker had to choose between introducing the new product and not introducing it without the benefit of the test-market information, he would introduce the new brand.

Expected Value of Perfect Information

If after getting the test-market information we find that p is less than p_B we will not, of course, introduce the new product and receive a profit of $0, while if after the test market we find that p is greater than p_B we will introduce the new product and obtain a profit that depends on p. Conditional profit after the test-market information has been received is shown as the heavy line in Figure 4. The conditional

FIGURE 4. *Conditional profit after test-market information*

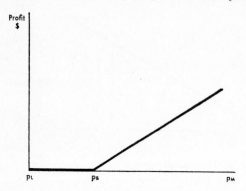

profits of introducing the new product prior to the test-marketing operation are shown as the heavy line in Figure 5.

Just as in the decision tree we found that the expected value of the research information was the difference between the expected profits of two branches of the tree, we find here that expected value of test-marketing information (with perfect prediction of p) = expected value of the set of points in Figure 4 minus expected value of the set of points in Figure 5. The value of the information, as before, is the difference between expected profit if we act after collecting additional information and the expected profit if we act without the benefit of additional information. In this case we subtract the set of points in Figure 4 from those in Figure 5 and take the expected value of the remainder. Thus the expected value of test-marketing information is the expected value of the function shown in Figure 6, where $k = \$10$ million is the slope of the profit function.

The expected value of test-marketing information in this case is $87,500 and (in general, when the probability assignment to p is "equally likely" between p_L and p_M and the prior expected value of p is greater than p_B) will be

FIGURE 5. *Conditional profit prior to test-market information*

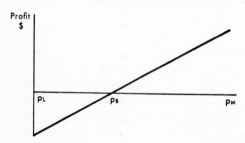

FIGURE 6. *Conditional losses for decision to introduce new product*

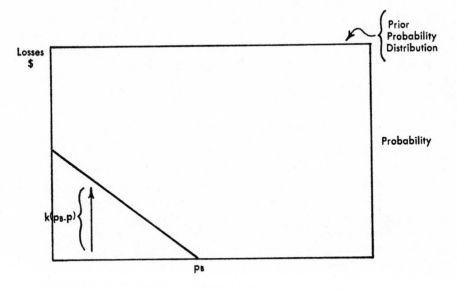

$$\frac{k(p_B - p_L)^2}{2(p_M - p_L)}, \tag{1}$$

where k = the increase in profit for each increase of .01 in p, that is, the slope of the profit function.[6] If the prior expected value of p is less than p_B, the best act prior to test-marketing will be not to introduce the new product. In this case the expected value of perfect information will be expected value of the set of points in Figure 7 and the expected value of perfect information is:

$$\frac{k(p_M - p_B)^2}{2(p_M - p_L)}. \tag{2}$$

Formula (1) applies when the decision-maker would choose to introduce the new brand if he had to choose between introducing it and not introducing it without additional information.[7] Its use does not require that the conditional profit function be linear in p for possible market share above p_B. It does require, however, that conditional profit, i.e., losses, be linear for market shares below p_B.[8] This is very important since ordinarily it will be much more difficult in practice to estimate

---

[6] This formula is obtained by integrating $k(p_B - p)f(p)$ over the interval (p_L, p_B). Formula (2) is obtained by integrating $k(p - p_B)f(p)$ over the interval (p_B, p_M), where $f(p)$ is the probability function $1/p_M - p_L$.

[7] This implies prior expected profit is positive.

[8] Conversely, when prior expected profit for the decision to introduce the new product is negative, it is required that conditional opportunity losses be linear for values $> p_B$.

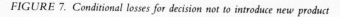

FIGURE 7. *Conditional losses for decision not to introduce new product*

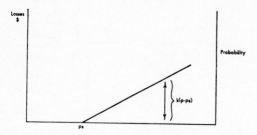

conditional profit for market shares above p_B than to specify losses for values below p_B. Also, it will ordinarily be reasonable to approximate conditional losses below p_B with a linear function. Thus formulas (1) and (2) provide a convenient method of establishing an *upper bound* on the value of marketing research information when (a) the decision-maker is certain that market share will lie in an interval bounded by p_L and p_M, but feels that each possible market share is equally likely and (b) conditional losses are linear below p_B for (1) and above p_B for (2).

It should be emphasized that formulas (1) and (2) determine the expected value of *perfect* information. If the information the decision-maker receives is less than perfect in the sense that knowing the outcome of the research investigation does not permit one to predict with certainty the true market share, the expected value of the information is necessarily less than that specified in formulas (1) and (2).

Prior Distribution

The expected value of perfect information depends crucially on the prior probability distribution of possible market shares. In theory there is an infinite variety of distributions that may, under given circumstances, reflect the decision-maker's best judgment and willingness to bet about market share. One distribution that is capable, with the proper choice of parameters, of fitting a large number of situations is the "normal" distribution.

If we use a normal distribution with mean = .26 and standard deviation = .046 to analyze the expected value of perfect information when conditional profits are as described in the previous example, we have the situation illustrated in Figure 8.

In this case the probability that market share is less than or equal to p_B is .06426 as compared to 1/4 with the equally likely distribution. Since the probability of loss is less in this case, intuition suggests that the expected value of perfect information should be less. When the normal prior distribution is used with characteristics determined by the parameters suggested above, the expected value of perfect information is $12,880, only about 15 per cent of the value in the equally likely

FIGURE 8. Conditional losses and normal distribution

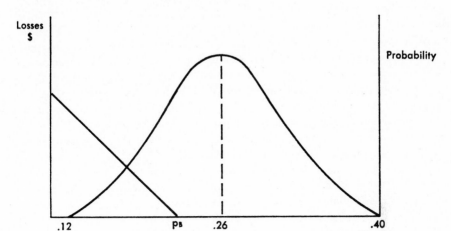

case. This example clearly demonstrates the importance of the prior probabilities in the analysis.

Summary and Conclusions

Funds are often appropriated for marketing-research studies without consideration of (a) monetary consequences of various possible acts and states of nature, or (b) the probability of choosing the "wrong" act. The decision theory approach outlined here provides a convenient method of formally analyzing all the relevant variables in order to decide whether or not to collect additional information before acting, and if so, how much the additional information is worth.

The decision model permits the decision-maker to utilize all the "information" he has at his command and to summarize this information in probability assignments and conditional profit estimates. One of the more important advantages of the formal analysis is that it provides a decision rule for each possible outcome of the proposed marketing research study.

In examining marketing research cases one is often struck with the fact that regardless of the outcome of the research project, the decision choice is unaffected or unclear. Formal analysis prior to the research may not only provide a better basis for evaluating a specific research proposal, but may also suggest a research design that would provide information which is more germane to the decision before management.

Exercises

6.1. Deluxware has developed a new electric machine for making homemade peanut butter. Preliminary consumer studies have indicated a favorable response. The marketing manager is inclined toward introducing the new product immediately on a small scale. However, his newly trained marketing research analyst recommends that additional market research be conducted to confirm the feasibility of its presentation. The marketing manager would be convinced of the value of his recommendation if additional information would point to greater profits. Based on the information from his initial studies, the manager is willing to consider three possible market shares obtainable from launching this product. If the market share is 12%, he expects discounted future profits of $8 million; if it is 5%, he believes profits will fall to $2 million; and if the market share is only 2%, he expects to incur a loss of $4 million. Using his experience and intuition, he assigns probabilities of 0.7, 0.1, and 0.2, respectively, to the states.

He also indicates that three possible outcomes of the test market are relevant: selling 20% or more, selling between 10% and 20%, and selling less than 10%. The probabilities of these possible outcomes conditional upon the states are given in Table 6.1.

TABLE 6.1. *Conditional probabilities of possible outcomes of test market*

	Outcomes		
States	Sell 20% or more in test (Z_1)	Sell 10–20% in test (Z_2)	Sell less than 10% in test (Z_3)
σ_1: market share = 12%	0.7	0.2	0.1
σ_2: market share = 5%	0.2	0.7	0.1
σ_3: market share = 2%	0.1	0.1	0.8

Assume that the cost of gathering additional market information is $30,000 and that you are the newly trained market research analyst.

1. How would you persuade your manager to follow your recommendation?
2. What is the value of the additional market information?
3. Specify the decision rule that you have employed in your analysis.

6.2. Beauty Queen is a medium-size manufacturer of ladies' hair spray. Its research team has successfully developed a new product believed to be decidedly superior to the current leading brand. Before introducing the new brand on the market, management proposes to conduct a consumer panel test to gather more information on the acceptability of the new product among potential customers. During the panel test, participants are asked to compare the new product with their present brand in three or more characteristics. Let Z be the percentage of superiority of the new product over the present brand in three or more characteristics, and let θ_i be the possible market share obtainable with the introduction of the new product. The expected profits and probabilities of occurrence of each of the three states are given in Table 6.2. In addition, management also assigns probabilities to the possible outcomes conditional upon the different market shares (see Table 6.3). The cost of the consumer panel test is expected to be $25,000.

TABLE 6.2. *Expected profits and probabilities of occurrence*

Market shares (possible states)	Discounted profits	Probabilities
$\theta_1 = 4\%$	-$20,000	0.25
$\theta_2 = 8\%$	$80,000	0.55
$\theta_3 = 12\%$	$450,000	0.20

TABLE 6.3. *Conditional probabilities of possible outcomes of consumer panel*

Outcomes	States		
	θ_1 (4%)	θ_2 (8%)	θ_3 (12%)
Z_1: less than 10% superior	0.65	0.20	0.15
Z_2: between 10 and 20% superior	0.25	0.55	0.20
Z_3: more than 20% superior	0.10	0.25	0.65

Based on this information,

1. What is the expected profit if the consumer panel test is conducted?
2. What is the expected profit if management decides to introduce the product without the consumer panel test?
3. What is the value of the additional information obtainable from the panel test?
4. Should management proceed with the consumer panel test? Specify the decision rule that you have used.

Marketing Investment Analysis   7

Paul F. Anderson

I. Introduction

It has long been recognized that many of the more important marketing decisions which a firm must face may be viewed as investment decisions [4, 10, 21, 22]. An investment may be defined as an outlay of cash in the current period which is expected to generate cash returns in future periods. As such, decisions to introduce new products, to commit more resources to sales territories, or to improve the long-term efficiency of distribution channels may all be classed as marketing investments. It is the intention of this paper to assess the current state of the art in marketing investment analysis and to explore the possible future directions in this area. The former task will involve a review of the marketing and traditional finance literatures, while the latter task will require an exploration of the leading edge of financial theory. The paper begins with a brief review and critique of contemporary procedures for analyzing marketing investments.

II. Contemporary Methods of Marketing Investment Analysis

Two basic methods of analyzing investment opportunities are popular in the marketing literature. The first may be referred to as the average rate of return on investment (ROI) approach.

Return on Investment

ROI is calculated as the ratio of the average annual net income generated by the project to the average investment in the project:

$$\text{ROI} = \frac{\text{average annual net income}}{\text{average investment}} \tag{1}$$

Investment opportunities whose return exceeds some predetermined cut-off rate are accepted, and all others are rejected.

Many variations on the form and use of this approach are to be found in the literature [10, 14, 21, 22]. In some cases cash flow or contribution margin is substituted for net income. In other cases, the return is calculated as a single rather

---

Adapted from "Marketing Investment Analysis" in *Research in Marketing*, Volume 4, J. N. Sheth, ed., Greenwich, CT: JAI Press (1980).

than a multiple period measure. In addition, ROI is frequently employed as a control as well as an evaluation tool.

There are at least two serious problems with the ROI approach to investment evaluation. Its first and foremost difficulty is that it ignores the time value of money. Projects are evaluated solely on the basis of their return to investment ratios. The rapidity with which returns are realized is not considered. Its second major problem is that ROI fails to consider the differential risk of investment projects. Investment rankings based on ROI alone can be misleading. Quite often high return opportunities carry with them high levels of risk. Clearly, a prudent marketing manager would wish to consider both risk and return in selecting among alternative investment strategies.

Discounted Cash Flow

The other major approach to the evaluation of marketing investments involves the use of discounted cash flow (DCF) techniques [3, 10]. There are two discounted cash flow procedures in the literature: the net present value (NPV) and the internal rate of return (IRR) methods. The NPV technique simply calculates the present value sum of the net cash flows resulting from a project:

$$\text{NPV} = \sum_{i=1}^{n} \frac{A_i}{(1+k)^i} \tag{2}$$

where NPV = the net present value of the project, A_i = the net cash flows resulting from the project in year i (this includes both inflows and outflows of cash), n = the expected life of the project in years, and k = the firm's weighted average cost of capital (WACC). The firm's decision rule is to accept the proposal if NPV is equal to or greater than zero. This implies that the return on the project equals or exceeds the firm's cost of capital.

The IRR method, on the other hand, solves the discounting formula for the rate which equates the present value of the cash inflows with the present value of the cash outflows. This is accomplished by determining k^* in equation (3):

$$0 = \sum_{i=1}^{n} \frac{A_i}{(1+k^*)^i} \tag{3}$$

where k^* is the internal rate of return on the investment. The firm should accept the project if k^* equals or exceeds the firm's cost of capital.[1]

Unlike the ROI approach, discounted cash flow methods take into account the time value of money. The discounting mechanism automatically adjusts for the differential timing of cash flows. Thus the present values or internal rates of return of projects with different cash flow configurations can be compared directly.

---

[1] Because of the "reinvestment rate" problem and the potential for multiple rates of return, the net present value method is considered to be theoretically superior to the internal rate of return model.

Another advantage of DCF over the return on investment approach is that the former employs cash flow as the return criterion. Cash flow, not net income, is the accepted measure of investment return [26]. An investment is essentially a commitment of immediate cash in anticipation of cash returns extending over some period of time. Cash is the important criterion, because only cash receipts can be reinvested in other projects or paid to stockholders as dividends. Net income, on the other hand, is an accrual accounting concept which results from an attempt to match expenses to benefiting periods regardless of when the actual cash outflow occurs [24].

Unfortunately, traditional discounted cash flow techniques do not consider the risk element in investment analysis. In order to deal with the problem of risk, various modifications of the DCF procedures have been suggested. Four of the more widely known approaches will be presented here.

Risk-Adjusted Hurdle Rate. The risk-adjusted hurdle rate approach is employed with internal rate of return methodologies. The technique involves a subjective adjustment of the firm's cost of capital to account for the riskiness of various investment projects [5, 25]. For example, assume that Firm J is considering four new-product investments represented by the letters A, B, C, and D. The expected internal rates of return for the new products are as shown below:

Product	IRR
A	18.7%
B	9.7%
C	14.0%
D	7.9%

In the traditional IRR approach, the firm would use its weighted average cost of capital (WACC) as the hurdle rate for each of the four products. Thus, if the WACC was 11.5%, products A and C would be accepted, and products B and D would be rejected.

However, management may believe that the riskiness of products A and C is such that a higher hurdle rate is necessary. Thus, a risk-adjusted rate of 16.0% might be applied as a cut-off criterion. With this approach, only product A would be considered an acceptable investment opportunity.

Risk-Adjusted Discount Rates. The risk-adjusted discount rate approach is formally equivalent to the risk-adjusted hurdle rate technique. Here, however, the risk-adjusted cost of capital becomes the discount rate used to determine the net present value of the investment alternatives [25]. All investment opportunities whose NPVs equal or exceed zero are accepted. Once again, this is equivalent to requiring the return on the project to equal or exceed the risk-adjusted cost of capital.

Certainty-Equivalent. The certainty-equivalent approach is generally employed with net present value methodologies. It involves the application of a risk-adjustment factor to the cash flows in the NPV formula:

$$\text{NPV} = \sum_{i=1}^{n} \frac{C_i A_i}{(1 + R_f)^i} \tag{4}$$

where C_i = the certainty-equivalent coefficient for year i, and R_f = the risk-free rate of interest (this is usually approximated by the return on short-term government securities) [25].

The certainty-equivalent coefficient can take on values between 0 and 1.00 and will vary inversely with the level of risk in the cash flows. The coefficient is determined by management's subjective risk preferences and may assume different values for different years. Thus, if management views risk as increasing over time, the certainty-equivalent coefficient will decline over the expected life of the project. The risk-free rate is used to discount the cash flows because the adjustment for risk takes place in the numerator. The riskless rate simply accounts for the time value of money.

Robichek and Myers suggest that the certainty-equivalent approach is theoretically superior to the risk-adjusted discount rate method [16]. They have demonstrated that the risk-adjusted discount rate implies increasing risk over time. While it is true that the assumption of increasing risk may be correct, they argue that certainty-equivalents allow management to explicitly consider the exact nature of the time pattern of risk.

Kotler's Risk-Return Criterion. The risk-return approach suggested by Kotler is conceptually similar to the capital asset pricing model approach to be discussed in a later section of this article [10]. Both approaches rest on the assumption that investment analysis is essentially a process of identifying the trade-offs between the risk and return of various investment opportunities.

In order to explicate the risk-return trade-offs, Kotler employs a graphical device similar to that shown as Exhibit 1. Here, rate of return is plotted along the vertical axis, and risk, as measured by the variance of return, is plotted along the horizontal axis.[2] Each point in this two-dimensional diagram represents the risk-return ordered pair of a potential investment project.

The risk-return space is divided into three decision regions. The area in the upper left is known as the GO region because management looks favorably upon projects with relatively high return and low risk. The cut-off line for the GO region has an intercept of 10 percent because this is the minimum return which management is willing to accept. The slope of the line represents management's subjective trade-off of risk for return. For example, if the slope of this line were 2.5, it would mean

---

[2] The rate of return and variance of a project are estimated subjectively by the decision maker.

EXHIBIT 1

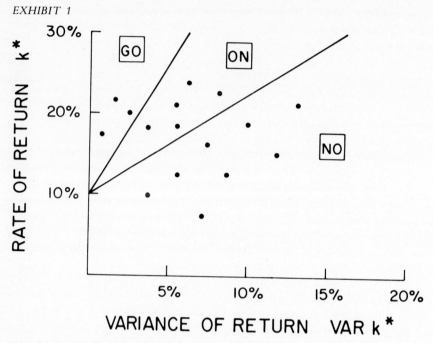

Source: Adapted from Philip Kotler, *Marketing Decision Making* (New York: Holt, Rinehart and Winston, 1971), p. 265.

that management requires an increase in return of 2.5 percent to compensate for a 1.0 percent increase in risk (variance).

The ON region contains projects with questionable risk-return profiles. Kotler suggests that additional marketing research be conducted on these proposals to clarify their risk-return potential. With additional information, management should be able to reclassify the projects in either the GO or the NO region. Investments falling in the NO region are deemed to be unacceptable to management and are rejected.

Of course, projects falling in the GO region must still be ranked in terms of their attractiveness. This is especially important if the firm operates under self-imposed capital rationing. Kotler suggests that this can be accomplished with reference to management's "utility function" for risk and return. If such a function can be identified, it is a simple process to rank-order the investments in the GO region.

Criticisms of Risk Analysis Methodologies

The four risk analysis methodologies presented above all have a number of potential limitations. One problem is that risk-adjusted rates and certainty-equivalents are highly subjective risk measures. Because of individual differences in risk preferences and estimating abilities, their application is likely to be inconsistent across projects and time periods. Indeed, there is always the danger that risk estimates may reflect the vested interests of various decision makers. Given the subjective nature of the task, it is not at all difficult to select and justify discount rates or certainty-equivalents which ensure the acceptance of "pet" projects.

A related problem is that these estimates reflect the preferences of management and are not necessarily those of the firm's stockholders. (This criticism also applies to Kotler's approach.) Ideally, investment decisions should be made in accordance with the risk-return preferences of the firm's shareholders. As the owners of the firm and the ultimate risk-bearers, it is the stockholders who should determine the levels of return they wish to attain and the risks they are willing to assume.

A second potential problem related to the Kotler model concerns the use of return variance as the risk surrogate. This is known in the financial literature as the total-project-risk approach [7]. Unfortunately, financial theorists are uncertain as to whether return variance is the appropriate risk measure for firm investment decisions. In a subsequent section, this issue will be reviewed and its implications for marketing investment analysis will be developed.

III. Corporate Goals and Marketing Investment Analysis

In the previous section, it was suggested that investment decisions should be made in accordance with the risk-return preferences of the firm's shareholders rather than its management. This view is widely held among financial theorists and is reflective of the fact that modern investment theory is built upon the assumption that shareholder wealth maximization is the firm's ultimate objective [6]. It should be noted that this is not necessarily the same as the objective of profit maximization. There are at least three significant problems with the profit maximization objective which make it a less than adequate criterion for investment analysis.

The first problem with profit maximization is its vagueness. The firm has a wide variety of profit measures which it could seek to maximize. For example, should the firm maximize the dollar amount of profits or earnings per share? What about return-on-equity versus return-on-assets? Should the firm focus on long-run or short-run profits? Finally, should accounting profits be measured or is cash flow more appropriate? The particular definition of profit employed has important implications for managerial decision making.

A second problem with the profit maximization criterion is that it cannot provide management with guidance in selecting alternatives which differ in the timing or duration of their cash flows. For example, should the firm invest in a project which returns $200,000 five years from now or one which produces $30,000 in each of the next five years? According to a pure profit maximization criterion, the former investment opportunity is the obvious choice. However, if the firm can reinvest the returns from the second alternative at a certain 15 percent, it will find that by the end of the fifth year it will have a total return of $202,271. Obviously, the firm must take into account the time value of money when evaluating investment opportunities.

A third, and possibly the most important, concern with the profit maximization criterion is that it does not consider the risk or uncertainty of investment returns. As noted previously, risk is frequently defined as the variability in the possible returns from a project [8, 26]. Exhibit 2 shows the probability distributions of the returns for two investment projects. Both have average expected annual returns of $5,000. However, the variability in the return of project Y is expected to be much greater than that of project X. Thus, project X is the preferred alternative on the basis of its lower level of risk. Application of a strict profit maximization criterion to this decision would not have differentiated between the two alternatives.

Because of the problems associated with the profit maximization objective, financial theorists have adopted the broader and more comprehensive objective of maximizing shareholder wealth. Maximization of shareholder wealth—i.e., maximizing the price of the firm's stock—provides the firm with the operational criterion it needs to make investment decisions. It is unambiguous; and, as will be demonstrated, it allows for the consideration of timing, duration, and risk differences in the returns of alternative investments.

It should be noted that the objective of share price maximization does not mean that management must make all decisions with one eye on the stock market ticker. Indeed, the short-term movements in stock prices are much too volatile to provide a useful guide for corporate action. Rather, what is implied by the wealth maximization criterion is that corporate investment decisions should be made according to a set of principles which are designed to ensure that shareholder wealth

EXHIBIT 2. Return distributions for two investment projects

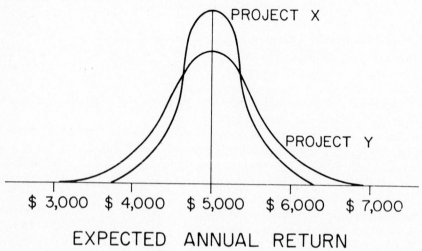

will be enhanced. These principles should be derived from the modern theories of investor and capital market behavior. In the following section, the traditional capital asset pricing model approach to these issues will be presented.

IV. Investor and Capital Market Behavior

In order to enhance shareholder wealth, the firm must understand the nature of investor behavior. In effect, it must have a theory of stockholder decision making. In 1952, Markowitz provided one such theory in his paper on portfolio selection [12]. The Markowitz approach eventually created a revolution in financial theory. Until recently his work has been viewed as the "theoretical substructure of finance" [20, p. 167].

Markowitz set out to develop a normative model of investor behavior in a security market in which participants are uncertain about future events. He noted that the tendency of investors to diversify their security portfolios cannot be explained by the traditional maxim that investors seek to maximize the discounted returns from their holdings. If this were true, investors would never diversify. Each market participant would hold only one security—the one which he believed would generate the highest discounted returns.

Markowitz suggested that diversification is essentially an attempt by risk-averse investors to lower their total risk exposure by purchasing a broad range of securities. The underlying assumption is that while some securities may fall upon hard times and their returns may decline, others will do well and will offset those stocks whose returns have fallen. The recognition that shareholders are concerned with risk as well as return led Markowitz to offer his "mean-variance" maxim in place of the maximization-of-discounted-returns rule.

This approach suggests that investors view uncertain security returns in terms of a probability distribution similar to those portrayed in Exhibit 2. Furthermore, investors are assumed to make their stock selection decisions on the basis of only two attributes: (1) the mean or expected value of the probability distribution of returns, and (2) the variance of the return distribution. The variance of returns is used as the risk surrogate—measuring as it does the variability in returns from some expected value. Markowitz assumes that investors make decisions on the basis of a single-period time frame, i.e., a week, a month, a year, etc. The expected return and variance are the investor's subjective estimates of these parameters during this single time period.

Markowitz noted that when securities are combined into a portfolio, the expected return on that portfolio is a weighted average of the expected returns on the component securities. However, the variance of the portfolio's return is not a simple weighted average of the variances of the individual securities. Portfolio variance is also a function of the correlation or covariances among the returns of the securities. Markowitz demonstrated that this fact allows investors to reduce portfolio variance without lowering the portfolio's return by combining securities which have less than perfect positive intercorrelations (as measured by Pearson's product–moment correlation coefficient) [8]. This procedure is referred to as Markowitz efficient diversification. In effect, by combining stocks with less than perfectly correlated returns, we find that a portion of each security's variation is cancelled by a complementary variation in the returns of other securities [13].

Once a portfolio is well diversified, its return becomes very highly correlated with the return on the security market as a whole. That is, the return on the portfolio tends to move in lock-step with the weighted average return of all securities in the market. This occurs because much of the variation in stock returns due to firm specific events (e.g., product failures, strikes, management errors, etc.) has been eliminated through Markowitz efficient diversification. The variability that remains is due largely to macroeconomic events which impact all securities (e.g., the business cycle). This variability is known as systematic risk. Systematic risk is the portion of a security's return variance which cannot be diversified away because it is more or less common to all securities. The firm-specific variance, on the other hand, is known as unsystematic risk and can be largely eliminated by diversification.

As a result, in a market in which Markowitz efficient diversification is the rule, investors are basically concerned with systematic risk. Since all investors hold fully diversified portfolios, additions to portfolios are evaluated solely on the basis of their systematic risk levels. Of course, securities differ with regard to the amount of systematic risk they bring to a portfolio. For example, a firm which manufactures consumer durables is much more likely to have its fortunes affected by the business cycle than the producer of a staple food item. Consequently, the systematic variability of the former's stock is likely to be greater than that of the latter.

The most widely used index of systematic risk is the so-called beta coefficient. This is simply the slope coefficient of a linear regression of the security's return (the dependent variable) on the market's return (the independent variable) for some "representative" number of periods:

$$R_{ij} = \alpha_j + \beta_j R_{im} \tag{11}$$

where R_{ij} = the return of security j during period i, α_j = the intercept coefficient for security j, β_j = the beta coefficient for security j, and R_{im} = the return on all market securities during period i. Since the returns of almost all securities are positively correlated with the return on the market as a whole, high positive beta coefficients indicate a high level of systematic risk.

For example, using data from the period 1959 to 1969, Weston has estimated that Chrysler Corporation's beta is approximately 2.94 [27]. This means that for every 1 percent change in the market return, the return on Chrysler's stock can be expected to change by 2.94 percent. Because of its high level of volatility vis-à-vis the market, Chrysler's stock is a relatively unattractive candidate for inclusion in a portfolio. Therefore, investors will bid Chrysler's price down (which is equivalent to bidding its return up) until its return is sufficient to compensate investors for assuming such a high level of systematic risk.

An opposite process occurs with low beta securities. Stocks with betas of less than one are known as defensive securities because they are particularly good candidates for inclusion in portfolios. Defensive securities tend to lower the systematic risk of fully diversified portfolios. As a result, these stocks are in high demand. This high demand for low beta securities pushes their prices up and drives their returns down. The adjustment process continues until the return on each security and portfolio in the market is commensurate with its systematic risk level. High-risk securities and portfolios will have relatively high returns, and low-risk securities and portfolios will have relatively low returns.

Sharpe demonstrated that when beta is used as the index of systematic risk, the risk-return relationship is not only positive, but also linear [23]. This linear relationship, known as the security market line (SML), is shown in Exhibit 3. Sharpe's equation for the security market line is given by:

$$E(R_j) = R_f + [E(R_m) - R_f]\beta_j \tag{12}$$

where $E(R_j)$ = the expected return on any security j, R_f = the risk-free rate of interest (often estimated by the return on U.S. Treasury bills), $E(R_m)$ = the expected return on all securities in the market (often estimated by the return on the Standard & Poor's 500-stock index), and β_j = the beta coefficient for security j. According to Sharpe, when the capital market is in a state of equilibrium—that is, when the competitive bidding process has adjusted the securities to their proper risk-return levels—all portfolios and securities in the market should plot on the SML. The security market line is, in essence, a model of capital market behavior. Since investors are assumed to make their decisions on the basis of two factors—expected return and systematic risk—the SML purports to describe the equilibrium prices of all securities in the market. Thus, the SML is frequently referred to as the capital asset pricing model (CAPM).

V. Marketing Investment Analysis and the CAPM

In theory, the applicability of the CAPM should reach far beyond the major stock exchanges. It has been noted that it should be possible to plot all income-producing assets in the risk-return space of Exhibit 3. As long as investors are free to enter any market they desire, the competitive process will ensure that the risk-return ordered pairs of all assets plot on the security market line. This includes stocks and bonds, Treasury bills, real estate, and even the capital investment projects of business firms.

Consider, for example, Firm J, whose securities plot on the SML as shown in Exhibit 3. From the viewpoint of the investors, Firm J is simply a collection of real and intangible assets (e.g., plant and equipment, patents, managerial acumen, brand franchises, etc.) held for the benefit of the shareholder. Firm J's systematic risk level is indicated by its beta coefficient, β'_j. The expected return on the firm's securities is given by $WACC_j$ (this is also the weighted average cost of capital for the firm).[3] Let us once again assume that Firm J is considering four new-product investments represented by the letters A, B, C, and D. Acceptance of a project requires an investment outlay to cover the research and development, production, and marketing of the product. The return on this investment is the estimated after-tax cash flow generated by the new product.

The expected return and risk levels for each project are shown in Exhibit 3. Note that projects A and B both plot above the security market line. This means that the return on these projects is in excess of that which is required to induce an investor to accept their risk levels. Since their returns more than compensate the firm for assuming the risk, acceptance of the projects will result in an upward revision in the firm's share price. Once the projects are combined with the firm's other assets, the firm's own risk-return ordered pair will be in temporary disequilibrium; i.e., it will plot above the SML. Investors will then act to restore equilibrium by bidding up the price of the firm's shares and lowering its expected yield to the security market line. Thus, all investors holding Firm J's shares just prior to the acceptance of projects A and B will realize a subsequent wealth increment due to the increase in share price [20]. On the other hand, projects C and D both plot below the SML. This means that their returns are not sufficient to compensate for their risk levels. Consequently, Firm J should reject these projects.

It may be instructive at this point to compare the CAPM's decision rules with those of the traditional weighted average cost of capital approach. The weighted average cost of capital (WACC) for Firm J is given by the horizontal dashed line in Exhibit 3. (Since Firm J is financed entirely with equity, its cost of capital is the return which stockholders require to induce them to accept Firm J's risk level.) In employing the cost of capital criterion, the firm accepts all investment projects whose returns exceed the WACC. As can be seen in Exhibit 3, this leads to decisions which are different from those generated by the market model. The WACC approach would accept project C and reject project B, while the market model would reject C but accept B. The difference, of course, is that the security market line adjusts for the differential risk of the projects and the WACC does not. Indeed, the WACC is only applicable for projects in the same "risk class" as the firm [20].

Proponents of the CAPM approach suggest that it offers important advantages over the traditional cost of capital or the various risk-adjustment approaches discussed earlier. First, it provides the firm with an objectively determined risk measure (the beta coefficient) which reflects the systematic rather than the total variability of project returns. Since only nondiversifiable or systematic risk is relevant to investors

---

[3] For simplicity, it is assumed that the firm is financed entirely with equity.

EXHIBIT 3. The security market line

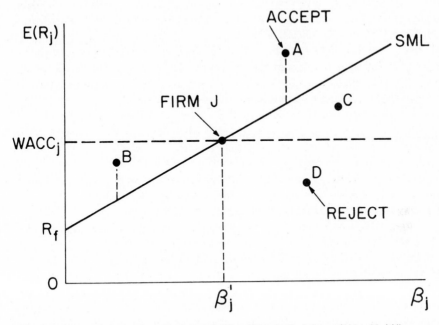

Source: Adapted from J. Fred Weston, "Investment Decisions Using the Capital Asset Pricing Model," *Financial Management*, Vol. 2 (Spring 1973), pp. 25–33.

who operate in Markowitz efficient security markets, beta becomes the "correct" risk measure for shareholder wealth maximizing firms. In addition, the CAPM's risk-return trade-off function represents the preferences of the firm's shareholders rather than those of management. Thus, the market model allows for the direct incorporation of shareholder preferences in firm investment decisions.

Operationalizing the Capital Asset Pricing Model

Even proponents of the CAPM approach to investment analysis realize that it is not without its operational difficulties. In particular, various measurement problems have limited its application in real-world settings. (Chief among these problems is the estimation of beta coefficients for investment projects.) However, some progress has been made in recent years in developing approaches which circumvent some of the problems [1, 2, 26, 27]. One such methodology will be presented here.

Consider the case of Firm J, which is trying to decide if it should enter a new product (product D) in an established market. Firm J does not now compete in this market but has developed product D as a technological spin-off from its main line of endeavor. After extensive marketing research covering such factors as market structure, consumer preferences, potential competitive reactions, available production and marketing resources, and a myriad of other factors, the firm has developed a ten-year revenue and profit forecast (it is expected that the product will have a ten-year life cycle). From this information, the firm determines the net after-tax cash flow which should result from the new-product venture. These cash flows are then entered into the traditional net present value discounting formula to determine the investment worthiness of the project:

$$\text{NPV}_d = \sum_{i=1}^{n} \frac{A_i}{(1 + R_d)^i} \tag{13}$$

where NPV_d = the net present value of the investment in product D, A_i = the net after-tax cash flow in year i, n = the expected life of the product in years, and R_d = the required rate of return for product D calculated from the SML.

Equation (13) is simply an updated form of the risk-adjusted net present value method. The only difference between this approach and the previous formulation is that the CAPM is used to generate the risk-adjusted discount rate. The discount rate R_d is calculated by using Sharpe's formula for the security market line [Eq. (12)]. Note that the components of Sharpe's equation are all market-wide constants. This implies that the required return for product D will be the same for every firm in the economy. While the cash flow expectations will vary from firm to firm (because of differences in marketing and production expertise, synergism, and so forth), the discount rate will be constant across firms.

With the exception of beta, the components of Sharpe's equation are easy to estimate. Both the risk-free rate R_f and the return on the market R_m can be estimated from published sources. Beta, on the other hand, is a more difficult matter. Unlike securities, new-product investments are not traded on stock exchanges. Thus, it is difficult to determine their potential levels of systematic risk.

One approach to the problem is to employ the average beta coefficient of a group of companies engaged exclusively, or almost exclusively, in the manufacture and sale of the product under consideration. Since systematic risk is largely a function of the response of a firm's product line to variations in economic activity, it is suggested that this surrogate approach should provide a reasonably good estimate of the product's beta coefficient.

Assume, for example, that the average beta of firms which market product D is approximately 1.9. If Firm J expects the return on the market to average 10 percent and expects the risk-free rate to be in the neighborhood of 4.4 percent, Sharpe's SML equation will generate a required return of 15 percent:

$$E(R_j) = R_f + [E(R_m) - R_f]\beta_j \tag{12}$$
$$15.0 = 4.4 + (10.0 - 4.4)1.9$$

This, then, becomes the rate at which the expected cash flows from product D are discounted in Eq. (13). The decision rule is to invest in the new product if its net present value is equal to or greater than zero. (This is equivalent to requiring product D's return to plot on or above the SML.) Alternatively, the internal rate of return for product D could be determined by using Eq. (3). If the IRR equals or exceeds R_d, the investment in the new product should be made.

A third approach involves the computation of risk-adjusted hurdle rates for each of the firm's existing product lines. This methodology has been employed at the Quaker Oats Company to determine the required rates of return on present products. Quaker's products range from ready-to-eat cereals and pet foods to industrial chemicals and restaurants. Employing a surrogate approach and a slightly modified version of the SML, Bower and Jenks determined individualized hurdle rates for four of Quaker's major product categories: grocery products, toys, industrial chemicals, and restaurants [1]. The rates ranged from a low of around 8 percent for restaurants to a high of almost 12 percent for chemicals. The significance of these rates is that they may be employed to evaluate any new investments in each of the firm's product lines. For example, if Quaker Oats wishes to expand its industrial chemical line, it knows that it must earn at least 12 percent on any new investments in this category. In addition, these rates may be employed as a control device to evaluate the ongoing performance of each of Quaker's product lines or product divisions. The major advantage here is that the required rates are tailored to the unique systematic risk levels of the various markets in which they compete.

Of course, it is not always a simple matter to estimate betas via the surrogate approach. In some cases, it will be difficult to find firms which deal exclusively with the product of interest. Indeed, in such instances it may be necessary to use a surrogate product which has similar systematic risk characteristics. For example, in calculating the individualized rates for Quaker Oats, Bower and Jenks reported difficulty in identifying wholly adequate surrogates for such products as pet foods, mixes, hot cereals, and industrial chemicals.

Another problem with the CAPM approach (or any other technique using DCF) concerns the need to estimate the net cash flows resulting from the investment. Cash flow is usually estimated by determining net accounting income and adding back depreciation and other noncash expenses. However, net accounting income can only be determined by fully allocating all costs to the new venture. The potential distortions which can result from the arbitrary allocation of marketing costs have been well documented in the literature [9, 14, 15]. Given the current state of the art in distribution cost accounting, the Sharpe model is probably more applicable to relatively "free-standing" marketing investments in which the costs of the venture are somewhat easier to separate from other marketing activities. Depending on the firm, this could include such a major marketing venture as the decision to introduce a new product, the decision to enter a new territory (or country), or the decision to acquire a new subsidiary. In addition, the CAPM has potential applications in the areas of new-product pricing, product line extension and abandonment, divisional control, and many others.

A final problem with the CAPM concerns its empirical testability. Roll asserts that the CAPM is a non-testable theory of capital asset pricing [17]. Ross, on the other hand, believes that a test of the CAPM is possible, but he recognizes that the problems involved will be formidable [19]. If the CAPM eventually proves to be a "degenerating research programme" [11], Ross has offered his arbitrage pricing theory (APT) as its logical successor.

The APT is essentially a multifactor version of the CAPM [18]. The arbitrage model is testable in principle if the factors which generate its returns can be identified. Unfortunately, the identification of these factors is an empirical task which is only just beginning. It may be many years before an operational version of the APT is available. In the interim, the lack of a decisive refutation of CAPM has allowed its proponents to offer it as the best alternative to non-discounted or subjective risk-adjustment methods.

References

1. Bower, Richard S., and Jenks, Jeffrey M. "Divisional Screening Rates," *Financial Management*, 4 (Autumn 1975): 42–49.
2. ———, and Lessard, Donald R. "An Operational Approach to Risk-Screening," *Journal of Finance*, 28 (May 1973): 321–327.
3. Cravens, David W.; Hills, Gerald E.; and Woodruff, Robert B. *Marketing Decision Making.* Homewood, IL: Richard D. Irwin, 1976.
4. Dean, Joel. "Does Advertising Belong in the Capital Budget?" *Journal of Marketing* 30 (October 1966): 15–21.
5. Donaldson, Gordon. "Strategic Hurdle Rates for Capital Investment," *Harvard Business Review*, 50 (March-April 1972): 50–58.
6. Fama, Eugene, and Miller, Merton H. *The Theory of Finance.* Hinsdale, IL: Dryden Press, 1972.
7. Findley, M. C.; Gooding, Arthur E.; and Weaver, Wallace Q., Jr. "On the Relevant Risk for Determining Capital Expenditure Hurdle Rates," *Financial Management* 5 (Winter 1976): 9–16.
8. Francis, Jack Clark, and Archer, Stephen H. *Portfolio Analysis.* Englewood Cliffs, NJ: Prentice-Hall, 1971.
9. Kirpalani, V. H., and Shapiro, Stanley J. "Financial Dimensions of Marketing Management," *Journal of Marketing* 37 (July 1973): 40–47.
10. Kotler, Philip. *Marketing Decision Making.* New York: Holt, Rinehart and Winston, 1971.
11. Lakatos, Imre. "Falsification and the Methodology of Scientific Research Programmes," in *Criticism and the Growth of Knowledge*, Imre Lakatos and Alan Musgrave, eds. Cambridge: Cambridge University Press, 1970, pp. 91–195.
12. Markowitz, Harry M. "Portfolio Selection," *Journal of Finance* 7 (March 1952): 77–91.
13. Modigliani, Franco, and Pogue, Gerlad A. "An Introduction to Risk and Return," *Financial Analysts Journal* 30 (March-April 1974): 68–80.
14. Mossman, Frank H.; Fisher, Paul M.; and Crissy, W. J. E. "New Approaches to

Analyzing Marketing Profitability," *Journal of Marketing* 38 (April 1974): 43–48.

15. "Report of the Committee on Cost and Profitability Analysis for Marketing," *Accounting Review Supplement* 47 (1972): 577–615.

16. Robichek, Alexander, and Myers, Stewart C. *Optimal Financing Decisions*. Englewood Cliffs, NJ: Prentice-Hall, 1965.

17. Roll, Richard. "A Critique of the Asset Pricing Theory's Tests: Part I," *Journal of Financial Economics* 4 (March 1977): 129–176.

18. Ross, Stephen A. "The Arbitrage Theory of Capital Asset Pricing," *Journal of Economic Theory* 13 (December 1976): 341–360.

19. ———. "The Current Status of the Capital Asset Pricing Model (CAPM)," *Journal of Finance* 33 (June 1978): 885–901.

20. Rubinstein, Mark E. "A Mean-Variance Synthesis of Corporate Financial Theory," *Journal of Finance* 28 (March 1973): 167–181.

21. Scheuble, Philip A., Jr. "ROI for New-Product Policy," *Harvard Business Review* 42 (November-December 1964): 110–120.

22. Schiff, J. S., and Schiff, Michael. "New Sales Management Tool: ROAM," *Harvard Business Review* 45 (July-August 1967): 59–66.

23. Sharpe, William F. "Capital Asset Prices: A Theory of Market Equilibrium Under Conditions of Risk," *Journal of Finance* 19 (September 1964): 425–442.

24. Spiller, Earl A., Jr. *Financial Accounting*. Revised edition. Homewood, IL: Richard D. Irwin, 1971.

25. Van Horne, James C. *Financial Management and Policy*. 2nd ed. Englewood Cliffs, NJ: Prentice-Hall, 1971.

26. ———. *Financial Management and Policy*. 4th ed. Englewood Cliffs, NJ: Prentice-Hall, 1977.

27. Weston, J. Fred. "Investment Decisions Using the Capital Asset Pricing Model," *Financial Management* 2 (Spring 1973): 25–33.

Exercises

7.1. The Peabody Electronics Company is considering two new-product ventures. Because of the rapid rate of technological innovation in this field, each is expected to have only a four-year product life cycle. It is estimated that engineering, tooling, product development, and other expenses would require an investment of approximately $118,080 to bring each product to the market. Based on market research surveys, the estimated cash flows for the new products are as follows:

End of year	Product X	Product Y
0	−$118,080	−$118,080
1	50,000	0
2	50,000	25,000
3	50,000	50,000
4	50,000	163,375

Weighted average cost of capital $(k) = 15\%$

Expected risk-free rate of interest $(R_f) = 8\%$

Expected return on S&P's 500-stock index $(R_m) = 20\%$

Beta coefficient for product X $(\beta_x) = 1.0$

Beta coefficient for product Y $(\beta_y) = 1.2$

1. Using the information given above, calculate for each product:
   a. the internal rate of return.
   b. the net present value (using the firm's weighted average cost of capital).
   c. the risk-adjusted net present value (using Sharpe's SML to determine the discount rate).
2. Based on your calculations, which new product would you recommend to Peabody?

7.2. The Salem Manufacturing Company is considering two new-product ventures. Each is expected to have a four-year product life cycle. It is estimated that development expenses would require an investment of approximately $100,000 to bring each product to the market. Based on market research surveys, the estimated cash flows for the new products are as follows:

End of year	Product X	Product Y
0	−$100,000	−$100,000
1	33,620	9,880
2	33,620	30,000
3	33,620	60,000
4	33,620	70,000

Weighted average cost of capital $(k) = 15\%$

Expected risk-free rate of interest $(R_f) = 10\%$

Expected return on S&P's 500-stock index $(R_m) = 24\%$

Beta coefficient for product X $(\beta_x) = 1.0$

Beta coefficient for product Y $(\beta_y) = 0.5$

1. Using the information given above, calculate for each product:
   a. the internal rate of return.

    b. the net present value (using the firm's weighted average cost of capital).

    c. the risk-adjusted net present value (using Sharpe's SML to determine the discount rate).

2. Based on your calculations, which new product would you recommend to Salem?

A Cost-Effectiveness Approach to Marketing Outlays

8

Arthur V. Corr

Marketing and distribution costs have recently begun to enjoy a new prominence. As they become an increasingly large part of the overall sales dollar, marketing costs become more and more critical to the success of a business enterprise. In fact, for many manufacturing companies, the cost to sell and distribute its products exceeds the cost to produce them.

The New Marketing Concept

The "new marketing concept"—which is at least twenty years old now—is the direct result of the mature economy. It reflects the new emphasis on the marketing function and a full recognition of its critical nature. The adoption of this concept has brought a reorganization of the corporate structure, and with it, a substantial amount of additional activities and responsibilities to the marketing function.

Traditionally in manufacturing companies the marketing or selling effort came at the end of the operating cycle after the goods were already produced. Usually the company was managed by the owner/founder who invariably had an engineering or mechanical background and an inventive bent. He designed the products initially, set up the manufacturing process and hired a salesman to sell the factory's production. So long as production was the limiting factor this worked fine, and unless the owner/manager was incompetent he managed to stay in business and make a profit.

Today we have, to a great extent, conquered the problem of production; we can make as many products as we can sell profitably. Business management is now spending more time and effort in determining what there is a market for: what do the customers want; in what sizes, shapes, colors and quantities; how much will they buy and at what prices.

Today, the emphasis on profitable sales rather than sales volume puts marketing at the beginning of the operating cycle. Market research tries to determine in advance the kinds of products that can be sold, their quantities and prices. Management then asks what it will cost to make and to sell (and whether it will be profitable enough) before the decision is made to produce it. Marketing comes in at the end of the cycle too: selling and distributing the products.

Reprinted by permission from *Management Accounting* (January 1976), pp. 33–36.

In recognition of its critical role in the economic success of the enterprise, several activities and responsibilities have been shifted to the marketing function. In more and more companies, marketing management is responsible for warehousing, inventory control, product design and development, as well as for product service, pricing, and credit and collection. In addition, marketing management is being given increased responsibility for financial objectives such as product line profitability, territory contribution, and in some cases, return on investment.

Order-Getting Costs

Marketing and distribution costs can be grouped into three broad categories: order-getting costs, order-filling costs, and marketing-administration costs. Our focus will be on the first category—the costs of order-getting activities.

Order-getting costs are the costs of activities carried on to bring in the sales orders. They include the costs of advertising and sales promotion, training and compensation of salesmen, and sales management and supervision. Order-filling costs are the costs of filling sales orders—warehousing, inventory handling, packaging and shipping, order processing, billing, and credit and collection. Marketing administration costs are the costs of marketing planning and organization, market research and forecasting, product design and development, and product line planning.

Marketing managers are responsible for determining how much can be spent profitably on these activities as a whole, and how much of the overall budget should be spent on the different kinds of order-getting activities. To act intelligently rather than to react blindly, marketing managers must be able to measure the profit impact of the various courses of action available to them.

Determining Profit Impact

Direct costing and contribution accounting are examples of decision-oriented techniques which enable the manager to develop profit-impact information without making extensive analyses and adjustments. Likewise, the adoption of standard cost systems and the extension of standards into the marketing area also contribute to the development of profit-impact information.

In order to appraise specific marketing outlays we must compare the benefit with the cost to determine the cost-effectiveness ratio. The relevant measure of the cost-effectiveness is the amount of profit added divided by the amount to be spent.

Consider, for example, a company preparing a special $100,000 advertising campaign which is expected to add $800,000 in sales volume. The marketing manager cannot appraise it properly and is not in a position to make a decision until he knows what the profit impact is going to be. Exhibit 1 illustrates the determination of the profit impact and the calculation of the cost-effectiveness ratio for the proposed advertising.

The increase in sales volume causes an automatic increase in the variable costs.

EXHIBIT 1. *Financial appraisal of special advertising*
(*in thousands of dollars*)

Additional sales revenue		$800
Standard variable cost of sales		
Production (45%)	360	
Marketing (10%)	80	
Total	440	
Marginal income		360
Incremental fixed costs		
Production	20	
Marketing-advertising	100	
Total	120	
Profit contribution before tax		240
Corporate income tax (50%)		120
Profit contribution after tax		$120

$$\text{Cost-effectiveness ratio} = \frac{\text{profit contribution}}{\text{advertising outlay}}$$
$$= \frac{120}{100}$$
$$= 1.2/1$$

The increase in the standard variable costs—production and marketing—is deducted from sales to get incremental marginal income. From this, any incremental fixed or period costs are deducted to get the profit impact before taxes. Finally, income taxes at 50 percent are deducted to arrive at the increase in net profit of $120,000. By relating this to the amount of the advertising outlay, $100,000, we get a cost-effectiveness ratio of 1.2 to 1.

Optimizing Marketing Outlays

The law of diminishing returns indicates that as spending for marketing activities is increased, there comes a point when the resulting profit contribution becomes less and less and finally becomes negative. A company therefore will benefit from increasing its marketing activities so long as the incremental impact on profits remains greater than zero, or, to put it another way, so long as the incremental cost effectiveness is greater than zero.

Exhibit 2 illustrates the impact of continued increases in marketing activities on a company's net profit.[1] It is essential that the analysis be done on an incremental basis because each increment of marketing expenses must be analyzed in terms of

---

[1] This analysis is based on holding other activities and costs constant while varying the order-getting activities in the form of marketing outlays. Provision, however, is made for proportionate increases in variable cost of sales, incremental fixed costs, and corporate income taxes.

EXHIBIT 2. Cost-effectiveness of marketing expenses (in thousands of dollars)

Marketing expenses	Profit contribution		Cost-effectiveness ratio	
	Net	Incremental	Average	Incremental
$5,000	$19,000	$	3.8	
6,000	21,000	2,000	3.5	2
7,000	24,000	3,000	3.4	3
8,000	28,000	4,000	3.5	4
9,000	30,000	2,000	3.3	2
10,000	30,000	—	3.0	—
11,000	29,000	(1,000)	2.6	(1)
12,000	26,000	(3,000)	2.2	(3)
13,000	21,000	(5,000)	1.6	(5)

its impact. In this example, we start our analysis at the $5 million level of marketing expense because management is not considering anything less. When spending for selling effort is increased to $6 million the net profit goes from $19 million to $21 million. Thus the one million increment in marketing outlays brings a two million increment in net profits—a cost-effectiveness ratio of 2 to 1. When spending is increased by another million, the cost-effectiveness ratio for that increment is 3 to 1 and so on. Based on this analysis, the company could profitably increase its marketing activities to the $9 million level, because each increment of cost up to that point has a positive cost-effectiveness ratio. Beyond that level, the cost-effectiveness ratio first becomes zero and then becomes negative. An examination of the net profit amount clearly shows there is no economic benefit to be gained by increasing marketing outlays beyond $9 million.

There are two important points to be noted about this method of analysis. First, only future costs and future revenues need to be considered for decision-making (we can't change the past). Second, the incremental approach is the relevant one. Exhibit 2 shows that the average cost-effectiveness ratio remains positive and substantial for all levels of spending, thus providing no indication as to the optimum level or the cut-off point. The incremental cost-effectiveness ratio, on the other hand, indicates clearly there is nothing to be gained economically from spending more than $9 million for marketing activities.

With such an analysis at hand, marketing management should argue strenuously for increasing total outlays only so long as the incremental cost-effectiveness is increasing, in this case up to $8 million. Up to that level each increment is more productive than the previous one.

Allocating the Marketing Budget

Up to this point we have been dealing with overall marketing expenses and we have developed an approach to help marketing management decide on how much should be spent for order-getting activities. Marketing management is also faced with the problem of allocating the available funds to the various kinds of order-getting costs: advertising, salesmen, and special promotions. The problem is how to allocate the budget to these activities so that the company's profit will be greatest. Here too we can use the cost-effectiveness approach and the cost-effectiveness ratio.

We must first determine what the impact on sales will be as the outlay is increased for each selling activity. Next, we use this information to calculate the impact on net profit. For companies with a direct costing system and current attainable standards, this is a relatively simple matter. The difficult part, which is the responsibility of the marketing manager, is measuring the impact on sales volume.

Exhibit 3 shows the profit contribution resulting from various outlays for each of the selling activities. It also shows the amount of profit and the cost-effectiveness ratio for every increment of cost for each activity.[2]

At the $500,000 expense level, advertising reaches a peak incremental cost-effectiveness ratio of 9 to 1. If the budget permits, however, the manager could continue to increase his profit contribution by increasing the advertising effort up to the $700,000 level. Increased activity beyond that point only adds costs; the cost-effectiveness ratio becomes negative.

The number of salesmen can be profitably increased up to an expense level of $600,000 for salaries and travel. This amount does not include salesmen's commissions; commissions are included in the variable marketing costs and deducted from sales to get the marginal income.

Each special promotion costs approximately $20,000. The six most productive promotions have positive incremental cost-effectiveness ratios, and thus would justify the related expenditures. Beyond those six, however, additional promotions are not profitable; their cost-effectiveness ratios are negative.

With this analysis of the incremental cost-effectiveness of the different kinds of selling activities, the manager is in a position to recommend and to justify an overall budget of $1,420,000 made up of:

Advertising expense	$700,000
Salesmen's expense	600,000
Special promotions	120,000

If the manager has to settle for a total budget of $1,080,000, he can use the cost-effectiveness information to determine the most productive way to allocate the funds. First he would allocate to each activity enough funds to reach the peak cost-effectiveness ratio. Then he would allocate the remaining funds so as to equalize the cost-effectiveness ratio from the last increment for each expense. That combination would generate the largest profit contribution, allocated as follows:

---

[2] For the purpose of this illustration, increments of $100,000 are assumed for advertising and for salesmen's expenses.

Advertising expense	$600,000
Salesmen's expense	400,000
Special promotions	80,000

The manager cannot improve the cost-effectiveness of the last increment of each expense by transferring it to another activity. For example, if he transfers $100,000 from advertising expense to salesmen's expense he gives up a cost-effectiveness ratio of 4 to 1 in return for one of 3 to 1.

The marketing manager must recognize the relationships between, and the inter-

EXHIBIT 3. *Cost-effectiveness of selling activities (in thousands of dollars)*

	Profit contribution	Incremental cost effectiveness	
		Amount	Ratio
Advertising			
$100	$200	$0	—
200	400	200	2
300	800	400	4
400	1,500	700	7
500	2,400	900	9
600	2,800	400	4
700	2,900	100	1
800	2,800	(100)	(1)
900	2,600	(200)	(2)
Salesmen's salaries and travel			
$100	$200	$0	—
200	600	400	4
300	1,400	800	8
400	1,900	500	5
500	2,200	300	3
600	2,300	100	1
700	2,300	0	0
800	2,300	0	0
900	2,200	(100)	(1)
1,000	2,100	(100)	(1)
Special promotions			
$20	$140	$140	7
40	240	100	5
60	320	80	4
80	400	80	4
100	460	60	3
120	480	20	1
140	470	(10)	(.5)
160	450	(20)	(1)

dependence of, the different selling activities. The effectiveness of the salesman is influenced by the amount of advertising and promotion and vice versa. The manager must, therefore, incorporate this knowledge into his analysis and he must exercise judgment in deciding on the overall amount and the mix of selling effort.

Conclusion

In this article we have identified the relevant approach and the appropriate economic measurement for planning and appraising marketing outlays: a cost-effectiveness approach based on incremental future costs and future revenues. It is not easy but it is the only valid method.

Decisions imply the future, and the future at best is not certain. Managers must therefore rely on estimates regarding the environment and the circumstances that are likely to prevail. The best approximations—even if they are rough—of future costs and revenues are more useful than precise measurements of the past.

Exercises

8.1. The marketing manager of the Action Company is preparing next year's budget. She is considering increasing the advertising budget as well as the budget for the sales force. An increase of $100,000 in advertising expenditures is expected to increase sales by $600,000. Each additional incremental increase of $100,000 for advertising is expected to generate only 80% of the sales increase resulting from the previous $100,000 incremental increase in advertising expenditures.

The sales force is paid on a mixed salary basis; i.e., the salespeople are guaranteed a fixed minimum salary of $10,000, and in addition a commission of 6% of generated sales. It is estimated that as additional salespeople are hired, total sales will increase as in Table 8.1.

TABLE 8.1

Additional salespeople	Expected increase in total sales
1	$120,000
2	220,000
3	300,000
4	360,000
5	400,000
6	420,000
7	420,000

The following conditions prevail:

Variable production costs amount to 40% of sales revenues.
Variable marketing costs amount to 15% of sales.
For every $100,000 increase in sales, a yearly increase of $10,000 in depreciation
  expenses will result because of the shorter expected life of machinery and plant
  as the production volume increases.
The corporate tax rate is 50%.

1. a. Construct a table showing the after-tax profit impact and the cost-effectiveness
      ratio of incremental increases in the advertising budget of $100,000 (up to a
      $600,000 budget increase).
   b. Construct a table showing the after-tax profit impact and the cost-effectiveness
      ratio of incremental increases in the sales force (up to seven additional sales-
      people).
   Treat parts a and b independently!
2. If you were the marketing manager and had no budget constraint:
   a. How much would you increase (if at all) the advertising budget?
   b. How many salespeople would you hire in addition to the present sales force?
   Treat a and b independently!
   c. How much would you increase the advertising and sales force budgets in total,
      and what would be the expected gain in after-tax profits? What is the average
      cost-effectiveness ratio resulting from the total increase in the above two
      budgets?
3. If you as the marketing manager could only expand the advertising and sales
   budgets by a maximum of $200,000 in total, how much would you allocate to
   each budget?

8.2. The marketing manager of Oswald & Sons is preparing the budget for the
forthcoming year. In order to increase profits, he is considering initiating various
promotions and advertising campaigns as well as a slight product modification
which he believes will improve the product. The following conditions prevail:

Variable production costs are 35% of sales.
Variable marketing costs amount to 10% of sales.
Without further expenditures on promotion and advertising, sales are expected
  to reach $1,000,000.
If sales exceed $1,000,000, additional machines will have to be leased. In terms of
  total sales, each additional machine represents a capacity increase of $50,000
  annually.
The annual charge for leasing each machine is $5,000.
The corporate tax rate is 50%.

Tables 8.2 and 8.3 reflect the marketing manager's estimates of the effects of
alternative expenditure levels.

TABLE 8.2. *Effects of promotions on sales*

Total promotion expenditures	Total estimated increase in sales
$ 30,000	$ 75,000
60,000	175,000
90,000	300,000
120,000	360,000
150,000	395,000

TABLE 8.3. *Effects of advertising expenditures on sales*

Total advertising expenditures	Total increase in sales
$ 50,000	$100,000
100,000	260,000
150,000	480,000
200,000	620,000
250,000	720,000
300,000	800,000
350,000	850,000

TABLE 8.4. *Effects of modifying the product*

Level of demand	Probability of level of demand	% change in all previous sales estimates[a]
Decreased demand	0.20	−20
No change in demand	0.20	0
Increased demand	0.60	+40

[a] The percentage changes in demand apply to the effects of both promotion and advertising expenditures, as well as the sales estimate corresponding to a zero advertising and promotion expenditure level.

In order to modify the product, investments representing $75,000 in annual costs will have to be made. According to market research, probabilities of change in the consumers' demand for the product are as shown in Table 8.4.

1. a. Given that it is decided not to modify the product, construct a table showing the after-tax profit impact and the cost-effectiveness ratios of incremental increases in promotion expenditures.
   b. Construct a table similar to that in part a for incremental increases in advertising expenditures.
   c. If there are no budget constraints, how much should be spent on promotions and advertising respectively?
   d. If the marketing manager faces a $240,000 budget constraint, how should he allocate the budget? (Assume zero opportunity cost of idle money.)
2. a. Given that it is decided to modify the product, construct a table showing the after-tax profit impact and the cost-effectiveness ratios of incremental increases in promotion and advertising expenditures (for all three possible states of nature!).
   b. Looking at what you have done in part a, determine the optimal expenditure levels for promotion and advertising respectively—given there is no budget constraint.
   c. What are the expected after-tax gains in profits to be derived from modifying the product? (In other words, isolate the effect of the "modification investment" from the promotion and advertising expenditure.) What is the "expected cost-effectiveness ratio" for this investment?

Recommendations for Further Reading

Hise, Richard T., and Robert H. Strawser. "Application of Capital Budgeting Techniques to Marketing Operations," *MSU Business Topics*, 18 (Summer 1970), 69–76.

A conceptual case can be made for the use of capital budgeting techniques in marketing, and a number of specific applications are proposed in the literature. But to what extent are capital budgeting techniques actually being used to make marketing decisions? To answer this question, a mail questionnaire was sent in 1969 to the 500 largest manufacturing firms in the United States. It was designed to: (1) reveal usage of four capital budgeting techniques (payback, average rate of return, present value, and discounted rate of return) in making marketing decisions; (2) ascertain in which decision areas these techniques were being used; (3) determine how such problems as dealing with risk, estimating useful life, and establishing the cost of capital were resolved; and (4) learn about special problems and overall user satisfaction. Though usage patterns by area of application and by technique differed markedly, considerable dependence on capital budgeting techniques was revealed, as well as a marked degree of satisfaction with them.

Ostalkiewicz, Clarence J. "Market Mix: The Key to Profitability," *Management Accounting (U.S.)*, 50 (January 1969), 28–30.

The firm's customer mix and its product mix are both determinants of its profitability. A computer-generated format is used to compare at the same time planned and actual product and planned and actual customer (or market) mixes. The system presupposes the establishment of a standard selling price higher than the current sales price, so that any reported price deviation will be a negative one. The reporting format used discloses each variation between planned and actual product or customer mixes. Such variances are expressed in percentage as well as dollar terms.

Schultz, Frank. "A Practical Marketing Model for Short- and Long-Range Planning," *Management Advising*, 10 (March-April 1973), 17–26.

Practical marketing models can increase the efficiency and effectiveness of marketing planning by dealing with such questions as the impact of a new competitor, the wisdom of cutting prices, and the profitability of launching a new brand. The procedures used by a consulting firm in developing such a model for a large consumer product division are spelled out in considerable detail. It is shown that such models need not be either excessively costly or unduly time consuming undertakings. The key determinants of system design were the kinds of questions that marketing managers had to resolve when either launching new products or evaluating possible new directions for existing items in the line. Current and future benefits associated with the introduction of such a model are also considered.

Stephens, H. Virgil. "A Profit-Oriented Marketing Information System," *Management Accounting (U.S.)*, 54 (September 1972), 37–42.

The system discussed is one which makes each sales area a profit center. After actual contribution to profit is compared with a predetermined plan, variances from the plan are analyzed as to cause. Individual salesmen's forecasts as to sales costs and revenues—modified as considered appropriate by higher levels of management—are used to generate budgeted profitability. The variance and performance reports generated include profitability by customer, by territory and by product, and an accounts receivable aging analysis. Each level of management is routinely furnished with the information it requires. Although it is also useful as a control device, the benefits of the system as a tool for more effective planning and direction should initially be emphasized.

Wills, Gordon, Christopher Martin, and Walter David. *Output Budgeting in Marketing*. Management Decision Monograph. UK: University of Bradford, Management Centre, 1972, 28 pp.

An output budget relates cost items to functions and corporate missions in a manner which makes clear what resources are being devoted toward what end. How output budgeting can be applied to corporate marketing and information systems is the subject of this monograph. Brand and venture management and increased concern with logistics are identified as forerunners of the total cross-country organization implied by output budgeting. Further, the corporate information mission is separately analyzed and then related to the product/market missions of the company. Criteria for selecting information goals and determining budgets are identified, and the manager's risk/expenditure trade-off function is introduced. Suggested cost-effectiveness measures for several information components are proposed. Examples from marketing explain and aid the development of the central concept.

Winer, Leon. "A Profit-Oriented Decision System," *Journal of Marketing*, 30 (January 1966), 38–44.

The PROD system advocated in this article involves the use of a return-on-investment approach to evaluating possible courses of marketing action. The cost of capital that must be considered by a marketing executive is defined to include the reciprocal of the price/earnings ratio. This figure is supplemented by an "add-on" covering the firm's fixed marketing expenses. Individuals' evaluations of such decisions as whether to introduce a new product, the price to charge, and which channels of distribution to use are then evaluated. Only those expenses related to the decision in question are considered, and future streams of revenue and expense are discounted by the cost of capital. The present value ratio is used as a basis of choosing among or ranking alternatives. Methods of allowing for risk and joint effects are also discussed.

PART III

Product

Opportunity Accounting for Product Line Decisions

9

Douglas P. Gould

The most significant evidence of aggressive management is its willingness to make decisions. The most significant measure of excellence of management is the quality of those decisions. Hesitancy in decision making often stems from an inability to ascertain or develop the decision alternatives and to quantify their effect.

Every business decision, to some extent or another, is a compound of risk, size of investment, return on that investment, and the time periods involved. One common area of decision making concerns the feasibility and desirability of adding a new product to the company's product line. The failure rate of new products, which has been estimated at between 80% and 90%, emphasizes the significance of this kind of decision, and the degree of potential error and risk which is attached to such decisions.

The financial and accounting functions are deeply involved in these decisions in such determinations as the following:

1. Costs to manufacture
2. Facilities requirements and costs
3. Potential product profitability
4. Capital investment requirements
5. "Payout" of investment
6. Return on investment
7. Pricing
8. Performance evaluation
9. Overhead apportionments
10. Interpretation of financial aspects to non-accounting personnel

Of necessity, projects are either aggressively pursued or abandoned, depending on the cost and profit data communicated to management. However, difficulties often result when conventional accounting approaches are used to evaluate such projects.

Decision Analysis

In order to provide a better approach to such problems and decisions related to them, a combination of analytical approaches is useful. Although the methods to

Reprinted by permission from *Management Accounting* (April 1969), pp. 33–38.

be discussed have wide application in many decision areas, an illustration of a new product decision provides a useful vehicle by which to explore several useful and related techniques. The related decision techniques to be explored include:

1. Price-volume curves
2. The marginal income concept
3. D.E.A.L (multiple break-evens)
4. Compounding
5. Discounted cash flow

The intent is to provide a meaningful basis of accumulating and analyzing the various data pertinent to the real yield of the new product program, and its profit effect on the company.

A cracker-barrel philosopher once noted that it was desirable to "trim your lamp so there is less smoke and more light." A comparable approach is here intended.

The Situation

Allen Manufacturing was a mature instrument company. For various reasons it had experienced declining volume and attendant profit decline in recent years. Profit-volume analysis of the overall company revealed the following annual structure, also shown graphically in Exhibit 1.

Fixed expense	$2,000,000
Marginal income rate	25%
Break-even point	$800,000,000
Objective	20% on invested capital, after tax

Marginal income is the amount available for the payment of all fixed expenses and for the provision of profits. It is found by subtracting the total variable expense from total sales income.

Fixed expenses are always expressed in dollars and are a function of time. They represent the cost of "being in business." Variable expenses are usually expressed as a percentage of the sales dollar or the direct labor dollar, and are a function of quantity. It follows then that the percentage difference between the sales dollar and the total variable expense will be the marginal income rate.

If the marginal income rate is low, say between 15 and 20%, large changes in volume are required to produce material changes in the profit and loss result. If large increases in volume are attained, additional working capital may be required faster than it is made available by the marginal income. In such a case, a business with inadequate working capital is liable to encounter financial difficulties.

When the marginal income ratio is high, say above 35%, large profits and an easy cash position result from comparatively small increases in volume above the

EXHIBIT 1. Break-even chart

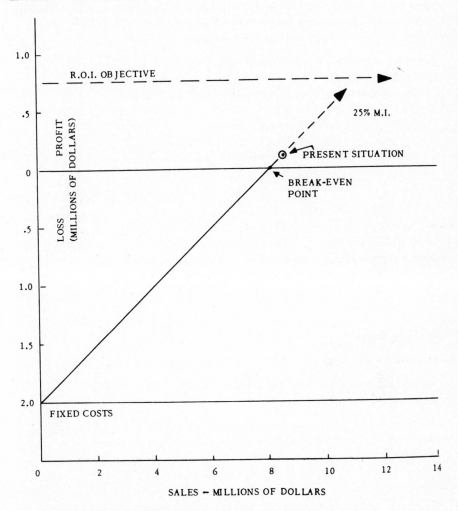

break-even point. Conversely, heavy losses will result from relatively small decreases as the volume falls below the break-even point.

Market Size and Prices

In its endeavor to improve profit, the company had embarked on a product development and acquisition program. One such product under consideration was a unique counting device felt to be superior to those currently on the market. Although application was somewhat specialized, it was felt that a fairly substantial market existed for the new product. In order to obtain a more reliable estimate of market size and prices actually existing in similar-purpose products, a market study was conducted which revealed the following situation:

1. An annual market of about 680,000 units
2. An average unit price of $5.80 at the manufacturer's level
3. Unit prices ranging from approximately $4.00 to $10.00
4. Evidence of a rising interest in similar-purpose products, plus evidence of unfavorable customer reaction to unreliability of lower priced units
5. Some price sensitivity in demand, across the product lines
6. A feeling that devices for this purpose priced in excess of $12.00 per unit (manufacturer's level equivalent) were "too high priced"
7. Somewhat less than a third of the units sold were priced over $9.00

Based on the performance of prototypes and nature of the competition, the company felt that it could rapidly achieve about a 10% penetration of the market with its present distribution, but that in all probability such penetration would be obtained in units in excess of the average price. Based on expected developments, the product life would approximate only five years.

Exhibit 2 shows a price/demand chart constructed from the information at hand.

Variable Cost

Cost estimates for the new product revealed a variable cost pattern as follows:

1. Low variable cost, per unit $5.10
2. High variable cost, per unit $5.60

No fixed burden of any sort was allocated to the product, as the objective was to determine the actual contribution to fixed overhead and profit which would result if the product were marketed. If a decision resulted to proceed further, any *new* fixed costs which would result from the program itself would be included in the program evaluation format. Such program fixed costs were estimated to range from $40,000 to $50,000 per year to gain the market share attempted.

Marginal Income

Because of the variable costs associated with the product, it was then necessary to develop the probable total marginal income dollars which would result if 10% of the unit market was obtained, at the indicated price-unit relationships shown in Exhibit 2.

The marginal income dollars per unit were developed by deducting both high

EXHIBIT 2. Price/demand chart

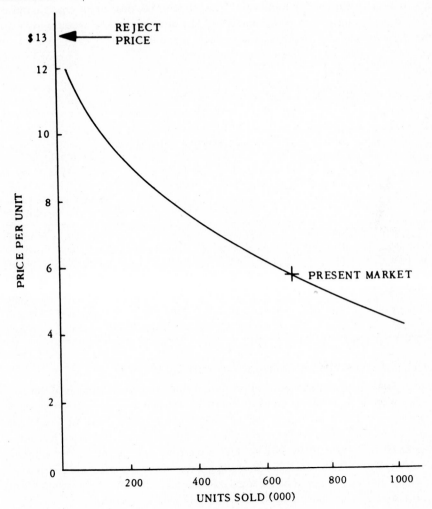

and low projected variable costs from the indicated sales prices, and by extending the result across the indicated number of units.

Table 1 summarizes this calculation. It is apparent that the marginal income dollars are optimized in the price range of $7.50 to $8.00 per unit. Exhibit 3 presents this information graphically.

Thus, a probable market of 40,000 to 50,000 units could be obtained if the manufacturer's realized price was as high as $7.50 to $8.00 per unit. Coupled with new program fixed costs of \$40,000 to \$50,000 per year to accomplish this objective, the total marginal income input of \$70,000 to \$96,000, depending on actual price and volume, appeared to be encouraging. The next step in the decision involved the development of a D.E.A.L. chart, using the multiple break-even principle to explore the effect of the range of prices, costs, volumes on the profit contribution likely to be obtained.

TABLE 1. *Marginal income per unit*

1	2	3	4	5	6
		M.I./unit			
	Units @ 10% of indicated	At high variable	At low variable	Total \$M.I. at stated market share	
Selling price/unit	market (000)	cost (\$5.60)	cost (\$5.10)	At high variable cost	At low variable cost
\$4.00	120	− \$1.60	− \$1.10	− \$182,000	− \$132,000
5.00	84	− .60	− .10	− 50,400	− 8,400
6.00	65	+ .40	+ .90	26,000	58,500
7.00	50	+ 1.40	+ 1.90	70,000	95,000
7.50	40	+ 1.90	+ 2.40	76,000	96,000
8.00	32	+ 2.40	+ 2.90	76,800	92,800
10.00	12	+ 4.40	+ 4.90	52,800	58,800
12.00	2	+ 6.40	+ 6.90	12,800	13,800

D.E.A.L. (Decision Evaluation and Logic)

The probable end result in terms of profit contribution of any decision of this type is a combination of ranges or likely limits of variable costs, selling prices, fixed program costs, sales volumes, and break-even points. The D.E.A.L. technique analyzes and summarizes the range effect of all of these factors, and permits a conclusion as to the likely end result, recognizing the extent of the extremes involved. The D.E.A.L. chart, in effect, superimposes and combines four break-even charts. Supporting it would be the usual schedules of detailed variable product costs (omitted here) and schedule of the net new program fixed costs.

Fixed costs directly associated with this program are noted in Table 2. These costs of a "time" nature would be incurred in addition to any existing common fixed costs, and in the event the program would be subsequently dropped, these time costs could be eliminated.

In addition, prior to the first year's sales, a one-time expenditure of \$50,000 would be incurred for a required re-layout of two departments, for outside engineering fees, and for specialized catalog material. These latter costs would be considered as a part of the investment analysis rather than as components of the ongoing D.E.A.L. analysis.

EXHIBIT 3. Marginal-income chart

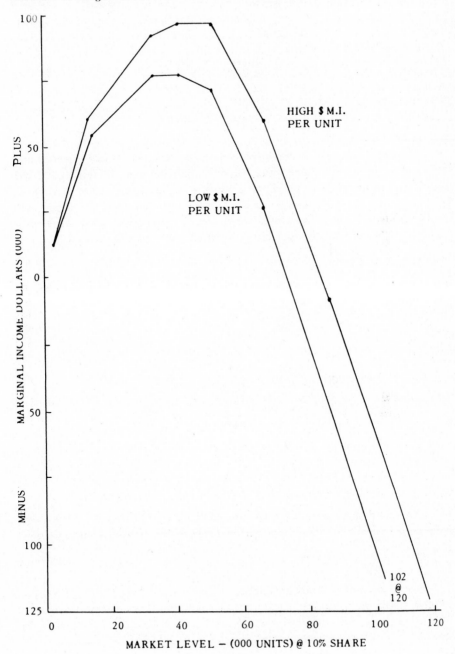

TABLE 2. *Summary of program fixed costs (annual)*

	Low	High
Depreciation—new equipment		
(investment $40,000)	$8,000	$8,000
Added engineering personnel	10,000	15,000
Added sales personnel	12,000	15,000
Advertising, trade magazine	10,000	12,000
Total	$40,000	$50,000

The specified ranges were considered reasonable. Selection of one value for any of several elements of volume, price, variable and fixed costs did not parallel the way things really happen. A technique which recognized that ranges of volume, cost, and break-even points were most likely to be encountered, and which expressed the profit contribution effects of those ranges in consolidated form, provides a rational and understandable appreciation of what might actually happen.

The D.E.A.L. Chart

Exhibit 4 was made to project the first full year of operation. On the break-even grid, the high and low fixed costs were noted. The range of marginal rates was determined in percentages as follows:

	High	Low
Sales price	$7.50	$7.00
Variable cost	5.10	5.60
$M.I./unit	$2.40	$1.40
M.I. ratio	$\dfrac{\$2.40}{\$7.50}$	$\dfrac{\$1.40}{\$7.00}$
M.I.%	32%	20%

Using the basic marginal income equation fixed expense/M.I. rate = break-even, it is possible at this point to determine the four applicable break-even points as follows:

$$1. \quad \frac{\text{Low fixed cost}}{\text{low M.I. rate}} = \frac{\$40,000}{.20}$$
$$= \$200,000 \text{ break-even}$$

$$2. \quad \frac{\text{High fixed cost}}{\text{low M.I. rate}} = \frac{\$50,000}{.20}$$
$$= \$250,000 \text{ break-even}$$

EXHIBIT 4. D.E.A.L. chart

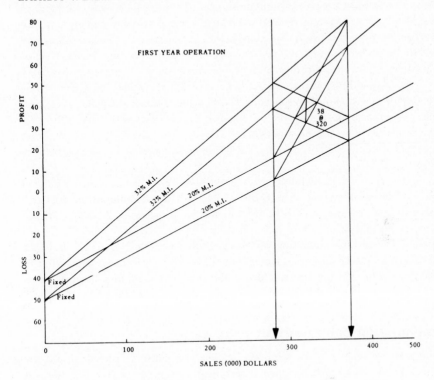

$$\frac{\text{Low fixed cost}}{\text{high M.I. rate}} = \frac{\$40,000}{.32}$$
$$= \$125,000 \text{ break-even}$$

$$\frac{\text{High fixed cost}}{\text{high M.I. rate}} = \frac{\$50,000}{.32}$$
$$= \$156,000 \text{ break-even}$$

Multiple Break-Even Chart

With a knowledge of these four points, the appropriate multiple break-even chart can be constructed by drawing the four lines through the appropriate break-even point to the associated fixed cost point.

The vertical volume ranges can be drawn as follows:

Minimum sales volume 40,000 units × $7.50 = $300,000
Maximum sales volume 50,000 units × $8.00 = $400,000

At this point it can be observed that when the program is operative, the combination of most unfavorable circumstances (i.e., highest fixed operating cost, lowest M.I.%, lowest volume dollars) would still result in a situation where a modest ($6,000 per year pre-tax) profit contribution would be obtained. The program could be said to slightly exceed a break-even situation on its own operating fixed costs even if everything approached the most unfavorable anticipated levels. On the other hand, if the opposite condition occurred (i.e., lowest fixed cost, highest marginal income rate and highest volume), the program could provide as much as $80,000 additional profit contribution, pre-tax, above the fixed operating costs in the first year.

The actual result would be somewhere between these extremes. The likelihood of approximating the high or low range limits can be determined through probability analysis.

In this instance the probabilities of one extreme or the other were considered equal, and the center point identified as $38,000 M.I. contribution at $320,000 annual first-year volume was to be used in further projections. A 26% marginal income rate would be expected under that assumption.

There is considerable discussion of "new product pricing." Actually, the price of the "program" is the significant factor. The entire program must provide sufficient return to warrant the investment. Hence the program itself must be subject to detailed analysis of its "return" possibilities over the expected life of the program.

Compounding Sales Growth

To this end, the sales growth from the chosen base must be presented and the marginal income yield of the *program* determined. In this case, a five-year life was anticipated, with a 10% annual sales growth rate. The sales growth compounded at 10% would be as in Table 3, anticipating zero sales the first or "get ready" year.

The "after tax" operating gain is then determined, using a 53% combined income and surcharge tax factor as shown in Table 4.

TABLE 3. Sales growth at 10%

Year	Sales 10% growth		Sales × M.I. % @ 26%		$M.I.		Less average fixed costs		Net $M.I. (rounded)
0–1	—		—		—		—		—
1–2	$320,000	×	.26	=	$ 83,200	—	$45,000	=	$38,000
2–3	352,000	×	.26	=	91,520	—	45,000	=	46,500
3–4	387,000	×	.26	=	100,620	—	45,000	=	55,600
4–5	425,920	×	.26	=	110,739	—	45,000	=	65,700
5–6	468,512	×	.26	=	121,813	—	45,000	=	76,800

TABLE 4. Operating gain

Year	Net $M.I. (pre-tax)		Tax @ 47%		After-tax $M.I. gain		Rounded value
0–1	0		—		—		—
1–2	$38,000	×	.53	=	$20,140	=	$20,000
2–3	46,000	×	.53	=	24,645	=	24,600
3–4	55,600	×	.53	=	29,468	=	29,500
4–5	65,700	×	.53	=	34,821	=	34,800
5–6	76,800	×	.53	=	40,704	=	40,700

Discounted Cash Flow

Calculations to this point have taken into consideration the prices, costs and profit-volume relationships involved in the new product, the range of values likely to occur, the planned sales and margin growth under expected operating conditions over the life of the program.

At this point the return on the investment must be developed and a decision must be reached on whether to accept or reject the proposed program. The discounted cash flow technique will be used for this purpose.

The effect of income taxes is considered, and depreciation is added back. Table 5 shows the calculation.

Various discount tables and assumptions can be employed with slightly varying results. In this instance, the present value of the cash flows over the life of the program is slightly less than the value of the investment in the year 0–1, at a rate between 27 and 28%, indicating that the proper rate of return is slightly less than

TABLE 5. Discounted cash flow from project

Year	M.I. gain after tax	Add = back depreciation	Total cash flow	Discount factors at 27%	Present values at 27%	Discount factors at 28%	Present values at 28%
			($50,000)				
0–1	—	—	(40,000)	.787	($70,830)	.781	($70,290)
1–2	$20,000	$8,000	28,000	.620	17,360	.610	17,080
2–3	24,600	8,000	32,600	.488	15,909	.477	15,550
3–4	29,500	8,000	37,500	.384	14,400	.373	13,988
4–5	34,800	8,000	42,800	.303	12,968	.291	12,455
5–6	40,700	8,000	48,700	.238	11,591	.277	11,055
					$ 1,398		(162)

Indicated rate of return 28%

the latter figure. At about 28% the present value of the discounted cash flows over the life of the program and the amount invested in the program would be approximately equal.

Value of the Analysis

As the company's profit plan objective in this case was 20% after tax on investment, the project would exceed the "par" established, and authorization could be given to proceed.

A sound "project description" has been provided for the product manager, in the form of a D.E.A.L. chart or charts, and he is in a position to gauge his progress against his approved plan as time goes by. This formal "pre-audit" for product additions forces attention to the key decision factors. Likewise, it forms a good basis for reviewing the degree of excellence of the decision at the termination of the program.

There is no real intention of "to the penny" accuracy, as some broad assumptions are obviously necessary. The intent is to consider the probable return on the investment, in time, with a rational consideration of all factors involved. To this end the several techniques used herein combine to provide a practical operational technique which can be readily employed to give greater dimension and accuracy to the profit aspects of decision making.

There can be considerable variation in the degree of sophistication surrounding the application of these and other useful techniques. The primary value is to approximate the real conditions likely to be encountered over the life of a given program, and to give proper direction to the decision maker. Most factors of the problem will change, if sufficient time passes. Unless there is a good record of the premises on which the original decision was based, the need for and effects of changes are very difficult to measure.

Exercises

9.1. Longrun Construction is contemplating adding a new compact ready-mix cement mixture to its product line. The market research group has conducted a study to obtain an estimate of market size and prices existing in similar products. The results were as follows:

1. An annual market of about 800,000 units.
2. An average unit price of $8.20 at the manufacturer's level.
3. Unit prices ranging from $6.00 to $14.00.
4. Evidence of rising interest in similar-purpose products.
5. Some price sensitivity in demand across product line.
6. Less than one quarter of the units sold were priced over $12.00.

TABLE 9.1. Unit-price relationships

Unit price	Units at 12% penetration (000's)
$ 6.00	140
7.00	110
8.00	85
9.00	69
10.00	50
11.00	35
12.00	20
13.00	15
14.00	5

TABLE 9.2. Profit-volume analysis of the overall company

Fixed expense	$2,500,000
Marginal income rate	30%
Break-even point	10,000,000
Investment policy	25% return, after tax

The group has also developed some unit-price relationships and a profit-volume analysis, which appear in Tables 9.1 and 9.2. Estimates of high and low variable costs are $6.90 and $6.50, respectively. Based on the prototype and the nature of the competition, the company estimated that it could achieve a 12% penetration of the market with its present distribution.

No fixed burden was allocated to the product, as the objective was to determine the actual contribution to fixed overhead and profit which would result if the product were marketed. However, if the decision is to proceed, any fixed costs will have to be included in the program evaluation. The cost of such a program is expected to range from $50,000 to $80,000 per year, of which $40,000 will be spent in equipment. In addition, the management estimates that outside consulting fees and plant safety requirements needed to accommodate the new process will amount to $85,000 the first year and $60,000 the second. The life of the product is expected to be five years.

1. In what unit price range are the marginal income dollars optimized? Show your calculations.
2. Calculate the marginal income ratios.
3. Using the basic marginal income equation $\dfrac{\text{Fixed expenses}}{\text{M.I. rate}} = \text{Breakeven}$, determine the four applicable break-even points.

4. How much pre-tax profit contribution would be obtained under the *most* and the *least* favorable circumstances?
5. Assuming that the probabilities of one extreme and the other are equal, calculate the net marginal income contribution at 29% marginal income rate. The sales figure corresponding to that figure will be your annual first-year volume which will be used in further projections.
6. Given the 12% sales growth objective set up by management, calculate a net marginal income dollar figure for the expected life of the product. Assuming a tax rate of 50%, calculate the after-tax marginal income dollar gain.
7. Using straight-line depreciation, do a discounted cash flow analysis of the project. What is the rate of return on the project? Does it meet the investment criteria of the company?

9.2. The X Company is contemplating the introduction of a new product. Variable costs are estimated at a low of $11.82 and a high of $12.16 per unit. Sales price is expected to be within the $14.50 to $15.35 range. Fixed costs associated with the product will vary from $50,000 to $80,000. To purchase the necessary equipment will cost $45,000. A one-time expenditure of $80,000 prior to the first year of operation will be required to comply with certain city regulations. The life of the product is expected to be five years.

1. Calculate the high and the low marginal income rates for the product.
2. Calculate the four break-even points.
3. If the minimum number of units that could be sold is 35,000 and the maximum is 45,000, calculate the profit contribution the product would make under the *most* and the *least* favorable circumstances.
4. Assuming an annual sales growth of 9%, calculate the sales for the next five years. A marginal income rate of 20%, corresponding to approximately $56,000 M.I. contribution, is expected for the first year.
5. Calculate the after-tax marginal income (tax rate of 50%). Using straight-line depreciation, do a discounted cash flow of the project. What is the expected rate of return?

Cannibalism and New Product Development

10

Roger A. Kerin   Michael G. Harvey   James T. Rothe

Inflation, slowed economic growth, resource shortages, and foreign competition are placing unprecedented pressures on product management. Properly or improperly, many firms appear to be focusing their efforts on opportunities that offer minimal market resistance. A. T. Kearney, Inc., noted recently that reformulated products directed toward existing markets have a substantially higher likelihood of success than product innovations directed at new markets.[1] While product line extension or repositioning strategies pose minimal risk of failure for the product being introduced, potential negative effects on existing products serving existing markets must be considered. These effects can be called product cannibalism. While some cannibalism may be planned or expected, considerable amounts of cannibalism may be an unexpected consequence of an improperly managed new product development process.

Examples of planned and unplanned product cannibalism abound. Earlier this year, Anheuser-Busch noted that 20–25 percent of the volume for its new brand, Michelob Light, would come from the existing Michelob brand because of the low-calorie appeal among current customers.[2] When General Foods introduced Maxim, linkages to the existing Maxwell House brand through packaging and promotion resulted in a loss of market share for the entire line. Similarly, Ford's introduction of the Falcon as a "new-sized Ford" at a lower price led consumers to substitute Falcons for existing Ford models.[3]

Cannibalism and New Products

The theoretical roots of product cannibalism can be traced to the cross-elasticity of demand theory. This theory suggests that the percentage change in the price of product A demanded will be influenced by the percentage change in the price of product B. The demand interrelationship of the two products may then be described as independent, complementary, or substitutable. In the case of product substitution,

---

[1] "The Breakdown of U.S. Innovation," *Business Week*, February 16, 1976: 46–60ff.
[2] "Anheuser-Busch, Inc., Has Another Entry in 'Light Beer' Field," *Wall Street Journal*, February 13, 1978: 4.
[3] William Copulsky, "Cannibalism in the Marketplace," *Journal of Marketing*, October 1976: 103–105.

Components of new product sales revenue

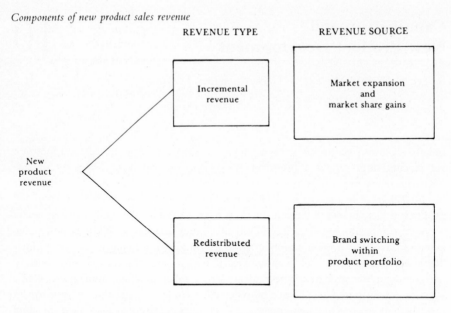

or cannibalism, a lowering of the price on product A will tend to decrease the quantity demanded for product B and effect a leftward shift in the demand curve for product B, providing "other things remain equal."

From a marketing standpoint, however, other things rarely "remain equal." Accordingly, an expanded interpretation of cross-elasticity of demand is necessary. In addition to price changes, physical and symbolic attributes of products, alternative means of promoting products, and potential end-use interchangeability between products must be considered. The Michelob Light, Maxim, and Falcon experiences illustrate these marketing effects.

As shown in the figure, new or reformulated products acquire their sales revenue from three sources: (1) new consumers who were not previously buyers of the product type, (2) consumers of competitive brands, and (3) consumers of an existing company brand who switch to the new or reformulated brand or product. The first two sources represent, respectively, incremental revenue for the product portfolio because of market expansion, and the capturing of competitors' market share. The remaining source represents "redistributed" revenue, or cannibalization, in that existing buyers are substituting one item for another in the company's product portfolio. Accordingly, product cannibalization has been defined as "the process by which a new product gains a portion of its sales by diverting them from an existing product."[4]

This process of sales diversion or redistribution of revenue has a subtle but

---

[4] James Heskett, *Marketing* (New York: Macmillan, 1976): 581.

managerially important consequence. Assuming that the change in profits earned by the existing product is negative because of substitution, this amount should be added to the incremental cost curve for the new or reformulated product.[5] The implication is clear. Sales and profit gains of new products at the expense of an existing product do not filter down to the bottom line. Rather, the loss of potential profits from a cannibalized product is a real cost that must be absorbed by the new product. The adage, "You can't have your cake and eat it, too," applies when cannibalism occurs.

These comments illustrate the importance of performing a marginal analysis on the new product and the modified character of the product portfolio within the context of present and forecasted market conditions. Incremental revenue, cost, and investment must be considered.

Fostering Cannibalism

The erosion of an existing product's share of the market through new product cannibalism may stem from management decisions, or it may be a necessary evil, given market conditions. Cannibalism becomes a problem when it provides no incremental competitive or financial benefit to the firm's product portfolio. Several managerial decisions appear to foster cannibalism of existing brand volume with no benefit to the firm:

- Strong top management pressure for growth from new products.
- Preoccupation with developing a full line of products in an attempt to achieve increases in overall market share in a product class.
- Inadequate positioning of new products, resulting in their seeking the identity of existing products.
- Unrealistic or excessive market segmentation, resulting in "two segments" with demands for identical product attributes or end-use needs.
- Aggressive promotional efforts reflected in sales representatives' overemphasis on new brands and neglect of existing products.

Product cannibalism by itself should not be viewed only negatively. Cannibalism by new products sometimes represents an outgrowth of effective and competitive product portfolio management. For example, a brand with cannibalism potential may be introduced to eliminate gaps in a product line that might be filled by competing offerings or to neutralize competitive inroads. In other words, it may be wiser to have buyers switching brands within a firm's product line than to have them switching out and purchasing competitive offerings. Viewed in this manner, preemptive cannibalism becomes a viable choice.

Bristol-Myers's introduction of Datril to compete with McNeil Laboratories'

---

[5] For an expanded discussion of this relationship, see "An Introduction to Multiple Product Analysis," in Eugene Singer, *Antitrust Economics: Selected Legal Cases and Economic Models* (Englewood Cliffs, New Jersey: Prentice-Hall, Inc., 1968): 177–186.

An example of product cannibalism

	A Existing product alone	Existing product	+	New product	=	B Products combined	Incremental analysis
Forecast total market units	15,000,000					18,000,000	
Forecast market share	5%					10%	
Forecast unit volume	750,000					1,800,000	
Source of volume:							
New customers	50,000			950,000		950,000	
Competitors' customers	200,000	100,000		100,000		200,000	
Cannibalized customers				200,000		200,000	
Repeat customers	500,000	450,000				450,000	
TOTAL	750,000	550,000		1,250,000		1,800,000	
Resulting market share		3.1%		6.9%		10%	
Unit price	$2.00	$2.00		$1.75			
Total revenue	$1,500,000	$1,100,000		$2,187,500		$3,287,500	$1,787,500
Gross margin/unit	$1.00	$1.00		$0.75			
Gross margin dollars	$750,000	$550,000		$937,500		$1,487,500	$737,500
Marketing expenditures and allocated overhead	$300,000	$300,000		$450,000		$750,000	$450,000
Profit before tax	$450,000	$250,000		$487,500		$737,500	$287,500
Investment	$4,500,000	$4,500,000		$1,000,000		$5,500,000	$1,000,000
Return on investment	10%	5%		48.7%		13%	28.7%

Tylenol appears to be a case in point. Bristol-Myers held a position of strength in the aspirin segment of the analgesic market with its Bufferin and Excedrin brands. However, this segment, while large, had plateaued in the mid-1970s. During the same period, the acetaminophen (noninflammatory compounds) segment of the analgesic market dominated by McNeil Laboratories had grown substantially, with a portion of the growth coming from former and potential aspirin users. Datril's introduction would hopefully attract aspirin switchers (that is, switching away from company brands) and top existing and potential acetaminophen buyers who would most likely purchase Tylenol. Therefore, even though Datril might cannibalize Excedrin and Bufferin, aspirin switchers would remain in the Bristol-Myers product line rather than being attracted to Tylenol.

IBM's introduction of the Series/1 minicomputer represents another possible application of preemptive cannibalism. Although the new product would compete in some respects with IBM's existing offering, the potential for attracting new buyers of competitive products as well as maintaining dominance in their product markets would offset any lost sales that might result.

Fiscal Consequences

An analysis of a hypothetical multiproduct firm serves to illustrate the fiscal consequences of product cannibalism. This firm has an existing product that was expected to capture 5 percent of a market forecasted at 15 million units, or 750,000 units. At a $2.00/unit price and a $1.00/unit gross margin, forecasted sales are $1.5 million with a $750,000 gross margin. Budgeted marketing expenditures plus allocated overhead total $300,000, which will provide a $450,000 profit before taxes and a 10 percent return on investment. An abbreviated pro forma income statement describing these figures is shown in column A of the accompanying table.

A new product is introduced that satisfies several, but not all, buyer requirements met by the existing product in addition to several other needs. The new product is priced at $1.75/unit, with a $.75/unit gross margin. The lower price and modified product benefits are expected to expand the market for this product type by 20 percent, to 18 million units. Both products combined are expected to capture 10 percent of the expanded market, or 1.8 million units, which represents a 240 percent increase over forecasted volume for the single existing product. Marketing expenditures plus allocated overhead for the new product are budgeted at $450,000. Incremental investment for the new product is $1 million. Most of the volume captured by the new product comes from market expansion because of the lower price and differentiated product benefit structure. However, slightly more than a 25 percent cannibalism rate occurs from the existing product.

Column B in the table shows the effects of the activities and events described for the existing product and the new product, individually and combined. Also shown is an incremental analysis comparing the existing product alone with the existing and the new product combined. Given the conditions of the example cited, the apparent new product profit is, in fact, much less when cannibalized volume at the existing product's contribution is subtracted. The apparent return on investment for the product line with the new product is inflated.

This example highlights several ramifications of product cannibalism:

- Without accounting for product cannibalism in new product introductions, new product volume and profits may be more illusionary than real.
- New product introduction examined in an isolated fashion, without also considering cannibalized volume, provides a distorted view of product line profits and return on investment.
- Market share growth for a product line resulting from new product introduction may represent Pyrrhic victories in terms of product line profitability and individual item volume.
- Both the amount and source of potential new product volume must be considered in product line planning to calculate the impact of cannibalism on product line profitability.

The table can also be used to illustrate the potential effects of preemptive cannibalism. Suppose in our hypothetical situation that the new product described was used as a retaliatory device to meet a competitor whose lower priced product was capturing a portion of the existing product's market share. If one considers the new product's cannibalized volume as potentially lost to the competitor, then these buyers are being kept by the firm, albeit at a lower return. If the new product were not introduced, 200,000 units would be lost, resulting in a 5 percent return on the existing product's investment. Even with cannibalism considered, the firm's new product will virtually preserve the return on investment percentage, thus showing the benefit of preemptive cannibalism.

Identifying Potential

The importance of identifying cannibalism potential in new product development cannot be overemphasized. Cannibalism effects should be considered throughout the product development process, beginning with concept testing and continuing through commercialization. Cannibalism potential can be identified during the concept evaluation stage, providing that product concepts are examined in light of end-use contexts rather than in an isolated, product-specific fashion. More specifically, product attributes should be evaluated in terms of their importance in satisfying a specific need. Louis Sharpe and Kent Granzin report that the analysis of product attributes in usage contexts enhances brand purchase predictions.[6] Edgar A. Pessemier and James Myers have recently developed promising research tech-

---

[6] Louis Sharpe and Kent Granzin, "Brand Attributes That Determine Purchases," *Journal of Advertising Research*, April 1974: 39–42.

niques that incorporate usage attribute criteria in concept testing.[7] Each offers a means for the early detection of potential cannibalism and possible end use interchangeability between products or concepts used in a specific situation.

Once the potential for cannibalism is recognized during the concept stage, the business analysis stage of the product development process should address the question of the source and amount of potential new product volume expected. Based on the concept test results, it would seem that the greater the similarity between product attributes in a particular use context, the greater the likelihood of expected volume coming from a competing brand or being cannibalized from an existing brand. Unfortunately, existing knowledge of consumer behavior precludes the exact specifications of the sources and amounts of new product volume. Therefore, judgmental scenarios examining alternative revenue sources and amounts in pro forma profit and loss statements as depicted in the table should be developed.

The question remains as to what level of cannibalism can occur and still warrant a "go" decision for the new product. According to William Reynolds, about 70 percent of Mustang sales in the car's introductory year were to buyers who would have purchased another Ford had the Mustang not been introduced; 30 percent represented incremental volume.[8] Cadbury, describing the recent introduction of a chocolate bar in England, reports that over 50 percent of its volume came from market expansion, with the remaining volume coming from existing company products.[9] Both products were considered successful introductions by their respective firms. The apparent diversity in cannibalism rates suggests that cost structure, degree of market maturity, and competitive appeal of alternative offerings will affect cannibalism rates and their importance to the sales and profitability of a product line and individual items. George Murray and Harry Wolfe have developed a potentially useful analytic model which combines a company's cost and profit structure with a qualitative assessment of consumer purchase patterns to determine an optimal product line.[10]

It is also possible to calculate the incremental unit volume necessary to overcome the effects of cannibalism. This measure can be used as a benchmark for evaluating market capacity and the quality of introductory marketing programs early in the business analysis stage. The expression is as follows:

Incremental volume to offset cannibalism effect =
      Cannibalized unit volume × ratio of the old and new product margins

Using figures from the previous example, the incremental new product volume

---

[7] Edgar A. Pessemier, *Product Management: Strategy and Organization* (New York: John Wiley & Sons, 1977): Chapter 5; James Myers, "Benefit Structure Analysis: A New Tool for Product Planning," *Journal of Marketing*, October 1976: 23–32.

[8] William Reynolds, "More Sense About Market Segmentation," *Harvard Business Review*, September-October 1965: 107–114.

[9] N. D. Cadbury, "When, Where, and How to Test Market," *Harvard Business Review*, May-June 1975: 96–105.

[10] George Murray and Harry Wolfe, "Length of Product Line," *California Management Review*, Summer 1970: 79–85.

necessary to overcome the effects of cannibalism is approximately 267,000 units: 200,000 units × $1.00 contribution/$.75 contribution. In other words, at the estimated cannibalism rate, the new product must generate an incremental volume from new and competitors' customers of 267,000 units to offset the loss of contribution dollars from the existing product. In effect, for this illustration, a 21 percent increase in incremental new product volume over forecasted levels would be required. Issues surrounding market capacity and the quality of the introductory product program assume a different light in this context.

Despite the insights garnered from pretests and preliminary volume forecasts, the best method for assessing the actual degree of cannibalism is a market test. Test markets afford the final opportunity for cannibalism research prior to commercialization of the new product. Cannibalism research at this juncture should focus not only on monitoring the new product but also on existing company products to determine whether new product volume is arising from existing products, the competition, or market expansion.[11] Knowledge of volume sources should assist in interpreting test market results and affect the "go" or "no go" decision.

Exercises

10.1. Brisco Tasty is a manufacturer of several breakfast cereal products. The total forecast market is 20 million units. "Good Morning Bran," an existing product of Brisco, was expected to capture 8% of this market. Of the unit volume forecast, 50% are repeat sales, 40% are derived from competitors' sales, and the remaining are new customers. The product is being sold at $1.80 per box (of 250 kg) and earns $1.00 in gross margin. A total of $700,000 is allocated toward marketing expenditures and overhead incurred for this product, which had required an initial outlay of $5 million.

Brisco is introducing a new product called "All Day Bran." The new product is priced at $0.30 less than "Good Morning Bran," with a gross margin of $0.85 per box (of 250 kg). With this new product in the market, the present market is expected to expand by 25%. Both products combined are expected to capture 15% of the new market.

However, with the new product, repeat sales from the existing product will decrease by some 25%. The new product is expected to cannibalize sales of some 800,000 units from the present product.

With the two products in the market, 300,000 competitors' customers are expected to still favor the existing product, while 340,000 of them will switch to the new bran.

---

[11] See Glen Urban, "A Mathematical Modeling Approach to Product Line Decisions," *Journal of Marketing Research*, February 1969: 40–47, for a description of a model designed to test distribution, advertising, and price cross-elasticities. Urban's model provides a conceptual and quantitative interpretation of interproduct substitution in a test market, and prescribes normative marketing mix strategies for new and existing products.

Marketing expenditures and allocated overhead are budgeted at $800,000. Incremental investment for the new product is $2.5 million.

Based on the above information,

1. What is the return on investment from the present product?
2. Show the incremental analysis, comparing the existing product alone with the existing and the new product combined.
3. Calculate the ROI for the product line with the new product, first without taking into account the effects of cannibalism and then taking the effects into account. How does this compare with the ROI for the existing product?
4. Calculate the incremental new product volume necessary to overcome the effects of cannibalism.

10.2. Nestlé is a manufacturer of several wheat and oats beverage products. The total market for such beverage drinks is forecasted at 35 million. Nestlé expected its leading brand, "Nestlé Chocolate," to capture 6% of this market. The forecast unit volume can be subdivided into three categories of customers—new, competitors', and repeat. The share of each group is 20%, 35% and 45%, respectively, of the forecast unit volume.

The product is currently being sold at $1.20 per tin (of 100 kg) and brings $0.80 in gross margin. Marketing expenditures and allocated overhead for this product total $800,000. Nestlé spent $4 million in capital investment for this beverage.

In the fall, Nestlé introduced a very similar beverage but with honey added, called the "Honey Milk Cocoa." It is being sold at $1.00 per tin and earns the company the same gross margin per unit as the present brand. This improved beverage is expected to expand the market by 10 million in unit volume and to capture a market share of 10% (for the products combined).

With this new product, 300,000 competitors' customers are expected to continue buying the existing brand, while 435,000 of them will buy the new brand. The number of repeat customers of the present product is expected to decline to 800,000, while the unit volume cannibalized by the new product is estimated at 1 million. Nestlé has a budget of $900,000 for marketing expenditures and allocated overhead for the new product. Incremental investment for the new product is $3 million.

Using the information above,

1. Calculate the return on investment from the present brand.
2. Show the incremental analysis, comparing the existing product alone with the existing and the new product combined.
3. Determine the ROI for the product line with the new product, first without taking into account the effects of cannibalism and then taking the effects into account. How does this compare with the ROI for the existing product?
4. Calculate the incremental new product volume necessary to overcome the effects of cannibalism.

A New Marketing Tool: Life-Cycle Costing

11

Robert J. Brown

> Life-cycle costing is a method of calculating the total cost of ownership over the life span of the industrial product. It can be especially useful in the marketing of industrial products that sell for high initial prices, but which provide long-run cost savings. This paper explains the life-cycle concept and its implementation.

Industrial products which find a market primarily on the basis of lowest initial cost are not necessarily those which cost the least in the long run. Costs incurred in the years after purchase may be significant, often far exceeding initial cost, and should be included in any purchase analysis. The method used to determine the total cost of a purchase over its life cycle or planning period is known as life-cycle costing. The purpose of this article is to explain the concept and use of life-cycle costing. The subject should be of interest to both buyers and sellers: to buyers so that they can better evaluate purchases, and to sellers so that they can better plan and market their products.

Life-cycle costing's most important use is in product analysis where costs expected over the asset's life are large relative to the purchase and installation costs. Factors of particular relevance are length of life and maintenance and operation costs. Initial cost will probably dominate for a short-lived asset while post-purchase costs will be more significant for long-lived assets. Where economies on maintenance and operation costs can be effected, LCC (life-cycle costing) can clearly demonstrate the savings. Examples of products on which LCC analysis is likely to be fruitful are: HVAC (heating, ventilation, and air conditioning) systems, pollution control equipment, heavy industrial equipment, farm equipment, earth movers, hospital facilities, computers, ceilings, floors, cables, cars, buses, telephone installations, etc.

Life-cycle costing is not a new concept. It has been used by the United States Department of Defense for a quarter century. What is new is the surge of interest in its use in the 1970s. The U.S. General Services Administration, Department of Health, Education and Welfare, National Aeronautics and Space Administration, Environmental Protection Agency, and other Federal agencies have now begun to avail themselves of LCC. Since 1974, seven states (Florida, Alaska, North Carolina, New Mexico, Washington, Texas, and Maryland) have passed laws requiring LCC analysis in the planning, design, and construction of state buildings.[1]

Reprinted by permission of the publisher from *Industrial Marketing Management*, vol. 8, pp. 109–113. Copyright 1979 by Elsevier North Holland, Inc.

[1] For a more extensive history of life-cycle costing, see Williams [2].

The primary cause of the increased emphasis on life-cycle costing has been inflation—in particular, the escalation of energy prices. Expected rising costs of labor, materials, oil, and other operating and maintenance elements give greater weight to post-purchase cost estimates vis-à-vis initial cost. The result is that life-cycle costing, which allows for both categories of costs, is becoming an essential evaluative technique.

The Method

There are two basic life-cycle costing methods: present value and average annual cost. The former reduces all dollar costs and benefits of a project to present value while the latter converts them to an average annual figure. If the length of life of competing projects is identical, both methods will rank the projects in the same order. However, the information obtained from both methods may be useful. For example, the present value method may reveal that equipment A will have a life-cycle cost of $10,000 less than B, while the average annual cost method will show that the average annual difference is only $200. The buyer may hesitate to incur an additional $10,000 cost to obtain a nonquantifiable benefit associated with B, but may have a changed opinion upon realizing that the difference averages out to only $200 a year.

If competing assets have different expected lives, the present value method is not appropriate without some adjustment for the difference. The average annual cost method may, however, be used for comparison. Information needed for LCC is as follows:

1. Initial cost: this will include the cost of delivery and installation.
2. Length of life: number of years of life or of the planning period.
3. Terminal value: this may be a benefit if it is a salvage value or a cost if it is a removal estimate.
4. Maintenance: average annual cost of maintaining the asset as well as any periodic replacement of parts.
5. Operation: average annual cost of energy, labor, materials, supplies, insurance.
6. Relevant taxes: investment tax credit, tax benefits from depreciation.
7. Discount rate: future costs must be discounted for the time value of money to the firm.
8. Escalation rate: estimated rate at which costs will grow as attributable exclusively to inflation.

Solving by the present value method is essentially the same as described in the capital budgeting section of any basic textbook on financial management (see, for example, [1]). The formula to be used for discounting a single value (e.g., the terminal value) is:

$$P = \frac{T}{(1+r)^n},$$

where r = buyer's cost of capital/discount rate, T = terminal value, n = length of life in years, and P = present value of T. If tables are utilized, T may be multiplied by the present value factor.

The formula for present value of a uniform annual series (e.g., maintenance and operation) is:

$$P = \sum_{t=1}^{n} \frac{C}{(1+r)^t},$$

where C = uniform annual cost and t = the year in which the cost is incurred. Present value tables will provide the factor for a uniform annual series.

If a cost is expected to escalate at rate e, the appropriate formula is:

$$P = \frac{a(a^n - 1)}{a - 1} C,$$

where $a = (1 + e)/(1 + r)$. A brief table of discount/escalation factors, developed by computer program, is provided in Table 1.

TABLE 1. *Present value factors for annual expenses that are escalating: life 20 years*

Discount rate	Escalation rate			
	5%	6%	7%	8%
6%	18.133620	20.000000	22.103420	24.477340
8%	15.075810	16.532210	18.165020	20.000000
10%	12.717780	13.867230	15.151140	16.588210
12%	10.874180	11.793080	12.815220	13.954010

Source: Author's computer program.

The discount rate to be used is the buyer's cost of capital. The buyer may be willing to provide the rate or the seller may estimate it.

Since expenses are tax deductible they should be multiplied by $(100\% - TR)$ where TR is the tax rate. The investment tax credit is the amount by which the Federal income tax is to be reduced. Depreciation is the annual amount by which the original cost is expensed and it provides a tax benefit of TR multiplied by the depreciation amount.

As an example of the use of LCC, take the case where a buyer is interested in

TABLE 2. Present-value method of solution[a]

	Model A	Model B
Initial cost[b]	$28,000	$26,000
Annual kWh consumption[c]	150,000	165,000
Operation and maintenance		
$(3,000 \times 12.71778 \times 0.52 =)$	$19,840	$19,840
Power		
$(150,000 \times 0.03 \times 15.15114 \times 0.52 =)$	35,454	—
$(165,000 \times 0.03 \times 15.15114 \times 0.52 =)$	—	38,999
Investment tax credit	(2,800)	(2,600)
Depreciation tax benefit		
$(28,000 \div 20 \times 0.48 \times 8.51355 =)$	(5,721)	—
$(26,000 \div 20 \times 0.48 \times 8.51355 =)$	—	(5,312)
Present value of costs	74,773	76,927
Present value differential in favor of A:	2,154	

[a] Benefits in parentheses.
[b] Includes sales tax, shipping, installation.
[c] Based on customers estimated operating needs.

Customer's annual discount rate: 10%. Life cycle: 20 yr. Estimated escalation rate of power: 7%. Estimated escalation rate of operation and maintenance: 5%. Investment tax credit: 10%. Customer's tax rate: 48%. Annual operation and maintenance cost of each model: $3,000. Power cost ($/kWh): $0.03. Depreciation method: straight line. Present worth factor for 20 yrs.: 8.51355.

purchase of a water chiller of 180-ton capacity. The manufacturer has two models (A and B) available, and the buyer wishes to choose between them on the basis of cost. Details on the two models and determination of the life-cycle cost of each are provided in Table 2. Although Model A has an initial cost $2,000 greater than B, A has a life-cycle cost $2,154 less than B.

If the present value has already been calculated, the average annual value may be found by multiplying by the capital recovery factor. The formula is:

$$A = \frac{r(1+r)^n}{(1+r)^n - 1},$$

where A is the average annual value to which a present value of $1 is equivalent.

In the compound interest tables, the capital recovery factor for 20 years at 10% is found to be 0.11746. The average annual cost of each type of equipment is:

A: $74,773 \times 0.11746 = $8,783
B: $76,927 \times 0.11746 = 9,036

If the present value has not been calculated, it may be easier to convert the costs and benefits to average annual values directly. However, escalated values must first be converted to present value (calculations are provided in Table 3).

TABLE 3. *Average annual-cost method of solution*

	Model A	Model B
Initial cost ($\times 0.11746$)	3,289	3,054
Operation and maintenance		
($19,840 \times 0.11746$)	2,330	2,330
Power		
($35,454 \times 0.11746$)	4,164	
($38,999 \times 0.11746$)		4,580
Investment tax credit		
(2800×0.11746)	(329)	—
(2600×0.11746)	—	(305)
Depreciation tax benefit		
($1400 \times 0.48 =$)	(672)	—
($1300 \times 0.48 =$)	—	(624)
Average annual cost	8,782	9,035
Average annual cost		
differential in favor of A:	$253	

The $253 average annual cost differential in favor of A leads to the same preference as the present worth method. The average annual cost method, however, provides a different perspective in quantifying the yearly cost. Whereas the $2,154 present worth differential could seem an impressive saving, it is possible that the decision maker would consider other benefits of Model B worth the additional $253 yearly difference.

Discounting

Anyone who has ever utilized the net present-value method for capital budgeting will recognize the application to LCC analysis. The only distinction is that LCC is the term generally applied to analysis of a subset of capital budgeting problems: projects that do not generate revenue. The latter may be divided into two types:

Type 1. Projects intended to produce economic benefits, e.g., devices to reduce the cost of labor or energy.

Type 2. Projects intended to produce benefits other than economic ones, e.g., pollution control equipment, public schools, defense installations.

The objective of LCC analysis of both Type 1 and Type 2 projects is cost minimization rather than revenue maximization.

Payback

Payback is the period required to recover initial outlay, and has traditionally been an important consideration for revenue-producing projects. Projects with attractive prospects simply won't be accepted by many firms unless the payback period is less than a prescribed minimum. Selling to such firms by LCC analysis may require some consideration of payback.

Type 1 assets provide economic benefits in the form of reduced costs and payback may be measured as the number of years it will take to recover initial outlay from the cost savings. Although a rough approximation may be obtained by dividing the annual savings into first cost—obtaining what may be termed the base payback period— this would ignore the time value of money and could over- or understate the payback period. A more accurate figure can be obtained if the payback definition is interpreted as the period needed to recover outlay from the cost savings *discounted*. This latter period may be termed the true payback period.

The true payback period will be the same as the base payback period if the cost savings escalate at the same rate as they are being discounted. For example, a new lighting system costing $12,000 and producing operating and maintenance savings of $3,000 a year will have a base payback of four years. If the savings escalate at 8% a year and are discounted at 8% a year, the true payback will be four years (see Table 4 for calculations). On the other hand, if savings escalate at 2% a year and the discount rate is 10%, the true payback is 4.98 years or $\simeq 5$ years (see Table 5 for abbreviated calculations).

Payback analysis may also be used for both Type 1 and Type 2 projects where the initial costs of competing projects differ and where the objective is to determine the time period required to recover the difference (assuming that the one with the higher first cost has the lower life-cycle cost). The water chiller problem can be used for illustration (Table 6).

The buyer now has three helpful pieces of information about the water chillers:

TABLE 4

Year			Annual return	Cumulative return
1	$\dfrac{3,000(1.08)}{(1.08)}$	$=$	3,000	3,000
.	.		.	.
.	.		.	.
4	$\dfrac{3,000(1.08)^4}{(1.08)^4}$	$=$	3,000	12,000

TABLE 5

Year		Annual return	Cumulative return
1	$\dfrac{3,000(1.02)}{(1.10)}$ =	2,781.82	2,781.82
.	.	.	.
.	.	.	.
.	.	.	.
4	$\dfrac{3,000(1.02)^4}{(1.10)^4}$ =	2,217.95	9,971.17[a]
5	$\dfrac{3,000(1.02)^5}{(1.10)^5}$ =	2,056.64	12,027.81[a]

[a] Interpolate to obtain 4.98 years.

TABLE 6

Initial cost of A $28,000 less 10% = $25,200
Initial cost of B $26,000 less 10% = 23,400
Amount to be recovered: $ 1,800

Year	Calculations[a]	Annual return	Cumulative return
1	$\dfrac{450(0.52)(1.07)}{(1.10)} + \dfrac{100(0.48)}{(1.10)}$ =	271.25	271.25
.	.	.	.
.	.	.	.
etc.			
	True payback $\simeq$ 7.5 yrs.		

[a] Annual savings on power = $450. Annual depreciation difference = $100.

(1) model A will have a life-cycle cost $2,154 less than B; (2) the average annual cost of model A will be $253 less than B; and (3) the true payback for the additional $2,000 initial cost of model A will be 7.5 years. In the light of this lengthy payback period, the cost advantage of A may seem of little consequence. In any case, however, the three bits of information are available to the buyer and should be helpful in decision making.

Conclusions

Life-cycle costing has value as a marketing tool for a great many individual products. Although its use is still limited mainly to building components and heavier equipment, it can be utilized fruitfully for lighter industrial goods and for many consumer goods, e.g., automobiles, appliances, home heating units, storm windows. The list of products to which it can be applied is virtually endless.

The term *life-cycle costing* is not yet a part of the vocabulary of the average citizen, but as the concept becomes better understood it will have an enormous impact on the buying and selling of industrial goods and services. As buyers integrate factors such as operating and maintenance costs and length of service into their purchasing decisions through LCC analysis, suppliers will be forced to consider these factors in product development, pricing, and marketing decisions. Some firms are already fully aware of LCC and utilize it in planning, buying, and selling, but widespread use of it has yet to be realized. In a society that is becoming increasingly cost-conscious and intolerant of inflation, suppliers who choose to ignore life-cycle costing risk negative economic consequences.

Appendix

An abundance of literature on LCC is available, but not readily accessible in textbooks or journals. The principal sources are United States Government documents. For those who wish to read further on the subject, a brief bibliography is provided. Works have been selected for conceptual and technical content as well as for their appended lists of further references.

> Department of General Services, *Florida Life Cycle Analysis Manual*, Tallahassee, Florida, March 1975.
> *Industrialization Forum*, Vol. 6, 1978. (Entire issue devoted to life-cycle costing.)
> K. G. Associates, *Life Cycle Cost-Benefit Analysis: A Basic Course in Economic Decision Making*, Dept. of Health, Education and Welfare, Washington, D.C. March 1976.
> General Services Administration, Federal Supply Service, *Life Cycle Costing: Procurement Case 1, Room Air Conditioners*, Washington, D.C., July 1975.
> American Institute of Architects, *Life Cycle Cost Analysis, A Guide for Architects*, 1977.
> U.S. Department of Commerce, *Life Cycle Costing Emphasizing Energy Conservation: Guidelines for Investment Analysis*, Washington, D.C., September 1976 (revised May 1977)
> Brown, Robert J., and Rudolph R. Yanuck, *Life Cycle Costing: A Practical Guide for Energy Managers*, The Fairmont Press, Atlanta, Georgia, 1980.

References

1. Philippatos, George C., *Essentials of Financial Management*, Chap. 4, Holden-Day, San Francisco, 1974.
2. Williams, John E., *Life Cycle Costing: An Overview*, Joint Conference of American Institute

of Industrial Engineers and American Association of Cost Engineers, Washington, D.C., October 5–6, 1977.

Exercises

11.1. The ABC Company, a manufacturer of energy-saver shower heads, wishes to develop a life-cycle costing presentation to demonstrate that its product can save both water and electricity. The head will sell for $28 and promises to save the average home 1,600 gallons of water each year. Water costs $2 per 1,000 gallons. It takes 0.11 kWh to raise the temperature of one gallon of water to shower temperature. Present electricity cost of $0.05 per kWh is expected to escalate at the rate of 8% a year.

Using a life of 20 years for the shower head and a discount rate of 10%, develop the presentation.

11.2. The XYZ Company, a manufacturer of solar panels for water heating, is preparing a life-cycle cost presentation to justify the purchase of its product. It will use the case of a homeowner who wishes to satisfy 60% of his family's hot water requirements by solar energy. Average daily usage is 68 gallons. The average temperature of the cold water supply is 55°F; it will be raised to 140°F.

Electricity costs $0.06/kWh, and the rate is expected to escalate at an average of 8% a year over the 20-year life of the system. 200,000 BTUs/sq. ft./yr. of collector is available in the particular geographical area. The installed cost of the system is $30/sq. ft. It is assumed that the buyer will be able to make use of the Federal income tax credit available, i.e., 40% of the first $10,000 of cost. A discount rate of 10% will be used.

Note that

1 gallon of water weighs 8.34 pounds.
1 BTU is the amount of heat required to raise the temperature of 1 pound of water by 1°F.
1 kWh is 3,416 BTUs.

Using the above information, how would you prepare the presentation?

Improving Product Abandonment Decisions

12

Paul W. Hamelman   Edward M. Mazze

Each year firms introduce new products into the market which are often researched as to potential market success, cost versus selling price, and efficiency of production. Once a product is launched, however, it blends in with existing products and becomes a part of the firm's total product line. One result of these product introductions can be an overpopulation of products for the firm. Therefore, an organized approach is needed to periodically review all of a firm's products in order to identify those which are no longer earning revenue in proportion to the efforts and resources required to produce and sell them. This article suggests such an approach, a Product Review and Evaluation Subsystem model called PRESS. This model helps to determine which product or products should be eliminated from a firm's total product line through the use of standard cost accounting data.

When firms abandon weak products they often do so to resolve an immediate problem. Too often, however, the focus is on products which are already known or suspected of being "dead." Some firms which have applied techniques of abandoning financially weak products have obtained substantial results.[1] An example is Hunt Foods who cut product lines from 30 to 3 during an eleven-year span, and yet increased sales from $15 million to $120 million.[2] Another company with $40 million in sales eliminated 16 undesirable products with a total sales volume of $3.3 million; over a three-year period, this action produced a 50% sales increase and a 20-fold increase in profit.[3] While some companies are beginning to apply scientific approaches to product deletion, a systematic and periodic analysis is not common in most organizations.[4] This may be due to lack of executive time devoted to product abandonment decisions, a false sense of financial security based on total product line profit analysis, resistance to changing the status quo, and internal problems such as determining who will make these decisions.[5]

Reprinted by permission from the *Journal of Marketing*, vol. 36 (April 1972), pp. 20–26, published by the American Marketing Association.

[1] Philip Kotler, "Phasing Out Weak Products," *Harvard Business Review*, Vol. 43 (March–April, 1965), p. 109.
[2] Same reference as footnote 1.
[3] Same reference as footnote 1.
[4] Same reference as footnote 1.
[5] D'Orsay Hurst, "Criteria for Evaluating Existing Products and Product Lines," in *Analyzing and Improving Marketing Performance*, Albert Newgarden, ed. (New York: American Management Association, Report Number 32, 1959), p. 92.

Approaches to Product Abandonment

Berenson presented a model for product abandonment which considered five major decision factors: financial security, financial opportunity based on phase of the product in its life cycle, marketing strategy, social responsibility, and the possibility of organized intervention against product deletion.[6] The first two criteria are readily quantified; the first relating to current profitability, and the second to potential for improvement of profitability based on phase of the product in its life cycle. Berenson suggested that a judgment-determined numerical scale could be established to accommodate the remaining three factors. He recommended assignment of subjective weights to reflect the degree of importance management attaches to each factor. The score for each category is then multiplied by the weighting factor, and the summation of the five weighted scores becomes the overall rating of the product under consideration.

Hurst proposed ten criteria for performing product abandonment analysis.[7] The criteria used were profitability, scope of product line, marketing efficiency, production efficiency, cost, price, value, quality, service, and competition. Three are quantified, the other seven being qualitative and subjective. The Hurst method includes many factors which have to be considered in making a product-deletion decision; however, no analytic method was suggested for performing this task. An analysis which attempted to incorporate each of these criteria becomes unwieldy and difficult to apply.

Kotler presented a planned product phase-out approach using PERT which approximates a quantifiable model. It enables a comprehensive review of the problems and opportunities related to product line analysis and deletion decisions.[8] He indicated that the costs of weak products go deeper than the profit statement. Additional burdens such as excessive management time, frequent inventory adjustment, short production runs, disproportionate advertising and marketing expenditures, and possible adverse goodwill attached to low-quality products are all costs which must be recognized.

Kotler proposed a six-step approach to product analysis and deletion. The first step consists of management preparing a data sheet for every company product and/or model. This sheet summarizes key statistics about the product for the last several years. The purpose of the data sheet is to provide information for judging whether the product is profitable or a candidate for deletion. Step two is the development of a computer program which scans the product data sheets (in the form of key-punched cards) for signs of weakness among the individual products. The next three steps are similar to the Berenson approach. A rating form is proposed

---

[6] Conrad Berenson, "Pruning the Product Line," *Business Horizons*, Vol. 6 (Summer 1963), pp. 62–72.
[7] Same reference as footnote 5.
[8] Same reference as footnote 1.

for detailed analysis of the deletion candidates. Management then assigns numerical scores to the categories on the form. Weighting factors are applied to the scores, and the weighted scores are summed to obtain an overall "product retention index." Product deletion decisions can then be made using a cut-off point in the retention index. Management must also evaluate such subjective considerations as product interaction, inventory level, and customer reactions which may overrule the action suggested by the index. Lastly, a management team develops policies and plans for phasing out "dropped" products.

The "PRESS" System

This article presents a computer-aided model for product abandonment decisions called PRESS (Product Review and Evaluation Subsystem).

PRESS is a flexible and adaptable system designed as a tool to assist management in identifying those products which are candidates for deletion. It is different from most product-abandonment models in that it is capable of coping with a company's total product line rather than a segment of products thought to be weak. Inputs to the system are standard cost accounting and marketing data, and outputs are ratios and other information relevant to the value of each product to the firm. The program for PRESS was written for a time-shared computer with teletype input and output. The advantages of a time-sharing system are that more business organizations can afford to use such a system. It also provides faster access to the computer, and more rapid return of the printouts are generally available.

The program consists of four integrated parts, PRESS I through IV. PRESS I contains the primary model and uses standard cost accounting and marketing performance data; while PRESS II, III, and IV perform analyses concerned with price changes, sales trends, and product interaction. These factors are essential considerations in product abandonment decisions.[9]

Data were obtained from the Devon Furniture Company to illustrate the use of the model.[10] At the time these data were prepared, Devon was considering pruning their product line for financial reasons. Devon had 552 different patterns in the line, but to facilitate the presentation of the PRESS model 25 products were selected for analysis.

PRESS I: Basic Data

The data shown in Table 1 represent the information required as inputs to the PRESS I model. The model is based on a variable cost accounting approach. The data show standard cost, unit price, and volume for the latest available period. Only

---

[9] James T. Rothe, "The Product Elimination Decision," *MSU Business Topics*, Vol. 18 (Autumn, 1970), pp. 45–51.

[10] Stanley S. Miller and David C. D. Rogers, *Manufacturing Policy* (Homewood, Ill.: Richard D. Irwin, Inc., 1964), pp.100–111.

costs that are a measured contribution toward the production and sales of a specific product are included as inputs for that product. Fixed overhead costs which are allocated against a product in proportion to some other factor such as direct labor hours are not included. Allocation of these charges is generally arbitrary and not a true measure of the costs associated with a specific product. Another reason for not considering fixed-facilities costs is that they are sunk costs and are not affected by the deletion decision. Thus, they are not pertinent to the product deletion decision and should not be included. Sales and administrative costs, on the other hand, are not sunk costs and could be included if they can be properly divided to identify effort chargeable to each product. This can be an important cost when, for example, high advertising expenses and excessive management attention are being devoted to keeping one of "yesterday's bread-winners" profitable. The PRESS I program permits entry of sales and administration costs, although zeros are shown in Table 1.

TABLE 1. Standard cost, price, volume data by products

Prod. no.	Unit mat'l cost $	Unit labor cost $	Unit varib. O. H. $	Unit sales price $	Unit quan. sold	Unit varib. S + A	Manufac- turing runs per yr.
801	39.32	32.17	19.04	180	189	0	2
802	27.71	40.17	21.91	170	186	0	2
803	22.17	47.47	23.71	120	141	0	2
804	21.09	57.12	29.17	130	29	0	2
805	7.09	16.75	8.90	104	82	0	2
806	13.07	17.44	7.93	60	291	0	3
807	41.71	37.74	19.91	215	104	0	2
808	28.82	39.11	15.42	200	97	0	2
809	14.25	21.42	12.75	59	502	0	2
810	47.17	39.77	18.02	200	390	0	1
811	24.40	42.70	21.35	150	207	0	1
812	33.13	61.74	33.07	190	402	0	2
813	17.74	14.42	9.47	57	607	0	2
814	14.42	23.44	12.24	125	72	0	1
815	19.77	30.14	17.13	175	109	0	1
914	30.88	24.36	16.00	130	154	0	1
917	21.16	45.91	29.56	171	35	0	1
922	14.86	49.22	26.67	140	17	0	1
923	9.27	16.57	10.61	68	160	0	2
926	16.38	5.63	2.60	45	65	0	1
927	13.02	13.87	8.07	58	869	0	3
951	21.21	10.69	6.32	65	197	0	2
952	34.52	61.28	44.87	242	32	0	1
959	34.69	31.06	22.83	150	156	0	1
960	6.75	11.84	7.82	54	168	0	1

This is because in the Devon case there was no basis for distributing sales and administration effort among different products based on data presented. When sales and administration costs are arbitrarily allocated by management on the basis of direct labor dollars, it will merely serve as a weighting factor on direct labor costs; use of these costs would not help the analysis. In this situation the cost entry is not made, and the program fills in zeros in that column.

Two assumptions were made in the design of this model. First, the available production factors can be utilized to produce any pattern in the line. A more sophisticated program definition can remove this limitation if necessary. Second, contribution margin has been selected as the primary criterion for comparing the value of the several products. This is a measure of the earning capability of each product. It does not, however, furnish information relative to the amount of resources required to produce that income. A more powerful comparison should include an adjustment for the use of the firm's facilities. This would put the comparison in terms of return on investment rather than on earnings alone.

Table 2 is a compilation of standard performance ratios for each product. This table is arranged in order of sequentially increasing product model identification numbers. The ratios shown are material cost to selling price (MC/SP), labor cost to selling price (LC/SP), product cost as a percentage of total plant labor costs (LC), variable overhead to selling price (VOH/SP), product variable overhead cost as a percentage of total plant variable overhead costs (VOH), and total dollars of variable cost. The percentages indicate how much labor and variable overhead become available for reemployment to other products should a product be eliminated. Thus, Table 2 includes the various data pertinent to product deletion decisions so that product comparisons can be made.

The basis for product comparisons in the PRESS model is called the Selection Index Number (SIN). The value of the SIN index is illustrated by the following example. If a product's contribution is 5% but it utilizes 10% of the firm's resources (facilities) to accomplish this, its effective contribution in terms of return on investment is small. The following formula is used to make this adjustment:

$$SIN_i = \frac{CM_i/\Sigma CM_i}{FC_i/\Sigma FC_i} \times (CM_i/\Sigma CM_i)$$

where:

SIN_i = selection index number for product "i"
CM_i = contribution margin for product "i"
FC_i = facilities costs for product "i"
ΣCM_i = summation of contribution margin of all products
ΣFC_i = summation of facilities costs of all products

or for the data above:

TABLE 2. *Performance ratios*

Prod.	MC/SP	LC/SP	PCT LC	VOH/SP	PCT VOH	Total VC
801	.22	.18	.02	.11	.02	90.53
802	.16	.24	.03	.13	.03	89.79
803	.18	.40	.03	.20	.03	93.35
804	.16	.44	.04	.22	.04	107.38
805	.07	.16	.01	,09	.01	32.74
806	.22	.29	.01	.13	.01	38.44
807	.19	.18	.03	.09	.03	99.36
808	.14	.20	.03	.08	.02	83.35
809	.24	.36	.02	.22	.02	48.42
810	.24	.20	.03	.09	.02	104.96
811	.16	.28	.03	.14	.03	88.45
812	.17	.32	.04	.17	.04	127.94
813	.31	.25	.01	.17	.01	41.63
814	.12	.19	.02	.10	.02	50.10
815	.11	.17	.02	.10	.02	67.04
914	.24	.19	.02	.12	.02	71.24
917	.12	.27	.03	.17	.04	96.63
922	.11	.35	.03	.19	.03	90.75
923	.14	.24	.01	.16	.01	36.45
926	.36	.13	.00	.06	.00	24.61
927	.22	.24	.01	.14	.01	34.96
951	.33	.16	.01	.10	.01	38.22
952	.14	.25	.04	.19	.06	140.67
959	.23	.21	.02	.15	.03	88.58
960	.13	.22	.01	.14	.01	26.41

$$\text{SIN} = \frac{.05}{.10} \times .05 = .025$$

Thus, since the product uses double the percent facilities it produces in revenue, the SIN number awards it one-half the value straight accounting analysis would have indicated. Conversely, a product whose proportional use of facilities is less than its percent contribution margin will show a higher SIN number than its unadjusted percent contribution margin.

The primary resources available to the firm are labor, variable overhead, sales and administrative expenses, plant and equipment, and working capital. Therefore, the deployment of these primary resources among alternative and competing products in the line expresses the firm's response to the market. As adjustments are made to the product mix, various amounts of resources become available for redeployment elsewhere. In the Devon case, the costs used in the PRESS model were labor, variable overhead, and the interest on the cash required to maintain the product's finished goods inventory. The time that a unit of any specific product is carried in inventory is computed as an inverse function of the number of manufacturing runs per year times the standard number of pieces per manufacturing run. A linear finished goods inventory depletion was assumed. While this technique is appropriate to the Devon situation, the PRESS model can accommodate the different inventory depletion patterns that are used in other industries. For compressed time periods, less than one year, curvilinear or erratic inventory depletion rules may be used.[11]

Table 3 lists for each product the total contribution margin (unit contribution times number of units sold), product contribution margin as a percentage of the 25 products' contribution margin, cost of facilities utilized, percent of the firm's

TABLE 3. Product rankings

Prod.	Total cont. mar. ($)	Pct. CM	Cost of fac. util. ($00's)	Pct. FU	SIN
810	37065.60	15.45	60.15	4.78	49.94
927	20021.80	8.35	22.16	1.76	39.56
812	24948.10	10.40	95.64	7.60	14.23
801	16909.80	7.05	52.19	4.15	11.98
813	9229.59	3.89	24.33	1.93	7.82
802	14919.10	6.22	62.77	4.99	7.75
815	11767.60	4.91	48.26	3.84	6.27
811	12740.90	5.31	65.27	5.19	5.44
807	12026.60	5.01	58.69	4.66	5.39
808	11315.10	4.72	55.25	4.39	5.07
914	9049.04	3.77	41.90	3.33	4.27
959	9581.52	3.99	55.62	4.42	3.61
951	5275.66	2.20	17.54	1.39	3.47
806	6273.96	2.62	25.59	2.03	3.36
805	5843.32	2.44	25.83	2.05	2.89
960	4635.12	1.93	20.00	1.59	2.35
923	5048.00	2.10	27.41	2.18	2.03
809	5311.16	2.21	34.53	2.74	1.79
814	5392.80	2.25	36.40	2.89	1.75
803	3757.65	1.57	71.73	5.70	.43
926	1325.35	.55	9.05	.72	.42
952	3242.56	1.35	107.88	8.57	.21
917	2602.95	1.09	76.53	6.08	.19
922	837.25	.35	76.63	6.09	.02
804	655.98	.27	86.82	6.90	.01
		100.00%		100.00%	

[11] Harvey M. Wagner, *Principles of Management Science* (Englewood Cliffs, New Jersey: Prentice-Hall, Inc., 1970), pp. 211–222.

resources being used to produce each product, and the selection index number (SIN). The table also lists the products in decreasing order of SIN numbers; the most profitable products are shown first, and the least profitable products appear at the bottom of the list. Therefore, the lowest SIN numbers are the most promising candidates for deletion. The point at which a product should be deleted is a management decision. In this situation, a SIN number of less than 1.0 is a definite indication of a marginal product. Among the factors that management should consider in selecting a cutoff point are contribution margin, the relationship of the product to other products in the line, existence of substitute products, and goodwill.

PRESS II: Price-Volume Relationships

PRESS II examines the effect of a price change on the contribution margin of specific products management wishes to examine. Since income in terms of contribution margin is being used as a primary criterion for the product abandonment decision, the possibility of improving a product's contribution margin by a price adjustment should be considered. For a specific percentage increase or decrease in the price of the product, the marketing manager is asked to predict the quantity of that product which he expects to be able to sell annually. Selective price increases or decreases are incorporated in the model; across the board price adjustments could be used if appropriate to the situation.

In effect, PRESS II looks at a narrow segment of the demand curve of each product to assist in evaluating whether current prices should be modified. Table 4 identifies those products whose contribution margin will be altered due to predicted quantity changes resulting from a change in price. However, the printout does not include products whose contribution margin would be unaffected by the proposed price change, nor are products included when no price change is being considered. The Devon Company is a prestige manufacturer of furniture. Thus, for illustrative purposes, products 801 and 802 were assumed to have an upward sloping demand curve within the range of prices considered. For both of these products, therefore, an increase in price was accompanied by an increase in the quantity sold. Along with the product number, the table includes the dollar value of the increase or

TABLE 4. Price strategy

Prod. no.	CM chg. in $'s	Quan. chg. in units	Unit labor chg.	Unit VOH chg.
801[a]	2891.78	5	160.85	95.20
802[a]	2581.80	4	160.68	87.64
803[b]	846.0	0	0	0

[a] Raised five percent.
[b] Lowered five percent.

decrease in contribution margin, the specific price action (raise or lower), and the expected increase or decrease in volume estimated by management, labor costs, and variable overhead costs. The last two items permit an evaluation of whether the requisite resources are available to implement the projected price strategy. PRESS II thus provides the marginal increment or decrement on total contribution margin based on management's price-volume projection.

The manager can use this information to review the entire product line or only that portion of the line that seems to be in trouble. He can adjust the percentage price increase, or decrease, that he wants to study on a product-by-product basis. After this is done, the original input data are adjusted accordingly for a reiteration of the PRESS I analysis.

PRESS III: Sales Trends

To judge the worth of a product based on performance at one point in time is shortsighted since each product has life cycle of several distinct stages. Historical data are available for each product, and use of these data to perform a series of PRESS I rankings of products could be informative. Products which continually appear near the bottom of the list would be candidates for deletion. Perhaps more important, however, is the need for data on *projected* performance in future time periods. PRESS III is designed to identify products which are likely to become good performers, as well as those which are in a period of decline.

In PRESS III, the program prints out the quantity of sales of each product for next year based on extrapolation from this and last year's sales. This is a convenient method for estimating demand using an exponentially weighted moving average.[12] A longer data base could be used for estimating future demand for products with relatively long life cycles; however, a shorter data base for some industries, such as furniture, is appropriate. In the Devon situation, the next-year quantity estimates for each product are automatically substituted for the original previous-period quantities. A new PRESS I analysis can be performed using these estimates. This produces a revised SIN listing for the total product line that shows the product rankings which would occur if the present trend of sales growth or decline continues.

This approach makes two assumptions. First, it assumes that selling price and all variable costs per unit of each specific product will not change from this year to next year. Since the primary reason for making this assumption is to permit calculation of next year's unit contribution, any variation from this first premise will not introduce major errors as long as the selling price remains the same number of dollars above variable cost as it was in the present year. Second, it assumes that total dollars spent next year on sales and administration cost allocations for a specific product will be the same as are being spent this year for that product, regardless of any change in the quantity of units sold. If management believes that cost changes

---

[12] R. G. Brown, *Decision Rules for Inventory Management* (New York: Holt, Rinehart, and Winston, 1967), pp. 292–295.

in some products will occur in a future period of time, they can be included in the PRESS analysis.

PRESS IV: Product Complementarity and Substitutability

In the multiproduct firm, some degree of complementarity and substitutability may exist between products. For example, at Devon Furniture, the sale of a bed would be likely to result in tie-in sales of one or more of the other items in that bedroom suite grouping. The elimination of one product could result in some loss of sales of another complementary product. If suitable substitutes are present in the firm's product line, a product abandonment decision might result in no loss in total sales. Kotler points out that total sales may even rise in such a situation.[13]

Up to this point, the manager has reviewed the effects of price change and/or sales

FIGURE 1. *Product complementarity and substitutability*

Product no. _____
Product name _____

If this product is deleted:

1. What product number will be sold instead?

Product number	Percent of units of deleted product which this no. will replace
a)	
b)	
c)	
d)	

Note: If less than 100% is shown, the remainder is assumed to be business which will be lost completely.

2. What tie-in sales on other product numbers will be lost?

Product number	Percent of units of presently sold product which will be lost if above product is deleted
a)	
b)	
c)	
d)	
e)	
f)	

---

[13] Same reference as footnote 1.

growth trends on each product number—in PRESS II and PRESS III. PRESS IV attempts to further improve the effectiveness of the basic model by introducing an adjustment to compensate for product complementarity and substitutability. This assessment is best made by the marketing manager with the aid of marketing research and is the final input to the PRESS cycle. Figure 1 illustrates one type of form which could be used to collect data on product complementarity and substitutability from salesmen, brand managers, or others sensitive to demand patterns for individual items in the product line. While this activity will require a significant amount of executive time, it forces a marketing judgment before the analysis is run. If, instead, the marketing manager were confronted with a list of potential product deletions which had not been adjusted for complementarity, he would focus on only a small portion of the product line and could tend to magnify the importance of loss of "full line coverage."

PRESS IV calculates a new factor known as RESIN. This is the original SIN value for each product (Table 3) adjusted upward for tie-in sales due to the product, and downward for any relacement sales which would result if the product were deleted. For example, if Product A is deleted, new SIN values are computed for Products B, C, and D if these will increase in sales upon deletion of A.

PRESS II, III, and IV organizes and quantifies the available subjective and historical data. The final step of PRESS IV is an automatic, stepwise product deletion iteration. This iteration begins with management's specification of a target reduction of one of the resource costs listed in Table 1. For example, assume that 20% of the firm's available labor costs has to be reduced to handle a new product which will be introduced. To satisfy this specification, PRESS IV will eliminate products one at a time, starting with the lowest RESIN number, until the labor costs reach 80% of their original value. A recalculation is made as each product is deleted, and new printouts of Tables 1, 2, and 3 are prepared. This process will continue until the 80% labor-cost level is reached, at which time a final printout is made, and the program will stop. This printout will also show the reduction in the other resources which have accompanied the reduction in labor costs.

Conclusion

The PRESS model described in this article is an approach for abandoning unprofitable products from a company's product line. The model is an extension of the earlier work by Kotler which consisted basically of the appointment of a high-level and broadly representative management team which holds meetings approximately once a year to set objectives and procedures for identifying weak products, to evaluate them, and to develop a phasing-out program for product pruning. In Kotler's approach, the executives use information which is processed on the computer. This system is expensive in executive time since each step in the system requires the executive to provide judgment inputs. Kotler's model was descriptive and did not present a specific example of how a product would go through the system. In addition, the system was designed to handle only single products.

A fully developed and updated cost accounting system is the critical requirement for PRESS. The number of products PRESS could handle at one time is limited to the accounting data available and the amount of management time necessary to provide estimates for the judgment parameters of the model. PRESS I and PRESS III programs use standard accounting data for inputs; PRESS II requires sales estimations at selected price levels using historical sales data. PRESS II could be restricted to marginal products with low SIN numbers. PRESS IV analyzes product complementarity and substitutability using a management rating form requiring subjective judgments.

The PRESS model differs from Kotler's approach in that it looks at the entire product line as well as individual products and requires less management judgment time. Kotler provided broad guidelines for his model; PRESS considers product line interactions and operational aspects of deletion decisions. The retention index suggested by Kotler yielded a single number indicating the degree of product desirability which is the sum of the weighted ratings on the product rating form that was prepared by the management team. This sum ranges from a maximum value of 7, if the product shows superior grounds for being retained on all counts, to a minimum value of 0, if the product shows minimal grounds for retention on all counts. The product rating form used by Kotler had seven different scales which were subjective. PRESS offers cutoff points for deletion decisions by a systematic review of SIN numbers. For example, products with a SIN number less than 1.0 are the ones that deserve special consideration for abandonment. The SIN number is based on a series of performance ratios using standard cost accounting data. The PRESS model also performs special analyses concerned with price changes, sales trends, and product interactions. These factors are all essential in making the product abandonment decision.

Exercises

12.1. Concourse Manufacturing, an auto parts company, was considering some cutbacks in its product line for financial reasons. Concourse has 168 different patterns in the line. The management wants to know how many of these products are producing a marginal contribution. (For the purpose of the exercise, standard performance ratios were computed for the 10 products in Table 12.1.)

1. Arrange the products in decreasing order based on their selection index number (SIN).
2. How many products do you think management should delete, and why?
3. What other factors should management consider in product deletion?

TABLE 12.1

Product #	Unit mat'l cost $	Unit labor cost $	Unit variable O.H. $	Unit sales price $	Unit quantity sold	Unit variable S + A	Cost of fac. util. ($00's)
499	23.69	11.36	5.98	79	380	0	22.12
565	6.35	21.59	10.27	73	507	0	20.95
566	17.83	19.72	9.66	92	283	0	25.76
567	45.11	36.18	17.28	146	112	0	45.26
568	28.26	30.71	13.38	140	35	0	37.80
569	23.14	39.25	18.42	160	24	0	46.40
624	19.42	12.64	7.91	78	391	0	19.50
625	8.51	15.93	10.63	65	82	0	14.95
626	32.68	61.89	44.05	198	157	0	47.52
627	17.19	10.52	6.34	65	196	0	18.85

12.2. The Westmore Co., a medium-size appliance company, has been battling against rising costs for the last two years. The company has at the moment 127 different patterns in the line. The management has just bought a copy of program PRESS and has decided to use it to see how many of its products are producing a marginal contribution. (For the purpose of the exercise, standard performance ratios were computed for the 12 products in Table 12.2.)

1. Arrange the products in decreasing order based on their selection index number (SIN).
2. How many products do you think management should delete? Why?
3. What other factors should management consider in product deletion?

TABLE 12.2

Product #	Unit mat'l cost $	Unit labor cost $	Unit variable O.H. $	Unit sales price $	Unit quantity sold	Unit variable S + A	Mfg. runs per year	Standard performance ratios					
								MC/SP	LC/SP	PCT/LC	VOH/SP	PCT/VOH	Total VC
501	45.38	39.11	24.09	216	176	0	1	.21	.18	.05	.11	.05	108.58
502	5.09	11.24	9.61	50	459	0	1	.10	.22	.02	.19	.02	25.94
503	34.37	62.15	32.54	202	184	0	2	.17	.31	.08	.16	.07	129.06
504	32.52	56.47	29.00	125	151	0	2	.26	.45	.07	.23	.05	117.99
505	13.17	24.21	6.96	82	276	0	2	.16	.30	.02	.08	.02	44.34
506	46.12	35.73	18.47	105	98	0	3	.44	.34	.04	.18	.04	100.32
507	29.34	32.76	26.29	121	134	0	1	.24	.27	.06	.22	.06	88.39
508	30.19	28.39	15.60	93	209	0	1	.32	.31	.04	.17	.03	74.18
509	26.51	43.17	28.13	164	397	0	1	.16	.26	.07	.17	.07	97.81
625	16.72	8.36	6.05	65	450	0	1	.26	.13	.00	.09	.00	31.13
626	9.89	26.18	15.32	97	264	0	2	.10	.27	.04	.16	.04	51.39
627	15.74	10.52	4.58	160	308	0	1	.10	.07	.01	.03	.01	30.84
643	35.51	16.18	13.91	171	65	0	1	.21	.09	.03	.08	.02	65.60
644	7.69	20.04	10.35	59	73	0	2	.13	.34	.02	.18	.02	38.08

Recommendations for
Further Reading

Gottlieb, Morris J., and Irving Roshwalb. "The 'Present Value' Concept in Evaluating New Products," in J. S. Wright and J. L. Goldstucker (eds.), *New Ideas for Successful Marketing*. Chicago: American Marketing Association Proceedings, No. 49, June 1966, 387–400.

Management needs to evaluate its portfolio of research projects and to select those likely to lead to new products. The evaluation methods developed make it possible to compare research investments with any other type of investment such as in marketing, in new buildings and/or facilities, and in the acquisition of companies. The criteria for the evaluation utilize the estimated cash flows. The technique recommended for computing the expected return of such an investment is the present value method of discounted cash flow analysis.

Konopa, Leonard J. "New Products: Assessing Commercial Potential," *Management Bulletin 88* (New York: American Management Association, 1966).

Emphasis is placed on the extent of corporate usage of a wide range of financial assessment techniques (break-even determinations, payout period calculations, and a variety of ROI approaches) in new product evaluation. More specifically, the author clearly and succinctly discusses the nature of each prominently employed method, illustrates how it can be applied, reports on that technique's actual frequency of usage by Fortune 500 companies, and, finally, comments on its relative strengths and weaknesses. The extent to which theory had outstripped practice is suggested by the fact that, as of 1965, only eighty-five of the 500 largest U.S. manufacturing firms reported that capital budgeting techniques were used when developing new products.

Kratchman, Stanley H., Richard T. Hise, and Thomas A. Ulrich. "Management's Decision to Discontinue a Product," *Journal of Acccountancy*, 139 (June 1975), 50–54.

Despite the benefits of a sophisticated product discontinuance program, the results of a recent survey reveal that the product elimination policies and practices of 96 of the nation's largest manufacturing firms are, generally, unstructured, unsophisticated and ineffective. The basic accounting data that management accounting personnel must furnish marketing for appropriate product elimination decisions is identified, as are a series of warning signals based on such data which might suggest that a given product is in trouble. The warning signals, however, presuppose agreed-upon performance standards, so that "below average" performance can be identified and the offending products "red flagged" for attention. Management accounting must participate in the development of such standards, see that primacy is assigned to financially oriented rather than marketing-oriented measures of performance, and also help estimate the effect of proposed deletions on the sale of other products in the line.

Lawson, William H. "Financial Concepts in New Product Development," *Financial Executive*, 33 (March 1965), 38–45, 59.

The key profit planning questions in the new product area are (1) how much current income should be spent on product development, and (2) what specific R&D opportunities will maximize the company's long-range profitability. Company objectives, competitive conditions, corporate capacity to absorb new products, and the need to establish a proper balance between immediate and long-term profits are the factors that should jointly influence the level of R&D expenditures.

The payback method, the internal rate of return approach, and an approximate evaluation of future cash flows are three possible methods of allocating R&D funds to specific projects. Prospective projects should then be ranked, with a cutoff point reflecting either a minimum rate of return or the exhaustion of available R&D funds. Effective expenditures to specific projects and periodic monitoring of the new product process prior to periods of major expenditure can also be tested with these tools to see whether such expenditures continue to appear justified.

Scheuble, Philip A., Jr. "ROI for New Product Policy," *HBR*, 42 (November-December 1964), 110–120.

An ROI approach to evaluating proposed new products is strongly advocated, and a method of making the necessary calculations is set out. A number of cost plateaus on both engineering and marketing sides of a proposed new product launch can be identified. ROI calculations should be updated as each such plateau is reached. Corporate revenue can be divided into three components and ROI separately calculated for the profit produced by old products, the profit from new products, and residual profit, which is treated as a return on the firm's investment in marketing. A monographic shortcut to determining ROI is also illustrated.

Silvern, David H. "Product Opportunity Analysis," *Management Accounting*, 50 (February 1969), 44–46.

In adequately evaluating a new product opportunity, one must consider (1) the cost of development, (2) its profit potential, (3) the time value of money, (4) the possibility of technical failure, and (5) the possibility that the market forecast might be wrong. A method of adjusting for technical or market failure based on the subjective probability estimates of the project engineer and the marketing man is presented. An illustration is provided in which (single value) estimates of revenue are first adjusted by discounting at the company's ROI objective. The resulting figure is further reduced when multiplied by a confidence rate of less than one. To allow for the possibility of technical failure, the discounted costs of achieving desired performance and service cost objectives are *divided by* the appropriate confidence of achievement figures. The procedure reveals both the desirability of product development and the length of development period that would be most profitable.

Stillson, Paul, and E. Leonard Arnoff. "Product Search and Evaluation," *Journal of Marketing*, 22 (July 1957), 33–39.

A great need exists for improved methods of new product search and evaluation. A sample list of seven criteria useful in evaluating a product's acceptance is proposed in this classic (1957) article. For any particular firm, however, distinct criteria may have to be developed. The degree to which a new product is unacceptable on any one criterion may be estimated by determining the cost to the firm of providing facilities or otherwise acting such that acceptance becomes possible. Consideration must also be given to the relationship between the proposed new product and the existing product line.

A three-stage method of product evaluation is proposed. The minimum acceptance level of gross sales is first determined. Next, the level of sales is analyzed with respect to its production planning, manufacturing facilities, manpower, and super-vision implications. Finally, a judgment is made as to whether these market and production requirements can be met. An example which also encompasses the question of how to arrive at an acceptable rate of return for the new product is provided.

Talley, Walter J., Jr. "Profiting from the Declining Product," *Business Horizons* (Spring 1964), 77–84.

The proper management of declining products can be a productive source of profits. Running-out the product, which involves cutting back all support costs to a bare minimum, is revealed as a policy that might well optimize profitability over the limited remaining life of that item. How one decides when such a strategy should be followed is discussed in considerable detail. It is pointed out that the profits possible from such "run outs" are often sufficient to finance an acquisition or support a new product's R&D program.

PART IV

Price

Probabilistic Bidding Models: A Synthesis

13

Wayne J. Morse

One of the most critical planning activities of many businesses is bidding for the opportunity to provide a product or service. The very existence of many firms depends upon a bidding strategy that produces both jobs and profits. Recently, a number of firms have employed probabilistic bidding models in an attempt to improve their bidding practices. Such models assist the decision maker in arriving at a bid price that has the optimal combination of probability of acceptance and profit if accepted.

A survey published in 1969 revealed that firms making use of probabilistic bidding models have a better record of successful bids than firms that do not. Yet, despite the importance of bidding and the favorable results obtained with probabilistic bidding models, the same survey revealed that only one-third of the firms engaged in competitive bidding use such models.[1]

There are at least two major reasons why probabilistic bidding models are not more widely used. First, the topic is a new one. More than one-half of the articles written on bidding have appeared since 1965.[2] Second, most of these articles have been either too specific or too esoteric to appear widely useful or usable. This article is an attempt to pull together the important aspects of probabilistic bidding into one coherent, intelligible model. Except where otherwise indicated, it is assumed that the objective of management is to maximize profits.

Basic Model

The underlying relationships in all probabilistic bidding models rest on the *size* of the bid, the expected profit if the bid is accepted, and the probability that the bid will be accepted. A high bid with a large expected profit has a low probability of being accepted in competitive situations. Conversely, a low bid, which has a high probability of being accepted, offers little or no profit. The basic objective of probabilistic bidding models is to find the optimum combination of profit if accepted and probability of acceptance. The optimum bid offers the highest expected profit.

From *Business Horizons* 18 (April 1975), pp. 67–74. Copyright 1975 by the Foundation for the School of Business at Indiana University. Reprinted by permission.

[1] S. Paranka, "The Pay-off Concept in Competitive Bidding," *Business Horizons* (August 1969), pp. 79–80.
[2] R. Stark, "Competitive Bidding: A Comprehensive Bibliography," *Operations Research* (March-April 1971), p. 484.

In mathematical notation the optimum bid is the one that maximizes the following equation:

$$E(X) = P(X)Z(X)$$

where

X = amount of the bid
$Z(X)$ = expected profit if accepted
$P(X)$ = probability of a bid of X being accepted
$E(X)$ = expected profit of a bid of X.

In the equation the expected profit equals the probability of winning with a bid of X multiplied by the profit associated with that bid. The basic problem in implementing probabilistic bidding models, such as the one represented by the equation, is estimating the probability that a bid will be accepted. In the absence of purchaser bias, this problem is one of estimating the probability of a bid being the lowest one submitted. The mathematical estimation of the probability is subject to two assumptions: (1) the competitor's estimates of direct costs bear a constant

TABLE 1. Relationship of XYZ's bids to ABC's estimated direct cost

Project	XYZ's bid	ABC's estimated direct cost	Percent
1	19,800	15,000	132
2	88,400	65,000	136
3	62,800	40,000	157
4	33,750	25,000	135
5	72,500	50,000	145
6	11,100	10,000	111
7	64,860	47,000	138
8	12,080	8,000	151
9	53,760	32,000	168
10	99,400	70,000	142
11	29,700	22,000	135
12	60,900	42,000	145
13	39,900	30,000	133
14	29,800	20,000	149
15	23,250	15,000	155
16	34,440	21,000	164
17	47,520	36,000	132
18	43,200	30,000	144
19	41,160	28,000	147
20	73,750	59,000	125

relationship to the bidder's estimates of direct costs, and (2) the competitor will act in the future as he has in the past.

The first assumption is reasonable if labor and material cost estimates of competing firms are consistently accurate (or inaccurate) and if labor and material costs are not subject to wide fluctuations across geographic areas. The second assumption may not hold over extended periods of time if the competitor responds to the bidder's behavior. Other factors, such as seasonal variations in work loads, may also weaken the second assumption. Several of these factors will be discussed later.

To demonstrate the basic model, use is made of two hypothetical competitors. The ABC company is considering bidding on a project against one known competitor, the XYZ company. Because the contract will be awarded to the lowest bidder, ABC wishes to determine the probability that its bid will be lower than XYZ's bid. The first step is to obtain information on previous relationships between ABC's estimated direct costs and XYZ's bids on similar projects. This is shown in Table 1. The second step is to analyze the data in Table 1 to determine the probability that XYZ will submit a bid higher than any given percent of ABC's estimated direct cost. The result of this analysis is presented in Table 2 and Figure 1.

FIGURE 1. *Probability of underbidding one known competitor*

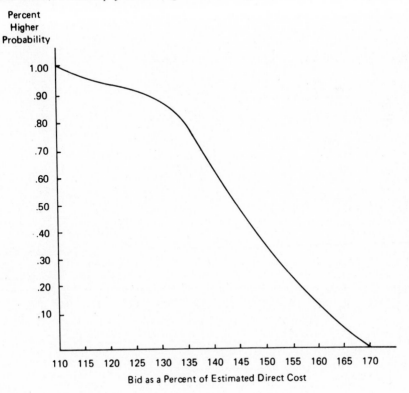

TABLE 2. Probability of underbidding one known competitor

Bid as a percent of estimated direct cost	Number of higher bids	Percent higher (probability of underbidding)
110	20	100
115	19	.95
120	19	.95
125	19	.95
130	18	.90
135	15	.75
140	11	.55
145	9	.45
150	6	.30
155	4	.20
160	2	.10
165	1	.05
170	0	.00

FIGURE 2. Relation between size of bid and contribution margin

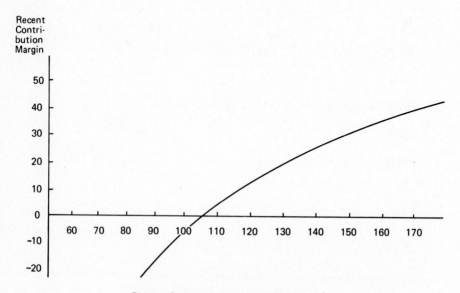

Bid as a Percent of Estimated Direct Costs

Because the contract will be awarded to the lowest bidder, the probability that XYZ will submit a bid higher than any given percent of ABC's estimated direct costs is also the probability that ABC will be awarded the contract when a contemplated bid is stated in terms of a percent of estimated direct costs. Accordingly, the probability that a bid will be successful can be readily determined from Table 2 or Figure 1.

If ABC submits a bid of 140 percent of estimated direct costs, then, as Table 2 and Figure 1 indicate, there is a 55 percent probability that such a bid will be lower than XYZ's bid. If ABC submits a bid of 110 percent of estimated direct costs, its bid almost certainly will be lower than XYZ's. However, a bid of 110 percent provides little contribution to profit and overhead. The relationship between the size of the bid as a percent of estimated direct costs and the contribution margin as a percent of the bid is shown in Figure 2.

As was previously stated, the optimum bid is the one that offers the highest expected profit. Because the model considers only direct costs, the operational definition of the optimum bid must be restated. *The optimum bid is the one that offers the highest expected contribution to profit and overhead.* The expected contribution margin of a bid is determined by multiplying the difference between the bid price and the estimated direct costs by the probability that the bid will be accepted. To determine the optimum bid, the contribution margin or contribution margin percent on each bid under consideration must be multiplied by the probability that the bid will be lower than a competitor's.

For example, ABC is considering bids of 130, 140, and 150 percent of estimated direct costs. Using the information given in Figure 2 and Table 2, the expected contribution margin percents of these bids are computed as follows:

$$(.23)(.90) = .21 \text{ for 130 percent}$$
$$(.29)(.55) = .16 \text{ for 140 percent}$$
$$(.33)(.30) = .10 \text{ for 150 percent.}$$

A bid of 130 percent of estimated direct costs has the highest expected contribution margin percent; it is the optimum bid. The expected contribution margin percents on other possible bids are shown in Table 3 and Figure 3.

Several Known Competitors

Thus far, consideration has been given to a situation in which the bidder has only one known competitor and no capacity constraints. A bidder usually has several known or unknown competitors, and he may have capacity limitations. The model can be extended to these situations.

Consider the case where there are several known competitors who act independently of each other. First, an analysis is made of the historic relationship between each competitor's bids and estimated direct costs. Then, the probability that each

TABLE 3. *Expected contribution margin percent when bidding against XYZ Company*

Bid as a percent of estimated direct cost	Contribution margin percent	Probability of acceptance	Expected contribution margin percent
110	9	1.00	9
115	13	.95	12
120	17	.95	16
125	20	.95	19
130*	23	.90	21*
135	26	.75	19
140	29	.55	16
145	31	.45	14
150	33	.30	10
155	35	.20	7
160	38	.10	4
165	39	.05	2
170	41	.00	0

*Optimal bid.

FIGURE 3. *Expected contribution margin percent when bidding against XYZ Company*

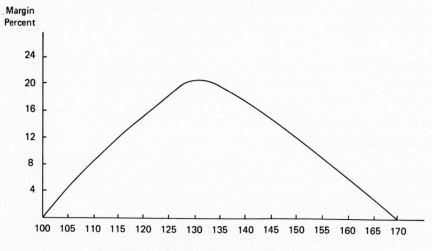

Bid as a Percent of Estimated Direct Costs

competitor will submit a bid that is higher than any given percent of estimated direct cost can be computed, as was done for the XYZ company in Table 2. Finally, the overall probability of underbidding all competitors and the expected contribution margin percent of a given bid can be determined.

(This analysis assumes that the competitors are acting independently and have acted so in the past. This assumption seems reasonable in most cases, especially when the competitors seldom submit bids on the same project because of capacity or geographic constraints. If the assumption is not appropriate, the competitors should be regarded as a unit and only their lowest bid on each past project considered. The analysis would proceed in a manner similar to that for one known competitor.)

For example, assume that the ABC company is considering bidding on a contract against three known independent competitors: DEF, TUV, and XYZ. After analyzing the past bids of these three competitors, the probability of underbidding each one when the bid is expressed as a percent of estimated direct costs is determined. These probabilities are shown in Table 4.

Next, the probability of underbidding all three is determined by multiplying the probabilities of underbidding each one. A bid of 140 percent of estimated direct costs has an 80 percent probability of being lower than DEF's bid; a 50 percent probability of being lower than TUV's bid; and a 55 percent probability of being lower than XYZ's bid, but only a 22 percent $[(.80)(.50)(.55)]$ probability of being lower than all three bids.

Finally, the expected contribution margin percent of a bid is computed by multiplying the probability of the bid being accepted by the contribution margin percent provided by the bid. A bid of 140 percent of estimated direct costs has a 22 percent probability of being accepted and provides for a contribution margin of 29 percent. The expected contribution margin of such a bid is 6.38 percent $[(.22)(.29)]$. Other

TABLE 4. *Probability of underbidding three known independent competitors*

Bid as a percent of estimated direct cost	Probability of underbidding			Overall probability of underbidding
	DEF	TUV	XYZ	
110	1.00	.98	1.00	.980
120	.98	.90	.95	.838
130	.95	.85	.90	.727
140	.80	.50	.55	.220
150	.40	.25	.30	.030
160	.20	.05	.10	.001
170	.05	.00	.00	.000

TABLE 5. *Expected contribution margin percent when bidding against three known independent competitors*

Bid as a percent of estimated direct cost	Contribution margin percent	Probability of acceptance	Expected contribution margin percent
110	9	.980	8.82
120	17	.838	14.25
130*	23	.727	16.72*
140	29	.220	6.38
150	33	.030	.99
160	38	.001	.04
170	41	.000	.00

* Optimal bid.

values are shown in Table 5. Once again, the optimum bid is 130 percent of estimated direct costs.

As the number of competitors increases, the probability that a given bid will be accepted decreases. However, the optimum bid does not necessarily decrease as the number of competitors increases.

One or More Unknown Competitors

The second extension of the model deals with the frequently encountered situation where either the identity or the number of bidders is unknown. One approach to this situation is to employ the concept of an "average" bidder. Past experience and judgment are used to determine the probability that a given bid will be lower than that submitted by an average bidder. The probability that a given bid will be lower than those submitted by n average bidders who act independently of each other is computed by raising the probability of underbidding an average bidder to the nth power.

For example, if XYZ is believed to be an average bidder and there are three unknown bidders, the probability that a bid of 130 percent of estimated direct costs will be lower than all other bids is $(.90)^3$ or 72.9 percent, and the expected contribution margin of such a bid is 16.8 percent $[(.729)(.23)]$. Other values are shown in Table 6. In the absence of capacity constraints, which will be considered later, the optimum bid may not be affected by the number of average independent bidders, although the expected contribution margin of the bid will be affected.

When the number of bidders is large or when the independence of the competitors' bids is doubted, the probability that a given bid will be accepted may be estimated by analyzing the relationship between the size of previously winning bids and estimated direct costs. This procedure has fairly limited data requirements. The

TABLE 6. *Expected contribution margin percent when bidding against three average independent bidders (XYZ is average bidder)*

Bid as a percent of estimated direct costs	Contribution margin percent	Probability of acceptance	Expected contribution margin percent
110	9	1.000	.9
120	17	.815	13.8
130*	23	.729	16.8*
140	29	.215	4.8
150	33	.027	.9
160	38	.001	.0
170	41	.000	.0

*Optimal bid.

results of its use will be satisfactory if the number of bidders on the type of project under consideration was large in the past and is expected to be large in the future.

However, neither the use of the concept of an average bidder nor the use of probabilities based on previously winning bids is recommended when a few competitors are known to act independently. In this case, knowledge of the bidding profile of a particular bidder may significantly affect the probability that a given bid will be accepted and the optimum bid.

Capacity Constraints

The final extension of the basic model to be discussed in detail is that of capacity limitations. Perhaps a bidder following a strategy of profit maximization is fortunate enough to find that he is being awarded more contracts than he has capacity to fill. In such circumstances, he could increase his profits by submitting higher bids. Although he would receive fewer contracts, he would earn a higher profit on each one.

For example, assume that the ABC company has been maximizing its expected contribution margin when bidding against companies DEF, TUV, and XYZ by constantly bidding 130 percent of estimated direct costs. Furthermore, assume that all of the contracts are approximately equal in size, that the contracts cannot be subcontracted, and that capacity cannot be expanded in the short run. Following this strategy, ABC has been winning 72 percent of the contracts it has bid on. ABC has a backlog because it has only enough capacity to fill 22 percent of the available projects.

ABC can operate at full capacity and increase the profit it earns on each awarded contract by designing its bidding strategy so that ABC submits low bids on approximately 22 percent of the contracts. Tables 4 and 5 indicate that this will be achieved with a bid of 140 percent of estimated direct cost. This method will increase the contribution margin on each bid won from 23 to 29 percent.

Conversely, if a bidder is temporarily operating below capacity because of seasonal fluctuations or other factors, he may consider sacrificing profits to keep his work force employed. The necessary bidding strategy can be determined once the bidder estimates the portion of the available contracts he must obtain to operate at full capacity. Ultimately, after comparing the costs of idle workers with the economic sacrifice required to keep them employed, he may decide not to operate at full capacity. However, he will have better information on which to base his decision.

Other Considerations

Despite the neatness of the foregoing analysis, probabilistic bidding models do not eliminate the need for professional judgment. Such models are merely one information source that is available to the decision maker. Many other factors, some quantifiable and some nonquantifiable, must also be taken into consideration.

Seasonal fluctuations affect the number of projects to be bid on and the number of bidders. The results of a recent study show that in the construction industry the largest number of contracts are let in the spring and summer, and the fewest number of contracts are let in the late fall and winter. Conversely, the average number of bidders per contract is lowest during spring and summer and highest in late fall and winter. As might be expected, the bids as a percent of estimated direct cost are highest in the spring and summer and lowest in the late fall and winter.[3]

The fluctuations in bids as a percent of estimated direct costs appear to be a function of the amount of capacity bidders have available. Bidding models for industries that display seasonal fluctuations in bids as a percent of estimated direct costs must be modified to take such fluctuations into account. (The analysis of the historic relationship between competitors' bids and estimated direct costs might be made for each season.)

Additional knowledge of a competitor's current condition might affect a firm's optimum bid. If a competitor has just been awarded a large contract, he may be less eager to receive another at once and may either submit a high bid or not bid. If it is anticipated that he will intentionally submit a high bid, he can be eliminated from the list of competitors.

In the construction industry, some consideration must be given to the proximity of the project in question to other projects currently under way. If a competitor has a nearby project, his estimate of direct costs may not bear the same relationship to the bidder's estimate of direct costs as it has in the past. The competitor would have lower transportation costs for equipment and the potential for more efficient utilization of personnel.

---

[3] J. Bocico, "Winter Best for Drawing Lower Bids," *Engineering News-Record* (November 6, 1969), p. 86.

The accuracy of cost estimates should also be considered. If little confidence is placed in the accuracy of cost estimates, the firm may want to submit a higher bid than would be indicated by the model in order to reduce the chance of incurring a loss. A number of writers have previously explored uncertainty in cost estimates.[4]

Data requirements may severely limit the usefulness of the model. Lists of prospective bidders and bid results may be obtained from the architect or engineer for a project or from a local construction newspaper. In other cases, bid results can be obtained at the bid opening. The *Commerce Business Daily*, published by the U.S. Department of Commerce, contains a daily list of contract awards by the U.S. government. However, the data required to use a probabilistic bidding model may not be available in all industries; and, in those in which data are available, a considerable period of time will pass before sufficient information can be accumulated to use the model.

This article has attempted to synthesize the important aspects of probabilistic bidding models. Such models aid the decision maker in arriving at a bid price that has the optimal combination of profit if accepted and probability of acceptance. In the past, firms employing probabilistic bidding models have had a better record of successful bids than firms that did not.

However, probabilistic bidding models, like other quantitative techniques, cannot replace the professional judgment of a decision maker. They are merely one source of useful information.

Exercises

13.1. The Veterans Association of Northwest City had been considering the addition of a new wing to their medical facilities for over two years. Disagreements regarding the exact allocation of the budget had postponed the final authorization. Hoping to avoid any more delays, the association decided to limit the bidding to civil contractors. The project would thus be awarded to the lowest bidder. This greatly limited the number of possible contenders. It was estimated that only five companies would be interested.

Lindenberg Construction & Engineering Ltd., a major employer in the area, would like to get the job. Lindenberg had used probabilistic bidding models in the past. It had files on the bidding activities of many of its competitors (see Table 13.1).

One of these, the Extant Company, had just been awarded a large contract, and so it was expected to submit a high bid. Three others were considered to be "average." Although the Lindenberg Company did not have files on these three,

---

[4] For example, see D. Hertz, "Risk Analysis in Capital Investments," *Harvard Business Review* (January-February 1964), pp. 95–106; R. Jaedicke and A. Robichels, "Cost-Volume-Profit Analysis Under Conditions of Uncertainty," *The Accounting Review* (October 1964), pp. 917–926.

TABLE 13.1

Project	Extant's bid	Astronomer's bid	Altamire's bid	Lindenberg's estimated costs
1	29,000	31,750	35,500	25,000
2	94,900	87,750	87,100	65,000
3	16,605	20,520	17,280	13,500
4	28,690	28,120	25,840	19,000
5	64,960	65,520	86,800	56,000
6	99,360	87,120	92,880	72,000
7	61,560	60,040	55,100	38,000
8	27,500	37,400	30,360	22,000
9	94,800	79,800	89,400	60,000
10	57,120	67,680	58,560	48,000
11	51,120	59,400	50,400	36,000
12	83,850	94,250	99,450	65,000

it estimated their behavior to be similar to that of Astronomer Inc., a company it had followed very closely. Astronomer itself would not be bidding. The fifth likely bidder, the Altamire Company, was an old rival.

1. Supposing that Lindenberg has no capacity constraints, what is the probability that the company will be awarded the contract if it submits a bid of 120, 125, 130, or 135% of its direct costs? These costs are estimated at approximately $55,000.
2. What is the expected contribution margin percent from each one of these bids?
3. Which one is the optimum bid? Why?
4. What other considerations, besides direct costs, should the Lindenberg Company take into account when submitting a bid? How can some of these change the bidding activities of its competitors?

13.2. The Albatross Company is considering bidding against the Marlowe Company for a project worth over $1 million. Since the contract will be awarded to the lowest bidder, the Albatross Company would like to determine the probability that its bid will be lower than Marlowe's. Direct costs are estimated at $450,000.

1. What is the probability of underbidding the Marlowe Company with a bid of 135, 145, or 150%?
2. What is the expected contribution margin percent from each one of these bids?
3. Which is the optimum bid? Why?

TABLE 13.2

Project	Marlowe's bid	Albatross's estimated direct costs
1	122,400	85,000
2	243,000	150,000
3	87,420	62,000
4	794,600	580,000
5	1,196,800	935,000
6	99,830	67,000
7	722,000	475,000
8	336,490	253,000
9	237,360	184,000
10	80,300	55,000
11	972,900	690,000
12	436,560	321,000
13	1,309,820	829,000
14	619,200	387,000
15	291,430	193,000

Pricing the Product Line During Periods of Scarcity

14

Kent B. Monroe   Andris A. Zoltners

A fundamental marketing decision problem is the determination of price for a product or service. Many factors complicate pricing decisions, such as cost per unit, competitor and buyer sensitivity to price, objectives of the firm, legal constraints, potential entry or exit of competing sellers, and the total product-service offering of the firm. The pricing literature has discussed in some detail each of these factors, except the total product-service offering of the firm. This has been neglected because of the attention given the problem of determining price for a single product or service. However, today most firms sell multiple products. Hence, there is a need to consider the effect total product-service offering has on pricing decisions.

Recently, a number of articles have suggested that the marketing manager must assume new responsibilities and develop alternative marketing approaches to cope effectively within a new economic environment (*Business Week* 1974a, 1974b; Guiltinan 1976; Guiltinan and Monroe 1974; Hanna 1975; Kniffen 1974; Kotler 1974; Kotler and Balachandran 1975; Oxenfeldt 1973). Moreover, it has become apparent that firms must develop positive and responsible pricing policies to respond to economic uncertainties, limited availability of productive resources and working capital, and changing government policies and regulations. Indeed, the business literature has documented some of these pricing responses: "delay-quotation" pricing, escalator clauses, eliminating low-margin products, unbundling of services, reducing or eliminating quantity discounts, establishing "one-price" policies.

Some of the above pricing responses directly affect the management of a product line. Indeed, a number of problems associated with unbundling low margin products, product-line price perceptions, and scarce resource capacity have been documented elsewhere (Guiltinan 1976; Guiltinan and Monroe 1974). The purposes of this article are to: (1) review the nature of the product-line pricing problem, its conceptualization, theoretical solutions, and practical approaches; (2) present a methodology for solving the simplest product-line pricing problem; and (3) develop a decision criterion for pricing the product line during conditions of resource scarcity.

Reprinted by permission from the *Journal of Marketing*, vol. 43 (Summer 1979), pp. 49–59, published by the American Marketing Association.

Nature of the Decision Problem

Generally, the firm has several product lines—groups of products that are closely related either because they are used together, satisfy the same general needs, or are marketed together. Within a product line there are usually some products that are functionally complementary to each other. For example, a photographic product line would include cameras, film, flashbulbs, projectors, screens, and other accessories. Different models are functional substitutes; whereas films, flashbulbs, and accessories are functionally complementary. Because of demand and cost interrelationships and because there are usually several price-market targets, the product-line pricing problem is one of the major challenges facing a marketing executive.

Conceptual Framework

Generally, a firm produces and distributes multiple products either because (1) the demands for the various products are interrelated, (2) their costs of production and distribution are interrelated, (3) both costs and demands are interrelated, or (4) multiple products enable the firm to appeal simultaneously to several diverse market segments (i.e., the products are neither demand nor cost related, but instead permit the firm to pursue expansion or diversification objectives).

Products are demand related if a change in price of a product, Q_1, induces buyers to change the quantity of their purchases of other products $(Q_2, \ldots, Q_n)$, along with changing their purchases of Q_1.

Similarly, products are related by production and distribution if a change in the quantity produced and distributed of a product, Q_1, results in a change in the costs of other products, $Q_2, \ldots, Q_n$.

The Theoretical Solution

Thus, if the firm's products are related by both demand and costs, the quantity of any particular product produced and sold affects both the revenues and costs of the other products a firm may sell. Hence, an adjustment in the price of a particular product to increase its net profit may or may not increase profits for the entire firm. In such situations, if the firm is interested in *maximizing contribution to profits*, it must consider not only the effect on revenues and costs of the particular product for which price is being adjusted, but also the changes in revenues and costs for all other related products.

Theoretically, the optimal solution for a multiproduct firm is to equate the adjusted marginal revenue with the adjusted marginal cost for each product. The adjustment required depends on the impact of the product's price and volume changes on the revenues and costs of the other products in the line. Table 1 provides the theoretical pricing solutions for the different possible situations.

If the products are demand related only, then some may be substitutes for each other while others may be complementary. A decrease in price for a complementary

TABLE 1. *Theoretical pricing solutions—product-line pricing*

Situation	Solution
Products not related (independent)	$MR_i = MC_i$
Products are demand related only	adjusted $MR_i = MC_i$
Products are cost related only	$MR_i =$ adjusted MC_i
Products are demand and cost related	adjusted $MR_i =$ adjusted MC_i
Products are demand related, but there is only a single "cost generating" product	$MR_i = MC_i$

Adapted from Palda (1971, p. 78).

product that leads to increased demand for that product also will increase the quantity sold of the products it complements. The reduced price for the complementary product also leads to a lower marginal revenue for that product. Therefore, the adjustment in the marginal revenue of this product is downward. On the other hand, for substitute products in the line, adjustments to marginal revenues and price are upward.

Similar results occur if the products are cost related. If the increase in quantity produced and sold of a product increases the costs of producing and distributing other products, then adjustments to their marginal costs and prices would be upward. On the other hand, if the costs of producing and distributing the other products are reduced, for example by qualifying for larger quantity discounts, then adjustments to their marginal costs would be downward.

As should be apparent, deriving optimal prices for each product is a complex optimization process requiring cost and demand information that simply is unavailable to the pricing decision maker. Moreover, despite the fact that demand and cost interrelatedness in a product line is typical today, the theoretical solutions have not been adequately specified, nor have the programming techniques been readily available. Finally, the estimation techniques for measuring demand interrelationships have been severely lacking.

Because of the inability to obtain reasonable estimates of product-line demand interrelationships, in practice, costs have provided the basis for product-line pricing. Primarily, the approach is to price products in proportion to their costs. Considerable controversy exists over whether full costs, incremental costs, or conversion costs should be used. Regardless of what is used, price frequently is determined by applying a percentage markup to each product's cost base. Hence, the pricing problem is reduced to determining the markup percentage. As a result of this practice, emphasis is placed on each product's margin (price-cost base), and the dynamic effects of price-volume-cost interactions are not always considered.

Finally, a number of constraints may exist that further complicate the problem.

Market constraints may exist in the form of buyer unwillingness to pay more than a certain amount, and in the form of existing competitive prices. Profit constraints may exist in the form of minimum acceptable rates of return or profit margins, and resources may not be available in sufficient volume for the firm to produce and sell the quantities of the products demanded. In each of these situations, the product-line pricing problem becomes a constrained optimization problem.

The Problem of Common Resources

The multiproduct firm typically uses joint or common resources to produce various product lines. Common plant, equipment, research and development facilities, and selling and administrative facilities may be used in the production and sale of products. Moreover, a critical or scarce common resource may be consumed in the product's production.

Because product prices must reflect competition and buyer reactions, as well as costs and corporate objectives, not all products make the same use of common resources per dollar of revenue or per dollar of out-of-pocket costs. However, it is important to consider the degree to which products (or special orders) use available resources (capacity) when determining prices. Otherwise, the firm may not be able to allocate resources in such a way as to obtain a desired level of contribution to profits.

During the 1973–1975 period, and again in 1979, the problem of scarce resources has existed. The lack of sufficient amounts of oil, for example, has hampered industries utilizing oil for energy or as a component in other products such as petro-chemicals. Recently, paper pulp has been in short supply, and there have been forecasts of other material shortages developing. A short supply of a resource common to several products introduces capacity constraints. The usual practice of cost-plus pricing to maintain profit margins will be inadequate when a firm is operating at capacity.

As shown in Table 1, there are five types of product-line pricing problems. Despite the ability to postulate a theoretical pricing solution for each pricing problem, the literature on product-line pricing contains few attempts to develop analytical models (Monroe and Della Bitta 1978).

Primarily, the multiple product problem has been handled as a production scheduling or product-mix problem. Typically, mathematical programming (usually linear programming) has been applied to fixed price versions of the model (P) given in the technical appendix. With a prespecified price in model (P), the decision problem is to determine the amount of product j to produce, q_j, subject to the assumed price-volume relationships, $f_j(p_j)$, and resource limitations, b_i. However, since the quantity, q_j, that may be sold is a function of price, a key marketing variable is exogenous to the model. Moreover as will be shown below, depending on the decision environment, the decision objective to maximize profit contributions may not be the optimal objective.

What is needed, therefore, is a solution procedure that incorporates price-volume estimates to determine price and product mix. The next section illustrates a solution procedure using a linear price-volume relationship. The technical appendix develops the theoretical justification for the procedure.

The procedure to be developed assumes no demand or cost interrelationships within the product line. Thus, the simplest product-line pricing situation will be presented, but price will be a decision variable. Moreover, the current economic constraint of scarce resources will be explicitly included in the analysis. There is no known (to the authors) published record for the solution to this pricing problem and, as observed in the next section, the lack of analytical attention to this problem has produced less than optimal decision prescriptions and practices.

An Analytical Pricing and Product-Mix Procedure

As the flow chart in Figure 1 suggests, the analysis begins with the marketing manager deciding either to maintain current prices without further analysis or consider an alternative price solution. If the decision is to consider alternative price solutions, the manager must decide either to specify a set of prices or to develop estimates of the price-volume relationships. The prices specified may be current product prices (which may be frozen) or contemplated product prices. The contribution-per-resource unit (CPRU) criterion to be defined below is used to allocate the common resources to the product line and thereby determine the current product-sales mix whenever a specific product price scenario is examined. If the manager wishes to analyze estimated price-volume relationships, then the price and product-mix model is used to determine a solution. In either case, the solution is considered in light of other environmental and marketing factors. When the solution is accepted, the analysis terminates and a decision is implemented. Otherwise, new estimates or prices are evaluated and the analysis continues as outlined in Figure 1.

To illustrate the application of this flow chart, a specific price scenario will be developed and illustrated. Then the price and product-mix model will be discussed.

Alternative Decision Criteria

As was observed above and as specified by the standard product-mix model, when prices are fixed (or predetermined), the firm should allocate resources and capacity to the products in such a way as to obtain a desired level of contribution to profits. Within the business literature a number of criteria have been discussed: contribution margin per unit, total contributions per period, proportion of resources required, or contribution-per-resource unit. (For ease of presentation, capacity and resource constraints will be considered as resource constraints.)

The pricing of special orders or the composition of the product strictly on unit or period contributions may result in the misallocation of available resources without obtaining the target contribution. In Table 2, Part A, the basic price and cost data

FIGURE 1. Decision flow chart of product-line pricing with scarce resources

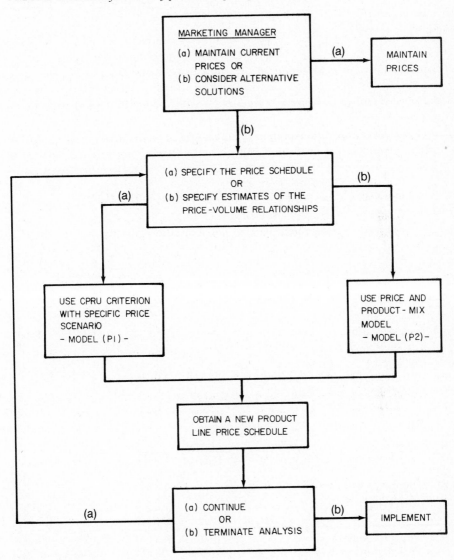

for a product line are provided. Table 2, Part B provides the demand forecasts, cost estimates, and required amount of common resource material necessary to meet the demand forecast.

As shown in Table 2, Part A, $1 per unit sold of product C is used to cover fixed expenses and contribute to profits. This unit contribution by product C is 24$^{¢}$ larger than B's unit contribution, and 41$^{¢}$ larger than A's unit contribution. However, in Table 2, Part B, it can be seen that because of total expected demand, the total dollar contribution is larger for product B, with product C ranked second, and product A, third.

In this illustration, two common resources—labor and material—are required to produce the three products. However, the mix of labor and material required to produce a unit of each product is quite different. Product A is relatively labor-intensive since 74.5% of its direct variable costs can be attributed to labor. Only 32.3% and 20% of the direct cost for products B and C is labor. Hence, products B and C require much more material input.

Now suppose this common material resource becomes scarce and the firm has

TABLE 2. Product-line contribution analysis

		A	B	C	Totals
			Product		
A.	Unit data				
	1. Price	$2.20	$3.00	$4.00	
	Variable costs:				
	2. Direct labor	$1.20	$0.70	$0.60	
	3. Direct materials	0.41	1.54	2.40	
	4. TOTAL	$1.61	$2.24	$3.00	
	5. Contribution $(1 - 4)$	$0.59	$0.76	$1.00	
B.	Data for planning period				
	6. Demand (units)	6,200	8,100	5,000	—
	7. Revenue (1×6)	$13,640	$24,300	$20,000	$57,940
	8. Direct labor (2×6)	$ 7,440	$ 5,670	$ 3,000	$16,110
	9. Direct materials (3×6)	2,542	12,474	12,000	27,016
	10. Contribution (5×6)	$ 3,658	$ 6,156	$ 5,000	$14,814
	11. Tons of material required	500	2,500	2,400	5,400
	12. Units per ton $(6 \div 11)$	12.4	3.24	2.083	—
	13. Tons per unit $(11 \div 6)$	.081	.309	.480	—
	14. CPRU $(10 \div 11)$	$7.32	$2.46	$2.08	—

been advised that it can acquire no more than 3,000 tons during the planning period. Furthermore, the world supply of this material is expected to be well below demand for at least several years. The firm must now consider the alternatives of reducing production of each product, eliminating a product and reducing production of the other products, or some reasonable combination of these choices. Clearly, the firm is faced with the problem of allocating the scarce resource to its products in the product line. Since, in theory, price has the role of allocating scarce resources, a positive price policy may be used to solve this allocation problem.

There are a number of criteria available for making the allocation decision: (1) the firm could allocate the common resource using *unit product contributions* (gross margin), (2) the allocation could be made by using *total contributions per product over the planning period*, (3) the scarce material could be rationed in *proportion to the resource requirements* given in the plan of Table 2, Part B, or (4) the firm could

TABLE 3. *Alternative resource allocations with resource constraints*

Resource allocation criteria	Resource units	Units produced	Total contribution	Reduction in contribution due to resource constraint
a. Contribution per unit:				
A	0	0	0	$3,658
B	600	1,944	$1,477	4,679
C	2,400	5,000	5,000	0
			$6,477	$8,337
b. Total product contribution per period:				
A	0	0	0	$3,658
B	2,500	8,100	$6,156	0
C	500	1,041	1,041	3,959
			$7,197	$7,617
c. Proportion of resources required:				
A	270	3,348	$1,975	$1,683
B	1,410	4,568	3,472	2,684
C	1,320	2,750	2,750	2,250
			$8,197	$6,617
d. Contribution-per-resource unit:				
A	500	6,200	$3,658	0
B	2,500	8,100	6,156	0
C	0	0	0	$5,000
			$9,814	$5,000

allocate the resource utilizing both the information on each product's unit contribution and how each product consumes scarce resources—*contribution-per-resource unit*.

As Table 3 shows, the effect of a resource constraint and constant prices is a reduction in total contributions for the period. Moreover, if either criterion (1) or (2) were adopted, it would be necessary to eliminate product A from the line. Allocation criterion (3) is the normal rationing procedure and is superior to both the unit and total contribution criteria in this example. Not only is total contribution to overhead and profits greater under the third alternative; it becomes unnecessary to eliminate a product from the line.

Product Contribution versus Resource Units

As demonstrated above, composing a product line strictly on gross contribution or margin may result in the exhaustion of available resources without obtaining the largest contribution possible. Essentially, neither approach considers how much of the scarce resource is consumed per unit of output.

As shown in Table 2, Part B, a ton of the resource material will produce 12.4 units of A, 3.24 units of B, and 2.083 units of C. The contribution per ton of material, as shown in Table 2, Part B, is greatest for product A, and least for product C. Consequently, when a resource is scarce, a method that allocates less of the resource to C and B and more to A improves contribution. Therefore, it is necessary to establish an allocation criterion that utilizes both the information on each product's unit contribution and how each product consumes scarce resources.

By shifting emphasis from product contribution to contribution-per-resource unit, it is possible to determine the resource allocation that maximizes contribution subject to the resource constraints. For the example product line, the calculations are shown in Table 2, Part B. Thus, it is apparent that product A has the highest CPRU (ton). When the resource is in limited supply, the decision rule should be to allocate resources to the profit segments with the highest CPRU. Using the CPRU criterion, Table 3 shows that product C, the highest priced, largest unit-margin product, is a candidate for elimination.

This illustration provides a fundamental principle: *When the volume of products that could be sold is greater than the resource capacity to produce these products, the largest contribution (and profit) results from producing those products that generate the greatest contribution-per-resource unit used.* A theoretical justification of the CPRU criterion appears in the appendix.

As shown in Table 2, Part B, when the capacity to produce is not constrained by the supply of resources or facilities, it is optimal to maximize the sum of the contributions per period over the product line. However, as illustrated above, the contribution margin is not applicable in all situations. Yet, the literature still discusses the relative emphasis placed on margins when identifying weak products or pricing the product line (*Business Week* 1974a; Hanna 1975).

The Price and Product-Mix Model

The analysis so far has centered on maintaining current prices. Maintaining current prices is appropriate when prices are frozen by government intervention, competition is intense, or buyers' reactions to price increases would be negative. Under those circumstances and when a scarce resource limits the firm's production capacity, the CPRU criterion is most appropriate.

It is also realistic that the firm may have pricing flexibility and the marketing manager may wish to analyze the effects of a price increase. If profitability is a decision criterion, then some products in the line could be repriced to improve their contribution-per-resource unit consumed. But, raising the prices of some or all of the products in the line can naturally be expected to reduce demand, and the pricing mechanism may serve to allocate demand. Some executives have confided to one of the authors that they followed such a pricing policy during the oil crisis of 1973–1975. Also, the reduction of product-line demand due to price increases leads to lower production requirements, thereby reducing the firm's demand for the scarce material.

Having already discussed the use of the CPRU criterion for specific prices, the price and product-mix model will be discussed next. This model has several modules, depending on the price-volume characterization. The linear price-volume relationship will be developed and illustrated.

Table 2 exhibits a single price-volume estimate for each of the three products. A linear price-volume relationship for each is shown in Figure 2. Such a relationship may be estimated in several ways (Darden 1968). One possibility is to make a second price-volume estimate for each product and join the two estimates with a straight

FIGURE 2. *Linear price-volume relationship*

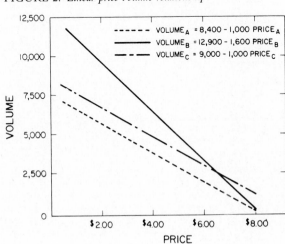

line. The relationships shown in Figure 2 were derived in this manner and are consistent with the current forecast.

As observed earlier, if prices are to be changed, then the standard product-mix model cannot be used, since it assumes prices are constant. Therefore, it is necessary to include a price-volume relationship in the model formulation. This relationship is included in model (P2) as $f_j(p_j)$, and replaces q_j of models (P) and (P1). Thus, price becomes the decision variable, as opposed to the quantity to produce. The result is that the formulation has been changed from a production scheduling problem to a marketing (pricing) decision problem.

Model (P3) shows the specific application of model (P2) when the price-volume relationship is assumed to be linear. The prices that enable this firm to achieve maximum total contribution subject to the single scarce resource can be found by solving the system of equations shown in the appendix. Solving the system for the three products ($k = 1, 2, 3$) using the demand relationships given in Figure 2 produces the prices, volumes, and total contributions shown in Table 4, Part A.

The firm may feel that such relatively large price increases are not desirable due

TABLE 4. *Optimal solutions, linear price-volume function, and resource constraints*

		Product		
	A	B	C	Totals
A. Without price constraints				
1. Price	$5.03	$5.27	$6.18	
2. Unit contribution	3.42	3.03	3.18	
3. Units produced (equals demand)	3,370.00	4,468.00	2,820.00	
4. Total contribution (2 × 3)	$11,525.40	$13,538.04	$8,967.60	$34,031.04
5. Resources required (tons)	271.80	1,379.00	1,353.60	3,004.40*
6. CPRU (4 ÷ 5)	$42.40	$9.82	$6.62	
B. With price constraints				
1. Price	$5.00	$5.00	$6.00	
2. Unit contribution	3.39	2.76	3.00	
3. Demand (units)	3,400.00	4,900.00	3,000.00	
4. Units produced	3,400.00	4,900.00	2,528.00	
5. Total contribution (2 × 4)	$11,526.00	$13,524.00	$7,584.00	$32,634.00
6. Resources required (tons)	274.19	1,512.34	1,213.47	3,000.00
7. CPRU (5 ÷ 6)	$42.04	$8.94	$6.25	

*Excess due to rounding the prices.

to potential loss of customer goodwill, relative competitive prices, and potential government intervention. Further, such a large price increase may dampen long-run demand, particularly if one or more of the products is in the growth stage of its life cycle (Guiltinan and Monroe 1974). The firm may also wish to have wider price differentials to maintain perceptual differences in the product line (Monroe 1973). Hence the solution technique provides the optimum solution and permits the firm to estimate the profit implications of moving to another solution because of realistic, but unquantifiable, marketing considerations.

The effect of adjustment of the optimal prices may be assessed using the CPRU criterion with the modified price scenario. For example, the firm may wish to consider the price scenario shown in Table 4, Part B. The firm believes the prices should be no higher than $5, $5, and $6 respectively; the marketing manager feels that these prices are realistic and suitable for both the firm's long-run objectives and environmental considerations. Total demand at these prices will exceed the firm's production capacity and it must allocate demand for product C. The solution shown in Table 4, Part B is the best product mix using the CPRU criterion *relative to the prices stated*. Table 4, Part B shows that the price constraint causes the total contribution (profit) to decline by $1,347.04. In general, the CPRU criterion provides the best solution when there are resource constraints and price ceilings.

Recent research on buyer's perceptions of price suggests that price-volume relationships may not be continuous and may not always be negative over all feasible prices. The acceptable price range concept suggests that several prices may be acceptable and that demand may be relatively price sensitive at specific, discrete prices (Monroe 1973). Indeed, the possibility of such a behavioral phenomenon and its price-volume implications have been discussed elsewhere (Kotler 1971; Monroe 1971). The acceptable price range concept also may imply that a part of the demand curve may bend backward and have a positive slope (Monroe 1971). The solution procedure illustrated above and formulated as model (P1) can be adapted to consider the price-volume relationships implied by behavioral price research.

Discussion

Noting that during times of scarcity, the firm is faced with problems of determining the optimum product mix and a set of profit maximizing prices, this article develops a criterion for these decisions. It has been shown that profits are largest when the firm produces those products and orders that generate the largest *contribution-per-resource unit used*. Further, as many firms have recognized, price can be used effectively to shift demand to the products with the largest CPRUs. However, when prices are changed, the quantity demanded changes and a new optimum product mix may result.

The structure of this decision problem is amenable to analysis using mathematical programming procedures. Taking a specific product-line example, the paper illustrates applying the CPRU principle using mathematical programming. Table 2 shows the type of data necessary to implement the procedure developed in this article. First, the manager or research staff must supply some price-volume estimates for the products at alternative and realistic prices. If a linear price-volume relationship is assumed, only two estimates for each product are necessary. If a nonlinear relationship is assumed, then several price-volume estimates for each product must be provided. Usually, a firm's periodic planning efforts provide and utilize some type of price-volume estimates.

The appropriate cost data to use are those costs that directly change as production and distribution volume change. To use full costs that include assigned overhead burdens precludes determining what costs actually change when volume changes. To ignore marketing and distribution costs affected by volume changes would not permit the analysis to indicate exactly what the profit implications will be. Therefore, the accounting data required are the direct product costs and the amount of the scarce resource needed to produce an order or product. Such data can be obtained from the firm's cost accounting system.

Further, by focusing on the objective of maximizing contributions to profits, the analytical procedure permits the manager to evaluate different scenarios including price guidelines and market reactions. Often the use of different scenarios provides the manager a type of sensitivity analysis in that the way prices and profits change given different situations can help the manager better understand the decision environment. Moreover, using contributions to profit as the decision criterion makes it easier to observe the dynamic price-volume relationships as the product mix changes (Monroe 1979).

The CPRU criterion is best used when productive capacity is constrained by a bottleneck. Factors causing the bottleneck might be machines, equipment, time, skilled labor, materials, or cash. For example, several years ago, the candy industry, because of high sugar prices, did not have the cash resources to acquire the necessary sugar tonnage to meet demand, thus constraining production and creating a bottleneck. Any industry or product line that depends heavily on a single resource would be particularly suited to use the criterion and analysis outlined in this paper. For example, product lines heavily dependent on petrochemicals, the paper industry, drugs, and fertilizers, all are dependent on critical materials.

It should be noted that the other elements of the marketing mix have been assumed constant in this paper. Indeed, price will not be considered in isolation by a well-managed firm. Price changes can affect the sales force and distributors. Advertising and promotion must be consistent with the pricing policy. However, when faced with scarce resources, price may become a dominant variable and may be treated as more than a mere parameter within the marketing planning process.

This paper has demonstrated the inadequacy of the gross margin criterion for product-mix and pricing decisions when the firm is operating at capacity due to resource constraints. It has been shown that the CPRU is a superior criterion and that pricing and production decisions may be enhanced using mathematical programming approaches. The data requirements are solvable and the solution technique is programmable. Because of these two features, the marketing manager would also find it convenient to interact with the computer via a terminal and test other profit-volume assumptions and their profit implications. With the information, estimates, and analysis a computerized procedure provides, the manager is better able to make a good price-product-mix decision.

Technical Appendix

This appendix provides the theoretical justification for the CPRU criterion and the formulation for the price and product-mix models.

Theoretical Justification for the CPRU Criterion

A firm wishing to price a product line and obtain the highest profit contribution is faced with the following optimization problem:

Model (P)

$$\text{maximize} \quad \sum_{j=1}^{n} (p_j - c_j) q_j \tag{1}$$

$$\text{subject to:} \quad \sum_{j=1}^{n} a_{ij}q_j \leqslant b_i \qquad \text{for all } i \tag{2}$$

$$0 \leqslant q_j \leqslant f_j(p_j) \qquad \text{for all } j \tag{3}$$

$$p_j \geqslant 0 \qquad \text{for all } j \tag{4}$$

where the decision variables are: p_j = price per unit of product j, q_j = number of units of product j produced and sold; and the model parameters are: n = number of products within the product line, c_j = direct variable costs of producing and distributing product j, a_{ij} = amount of resource i consumed per unit for product j, b_i = amount of resource i available for the planning period, $f_j(\cdot)$ represents the price-volume relationship for product j.

The objective function (1) reflects the firm's desire to maximize profit contribution. Constraints (2) insure that operating constraints are met. These constraints may be due to insufficient equipment capacity, raw material and labor availability, cash constraints, as well as corporate goals for market share and growth. Constraints (3) specify that the firm will not produce any more than it can sell, and constraints (4) insure that all product prices are positive.

In the simplest case, model (P) assumes no demand and cost interactions. That is, the demand for product j and cost of product j are not affected by the price of any of the other products.

For specified prices p_j and production capacities b_i, model (P) can be used to determine the production levels for each of the firm's products. This production problem has been referred to in the literature as the product-mix problem (Byrd and Moore 1978; Wagner 1969). From a practical point of view, capacity constraints (3) are usually nonbinding. For example, a firm can usually expand capacity by purchasing additional machines, adding a supplementary shift, or increasing working capital through borrowing.

Occasionally, as demonstrated in 1973–1975, a single resource (such as a raw material) can impose a binding constraint on operations. Whenever this happens, the firm is faced with the following singly constrained decision problem:

Model (P1)

$$\text{maximize} \quad \sum_{j=1}^{n} (p_j - c_j)q_j \tag{5}$$

$$\text{subject to:} \quad \sum_{j=1}^{n} a_j q_j \leqslant b \tag{6}$$

$$0 \leqslant q_j \leqslant f_j(p_j) \qquad \text{for all j} \tag{7}$$

$$p_j \geqslant 0 \qquad \text{for all j} \tag{8}$$

Constraint (6) represents the single resource confronting the firm. The firm must decide how to allocate this resource across the product line. The firm has two pricing options. Either it can maintain price and allocate the resource in the most effective way, or it can increase price and allow the anticipated decrease in demand to allocate the scarce resource.

If the firm decides to maintain current prices, then the optimal allocation of the resource can be obtained by solving model (P1) with the current price structure. The optimal solution to model (P1) is precisely the CPRU solution:

$$q_j = f_j(p_j) \qquad \text{for } j = 1, 2, \ldots, r-1 \tag{9}$$

$$q_r = b - \sum_{j=1}^{r-1} a_j q_j \tag{10}$$

$$q_j = 0 \qquad \text{for } j = r+1, \ldots, n \tag{11}$$

where (a) the products are ordered according to decreasing CPRU ratios, i.e.,

$$\frac{p_1 - c_1}{a_1} \geqslant \frac{p_2 - c_2}{a_2} \geqslant \ldots \geqslant \frac{p_n - c_n}{a_n}$$

and (b)

$$\sum_{j=1}^{r-1} a_j \leqslant b \text{ and } \sum_{j=1}^{r} a_j > b. \tag{12}$$

Price and Product-Mix Models

The CPRU criterion is appropriate when the firm must determine the best allocation of a single scarce resource in terms of a fixed product-line price schedule. Alternatively, if the firm increases price to dampen demand, it is faced with the following decision problem.[1]

Model (P2)

$$\text{maximize} \qquad \sum_{j=1}^{n} (p_j - c_j) f_j(p_j) \qquad\qquad (13)$$

$$\text{subject to:} \qquad \sum_{j=1}^{n} a_j f_j(p_j) \leqslant b \qquad\qquad (14)$$

$$p_j \geqslant 0 \qquad\qquad \text{for all } j \qquad\qquad (15)$$

$$f_j(p_j) \geqslant 0 \qquad\qquad (16)$$

This model has several variations, depending on the price-volume characterization. The case of linear price-volume relationships is developed and illustrated in this section. Using the La Grange multiplier technique, an optimal closed-form product-line pricing schedule can be determined for the linear case. For more complicated demand functions, model (P2) can be discretized and solved as an integer program. The integer programming formulation of (P2) was actually used in the pricing system described in Figure 1 because it accommodates a variety of demand functions.

Assuming linear demand functions, $f_j(p_j) = \alpha_j - \beta_j p_j$, model (P2) becomes:[2]

Model (P3)

$$\text{maximize} \qquad \sum_{j=1}^{n} \{(\alpha_j + c_j \beta_j) p_j - \beta_j p_j^2\} \qquad\qquad (17)$$

$$\text{subject to:} \qquad \sum_{j=1}^{n} (-a_j \beta_j) p_j \leqslant b - \sum_{j=1}^{n} a_j \alpha_j \qquad\qquad (18)$$

$$\frac{\alpha_j}{\beta_j} \geqslant p_j \geqslant 0 \qquad\qquad \text{for all } j \qquad\qquad (19)$$

The prices that will enable this firm to achieve maximum total contributions subject to the single resource constraint can be found by solving the following system of equations:

$$(2a_n \beta_k \beta_n) p_k - (2a_k \beta_k \beta_n) p_n = (\alpha_k + c_k \beta_k) a_n \beta_n - (\alpha_n + c_n \beta_n) a_k \beta_k \qquad (20)$$
$$\text{for } k = 1, \ldots, n-1$$

$$\sum_{j=1}^{n} (-a_j \beta_j) p_j = b - \sum_{j=1}^{n} a_j \alpha_j {}^{3} \qquad\qquad (21)$$

For the example of Figure 2, the following equations were derived:

---

[1] It can be shown that $q_j = f_j(p_j)$ is an optimal solution to (P2) when $f_j(p_j)$ is monotone nonincreasing.

[2] Models (P1), (P2), and (P3) can be extended to incorporate multiple resources. These extensions will not be presented in this paper.

[3] An adjustment to the solution will have to be made whenever there exists an optimal price, p_j, that violates its boundary conditions.

$$9{,}600 \ \text{price}_A \qquad\qquad -1{,}620 \ \text{price}_C = 38{,}328$$
$$15{,}360 \ \text{price}_B - 9{,}888 \ \text{price}_C = 19{,}795.2$$
$$80.65 \ \text{price}_A + 493.82 \ \text{price}_B + \ \ 480 \ \text{price}_C = 5{,}978.9$$

The procedure for finding optimal prices in the linear price-volume case has the same degree of difficulty as solving a system of equations having as many equations and unknowns as there are products whose prices are to be determined. In the current example, demand for each product is independent of demand for the other two products.

Solving this system of equations for products A, B, and C yields the prices, volumes, and total contribution found in Table 4.

References

Business Week (1974a),. "The Squeeze on Product Mix" (January 5), 50–55.

———, (1974b), "Pricing Strategy in an Inflation Economy" (April 6), 43–49.

Byrd, Jack, Jr., and L. Ted Moore (1978), "The Application of a Product Mix Linear Programming Model in Corporate Policy Making," *Management Science*, 24 (September), 1342–1350.

Darden, Bill R. (1968), "An Operational Approach to Product Pricing," *Journal of Marketing*, 32 (April), 29–33.

Guiltinan, Joseph P. (1976), "Risk-Aversive Pricing Policies: Problems and Alternatives," *Journal of Marketing*, 40 (January), 10–15.

———, and Kent B. Monroe (1974), "Making Sound Pricing Decisions in the Current Economic Environment," *Executive Scene*, 3 (October), 11–16.

Hanna, Nessim (1975). "10 Ways Inflation-Recession Challenge Marketers with Pricing Responsibilities," *Marketing News*, 8 (February 28), 4.

Kniffen, Fred (1974), "'Stagflation' Pricing—Seven Ways You Might Improve Your Decisions," *Marketing News*, 8 (November 15), 4–5.

Kotler, Philip (1971), *Marketing Decision Making: A Model Building Approach*, New York: Holt, Rinehart and Winston.

——— (1974), "Marketing During Periods of Shortage," *Journal of Marketing*, 38 (July), 20–29.

———, and V. Balachandran (1975), "Strategic Remarketing: The Preferred Response to Shortages and Inflation," *Sloan Management Review*, 17 (Fall), 1–17.

Monroe, Kent B. (1971), "Measuring Price Thresholds by Psychophysics and Latitudes of Acceptance," *Journal of Marketing Research*, 8 (November), 460–464.

——— (1973), "Buyers' Subjective Perceptions of Price," *Journal of Marketing Research*, 10 (February), 70–80.

——— (1979), *Pricing: Making Profitable Decisions*. New York: McGraw-Hill.

———, and Albert J. Della Bitta (1978). "Models for Pricing Decisions," *Journal of Marketing Research*, 15 (August), 413–428.

Oxenfeldt, Alfred R. (1973), "A Decision Making Structure for Price Decisions," *Journal of Marketing*, 37 (January), 48–53.

Palda, Kristian S. (1971), *Pricing Decisions and Marketing Policy*, Englewood Cliffs, NJ: Prentice-Hall, Inc.

Wagner, Harvey M. (1969), *Principles of Operations Research*, Englewood Cliffs, NJ: Prentice-Hall, Inc.

Exercises

14.1. This problem requires the use of Tables 2 and 3 and Figure 2 in the preceding reading. If the firm wishes to maintain the prices shown in Table 2, the best decision is to use the CPRU criterion and suspend production of product C. However, the marketing manager may feel that the product is necessary to complete the product line, or that demand for product C will grow in the near future. Therefore, the firm should consider repricing products B and C to increase their relative CPRUs.

1. The first step would be to compute new selling prices for B and C that provide for CPRUs equal to that for product A. Assuming no demand effects, compute what the new selling prices for B and C must be so that their CPRUs equal $7.32.
2. Using the linear price-volume relationships given in Figure 2, compute the estimated sales volume for B and C. Using Table 3 as a guide, prepare a planning summary for the product line. What resources will be required to supply this sales volume?
3. Describe the situation depicted in your planning summary. What should be the firm's next step? What factors should the firm consider before taking the next step?

14.2. The CPRU criterion may also be used when a firm is not operating at capacity or is faced with a shortage of critical resources. When the CPRU criterion is used for setting prices, it provides a means of maintaining consistency over customers, product lines, or special orders. This problem involves the application of the CPRU criterion to the pricing of a special order.

A special order occurs when an established customer places an order for a quantity different from the normal one, when a nonregular customer places a one-time-only order for a substantial quantity, or when an order is placed for a product not usually produced by the firm but which the firm has the capability of producing. In each of these situations, the firm must establish a price that is consistent with prices for regular products and customers as well as being acceptable to the originator of the special order.

Assume that the Ashley Company normally sells a product in a standard order of 500 units. The basic cost and contribution data for a standard order are given in Table 14.1. On a standard order of 500 units, the firm needs 10 hours to set up the production equipment to make the production run. Labor costs for a setup are $10.00 per hour. The standard hourly rate for the machine used in the process is $10.00, and five units can be produced per hour. A standard order of 500 units currently is priced at $20.00 per unit.

Suppose a nonregular customer approaches the firm with an offer for a one-time-only order for 1,000 units. This potential customer is aware that a standard

TABLE 14.1. *Data for standard order (500 units)*

1. Revenue at $20.00 selling price		$10,000
2. Variable manufacturing costs		
Setup cost (10 hours @ $10/hour)	$100	
Machine cost (100 hours @ $10/hour)	$1,000	
Materials ($3.00 per unit)	$1,500	
Labor ($3.00 per unit)	$1,500	4,100
3. Contribution		$5,900
4. Total hours (10 hours + 100 hours)		110
5. CPRU per hour (3 ÷ 4)		$53.64

order is 500 units at a per unit price of $20.00; however, the customer asks for a price quotation.

1. Why do you think the customer asked for a price quotation?
2. Assume that the firm has the capacity to handle this special order, but that it wishes to be consistent in its price quotation relative to the price that is quoted to its regular customers. Determine a potential unit selling price for the special order that maintains the CPRU per hour at $53.64.
3. What other factors should the firm consider before quoting a specific price for this special order?
4. What price would you quote? Why?

An Alternative to Transfer Pricing

15

Peter Mailandt

A decentralized corporate organization is commonly recognized as the most effective structure to serve the needs of large multiproduct, multiservice companies. The subdivision of a corporation into separate, largely autonomous profit and cost centers accomplishes many purposes. Two of the most important ones are:

> To stratify the wide spectrum of markets served, products manufactured, and services offered into segments, each one of which is reasonably transparent when (1) evaluating markets, products, processes, and services; (2) identifying, isolating, and solving problems; and (3) locating and exploiting opportunities.
> To provide a proving ground for managers who, to various degrees, are free to exercise authority over sources of input, level of output, application of people and capital resources, and financial and long-range planning.

Establishing separate profit centers means setting up distinct accounting entities to control and to evaluate the profit centers' internal operations in accordance with the company's overall goals and objectives.

The existence of two or more profit centers or autonomous divisions frequently gives rise to controversies among operational units. The two main areas of interdivisional friction are readily identified as the allocation of corporate and joint cost among benefiting divisions, and the establishment of intracompany transfer prices. This article deals with the problem of intracompany transfer pricing. The need for transfer prices has been recognized by virtually all large companies. As Joel Dean observed twenty years ago, trying to operate without transfer prices would severely jeopardize effective decentralization and would avoid no problems.[1] In this article, I will propose a new approach to transfer pricing that promises to overcome many of the problems and controversies associated with conventional transfer pricing methods. (To aid the reader, a list of terms used in this article and their definitions is provided in the accompanying "box.")

---

[1] National Industrial Conference Board, *Interdivisional Transfer Pricing*, Business Policy Study No. 122 (New York: National Industrial Conference Board, 1967).
Joel Dean, "Decentralization and Intracompany Pricing," *Harvard Business Review* (July-August 1955).

The following is a list of definitions of terms used in this article.

Product includes services, components, subassemblies as well as finished goods.

Division is a profit or cost center that is autonomous within a company with respect to procuring input products from internal or external sources.

Transfer price refers to the price at which a product unit is transferred from one division to another.

Total cost is the sum of all direct, indirect, and allocated costs and expenses incurred by and allocated to the division. In effect, the concept presented calls for identical cost allocation for products sold within and outside the company.

Division profit margin is the ratio of pretax profit to sales realized by the division.

Product profit margin is the profit margin the selling division would realize if it were to sell its product in a competitive, uncontrolled outside market. If no applicable outside market can be identified, a substitute "product profit margin" can be established, as outlined in the text.

Cost markup is the supplying division's percent markup from total cost to arrive at the transfer price.

Market price discount is the percent rebate from the market price at which the product is transferred to the purchasing division.

Margin distribution index is the relative distribution of the product profit margin between the selling division and the buying division.

The following example illustrates the terms defined: The *total cost* of a *product* to the supplying division is assumed to be $8.40. The comparable market price is $12.00, so that the *product profit margin* is $3.60 or 30 percent.

If the *margin distribution index* is set at 2, for every two dollars of profit made by the supplying division, the buying division will be allowed a one-dollar discount from the market price. The *transfer price* is therefore set at $10.80, the *cost markup* is $2.40 or 28.6 percent, and the *market discount* is $1.20 or 10 percent. The supplying *division profit margin* is 22.2 percent.

Purpose of Transfer Pricing

Divisions of highly integrated companies typically engage in lively trade with one another, and the effect of transfer prices can be seen in most facets of operations and planning. Decisions at division level as to what products to manufacture at what quantities frequently depend on the profitability of individual products relative to each other. Production of goods whose costs are expected to rise is favored by transfers at cost-plus; products with good cost reduction potential are promoted when transfer prices are tied to the market.

Transfer price–dependent profitability considerations will influence make-or-buy, and may influence capital expenditure decisions at the division level, but this influence may not bring about sensible performance improvement programs at the division level unless an adequate incentive is provided for the burdened profit center. Sound transfer pricing practice should allocate profits among the participating divisions so that the profits are permitted to settle where the money has been earned. This serves two purposes; first, potentially unprofitable business units can be identified and top-level attention focused on the problem areas. Second, an objective appraisal of division performance can be complemented by an objective appraisal of the manager's performance.

Although participants readily agree that sound transfer pricing policy is a key to effective business decisions, two divisions trying to protect their own interests in their interactions often find the individual requirements on transfer prices to be contradictory. The transfer price is forced into the role of being a servant for two masters. How can the need for fair financial representation of intracompany transactions be satisfied without compromising the need for effective control and for providing incentives for performance improvement in the participating organizations?

Little hope can be held for a cost or cost-plus pricing scheme that disregards market value. Nor can there be much hope for a market-value-related transfer price that rejects cost considerations. Market- and cost-oriented views both must enter into developing sound intracompany transfer prices. When this is done, a relatively simple pricing scheme such as the one I am proposing can accommodate the competing interests of the interacting division as well as comply with the control and performance incentive objectives of the total enterprise.

A New Approach

The new concept is basically simple. Once a year a transfer price is agreed upon by the interacting divisions through negotiation. The negotiation, in effect, focuses on allocating the margin between the supplying division and the buying division by setting the transfer price at a level above total cost but below market price. The transfer price relative to the total cost incurred by the supplying division and relative to the comparable market price will yield the cost markup and the market price discount, respectively. If one starts with the cost markup and the market price discount, calculation of the "product margin distribution index" is as follows:

$$\text{product margin distribution index} = \frac{\text{cost markup \% }(100 - \text{market discount \%})}{\text{market discount \% }(100 + \text{cost markup \%})}$$

(A)

In the proposed method, the distribution index for the product margin is held constant throughout a designated future period. Changes in the product margin due to changes in the costs incurred by the supplying division or due to changes in the comparable market price will affect the transfer price. However, the index that characterizes the distribution of the product margin between the interacting divisions will not be allowed to change. This "automatic" adjustment of the transfer price to account for changes in cost or market price is the central feature of this intracompany transfer pricing method. Other aspects will be highlighted below.

The lower and the upper limits of a transfer price are, respectively, the total cost to the supplying division and the comparable market price of the product. The total cost associated directly and indirectly with the product is usually well known,

Effects of changes in cost and market price

	Bench mark					
	1	2	3	4	5	6
List or market price ($)	10.00	10.00	12.00	10.00	9.00	12.00
Transfer price ($)	9.00	8.67	10.33	9.33	8.33	10.80
Total cost ($)	7.00	6.00	7.00	8.00	7.00	8.40
Cost markup factor	.286	.476	.477	.167	.190	.286
Market price discount factor	.100	.133	.139	.067	.074	.100
Margin distribution index	2.0	2.0	2.0	2.0	2.0	2.0
Product profit margin	30.0%	40.0%	41.7%	20.0%	22.2%	30.0%
Supplying division profit margin	22.2%	30.8%	32.3%	14.3%	16.0%	22.2%
Market price discount	10.0%	13.3%	13.9%	6.7%	7.4%	10.0%
Change in overall margin from column 1	—	+33.3%	+39.0%	−33.3%	−26.0%	0.0%
Change in supplying division margin from column 1	—	+38.7%	+45.5%	−35.6%	−27.9%	0.0%
Change in market discount from column 1	—	+33.3%	+39.0%	−33.3%	−26.0%	0.0%

since alternative transfer price methods based on cost, as well as an effective cost control system, are dependent on accurate cost information. Establishing a comparable market price is less objective and, therefore, more difficult in instances where published or other market price data are unavailable. One of the following methods is then suggested:

1. Identify a product within the company's portfolio for which total cost and market price are available and which relates well with the product under consideration in terms of markets served, product and process technology used, and unit/dollar volume sold. The profit margin of the identified product can be substituted for the profit margin of the product under consideration.
2. If no related product can be identified, the division's overall profit margin on outside business can be taken as the profit margin of the product under consideration.

With the total profit margin established, either directly or indirectly, the task remains to decide the margin distribution index. In his article on intracompany pricing, Joel Dean offers strong arguments in favor of determining transfer prices by negotiation where all parties are fully informed, are knowledgeable, and are free to deal with the outside. The margin distribution index is then calculated from the agreed transfer price.[2]

Why should the transfer price be more than cost? To provide for a profit to the supplying division and with it a performance measure. Why should the transfer price be less than market price? To provide the buying division with the financial incentive to purchase inside and thus contribute to a volume-related reduction of cost per unit. Savings are also realized by the buyer in the form of reduced purchasing activity, reduced receivables, and reduced inventory risk—all commonly associated with intracompany purchases. In the annual negotiation of the index, all contributing factors must be weighed carefully, so that the index will not be subject to change.

How It Works

To illustrate the proposed pricing concept and its positive features, some of which are not shared by other frequently used transfer pricing schemes, a numerical example is given in the accompanying table. It shows the impact of changing costs and shifting market prices on the transfer price.

At the time of the annual transfer price negotiation, the total cost of a particular product is $7.00, and the comparable open market price is $10.00. Negotiations resulted in a margin distribution index of 2, indicating that for every margin of two dollars to the supplying division, the transfer price is one dollar less than the

[2] Joel Dean, "Decentralization and Intracompany Pricing," p. 2.

market price. Accordingly, the first column in the table shows a transfer price of $9.00. Also shown are: the product profit margin, 30%; the supplying division profit margin, 22.2%; and the market price discount to the buying division, 10%. Each subsequent column in the table shows the effect of changing cost or price levels on the transfer price, the cost markup and margin claimed by the supplier, and the market discount taken by the buyer. A decrease in cost by one dollar (column 2) lowers the transfer price by $.33 to $8.67. The margin for the supplier and the discount to the buyer increase by 38.7% and 33.3%, respectively, with respect to column 1 data. A rise in market price without a change in cost level (column 3) increases the transfer price so that both divisions expand their margins. An increase of cost without a market price move (column 4) penalizes the supplier more than the buyer. Column 5 represents a situation where a rise in cost is accompanied by a decline in market price, causing margin deterioration for both participants. A 20% rise in cost coupled with a market price increase by a like percentage (column 6) raises the transfer price symmetrically, preserving margin and discount percentages.

Major Advantages

The quality and usefulness of any intracompany pricing method can be measured by how well it satisfies each of the following four requirements.

1. *Transfer pricing must be easy to manage and to administer.* The proposed method calls for negotiation, say, once a year to set the margin distribution index for the subsequent twelve months. The negotiation may or may not be time-consuming, depending on the complexity of the business and the people involved. After the index has been agreed upon, the impact on the transfer price of any changes in cost or market price level can be readily calculated by the administrative staff without management involvement. Updates of the transfer price can be made according to a fixed timetable or whenever changes warrant revisions.
2. *The transfer price method must provide a way to measure a division performance.* The proposed transfer pricing method permits divisions to retain a share of the financial benefits derived from effective cost reduction efforts. Inversely, poor cost control is reflected in decreasing margins if the cost increases cannot be passed on to the market. Consequently, division-level profits in relation to sales are good indicators of the division's operational performance and the manager's contributions to the company's overall profit objectives.
3. *Transfer pricing must promote continuous performance improvement.* The proposed method rewards effective cost control, successful product or process improvement, and skillful marketing efforts by increasing the profit margin at the organizational level where improvements are implemented.
4. *Transfer pricing must be fair to all participants and flexible in times of change.* The

proposed pricing method permits adjustment of the transfer price to equal total cost (index = 0) or to approach the market price (index is very large) and can thus accommodate all interdivisional preferences, corporate guidelines, or regulations of government agencies, without changing the concept or super-imposing other pricing methods on the proposed one. Since interdivisional pricing changes are relatively easy adminstrative tasks—the margin distribution index remains unchanged—market price changes can be accommodated quickly and fairly with minimum disruption and without a departure from the previously agreed upon guidelines.

Implementing the Concept

The "arms-length" negotiation of interdivisional transfer prices assures independence of operating entities and leads to meaningful ways to measure business performance. Control of cost has to be complemented with control over price to an extent that is acceptable to the trading partners. Only then do financial results of operations fairly reflect managerial skill as well as the division's and the product's contributions to overall corporate success or failure. Developing and promoting skills of negotiation at the division level can only enhance the competitive position of a company in the marketplace.

Not surprisingly, opposition to arms-length price bargaining is most often voiced by managers who fear exposure of inadequacies in the area of negotiation. A popular argument is that a policy of transfer price bargaining is a time-consuming, never-ending process. However, the proposed method calls for negotiations only once a year or even less frequently, since changes in cost or market prices can be accommodated administratively and do not require new bargaining. The arms-length negotiations do require the participants' full knowledge of the total cost to the supplying division as well as the competitive market price of a like product.

The bargaining could focus on establishing a transfer price, which would in turn permit calculation of the margin distribution index:

$$\text{margin distribution index} = \frac{\text{transfer price} - \text{total cost}}{\text{market price} - \text{transfer price}} \quad \text{(B)}$$

Or the negotiations could lead to an agreement as to how the margin should be divided between the trading divisions. For example, the accord may call for twenty cents to the supplying division for every dollar to the buying division, fixing the margin distribution index at .2. The resulting transfer price would then be:

$$\text{transfer price} = \frac{\text{margin distribution index} \times \text{market price} + \text{total cost}}{1 + \text{margin distribution index}} \quad \text{(C)}$$

This formula would also be used when events subsequent to the agreement on the margin index change the total cost or the market price, calling for corresponding recalculation of the transfer price.

The equations in this section and the numerical example show that the transfer price follows movement of cost as well as market price changes in a compensating manner. On the one hand, manufacturing cost increases cannot be passed on in total to the next division as in the cost or cost-plus transfer price method. On the other hand, effects of market price changes will be shared by all participating divisions. The far-reaching consequence of this is that divisions at all formation stages will become rightfully concerned about the structure and dynamics of cost components and the market environment of the products with which the divisions are involved.

The proposed transfer pricing method, which distributes the available product margin between the exchanging divisions, offers—at the cost of only slightly increased complexity—a number of operational as well as planning advantages. Operationally, the financial statements of divisions engaging in considerable in-house trading are heavily influenced by the transfer price policy guidelines. The proposed method permits top management to rely on financial statements as bases for performance appraisals to a larger extent than would be warranted with the conventional transfer pricing methods. Also, comprehensive planning and forecasting processes in divisions should involve reviews of cost as well as price structure of products and services. The constant margin distribution index transfer pricing method requires the incorporation of cost as well as price considerations in business projections. This expanded planning scope should lead to an increased awareness of the company's overall profitability and competitive position by managers at all levels.

Exercises

15.1. Transfer pricing negotiations used to be dreaded at Bits and Britz Int'l., a toy manufacturing company. Intracompany transfer pricing always caused a lot of friction among division heads. Last year the company decided to experiment with a new method called the product margin distribution index (PMDI). Once the parties concerned agreed on a distribution ratio, that ratio would remain constant despite changes in either production costs or market prices. The new method proved effective in reducing disputes and time spent at the bargaining table.

This year's meeting was expected to be a review of the systems for most members. One of the more experienced managers offered to demonstrate the method to a couple of newcomers.

Suppose you are this experienced manager. How can you arrive at the PMDI once you agree on a transfer price? How can you use the PMDI to set new transfer

TABLE 15.1

	1	2	3	4	5	6
Market price ($)	48.00	52.00	50.00	48.00	48.00	45.00
Transfer price ($)	46.55					
Total cost ($)	42.20	42.20	45.00	45.00	40.00	42.20

prices if there is a change in either production costs or market prices? Use the data provided in Table 15.1 for your illustration.

1. What is the product margin distribution index for case 1?
2. Taking PMDI for year 1, calculate, for each subsequent case,
   a. transfer price.
   b. cost markup factor.
   c. market price discount factor.
   d. product profit margin.
   e. supplying division profit margin.

15.2. The total cost of a steel belt at the J. R. Rubber Company at the time of the annual transfer price negotiation was $5.00. The comparable price for the same product in the open market was $7.50.

Negotiations resulted in a margin distribution index of 1.5, which meant that for every margin of $1.50 to the supplying division, the transfer price would be $1.00 less than the market price. The market price for that type of steel belt is not very stable, however. Fluctuations of plus or minus 10% of the actual price are expected.

1. Calculate transfer pricing, cost markup factor, product profit margin, and market price discount for the actual price and the proposed new prices.
2. How will the supplying division and the buying division be affected if the total cost increases by 20% and the open market price remains the same—i.e., $7.50?

Recommendations for
Further Reading

Brooks, Douglas G. "Bidding for the Sake of Follow-On Contracts," *Journal of Marketing*, 42 (January 1978), 35–38.

Many firms face bidding situations in which follow-on contracts are likely and the firm winning the initial contract is also favored to win any subsequent contracts. A method proposed earlier by the author to determine the markup on materials and the direct labor necessary to meet any target return-on-objective is reviewed. However, a lower price could be bid on an initial contract if the probability was high that a follow-on contract could be won at a higher level of profitability. The problem then becomes one of determining which combination of initial bid and follow-up bid would generate an expected rate of return equal to the firm's target. How such information could be obtained after due allowance is made for the probability of actually obtaining the second contract is illustrated.

Brooks, Douglas G. "Cost-Oriented Pricing: A Realistic Solution to a Complicated Problem," *Journal of Marketing*, 39 (April 1975), 72–74.

A case is made for cost-oriented pricing and a method proposed that is particularly appropriate to a firm with fixed capacity, a target rate of return objective, and a sales volume that can be estimated with some reliability. The value of this method lies in the ease with which typical pricing decisions can be made at relatively low levels in the organization. The first step involves calculating the present value of fixed expenses, direct labor and materials, and target gross income on operations. The percentage markup over direct labor and material cost necessary to cover fixed expenses and target gross income can then be derived. Use of this standard markup greatly simplifies the pricing and, it is suggested, often proves far superior to more complex methods.

Dearden, John. "Interdivisional Pricing," *Harvard Business Review*, 38 (January–February 1960), 117–125.

Inefficient interdivisional pricing is a cause of wasted production and lower profits. Four actual cases are cited to illustrate how profits are lost by inadequate internal pricing systems. Methods which have been used to establish and administer successful systems of interdivisional pricing are then described. Four special problems that might arise are next given attention and solutions to such problems suggested. One such area of concern is that of the interdivisional pricing relationships that should exist between manufacturing divisions and a separate marketing division.

Green, Paul. "Bayesian Decision Theory in Pricing Strategy," *Journal of Marketing*, 27 (January 1963), 5–14.

Traditional techniques rarely consider alternative states of nature, let alone assign prior probabilities to their occurrence; neither do they test the sensitivity of expected outcomes to variations in basic assumptions. The Bayesian model, in contrast, forces a more rigorous approach and offers a device for quickly finding the financial implications of assumptions about the occurrence of alternative states of nature. Its sophisticated approach to data collection requirements provides a flexible means of facilitating dynamic marketing planning and effective pricing. Exactly how Bayesian statistics could be employed in pricing is demonstrated by means of a detailed, illustrative application.

Lynn, Robert A. "Unit Volume as a Goal for Pricing," *Journal of Marketing*, 32 (October 1968), 34–39.

Most product pricing systems are based on profit objectives. In some cases, however, unit volume is and should be the planning objective that shapes the price decision. Conditions when this is true are outlined when high unit volume is accepted as a goal for pricing. A price consistent with this objective can be established even in the face of an uncertain response on the part of competitors. How this might be done is illustrated. Public policy implications of such action are then reviewed.

Paranka, Stephen. "Competitive Bidding Strategy," *Business Horizons*, 14 (June 1971), 39–43.

Little has been written on pre-bid analysis of bidding strategy. A procedure is herein developed for a screening method whereby a company can decide whether or not to develop a competitive bid.

The bidder first defines his objectives and those of his competitors. He then considers the criteria of capacity, competition, follow-up, quantity, desired delivery, and profit. A weight reflecting importance and a rating reflecting its firm's strength or availability in this area are assigned to each of these factors. The sum of the product of multiplying all weights by the assigned rating was used to compare the value of various bids. Two case studies are used to illustrate the method.

Simmonds, Kenneth. "A Model for Marketing and Pricing Under Competitive Bidding," in F. E. Webster (ed.), *New Directions in Marketing*. Chicago: American Marketing Association Proceedings No. 48, June 1965, S9–S22.

Key features of a decision model for selection and pricing of bids are presented. The model integrates consideration of bid preparation costs and production capacity, outstanding orders, volume and profitability of present and future opportunities, variable bid features, advantages that carry over to later bid, and the costs of under or over capacity.

Starting with the decision to prepare a bid, aspects involved in forecasting profitability, measuring availability of capacity, and comparing opportunities are joined into a decision framework for the optimum combination of bids and prices. The emphasis is on maximizing the total expected contribution, before fixed costs, to overhead and profits rather than on maximizing expected markup.

Van Dyke, James E., Kenneth J. Roering, and Robert J. Paul. "Guidelines for Competitive Bidding," *Journal of Purchasing and Materials Management*, 11 (Fall 1975), 27–31.

Although price is recognized as a major variable in any purchase transaction, little progress has been made toward rational pricing decisions. Competitive bidding per se does not necessarily assure the lowest possible price. Methods are recommended for the improvement of competitive bidding models. It is suggested that purchasers develop a profile of the bidding behavior of each supplier. Suppliers in turn can construct a curve reflecting the sensitivity to price and nonprice variation of each buyer at each price level. Also, both buyers and suppliers can develop a better understanding of negotiating skills. Methods of incorporating bidding costs into bidding models and handling sequential or otherwise linked bids must also be developed.

Walker, Arleigh W. "How to Price Industrial Products," *Harvard Business Review*, 45 (September–October 1967), 125–132.

Industrial product and construction company executives often lose many opportunities for winning profitable bids because of erratic pricing. A price level/market share curve has been designed to help such executives bid more accurately, determine whether or not to pursue a larger share of market, and minimize profits lost through inexact pricing. Mathematical probabilities are used to determine the impact of even small price changes on the chances of winning. The market price level is presumed to be the mean of the entire group of bids. Lower and higher bids form a band of prices. Postulating success probabilities at various price levels enables the plotting of a market share against each market price level and generates a price level/market share curve which helps management price its products.

Wentz, Theodore E. "Realism in Pricing Analyses," *Journal of Marketing*, 30 (April 1966), 19–26.

Examination of the competitive pricing problems of both a toy manager and a company producing abrasive grains demonstrates the detrimental effect that ready-made pricing formulas, especially those based on full-cost plans, could have on profits. Specific pricing problems in each industry are explored in a way that indicates the importance of industry structure and customer characteristics in setting price. The case is also made for considering only incremental costs when setting prices. The method used to estimate possible profit contributions under varying sets of circumstances is discussed in some detail. Estimating how volume will vary with price is the key component of the form of analysis used. Projected price, cost and profit estimates under varying sets of circumstances are presented in tabular form. The actual figures employed have been coded but not in a way that distorts underlying relationships.

Wood, D. "A Decision System for Competitive Bidding," *European Journal of Marketing*, 5 (Winter 1971/72), 168–177.

Successful competitive bidding strategies require constant adaptation to a steadily changing corporate and marketing environment. A "real time" decision system that facilitates such adaptation is first proposed and then placed in the context of the firm's overall structure and its prevailing competitive strategy. The benefits arising out of the construction of such a decision system are threefold. First, a major contribution is made to understanding the systems nature of the bidding process. Such an approach also helps to unravel the relationship between work loads, throughput and profitability. Finally, it allows new methods of bidding to be adopted as conditions change. Simulations will also reveal the costs and benefits of removing any constraint on a firm's performance.

Wotruba, Thomas R., and Robert H. Nelson. "Evaluating Pricing Alternates for a New Product: The Gaslight Case," *Akron Business and Economic Review*, 4 (Summer 1973) 9–14.

Survey data is used to evaluate alternate pricing approaches under consideration by a utility planning to market outdoor decorative gaslights. The basic pricing choice was between selling and leasing. Two possible purchase prices, a variety of monthly rental figures, and three levels of installation charge were under consideration. The weaknesses of a questionnaire approach to estimating price-quantity relationships were recognized and efforts made to deal with these problems. The data obtained is used to produce demand curves reflecting the sensitivity of demand to price. Net revenue figures are generated by first multiplying, for each approach under consideration, expected demand times price and then deducting all relevant costs. With appropriate modifications, the technique is believed applicable to a wide range of pricing decisions.

PART V

Credit, Discount
Leasing, and Forward Buying

Credit Risks and Opportunities

16

Robert M. Kaplan

It is surprising how many credit managers say with pride that their companies are renowned in their industries, by customers and competitors alike, for having a very stringent credit policy. These companies, however, are not maximizing profits (unless they are operating at capacity), are creating an umbrella under which competition is invited, and are probably causing considerable frustration in the sales force.

While the marketing department's objective naturally is sales maximization, the credit department's objective is credit loss minimization. The former wants to sell to everyone, and the latter wants to extend credit to just the "gilt edge" accounts.[1]

This article presents an approach for reconciling these opposing attitudes by using the credit function as a sales tool as well as a financial tool.

Before the sales department can make use of the credit department, however, the credit department must establish guidelines for the granting of unsecured trade credit. To this end, I will propose a method of analyzing credit risks in terms of the company's products and overhead.

Economists tell us that profits are greatest when marginal costs equal marginal revenue (assuming marginal costs are increasing and average variable costs are less than marginal revenue) and that a company will continue to increase profits by increasing sales as long as marginal costs are less than marginal revenue. Management, in its quest to maximize profits, has been attempting to use this aspect of microeconomic theory in many functions. For example, advertising is questioned as to whether it is bringing in more profit than it costs, and other sales expenses are questioned accordingly. One area where this approach can be used, but has not been, is credit management.

True Marginal Cost

The quantification of the left side of the equation, marginal costs, is not very difficult; but, unfortunately, credit managers often consider the marginal cost of

[1] For a survey of current trade credit policies, see Merle T. Welshans, "Using Credit for Profit Making," HBR January-February 1967, p. 141.

EXHIBIT 1. *Sample income statements*

	Before bad debt loss	After bad debt loss
Sales	$1,000.00	$1,000.00
Cost of goods sold	600.00	600.00
Gross margin	400.00	400.00
Selling, general, and administrative expenses	300.00	300.00
Bad debt expense	—	50.00
Net profit before taxes	$100.00	$50.00

credit losses to be the amount of the account written off, and claim that bad debt losses come right out of profit. A sample income statement, before and after writing off a bad debt, shows the basis for this claim (Exhibit 1).

In this case the net profit before taxes has been reduced by $50, the same amount as the credit loss. This is a true income statement when there is an opportunity loss expense to be considered—that is, if the choice had been available to sell to an account from which payment was certain. In this discussion, however, I am analyzing cases in which a company (perhaps with excess capacity) must decide whether to sell to an account whose ability to pay for the merchandise is less than certain or not to sell the product at all.

Consider such an instance. In the example shown in Exhibit 1, the company sold the product for $50, but not all of that amount was out-of-pocket cost. The company built a profit into the price, as well as an allocation for fixed expenses which would have been incurred regardless of whether the product was produced. Exhibit 2 shows a breakdown of the sale price into its components.

The correct income statements for the company, then, would be as shown in Exhibit 3.

EXHIBIT 2. *Analysis of sale price*

Sale price	$50.00
Variable costs:	
Manufacturing	$20.00
Marketing	10.00
Contribution to overhead and profits	$20.00

EXHIBIT 3. *Correct income statements*

	Sale is not made	Sale is made and account proves uncollectable
Sales	$950.00	$1,000.00
Cost of goods sold	580.00	600.00
Gross margin	$370.00	$400.00
Selling, general, and administrative expenses	290.00	300.00
Bad debt expense	—	50.00
Net profit before taxes	$80.00	$50.00

If the sale of $50 to the potentially bad account was not made, the gross sales would be lower by a like amount, the profit on the sale would not be previously counted and then subtracted, and all the manufacturing expenses would not have been incurred.

If the sale was made, and the account proved uncollectable, the cost to the company would be the difference between the $80 profit that would have been made without the sale and the $50 profit realized after the account was written off—that is, $30. The value of the variable costs, not the amount of the account written off ($50), therefore represents the marginal cost of the sale ($MC = \$30$).

Calculating MR

Marginal revenue (MR) is the extra revenue a company will receive if it makes the sale and the customer pays.

Probability of Payment

The decision whether to grant credit to a customer cannot be made by simply equating marginal cost with marginal revenue, since obviously the economist's decision rule—that a company should continue to make sales to increase profits as long as marginal costs are less than marginal revenue ($MC < MR$)—would lead one to grant credit to all potential customers whenever the selling price was more than the variable cost to produce and market the goods.

Another consideration which a company must incorporate into the analysis is the probability of receiving payment for the sale.[2] Whether a high or low probability of payment is assigned obviously will influence the extension of trade credit. (There are cases where payment is received before production, but then the probability of payment is 100%, or the products are not made. The following analysis is useful if the vendor must obligate himself financially before receiving payment to be sure of having the raw materials for the contract.)

I will discuss two approaches to the calculation of payment probabilities. The first emphasizes the *minimum value* that can be realistically expected from a forced sale of the assets in case of bankruptcy. The second method considers the *most likely value* to be received if liquidation proves necessary. The former method is more conservative.

First, however, I must interject a word of caution. In each of the proposed methods, the basis for calculation is the customer's balance sheet. This, unfortunately, provides a picture of the books of account only on a specific date and fails to recognize the customer's dynamic nature.[3] Changes in the accounts are very important and should be considered, for by the time the account is due for collection, the balance sheet structure may have changed considerably, thus offering a different probability of payment.

When assessing each asset account in the balance sheet, the credit department should also make an estimate as to the probable balance or value of the account and the liquidation values of its components at the time of collection, as opposed to the present. Undoubtedly this will be quite difficult to "guesstimate"; usually the most recent financial statement will have to be relied on.

Normally the fixed asset accounts will not vary in valuation as much as the more liquid assets; but, on the other hand, the more "fixed" the asset, the less chance there is that it will be quickly saleable, except at a considerable discount from what could be realized if one did not have to sell in a hurry.

When assessing the balance in each asset account, particularly with the more fixed assets, a prime consideration is that often the book value may bear little relation to the actual market value. This is usual in cases where rapid depreciation charges have been allowed against an asset or where an asset has been fully depreciated on the books but still has some value in the marketplace.

Minimum Value ...

From an analysis of the potential customer's asset accounts, the vendor's credit department can calculate the minimum amount of cash that could be realistically expected from each asset in the event of a forced sale. If, after satisfaction of all prior claims, enough cash remains from liquidation to pay all creditors, the probability of collecting the account is, of course, 100%. The usual expectation,

---

[2] I wish to express my thanks to David Promislow of the Department of Mathematics, University of British Columbia, who assisted in explaining the mathematics for this concept.

[3] For a different development of this point, see Edward C. Bursk, "View Your Customers as Investments," HBR May-June 1966, p. 91.

however, is for somewhat less than 100% recovery.

If the vendor adopts a conservative credit policy, the ratio of the lowest amount that can be expected by the general creditors (after payment of all prior claims) to the total general liabilities gives the probability of payment to the creditor. This probability should then be the weight used to calculate the expected value of the marginal revenue. For example:

If the residue available to the general creditors is $200, and the outstanding general liabilities total $400, then $200 ÷ $400, or 50%, is the amount which can be expected on collection of this account.

... and Most Likely Value

A more realistic method than minimum value is the expected value drawn from a probability distribution on the sale of the assets at prices above the minimum certainty level.

Consider, for example, a building valued on the balance sheet at $10,000 (net of depreciation) and assigned by the vendor a minimum cash value of $7,500. Credit management has made the following judgments:

While there is 100% certainty that 75% of the net value of the structure, or $7,500, can be realized, there is only a 70% chance of getting more than $8,000, a 45% probability of selling it for at least $8,500, a 25% chance of receiving more than $9,000, a 10% possibility of at least $9,500, and a zero probability of selling the building for more than $10,000. (For the sake of simplicity, I have set the net book value as the maximum that could be realized.)

From this cumulative distribution, a frequency distribution can be developed to show the probabilities of receiving the incremental amounts over the $7,500 certainty level. The chances of receiving from:

$$
\begin{aligned}
\$ \quad 0 \text{ to } \$ \ 500 \text{ more is } (1.00 - .70) &= .30 \\
500 \text{ to } \quad 1,000 \text{ more is } (.70 - .45) &= .25 \\
1,000 \text{ to } \quad 1,500 \text{ more is } (.45 - .25) &= .20 \\
1,500 \text{ to } \quad 2,000 \text{ more is } (.25 - .10) &= .15 \\
2,000 \text{ to } \quad 2,500 \text{ more is } (.10 - .00) &= .10
\end{aligned}
$$

The expected value of the extra amount is calculated by multiplying the midpoint or average (the most representative amount) of each group by the probability of receiving it and then totaling the results:

$$
\begin{aligned}
.30 \ (\$ \ 250) = \$ \quad & 75.00 \\
.25 \ (\quad 750) = \quad & 187.50 \\
.20 \ (\ 1,250) = \quad & 250.00 \\
.15 \ (\ 1,750) = \quad & 262.50 \\
.10 \ (\ 2,250) = \quad & 225.00 \\
\hline
\text{Expected value} \quad & \$1,000.00
\end{aligned}
$$

Adding $1,000 to the $7,500 minimum value gives the most likely value—in the case of a forced sale—for the building, $8,500.

Using calculus, such a continuous probability distribution is figured thus:

Let F(x) equal the probability that the amount collected will be less than, or equal to, x. If a is the minimum amount that will be collected (e.g., a = $7,500 in the just-mentioned example) and b is the maximum amount (e.g., b = $10,000 in the example), then F(x) will be a strictly monotonically increasing function defined for $a \leqslant x \leqslant b$ with $F(a) = 0$ and $F(b) = 1$. Suppose that F(x) is a continuously differentiable function of x, then from probability theory the expected value can be calculated as follows:

$$\text{Let } f(x) = \frac{d}{dx}F(x)$$

$$\text{Expected value} = \int_a^b x\, f(x)\, dx$$

Completing the Formula

Once the analysis has been made for each asset and the prior liability claims subtracted from the total expected cash value, the probability of the account paying can then be calculated as it was by the minimum value method. If, for example, the general creditors claim $400 and the residual expected cash is $200, then the most probable amount that can be expected from this account is 50% of the yield from the sale. If the sale is for $1,000, then 50% of $1,000 equals $500, which is the expected value of the marginal revenue in this case.

In calculating the marginal costs and marginal revenues, the vendor must consider factors other than those already discussed. For example:

Possible collection charges—Some probabilities can be assigned to this uncertainty, and the expected value added to marginal costs already figured for producing and selling the goods.

A number of products, with different gross margin percentages, in one sale—The marginal costs for the sale are the total marginal costs for the various products; similarly, the marginal revenue for the sale is the sum of each product's marginal revenue.

Once all the probabilities are included in the calculation, the credit department can use a modification of the economist's equation MC = MR to determine whether the sale should be made. This modification considers the expected value of the marginal revenue (MC = EV of MR). Continuing my example:

Assume that the vendor's marginal cost in a proposed sale is $600; the sale price, or marginal revenue, is $1,000; and the expected value of collection is 50%. Then MC > EV of MR ($600 > .50 × $1,000), and credit should not be granted. If the expectancy of payment were 70%, then MC < EV of MR ($600 < .70 × $1,000), and credit should be extended.

In cases where MC = EV of MR, management must make a further judgment. It should weigh other factors, such as the long-term potential of the account, the consequences of losing the account to a competitor (perhaps permanently), and the effects on other sales. These factors may override the consideration of making a profit on any one sale.

Management may find it useful to figure the break-even point, based on the ratio between marginal cost and selling price, and then assess prospective debtors against these "points of indifference." If, for example, the break-even point is 60% and the chance of collecting from a potential prospect is 70% (EV = .70), then credit should be granted.

In cases where a number of products are being considered for sale to this account, a weighted average of the products' points of indifference should be used. For instance:

> Product line A (with 85% break-even point) = 50% of sale.
> Product line B (with 75% break-even point) = 25% of sale.
> Product line C (with 70% break-even point) = 25% of sale.

Then:

$$.50 \times .85 = .4250$$
$$.25 \times .75 = .1875$$
$$.25 \times .70 = .1750$$
$$\text{Weighted average} = .7875 \text{ or } 78.75\%$$

And since EV = .70, or 70%, credit should not be extended to this customer.

This method of analyzing credit risks is, as I said earlier, a static one, since it depends on analyzing the account's balance sheet. One way to take into consideration the dynamic nature of accounts is to build into the equation a factor greater or less than 1.00, depending on whether the latest income statement—or some other information more current than a balance sheet—gives rise to optimism or pessimism about the creditor's prospects. A 1.1 factor could represent a 10% improvement in the company's profit position. In a situation, for example, where it was earlier determined that:

$$\text{EV of MR} = .60 \times \$1,000 = \$600$$

it could now be recalculated as:

$$\text{EV of MR} = .60 \times \$1,000 \times 1.1 = \$660$$

A 10% decline in profits, or increase in losses, would be represented by a .9 factor.

I should caution that building in such a qualification is subjective, particularly if the new information is based on relatively short-term results, such as a quarterly income statement. But it may be useful in evaluating potential creditors and accounts with which a vendor has done some business in the past. The vendor, of course, is also free to introduce other interpolations into the equation, such as a "management capability" index to qualify the account's prospects in the event of a change of management or departure of a key employee. Needless to say, this calculation would be even more subjective than the "profitability" index.

Credit as a Sales Tool

Most companies look on credit as a service to their customers, but often it can be used to cultivate demand and promote sales. The question to be asked is: How much does the company stand to gain by making the sale versus how much it will lose if the account is not collected? My previous analysis suggests that a major consideration in granting credit should be the contribution to overhead and profits of the products to be sold. This is quite different from present credit policies that place the emphasis solely on the customer's ability to pay. But if maximum profits are the objective, the contribution of the various products should be a factor in the credit-granting decision.

If a product has a relatively high gross profit margin, it can, and should, be sold to higher credit risks than products with a lower contribution to overhead and profits. This will create a situation where some products could be sold to a certain account while other products should not be sold to that account. However, the situation will also be created where the sales force can sell selected products or product lines to customers to whom they were not able to sell previously—because of their poor credit rating. The new accounts will increase the company's sales and profits; and as these accounts improve their credit rating, the sales force will be able to sell other products to them. Without this initial "foot in the door," in a situation where a prospect's credit improves, the salesman could lose the opportunity to service the account, possibly because the competition has the account "sewn up" or because the prospect is unwilling to do business with a company that previously would not extend him credit.

Another consideration is the fact that often the only competitive advantage a company has is its credit terms. If, as is often the case, its competitors' products can do the job equally well, cost about the same, and have comparable service arrangements, the credit terms can decide who makes the sale.

Many companies with seasonal business operate at or near capacity during only part of the year. But they often deem it necessary to retain key staff (or complete staff) to ensure the availability of a good labor force for future needs. The labor costs (or at least part of them) in the products produced during periods of excess capacity, for the sake of the credit-granting decision, should be included as fixed expenses. This would allow credit to be used in expanding markets by granting it to riskier accounts, since the marginal costs would be lower than with products made during "normal" times.

Aggressive companies often provide for a certain cost for credit (that is, losses), just as they do for advertising and for personal selling, in launching a new product or stimulating increased sales. In such cases they can concede a credit cost for demand cultivation and can control the cost by building it into their marginal cost. Consider this example:

The management of Company A decides that it would be less expensive to develop demand for a new product by granting easy credit than by putting the same amount of money into advertising. It budgets $100,000 for this purpose to sell 10,000 units in the first year. One half of the units can be sold to good credit accounts, but the remainder must be sold to poorer credit risks. The company apportions the "promotional" dollars to the 5,000 units to be sold to the high-risk accounts ($20 per unit). In calculating whether credit should be granted to a particular account, if the expected value of the marginal revenue is not less than $20 below the marginal cost, credit should be granted. (Another way to establish the cut-off point for credit is to subtract the $20 from the marginal cost side of the equation.)

This approach may be taken in other situations, such as sales maximization, with a minimum level of profit. Here management should calculate the desired profit level and then figure the sales necessary to reach that level. If the company raises its sales target, the contribution from sales above the amount calculated to reach the desired profit level could be spent entirely on promotional activities, with credit allocated its share of this amount.

This proposed method of credit analysis requires a great deal of cooperation among the vendor's departments. The production and accounting departments must furnish the credit and marketing departments with figures on the marginal costs involved in turning out the various products. The sales department must supply the credit department with data on present and potential customers, including their financial position and the caliber of management, and frequently the sales force can venture predictions on the future of these companies. Before a salesman approaches a prospect, he must know the possibility of collecting on the account.

The production department often can be a key factor in imaginative use of credit. For example, the sales force may feel that a product has great potential, but sales have fallen short as the result of a credit constraint caused by high variable costs and relatively low chances of collecting on the accounts. Furnished with a forecast of how many more units could be sold at different variable cost figures, production may be able to reduce marginal costs by investing in more specialized equipment. Of course this would raise the capital investment, but it also would permit credit to be granted to more customers.

Conclusion

Sophisticated management should regard the credit function as a promotional tool as well as a financial tool, and should judge the performance of this function as efficient only when these two aspects are brought into a balance that will maximize profits. It should be an obligation of the credit department to analyze credit risks according to the probability of payment, in relation to the increased cost to the company of producing the goods for those accounts. Companies making creative use of credit will become more aggressive competitors in keeping and expanding their shares of markets.

Exercises

16.1. Davinson Company is evaluating its credit policy (See Table 16.1).

A breakdown of the "bad accounts" revealed that of the $140,000 in sales, variable costs amounted to $80,000, of which $55,000 were in manufacturing and $25,000 in marketing.

1. What would net profit before taxes have been if Davinson Company had not sold to the "bad accounts"? (Assume that it would have been possible to identify these accounts before sales were completed.)
2. What would the contribution to overhead and profits have been had the $140,000 been collected?
3. What is the actual dollar loss Davinson Company incurred as a result of the bad debt?
4. Davinson Company estimates that if it tightens credit to customers in cases where the expected value of the marginal revenue is greater than the marginal cost of the sales, total sales will decrease by 5%, while bad debts will decrease by 50%. Assuming that the respective costs will decrease proportionally—except selling and administrative expenses, which will remain at the same level—should credit be tightened as proposed?

16.2. Davinson Company's records show that three customers account for more than 50% of the total bad debt. Customer A accounts for $35,000, customer B for $30,000, and customer C for $25,000. The company would like to eliminate some

TABLE 16.1. *Davinson Company income statement 1980*

Sales	$1,500,000
Cost of goods sold	850,000
Gross margin	$ 650,000
Selling, general and administrative expense	$ 400,000
Bad debt expenses	$ 140,000
Net income (before taxes)	$ 110,000

of these accounts and thus reduce its losses due to bad debts. Based on the data that appear in Exhibits 1, 2, and 3, which account(s) do you recommend that the company drop, and why?

EXHIBIT 1: *Customer A Profile*

Family-owned business. Strong but old president. Succession problems foreseeable.
   Total tangible assets valued at $30,000 (net of depreciation); liability claims of $45,000. Davinson's MC in this sale was $20,000.
   While there is 100% certainty that 67% of the net value of the assets or $20,000 can be obtained, there is only a 60% chance of getting more than $22,000, a 40% chance of selling for at least $24,000, a 25% chance of getting more than $26,000, a 10% chance of getting more than $28,000, and a zero probability of selling for more than $30,000.

EXHIBIT 2: *Customer B Profile*

Small firm. Young management.
   Total tangible assets valued at $50,000 (net of depreciation); liability claims of $60,000; minimum cash value of the assets, $40,000.
   Davinson's marginal cost in this sale was $17,000.
   Davinson estimates that there is a 70% chance of getting more than $42,000 for the assets, a 45% probability of selling them for at least $45,000, a 20% chance of obtaining at least $47,000, a 5% chance of getting at least $49,000, and a zero probability of selling them for more than $50,000.

EXHIBIT 3: *Customer C Profile*

A drug manufacturing company in the process of expanding.
   Total tangible assets valued at $100,000 (net of depreciation); minimum cash value of the assets, $80,000; liability claims of $150,000.
   Davinson's marginal cost in this sale was $14,000.
   There is a 70% chance of getting more than $85,000 for the assets, a 50% chance of selling them for at least $90,000, a 30% probability of getting more than $95,000, a 15% chance of selling them for at least $98,000, and a zero probability of selling them for more than $100,000.

1. What is the expected value of the extra amount to be obtained above the minimum sales price of the assets in each case?
2. Calculate the most likely value to be obtained from the sale of the assets in each case.
3. What is the EV of the MR for Davinson Company in each case?

A Flexible Approach to Determining Financial Terms of Sale

17

Michael Levy   Dwight Grant

Recent articles [1, 2] state that many companies are experiencing a slowdown in the payment of bills by their customers. Higher interest rates and pressures created by inflation are cited as the main reasons for this change in customer payment patterns. By forgoing traditional discounts for early payments,[1] customers increase their use of their suppliers' funds as a source of capital; this is occurring with increasing frequency. Customers are opting for the second of the two alternatives, late payment of the full amount of the invoice, rather than early payment with a discount. This change in the traditional payment pattern has both negative and positive effects. It increases the time that the seller is a lender and the interest expense associated with that activity. On the other hand, the buyer pays more by forgoing the discount. This article considers the trade-off between these effects and illustrates how terms of sale can be used as an element of a firm's logistics and marketing strategy.[2] More specifically, a method of setting terms is described such that the seller receives the same "real" price, but the buyers are given a choice of terms, some of which are likely to be better than those they are currently being offered. The second objective is to provide buyers with a rational approach for choosing among the terms alternatives offered by suppliers.

Setting Terms

The following discussion first briefly describes previous approaches to establishing financial terms of sale. An approach for offering a set of alternative terms is then described. Guidelines for establishing minimum and maximum payment periods are described and the section closes with suggestions for determining when and by how much terms should be changed when there are changes in the environment.

Background

Several papers have proposed procedures for establishing optimal terms policies from the seller's point of view. For example, a model developed by Beranek [4]

Reprinted by permission of the publisher from *Industrial Marketing Management*, Vol. 10, pp. 11–16. Copyright 1981 by Elsevier North Holland, Inc.

[1] Typical of these discounts are 2/10/net 30. In this case the buyer may take a 2% cash discount from the stated invoice price if payment is made on or before the tenth day following the date of invoice. If the buyer does not pay by that date, the full invoice price is due on the thirtieth day.

[2] A theoretical presentation of the arguments found here is Ref. 3.

utilizes classical economic pricing theory. For financial terms of sale policy to be profitable to the seller, the elasticity of demand with respect to "terms" must increase demand sufficiently to overcome the lower per unit profit resulting from the cash discount and the extended payment period. Other papers have focused on the present value of cash flows approach. Anderson [5] discusses this question particularly in terms of the measurement of risk and the interface between marketing and finance. In another recent analysis, Hill and Riener [6] developed a more detailed approach to the determination of a cash discount policy. Their model employs a net present value approach to determine the maximum feasible cash discount given: the timing of payments, change in sales, variable costs, the proportion of sales expected to be paid with a discount, the bad debt loss rate, and the seller's cost of funds. Their approach can be used to develop an optimal cash discount if the functional relationships between the size of the cash discount and the other factors just listed can be established. This and other articles [5, 7–11] tend to concentrate on the individual seller's decision without regard to the potential actions and reactions of the buyers. Ignoring or failing to specify the environment in which the sale occurs and the circumstances of the buyers is a potentially important omission.

Defining a Set of Terms

An attempt by the seller to implement a financial terms of sale policy without regard to the buyer may cause that buyer to become disenchanted. The seller should then develop an optimal cash price and determine a terms of sale policy such that he will receive the same present value of revenue whether it is a cash sale or a sale with payment on the tenth day, thirteenth day, or any other. Buyers can then choose the most beneficial terms option from their perspective. Sellers will receive equal present value if they systematically adjust the cash discount percentage and the discount period (the number of days that are allowed the buyer before the discount invoice is due for payment) to reflect the appropriate cost of funds. This cost relates to both the riskiness of the customer and the length of the credit period. That is, the riskier the receivable and the longer the credit period, the higher the cost of offering credit will be. This cost of funds will be referred to as the "cost of capital."

Examine a situation in which a firm sells a product for $100 and offers terms of 2%/10 days/net 30. If payment is made on the 10th day, and the cost of capital is 15% annual or 0.04% per day, the present value revenue of the $100 sale is calculated using the following simple net present value formula:

$$PV = 100(1 - x)/(1 + i)^n, \tag{1}$$

where PV is present value; x is the discount, in decimal form, which is applicable on the nth day; and i is the cost of capital per day. Using this formula, the present value is 97.61. Since the firm wants to realize the same net present value for other

FIGURE 1. Equal net present value discount/discount period combinations

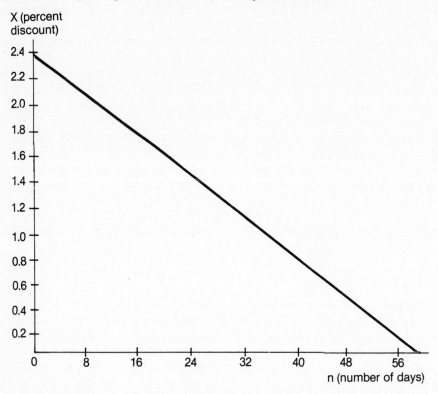

discount/payment date combinations, we can rearrange the formula to solve for the cash discount (x) for any payment date:

$$x = 1 - (PV(1 + i)^n/100). \qquad (2)$$

For example, if we want to receive the same net present value with a 5-day discount period, we could offer a 2.2% cash discount. Likewise, we could offer a 2.4% discount for payment on the invoice date, or no discount and payment in full on day 60. In fact, there are an unlimited number of discount/payment date combinations, some of which are illustrated along the curve in Fig. 1. The slope of this curve is determined by the cost of capital.

The Earliest Discount Period

The seller must define the range of discount periods to reflect both logistics and financial risk considerations. The earliest discount period is defined by the seller's logistics system. It is possible for a seller to create and mail an invoice as early as the date an order is received. However, the elapsed time from receipt of the purchase order by the seller until the merchandise is received by the buyer could extend from several days to several weeks, depending upon his logistics system. The seller must then start the discount period after the buyer has a chance to receive the merchandise.

Rationale for Limited Credit Extension

The example developed earlier indicated that the seller would get the same net present value for a sale given a 2%/10 day policy or no discount with payment due on the sixtieth day. Then is there any rationale for the prevalent terms which end at 30 days? Should the seller be granting terms of 60 days or even longer? To answer these questions, we must consider the risk associated with granting terms. Because the goods sold will provide collateral protection only for the length of one inventory turnover period of the buyer, the seller will be unwilling to finance the buyer much beyond the time the goods are resold. This provides a natural limit to the period over which credit is extended.

In fact, the influence of risk may be more gradual but even more important than just suggested. Later payment is likely to be viewed by sellers, and by their sources of capital, as creating a higher level of risk. First, there is the simple reality that there is more time for adverse incidents to occur the longer an account is outstanding. In addition, the seller may view the buyer's delay of payment as a signal indicating a lower degree of credit worthiness than was originally assumed. This is particularly true if the buyer is offered a generous inducement, as is the case with 2/10/net 30 which provides an implicit annual return of 36%,[3] to pay early but declines. If risk does increase with the time elapsed before payment is received, then the seller's cost of capital will also increase.

This impact is illustrated by modifying Fig. 1 appropriately in Fig. 2. The curve becomes steeper as the number of days before payment is received increases because the seller increases i, the cost of capital per day in Equation (1), to reflect the increased risk.

When and How Much to Change Terms

The seller should adjust terms to reflect changes in the cost of funds caused by the economic environment. To avoid creating ill will, new policies should be implemented prior to rather than in response to any substantial change in the payment pattern of customers. Otherwise, the seller will be perceived as trying to coerce the buyers to reverse their late payment behavior rather than encouraging them to maintain their previous patterns. Currently it appears that many sellers are not adjusting terms to reflect higher costs of funds. Therefore, buyers are taking advantage of the fact that inflation and high interest rates have made it relatively

---

[3] This is based on the simple interest approach that 2% for 20 days is equivalent to $2(360/20) = 36\%$ for 360 days, or 1 year.

FIGURE 2. *Discount/discount period combinations reflecting changing risk*

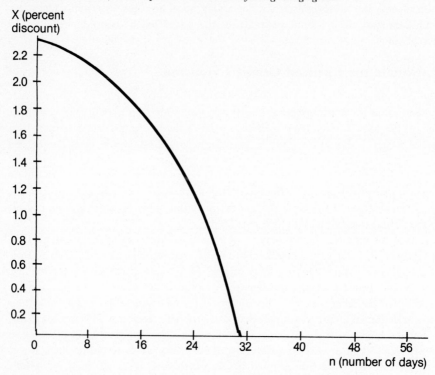

more advantageous to forgo the early payment discount and delay payment. Although sellers are bemoaning this situation, in the future they can anticipate and avoid the problem. Since the high interest rates that encourage late payment are tied to inflation, the seller should incorporate more generous terms into a price increase occasioned by inflation.

To illustrate this simultaneous price/terms adjustment, consider the following example. A firm has been offering terms of 2/10, 1.7/15, 1.3/20, 0.8/25, and net 30. Thus a $100 purchase can be paid for with $98 at day 10, $98.30 at day 15, or $100 at day 30. All of these terms are perceived as having identical worth[4] by the seller. That is, they are all on a curve similar to that depicted in Fig. 2. For the periods day 10–15, 15–20, 20–25, and 25–30, the implicit annual interest costs of delaying payment are 21.6%, 28.8%, 36%, and 50.4%, respectively.[5] Note that the

---

[4] By "identical worth" we mean that the seller views all of these terms equally, but they do not have the same net present values, since the increased risk of extending the payment period is reflected in a higher cost of capital.
[5] Each of these values is calculated in the same way. By paying at day 15 instead of day 10, a customer forgoes a 0.3% discount for 5 days. Using the simple interest approximation, this is equivalent to an annual rate of 0.3(360/5) = 21.6%.

costs of delaying payment increase sharply, to reflect a perception of increased risk as payment is delayed.

Suppose that the seller's cost of capital increases in response to inflation and higher interest rates. The terms should be adjusted to reflect that change and done so in a way that will minimize hard feelings from customers. Since prices will be increased to reflect the effects of inflation, the seller can simultaneously increase prices and also increase the discount for early payment in such a way as to achieve both a higher cash price and increasingly less attractive terms as payment periods get longer. This can be illustrated by extending the example. Let the desired increase in price at day 10 be 8.9%. The seller can increase its price for $100 of goods to $110 and also improve terms to 3/10, 2.5/15, 1.8/20, 1.0/25, and net 30 (compared to the 2/10, 1.7/15, 1.3/20, 0.8/25, and net 30 offered previously). Thus, if payment is made at day 10, the firm will receive $106.70, which is approximately 8.9% more than $98, the former day 10 price. Furthermore, the costs of forgoing discounts are now significantly higher, i.e., 36%, 50.4%, 57.6%, and 72% for the periods day 10–15, 15–20, 20–25, and 25–30, respectively. Therefore, the customers are further induced to pay early. In effect, the price increase was "higher" than desired, but this "excess" is offset by the "more generous" terms.

Taking Terms

Up to this point we have concentrated on the seller's terms strategy. Since the second stated objective of this paper was to provide buyers with a rational approach for choosing among the terms alternatives offered by suppliers, our attention is now turned to this problem.

Assuming the buyer's cost of capital is different from that of the seller, the net present value for the alternative terms will also be different. This assumption is reasonable if the seller is a large publicly owned firm and the buyer is a small privately owned firm that suffers inferior access to capital markets. In this case, the buyer's cost of capital would probably be higher than that of the seller. For example, the large company can raise money by issuing commercial paper, additional equity, or by borrowing from large groups of city banks. On the other hand, the small private concern may be restricted to a set of local banks and may avoid equity issues because of control considerations.

For ease of discussion, let us continue with the example developed previously in which the seller has just taken a price increase and changed terms to the more advantageous 3/10, 2.5/15, 1.8/20, 1.0/25, and net 30. Assume the buyer's cost of capital is twice that of the seller, that is, 0.08% per day or approximately 30% annually. Using Equation (1), the net present values of $100 of sales are $96.22, $96.34, $96.64, $97.04, and $97.63 for terms of 3/10, 2.5/15, 1.8/20, 1.0/25, and net 30 respectively. Terms of 3/10 clearly offer the buyer the lowest cost purchase.

Now let's consider another set of terms from another firm. Assume this company is offering 2/10, 1.6/20, 0.5/30, and net 31. The present value of these terms for a firm with a 30% cost of capital (0.08%/day) is $97.22, $96.83, $97.11, and $97.55, respectively. In this case the 1.6/20 day terms are most attractive, since the present value is lower than the other three alternatives.

Using the net present value formula in Equation (1), buyers can evaluate any set of terms and choose the discount/payment period combination which has the lowest present value cost. This procedure can also be used to evaluate vendors. For example, if two firms are selling products which are virtually identical in every aspect except for price and terms, that is, a commodity, then buyers can rationally choose the vendor offering the lowest present value cost.

Conclusion

A net present value approach has been described for setting terms of sale. A set of terms should be offered to customers, each having the same value to the seller, but offering a choice to the buyer. The shortest payment period in the terms policy should be of sufficient duration so that buyers may receive the merchandise before it is due for payment. The duration of the payment period should be influenced by the additional risk associated with extending credit much beyond one inventory turnover period of the buyer. In light of the current economic siutation in which we see high interest rates and rapid price escalations, sellers can use financial terms of sale as an integral element of a firm's pricing strategy. The impact of price increases can be softened and at the same time customers can be induced to pay early. Finally, customers can rationally choose between various terms policies by isolating the lowest net present value price offered.

References

1. Signs of a Slow-Pay Syndrome, *Business Week*, p. 60 (July 23, 1979).
2. Slump Leads Firms to Lag in Paying Bills; Creditors Try Range of Strategies to Cope, *The Wall Street Journal*, p. 42 (June 25, 1980).
3. Levy, Michael, and Grant, Dwight, Financial Terms of Sale and Control of Marketing Channel Conflict, *Journal of Marketing Research* 17, 524–530 (November 1980).
4. Beranek, William, *Analysis for Financial Decisions*, Richard D. Irwin, Homewood, IL, 1963.
5. Anderson, Paul F., The Marketing Management/Finance Interface, *1979 Educators' Conference Proceedings*, American Marketing Association, Chicago, 1979, pp. 325–29.
6. Hill, Ned C., and Riener, Kenneth D., Determining the Cash Discount in the Firm's Credit Policy, *Financial Management* 8, 68–73 (Spring 1979).
7. Atkins, J., and Kim, Y., Comment and Correction: Opportunity Cost in the Evaluation of Investment in Accounts Receivable, *Financial Management* 6, 71–74 (Winter 1977).
8. Dyl, E., Another Look at the Evaluation of Investment in Accounts Receivable, *Financial Management* 6, 66–70 (Winter 1977).
9. Kim, Y., and Atkins, J., Evaluating Investments in Accounts Receivable: A Maximizing Framework, *Journal of Finance* 33, 405–12 (May 1978).

10. Walia, T., Explicit and Implicit Cost of Changes in the Level of Accounts Receivable and the Credit Policy Decision of the Firm, *Financial Management* **6**, 75–78 (Winter 1977).
11. Wrightsman, D., Optimal Credit Terms for Accounts Receivable, *Quarterly Review of Economics and Business* **9**, 59–66 (Summer 1972).

Exercises

17.1. The purchasing agent for the J. T. Forging Company of Fort Worth has received bids to supply her firm with $\frac{3}{4}''$ steel bars. She believes that the competing firms will provide steel of identical quality, and that they are equally prompt in delivering their products. Consequently, their bids differ primarily with regard to price. The Ocat Steel Company has offered to sell the steel for $200 per ton. The terms are 2/10/net 30. Yoder Steel has bid $198 per ton and offers terms of 0.75/5/net 30.

According to the vice-president for finance of J. T. Forging, the purchasing agent should consider her cost of capital to be 20% per year.

1. What is the effective cost of capital per day if it is 20% per year?
2. Find the present value cost of each payment alternative.
3. From which company should J. T. Forging buy its steel? Would you take the discount? Why?
4. If you purchased from the other company, would you take the discount? Compare this decision with that made in question 3 and explain the difference.

17.2. Yoder Steel Manufacturing Company is offering $\frac{3}{4}''$ steel bars for $198 per ton with terms of 1/5/net 30. A major competitor, Ocat Steel Company, is currently pricing its $\frac{3}{4}''$ steel bars at $200 per ton with terms of 2/10/net 30. The sales manager of Yoder Steel is convinced that his product is of identical quality, and his firm is providing equally prompt delivery as Ocat Steel. However, he has noticed a trend for his customers to switch to Ocat Steel. Yoder's sales manager believes he can counter this trend by offering an extended-payment option to his customers because he thinks his cost of funds is lower than his customers' and his competitors'. He estimates his customers' cost of funds at 0.05% per day.

1. What cost of capital per day is implied by the terms Yoder is currently offering?
2. If Yoder accepts payment on day 60, what should be the company's price of steel if we assume that the cost of capital does not change? Is this a good assumption? Explain your view.
3. If Yoder offered the price you estimated in question 2, would the customer choose it?
4. If Yoder knew the size of its customers' cost of capital, what prices would it offer at days 5, 10, 30, and 60, in order to be competitive with Ocat Steel? What is the worth to Yoder, in present value terms, of each of these prices? Briefly discuss the relationships you observe and relate them to question 2 above.

Industrial Lease Marketing 18

Paul F. Anderson   William Lazer

More than 30 years ago, Russell B. McNeill warned readers of the *Harvard Business Review*:

> There is danger ... that adequate attention may not be given to one marketing device, not customarily considered, which is particularly useful in the distribution of many kinds of equipment: the lease or rental agreement...[1]

That statement was prophetic. While leasing, particularly financial leasing, has become an important technique in marketing industrial equipment, scholarly investigation and research have not kept pace.

While solid statistics on the volume of industrial leasing do not exist, Brigham estimates that equipment leasing grew at a rate of 30% a year during the decade of the 1950's.[2] Estimates for 1975 place the original cost value of industrial equipment on lease in the neighborhood of $80 billion.[3] The current annual rate of growth in leasing is estimated to be 15% to 20%,[4] and it is predicted that approximately one-fifth of all new capital equipment acquired in 1977 will be leased.[5] While the majority of these leases will be written by manufacturing firms, independent and bank lessors are expected to account for a growing proportion.

Types of Leases

A lease may be defined as a contract by which the owner of an asset (the lessor) grants the right to use the asset for a given term to another party (the lessee) in return for a periodic payment of rent. Leases may be grouped into two broad categories, financial leases (also called full-payout leases) and operating leases:

Reprinted by permission from the *Journal of Marketing*, Vol. 42 (January 1978), pp. 71–79, published by the American Marketing Association.

[1] Russell B. McNeill, "The Lease as a Marketing Tool," *Harvard Business Review*, Vol. 22 (Summer 1944), pg. 415.
[2] Eugene F. Brigham, "The Impact of Bank Entry on Market Conditions in the Equipment Leasing Industry," *National Banking Review*, Vol. 2 (September 1964), pg. 12.
[3] Telephone interview with Mr. Thomas W. Eck, Assistant Executive Secretary, American Association of Equipment Lessors, July 28, 1976; Frost & Sullivan, *Equipment Leasing Market*, Report No. 382 (New York: 1976).
[4] Ibid.
[5] Peter Vanderwicken, "The Powerful Logic of the Leasing Boom," *Fortune*, Vol. 88 (November 1973), pg. 136.

Financial leases are typically long- or intermediate-term, noncancellable contracts which are fully amortized over their basic term (i.e., the sum of the lease payments equals or exceeds the original purchase price of the asset). Generally, the lessee pays all of the operating expenses of the equipment and assumes all liabilities connected with its use. Under competitive pressures, however, the lessor may be induced to cover such operating costs as insurance, maintenance, and property taxes. Financial leases frequently include a purchase option which may be exercised at the termination of the contract. In most cases, the agreement will stipulate the purchase option price as the asset's fair market value at the end of the lease term.

Operating leases are usually short-term, cancellable contracts which are not fully amortized. In an operating lease, the lessor assumes most or all of the expenses and liabilities associated with ownership of the equipment. This type of lease usually does not include a purchase option. Its primary purpose is to provide the lessee with equipment which is only needed for short periods of time. Rates on operating leases are generally high relative to financial leases in order to compensate the lessor for assuming the operating costs and the risks of obsolescence. Our focus is on *financial* leases.

Financial Context

The existing literature on leasing is sadly outdated, and the conventional wisdom of early research has remained largely unchallenged.[6] Contemporary authors simply repeat the conclusions of prior researchers.[7] The result, unfortunately, is a literature which is both inadequate and inaccurate.

Published articles on lease marketing have two main limitations: *First*, they fail to recognize that the full-payout lease is essentially a financial device whose benefits are primarily economic. *Second*, they fail to recognize the true nature of the potential economic advantages of financial leases and, instead, tend to focus on questionable benefits.

This misdirection stems largely from unwillingness, or inability, to analyze leasing within the context of contemporary financial theory. Many of the so-called

---

[6] McNeill, same as reference 1 above, pp. 415–30; Francis A. Babione, "Marketing Equipment by Leasing," Ph.D. dissertation, Ohio State University, 1949; Wilford John Eiteman and Charles N. Davisson, *The Lease as a Financing and Selling Device* (Ann Arbor: School of Business Administration, University of Michigan, 1951); Bruce E. MacNab, "The Lease as a Device to Market Equipment," M.B.A. thesis, Ohio State University, 1959; Alvin J. Bytwork, "The Effectiveness of Alternatives to Purchase in the Marketing of Construction Equipment Through Distributors," Ph.D. dissertation, Michigan State University, 1959; Peter D. Bennett, *Marketing Aspects of Capital Equipment Leasing* (Austin, TX: Bureau of Business Research, University of Texas, 1961); and R. A. Perkins, "Leasing as a Marketing Tool," in *Leasing of Industrial Equipment* (Washington, D.C.: Machinery and Allied Products Institute, 1965), pp. 40–51.

[7] William J. Stanton, *Fundamentals of Marketing*, 4th ed. (New York: McGraw-Hill Book Company, 1975), pp. 154–55; Thomas A. Staudt, Donald A. Taylor, and Donald J. Bowersox, *A Managerial Introduction to Marketing*, 3rd ed. (Englewood Cliffs, NJ: Prentice-Hall, 1976), pp. 434–35; Richard M. Hill, Ralph S. Alexander, and James S. Cross, *Industrial Marketing*, 4th ed. (Homewood, IL: Richard D. Irwin, 1975), pp. 231–32; George Risley, *Modern Industrial Marketing* (New York: McGraw-Hill Book Company, 1972), pp. 217–18; and J. H. Westing, I. V. Fine, and Gary J. Zenz, *Purchasing Management*, 4th ed. (Santa Barbara, CA: Wiley-Hamilton, 1976), pp. 504–7.

"non-financial" advantages of leasing simply do not hold up in the face of the empirical and theoretical findings of finance.[8]

A Product Augmentation Strategy

Since industrial equipment manufacturers have the option of leasing indirectly through an independent or bank lessor, why would they become involved in the direct leasing of their products? The answer seems fairly straightforward. Leasing broadens a company's product and services offering and expands its opportunity for profit.

When a manufacturer sells an industrial product, the customer is provided with a different set of benefits than he can receive if he leases the same product. For any given product, the physical attributes, the use services, and the acquisition services are the same for both leasing and purchasing. The critical difference between the two lies in the financial services provided. A lease arrangement has the potential to provide the lessee with economic benefits not available through outright purchase.

Leasing, then, is a product augmentation strategy.[9] A manufacturer's product and services mix is augmented by the additional benefits, largely economic in nature, available to customers through leasing. To develop a successful lease marketing program, these benefits must be fully understood by manufacturers.

The potential economic benefits of financial leases may be identified by modeling the financial decisions facing both the lessee and the lessor. The model used in this article has been developed in accordance with modern financial theory and represents the culmination of theoretical developments over a period of more than two decades.[10]

Economic Benefits

To understand the lessee's economic benefits, one should consider the nature of the financial decision facing both parties to a lease.[11] In this regard, the lessee and lessor represent different sides of the same coin. This is demonstrated by the two decision equations shown in Exhibit 1. The lessee's decision should be based on the present value sum of the costs and benefits of the lease. The costs of the lease include the

---

[8] This is not to say, however, that some firms do not consider "non-financial" issues in making leasing decisions. Recent research suggests that these factors may play a part in the leasing decisions of some corporations. See Paul F. Anderson and Monroe M. Bird, "The Industrial Leasing Decision," Working Paper, Virgina Polytechnic Institute and State University, 1977.

[9] Theodore Levitt, *Marketing for Business Growth* (New York: McGraw-Hill Book Company, 1974), pg. 14.

[10] For a review of the literature on lease versus purchase models, see Anderson, same as Note above.

[11] This section owes much to Timothy J. Nantell, "Lessor's Pricing Decision, An Indifference Theorem, and the Evaluation of Lease vs. Buy Algorithms," paper presented at the Financial Management Association meetings, Montreal, Canada, October 1976; Merton H. Miller and Charles W. Upton, "Leasing, Buying and the Cost of Capital Services," *Journal of Finance*, Vol. 31 (June 1976), pp. 761–86; Wilbur G. Lewellen, Michael S. Long, and John J. McConnell, "Asset Leasing in Competitive Capital Markets," *Journal of Finance*, Vol. 31 (June 1976), pp. 787–98; and Stewart C. Myers, David A. Dill, and Alberto J. Bautista, "Valuation of Financial Lease Contracts," *Journal of Finance*, Vol. 31 (June 1976), pp. 799–819.

EXHIBIT 1. *The lessee and lessor decision models*

Equation 1: The lessee's lease versus purchase decision model

$$NAL = A - PV_r(R) - PV_r(tD) + PV_r(tR)$$
$$- PV_r(tI) + PV_r(C) - PV_r(tC) - PV_k(V_n)$$

where

NAL	= the net present value advantage of the lease,
A	= the cash purchase of the asset,
PV_r	= an operator representing the present value of a given cash flow at r percent,
PV_k	= an operator representing the present value of a given cash flow at k percent,
n	= the lease term in years,
r	= the discount rate appropriate to the risk of the respective cash flows,
k	= the discount rate appropriate to the risk of the after-tax salvage value,
R	= the annual lease payments,
t	= the lessee's marginal income tax rate,
tD	= the tax shield provided by the annual depreciation expense,
tR	= the tax shield provided by the annual lease payments,
tl	= the tax shield provided by the annual interest charges on a loan used to finance the purchase,
C	= the portion of the annual pre-tax operating costs of the equipment which will be paid by the lessor,
tC	= the tax shield provided by the operating costs, and
V_n	= the expected after-tax salvage value of the equipment at the end of year n.

Equation 2: The lessor's pricing model

$$NRL = -A' + PV_r(R') + PV_r(t'D') - PV_r(t'R')$$
$$+ PV_r(t'I') - PV_r(C') + PV_r(t'C') + PV_k(V'_n)$$

where the primes over the previously defined variables represent flows to the lessor, and

NRL	= the net present value return to the lessor
A'	= the cost of the asset to the lessor (for a manufacturer lessor, this would be his opportunity cost, i.e., the asset's purchase price),
t'	= the lessor's marginal income tax rate,
t'R'	= the taxes payable on the lease revenue

---

lease payments cash outflow; the forgone tax shields resulting from depreciation, interest and operating expenses; and the sacrifice of the asset's salvage value.

Only the lease payments represent an out-of-pocket cash flow. The others are opportunity costs. They represent cash inflows or cash savings which would be available only if the firm purchased the asset; thus, they are forgone if the firm decides to lease. For example, the tax shields represent the reduction in income tax liabilities resulting from the fact that depreciation, interest, and operating costs are deductible expenses under the present Internal Revenue Code.[12]

The benefits of the lease include the avoidance of the cash purchase cost of the asset and the operating expenses absorbed by the lessor, as well as the tax shield

---

[12] Prentice-Hall 1975 Federal Taxes, par. 11,005.

provided by the lease payments. A positive net present value advantage to leasing (NAL > 0) indicates that the cash flow benefits of the lease exceed its cash flow costs. The lessee's decision rule, then, is to lease the asset if NAL > 0 (assuming that such an investment is sound from a capital budgeting standpoint).

The lessor's decision model is simply the mirror image of the lessee's model. Since cash outflows faced by the lessee are cash inflows faced by the lessor, and vice versa, the lessor's return computation is just the lessee's present value equation with the signs reversed (see Exhibit 1). This is, in effect, the lessor's pricing model. The lessor's task in pricing is to set the lease rate such that the net present value return of the lease (NRL) is maximized, subject to the constraints imposed by competition in the capital markets. On the other hand, the lessee's task, given this rate, is to decide whether to lease or purchase.

Portraying the two decision tasks in this form allows us to pinpoint the sources of potential benefits to the lessee. There are actually two major categories of potential economic benefits. The first results from cash flow savings which are available to the lessor but not to the lessee. If the lessor chooses to pass on all or a portion of these savings in a reduced lease rate, the lessee will lower his acquisition costs by leasing rather than purchasing. The second source of economic benefits results from differential expectations as between the lessor and lessee.

Cash Flow Savings

The first potential cash flow savings may result if the lessor's acquisition cost, A′ in Equation (2), is less than the acquisition cost to the lessee, A in Equation (1). This could occur because of quantity discounts available to non-manufacturer lessors, or because of a tax benefit available to the lessor but not the lessee. An example of the latter is the investment tax credit (ITC).

Sharing Tax Credit

Because the ITC represents a credit against a tax liability, firms with low or heavily sheltered earnings may not have sufficient taxable income to use the full amount of the credit if they purchase a piece of equipment. Moreover, the Internal Revenue Code places a limit on the amount of the credit which may be taken in any one year.[13] On the other hand, a lessor may be able to utilize the full amount of the credit and thereby lower the effective acquisition cost of the asset. To the extent that this saving is passed on in a lower lease rate, an economic benefit accrues to the lessee.

A numerical example will be employed to demonstrate this potential advantage. Two cases will be considered. In the first, the indifference case, it is assumed that

---

[13] Prentice-Hall Federal Tax Course 1976, par. 2050 (1976).

the lessor and lessee face identical cash flows and employ identical discount rates in calculating their net present values. In the second case, the impact of the investment tax credit is considered.

The following values are assumed for the indifference computations:

$$\begin{aligned}
\text{Purchase Price} &= A = A' = \$15,000 \\
\text{Lease Rate} &= R = R' = \$4,200 \text{ per year} \\
\text{Lessor's Costs} &= C = C' = \$1,600 \text{ per year} \\
\text{After-Tax Salvage} &= V_n = V'_n = \$1,119
\end{aligned}$$

It is further assumed that the lease term is five years and that the lessee and lessor will both fully depreciate the asset over this period by employing the sum-of-the-years'-digits method. Purchase financing for both parties is assumed to be a bank term loan in the amount of $15,000, to be repaid over a five-year period at 8% interest. Finally, a risk-adjusted discount rate of 4% (the after-tax cost of debt) is assumed for the contractual lease payments, the tax shields, and the operating expense flows. A risk-adjusted rate of 12% is assumed for the salvage value. (Discount rate determination for lease versus purchase analysis is discussed by Anderson and Martin.)[14]

As can be seen from the calculations for the indifference case in Exhibit 2, when the lessee and lessor face identical cash flows and discount these flows at the same rates, there is no incentive for either party to enter into the transaction. Since the NAL and the NRL are both zero, neither side will gain (or lose) by signing the lease contract. This represents the point of indifference for the lessee and the lessor.

The computations in the bottom portion of Exhibit 2 represent the introduction of the investment tax credit. It is assumed that the lessee has sufficient other income to employ the lease payments' tax shield but is unable to use the tax credit. It is further assumed that the lessor's use of the credit is unencumbered.

Under the present tax laws, the allowable credit for an asset with a five-year useful life is 6.67%.[15] Thus, the total amount of the credit is $15,000 × .067, or $1,000. The present value of this flow to the lessor is $962 (discounted at 4% for one year). As such, the lessor's net acquisition cost is $15,000 − $962, or $14,038.

Now, what happens if the lessor decides to pass on a portion of his $962 savings by lowering the lease rate to $4,100? Both parties to the transaction will gain. The net present value advantage of leasing to the lessee increases from zero to $223. And the lessor will still gain, but by less; his net present value return decreases to $739. Note that the two present values sum to $962—the total advantage available

---

[14] Paul F. Anderson and John D. Martin, "Lease vs. Purchase Decisions: A Survey of Current Practice," *Financial Management*, Vol. 6 (Spring 1977), pp. 41–47; and John D. Martin and Paul F. Anderson, "A Practical Approach to the Lease vs. Purchase Problem," Working Paper, Virginia Polytechnic Institute and State University, 1977. A more theoretical approach is to be found in Lawrence D. Schall, "The Lease-or-Buy and Asset Acquisition Decisions," *Journal of Finance*, Vol. 29 (September 1974), pp. 1203–14.

[15] Tax Course 1976, same as reference 13 above.

EXHIBIT 2. *Numerical example for equations (1) and (2)*

End of year[a]	Purchase price $A = A'$	Lease payments $R = R'$	Depreciation[b] tax effect $tD = t'D'$	Lease payments tax effect $tR = t'R'$	Interest tax effect $tI = t'I'$	Operating costs $C = C'$	Operating costs tax effect $tC = t'C'$	After-tax salvage $V_n = V'_n$
0	$15,000							
1		$ 4,200	$2,500	$ 2,100	$ 600	$1,600	$ 800	
2		4,200	2,000	2,100	498	1,600	800	
3		4,200	1,500	2,100	387	1,600	800	
4		4,200	1,000	2,100	268	1,600	800	
5		4,200	500	2,100	140	1,600	800	$1,119[c]
Total	$15,000	$21,000	$7,500	$10,500	$1,893	$8,000	$4,000	$1,119

Indifference case:

NAL =	+$15,000	−$18,698	−$6,852	+$ 9,349	−$1,725	+$7,122	−$3,561	−$ 635 = 0
NRL =	−$15,000	+$18,698	+$6,852	−$ 9,349	+$1,725	−$7,122	+$3,561	+$ 635 = 0

Investment tax credit case:

NAL =	+$15,000	−$18,252[d]	−$6,852	+$9,126[e]	−$1,725	+$7,122	−$3,561	−$ 635 = $223
NRL =	−$14,038	+$18,252[d]	+$6,852	−$9,126[e]	+$1,725	−$7,122	+$3,561	+$ 635 = $739

[a] All cash flows occur at the end of a year
[b] Tax rate = 50 percent.
[c] Discounted at 12 percent.
[d] PV of $4,100 at 4 percent for 5 years.
[e] PV of $2,050 at 4 percent for 5 years.

as a result of the tax credit. The two parties have simply divided an economic advantage available under the existing tax laws.

In practice, the exact division of any economic advantage will be determined by the relative bargaining power of the parties and the nature of competition in the leasing market. Obviously, the task of the lease marketer is to offer the potential lessee enough of the tax savings to induce him to enter into the lease agreement, but not so much as to reduce the lessor's return below an acceptable level. This may involve some hard bargaining and some careful forecasting on the part of the lessor.

Example: Multimillion Dollar Deal

One of the largest leasing deals ever consummated involved the 1973 acquisition of a $110.7 million aluminum-reduction mill by the Anaconda corporation.[16] Anaconda was motivated to lease the facilities because of a huge loss carry-forward resulting from the expropriation of its Chilean copper mines by the Allende government. The write-off totalled $356.3 million and could be used to offset tax liabilities for ten years. As a result, Anaconda expected low effective tax rates for most of the ten-year period. This meant, of course, that they would be unable to employ the full amount of the investment tax credit or the interest and depreciation tax shields resulting from a purchase of the mill.

Thus, Anaconda began looking for a leasing deal which would allow them to reap the kind of tax advantage demonstrated in Exhibit 2. After almost a year of negotiations, U.S. Leasing International assembled a consortium of five banks (headed by Manufacturers Hanover Trust Company) and a large finance company (Chrysler Financial Corporation) to underwrite the lease. Anaconda acquired the facility on a 20-year lease which called for lease payments totaling $187.4 million. However, because of the tax aspects, the company expected to save $74 million by leasing rather than purchasing.[17] An independent assessment of the lease terms by Myers, Dill, and Bautista supported the firm's contention that it would benefit from the lease.[18] Indeed, their figures suggest that Anaconda was able to extract the majority of the available tax benefits from the lessors.

Of course, calculations on both sides of the transaction are subject to forecast error. An increase in copper prices, a change in corporate tax rates, or a decline in the mill's residual value could all affect the profitability of the transaction. Consequently, lease marketers must build a margin for error into their forecasts and must be sure that this is reflected in the final lease rate which is negotiated.

Tax advantages which lower the lessor's acquisition costs are one of the more

---

[16] Vanderwicken, same as reference 5 above; and Myers, Dill and Bautista, same as reference 11 above.
[17] Vanderwicken, ibid., pg. 136.
[18] Myers, Dill and Bautista, same as reference 11 above, pp. 807–11.

important sources of cash flow benefits in leasing. However, other cash flow savings may also be important.

Sharing Operating Costs

Thus an economic advantage may result if the lessor incurs a portion of the asset's operating costs. In such a situation, it is possible that the operating costs to the lessor, C' in Equation (2), may be less than those which would have to be incurred by the lessee, C in Equation (1). This may occur because the lessor is able to attain economies of scale in the provision of repair, maintenance, and management services for a particular type of equipment or a specific group of lessees. Of course, manufacturer lessors would have a clear advantage over nonmanufacturers in the realization of these economies because of their greater degree of specialization and technical expertise.

Differential Depreciation Periods

Another cash flow benefit can occur if the lessor is able to depreciate the asset over a shorter time period than the lessee. The larger depreciation charges over a shorter period of time will result in a greater depreciation-generated tax saving in the lessor's return equation. Differential depreciation periods could result from a situation in which the lessor uses the lease term as the estimated useful life of the asset while the lessee employs the Class Life Asset Depreciation Range option.

Under the Class Life ADR system, firms are allowed to choose a range of depreciation lives for each type of asset owned by the firm. The Asset Depreciation Ranges are determined by the Internal Revenue Service. Once a firm has elected to use the ADR system for a particular type of equipment, all assets falling within the guideline class must be depreciated under the ADR systems during the year of the election.[19] To the extent that the lessor's depreciation period (the lease term) is less than the ADR, the potential for an economic benefit exists. It is unlikely, however, that a significant advantage could be generated through the use of different depreciation lives.

In most instances, the useful economic life and the ADR life will be very close, and any attempt by the lessor to write off the asset over a period which is substantially less than its useful economic life could be disallowed by the IRS.[20] The lessor should nevertheless be alert to the possibility of differences in depreciation schedules.

Differential Tax Shields

Still another potential benefit of leasing may occur if the interest tax shield available to the lessor $(t'I')$ is greater than the interest tax shield (tI) available to the lessee.

---

[19] Tax Course 1976, same as reference 13 above, par. 2032–34.
[20] Ibid., par. 2000–2005 and 2032.

This will result if the lessor is able to "leverage" the acquisition of the asset to a greater extent than the lessee; that is, if the lessor is able to finance a greater proportion of the asset's cost with debt capital. (This assumes that the lessor and lessee will face similar rates of interest on term loans used to finance the purchase of the asset.)

The lessor may be able to obtain greater leverage because the asset's acquisition may actually lower the financial risk of the firm. Martin and Anderson have demonstrated that a revenue-generating asset may create debt capacity by virtue of the fact that its acquisition affects the level and volatility of the firm's cash flows.[21] That is, the asset may alter the mean and variance of the firm's cash flows in such a way as to reduce the probability of insolvency. If the probability of insolvency is reduced, additional debt may be incurred up to the point at which the risk of insolvency reaches its former level.

Given the fact that the asset generates relatively riskless flows to the lessor and relatively risky flows to the lessee, it is quite possible that the lessor will be able to obtain a leverage advantage vis-à-vis the lessee.

Differential Tax Rates

A final cash flow savings benefit may result if the tax rate of the lessor is higher than that of the lessee. To the extent that these savings are passed on in a lower rental, the lessee benefits. It should be noted, however, that a higher tax rate does not guarantee a cash flow savings for the lessor. While a higher rate increases the taxes which must be paid on the lease revenue $(t'R')$ and any realized gain on the salvage value (V_n'), it also increases the tax shields available from depreciation $(t'D')$, interest $(t'I')$, and operating costs $(t'C')$. Thus, the actual cash flow impact will depend upon the relative magnitude of the flows, the length of the lease, and the discount rates employed.

Generally, given normal lease terms, a higher tax rate will increase the return to the lessor. Where reasonably competitive conditions prevail in the capital markets, there is a good chance that all or part of this tax advantage will be passed on to the lessee. Indeed, competitive pressures should insure that any cash flow savings available to the lessor will be passed on to the lessee.

Benefits from Differential Expectations

The second major category of potential economic benefits results from differential expectations as between the lessor and lessee.

---

[21] John D. Martin and Paul F. Anderson, "Financial Risk, Debt Capacity and the Lease vs. Purchase Decision," Working Paper, Virginia Polytechnic Institute and State University, September 1976; and John D. Martin and David F. Scott, Jr., "Debt Capacity and the Capital Budgeting Decision," *Financial Management*, Vol. 5 (Summer 1976), pp. 7–13.

Forecasting Salvage Value

In determining his net return, the lessor may forecast a higher salvage value than the lessee. To the extent that his salvage value estimate exceeds that of the lessee, the lessor will anticipate a higher return on his investment. This, in turn, will allow him to reduce his rental charge to the lessee.

Manufacturer lessors, in particular, may be able to capitalize on this advantage because of their specialized knowledge of the leased equipment. In addition to their superior ability to forecast the secondary market, manufacturers may be able to realize economies of scale in the reconditioning and sale of the asset once its original lease terminates. Indeed, they may be able to extend the useful economic life of a piece of equipment through a combination of expert maintenance and marketing.[22]

Perception of Risk

A related advantage can occur if the lessor perceives less risk in the salvage value cash flow than the lessee. In accordance with contemporary financial theory, the discount rates in Equations (1) and (2) vary with the risk of their respective flows.[23] The greater the perceived risk of the cash stream, the greater the discount rate. Thus, if the lessor views his salvage estimate (V_n') as being less risky than the lessee's estimated salvage (V_n), the lessor's discount rate will be lower than the lessee's, and the net present value return to the lessor will be higher. This allows for the possibility that the increased return will be passed on in a lower lease rate.

Again, manufacturer lessors would be in the best position to capitalize on this potential benefit. Indeed, financial institutions, which do not have specialized knowledge of the equipment and do not have the capability of realizing economies in its reconditioning and disposal, may actually perceive greater risk in these cash flows. Thus, banks and independent leasing companies may tend to be at a competitive disadvantage with regard to this potential leasing benefit.

"Underpricing"

An economic advantage of leasing will also result if the lessor is willing to "underprice" alternative debt capital suppliers, i.e., banks. (In most instances, if the lessee purchases the asset, it will be financed with a bank term loan.) Underpricing may be possible because the lessor considers his security position to be superior to that of a bank, since the lessor retains title to the asset.[24] On the other hand, it may simply represent a competitive pricing tactic designed to gain market share at

[22] J. Fred Weston and Eugene F. Brigham, *Managerial Finance*, 5th ed. (Hinsdale, IL: Dryden Press, 1975), pg. 483.

[23] James C. Van Horne, *Financial Management and Policy*, 3rd ed. (Englewood Cliffs, NJ: Prentice-Hall, 1974), pg. 137; Eugene F. Fama and Merton H. Miller, *The Theory of Finance* (Hinsdale, IL: Dryden Press, 1972), pp. 276–304; and William F. Sharpe, *Portfolio Theory and Capital Markets* (New York: McGraw-Hill, 1970), pp. 77–95.

[24] Nantell, same as reference 11 above, pg. 14.

the expense of lenders. Also, the lessor may sometimes be able to attain economies of scale in financing his leased equipment inventory, and, if so, may be able to undercut the lessee's cost of debt capital.

The foregoing analysis should underscore one point. If the lessor and lessee face identical cash flows and perceive identical risks in these flows, the only economic advantage of leasing results from the lessor's willingness to underprice lenders. Given competitive conditions in the capital markets, however, it is unlikely that lessors could maintain a long-run strategy of underpricing alternative sources of financing. Thus, the long-term viability of leasing depends upon the lessor's ability to provide the lessee with *real economic benefits*, in contrast to so-called "non-economic" or operating advantages of leasing. (When analyzed, in most instances these so-called operating advantages simply become variants of economic claims.[25])

The Marketing Financial Analyst Concept

The preceding analysis underscores the importance of featuring economic benefits in the marketing of financial leases. Unfortunately, not many industrial sales representatives have the requisite financial training and background to effectively market the economic benefits of equipment leasing. Industrial equipment salesmen are usually specialists in the technical features rather than the financial aspects of their product and service offerings.

This would not be as serious a problem if industrial consumers were fully capable of analyzing the economic advantages of leases. Unfortunately, a recent survey indicates that even many large corporations are employing techniques of financial analysis which are biased against leasing.[26] These firms often use outmoded lease versus purchase analysis models which are inconsistent with contemporary financial theory. The methodologies which they employ fail to give appropriate weight to the potential economic benefits of leasing. It becomes imperative, therefore, that manufacturer lessors take the initiative in marketing the financial aspects of their leases.

The most significant problems involved in implementing an aggressive lease marketing program will concern the organization and staffing of the "sales" force. Larger industrial marketers may find it profitable to create a financial specialist position within the sales organization. This specialist would act as a marketing financial analyst. The analyst would be a member of a sales team with responsibility for "selling" the economic benefits of leasing.

Such an analyst must be capable of interfacing with controllers, financial analysts, accountants, tax specialists, and other financially oriented "influencers" within the

---

[25] Anderson, see Note, p. 294.
[26] Anderson and Martin, same as reference 14 above.

buying center.[27] The person should possess exceptional communications skills and have a solid background in corporate finance, accounting, and marketing.

The marketing financial analyst would be under the direction of the manager of a sales team or the sales branch manager and would have the primary function of making financial presentations to customers on the economics of leasing. The analyst would also work with members of the customer's financial staff to determine the economic impact of the acquisition decision. In this regard, he would operate much like a financial consultant, analyzing the firm's current decision models and suggesting alternative approaches which more accurately reflect the true economic benefits of leasing.

The analyst could also give advice on matters related to taxes, accounting, legal considerations, or any other issues related to asset acquisitions. In short, the marketing financial analyst would provide the customer with a full range of consulting services and financial information designed to encourage acceptance of the firm's leasing program.

This approach appears to be gaining some adherents within industry. For example, Xerox Corporation has created a specialist position in its sales organization known as Consulting Service Representative (CSR). The position is similar in concept to the marketing financial analyst. In addition to providing a wide range of product-related consulting services, the CSR works with members of the customer's financial group in analyzing the economic aspects of lease and rental options. Generally, these representatives focus on the larger, multiple-installation customers who require more elaborate technical and financial services. Xerox has also created a financial specialist position to aid customers who express a preference for purchase rather than lease. The Sold Equipment Representative (SER) provides the customer with assistance in analyzing the financial aspects of both installment sale and outright purchase.

Both types of specialists operate at the district office level and are called in to work with area office sales representatives as their services are required. The individuals selected for these positions are former sales representatives who have established a good sales record and have demonstrated an aptitude for the financial aspects of placing business equipment. In addition, each representative receives special training for this position before being assigned to a district office.

Impact on the Marketing Mix

The implementation of a lease marketing program will impact various elements of the marketing mix.

---

[27] Frederick E. Webster, Jr. and Yoram Wind, *Organizational Buying Behavior* (Englewood Cliffs, NJ: Prentice-Hall, 1972), pp. 77–80.

Promotional Programs

The objectives of the promotional campaign, the message strategy, and the promotional media employed will all be affected. The firm's promotional program must be redirected to communicate not only the technical advantages of the product, but also the economic advantages of leasing. It will likely necessitate redirecting the firm's promotional effort from traditional targets, such as purchasing agents and production engineers, to other participants in the lease-purchase decision process, particularly some members of the financial staff. In addition to communicating the economies of leasing, the firm's message strategy must attempt to dispel negative attitudes that buying center members may have concerning leases. (A recent survey suggests that many corporate decision makers have negative or neutral attitudes toward leasing.[28] This suggests the need for informational campaigns designed to confront the various objections to leasing on a point-by-point basis.)

Pricing Strategy

Pricing presents a unique problem for the manufacturer lessor because both a sale price and a lease rate must be determined for the same product. One approach is to set the lease rate and purchase price such that they generate the same rate of return over the product's useful economic life. Alternatively, the rates may be set so as to encourage either leasing or purchasing, depending upon the desired outcomes and market conditions.

A manufacturer may feel that a high lease-to-purchase ratio generates closer contact between the lessee and the manufacturer's sales force. He may believe that this will lead to lease renewal business or increased sales of other products in the company's line.

Or, a firm may wish to encourage leasing in an attempt to "tie" the lessee firm to the company's product line. The use of incentives such as lease credits may encourage the lessee to trade up within the lessor's line as capacity or needs require. This technique is used by many business equipment manufacturers who allow their customers to apply a portion of the payments on presently leased equipment toward the purchase or lease of larger and more expensive models.

Some manufacturers, on the other hand, may wish to set relatively high lease rates to encourage outright sale. Leasing requires the financing of leased equipment inventories and can place a severe cash flow drain on a company. Fruhan estimates that in the computer industry it requires $1.20 in firm capital to support $1.00 in annual shipments.[29] Indeed, it has been suggested that inability to meet the heavy capital requirements of the industry was one of the major factors in the decision

---

[28] Anderson and Bird, same as reference 8 above.

[29] William E. Fruhan, "Pyrrhic Victories in Fights for Market Share," *Harvard Business Review*, Vol. 50 (September–October 1972), pp. 100–107.

to abandon the RCA and General Electric computer ventures.[30] Thus, certain manufacturers may find it prudent to maintain a lower lease-to-purchase ratio.

Product Quality & Maintenance

Manufacturers may find that leasing also affects the maintenance service and product quality elements of the marketing mix. For example, Wehle found that many firms expect better maintenance and installation service on leased equipment.[31] If these expectations are not fulfilled, the lessor may lose the opportunity for both lease renewal and new lease business.

From the standpoint of long-term profitability, the lessor has a vested interest in maintaining high standards of product quality and maintenance service. As the product moves through its life cycle, the lease renewal revenue it generates will be proportionate to its expected useful life. Clearly, high quality standards and expert maintenance will allow the manufacturer to stretch the period of useful service. Proper maintenance will also facilitate the sale or lease of the product as secondhand equipment after the original lease has expired. Thus, the equipment may be able to generate a reasonable return through the maturity and decline stages of its life cycle.

Summary & Conclusions

In the final analysis, the long-term profitability of a manufacturer's leasing program will depend upon how well the firm markets the economics of leasing. We have argued here that the lease is essentially a financial device which provides the industrial customer with a set of benefits that are primarily economic in nature. It is essential that the lessor's organization fully understand the nature of these economic benefits if a successful lease marketing program is to be developed.

In this regard, the recruitment and training of financially oriented sales personnel is of utmost importance. In addition, the marketing organization as a whole must be aware of the unique problems created by the implementation of a leasing program. Decisions in the areas of promotion, pricing, product quality, and maintenance service are of particular significance in the success of such a venture.

Note: Some of the material in this article will appear in Paul F. Anderson, *Financial Aspects of Industrial Leasing Decisions: Implications for Marketing* (East Lansing, MI: Division of Research, Graduate School of Business Administration, Michigan State University, forthcoming).

---

[30] Ibid.
[31] Mary M. Wehle, "Lessee Decision Criteria and Accounting Implications," Ph.D. dissertation, Harvard University, 1972, pg. VI-45.

Exercises

18.1. The Walker Truck Leasing Company is about to enter into negotiations with the Lynn Construction Company concerning the leasing of a new truck.

1. Given the data below, find the minimum annual lease payment Walker would be willing to accept (i.e., find the lease payments that make Walker's net present value equal to zero):

Cost of truck to Walker = $27,000;
Length of lease = 4 years;
Operating costs to be paid by Walker = $1,800 per year;
Expected after-tax salvage value at the end of the fourth year = $6,000;
Pre-tax cost of debt capital = 10%;
Investment tax credit = $900;
Income tax rate = 50%.

Sum-of-the-years'-digits depreciation schedule

End of year	Depreciation
1	$10,800
2	8,100
3	5,400
4	2,700
	$27,000

Interest payment schedule on $27,000 term loan

End of year	Interest
1	$2,700
2	2,118
3	1,478
4	774
	$7,070

Assume that all cash flows occur at the end of the year. (Assume too that the purchase price and investment tax credit flow occur at the end of year zero; i.e., the beginning of year one.) Use a discount rate of 15% for the salvage value flow and a rate of 5% for all other cash flows.

2. Given the following figures, find the maximum lease payments Lynn would be willing to make (i.e., find the lease payments that make Lynn's net present value equal to zero):

Cost of the truck to Lynn = $30,000;

Length of lease = 4 years;

Operating costs that would have to be paid by Lynn if it purchased the truck = $2,000 per year;

Expected after-tax salvage value at the end of the fourth year = $3,000.

18.2. Jeff Dale, administrator at Martin Memorial Hospital, is very upset. The chief radiologist has just threatened to take his expertise to another hospital if Martin Memorial fails to acquire a new piece of radiation therapy equipment, the XR7. Mr. Dale had originally planned to purchase the XR7, but having recently read an article on the economic benefits of leasing, he is no longer convinced that purchasing the XR7 would be in the best interest of the hospital. To make matters worse, Magic Medical Leasing Company has indicated that it is willing to negotiate a contract and suggested that Mr. Dale calculate the lease payments the hospital would be willing to pay. Mr. Dale has no idea how to calculate the lease payments.

1. Given the following figures, find the maximum lease payments Martin Memorial would be willing to make (i.e., find the lease payments that make Martin Memorial's net present value equal to zero):

Cost of the XR7 to Martin Memorial Hospital = $60,000;

Length of lease = 5 years;

Operating cost that will have to be paid by Martin Memorial if it purchases the XR7 = $1,000 per year;

Expected after-tax salvage value at the end of the fifth year = $10,000;

Pre-tax cost of debt capital = 8%;

Investment tax credit = $4,000;

Income tax rate = 50%.

Sum-of-the-years'-digits depreciation schedule

End of year	Depreciation
1	$20,000
2	16,000
3	12,000
4	8,000
5	4,000
	$60,000

Interest payment schedule on $60,000 loan

End of year	Interest
1	$4,800
2	3,982
3	3,098
4	2,143
5	1,113
	$15,136

Assume that all cash flows occur at the end of the year. (Assume also that the purchase price and investment tax credit flow occur at the end of year zero, i.e., the beginning of year one.) Use a discount rate of 14% for the salvage value flow and a rate of 6% for all other cash flows.

2. Given the following figures, find the minimum annual lease payment Magic Medical would be willing to accept (i.e., find the lease payments that make Magic Medical's net present value equal to zero):

Cost of XR7 to Magic Medical = $54,000;
Length of lease = 5 years;
Operating costs to be paid by Magic Medical = $900 per year;
Expected after-tax salvage value at the end of the fifth year = $20,000;
Pre-tax cost of debt capital = 8%;
Investment tax credit = $3,600;
Income tax rate = 50%;

Sum-of-the-years'-digits depreciation schedule

End of year	Depreciation
1	$18,000
2	14,400
3	10,800
4	7,200
5	3,600
	$54,000

Interest payment schedule on $54,000 term loan

End of year	Interest
1	$4,320
2	3,584
3	2,788
4	1,929
5	1,002
	$13,623

Assume that all cash flows occur at the end of the year. (Assume also that the purchase price and the investment tax credit flow occur at the end of year zero.) Use a discount rate of 14% for salvage value and a rate of 6% for all other cash flows.

Forward Buying for Profit Maximization

19

J. E. Tusing   R. E. Moll

Forward buying is a term that refers to acquiring materials well in advance of the time when the material may actually be needed. This kind of purchase can be made for a number of reasons, such as pending price increase, a potential supply shortage or unusual manufacturing logistics. Many factors influence the extent to which forward buying can be practiced. The stability (perishability) of the purchased material is probably the most important factor. Where material stability is not a problem, further considerations need to be made: Will demand for the material change significantly in the near term? Are funds available to finance forward purchases? Are materials-handling equipment and warehousing facilities available if necessary? Having satisfied questions like these, a conscientious buyer can maximize corporate assets utilization through forward buying techniques.

This article will focus on the use of forward buying in anticipation of a price increase. Forward buying in this case is done to minimize the impact of a price increase, which is another way of effectively delaying the price increase for a period of time.

To what extent (in terms of amount of material or forward period of time) should forward buying be done? It should be done to the extent that it maximizes asset utilization—the net savings accrued as a result of the forward purchase is maximized against having made no forward purchase at all.

How does a purchasing agent determine how far ahead to buy? One would expect the net savings obtained to first increase with each increment purchased, due to low price advantages. Then, as additional increments are purchased, the savings should decline, due to cost disadvantages.

To do the job well, the purchasing agent must be able to identify the purchase quantity that generates the maximum savings. In order to identify the maximum savings, an equation must be developed which describes the various cost factors and savings. The basic equation is:

$$\text{net savings} = \text{gross savings} - \text{costs} \qquad (1)$$

where

gross savings =
$$\text{units purchased} \times (\text{new delivered price/unit} - \text{old delivered price/unit}) \quad (2)$$

and costs are those resulting from the forward purchase.

From *Business Horizons* (December 1976), pp. 82–86. Copyright, 1976, by the Foundation for the School of Business at Indiana University. Reprinted by permission.

The costs arising from the hedge can vary with the situation. By including all expected costs, a general equation can be developed. It can then be simplified when desired by setting the appropriate cost coefficients to zero.

One cost which always appears is the inventory carrying cost. This is the same concept that appears in the classical EOQ formulation:

inventory carrying cost = average units on hand over the hedge period
$\qquad$ × old price per unit
$\qquad$ × inventory carrying cost/mo.
$\qquad$ × number of months the hedge will last $\qquad$ (3)

If a public warehouse must be used to store the hedged material, additional costs are incurred which are incremental to the hedge. Specifically these can be:

additional freight cost = freight/unit × units purchased $\qquad$ (4)

in/out cost = in/out rate per unit × units purchased $\qquad$ (5)

storage cost = storage rate per unit per month
$\qquad$ × average units on hand over the hedge period
$\qquad$ × number of months the hedge will last $\qquad$ (6)

The final cost included in the general equation is the risk of something going awry:

risk cost = risk per unit × units purchased $\qquad$ (7)

The risk per unit can include the incremental costs that a large forward purchase might yield. These include obsolescence risk, risk of damage during storage, and the risk that the price will decline during the hedge period. If there is a chance the price will increase again during the hedge period, that factor can be considered as a negative risk cost (or additional savings).

Having quantified the gross savings and costs, it is a simple mechanical task to solve for the optimum hedge quantity (see Appendix). The optimum hedge quantity is described by the equations:

number of months to hedge =
$$\frac{(\text{new price/unit} - \text{old price/unit} - \text{freight/unit} - \text{in/out/unit} - \text{risk/unit})(\text{risk/unit})}{[(\text{interest rate/month} \times \text{old price/month}) + \text{storage cost/unit/month}]}$$
$$(8)$$

units to be hedged = number of months to hedge (equation 8) × unit demand/month
$$(9)$$

An example for using this equation will now be given, using the following data:

Consumption = 100,000 pounds/month
Inventory carrying cost = 2%/month

Freight rate from public warehouse = $.003/lb.
In/out cost at public warehouse = $.0009/lb.
Storage cost at public warehouse = $.001/lb./month
Old delivered price = $0.70/lb.
New delivered price = $0.77/lb.
Risk cost estimate = $0.01/lb.

Substituting these various values into equation (8) yields the following hedge period that will maximize savings:

$$\text{number of months} = \frac{(.77 - .70 - .003 - .0009 - .01)}{[(.02 \times .7) + .001]}$$

$$= 3.74$$

The actual quantity to be hedged is then determined by substituting 3.74 and the consumption value into equation (9):

hedge quantity = 3.74 months × 100,000 lb./mos. = 374,000 lb.

The net savings likely as a result of this hedge can then be calculated by substituting the hedge quantity back into equation (10) (see Appendix) and solving.

In this example, the substitution of the various factors yields a net savings of $10,491. Additional savings may be generated if the hedge quantity moves the old price to a lower level as a result of quantity purchase price breaks. This serves to increase the old price/new price differential for subsequent recalculation of the hedge as described above.

This hedge model assumes uniform consumption of the hedged material over the hedge period. Thus, it should not be used to hedge a material which is used infrequently or which has a highly seasonal usage pattern. Those materials must be handled on an individual basis.

The use of this forward buying model has several advantages:

It ensures that the actual quantity hedged generates savings which are reasonably close to the maximum.
It ensures that within an operating unit where many purchasing agents may be involved, all are using the same hedge procedure.
It is conceptually easy to understand.
The calculations are easy.
It is easily put onto a programmable calculator which dramatically simplifies its use.
The data required are easily obtained.
If a hedge is undertaken for nonprice reasons, such as shortages, this equation quantifies the cost of taking that forward position.
A purchasing clerk can analyze hedge opportunities, leaving more time available for the professional buyer.

The model for hedging, proposed by Dennis A. Kudma, is conceptually similar to the model described here.[1] The major advantage offered by this model is the ability to consider other cost factors besides the inventory carrying cost. In the everyday decision-making atmosphere under which the typical buyer operates, all these real costs, such as warehousing, risk, and so forth, play a major role in formulation of a forward buying plan. Secondarily, the formulation and proof of the model in this article is more straightforward.

The hedging procedure discussed here was developed in the Coatings and Resins Division of PPG Industries, Inc., in 1975 to meet a perceived need. During the 1974 shortage period, changes in price occurred but there were no opportunities to buy ahead to effectively delay price increases. Even though material supplies became less restrictive in late 1974 and early 1975, certain materials continued to increase in price. Thus, forward buying became possible. During 1975, excessive management efforts were expended in developing appropriate hedge strategies for a limited number of materials while many other opportunities were overlooked due to lack of manpower.

The goal of the effort that produced this hedge equation was to produce a method that could be used easily and could be conceptually understood by materials-managing personnel at the division's manufacturing locations. Due to the large number of raw materials in inventory among the various plants, it is generally beyond the capability of the general office staff to be directly involved in all local hedge opportunities. Only for those materials where divisional strategies exist should the general office staff get involved.

The model has been used extensively by the Coatings and Resins Division in planning preprice-increase purchases since late 1975 and is now accepted as the key determinant of hedge quantity purchases. The concept has been introduced to the materials-managing personnel at all division manufacturing locations worldwide. Actual determination of the hedge quantity is facilitated by use of programmable calculators. Each location has developed its own cost parameters depending upon the availability of on-site storage space. Where public warehousing is required, the incremental charges are readily available from itemized invoices or upon request from the warehouse management.

The first major use of the equation occurred early in 1976 when producers of Titanium Dioxide, a key pigment for coatings, announced a price increase from 43.5¢/lb. to 46.5¢/lb. Large quantities of this material are needed by the Coatings and Resins Division. Using the model, it was determined that the various plants should prepurchase quantities adequate to last from 2.5 to 3.9 months. The accompanying table indicates the range of values used for each variable. This hedge yielded the

---

[1] Dennis A. Kudma, *Purchasing Managers' Decision Handbook* (Boston: Cahners Books, 1975).

Forward Buying Determinations

Applying the equations explained in the article, PPG Industries, Inc., used the following data to determine how much of a certain material to buy before price increases went into effect.

		Incremental warehousing charges—$/lb.					
Location	Price increase $/lb.	In/out	Inbound freight	Storage/ mo.	Obso- lescence risk/lb.	Inv. carry cost/mo.	Forward quantity: number of months' supply
A	.030	0	0	0	N.A.*	N.A.	3.9
B	.030	.00071	.00210	.00021	N.A.	N.A.	3.4
C	.030	.00048	.0007	.00044	N.A.	N.A.	3.7
D	.030	.00350	0	.00084	N.A.	N.A.	3.0
E	.030	.00210	.00400	.00100	N.A.	N.A.	2.6
F	.030	.00320	.00400	.00100	N.A.	N.A.	2.5
G	.030	0	0	0	N.A.	N.A.	3.9

*Not available for publication.

division a net savings in the low six figures. Note in the table how hedging is significantly affected by local public warehousing costs, where applicable.

The equation has been used in other ways. From time to time spot quantities of materials become available. Depending upon the circumstances applicable to that material, the offering price may be different from the normal market price. This model allows for determination of rapid, reliable estimates of the savings or costs involved in purchasing that spot material. For example, on one occasion a spot material was offered at below the normal purchase price. At the same time, purchasing management was anticipating a market price increase to occur within several months' time. Using this model, it was a simple matter to allow for a negative risk factor and thus build into the decision the future price increase—a two-fold justification for the purchase. The estimated cost savings were in the low five figures.

During the introduction of the hedging concept to plant personnel, it became apparent that application of the theory to actual day-to-day opportunities was limited because manual calculations were somewhat tedious. On a typical opportunity, as much as fifteen minutes to one-half hour was expended by the time all the calculations were made and revalidated for mathematical correctness. This tedium and need for manual revalidation was dramatically reduced through use of a small, hand-held, programmable calculator. Having gathered the necessary input data, the actual determination is completed easily in less than two minutes, including the validation process.

A problem confronting one new to this concept is to be able to separate the incremental costs applicable to the hedging process itself from those which would be incurred in a nonhedging environment. Those incremental costs are traded off against the incremental savings in this hedging model to yield the proper decision. One other consideration is to correctly segregate those incremental cost factors between time-dependent and time-independent categories. Storage charges and inventory carrying costs are of the time-dependent type, whereas one-time costs such as in and out charges at a public warehouse or inbound freight from a warehouse are independent of time but directly related to the quantity. All cost factors, whether or not they are time dependent, can be properly categorized for use with this model.

This model has proven to meet all the goals of the original development effort. It is easily used in a consistent manner by a large number of people with diverse backgrounds. Plant level use of this model has also released general office staff time for other functions.

Appendix: Solution of the Hedge Equation to Determine Optimum Savings

$$\text{net savings} = (NP - OP) \times TU - INVavg \times OP \times IR \times MON$$
$$- (FRT + IN/OUT + RISK) \times TU - INVavg \times STORE \times MON \tag{10}$$

where:

NP = new price
OP = old price
TU = total units purchased
$INVavg$ = average inventory in units
IR = interest rate per month
MON = number of months the hedge quantity will last
FRT = inbound incremental freight cost/unit
IN/OUT = in/out cost per unit
$RISK$ = risk cost per unit
$STORE$ = storage cost per unit per month

Two simplifications can be made to the equation:

$$MON = \frac{TU}{C} \tag{11}$$

where C = the units consumed per month and

$$INVavg = \frac{TU}{MON} \tag{12}$$

Substituting (11) & (12) into (10) we obtain

net savings $= (NP - OP) \times TU - \frac{1}{2} OP \times IR \times TU^2/C - FRT \times TU$
$$- IN/OUT \times TU - STORE \times \tfrac{1}{2} TU^2/C - RISK \times TU \qquad (13)$$

Rearranging and combining terms in the last equation further simplifies to:

net savings $= (NP - OP - FRT - IN/OUT - RISK) \times TU$
$$- \frac{TU^2((OP \times IR) + STORE)}{MON(C)} \qquad (14)$$

To find the maximum savings, equation (14) is differentiated with respect to TU and is set equal to zero:

$$\frac{d \ net \ savings}{d \ TU} = 0 = (NP - OP - FRT - IN/OUT - RISK)$$

$$- \frac{2TU}{2C}((OP \times IR) + STORE) \qquad (15)$$

Solving (15) for TU/C yields:

$$months = \left(\frac{TU}{C}\right) = \frac{NP - OP - FRT - IN/OUT - RISK}{(OP \times IR) + STORE} \qquad (16)$$

This is identical to equation (8).

Exercises

19.1. Artex Corporation, a major construction company, had successfully bid on the construction of a large condominium near a shopping center outside Vancouver. The project was scheduled to be finished in 12 months, which under normal circumstances would have given the contractor sufficient time. However, Artex was experiencing delays in shipment from its principal steel supplier, who explained that the problem was the result of strikes and other work stoppages in the steel industry in general; business would return to normal when terms of settlement were reached with the workers and a price increase was agreed upon.

Artex needed an average of 200 short tons of steel (structural shapes) per month in order to meet all of its requirements. The price of structural shapes was $0.12 per pound and was expected to rise to $0.15 per pound F.O.B. destination.

In view of the situation, the purchasing manager was considering forward buying; thus he would postpone the price increase for a time and, by ordering in advance of need, be assured that a supply of steel would be on hand to meet his requirements.

The company's warehouse was operating at almost full capacity. Any purchases above and beyond the normal amount would have to be stored in a public warehouse. The purchasing manager had estimated the costs of using this storage facility as follows:

Inventory carrying cost = 2.25%/month
Freight rate from public warehouse = $0.005/lb.
In/out cost of public warehouse = $0.002/lb.
Storage cost at public warehouse = $0.003/lb./month

The risk cost involved in such a purchase was estimated at $0.005/lb.

1. Compute the hedge period and the actual quantity to be hedged that will maximize savings.
2. What is the maximum savings that can be generated from this forward purchase?

19.2. The general manager of Tops Food Markets Corporation, a chain of eight retail food markets in the northeastern part of the United States, was convinced that the price of instant coffee would soar in the next few months. Normal consumption of instant coffee for the chain was about 50 cases per week. However, she estimated that consumption would decrease if the price went up, and that the weekly requirement would drop to approximately 40 cases. At that time the price of instant coffee was $63.00/case; she was sure that it soon would go up to at least $75.00/case.

She decided to explore the advisability of buying a reserve stock to last a few months and thus in effect delay the price increase.

Since she had no warehouse space available, she would be obliged to use a public warehouse. She estimated the costs as follows:

Inventory carrying costs = 1.25%/month
Freight rate from public warehouse = $0.0020/case
In/out charge by public warehouse = $0.0035/case
Storage cost at public warehouse = $0.25/case/month

The risk cost involved in such a purchase was practically nil. She conservatively estimated it at $0.05/case.

1. Calculate the hedge period and the quantity that will maximize her savings.
2. What is the maximum savings that can be generated from this forward purchase?

Recommendations for Further Reading

Andrews, Victor L. "The Credit Manager in the Capital Rationing Process," *Credit and Financial Management*, 73 (August 1971), 26–28ff.

Credit managers should play a pivotal role in the management of company funds for greater profitability. They should use the opportunity cost of money—the return that could be earned in an alternative—to ration the amount of funds committed to receivables. Subjecting the investment in receivables to tests of profitability requires that sales, cash flows and supporting inventory costs be estimated. The discounted cash flow technique can then be applied to generate a rate of return. Credit scoring techniques such as discriminant analysis should be applied to trade credit analysis. Also, marker chain analysis can aid in the estimation of expected collections per period and of total funds committed to receivables.

Bartels, Robert. "Credit Management as a Marketing Function," *Journal of Marketing*, 28 (July 1964), 59–62.

A change in attitudes and a more sophisticated approach to credit management can open the way for credit to be better employed for the achievement of marketing objectives. For the seller, a credit operation is not merely the financing of an asset but also the financing of markets. A number of marketing objectives that can be achieved through further development of the seller's credit function are identified. The actual division of credit responsibility within the organization should reflect that function's relationship to the firm's marketing objectives. It should also be recognized that the credit function can be shifted to outside specialists such as credit card companies.

Crowther, John F. "Rationale for Quantity Discounts," *Harvard Business Review*, 42 (March-April 1964), 121–126.

Quantity discount schedules vary greatly between firms and are often arrived at in a nonrational manner. Here a rational method is presented which takes into account both the buyer's and the seller's costs. The buyer's costs are minimized by the purchase of "economic order quantities." These costs are those of placing individual orders and of carrying inventory. Unlike the buyer's cost, the seller's cost continues to decrease as order size increases. Moreover, for a range beyond the economic order quantity, the added savings to the seller exceeds the added cost to the buyer. But few sellers are always clear as to when the extent of the discount they offer will compensate the buyer for the added cost. An example fully illustrates the logic of this method of determining how great a discount sellers should offer.

Davis, P. Michael. "Marginal Analysis of Credit Sales," *Accounting Review*,
    41 (January 1966), 121–126.

Management is concerned about the possible loss of sales resulting from a credit
policy that is too restricting. On the other hand, high bad debt losses may be
caused by an easy credit policy. A marginal analysis model can be helpful in resolving
this conflict. Marginal cost equals marginal revenue at that point where cost of
goods sold, stated as a percentage of the selling price, plus the probability that the
account will never be collected equals one. The inclusion of various other costs is
discussed and reasons given why they need not be considered. It is also pointed out
that several nonquantitative factors, such as availability of goods and the status of
competition, must also be taken into account when deciding whether or not to
offer credit.

Fox, Harold W. "A Dynamic Perspective for Credit Analysis," *Credit and
    Financial Management*, 79 (January 1977), 31–39.

Each of the stages in a product's life cycle requires different credit norms and
offers suppliers different profit opportunities. Credit managers should use the product
life cycle concept as a supplement to their more traditional methods of customer
credit evaluation. Traced out are the differences in credit needs and in desirable
vendor policies as an industrial customer's new product proceeds through the typical
life sequence of precommercialization, introduction, growth, maturity and decline.
Product life cycle thinking is advanced as a method of broadening a credit manager's
understanding of customer needs in a way that indicates when such needs can
profitably be satisfied.

Fox, Harold W. "Product Life Cycle—An Aid to Financial Administra-
    tion," *Financial Executive*, 41 (April 1973), 28–34.

The familiar product life cycle is reviewed but in a manner that emphasizes both
the financial stresses associated with each stage in the process and the response of
financial officers that would be most appropriate. The cash flows and profits
associated with each stage must be determined, as must the corporate financing
practices (e.g., borrowing in anticipation of future profits) that might be in order.
The need for a balanced mix of products at various stages in the life cycle is stressed.
Life cycle thinking is also advocated because of its integrating effect and its tendency
to close the perceptual gaps between financial officers and operating managers.

Frantz, Kenneth E., and Jerry A. Viscione. "What Should You Do About Cash Discounts?" *Credit and Financial Management* (May 1976), 30–37.

A recent survey generated responses from 168 manufacturers (28% of the total sample) who are active in six industries that vary greatly in terms of the importance of accounts receivable as a percentage of total assets. The results suggest that more attention should be paid to the feasibility of eliminating cash discounts as a means of improving corporate profits. The revenue sacrificed by cash discounts expressed as a percentage of net profit emerges as a very significant figure. It averages, for example, 28% for firms taking a 2% discount. An analysis of each respondent's estimate of the extent to which sales would decline were cash discounts eliminated suggests that if these estimates are reliable and certain possible biases are accepted as offsetting in direction, most of the firms that now report offering a 2% cash discount would increase their profitability by eliminating such discounts. Though the conclusions of the study are tentative, the need for a careful evaluation of cash discount policies clearly emerges.

Schwab, Richard J. "A Contribution Approach to Transfer Pricing," *Management Accounting*, 56 (February 1975), 46–48.

Transfer pricing is a vital element in the management of decentralized firms. To be effective, such a pricing system must promote goal congruency, provide an equitable basis for evaluating the performance of divisional management, and still preserve the autonomy of each division. When a competitive "open market" exists for the transferred goods, the transfer price can be the market price, or it can be negotiated on the basis of that price. A method of transfer price setting based on contribution margin is proposed for situations in which no market price exists. This method is believed to meet the effectiveness criteria mentioned above. It requires, however, that the firm have a standard cost system based on products, that it conduct variance analyses along departmental lines, and also that it know the contribution margin of each product line.

PART VI

Promotion and
Distribution

The Determination of Advertising Budgets for Brands

20

Kurt H. Schaffir   Earle W. Orr, Jr.

Methods of budgeting advertising expenditures are generally a mixture of fact and fancy. The factual portion often includes a historical comparison of advertising expenditures to sales and profits for one's own product and also for competitive products, where available. These comparisons tend to be used mainly to verify the fact that it is established practice to budget some fixed percentage of sales—perhaps ten per cent—for advertising. This percentage may then be viewed as a starting point for applying the more subjective aspects of the budgeting procedure, which involve considerations of market objectives, use of promotional devices other than advertising, possible action by competitors, and so forth.

It is recognized that the historical percentage approach leaves much to be desired: if accepted at face value, it would tend to perpetuate past practice whether it be right or wrong, and would fail to allow for the different needs of different products or brands in a line except insofar as these are already reflected in past decisions. But in the absence of compelling reasons to deviate, the ratio of advertising expenditures to sales dollars established by company history or industry tradition remains a major factor in evaluating advertising budgets.

In view of the sizable expenditures often involved, there is considerable incentive to devise a better approach for analysis and interpretation of historical data, preferably one which would reasonably reflect the presumed relationship between advertising action and sales effect.

Advertising is, of course, only one of many factors influencing sales, and often not the dominant one. Even where it is a major factor, its effect is not instantaneous, and is likely to be obscured by other concurrent happenings. Nevertheless, the search for evidence of a positive relationship between advertising expenditures and sales or profits is of continuing concern to those responsible for the establishment of advertising budgets.

For reasons which will be more fully discussed, the results to date of this search have been largely disappointing, and while this paper offers some positive findings for one particular product line, these do not alter the basic fact that the determination of advertising budgets remains primarily a matter not of science but of judgment based

Reprinted from the *Journal of Advertising Research*, Vol. 3, No. 1 (March 1963), pp. 7–12. © Copyright 1963, by the Advertising Research Foundation.

on experience. A more scientific approach may prove useful, however, if it is properly integrated with other conventional methods.

Efforts in this area have unfortunately often involved complex mathematical formulations which are difficult to interpret and impossible to verify. Urging the adoption, on the basis of their logical merits alone, of complex and time-consuming methods which are inadequately supported by evidence is unreasonable, and has caused many practitioners to reject these methods altogether. A better approach would be to identify the basic elements of scientific method which can be useful, and to apply them, with judgment, to the degree supportable by such limited evidence as we possess. This paper represents an effort in this direction, with the objective of defining a quantitative relationship between advertising expenditures and sales which is:

1. broad enough to offer promise of being verifiable;
2. simple enough to be generally understood and efficiently applied;
3. in agreement with our general knowledge of the economic characteristics of advertising;
4. logically complete and internally consistent; and
5. hopefully a moderate but significant improvement over simple historical ratios.

A method designed to serve as a guide in determining advertising budgets for brands—or for categories of products—will be outlined, and its application to empirical findings obtained from the sales and advertising data of a firm in a consumer goods industry will be described.

Problems of Measurement

In some industries, analysis of sales-advertising relationships may best proceed along brand lines. In others, such as the cigarette industry, it may be advantageous also to consider *categories* of products (e.g., regulars, filters, kings, menthols, etc.) as a basis for identifying such relationships.

In either case there are many obstacles in trying to extract quantitative relationships from historical data on advertising; the principal problems are:

1. Data on advertising expenditures, as well as sales, are subject to error in reporting.
2. Differences from year to year are small in relation to total annual quantities.
3. Expenditures are not necessarily a good measure of the value of advertising.
4. Advertising-to-sales relationships are distorted and obscured by other factors such as price and quality changes, or dealer allowances.

To find a relationship, it is generally necessary to work with large aggregates of numbers. The analysis described here is based on yearly totals for each of seven regions, but because of inaccuracy in the data (which will be avoided in the future) further aggregation was necessary. For each of the four brand categories which make up the market, the total advertising expenditures for each of two two-year periods (1952–53 and 1959–60), separated by five years, were determined, and a ratio computed, by region, of 1959–60 expenditures divided by 1952–53 expenditures. Similar ratios were calculated for total sales revenues, again for each of the four categories and seven regions, using the same two two-year periods. The two sets of ratios were then plotted one against the other (see Figure 1).

Other formulas can be used, of course, but the calculations shown here will serve to illustrate the basic merits of a quantitative approach.

FIGURE 2. *Adjusted ratios of 1959–60 to 1952–53*

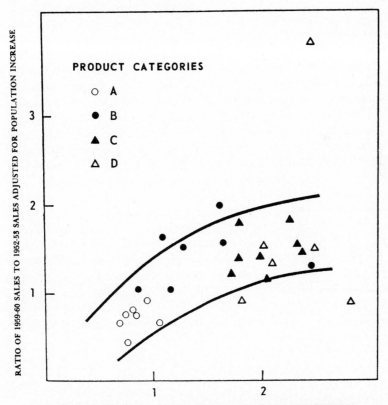

RATIO OF 1959-60 ADV. EXPENDITURES TO 1952-53 ADV. EXPENDITURES
ADJUSTED FOR TOTAL ADVERTISING DOLLAR INCREASE

Relationship of Diminishing Returns

The data plotted in Figure 1 suggest that sales increase as advertising expenditures increase, but the return in sales dollars per advertising dollar is less for large increases in advertising than it is for small increases. In other words, it is a situation of diminishing returns. Thus we cannot estimate the next period's sales simply by multiplying the present period's sales by the ratio of the next period's advertising to this period's. Instead, this ratio must be modified in two ways.

First, in order to show the gradually diminishing effectiveness of advertising, an exponent (denoted by a) is applied to the advertising ratio (next period's advertising divided by this period's). If a were equal to 1, sales would increase proportionately with advertising. If a were greater than 1, sales would increase more than proportionately with advertising. Under either of these circumstances, advertising would not be subject to the law of diminishing returns. Common sense tells us that a must be less than 1.

Secondly, after modification by the exponent, the advertising ratio must be further adjusted through multiplication by a coefficient b. If this adjustment were not made, our relationship would tell us that the next period's sales will equal this period's sales whenever the next period's advertising expenditure is equal to this period's expenditure. In general, this will not be true. If it is true in a specific instance, then for that particular case the value of b will be 1. If b is less than 1, then constant advertising expenditures from period to period will result in decreases in sales from period to period. Or, if sales are to be maintained from period to period, advertising expenditures would have to be increased from period to period. Eventually these expenditures would become prohibitive unless the value of b changes in the meantime. Hence if the coefficient b for a given brand is less than 1, either the brand is a dying brand (in a given geographic area) in terms of inherent consumer acceptance, or else competitors are significantly increasing their advertising on a brand which is a close substitute when the two brands are advertised on a comparable scale.

If b is greater than 1, then a constant level of advertising from period to period will produce increased sales; or, sales could be maintained even if advertising expenditures were to be decreased slightly. Thus if b is greater than 1, the brand is growing in popularity (in some geographic area) to some degree independently of advertising expenditures, or possibly because advertising has been decreased on a competitive brand.

This general relationship between sales and advertising can be summed up concisely by the following equation:

$$S_1 = bS_0(A_1/A_0)^a; \ 0 < a < 1$$

where S_1 symbolizes sales in the next period; S_0, sales in the current (base) period; A_1, the advertising budget for the next period; and A_0, the advertising budget in the current (base) period. Only S_1 and A_1 are variables, once the statistical determination of the sales-to-advertising relationship has been completed.

If this seems excessively simplified, it is mainly because the available data will not support any more complex formulation. This simple description of the advertising-to-sales relationship is, however, logically consistent and can provide considerable information on how future budgets may be set.

To sum up, the numbers a and b, which are given specific numerical values (for particular product categories in particular regions) in the statistical analysis of the historical data, have imbedded within them the following characteristics of the brand's market or markets:

1. The susceptibility of consumers to additional doses of advertising.
2. The growth, stability, or decline in popularity of the inherent qualities of the brand.
3. The effects of competitors' advertising on sales of the company's brands.

Whenever one or more of these characteristics changes appreciably, the values of a and/or b will also change. It is therefore desirable that the sales-to-advertising relation be re-evaluated periodically.

An Example

For Category D in the North Central Region, the values of a and b, estimated statistically, are 0.71 and 1.00, respectively. We also have the following information for a specific brand within Category D.

1. Annual sales in the North Central Region in the base period $100,000
2. Advertising in the North Central Region for the base period $6,000
3. Selling price in North Central Region $75/unit
4. Cost of sales $40/unit
5. Cost of administration and selling, excluding advertising $27.50/unit

Thus there is available for advertising and profit:

$$75 - (\$40 + \$27.50) = \$7.50/\text{unit}$$

And total variable costs, exclusive of advertising, are equal to nine-tenths of sales.

$$\$67.50/\$75.00 = 0.9.$$

Profits in the base period were as follows:

$$\$100,000 - \$90,000 - \$6,000 = \$4,000.$$

With this information, it is possible to construct the data of Table 1. Given the level of sales and advertising for the base period, the second column of Table 1 shows the

TABLE 1. Projected effect of advertising expenditure on sales and profits, for one year

Advertising expenditure	Sales	Total cost excluding advertising	Profit after advertising
$ 4,000	$ 75,000	$ 67,500	$3,500
6,000*	100,000	90,000	4,000
8,000	122,600	110,400	4,200
10,000	143,700	129,300	4,400
12,000	163,500	147,200	4,300
14,000	182,500	164,200	4,300
16,000	200,600	180,600	4,000

* Actual results of "base" year, on which calculations are based.

projected sales response, based on the equation given in the preceding section, with $a = 0.71$ and $b = 100$. The third column lists the total variable costs exclusive of advertising, and the fourth column the projected profit after advertising expenditures.

Table 1 suggests that if the $6,000 advertising expenditures of the "base" year were doubled to $12,000, sales would increase by only about 60 per cent (from $100,000 to $163,500) in accordance with the effect of diminishing returns. More important, profits would rise only about 7 per cent (from $4,000 to $4,300). We may reasonably have doubts as to the accuracy of these numbers, and be satisfied to state broadly that a 5 to 10 per cent increase of profit seems obtainable with a 50 to 150 per cent increase in advertising; or more broadly, that the evidence favors an increase in advertising rather than a decrease, provided the present profit margin is satisfactory.

This approach lends itself not only to evaluation of budgets for individual products or brands, but also to comparisons between brands and allocation of funds among them. A comparison of three different brands is shown in Table 2.

The "best" results would apparently be obtained by spending $10,000 on Brand A, $10,000 on Brand B, and $12,000 on Brand C. If the total advertising budget is to be limited to that of the base year, however ($6,000 + $6,000 + $16,000 = $28,000), the best allocation would be $10,000 for A, $10,000 for B, and only $8,000 for C.

Such analysis provides management with alternatives which may be useful whenever total funds available for advertising are less than the sum of the budgets for each brand product category determined by the procedure, or whenever a minimum profit return per dollar spent on advertising has been established. If the resulting profit for a brand does not provide, in the judgment of management, an adequate return on investment in inventories or facilities specifically associated with the brand,

TABLE 2. Comparison of alternative budgets

Advertising expenditure	Profit after advertising		
	Brand A	Brand B	Brand C
$ 4,000	$3,500	$ 6,200	$7,000
6,000	4,000★	8,200★	7,500
8,000	4,200	10,000	7,700
10,000	4,400	12,000	7,800
12,000	4,300	11,700	7,900
14,000	4,300	10,500	7,800
16,000	4,000	9,800	7,500★

★ Base year results.

then, barring possible profit improvements through adjustments in pricing or costs, the best alternative may well be the discontinuance of the brand. This alternative would become increasingly attractive if periodic review of the sales-to-advertising relationship indicated a continuing inadequate performance.

Summary of Method

This method provides, then, a rough guide for determining whether current advertising expenditures are in the right range, and for finding a reasonable allocation of specified advertising funds among several brands. It uses information normally available on each brand's preceding year's experience as to sales, profits, and advertising expenditures.

In addition, an analysis is made of historical data on sales and advertising. For the purpose of this analysis, several brands and, where applicable, several regions for each brand are evaluated to determine whether, based on judgment, their sales may be expected to respond in a roughly similar manner to changes in advertising expenditures. If so, the corresponding historical data are analyzed as a single group to arrive at estimates of two constants or factors.

The first factor (*a*) measures the way in which increased advertising expense leads to diminishing returns in sales. The second factor (*b*) measures what happens to sales from one year to the next if advertising expenditures are held constant.

These two factors are then applied to each brand in each region, to estimate the effect on profits of changes in advertising from the present level to a higher or lower one.

This method assumes that there will be no significant changes, from the preceding year to the next, in such factors as:

Product quality or appearance.

Price, relative to competitors'.

Effectiveness of advertising per dollar spent by virtue of changes in concept, copy, or media.

Use of other promotional devices.

Introduction of other competitive products.

Competitive effort by others, except insofar as this is part of a general continuing trend.

Where a change in one of these factors is expected, an appropriate adjustment in advertising budget must be made. Very often, however, although such changes are deemed possible, they cannot be predicted. In these cases, the method proposed here should suggest a reasonable budget level.

Area of Application

It should be borne in mind that the application of this approach is limited to instances where substantial experience exists over a period of years. New brands or brands not previously advertised could not be handled; nor would it be reasonable to apply this method where a product has recently undergone drastic changes in character, price, or marketing approach. It is adapted more to the task of reviewing or screening brands which have been marketed in roughly the same way over some period of years.

For the moment, budgets arrived at through the allocation procedure described here will be useful as a basis for comparison. Where present budgets differ drastically from those suggested by this procedure, the latter may be taken as an indication of the direction in which future changes may be made.

This procedure cannot be, and is not intended to be, applied blindly. Its purpose is to provide a basis for *testing* budget allocations for consistency with the relationships developed in this study and with each other. Consistently applied over a period of years, this procedure should lead to a better understanding of sales–advertising relationships.

Exercises

20.1. Sunlife is an established company, selling fresh milk in the Southern California region. It has reviewed its annual performance and is currently allocating funds for advertising in the next fiscal year for its two leading brands, "Daisy Milk" and "Rose Milk." Past sales and advertising expenditure records have indicated diminishing returns from advertising. Sunlife has estimated that sales fluctuate proportionally to $(A_1/A_0)^{68}$, where A_1 is the advertising budget in the period in which sales are attempted to be forecasted and A_0 represents the previous period's advertising

TABLE 20.1

	Daisy Milk	Rose Milk
Sales per year (bottles)	14,000	20,000
Unit price	$0.80	$0.96
Cost of sales	$0.50	$0.70
Selling and administrative expenses (excluding advertising)	$0.14	$0.10
Advertising in the Southern California region in 1980	$1,000	$2,000

budget. At the same time, the company also estimated that if advertising is kept at a constant amount, sales are likely to remain unchanged from 1980. Basic costs and sales data for the two brands for 1980 are given in Table 20.1.

Given that the company plans to spend no more than $7,000 on advertising for the two brands in the next year, how should it allocate its funds optimally between "Daisy" and "Rose" to maximize profits? (Carry out your calculations for advertising expenditures from $1,000 to $7,000 in increments of $1,000.)

20.2. Healthcare is a leading company in the sale of two brands of soap, "Fresh" and "Dewdrops." Its advertising and promotion department is presently reviewing the annual advertising budget allocated to each brand. Past sales and advertising expenditure records have indicated diminishing returns from advertising. Healthcare has estimated sales to fluctuate by a factor equal to (A_1/A_0), where A_1 is the advertising budget in the period for which sales are to be forecasted and A_0 represents the previous period's advertising budget. If the advertising budget is maintained at a constant amount annually, sales are not expected to differ from those of previous years.

The department has collected the data in Table 20.2 to be used in determining the best allocation of advertising expenditures between the two brands, with a target budget of no more than $2,000 above the amount spent on advertising (for the two brands) in the base year.

TABLE 20.2

	Fresh	Dewdrops
Annual sales	$20,000	$40,000
Unit price	$1.00	$1.20
Cost of sales	$0.55	$0.80
Selling and administrative expenses (excluding advertising)	$0.25	$0.22
Advertising in the base year	$3,000	$4,000

Using the above information, decide what is the best way to allocate the budget between the two brands. (Calculate using advertising expenditures from $2,000 to $7,000, in increments of $1,000.)

A Quantitative Method for Structuring a Profitable Sales Force

21

C. Davis Fogg   Josef W. Rokus

The structure and composition of a sales force varies widely from one company to another. Authorities on sales force management agree that each sales force must be structured to fit the unique needs of the company and its management.[1] This article describes a quantitative method to define the most profitable type of sales force (such as direct factory controlled, independent representatives, mixed representatives and direct sales forces, or sales forces shared with other companies or divisions), to calculate the number of salesmen of each type and the management structure needed to control them, and to calculate the maximum potential profits from each type of sales force evaluated.

This method should prove particularly valuable to sales and marketing managers faced with the need to establish a new sales force for new products, to restructure and reevaluate old systems in response to changes in volume or profitability, and/or to combine and restructure sales forces when companies are being merged and their products can be sold to the same customers through the same distribution channels. While the method is illustrated here with an example for a noncapital industrial good, it can be easily modified and used to effectively structure selling efforts in other industries such as capital goods, consumer durables, and nondurables.

The Method

The method specifically takes into account the following key factors which affect both sales volume and profit: (1) *market penetration* and, consequently, sales, which vary from one type of sales force to another and depend on the quality, strength, and type of competitive sales forces; (2) *selling costs*, which depend upon the type of sales force chosen; and (3) *manufacturing costs*, which vary with sales volume.

The measure of profitability used to distinguish between alternate sales forces is *contribution to operating margin*, which is defined as follows:

$$COM = GM - SC$$

Reprinted from *Journal of Marketing*, Vol. 37 (July 1973), pp. 8–17, published by the American Marketing Association.

[1] See, for example, John C. Aspley, *Sales Manager's Handbook*, 7th ed. (Chicago: Darnell Corp., 1956); J. Russell Doubman, *Fundamentals of Sales Management* (New York: F. S. Crofts and Co., 1937); Paul H. Hystrom, ed., *Marketing Handbook* (New York: The Ronald Press Co., 1948).

where:

    COM = contribution to operating margin
    GM   = gross margin = net sales − manufacturing cost of goods sold
    SC   = direct cost of the sales force, including salaries, travel and other expenses,
              management overhead, training, etc.

This definition of profit includes only those factors which are directly influenced by the sales force and method of selling.

This analytical method assumes that a nationwide or multi-territory sales force will be established. The steps in the analysis are discussed below and summarized in Figure 1.

FIGURE 1. *Schematic flow of steps in defining the most profitable sales force*

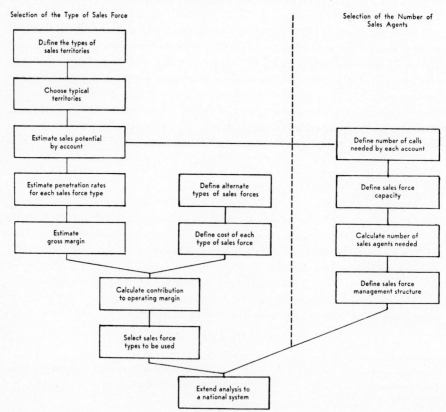

Selection of the Type of Sales Force to Be Used

The first step is to *define the sales territories*, that is, to define the types of sales territories to be evaluated. Sales territories usually fall into two categories: (1) *major territories*, where there are a large number of accounts with high potential in a relatively small geographic area; and (2) *minor territories*, where there are a small number of accounts in a relatively large geographic area.

After the sales territories have been defined, the manager should *choose one typical territory* of each type for further analysis. He should then *estimate the sales potential by account* by identifying all accounts in the typical territory and defining the sales potential for the product being considered in each account. Sales potential may be based on current data or on forecasts of future sales using historical information and expected growth rates.

The next step is to *define the alternate types of sales forces available*. For example, two common types are direct factory salesmen and commissioned manufacturers' representatives. Subsequently, the manager should *estimate the ultimate penetration* of each type of sales force at different size accounts and *define the cost of the sales force* for each type of sales force considered.

The last three steps involve *estimating the gross margin* for each product line to be marketed at different volume levels, *calculating the contribution to the operating margin* expected from each sales force alternative, and, finally, *selecting the sales force types* which make the maximum contribution to operating margin.

Selection of the Number of Sales Agents of Each Type for the Typical Territory

This second part of the method under discussion, the selection of the number of sales agents, involves four major steps. First, the manager must *define account needs*, that is, sales force time and calls per week required by each account. Second, he should *define sales force capacity*, which is the time available and geographic coverage of each type of salesman being used. The third step requires the calculation of the *number of salesmen of each type* which will be needed, and the fourth calls for the definition of the *management structure* needed to manage the typical territory.

Extension to a Larger Area System (Regional or National)

Once the type of sales force is chosen for the typical territories, all other territories of each type can be easily and quickly evaluated by (1) defining the number of accounts in the territory, (2) defining their potential using data generated during the typical territory analysis, and (3) repeating the steps indicated above to determine the number of sales agents and the sales management structure.

Application of the Method

The following example is based on work done in restructuring sales forces for passive electronic components such as resistors and capacitors. The method has been used both to restructure an existing sales territory and to aid in combining the sales forces of a major company and a recent acquisition. The numbers used in the example are fictitious, but they are realistic for passive electronic components.

Objective

The objective of this analysis is to define the most profitable, practical national sales force to handle two passive electronic components—product X and product Y. In this example, the two products are already being successfully sold to the same market, and some knowledge of the market and customers exists.

Selection of the Type of Sales Force

Territory Definition.   There are two types of territories for electronic components. *Major territories* are characterized as geographically compact with a large number of accounts; broad distribution of account sizes; major sales potential; and different types of accounts—e.g., military, consumer, data processing, and telecommunications. Typical major territories would be New England, New York—Long Island, and Los Angeles. *Minor territories* are characterized as geographically dispersed with a small number of customers in a large area, a long travel time between accounts, and a moderate to small sales potential. Parts of the southeastern United States, such as Georgia, Florida, Alabama, and Mississippi, might be classified as minor territories. There may be additional types of territories for products other than electronic components, for example, intermediate territories with moderate account density and potential or isolated cities with a few large high-potential customers.

Choice of Typical Territory.   So that the method of restructuring the sales force can be confidently applied throughout the market, the territories selected as typical should be representative in geographic concentration of accounts and travel time between accounts; average number of accounts; size distribution of customers (the percentage distribution of customers from small to large); and the type of customer—military, industrial, consumer, or special (accounts requiring intensive sales force attention to design components into new products). This example will deal only with major territories. A fictional territory has been selected that is typical of the major territories.

Estimate of Sales Potential by Accounts.   Two types of data are needed to estimate sales potential by account: a complete list of accounts in the territory and potential sales at each account for products X and Y.

A *list of potential accounts* (account census) was compiled from three sources:

accounts that are currently customers, a list of accounts from current or potential distributors, and directories listing accounts buying and manufacturing electronic components and equipment.[2]

The *potential sales for each account* can be determined as follows. For large accounts with high potential, this information can often be obtained from the existing sales force and distributors. Salesmen, contrary to common opinion, can be good market researchers if trained to ask the right questions of the proper respondent and if well supervised in the collection and interpretation of data. The potential for other accounts (or the potential for all accounts if not currently selling in this market) is obtained by one of two methods. The first is the use of *sample surveys* which group accounts into discrete categories based on total sales or number of employees, sample-survey each group to determine their potential, and extrapolate the sample to all accounts. The second is *an input/output method* which obtains the input/output coefficient for products X and Y. This coefficient is defined as follows:

$$\text{I/O coefficient} = \frac{\text{dollar consumption of a product}}{\text{dollar sales of equipment using the product}}$$

Multiply this coefficient by the dollar equipment sales of each account to obtain the account's sales potential. Account equipment sales are available from directories such as the two cited.[3]

Input/output coefficients are available from three sources: (1) *historic sales* to accounts, where their potential and sales of finished goods are known; (2) *sample survey* of a few accounts of various types to define the I/O coefficient; and (3) *published services* such as Quantum Science's MAPTEK Data Base,[4] which lists the I/O coefficient for a wide variety of electronic components and equipment types.

The total sales potential for each account equals:

$$(\$ \text{ equipment sales}) \times (\text{I/O}_X + \text{I/O}_Y)$$

Once the potential for each account is calculated, the accounts are ranked by sales potential, and the total potential in each group is summarized for further analysis. See Table 1 (Columns 1, 2, and 3).

Definition of Alternate Types of Sales Forces Available.   For passive electronic components, the alternative types of sales forces available are: *direct salesmen*—salesmen employed exclusively by the manufacturer to sell his product; *manufacturers' representatives*—independents who represent a number of noncompeting manufacturers for a commission on sales; and *mixed*—a combination of direct men plus

---

[2] Examples of such directories in the electronics field are: *Electronic Marketing Directory* (New York: National Credit Office, 1971); and *The Electronic Engineer* (Philadelphia: Chilton Publications, 1968).

[3] Same reference as footnote 2.

[4] *MAPTEK Strategy Study—Component Industry* (New York: Quantum Science Corp., 1969) and *Component Industry* (New York: Quantum Science Corp., 1971).

TABLE 1. *Calculation of contribution to operating margin of a direct sales force*

(1) Account potential ($000)	(2) No. of accts.	(3) Sales potential (1 × 2) ($000)	(4) Calls/ acct. per year	(5) Total calls needed (2 × 4)	(6) Cost/ call ($)	(7) Total cost ($)	(8) Ave. pene- tration (%)	(9) Ex- pected sales ($000)	(10) Ave. G.M. per- centage (%)	(11) Ave. G.M. (10 × 9) ($000)	(12) COM (11 − 7) ($000)	(13) COM per acct. (12 ÷ 2) ($000)
800 –1,200	1	1,000	50	50	110	5,500	40	400	39	156	150.5	150.5
500 – 800	1	650	50	50	110	5,500	40	260	39	101	95.5	95.5
300 – 500	3	1,200	50	150	110	16,500	40	480	39	187	170.5	56.8
100 – 300	6	1,200	45	270	110	29,700	40	480	39	187	157.3	26.2
50 – 100	7	525	35	245	110	26,950	35	184	41	75	48.1	6.9
25 – 50	22	825	35	770	110	84,700	35	289	41	118	33.3	1.5
12 – 25	14	259	20	280	110	30,800	35	91	41	37	6.2	.46
6 – 12[a]	18	162	10	180	110	19,800	30	49	43	21	1.2	.06
3 – 6	28	125	6	168	110	18,480	30	38	43	16	(2.5)	(.09)
1.5– 3	25	56	6	150	110	16,500	30	17	43	7	(9.5)	(.38)
0.5– 1.5	21	21	6	126	110	13,860	30	6	43	3	(10.9)	(.52)
0 – 0.5	80	20	6	480	110	52,800	30	6	43	3	(49.8)	(.62)
								2,299		912	589.9	

[a] No calls would be made below this level for an all-direct organization, although the indicated number of calls would theoretically be necessary to adequately service the small accounts.

representatives, with the direct man usually handling the largest accounts, and the representative handling the remainder.

In addition, electronic component distributors are the principal means of selling to small accounts and providing rapid delivery of small quantity purchases to medium-large accounts. They do not, however, have the time or knowledge to effectively sell an end customer on using a specific manufacturer's product line and are, therefore, not a practical alternative to representatives or direct salesmen in this industry. The time and cost of servicing and motivating the distributor must, however, be included when evaluating alternate sales forces.

Penetration by Type of Sales Force and Size of Account.   Market and account penetration varies according to three key factors. The first factor is the *type of salesman*. For example, representatives are usually less effective than direct salesmen, particularly for large accounts that buy on contract. Second is the *size of the account*. Penetration tends to be lower at smaller accounts irrespective of the type of sales force used. Small accounts usually get less sales force attention than large accounts and are, therefore, more easily picked off by competitors who are particularly aggressive at certain times or by competitors who have been selling to them on a personal basis for a number of years. The final consideration is *competition*. The quality and strength of competition is evaluated by the quality and strength (number) of salesmen, the historic penetration (it is difficult to budge someone who is well established unless you have an advantage), product quality and uniqueness, and service.

The following sources are used to estimate the maximum penetration that can be obtained with each kind of sales force: (a) *history*—historical results if the company has been selling in this market; (b) *competition*—the results obtained by competitors who use different types of sales forces; and (c) *similar noncompetitors*—results of non-competitors selling a similar product and using different types of sales forces.

The probable penetration for each method is obtained by subjectively lowering the maximum penetrations to account for the quality, strength, and typical sales force used by competitors.

Table 1 (column 8) and Table 2 (column 5) contain estimates of probable penetration for products X and Y by account size and for both representative and direct sales organizations.

Cost of the Sales Forces.   Representatives are paid a straight commission on sales, usually 5%–10%, when given complete responsibility for a territory. Commission rates go up if key large accounts are taken away and handled by direct salesmen. On the other hand, a direct salesman costs approximately $34,000 per year and can make approximately 310 customer location calls per year. The cost per customer call is $110 and includes salary, direct sales management overhead, travel and expenses, fringe benefits, and the cost of servicing distributors.

The total cost of servicing an account equals the cost per call times the number of calls that a salesman must make on an account to adequately service it. In general, the

TABLE 2. *Calculation of contribution to operating margin for an all-representative organization*

(1)	(2)	(3)	(4)	(5)	(6)	(7)	(8)
Account potential ($000)	No. of accts.	Ave. sales potential per account ($000)	Total potential (3 × 2) ($000)	Ave. penetration (%)	Expected sales ($000)	Ave. G.M. (%)	Ave. G.M. ($000)
800 –1,200	1	1,000	1,000	30	300	39	117
500 – 800	1	650	650	30	195	39	76
300 – 500	3	400	1,200	30	360	39	140
100 – 300	6	200	1,200	30	360	39	140
50 – 100	7	75	525	30	158	41	65
25 – 50	22	37.5	825	30	248	41	101
12 – 25	14	18.5	259	30	78	41	32
6 – 12	18	9.0	162	25	40	43	17
3 – 6	28	4.5	126	25	32	43	14
1.5– 3	25	2.25	56	25	14	43	6
0.5– 1.5	21	1.00	21	25	5	43	2
0 – 0.5	80	.25	20	25	5	43	2
					1,794		

[a] Percentage rate times expected sales (column 6).

number of calls per customer location per month and the time a salesman (direct or representative) spends on an account will increase (a) the larger the account or its potential, (b) the more complex the product and more frequent the product redesign, (c) the more frequently orders are placed, and/or (d) the larger the number of lines handled. Column 4 of Table 1 indicates the average number of calls required to adequately service accounts of different potential.

Data on the number of calls needed is obtained from *historical data* where accounts have been adequately serviced and penetrated and from *sample surveys* of customers.

Gross Margin Estimates.   Column 10 of Table 1 gives the estimates of gross margin as a percent of sales by account size and total sales volume range.

Calculation of the Contribution to Operating Margin.   The cost and contribution of each alternative sales force can now be calculated. These calculations are shown in Table 2.

Direct Sales Force. The contribution to operating margin of a direct sales force is $589,900 per year. This is calculated in Table 1 according to the following formula:

$$\text{COM} = \sum_{1}^{n} \{[\text{account potential} \times \text{number of accounts} \\ \times \text{percent penetration} \times \text{percent gross margin}] \\ - [\text{number of accounts} \times \text{calls year} \times \text{cost/call}]\}$$

(9) Cost ($000) commission rate[a]			(10 COM ($100) (8) − (9) commission rate			(11) COM/Acct. ($000) (10) ÷ (2) commission rate		
5%	7%	9%	5%	7%	9%	5%	7%	9%
15.0	21.1	27.0	102.0	96.0	90.0	102.0	96.0	96.0
9.8	13.6	17.6	66.2	62.4	58.4	66.2	62.4	58.4
18.0	25.2	32.4	122.0	114.8	107.6	40.7	38.3	35.9
18.0	25.2	32.4	122.0	114.8	107.6	20.3	19.1	17.9
7.9	11.0	14.2	57.1	54.0	50.8	8.2	7.7	7.3
12.4	17.3	22.3	88.6	83.7	78.7	4.0	3.8	3.6
3.9	5.4	7.0	28.1	26.6	25.0	2.0	1.9	1.8
2.0	2.8	3.6	15.0	14.2	13.4	0.8	0.8	0.7
1.6	2.2	2.8	12.4	11.8	11.2	0.44	0.42	0.40
0.7	1.0	1.3	5.3	5.0	4.7	0.21	0.20	0.19
0.3	0.4	0.5	1.7	1.6	1.5	.080	.076	.075
0.2	0.4	0.4	1.8	1.6	1.6	.023	.020	.020
			622.2	586.6	550.5			

where:

$$n = \text{account-potential-size group}$$
$$COM = \text{contribution to operating margin}$$

Representatives Only. The contribution to operating margin for an all-representative organization is:

Commission rate	COM ($000)
5%	622.2
7%	586.6
9%	550.5

The contribution to operating margin is computed according to the following formula (see Table 2):

$$COM = \sum_{1}^{n} \{[\text{average account potential} \times \text{number of accounts}$$
$$\times \text{percent penetration} \times \text{percent gross margin}]$$
$$- [\text{sales} \times \text{commission rate}]\}$$

The calculations of Tables 1 and 2 were performed using two time-sharing computer programs.

Representatives + Direct. The objective in a mixed system is to define the individual account size (break-even point) where the contribution to the operating margin of a representative force equals that of a direct sales force. Above the break-even account size, a direct force normally has a higher contribution to operating margin; and below this point, the representative's contribution is usually higher.

FIGURE 2. *Contribution to operating margin for a single account of a direct sales force and representatives*

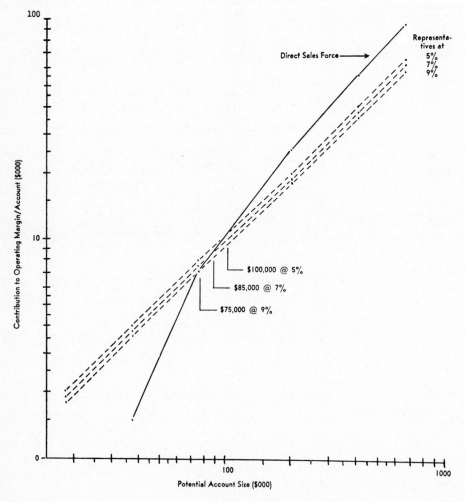

The break-even point is a function of the representative's commission rate. Figure 2 plots contribution to operating margin for a *single account* of a direct force versus a representative force at various commission rates. The data for the calculations are shown in Table 1 (column 13) and Table 2 (column 11). The contribution to operating margin at each break-even point is:

Commission rate	COM ($000)[a]	Representatives given accounts with sales potential less than or equal to ($000)
5%	785	100
7%	772	85
9%	761	75

[a] The contribution to operating margin would be the same for the three commission rates if the account size groups were further broken down.

Selection of the Sales Force to Be Used.   Figure 3 compares the total contribution to the operating margin of: a direct sales force; a representative force at 5%, 7%, and 9%; and a mixed representative-direct sales force at various commission rates. The choice is clearly to have a mixed sales force if representatives can be obtained under any of the following conditions:

Commission rate	Representatives given accounts with sales potential less than or equal to ($000)
5%	100
7%	85
9%	75

The key question at this point is whether or not there are enough accounts to generate sufficient revenue to attract a good representative at any combination of account sizes and commission rates. Commissions must be high enough to attract a good representative (or representatives) and place the product line among the representative's top three-to-five revenue earners so that it will get adequate attention.

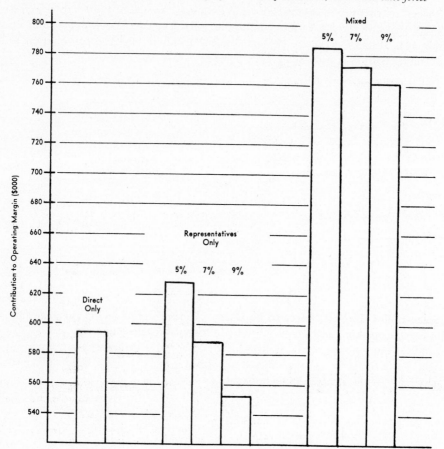

FIGURE 3. *Contribution to operating margin for direct, representative, and mixed sales forces*

The following table summarizes the revenue which the representatives will receive at various commission rates:

Commission rate	Representatives given accounts with sales potential less than or equal to ($000)	Number of accounts	Commission ($000)
5%	100	215	29
7%	85	214	33
9%	75	212	45

The next step is to find a representative (or representatives) who will handle the territory for one of the above commission rate-account size combinations. In the remaining calculations, it is assumed that a representative will take all accounts below $100,000 in sales potential at a 5% commission rate.

Determination of the Number of Sales Agents

Representatives. The number of manufacturers' representatives needed depends on the size of the geographic territory. Ideally, the fewer firms one has to deal with, the better. Regardless of the number of representatives necessary to cover the territory, it is extremely important to insure: (1) that the representative has enough salesmen to cover all of the territory's accounts; (2) that the salesmen currently call on the accounts being assigned with adequate frequency (particularly the smaller accounts); (3) that the potential revenue from the products ranks high (within the top five) in the representative's list of money earnings; and (4) that the reputation and quality of the sales force is consistent with criteria for these factors. In this case, it is assumed that one firm of manufacturers' representatives is selected.

Direct Sales Force. Once a representative is selected, the required number of direct men can be calculated.

Definition of Account Needs. The eleven customers with sales potentials *over* $100,000 will require 520 location calls per year as shown in Table 1.

Sales Force Capacity. In a major territory, a direct salesman can handle approximately two location calls per day or a total of 310 location calls per year. This call capacity allows time for managing distributors, salesman training, salesman sick days, salesman vacations, sales meetings, paperwork, plant visits, and the like, as well as assisting the representative and distributors with their customers. This call capacity assumes that the representative is managed by a district manager and not by the direct (company) salesman.

Number of Salesmen Needed. The number of direct salesmen needed $=$

$$\frac{\text{total calls required/year}}{\text{salesman's call capacity/year}} = \frac{520}{310} = 2$$

Management Structure. A single manager can normally handle approximately five direct men or seven representatives. The management needed for this territory is 0.5 man calculated as follows:

$$\frac{\text{number of direct men}}{5} + \frac{\text{number of representatives}}{7} = \frac{2}{5} + \frac{1}{7} = 0.5$$

The management of this territory can thus be combined with that of another.

Optimum Territory. The optimum territory involves:

(a) *Supervision*: 0.5 man.
(b) *Direct men*: two who will supervise distribution and handle key accounts above $100,000 in sales potential.
(c) *Representatives*: one firm handling accounts less than $100,000 in volume at a 5% commission rate.
(d) *Potential*: the territory should ultimately contribute $785,000 to operating margin after sales and plant expenses but before other expenses.

Extension to Other Major Territories

If a representative major territory was selected for the first analysis, a detailed analysis is not needed for the other major territories. Instead, the process can be simplified into three major steps. First, estimate each account's potential on the basis of knowledge or extrapolation using input/output ratios developed in the typical territory analysis. Second, split accounts between direct and representative organizations based on their potential and on the commission rate-account-size combinations shown to be most profitable during the analysis of the typical territory. Third, define the number of direct men and supervisors needed.

Minor Territories

An analysis similar to that described for major territories can be done for minor territories.

Managerial Implications of the Method

General Cautions in Using the Method

There are two key cautions to observe in applying the method described in this article. First, the numerical results should be used as a guide for decision making and not as the absolute rule. Other qualitative factors that could change the decision in each territory should be identified and considered—factors such as the strength of competition or the availability of a particularly good salesman or representative in a specific territory. For example, the analysis may indicate that a territory should be handled by a direct salesman, but the availability of a particularly effective representative with established account relationships well might reverse the decision. The representative may be able to achieve above-average account penetration and be more profitable than a direct salesman. Or the analysis may indicate one level of sales force strength while particularly strong competition may practically dictate a higher, less profitable, level. Second, it must be recognized that territories may change in the future—in the number of accounts, their potential, the number and strength of competitors, and so on. The manager should attempt to base his analysis on anticipated future conditions and be prepared to redo the analysis if market conditions change.

Considerations Involved in Changing Sales Forces

If this type of analysis is being used to restructure or merge two sales organizations, the following qualitative factors should be considered *before* recommended changes are implemented.

1. *Special relationships* which may exist between some customers and specific salesmen or representatives which might be damaged by transferring the account.
2. *Utilization of direct salesmen (if any)*. A company will probably be reluctant to drop most of its experienced salesmen in favor of representatives or vice versa unless application of the above analysis points overwhelmingly to such a decision.
3. *Control*. A direct sales force is usually easier to control than representatives. Management must decide how much control it will relinquish in moving towards a mixed sales force.
4. *Short-term sales loss*. In most cases, any significant changes in sales force structure will result in a short-term sales loss. The significance of this loss must be evaluated.
5. *Flexibility*. Because it is difficult or even impossible to restructure the sales force repeatedly, thought must be given to how any possible future changes will be affected by the present decisions. For example, if a company drops most of its representatives now it will find it cannot rehire those dropped (or maybe any others) should it decide again to sell through representatives in the near future.
6. *Design-in*. If a company's sales are heavily dependent on getting its products designed in (intensive engineering selling to get a customer's engineers to specify a product in a piece of equipment), the question of how well this design-in can be accomplished using representatives or direct salesmen must be considered.

Applying the Method to Other Industries

There are four keys to success for the sales or marketing manager interested in applying this method to other industries. First, he should identify and assess the effectiveness of all selling methods available—representatives and direct salesmen are not necessarily the only alternatives.

Second, he should carefully classify and group customers into homogeneous groups by the *type* of selling effort necessary to service them. If there are several classes of end customers that must be serviced by several different types of salesmen, a complete analysis may have to be run for each class of end customer. For example, in selling electronic components the same general purpose representative or salesman can service all classes of customers—manufacturers of television sets, missiles, telecommunications equipment, computers, electronic instruments, and the like. In selling computers, however, salesmen may have to specialize by major class of customer—such as manufacturing, utilities, airlines, educational institutions, or financial firms—because of the specialized technical knowledge needed to serve each industry.

Third, he should look carefully at the geographic distribution of his customers.

There may be more than the simple major and minor territories found in the electronic components business, and an analysis may have to be run for each type of territory.

Finally, the role of physical distributor should be carefully evaluated. The distributor may play an important part in selling (not just distributing) a specific manufacturer's brand to the end customer.

Comparison with Other Methods

There are three other methods typically used to structure a sales force: (1) "seat of the pants"—guessing what is needed based on precedent or "gut feel"; (2) duplicating what the competition has done; and (3) evaluating alternative sales forces on cost alone to minimize the cost of serving known accounts.

The method presented in this article has a number of advantages over other methods. First, it *focuses on profit* and not cost. Sometimes the more expensive selling method is more profitable because of its ability to get higher market penetration, higher sales volume, and higher profit volume and margins. Second, it *accounts for all sales controlled factors influencing profitability*. It gives the sales manager reasonable certainty that he has reached the right decision by forcing him to think about all of the factors affecting sales force profitability: number of accounts, account potential, penetration ability of alternate selling methods, cost of each selling method, overhead expenditures, and so on. Third, it *helps choose the optimum sales force, thereby minimizing risk* of lost sales and profits due to too little selling effort and subsequent poor market penetration or poor profitability due to a selling effort that is larger and more expensive than warranted by the territory potential. Finally, it *forces in-depth knowledge of territories by salesmen* who must provide information for the analysis. This alone can force salesmen out of stale, comfortable call patterns and stimulate them to seek new business.

The method has three distinct disadvantages over less rigorous methods: (1) *it requires extensive quantitative information* about the market; (2) it generally takes more *time and money* to execute; and (3) it *must be repeated* occasionally—every two to four years or when market conditions change significantly—to be effective.

Future Implications

The analytical method presented in this article can be expanded to become the basis for a sales force information and control system. The system would have four objectives: first, establish the optimum sales force; second, measure market penetration and profit performance against predicted goals, territory by territory; third, identify problem territories so that corrective action can be taken to improve performance; and fourth, reevaluate the selling effort on a periodic basis and change the sales force if required by changes in the market.

Accomplishment of these objectives requires an extensive computer model based on the analytical method presented, an annual or biannual account census to update the market information in the model, and a computer program to periodically compare actual results versus those predicted by the model.

Summary

The method for structuring a sales force described in this article quantifies most of the factors which must be considered in deciding how a company's products are to be sold. Traditionally, such decisions have been based on qualitative factors without any explicit determination of how the various alternatives would affect operating margin dollars. The method presented here permits a company to consider variously structured sales forces to arrive at the structure which will maximize its operating margin.

Exercises

21.1. Prochemco, a well-known manufacturer of dyes, was experiencing a sales decline in its major product line, the P–Ch compound. Anxious to reverse the trend, management decided, among other measures, on an evaluation of its sales structure.

The company had always employed direct factory salespeople; however, in the last few years some of its competitors had switched to a mixed force. Management wanted to analyze the different types of sales forces available; they would then select the one that would make the maximum contribution to operating margin. They requested salespeople's input in order to determine the typical territory. Estimates of the sales potential were obtained from company records, industry surveys, competition, and other sources. (See Table 21.1 for relevant data.)

TABLE 21.1. Typical territory

Acct. potential ($000)	No. of accounts	Calls/acct. per year	Average penetration (%) with direct force	Average penetration (%) with representatives	Estimate of average G.M. as % of sales
700–1,000	1	40	30	20	30
500– 700	2	40	30	20	30
200– 500	5	30	25	20	32
100– 200	8	30	25	20	32
50– 100	20	20	20	15	35
10– 50	40	8	20	15	35
0– 10	70	4	20	15	35

Cost per customer call is estimated at $125.

A representative force can be obtained on a 5%, 8%, or 10% commission rate.

1. Calculate the contribution to operating margin using a direct sales force and using a representative force at the various commission rates.
2. If the company decides to follow competition in employing a mixed force, which accounts should be handled by representatives?
3. Based on your results, should the company change its present sales structure? Why, or why not?
4. What are some of the considerations that must be taken into account when changing a sales force?

21.2.   The Sobi Company, a subsidiary of a large Japanese multinational corporation, had recently merged with a small midwestern appliance company. Although the acquired company used primarily a direct sales force, Sobi's management felt that a mixed sales force might be more profitable. The vice-president in charge of sales agreed and decided to investigate. He requested all the sales records for a typical territory. Additional information was obtained from salespeople's questionnaires, company records, industry surveys, and the like. With the help of experts in the field he and members of his staff sifted through the data to obtain the information in Table 21.2.

TABLE 21.2

Acct. potential ($000)	No. of accts.	Calls/acct. per year	Average penetration (%) with direct force	Average penetration (%) with representatives	Estimate of average G.M. as % of sales
300–500	2	30	40	25	35
200–300	5	30	40	25	35
100–200	6	30	40	25	35
75–100	10	20	30	25	38
50– 75	25	20	30	25	38
25– 50	30	10	25	25	38
15– 25	50	6	25	20	38
10– 15	60	6	25	20	40
5– 10	75	3	25	20	40
0– 5	90	2	25	20	40

The cost per customer call by a salesperson is $115. This includes salary, direct sales management overhead, travel expenses, fringe benefits, and the cost of servicing distributors.

Representatives are paid a straight commission on sales, usually 5% to 10%.

1. Calculate the contribution to operating margin using a direct sales force and using a representative force at 5%, 7%, and 10%.
2. Calculate the contribution to operating margin per account using the different types of sales forces. Based on your results, which accounts should be handled by direct salespeople, and which should be handled by representatives?
3. Should the company employ a mixed sales force, or should it stick to direct salespeople? Justify your answer.

Sales Recruiting— A Major Area of Underinvestment

22

René Y. Darmon   Stanley J. Shapiro

Introduction

Given the substantial and ever increasing costs of personal selling, it is not surprising to find a rapidly growing literature dealing with more nearly optimal methods of designing sales territories [1], structuring sales forces [2], and allocating sales effort [3]. Similarly, practitioners remain vitally interested in such traditional concerns of sales management as recruitment, selection, training, compensation, and control; and research continues to be conducted in these areas. However, one important area—the amount that firms should be prepared to spend first in generating a pool of applicants for sales positions and then in selecting from among that pool the salesmen to be hired as replacements or net additions—has received scant attention. This article deals with that gap in the analytical literature of sales management by demonstrating a method of determining "how much should be spent" on recruiting and screening candidates for the sales force [4]. Application of the method being proposed to a hypothetical but nevertheless realistic set of circumstances suggests that many major corporations may be spending far less than they should on sales force recruitment and selection.

XYZ Corporation—Recruitment Expenditures and Sales Force Performance

Let us begin by examining the "fact pattern" of sales force recruitment at XYZ corporation, a manufacturer of industrial supplies. We could expect XYZ to sell directly to very large accounts as well as through distributors. The firm could quite conceivably have 240 sales representatives, each assigned to a separate district or territory. One might further presume that the turnover rate of the sales force has been averaging 20%, with the average salesman therefore spending five years with XYZ.

Given the high cost of training industrial salesmen and a steadily rising cost-per-call ratio, XYZ is taking a number of steps to reduce sales force turnover. No change is anticipated, however, in the amount spent on recruiting applicants or actually selecting the fifty sales representatives hired each year. XYZ now spends $60,000 a year, or about $1,200 per sales representative, on just the variable or out-of-pocket expenditures associated with sales force recruitment and selection. Most XYZ executives believe that $1,200 per representative is more than enough for the task being performed. But is $1,200 a sales representative the right amount to be spending? Could it be too much or too little? To answer these questions, we don't have to know much more about XYZ corporation or any firm like it. Also, the information required is likely to be either already on hand or extremely easy to collect.

Let us assume that XYZ spends $40,000 of the $60,000 mentioned above in generating annually a pool of 1,000 applicants for the fifty positions to be filled. Also, the firm's executives might well have estimated that any reasonable number of additional applicants could be generated at a constant marginal cost of $50 for each such applicant. Of course, every applicant for a sales position with XYZ is not screened, tested, and interviewed. On the average, only 200 of the 1,000 applicants in the pool are treated as serious candidates. A considerable amount of executive time is obviously spent on this evaluation process. However, the out-of-pocket or variable costs associated with the screening of serious candidates total $20,000 or approximately $100 per candidate.

Each of the 200 serious candidates for a sales position with XYZ is assigned a numerical rating on a scale running from 0 to 100. That scale, in turn, has five components—each worth a maximum of twenty points. These components include the family profile reflected on the application form, the candidate's letters of recommendation, his or her face-to-face interviews with XYZ's sales executives, past work experience, and the results of a sales aptitude test. Each candidate is rated by five different individuals. The weighted average score of all candidates taken as a group is 60 (with 95% of the candidates falling between 30 and 90), but successful candidates offered positions typically amass an average score of 70.

XYZ executives have evaluated a large number of candidates over the years and are using fairly standardized rating guides. Consequently, the point scores individually assigned each candidate by the five evaluators do not differ a great deal. In 95% of the cases, for a candidate with an average score of 50, the highest point score received would be a 55 and the lowest 45. The same spread among evaluators is all one finds (65 on the low side and 75 on the high side) when an average or mean score of 70 is obtained by an applicant.

Obviously, the fifty sales representatives hired each year are not equally productive. Some generate far more profit for the company than others. The XYZ sales management staff, however, is primarily concerned with minimizing the number of "losers" or "mistakes" who slip through the screening process. Since, on the average, only two out of the fifty salesmen hired each year turn out to be "losers," XYZ considers its screening technique as 96% effective. "Losers" are terminated at the end of their first year of employment, and, on the average, they reduce profits by $10,000. In contrast, the median "acceptable" salesman—some forty-eight out of the fifty hired each year—generates during his average five-year life with the company a profit before taxes of $20,000 per year.

Such are the facts and figures associated with XYZ's recruitment effort and the performance of its sales force. The type of information presented above should be recognized as typical of what any large corporation would routinely generate. But what conclusions, if any, can be reached as to whether the $60,000 being spent by XYZ to generate applicants and evaluate candidates is too much, not enough, or about right?

Given the facts presented above, the authors maintain that XYZ should be spending not $60,000 but $241,000 if sales executives wish to maximize the firm's profits. An expenditure of this amount would result in the firm's generating not 1,000 applications each year but 3,586 such applications. Some 717 applicants, a figure also approximately 3.6 times the number of applicants (200) now being so considered, would be evaluated as serious candidates for the fifty available positions.

On what basis have those conclusions been reached? What makes us so sure XYZ is underspending? Our findings are generated by a statistical decision theory technique adapted from an approach originally developed by Gross to determine the number of different advertisements that should be created before one was chosen for use in a campaign [5]. The essentials of this modified approach are described below, with the relevant information previously presented on the XYZ corporation being used in the analysis.

Toward a More Nearly Optimal XYZ Expenditure

The approach in question builds on the assumption that a sales manager would hire better quality recruits if he started with a larger pool—say, 2,000 rather than 1,000 applicants from which to select the fifty salesmen he needs. More specifically, the procedure estimates the additional profit that can be expected from the resulting improvement in the quality of the fifty sales recruits subsequently chosen. Steps should be taken to increase the pool of applicants as long as the expected profits from better quality recruits are sufficient to cover the additional costs of recruitment and selection.

Only five quantities need to be estimated in order to determine the "optimal" size of applicant pool and the number of those applicants who should be interviewed:

1. The marginal cost of generating additional applicants for available sales positions (g).
2. The marginal cost of interviewing, screening, and processing each applicant considered as a serious candidate (c).
3. An estimate of a reliability index (between 0 and 1) of the recruiting process, representing the extent to which the process would yield the same results if it were repeated a large number of times on the same candidates and under the same conditions (R).

4. An estimate of a validity index (between 0 and 1) of the recruiting process, representing the extent to which the process leads to good decisions (r).
5. A measure of the dispersion of the expected profit outlook of the population of potential applicants for sales positions (s).

These five numbers are used to compute a single quantity (K), such that $K = (c + g)/sRr^1$. Then, K is compared to a statistical quantity (E_p), which is a previously tabulated function of the proportion (p) of candidates to be hired out of a pool of applicants [4]. The solution is the largest p for which E_p is larger than K. A formal demonstration of the entire procedure is found in a previously published paper of the senior author [4].

In the case of XYZ, the marginal cost (g) of generating each additional applicant was estimated at \$50. The expected cost of screening, testing and interviewing an additional applicant is \$100 × 0.2 = \$20, because only two out of every ten additional applicants will actually be treated as serious candidates for a position.

A joint estimation of reliability times validity (the product of Rr) can be based on the company's own records of the subsequent success or failure of sales recruits [4]. Obviously, the degree of sales force failure reflects the lack of validity and/or reliability of the recruiting process. The joint estimate is based on two proportions (n) and (m). We define n as the proportion of applicants who were hired in the past, this being, in the case of XYZ, $50/1,000 = 0.05$. Similarly, m is the proportion of applicants who were hired but who turned out to be "losers." As far as XYZ is concerned, $m = 2/1,000 = 0.002$. The product Rr is estimated as $Rr = 1 - m/n(1 - n)$, i.e., $Rr = 1 - 0.002/(0.05)(0.95) = 0.958$. This high value suggests that XYZ is using a very valid and reliable procedure for selecting its salesmen.

This estimate is somewhat corroborated by a measure of the reliability R of the selection procedure which can be generated in a different manner. The range within which 95% of the scores of individual candidates across evaluators would fall (assuming a normal distribution) can be estimated to encompass about 4 standard deviations. Thus, the standard deviation of this distribution in the reported example can be estimated as $10/4 = 2.5$. In the same way, the dispersion of all the candidates' average scores can be estimated as $(90-30)/4 = 15$. According to the definition of the reliability index provided by Gross [5], $R = [1 - (2.5)^2/(15)^2]^{\frac{1}{2}} = 0.986$. Assuming this reliability estimate can also be extended to the screening procedure, the validity index can be estimated at $0.958/0.986 = 0.972$. These figures reflect the high success rate of XYZ in selecting effective salesmen from the pool of applicants.

The efficiency measures of all possible applicants (whether interviewed or not) in terms of expected profit dollars are assumed to be normally distributed. In the past, XYZ has successfully selected salesmen who would be found in the furthest 4.8% of

---

[1] This applies to the case where, as for XYZ, the marginal generating and recruiting costs are constant. More general formulas can be found in the original article.

FIGURE 1. *Estimation of the dispersion of the efficiency distribution*

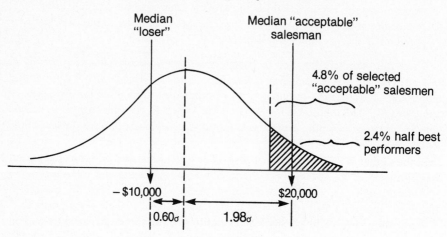

the right hand of this distribution. This is shown in Fig. 1. Consequently, a median XYZ salesman who brings in about $20,000 profit before taxes per year should stand at about 1.98 standard deviations from the mean of the efficiency distribution. But what about the "losers" who average a yearly loss of about $10,000? If they are randomly scattered in the rest of the distribution, their median should stand at about −0.06 standard deviation from the mean. This may well be a very conservative estimate, since it is reasonable to assume that losers who also went through the screening process will not be found throughout the entire efficiency range. Rather, they should also have a tendency to be clustered toward the right of the distribution. Consequently, the difference between the two median performance levels of successful and unsuccessful salesmen ($20,000 + $10,000 = $30,000) should encompass 1.98 + 0.06 = 2.04 standard deviations of the efficiency distribution. This leads to an estimate of $s = \$30,000/2.04 = \$14,706$.

As suggested previously, the five aforementioned estimates are used to compute the quantity $K = 70/(0.958) (14,706) = 0.00497$. According to the tabulated values of E_p, [4] this corresponds to a proportion p of 0.01394 salesmen to be hired. Because XYZ needs fifty salesmen each year, this proportion implies a pool of 50/0.01394 = 3,586 applicants. The profits that can be expected from this proposed solution are shown in Table 1.

An analysis of this table shows that the budget necessary to generate and process this number of applications is $241,000, more than four times the present expenditure level. However, the forty-eight "acceptable" salesmen ultimately selected can be expected to generate an average of not $20,000 but rather $27,059 in profits each year. After taking into account increased recruiting costs, this improvement in sales force

TABLE 1. Comparison between the profit outlooks of the present situation and the proposed solution

	Present situation			Proposed solution			
	No.	$ unit	$ total	No.	$ unit	$ total	% increase
Recruiting costs							
Applicants	1,000	40	40,000	1,000	40	40,000	
Additional applicants	—	—	—	2,586	50	129,300	
	1,000		40,000	3,586		169,300	
Interviews	200	100	20,000	717	100	71,700	
Total			60,000			241,000	+301.7
Profits before taxes of new salesmen (1st year)							
"Acceptable" salesmen	48	20,000	960,000	48	27,059	1,298,832	
"Losers"	2	(10,000)	(20,000)	2	(10,000)	(20,000)	
Total	50		940,000	50		1,278,832	
Additional recruiting costs						(181,000)	
Total			940,000			1,097,832	+16.8

productivity should still yield a 16.8% increase in profits before taxes *for the first year alone*. This profit increase should last over the average of five years that each salesman spends in the sales force. Similarly, if the new procedure is used for recruiting salesmen in subsequent years, the fifty salesmen selected in each of the next four years should also prove 16.8% more effective as profit generators than would otherwise have been the case.

Cautions and Conclusions

Few analytical techniques are without shortcomings, and this one is no exception. First, it may be argued that our solution is not truly "optimal" because it relies on judgmental estimates of the parameters. Alternately, a marked increase in the size of the pool of applicants may put such a strain on managerial time that either the marginal costs of recruitment and evaluation would increase rapidly or fixed costs would be adversely affected. While both criticisms would be valid, they are in themselves not sufficient to cause us to reject findings that so clearly indicate that a marked increase in XYZ's sales force recruitment and selection budget is definitely in order. Indeed, are such results surprising when one considers that corporate recruiting costs are usually relatively minor in comparison with the flow of profits that more effective salesmen selected from a larger pool of applicants are likely to generate?

Although XYZ is a hypothetical corporation, it is by no means an atypical one. The kinds of information needed to use the approach outlined above could be routinely generated by every major firm. It seems likely that most of these organizations would be revealed as underspending in an area where increased corporate outlays would be one of the wisest marketing investments that could be made.

Appendix to Article: How to Find *s*

Of the 1,000 applicants, only forty-eight proved successful (4.8%), and the median profit generated by the successful salespeople was $20,000; 97.6% of the applicants would have generated less than $20,000 in profit had they been hired. In terms of standard deviations, the median successful salesperson should lie 1.980 to the right of the mean of the distribution.

Since the "losers" are assumed to be randomly scattered in the rest of the distribution, the median "loser" should be located in the middle of the remaining 95.2% of the distribution—i.e., at 47.6 (95.2 ÷ 2) and 2.4% to the left of the mean (50 − 47.6 = 2.4%). In terms of standard deviations, the "median loser" who generated $10,000 in profits should therefore lie -0.06σ to the left of the mean.

Now, to find the dollar amount that corresponds to a single standard deviation

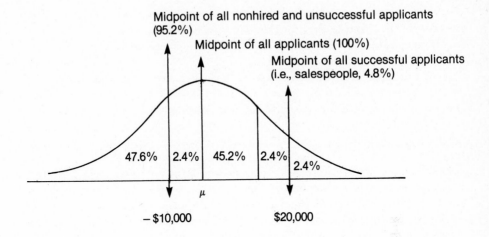

Midpoint of all nonhired and unsuccessful applicants (95.2%)

Midpoint of all applicants (100%)

Midpoint of all successful applicants (i.e., salespeople, 4.8%)

47.6% | 2.4% | 45.2% | 2.4% | 2.4%

μ

$-\$10,000$ $\$20,000$

(σ), one has to divide the difference in dollars and the corresponding difference in standard deviation between the median successful salesperson and the median "loser":

$$\sigma = \frac{\$20,000 - (-\$10,000)}{1.98 - (-0.06)} = \frac{30,000}{2.04} = \$14,706$$

References

1. See for instance Hess, Sydney W., and Samuels, Stuart A. Experiences with a Sales Distributed Model: Criteria and Implementation, *Management Science*, 41–54 (December 1971); Leonard M. Lodish, Sales Territory Alignment to Maximize Profits, *Journal of Marketing Research* 30–36 (February 1975).
2. Fogg, C. Davis, and Rokus, Joseph W. A Quantitative Method for Structuring a Profitable Sales Force, *Journal of Marketing* 8–17 (July 1973).
3. Beswich, Charles E. Allocating Selling Effort via Dynamic Programming, *Management Science* 667–668 (March 1977); Lodish, Leonard M. Callplan: An Interactive Salesman's Call Planning System, *Management Science* 25–40 (December 1971).
4. Darmon, René Y. Sales Force Management: Optimizing the Recruiting Process, *Sloan Management Review* 47–59 (Fall 1978).
5. Gross, Irwin. The Creative Aspects of Advertising, *Sloan Management Review* 83–109 (Fall 1972).

Exercises

22.1. Nutrimetics is a manufacturer of cosmetics made from natural fruits and plants. Since its inception eight years ago, the company has been growing steadily. Its distinctive competence lies in its unique personal selling to beauty and hair salons.

However, the recent high turnover in its sales representatives is causing management worry over the effects on profits of the high costs of training these sales beauticians.

Nutrimetics has solicited the advice of Walter Consultants concerning a better way of recruiting and selecting its sales team.

Each year the company spends a total of $80,000 to hire fifty-four sales representatives. Of this sum, 75% is expended in generating a file of 1,000 applications, while the remaining sum is used for screening and interviewing some 250 applicants to be considered as serious candidates. The company estimates that each additional application will increase costs by 10%. Past records of the performance of the sales force have shown that the salespeople are not all equally productive. During their term of contract with the company, about fifty of the fifty-four sales representatives generate a profit before taxes of $24,000 per year. The company incurs a loss of $9,000 annually on each of the other members of the sales team.

Assuming that you are one of the Walter Consultants, how would you advise Nutrimetics on the following? [The tabulated values of E_p are shown in Table 22.1. Note that the values in the cells are the K values (as explained in the article), while the corresponding p values are given along the side column and top row.]

1. The optimal amount to be spent in recruiting and selecting the fifty-four sales representatives.
2. The new number of applications desired and the corresponding number to be interviewed.
3. The new profit level expected to be generated from these sales representatives during the first year. Show a comparison of the present and the new profit situation.

22.2.   Koodic is a manufacturer of mini movie cameras. The growth of the company had been dramatic until the last two years, when profits took a sharp plunge because of the high turnover in its sales force.

The company has sought the help of Marshall Consultants in designing a more effective sales force recruitment program and has provided the relevant information to enable Marshall's consultants to analyze the case. The company has spent $75,000 annually to hire forty-five salespeople; $50,000 is actually spent in generating a total of 800 applicants, 200 of whom are seriously interviewed and screened for the positions, each at a cost of $125. Each additional application to be generated will cost the company 20% more. Past records of the performance of the sales force have shown that forty of the forty-five salespeople earn for the company an average profit before taxes of $30,000, while the other five reduce profits by $10,000 annually.

If you were one of the Marshall Consultants, how would you advise Koodic on the following? (The tabulated values of E_p are shown in Table 22.1. Note that the values in the cells are the K values, while the corresponding p values are given along the side column and top row.)

TABLE 22.1. *Increase in the expected value of the average best draws (dE_p) when a proportion (p) of observations is selected from a sample of size n from a unit normal distribution*

					Second decimal place of p					
p	0.00	0.01	0.02	0.03	0.04	0.05	0.06	0.07	0.08	0.09
0.0	—	0.003	0.008	0.013	0.018	0.023	0.028	0.034	0.040	0.045
0.1	0.051	0.057	0.063	0.069	0.076	0.082	0.088	0.095	0.101	0.107
0.2	0.114	0.121	0.128	0.136	0.143	0.148	0.155	0.161	0.167	0.175
0.3	0.181	0.188	0.195	0.202	0.208	0.215	0.222	0.228	0.236	0.242
0.4	0.249	0.255	0.261	0.268	0.275	0.281	0.288	0.294	0.301	0.308

1. The optimal amount to be spent recruiting and selecting the forty-five salespeople.
2. The new number of applications desired and the corresponding number to be interviewed.
3. The new profit level expected to be generated from these sales representatives during the first year. Show a comparison of the present and the new profit situation.

Distribution System Analysis: A Problem in Capital Budgeting

23

John R. Grabner, Jr.   James F. Robeson

Business logistics has proven to be a fertile field for the application of many of the techniques and tools of analysis provided by operations research. Linear programming, queuing theory, game theory, E.O.Q. models, etc., have all received widespread attention and have shown themselves to be of value to distribution managers. Indeed, simulations utilizing the more sophisticated of these algorithms may well be the only effective way of dealing with the multi-dimensional problems in distribution analysis.

Perhaps the most basic yet most complicated problem which distribution managers face is that of selecting a system, or systems, for the physical distribution of products.[1] Several models have been developed to help managers as they seek to arrive at a solution to this problem. However, it appears that the greater majority of these models have used decision criteria based almost exclusively on costs. In particular, they usually utilize cost minimization rather than profit maximization as the objective function.

The need for more broadly based decision models has not gone unrecognized, nor has the profit criterion been completely ignored in existing models. Models utilizing cost minimization as the criterion function sometimes deal indirectly with revenue by classifying revenues which could have been achieved but were not as a "cost of lost sales." The purpose of this paper is to present some suggestions for enlarging the conventional scope of distribution analysis to include an explicit consideration of profits and the return which they represent on investment.

The Total Cost Model

The most widely used model for evaluating distribution systems is probably the so-called total cost model. This model permits the manager to examine the inter-dependence of the costs associated with each physical distribution system.[2] It is a

From *Business Logistics: Problems and Perspectives*, David McConoughy, ed. Los Angeles: University of Southern California Research Institute for Business, 1969, pp. 143–156.

[1] The scope of this paper is limited to a discussion of physical distribution systems. However, in most instances, the comments apply equally well to similar aspects of systems of physical supply.

[2] The description of the total cost model which follows is based largely on material found in the following sources: Edward W. Smykay, Donald J. Bowersox and Frank H. Mossman, *Physical Distribution Management* (New York: The MacMillan Co., 1961), 73–87; J. L. Heskett, R. M. Ivie and N. A. Glaskowsky, *Business Logistics: Management of Physical Supply and Distribution* (New York: Ronald Press Co., 1964), 454–69; and H. T. Lewis, J. W. Culliton and J. D. Steele, *The Role of Air Freight in Physical Distribution* (Boston: Division of Research, Graduate School of Business Administration, Harvard University, 1956).

useful technique for approximating the magnitude of the change which might take place in total physical distribution costs as various elements in the distribution system are altered. Some of the elements which are often amenable to alteration include the mode of transportation; type (public or private) of transportation; inventory levels; and the types, locations and numbers of plants and warehouses. Total cost analysis is primarily concerned with the trade-off in costs which occurs as these and other elements are varied.

The concept of cost trade-offs can perhaps best be illustrated by examining the interrelationships between inventories and the transportation system. Inventory carrying costs are often a substantial part of a firm's fixed costs of distribution while the cost of transportation usually constitutes a significant portion of variable distribution costs. As a firm utilizes slower methods of transportation it increases its order cycle time and thereby increases fixed costs per unit because it must carry larger quantities of inventory in order to fill the same level of orders. But, slower forms of transportation typically cost less, which results in decreased variable costs. Therefore, in many distribution systems it seems reasonable to expect variable costs per unit to decrease as total fixed costs increase.

In order to implement the total cost model, the costs associated with each physical distribution system must be divided into their fixed and variable components. Simplified linear cost equations may then be written for each alternative in the following form.

$$TC = F + V \cdot (X)$$

where

$$TC = \text{total cost}$$
$$F = \text{fixed cost}$$
$$V = \text{variable cost per unit of volume}$$
$$X = \text{sales volume (units).}$$

Once the total cost equations have been developed they may be graphed in the manner illustrated in Figure 1. The Y intercept is given by the fixed cost of the system (F) and the slope of each curve is represented by variable costs per unit of volume (V). The conclusion reached earlier, that it is reasonable to expect variable costs to decrease as fixed costs increase, means that it is quite likely that two or more of these curves will intersect.

The total cost curves for each of the physical distribution systems can now be examined to determine which one yields the lowest total cost for distributing each of various levels of forecasted sales. In Figure 1 Alternative I is lower in total cost than any other for volumes up to 10,000 units. At exactly 10,000 units the firm is indifferent as to whether it utilizes System I or System II. In similar fashion, System II would be specified for sales from 10,000 to 12,500 units, System III for volumes from 12,500 to 15,000 and System IV for quantities in excess of 15,000 units.

FIGURE 1. *Graphic presentation of the total cost model*

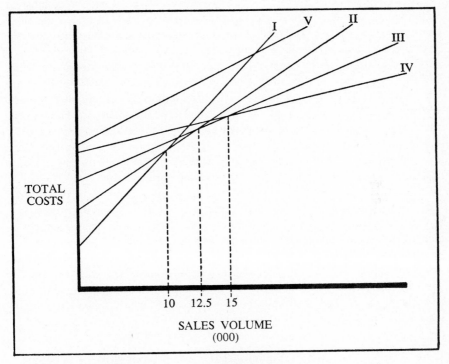

Logistics System #	Total Cost Equation (000)
I	TC=2.0+.30X
II	TC=3.5+.15X
III	TC=4.5+.07X
IV	TC=4.8+.05X
V	TC=5.5+.18X

It is possible for one alternative to have a higher fixed cost than another and also have higher variable costs. System V in Figure 1 is characteristic of such a condition. Since at any volume there would always be another system capable of distributing the product at a lower total cost, such systems are omitted from further analysis.

Limitations of Cost Oriented Models

The total cost model is a useful tool of analysis. However, it has several inherent limitations. It assumes that fixed and variable costs can be clearly identified, that there is a straight line relationship between costs and volume, and that there is a constant average shipment size for goods moving between two points.[3] These limitations certainly reduce the effectiveness of cost based models as an aid to decision making, but their most serious shortcomings appear to be the absence of *explicit* consideration of: (1) the effects which the various levels of customer service provided by each physical distribution system might have on demand, (2) the different levels of investment which may be required to implement each physical distribution system, and (3) the time value of the savings generated by these various investment outlays.

The foregoing criticisms of the total cost approach do not imply that the approach is without merit. Indeed, most users of the technique are undoubtedly well aware of these as well as perhaps other limitations. Recognizing this, one might well wonder why additional attention has not been given to overcoming these limitations.

Ideally, the total cost model should be expanded to a total profit model in which demand effects as well as cost effects are considered. Further, the model should provide a means of incorporating the magnitude and timing of the capital investments required as well as the cost and revenue streams associated with a particular distribution system. These changes can be accomplished by utilizing return on investment rather than total costs as the decision criterion for choosing among alternative physical distribution systems.

The Apex Company: An Illustrative Comparison of Return on Investment and Total Cost Analyses

To demonstrate the similarities and differences of the return on investment and total cost techniques as they apply to the evaluation of alternative distribution systems, let us consider the case of the Apex Company, a hypothetical firm. Apex presently maintains field stocks at 30 public warehouses scattered throughout the country. The public warehouse stocks are replenished from the company's main warehouse located at its only plant. Shipments are made in truckload lots to the public warehouses and deliveries are made from the warehouses either by local cartage firms or by l.t.l. shipments. When items are ordered which are not in stock at a particular warehouse, the item is back-ordered and shipped to the warehouse either from the plant warehouse or from stocks at one of the other public warehouses.

The company's distribution manager is considering two proposals for restructuring the present distribution system. Proposal A involves establishing three

---

[3] Heskett, Ivie and Glaskowsky, *op. cit.*, p. 468.

TABLE 1. *Operating characteristics of Apex's present and proposed physical distribution systems (all dollar figures in thousands)*

Characteristics	Present system	Proposed systems	
		A	B
Warehouse replenishment time	16 days	8 days	8 days
Average customer order cycle time from warehouse stocks	5 days	5 days	4 days
Average customer order cycle time for backorders	25 days	18 days	16 days
Proportion of total orders backordered	25%	10%	8%
Proportion of backorders cancelled	20%	20%	20%
Lost sales (% of total orders)	5%	2%	1.6%
Annual operating expenses: production, sales and general administration expenses	$2,000 + .80NS[a]	$2,000 + .80NS	$2,000 + .80NS
Physical distribution expenses:			
Transportation and warehousing	$285 + .052NS	$310 + .038NS	$325 + .030NS
Inventory carrying costs[b]	60 + .055NS	40 + .003NS	50 + .004NS
Depreciation (buildings and equipment)	10	40	52
General physical distribution administrative expense	25	35	40
Order handling	15	40	50
Total physical distribution expenses	$395 + .057NS	$465 + .041NS	$517 + .034NS
Investment required:			
Inventories	$300 + .025NS	$200 + .015NS	$250 + .020NS
Warehouses (new)		500	600
Equipment (new)		300	400
Land		75	100

[a] NS = net sales. Net sales = total orders received − cancelled back orders.

[b] Annual inventory carrying costs are assumed to be 20% of the book value of inventory. The inventory carrying cost equation was derived by multiplying the inventory figure (found in the investment required part of the table) by .20.

strategically located distribution centers and virtually eliminating the stocks held at public warehouses. These centers would be served by rail from the plant warehouse and shipments to customers would be made via motor carrier. A new order processing system would also be installed in conjunction with the new centers in order to reduce the replenishment cycle between the distribution centers and the plant warehouse.

Proposal B is identical with A except that it entails the use of four distribution centers rather than three. The effect which the present and each of the proposed systems is expected to have on sales, costs, inventories and fixed assets is shown in Table 1.

A five-year projection of the operating results from the current and the proposed systems is shown in Table 2. Apex executives, acting on the basis of market research information and past experience, estimate that the improved customer service resulting from fewer backorders and shortened times for filling backorders in Proposals A and B will generate an increase in sales over those that could be expected if the present system is retained. Under Proposal A they estimate that gross orders would be 2% greater than under the present system during the first two years it is in operation and about 1% greater during each of the succeeding years. The decrease in orders after the second year reflects a belief on the part of Apex's management that their competitors will initiate retaliatory measures in response to Apex's improved service levels.

Under Proposal B, sales would be 2.5% greater during the first two years and 1% greater during the remaining three years of the planning period.

The cost figures shown in Table 2 were projected on the basis of the relationships between the various types of expenses and the net sales shown in Table 1.

If either total costs or total profits are used as the criterion to decide among the three alternatives, the results would be as follows:

	Total costs over 5 years (000)	Total profits over 5 years (000)
Present system	$7,931	$1,484
Proposal A	6,806	2,514
Proposal B	6,322	2,832

From this analysis it appears quite obvious that either Proposal A or B would be preferable to the present system over the next five years. Further, Proposal B would also appear to be preferable to A because the firm will realize greater profits over the period with it. The greater profits in System B reflect lower operating costs, an increased level of gross sales due to better service and a smaller proportion of lost sales.

However, let us now expand the scope of the analysis to consider three additional factors: (1) the investment required to implement each of the proposed systems; (2) the net cash flows generated by the present and proposed systems; and (3) the present value of the savings which it is estimated will be realized from implementing the proposed systems. This expanded analysis is shown in Table 3.

Each of the proposed systems requires a certain initial investment for warehouses, equipment and land. The investments required to implement Proposals A and B are $875,000 and $1,100,000 respectively.

As shown in Table 2, both of the proposed systems increase profits by reducing distribution costs and by increasing sales volume. (The sources of the increased profitability are summarized in the first five lines of Table 3.) However, profits are only one aspect of the returns to be realized from an investment. Even more important are the differences that will be realized in net cash flows in each year of the planning period. The importance of cash flows stems from the fact that the amount of money a firm has available for operations and investment is determined by its cash flow rather than by profits alone.

The net cash flow realized from a project in a given year is composed of the after tax profits it generates plus the sum of any non-cash expenses charged against it for tax purposes and any changes it makes possible in the amount of funds invested in assets. In the case of the Apex Company, the non-cash expenses consist of the depreciation on the new buildings and equipment required to implement the proposed changes. The depreciation is charged as an operating expense for tax purposes but does not actually result in a cash outflow. Therefore, the depreciation charges represent funds that are actually available for other uses.

Either of the proposed systems will enable the company to substantially reduce its investment in inventories. Since these funds are available for other uses, they should also be counted as part of the returns realized from changing the distribution system. The differences between the total funds available if one or the other of the proposed systems is adopted and what will be available if the present system is retained are summarized on the line titled "Net increase in funds available" in Table 3.

As is true in many companies, the Apex Company has a variety of other possible uses for its investment funds in addition to the revamping of its distribution system. After considering the risk involved in changing distribution systems and the returns that might be realized from other investment projects, top management has determined that the company must realize at least a 20% return, after taxes, on any major investment in its distribution system. Thus, the ultimate purpose of analyzing the return on investment is to determine whether the returns from either of the proposed systems will meet this criterion.

In order to properly evaluate the returns from the project the company should first recognize the time value of money; that is, that returns realized in the future are

TABLE 2. *Total cost and total profit analysis of Apex Company's present and proposed physical distribution systems (thousands of dollars)*

| | Present system | | | | | Proposed systems A | | | | | B | | | | |
| | Year | | | | | Year | | | | | Year | | | | |
	1	2	3	4	5	1	2	3	4	5	1	2	3	4	5
Total orders received[1]	$20,000	$21,000	$22,000	$23,000	$24,000	$20,400	$21,420	$22,220	$33,230	$24,240	$20,500	$21,525	$22,220	$23,230	$24,240
Orders cancelled	1,000	1,050	1,100	1,150	1,200	408	428	444	465	485	328	344	356	372	388
Net sales	$19,000	$19,950	$20,900	$21,850	$22,800	$19,992	$20,992	$21,776	$22,765	$23,755	$20,172	$21,181	$21,864	$22,858	$23,852
Production, sales & general administrative expenses	17,200	17,960	18,720	19,480	20,240	17,994	18,794	19,421	20,212	21,004	18,138	18,945	19,491	20,286	21,002
Total physical distribution costs	1,478	1,532	1,586	1,640	1,695	1,285	1,326	1,358	1,398	1,439	1,203	1,237	1,260	1,294	1,328
Net profit before tax	$ 322	$ 458	$ 594	$ 730	$ 865	$ 713	$ 872	$ 997	$ 1,155	$ 1,312	$ 831	$ 999	$ 1,113	$ 1,278	$ 1,442
Tax (50%)	161	229	297	365	432	356	436	494	572	656	416	500	556	639	721
Net profit after tax	$ 161	$ 229	$ 297	$ 365	$ 433	$ 357	$ 436	$ 493	$ 573	$ 656	$ 415	$ 499	$ 557	$ 639	$ 721

Source: Derived in part from Table 1. Order cancellations, production, sales and general administrative expenses, physical distribution costs and the investment required in inventories were obtained by multiplying net sales volume by the equation shown in Table 1 for the relationship between these factors and net sales volume.

[1] Total orders received for System A assumed to be 2% greater than present system in years 1 and 2 and 1% greater each year thereafter. Total orders received for System B assumed to be 2.5% greater than present system in years 1 and 2 and 1% greater each year thereafter.

TABLE 3. *Return on investment analysis of Apex Company's proposed physical distribution systems (thousands of dollars)*

| | Proposed System A | | | | | Proposed System B | | | | |
| | Year | | | | | Year | | | | |
	1	2	3	4	5	1	2	3	4	5
Physical distribution cost savings[a]	$ 193	$206	$228	$242	$ 256	$ 275	$295	$326	$346	$ 367
Contribution margin on sales gained by better service[b]	158	166	139	145	152	195	205	160	167	175
Total increase in before tax profits due to improved physical distribution service	351	372	367	387	408	470	500	486	513	542
Tax (50%)	175	181	184	194	204	235	250	243	256	276
Net increase in after tax profits due to improved physical distribution service	$ 176	$181	$183	$193	$ 204	$ 235	$250	$243	$257	$ 276
Add:										
Depreciation and capital recovery[c]	40	40	40	40	715	52	52	52	52	836
Difference in average annual inventory levels[d]	275	279	290	298	309	122	120	130	134	138
Annual net increase in funds available if system adopted	$ 491	$500	$513	$531	$1,228	$ 409	$422	$425	$443	$1,250
Discount factor (20% annual rate of return required on this type of investment)	.833	.694	.579	.482	.402	.833	.694	.579	.482	.402
Present value of annual net increase in funds available[e]	$ 403	$347	$297	$256	$ 494	$ 341	$293	$246	$214	$ 502
Present value of total increase in funds available	$1,797					$1,596				
Total initial investment required	875					1,100				
Profitability index[f]	2.05					1.45				

Source: Derived from Tables 1 and 2.

In the following footnotes let i = any year in the planning period, j = any one of the proposed distribution systems, and p = the present distribution system.

[a] $TDCS_{ij} = TDC_{ip} - TDC_{ij}$ where $TDCS_{ij}$ = total distribution cost savings and TDC = total distribution costs.

[b] $CMSG_{ij} = (NS_{ij} - NS_{ip})(1 - x_j NS_{ij})$ where CMSG = contribution margin on sales gained by better service, NS = net sales, x = sum of variable portions of production, sales, general administrative and physical distribution costs, and $(1 - x_j NS_{ij})$ = contribution margin, i.e., the percentage of net sales that is available for covering overhead expenses and contributing to profit. In this particular example: $CMSG_{iA} = (NS_{iA} - NS_{ip})(1 - .841) = (NS_{iA} - NS_{ip})(.159)$ and $CMSG_{iB} = (NS_{iB} - NS_{ip})(1 - .834) = (NS_{iB} - NS_{ip})(.166)$. This factor measures the opportunity cost of retaining the present system. It indicates the amount of funds each of the proposed systems will make available that will not be available if the present system is retained. This amount is measured by the increased sales volume expected less the variable expenses that will be incurred in generating the additional volume.

[c] The warehouses, equipment and land purchased for the new system will have economic value at the end of the planning period. Therefore, we have assumed that these assets can be resold, if need be, for their depreciated book value at the end of the five-year planning period. This element of capital recovery accounts for the large increase in cash flow in year 5.

[d] $DAAI_{ij} = I_{ip} - I_{ij}$ where DAAI = differences in average annual inventory investment and I = average annual inventory investment. I, for each system, present and proposed, was computed using the relationship between inventories and net sales shown in Table 1.

[e] Sum of present values of annual net increases in funds available.

[f] Profitability index = $\dfrac{\text{present value of total increase in funds available}}{\text{total initial investment required}}$

361

not as valuable as money "in hand" at the present. If a 20% return on investment is required, returns of $1,000 realized one year from now would presently be worth $833, and realizing $1,000 five years from now would be worth $402 at present. Stated differently, the company is willing to invest $833 today in order to realize $1,000 one year from now and $402 today in order to realize $1,000 five years from now. The discounted value of the savings generated by each of the proposed systems is shown on the line titled "Present value of net increase in funds available" in Table 3.

Recognition of the time value of money is important, as different projects often have different time patterns of returns. In order to accurately compare projects that produce substantial savings in the early years of their lives and diminish as time goes by with projects that produce larger savings with the passage of time, it is necessary to express the savings in common terms. Reduction of all funds flows to their present value makes it possible to accurately appraise the relative values of the varying patterns of returns.

The final step in appraising the relative desirability of the proposed systems involves the determination of a profitability index. This is a ratio of the present value of the stream of funds that will become available as a result of the change in distribution systems to the present value of the total investment required to implement the change. So long as the index is greater than 1.00, the project more than satisfies the return criterion. If the index value is less than 1.00, the proposed system will fail to yield the required return.

On the basis of the foregoing analysis note how the desirability of the two proposed changes in distribution systems has changed:

	Proposal A	Proposal B
1. Present value of total increase in funds available over the planning period	$1,797	$1,596
2. Total initial investment required (obtained from Table 1)	875	1,100
3. Profitability index (1 ÷ 2)	2.05	1.45

In Apex's case, both projects have a profitability index greater than 1.00. System A's index is 2.05, which indicates a return in excess of 40% per year after taxes, and System B's index is 1.45, a return of approximately 29% per year after taxes. Note, however, that now System A is the preferred system due to its higher return. This conclusion is in direct contradiction to that which was indicated by total cost or total profit analysis. System B was the most desirable alternative on the basis of cost savings and profits.

The basic reason for the reversal in the rankings of the alternative systems is the differing intensities with which capital is used. In order to generate higher dollar profits, System B required substantially greater quantities of capital. While System A generated smaller dollar profits, it produced more dollars of cash flow per dollar of invested capital than did System B.

The savings in cash flow made possible by System A makes substantial quantities of funds available for other investment opportunities. So long as these "extra" funds are invested in projects earning acceptable rates of return, the company will earn greater total profits if it adopts System A rather than System B.

Summary

The major differences between total cost techniques, as they conventionally have been used, and return on investment center around the treatment of demand, investment and cash flows.

The effects of distribution service levels on demand are often ignored or assumed away as being too difficult to determine in total cost analyses. This is not overly surprising, as the original impetus behind the total cost approach was to evaluate the impact of changes in logistics or physical distribution methods upon costs in other areas of the firm. Thus, demand effects were at best a secondary consideration. The pre-occupation with costs is lessened somewhat by couching the analysis in a return on investment framework. In order to determine the return on investment it is necessary to first determine the profitability of a proposed project. Profit can be affected by increasing demand as well as by reducing costs; thus the analyst is encouraged to explicitly estimate demand effects in order to come up with an accurate approximation of expected returns.

Even more importantly, the amount of capital required to implement a change and the total funds which the change is expected to generate are explicitly included in return on investment analysis. This provides a means of measuring the capital productivity of a project. A company will realize the largest possible returns from a given amount of capital by investing in those projects having the greatest returns, i.e., those which generate the greatest number of dollars of returns for each dollar invested.

Total cost analysis, as often described and practiced, does not take capital productivity into account.[4] Use of this technique may thus result in a less "efficient" use of capital by leading to investment in distribution systems which require disproportionate amounts of capital to generate cost savings. The result, in some cases, may be lower *total* profits for the firm than what might otherwise have been realized.

---

[4] In the theoretical investment analysis literature, total cost models encompass the cost of capital of all assets committed to a particular investment project. Thus, they are an alternate form of return on investment models. Many of the total cost models discussed in the physical distribution and logistics literature recognize the cost of capital of carrying inventory but ignore the capital cost of other assets committed to distribution activities. The costs which they consider are primarily the operating costs associated with the systems being considered rather than the total economic costs associated with the system.

A cursory examination of return on investment might cause one to think that it is not an appropriate tool for use in situations involving minimal capital expenditures. This is especially true when changes in organization or in operating practices are being considered. While these types of changes often involve very little capital outlay, they may result in substantial cost savings.

However, if one examines these situations more closely the relevance of return on investment analysis becomes evident. The impact of organizational or procedural changes on the firm's cash flow should be carefully considered and the returns from any such change should be expressed in terms of cash flow rather than just cost savings (assuming the two are different). Another factor which is frequently overlooked is that the expenditures needed to implement those changes which appear to be most desirable are actually investments. That is, they will not be incurred unless the proposed change is adopted. If the firm uses total costs as the criterion for deciding whether or not to change existing methods it may ignore the "hidden" capital costs involved in making the changeover. Even if the costs of implementing the change are compared with (expected) cost savings, the basis of decision is often whether or not the savings exceed the implementation costs. This, of course, completely overlooks the fact that the costs involved in implementing a procedural or organizational change constitute a use of funds which otherwise might have been invested in some other income-producing activity or asset. If the money spent analyzing and implementing the change would have yielded a greater return in some alternative use, the firm's total profits would have been increased if the change in distribution methods had not been made.

Thus, return on investment analysis is applicable anywhere that total cost analysis can be used. In situations where the firm is confronted with definite limits on the funds available for investment, return on investment analysis certainly appears to be a better criterion than total cost for deciding among alternative uses of those funds. The same reasoning is true for the distribution manager who may be allocated a specified amount of money to be spent at his discretion on physical distribution operations.

Finally, the return on investment framework encourages the distribution analyst to examine the effects which changes in distribution methods may have on all accounts in both the profit and loss statement and the balance sheet. This information should enable the decision maker to more effectively assess the actual impact of his decision upon the firm's operations than if he examined only the data generated on the basis of total cost analysis.

The arguments set forth in this paper should not be construed as a condemnation of the usefulness of the total cost analysis. Its use does not always necessarily lead to overstating the relative importance of improvements in distribution systems. If anything, the result has often been to understate the importance of such improvements. Many companies have succeeded in substantially reducing the amount of assets invested in physical distribution activities while reducing the operating costs of the system. As a result, the improvement in the rate of return on investment realized on assets committed to physical distribution may be even more dramatic than the cost savings by themselves.

Exercises

23.1. The Apex Company is attempting to determine whether it should drastically restructure its physical distribution system. The company presently distributes its products through thirty public warehouses located in major markets throughout the United States. The throughput of the various warehouses is approximately equal. The warehouses are supplied by truck, with most warehouse shipments made in truckload quantities. Shipments from warehouses to customers are made via local cartage companies and l.t.l. freight. Items out-of-stock in a warehouse are typically back-ordered and included in the next replenishment order sent to the warehouse.

Apex's distribution manager is considering two similar proposals for changing the present system. One involves shifting to four regional distribution centers operated by public warehousers. The other is identical in most respects except that Apex would own and operate the regional distribution centers.

The key operating characteristics of the present and proposed systems are included in Table 23.1. Management has established a five-year planning horizon for the company and has established a criterion of a minimum 25% return on investment after taxes for considering new investment. A 50% tax rate is assumed.

1. How should Apex's distribution manager approach the task of analyzing the desirability of the proposed changes?
2. Should either of the proposed systems be adopted? If so, which one? Why?
3. Would the relative desirability of the two proposed systems change over time? Why? (All numbers rounded to the nearest 1,000.)

23.2. The Norway-based Brynje Company is attempting to revise its U.S. physical distribution system. Brynje makes textiles and garments of high quality for recreational purposes. Being a market leader in this sector, it presently operates fifty warehouses throughout the U.S. Shipments are made mainly by truck. Items out-of-stock in a warehouse are typically back-ordered and included in the next replenishment order sent to the warehouse.

Two proposals for an alternative system exist (Table 23.2). The planning horizon is five years, and the return on investment criterion is 20% after taxes. (Assume a 50% tax rate.)

Which system would you recommend, using the analysis methods in the article? Use whole numbers only (no decimals).

TABLE 23.1. *Operating characteristics of Apex's present and proposed systems*

System characteristics	Present system	Proposed systems	
		Public	Private
Number of warehouses	30	4	4
Average warehouse replenishment time	18 days	8 days	8 days
Average customer order cycle time from warehouse stocks	5 days	5 days	5 days
Average customer order cycle time for back orders	25 days	15 days	15 days
Proportion of total orders back-ordered	25%	10%	10%
Proportion of back orders canceled	20%	20%	20%
Average sales value per case	$30.00	$30.00	$30.00
Average inventories (as percent of sales in cases)	0.33%	0.25%	0.25%
Estimated sales—1st year			
Cases	1,00,000	1,030,000	1,030,00
Dollars	$30,000,000	$30,900,000	$30,900,000
Estimated sales growth per year			
Cases	30,000	31,000	31,000
Dollars	$900,000	$930,000	$930,000
Production, sales and general administrative costs	$3,000,000 + $15.00C[a]	$3,000,000 + 15.00C	$3,000,000 + $15.00C
Physical distribution expenses:			
Average transportation cost to warehouse	$0.70C	$0.40C	$0.40C
Average transportation cost from warehouse	$0.35C	$0.50C	$0.50C
Average warehousing costs—public			
Handling	$0.11C	$0.10C	
Storage (annual)	$0.30C	$50,000 + $0.25C	
Clerical	$75,000	$60,000	

Insurance	$0.02C	$0.02C
Loss, damage, and obsolescence	$0.20C	$0.15C
Total public warehousing costs	$75,000 + $0.63C	$110,000 + $0.52C
Annual warehousing cost—private		
Labor			$200,000 + $0.05C
Administration			$80,000
Clerical			$80,000
Loss, damage, and obsolescence			$0.15C
Operating costs			$60,000 + $0.01C
Insurance			$25,000 + $0.01C
Depreciation			
Buildings (20-year life)			$50,000
Equipment (5-year life)			$15,000
Total private warehousing costs			$510,000 + $0.22C
Communication cost	$30,000	$60,000	$60,000
Physical distribution administration	$60,000	$60,000	$75,000
Total physical distribution costs	$165,000 + $1.68C	$230,000 + $1.42C	$720,000 + $1.12C
Investment required:			
Inventories[b]	0.331($3,165,000 + $16.33C)	0.251($3,230,000 + $15.92C)	0.25($3,720,000 + $15.62C)
Buildings			$1,000,000
Equipment			$75,000

[a] C = per case.
[b] *Inventory investment value* is composed of the sum of production, sales, administrative, transportation to warehouse, and warehousing costs.

TABLE 23.2. Operating characteristics of Brynje's present and proposed systems

System characteristics	Present system	Proposed systems	
		A	B
Number of warehouses	50	25	20
Proportion of total orders back ordered	25%	10%	10%
Proportion of back orders canceled	20%	10%	10%
Estimated sales—1st year dollars	$1,000	$1,100	$1,100
Estimated sales growth per year dollars	100	200	100
Production, sales, and general administrative costs	$200 + 0.25NS^a$	$250 + 0.20NS$	$350 + 0.10NS$
Total physical distribution costs	$50 + 0.10NS$	$40 + 0.05NS$	$45 + 0.04NS$
Investment required Inventories	$200 + 0.02NS$	$100 + 0.10NS$	$150 + 0.01NS$
Buildings and equipment	—	1,000	800
		(Expected life 20 years)	

All numbers are in thousands.

[a] NS = net sales.

Recommendations for Further Reading

Advertising/Sales Promotion

Dean, Joel. "Does Advertising Belong in the Capital Budget?" *Journal of Marketing*, 30 (October 1966), 15–21.

Should advertising be budgeted as an expense or as an investment? Most promotional investments have an indeterminate economic life. For instance, brand acceptance "planted in the head" of a teenager by TV may influence his purchases in either the short or the long term. Uncertainty as to the duration of the resulting benefits does not make the promotional outlay any less an investment. The economic case for an investment approach to the advertising budget is laid out. Discounted cash flow (DCF) analysis is suggested as the financial yardstick most appropriate for promotional investments. Putting advertising into the capital budget opens the way for a research approach that will permit proposed investment in advertising to fight for funds on a far more rational basis than is customarily the case.

Deutsch, Leonard L., and Paul J. Meranti, Jr. *The Use of Profitability in Managing Field Sales Operations.* New York: Sales Executive Club of New York, Inc., 1974, 83 pp.

Marketing management is interested in accounting systems that provide information on the profitability of the selling effort in a manner that can be used for more effective direction and control of field sales operations. This study reports on the experience that twenty firms, representing a cross section of size and industry classification, have had with such accounting systems. Each firm's experience has been analyzed to demonstrate both the benefits and the problems arising out of its use of a particular system. Emphasis is placed on the methods used to keep the goals of the field sales force compatible with the overall profit goals of the firm. Some of the recommendations with reference to field sales operations are:

1. Profit center reporting is superior to expense reporting for internal control.
2. For decision making, the system should report incremental revenues and costs. (The most effective measure of incremental revenue is the contribution after variable manufacturing, distribution and field sales cost.)
3. ROI analysis is useful. The asset base for computation of ROI should include accounts receivable, identifiable inventories, and fixed assets such as automobiles, furniture and fixtures.

Domin, William M., and Jack Freymuller. "Can Industrial Product Publicity
be Measured?" *Journal of Marketing*, 29 (July 1965), 54–57.

Various quantitative methods are being used to demonstrate the relative effectiveness of an industrial publicity program. The first approach involves determining the
amount of such publicity obtained by measuring such factors as the column inches
appearing, the equivalent number of pages of publicity received, the total audience
exposure or total circulation of all publications in which such literature appeared, and
the number of inquiries generated. The second approach, building upon the first,
determines the cost per unit of publicity obtained, with the units being expressed in
inches, pages, audience exposure, or inquiries, and the cost being the total publicity
budget. Finally, unit publicity costs can be compared with the cost of other
promotional components such as paid advertising. This is done through the employment of an index of publicity performance which equates the worth of a page of
publicity with the average cost of a page of advertising.

Fulmer, Robert M., "How Should Advertising and Sales Promotion Funds
Be Allocated?" *Journal of Marketing*, 31 (October 1967), 8–11.

Allocating sales promotion dollars on an equal per case basis tends to generate
disproportionately large spending per thousand potential customers in areas where
the brand is already strong and trade support is more easily generated. Less developed
sales territories, in contrast, receive relatively fewer promotional dollars per thousand
prospects merely because the equal per case system is employed. An argument is made
for distinguishing between the level of spending required to sustain a brand and
protect its franchise where it is already strong and the somewhat heavier volume of
developmental dollars that should be spent in areas where the brand is now relatively
weak but where there appears to be no insurmountable barriers to increasing these
sales and market shares. When such barriers do exist, maintaining the present level of
promotional spending may be revealed as entirely in order.

Kelley, Richard J., *The Advertising Budget: Preparation, Administration and
Control*. Edited by H. A. Ahlgren. New York: Association of National
Advertisers, 1967, 290 pp.

How advertising expenses can be related to profits is a problem receiving steadily
increasing attention. There is a heightened demand for judgment supported by facts
in the preparation of advertising plans and budgets. This book synthesizes then
current practices in this field. It also provides the advertising manager with a guide for
establishing and maintaining a sound budgetary control system for advertising. This
text contains many short articles on how particular companies handle different
financial facets connected with the advertising function, media expenditures, and
advertising agencies.

Lilien, Gary L., A. J. Silk, J. M. Choffray, and M. Rao, "Industrial Advertising Effects and Budgeting Practices," *Journal of Marketing*, 40 (January 1976), 16–24.

In the field of industrial advertising, some insight is available into the existence of economies of scale, threshold effects, and the interaction of marketing mix components. Also the evidence suggests that industrial advertising and personal selling perform complementary and synergistic roles. However, much remains to be learned, and current budgeting practice reflects this lack of knowledge about response to advertising. The literature is reviewed and a need pointed out for a better understanding of how industrial advertising expenditures can be more effective.

Margolis, Milton J., "How to Evaluate Field Sales Promotion," *Journal of Marketing*, 24 (July 1963), 42–46.

Although sales promotion budgets continually grow in importance, the vast majority of companies are not attempting to evaluate their sales promotion efforts. A case is made for a commitment to evaluation even though it is recognized that available evaluation techniques are far from perfect. A systematic evaluation procedure is outlined and a standard evaluation, requiring a comparison of estimated and actual results, presented. Finally, a case study is then provided of how that form could be employed to evaluate a specific promotion.

Strang, Roger A. "Sales Promotion—Fast Growth, Faulty Management," *Harvard Business Review*, 54 (July–August 1976), 115–124.

Expenditures on sales promotion are now greater than those on advertising and are continuing to grow at a faster rate. However, few companies know how much they are spending on promotion, presently attempt to determine how effective past promotional efforts have been, or even have long-term corporate policies in this area. Revenue and costs are often not being allocated in a manner that facilitates appropriate decision making. A practical step-by-step guide that could markedly improve the management of promotion activities is proposed.

Sales Management

Bird, Monroe M.; Edward R. Clayton, and Lawrence J. Moore. "Sales Negotiation Cost Planning for Corporate Level Sales," *Journal of Marketing*, 37 (April 1973), 7–13.

An attempt is made to show how corporations can exercise tighter control over the sales negotiation costs which for industrial firms often represent such a significant percentage of total sales costs. A sales negotiation planning model utilizing a simulation approach is described. This method provides a means of estimating the chances of success when entering into negotiations for a large sales contract. It also yields cost and time statistics with associated distributions. Such estimates should be quite valuable to the selling firm in first analyzing and then improving the level of efficiency of the entire negotiation process. Moreover, the method is a relatively simple one in both concept and application.

Hall, William P. "Improving Sales Force Productivity," *Business Horizons*, 18 (August 1975), 32–42.

Knowledge of the ratio of sales cost to territorial sales is informative. Information on actual revenues and sales expenditures is even more useful. Such inputs make it possible first to draw an industry cost-volume relationship and then to plot the location of each competitor. Cost ratios higher than the industry average suggest an opportunity for substantial economies. A straight commission compensation system should be recognized as a fixed cost component when one calculates the sales-to-selling-cost ratio. Opportunities for improved sales force productivity at the territory level include a time and duty study, more effective classification of customers in terms of potential, and a salary plus incentive form of compensation. Other factors contributing to productivity include job specialization and/or job simplification, a relevant organizational structure, a good sales productivity planning program, and adequate analysis both of territory potential and customer profitability. The nature of potential benefits and implication problems of a sales productivity audit are also discussed.

Robertson, Leon H. "Profitability Commission Plans Relating Sales Compensation to Profitability," *Management Accounting*, 49 (June 1968), 39–45.

How can one redesign the sales commission structure in a way that encourages sales of more profitable items without increasing the amount paid in commissions? It is shown that the optimum approach, from both the firm's and the salespeople's view, is one which sets the commission rate as a fixed percent of *gross profit* for all levels of gross profit. A constant level of commission expenditures will be maintained, and the sales force is encouraged to sell the most profitable items. Such a compensation structure also meets all the other postulated objectives of simplicity, objectivity, and ease of implementation.

Schiff, J. S., and Michael Schiff. "New Sales Management Tool: ROAM," *Harvard Business Review*, 45 (July-August 1967), 59–66.

Incremental revenue and cost analysis is insufficient in deciding 1) whether to expand or contract in a market, or 2) whether to change either the composition of the product line or the size of the sales force. The amount of working capital— more precisely, the effect of the proposed change on accounts receivable and inventory

—must be considered. Indeed, commitments of working capital are generally far more fixed than commitments of so-called fixed assets, since the latter are customarily amortized, while the former are not. Once the additional investment in inventory and accounts receivable is recognized, one can calculate the ROAM (return on assets managed) of each proposed venture. Such an approach helps convert "old line" sales managers into more knowledgeable business managers.

Vizza, Robert F. "ROTI, Profitable Selling's New Math," *Sales and Marketing Management* (May 24, 1976): Special Report on Time and Territorial Management, 17–22.

A return on time invested (ROTI) approach reveals how much time and how many calls can be invested in any account. By comparing the present ROTI on all accounts in the territory, the selling effort can be redirected in a more productive fashion. The first step in measuring ROTI is to place a value on an hour of time on either a cost basis or a break-even sales volume basis. How one determines the direct selling costs associated with an hour's selling and the sales volume that must be sold during each hour of face-to-face selling is illustrated. ROTI is determined by dividing gross margin for that account by the cost of the time invested. ROTIs greater than one are profitable and less than one unprofitable. Relative ROTIs for different accounts indicate their comparative value.

Winer, Leon. "A Sales Compensation Plan for Maximum Motivation," *Industrial Marketing Management*, 5 (March 1976), 29–36.

The development of a highly motivating sales compensation plan is traced over a period of eight years. The system is shown to have evolved in response to such factors as efforts to improve both profitability and motivation, personnel problems, and new developments in the marketplace. Each of the specific changes made in the plan is briefly discussed and then illustrated in graphic form. Indeed, a firm's sales compensation plan is never in "final" form but rather must respond to changing conditions. A case is also made for subjecting proposed compensation plans to computer simulation before their actual implementation.

Channels/Physical Distribution

Buxton, Graham. "Accounting for Channel Costs in Marketing Logistics System Selection," *International Journal of Physical Distribution*, 5 (Number 3, 1974), 157–164.

Any marketing logistics system has a marketing channels management component as well as a physical distribution facilities component. In order to derive optimum solutions for the firm's distribution problems, the interrelationships that exist between the two areas must be recognized. The framework developed here integrates both marketing channel and physical distribution cost considerations. Alternative marketing channel systems are evaluated by assigning weights and performance ratings to behavioral and structural factors. The resulting evaluations are then used to adjust each channel's sales efficiency at the retail level and/or to assess the extra costs required to raise that channel's efficiency.

Lalonde, Bernard J., and Douglas M. Lambert. "Inventory Carrying Costs: Significance, Comments, Means, Functions," *International Journal of Physical Distribution*, 6 (Number 2, 1975), 51–63.

Inventory carrying cost estimates can only be determined by examining a number of different cost components. A new method that can be used by managers to determine the true cost of carrying inventory is outlined. In addition to providing a framework that can be applied operationally, this article explores some specific uses of more accurate information on inventory carrying cost.

Lambert, Eugene W., Jr. "Financial Considerations in Choosing a Marketing Channel," *MSU Business Topics*, 14 (Winter 1966), 17–26.

Selection of a marketing channel is usually considered to be a marketing decision. However, the shorter the marketing channel and the fewer the number of middlemen involved, the greater the financial burden on the manufacturer. Selection should thus be based on the estimated rate of return on the varying amounts of capital required to use different types of channels. A comparison must also be made between the anticipated earnings on capital used by present or proposed marketing channels and the firm's cost of capital. Finally, the alternative of shifting funds now invested in short or selective marketing channels to manufacturing must also be recognized. Unless the firm using relatively capital-intensive channels can earn more than both the cost of its capital and the returns available from employing additional funds in manufacturing, it should use a longer channel which shifts marketing responsibilities and costs to middlemen.

Lewis, Richard J. *A Logistical Information System for Marketing Analysis.* Cincinnati: South Western Publishing Co., 1970, 120 pp.

The uniqueness of marketing is identified as the problem of overcoming spatial influences in both the demand-obtaining and order-servicing activities. Since several of marketing's costs and all its revenues are generated outside the firm's centralized operations, the marketing manager has to control geographically dispersed activities, costs and revenues.

The postulated answer is to integrate internal marketing records into an information system based on geographic control units. The specific nature of distribution costs and cost control is discussed in context. Employment of a system of geographic grid blocks which can be restructured into control unit blocks is proposed. Use of these grid blocks for area determination based on total sales, products shipped, and sales by product or customer type provides marketing management with a tool for evaluating and controlling geographically dispersed activities.

Lewis, Richard J., and Leo G. Erickson. "Distribution Costing: An Overview," in *Distribution Systems Costing: Concepts and Procedures*. Columbus, Ohio: The Ohio State University, 1973, 1–27.

The natural expense to functional expense to segment method of distribution cost accounting is criticized primarily for being an after the fact analysis in large part shaped by data and control unit availability rather than a system designed to facilitate effective decision making and control. An ideal information system is shown to be one which recognizes the interrelationship between demand obtaining (marketing-oriented) and demand servicing (physical distribution relations) costs and activities. Costs, revenues, and potential are presented as the essentials of such a planning and control system. The approach taken to variance analysis also allows for the interdependence of the components of the firm's marketing effort. Functional costs are better allocated to a particular customer in a given location buying a specific product mix than separately to products, customers and territories. A case is made for establishing the post of physical distribution controller, a position concerned with far more than merely minimizing physical distribution costs.

Peters, Richard D. "Distribution Profit Measurement," *Management Accounting*, 54 (August 1972), 47–48.

This brief article spells out both the nature and merits of a new profitability measure for assessing comparative distributor performance. This measure, gross trading margin per inventory dollar invested, or GTM/IDI, provides meaningful comparative data without requiring detailed knowledge of the dealer's financial position. It also incorporates sales volume, gross profits, inventory investment, and inventory turnover in a single measure of performance.

Schiff, Michael. *Accounting and Control in Physical Distribution Management*. Chicago: National Council of Physical Distribution Management, 1972, 217 pp.

Marketing policy and tactics have a fundamental controlling influence on the design and operation of physical distribution (PD) systems. PD is defined as the group of functions associated with the storage of goods from the time they are identified as finished to the time when they are delivered to the customer. The study discussed was based on a sample of 14 large companies selected for their size, their representativeness, and the relatively advanced development of their physical distribution activities.

This in-depth study reveals the following conclusions: (1) financial profit reporting as it relates to physical distribution needs improvement; (2) in a number of companies, cost reporting with PD has been developed to a point permitting effective control and making available relevant information for decision making; and (3) the real gap is not in PD cost information, but in the evaluative systems currently used. The reward system in marketing does not focus on profit performance after the deduction of relevant PD costs.

Schiff, Michael. "Distribution Cost Management and Control," *Price and Inventory Management*, 17 (First Quarter 1976), 26–40.

What should be included as a distribution cost? How should distribution costs be classified in external reports? Is a distribution cost a period or product cost? These problem areas are first recognized and then discussed within the context of the external reports accountants must provide owners and creditors. The type of internal reporting of greatest use to managers concerned with decision making and control is next considered.

Particular attention is paid to issues affecting the appropriate allocation of distribution costs to such marketing segments as geographic units, alternate channels, customers and products. Other issues considered are the imputed interest, or opportunity cost, of money tied up in inventories and the impact on working capital requirements of the interface of credit and inventory management. One weakness of marketing control that emerges is in the area of the increased demand for physical distribution services associated with inappropriate sales force commitments to customers.

Weigand, Robert E. "The Accountant and Marketing Channels," *Accounting Review*, 38 (July 1963), 584–590.

Financial analysis can be helpful in at least two major aspects of the management of the firm's marketing channels. An emphasis on the present or prospective dealer's financial capacity is useful in determining whether market intermediaries have the financial resources necessary to perform the range of services expected of them. Financial data that reveal that a manufacturer's product line is more profitable for a dealer or distributor than that of competitors or other producers competing for the same shelf space is also helpful. The analyst who furnishes such information must be able to marry marketing and finance. In many organizations, but by no means all, the firm's accountants will be the logical ones to carry out the necessary studies.

PART VII

Segmental Costing and
Customer Worth

Calculating the Dollar Value of a Customer

24

Julian Simon

How much is it worth to you to get an additional customer? The calculation of the answer to this question is the most important calculation a mail-order merchant makes, and this calculation is what this chapter is about.

The calculation of the value of a customer may be done more precisely in the mail-order business than in any other line of business. And yet, there are many (even many successful) mail-order firms that have never made this calculation correctly, as may be seen in the interviews with mail-order firms frequently reported in *Direct Marketing*.

Knowing the value of a customer is crucial because this information helps you find the break-even point for the number of responses to a space advertisement or mailing-list campaign that are necessary for you to make money rather than lose money. Once you have correctly calculated the value of a customer, you only need to estimate the number of new customers you will get from the ad or mailing (and know the cost of the space ad or the mailing) to decide if that space ad or mailing should be undertaken.

The value of a customer is the total *profit* he will bring you. Not the *volume*, mind you, but the profit. You certainly would not pay me $2 to bring you a customer who will give you $10 in volume but only $1 in profit. But if you had a high-margin business and $10 volume gave you $4 profit, you *would* pay me $2 to bring you in a customer who would spend $10. In fact, you'd be willing to pay me almost $4 for him or her.

Three elements enter into the calculation of the dollar value of a customer: (1) The dollar amount of revenue you expect to get from the customer in each year; (2) the cost to you of filling the order; and (3) your "cost of capital"—that is, the worth to you today of a dollar in net revenue next year or 2 years from now.

There are good customers and poor customers, and obviously the good customers are worth more than the poor customers. But we're talking now of *average* customers. When you first get a *new* customer, you can't tell whether he or she will be a good customer or not.

For a one-shot deal—say, a camera sold by Bell & Howell from a Diners Club list mailing—the calculation of the value of a customer is reasonably simple. The revenue from the first sale is all that Bell & Howell will get from the customer. And the costs of the camera are relatively easy to figure because they will all be incurred immediately. And you do not need to know the "cost of capital" because all the revenues and costs will occur within a short time, and there is no "interest" to be paid while waiting for your money. So the value of a customer to Bell & Howell is simply the sales price minus the cost of goods sold and the cost of servicing the order. (Notice that the cost of the advertisement that solicits the customer is *not* included in this calculation of the value of the customer.)

Even in this simple case one can err badly by forgetting some important costs, but we'll assume that the costs are figured correctly.

The main complication in calculating the dollar value of a customer arises when a substantial portion of your business is repeat business—as is the case for almost all successful mail-order businesses. When a substantial number of customers buy more than one time, the value of a customer derives not only from his first purchase but also from the subsequent purchases he is likely to make. If you ignore the subsequent purchases, you will arrive at a wrong calculation and too small a customer value. That will cause you to forgo some valuable customer volume, and in fact may lead you to decide that a whole line of business is unprofitable when in fact it is profitable. For example, if magazine publishers did not include repeat business in their value-of-a-customer calculations on subscription campaigns, they would never solicit *any* subscriptions by mail.

We'll proceed with several examples. We'll begin with the simplest possible example of a typist who solicits business by advertising. Then we'll go on to a common sort of repeat-business situation, a mail-order drug firm. Then we'll wind up with a calculation from a magazine's subscription campaign that looks more complicated but still is fundamentally the same calculation.

The Value of a Customer to Various Businesses

Let's begin with a very simple example—the case of a typist who wants to get typing work to do at home. The reason for beginning with such a simple case is that the method needed to handle this kind of problem is straightforward and almost obvious. Yet it is the same method needed for major mail-order advertising campaigns.

Assume that Judith, your wife or girl friend, wants to make money typing at home. She realizes that she must advertise in order to obtain jobs. The question is: Where and when should she advertise?

We must begin by collecting some information. Does Judith type fast enough to make a profit? She announces to us that if she cannot net at least $1.25 per hour from typing, she prefers to read mystery novels instead. Next we must find out whether she can type fast enough to earn at least her "opportunity cost" of $1.25 per hour. Judith wisely *experiments* to determine her cost of production. She clocks herself typing some average material and determines that she can do five pages per hour on the average. If we assume for the moment she will charge the going rate for average-quality work—40 cents per page in this town—she can hope to gross $2 per hour, not counting any possible costs of advertising promotion.

A notice on a college-dormitory bulletin board is Judith's first advertising. In the first week she gets one call, which results in her typing a four-page paper. On this evidence, she sensibly concludes that while the bulletin-board notice may produce some business, it will not produce *enough* work to keep her busy. This is frequently the case for advertisers. A particular advertising vehicle may produce business very cheaply—in this case, at practically no cost at all—and therefore be very profitable. But one must also use less efficient advertising vehicles to get more business and increase *total profit*.

Judith now considers placing advertisements in both the college daily and the town newspaper. At this point, she must begin to think in a more businesslike way. Which of the two papers is likely to bring in the most business per dollar of cost?

One source of information about an advertising vehicle's potential is observation of what other firms—other home typists, in this case—are doing. Judith observes that there are many advertisements for home typists in the college newspaper's classified section but just one ad in the town newspaper. She therefore wisely decides to imitate the other typists, and she places a classified advertisement in the college paper.

Now that Judith has run her advertisement in the college newspaper for a week's trial, she must calculate whether the advertising is profitable or not. Judith paid out $2.50 for the week's classified advertising, and she obtained two customers from it. She can directly link the customers to the advertising for these reasons: (1) She has not publicized her services in any other way; and (2) when they called, both customers said they had read her advertisement in the paper. One customer's business amounted to $3 worth; the other's was $1. This required a total of 2 hours' typing. Judith then figured this way:

Production expenditures:	
2 hours' labor × $1.25	$2.50
Advertising expenditures	$2.40
Total cost	$4.90

The total cost of $4.90 exceeded her first week's sales of $4. Hence she figured that the advertising was a losing proposition and she decided to advertise no more.

But the following week one of her customers returned with another $2 worth of business, reducing the apparent loss on the initial advertising. Clearly Judith must somehow take account of the long-run effect, the *repeat* sales that the advertisement generates.

What is needed here is an estimate of how much business our home typist can expect to get from an *average customer in the long run*. But instead of waiting many months to collect this information, Judith wisely consults a friend who is experienced in home typing. Her friend tells her that on the average, a customer yields $10 worth of business before leaving town or graduating or buying a typewriter or otherwise ceasing to patronize the typist. Some customers provide less than $10 worth of business, of course, and others more; $10 is an average. Judith can now estimate that her first week's advertising brought in $20 worth of business (two customers multiplied by the $10 long-run estimate for the average customer), and she can now figure the overall profitability of the advertising this way:

Total sales (gross revenue)	$20.00
Production expenditures for $20 business:	
10 hours × $1.25	$12.50
Sales minus production cost	$ 7.50
Advertising expenditure	$ 2.50
Sales minus production cost minus advertising cost	$ 5.00

The advertising now is seen to be profitable because the sales revenue less the production cost exceeds the cost of the advertising. So the typist decides to rerun the advertisement in the next issue of the college newspaper. So we see that correct figuring leads to a decision opposite to that of her earlier naive figuring.

The value of a customer enables us to quickly determine whether any given advertisement is above or below the break-even point of profitability. The value of a typing customer can be estimated as sales minus labor expenditure. That is, $10 - (5 \times \$1.25) = \$3.75$. The labor cost is estimated at 5 hours on the basis of the experimental data which showed that Judith types an average of five pages per hour. The concept of the value of a customer is then used this way: Any unit of advertising that produces customers at a cost of $3.75 or less per customer is profitable; otherwise, it is unprofitable. For example, our gal's original advertisement produced two customers estimated to be worth a total of $2 \times \$3.75 = \$7.50$, for an advertising expenditure of $2.50. This suggests that her first advertisement was profitable.

In following weeks the repetitions of her advertisement produced an average of only one and one-half new customers per week, but since the value of one and one-half customers ($1.5 \times \$3.75 = \$5.62$) is considerably greater than the $2.50 weekly cost, the advertising still is profitable on the average, indicating that she should continue to run the advertisement.

The value of a customer provides a standard against which to compare the results from any medium as well as any advertisement.

Before we leave Judith, our home-typing friend, and move on to more complex problems, a few of her other management decisions deserve to be mentioned.

Other decisions for the home typist are *how large* an advertisement to run, and *how many* advertisements to run in various media. These decisions depend on the extent to which she really wants to set up a business. If she wants to do no more than obtain work for herself for 8 hours a day or less, these questions may not arise. But if she really wants to start a business, employ other typists and job out the work, she will need to run bigger advertisements and more of them. The decision rule in every case is the same as before: Does the added unit of advertising produce enough customers so that, when multiplied by the long-run value of a customer, the cost of the added unit of advertising is exceeded?

Now let's move on to the actual (but camouflaged) case of Home Sewing, Inc., a firm that sells sewing materials by mail. Home Sewing obtains customers with a special introductory offer at $3 in space advertisements. Its records show that 30 percent of those introductory customers buy again from the line of regular merchandise. And on the average, 40 percent of customers who buy regular merchandise once then buy a second time; 40 percent who buy a second time then buy a third time, and so on. The average size of subsequent orders is $10. Home Sewing figures that the total costs of servicing a customer (the goods, shipping and everything else except the cost of advertising) amount to 70 percent of the sales price for the introductory offer, and 50 percent thereafter. The average time between orders is 6 months, and over that period the cost of money to the firm is 10 percent, so $1 received 6 months hence is worth about 90 percent of $1 (90 cents) now.

The value of a new customer to Home Sewing can be figured as follows: ($3 introductory-offer revenue − .70 × $3 cost to the firm of introductory offer) plus (.3 probability of repeating from introductory offer) times ($10 second-order revenue − .50 × $10 cost of second-order) times (.9 to allow for the cost of money over half a year) plus (.4 × .3 probability of repeat from second order) times ($10 third-order revenue − .5 × $10 third-order cost) times (.9 × .9 to allow for the cost of money over two 6-month periods), and so on for subsequent periods.

That is,

$$\text{Value of new customer to Home Sewing} = (\$3 - \$2.10) + .3(\$10 - \$5)(.9)$$
$$+ (.4 \times .3)(\$10 - \$5)(.9 \times .9) \ldots$$
$$= \$.90 + \$1.35 + \$.49 \ldots$$
$$\approx \$2.74 + \ldots$$

So the value of an additional customer to Home Sewing is about $2.74. Actually, the value is considerably higher, because subsequent orders have not been figured in. But it is clear from inspection of the figures that the value now of additional future orders is really quite small—so small that their calculation is hardly worthwhile.

Now let us see how the value of a customer changes if one of the elements is different. Let's say (as actually happened) that this firm found on further inspection that the reorder rates were higher than originally thought—the reorder rate is really 40% (that is, .40) from the introductory offer to the second order, and 49% (that is, .49) for subsequent reorders. The value of a customer then is:

$$\text{Value of a customer} = (\$3 - \$2.10) + .4(\$10 - \$5)(.9)$$
$$+ (.49 \times .4)(\$10 - \$5)(.9 \times .9) \ldots$$
$$= \$.90 + \$1.80 + \$.80 +$$
$$\approx \$3.50 +$$

For practice, another change: Let us calculate the value of a customer to Home Sewing under a third set of conditions. Assume the firm found that its costs for subsequent orders were only 45 percent rather than 50 percent. So:

$$\text{Value of a customer} = (\$3 - \$2.10) + .4(\$10 - \$4.50)(.9)$$
$$+ (.49 \times .4)(\$10 - \$4.50)(.9 \times .9) \ldots$$
$$= \$.90 + \$1.98 + \$.88$$
$$\approx \$3.76$$

Before the death of *Life* a few years ago, its circulation director supplied excellent data on *Life*'s circulation advertising results, summarized in Table 1. Like every other magazine and like other repeat-business mail-order firms, *Life* could never

TABLE 1

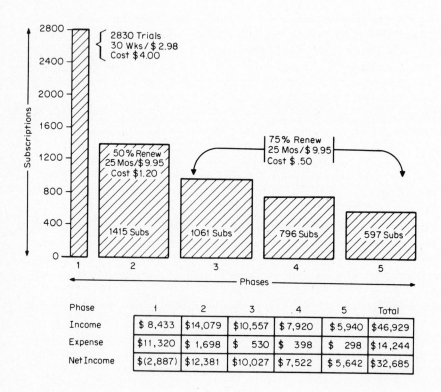

Phase	1	2	3	4	5	Total
Income	$ 8,433	$14,079	$10,557	$7,920	$5,940	$46,929
Expense	$11,320	$ 1,698	$ 530	$ 398	$ 298	$14,244
Net Income	$(2,887)	$12,381	$10,027	$7,522	$5,642	$32,685

have been profitable if it had depended on the revenue from the first orders. For the sample shown, the first year the net *loss* was $2,877. But by the end of 5 years, the profit was $32,685.

Assume for the moment that "fulfillment" costs of producing and distributing the magazine equaled the revenue from advertising—a pretty good assumption for mass consumer magazines. Then figure how much *Life* could afford to spend for a new customer in this way:

1. Subscription revenue from an *average* customer during the "life" of the customer equaled

$$\$46,269 \div 2,830 = \$16.35$$

2. The total cost of soliciting *renewals* for a group of customers divided by the number of original customers in the group equaled

$$\frac{\$1,698 + \$530 + \$398 + \$298}{2,830} = \$1.03$$

3. The most that the magazine should have spent to get a customer, then, was

$$\$16.35 - \$1.03 = \$15.32$$

Note how, after the trial-period renewal, customers fell away at about 25 percent *each year*. It will be true for practically every mail-order business that a constant *percentage* of a group of customers will drop out each year. Once you have estimated the customer fall-off rate for one year for your business, you have a terrifically valuable tool for future planning.

How to Estimate Repeat Rates

But, you ask, how does one know what the repeat rates will be? Sometimes the repeat rate is very easy to learn, sometimes a bit harder. An easy example: Once I sold monthly flower subscriptions by direct mail. After the first experimental month, I immediately saw that fifteen of twenty-five (60 percent) of my introductory-offer customers signed up for another month at the regular rate. And at the end of the second month, I found that eleven of fifteen (about 73 percent) bought again. That was enough information for me to make a rough estimate of how the business would do in the future. Of course my samples were small, and at first I had no evidence about subsequent repeats after the first repeat. But after a few more months I had accumulated solid evidence from bigger samples, and I had information about the repeat rates after the first repeat. My initial estimates were not far off, and they certainly were accurate enough to work with.

Now let's take the case of a camouflaged fishing-equipment firm, Doog and Doog, two friends of mine who have been in business for about 4 years as of the date we are making the analysis, March 1974. Doog and Doog had never estimated their repeat rates as of the date they called me in as a consultant. But they had kept all their old orders in boxes. So we sorted out all the customers whose names started with B or R, as a rough way of taking a sample of the buyers who had *first* ordered merchandise in January, February and March of 1971. (We could tell which customers were ordering for the first time because they were buying the introductory offer. All the other B and R orders we put aside.) Then we checked to see how many times each of them ordered again. We found that of the 110 first-time B- and R-named buyers in January through March of 1971, the following were the repeat-purchase records:

Total sample: 110 buyers. Of these,

26 (24 percent) reordered once only	representing 26 orders
12 reordered twice	representing 24 orders
4 reordered 3 times	representing 12 orders
3 reordered 4 times	representing 12 orders
1 reordered 5 times	representing 5 orders
Total buyers 46	Total orders 79

(You may think that it cost a lot of work and money to go back through 18 months' worth of old orders to get this information. It was a bit of a nuisance, and now the firm has learned that it makes sense to keep records in better form; in their case, the Doogs are now ready for a modern punched-card system. But even so, the total cost of studying the back orders was only a few hundred dollars, and the information gained is worth much more than that to Doog and Doog in future added profit.)

If the firm has kept good records of customer purchases in the past—say, on index cards—the job is much simpler. All one then need do is take a random sample of, say, 300 people who first bought between 3 and 5 years ago, and study their purchases over 3 years from the date of first purchase. (Use a longer period if the firm's repeat business extends a very long time, as is the case with magazine subscriptions.) If the firm's records are on punched cards or tape, the firm can even work with *all* the customers in that category with no extra effort.

The best way to take a fair random sample from index-card records is as follows:

To make things simple, we shall assume that the future ends after 3 years. Anything you take in after that is gravy, a margin for error. For several economic reasons this won't distort our calculations very much.

If you have been in business over 3 years, the figuring is a breeze. All you have to do is take a sample of people who bought from you over 3 years ago, and see how much they purchased in the first 3 years after you first heard from them. Use a ruler to make a mark at equal intervals in your customer files so that there are *300 equal intervals.* This saves you the trouble of counting off the cards. Take the first customer's card *over 3 years old* that comes after each mark.

If you have been in business only a short time, you can *estimate* the same data by first figuring out how the average customer's purchase frequency drops as time goes on. Then you project the effect for a 3-year period. Better get some help from a statistician on this. Actually, this procedure is especially vital for new businesses. It is only in this way that you can accurately decide whether you are making or losing money.

IMPORTANT: You *must* sample *both* the customers who are still active *and* those who are now in your inactive or "dead" file. If, by some unfortunate accident, you have thrown away the records of inactive customers, you will need a procedure slightly more complicated than we have space to describe here. Any statistical consultant should be able to set up a satisfactory procedure for you in a few hours.

I can't tell you the *exact* size of the proper sample for your business. But 300 customers should be more than enough in most cases, and a sample a little too big won't cost you much extra.

The value of a customer then is calculated as follows:

1. Take a *fair* (random) sample of the names of 300 customers—active and inactive—who first bought over 3 years ago.
2. Add up the total amount they have purchased in the 3 years from the date of first purchase.
3. Divide by 300.
4. Multiply by your average profit margin (in percent).

The figure you come out with is the amount it is worth to you to *get a customer onto your books*. Never lose an opportunity to get a customer for anything less than that cost.

The procedure described here should not cost you more than $400 including clerical time, no matter how big your list is. (And if your business has progressed to the point where the customer records are on punched cards or electronic tape, the job is even less expensive.) I practically guarantee that the information will increase your future profit by many thousands of dollars, if your business is any size at all.

Using the Value of a Customer

The dollar value of a customer is used in decision making as follows: Any advertisement or list for which the expected result of this multiplication [(number of customers) times (value of a customer)] is greater than the cost of the ad or mailing should be run. But if the cost of the ad is greater than the expected number of customers multiplied by the value of a customer, the ad or mailing should not be done.

Remember that you are interested not only in the *frequency* of reorders, but also in the *dollar amounts* of reorders. Calculate the dollar size of reorders *separately* for first reorders, second reorders, etc. In the example above, the amount of the reorder is the same for each reorder, but in many cases the amount is different, averaging higher (or, less often, lower) with subsequent purchases.

Remember that from the expected *revenue* of a customer, you must subtract the *cost* of servicing these orders, or else your calculations will overstate the value of a customer.

Often it is useful to refine the calculation of the value of a customer to take into account the value of his particular first order. This refinement can be worthwhile because customers tend to vary much more in the size of the first order than in subsequent orders, and because the money from the first order is received immediately and hence has higher value to you per dollar than future revenue.

Here is an example of how the calculated value of a customer depends upon the first-order size for the sewing-materials firm:

TABLE 2

If first order is:	Firm can pay, to get the order
$ 3.00	$3.00
3.50	3.20
4.00	3.45
4.50	3.65
5.00	3.90
5.50	4.10
6.00	4.35
6.50	4.55
7.00	4.80
7.50	5.00
8.00	5.25
8.50	5.45
9.00	5.70
9.50	5.90
10.00	6.15

It is amazing and sad to see how much profit mail-order firms forgo by not correctly estimating and using the value of a customer. For example, a large mail-order shoe firm was asked about its mailing-list rental policy:

Q. What rate of returns from your mailings do you consider a good point?
A. We happen to break even at 1.8%. We rent anything that goes over that. By break even, I mean it pays off in the first mailing. We don't rent a list that pulls less than that because it goes into a loss position and we don't like that. Although in a long test, it might be worth doing, we like to have short term profits.

Q. In other words, you won't take a 1.5% return and hope you get repeat orders which will then make it worthwhile?

A. We do not have to do this right now. I think it might be acceptable, but not necessary.

I am absolutely sure that if this firm took into account the value of the customers after the initial order, it would greatly increase its profit by renting more lists and increasing its volume.

Exercises

24.1. The Singapore Book Club, a mail-order pocket book firm operating in Singapore and Malaysia, obtains its customers by offering a special introductory order of the five bestsellers of the year for only $1.75, plus handling and postage charges. The club's records show that 20% of those customers who purchase the introductory package buy again from the list of regular books. On the average, 65% of the customers who buy books once at the regular price buy a second time; 85% of those who buy a second time buy a third time, and so on. The total cost of servicing a customer (excluding advertising) is approximately 90% of the sales price for the introductory offer and 44% thereafter. The average size of orders shipped is $8.20. The average time between orders is four months. The cost of money to the club for that period of time is 8%.

How much is each new customer worth? The value of the customer should be calculated on the basis of the expected value up to the fourth regular purchase.

24.2. The Atlantis Book Club, a mail-order pocket book club operating in Atlanta, attracts its customers with a special introductory order of the five bestsellers of the year for only $2.00, plus handling and postage charges. The club's records show that 25% of those customers who purchase the introductory package buy again from the list of regular books. On the average, 60% of the customers who buy books once at the regular price buy a second time, 80% of those who buy a second time buy a third time, and so on. The total cost of servicing a customer (excluding advertising) is approximately 90% of the sales price for the introductory offer and 40% thereafter. The average size of each subsequent order is $7.50. The average time between orders is three months. The cost of money to the club for that period of time is 5%.

How much is each new customer worth? The value of the customer should be calculated on the basis of the expected value up to the fifth regular purchase.

Marketing Cost Analysis: A Modularized Contribution Approach 25

Patrick M. Dunne   Harry I. Wolk

In recent years, an increasing use of accounting information for planning, controlling, and evaluating the firm's marketing performance has been advocated in the literature.[1] Some of this published material is very sophisticated, and indeed there is almost no limit to how far one can go in analyzing the effectiveness of marketing operations by accounting techniques. At the same time, it is truly astounding that many marketing managers do not use even some of the more elementary accounting tools that are available.

The authors know of one company where Product X was generating an annual profit of $800,000, and Product Y was losing money at the rate of $600,000 per year—and management was totally unaware of the situation, just pleasantly happy to be making $200,000! They were simply astounded when a little accounting by product line revealed Product Y to be such a drain.

Not quite that elementary, but still well within the grasp of non-accounting trained managers, is the *modular contribution margin income statement*. This technique spotlights the behavior of controllable costs and indicates each segment's contribution to profit and indirect fixed costs. It is a very useful tool for marketing managers who are concerned not only with the efficiency of the operation for which they are responsible, but also with the profitability of the product, various territories, channels, types and sizes of customer, etc.

In order to generate accounting information for specific market segments, a detailed data base is a necessity. All transactions entering the system must be classified

Reprinted by permission from the *Journal of Marketing*, Vol. 41 (July 1977), pp. 83–94, published by the American Marketing Association.

[1] For example, "Report of the Committee on Cost and Profitability Analyses for Marketing," *The Accounting Review Supplement* (1972), pp. 575–615; W. J. E. Crissy, Paul Fischer, and Frank H. Mossman, "Segmental Analysis: Key to Marketing Profitability," *Business Topics* (Spring 1973), pp. 42–49; V. H. Kirpalani and Stanley J. Shapiro, "Financial Dimensions of Marketing Management," *Journal of Marketing*, Vol. 37, No. 3 (July 1973), pp. 40–47; Leland L. Beik and Stephen L. Buzby, "Profitability Analysis by Market Segments," *Journal of Marketing*, Vol. 37, No. 3 (July 1973), pp. 48–53; Frank H. Mossman, Paul Fischer and W. J. E. Crissy, "New Approaches to Analyzing Marketing Profitability," *Journal of Marketing*, Vol. 38, No. 2 (April 1974), pp. 43–48; Merritt J. Davoust, "Analyzing a Client's Customer Profitability Picture," *Management Adviser*, May-June 1974, pp. 15–19; Harry I. Wolk and Patrick M. Dunne, "Modularized Contribution Margin Income Statements for Marketing and Physical Distribution Analysis," *Research Issues in Logistics*, James F. Robeson and John Grabner, eds. (Columbus: The Ohio State University, 1975), pp. 199–210; Stephen L. Buzby and Lester E. Heitger, "Profit Oriented Reporting for Marketing Decision Makers," *Business Topics*, Summer 1976, pp. 60–68; Richard L. Lewis and Leo G. Erickson, "Distribution System Costing: An Overview," *Distribution System Costing: Concepts and Procedures*, John R. Grabner and William S. Sargent, eds. (Columbus: The Ohio State University, 1972), pp. 1–30.

and coded so that costs can be matched with revenues at desired aggregation levels for different combinations of relevant factors. But the payoff is usually worth the effort. The modular contribution margin approach to marketing analysis enables management (a) to judge the profitability of a specific marketing mix in a specific area and (b) to decide whether or not to take action to change it.

Case Example

Consider the D-W Appliance Company, a small appliance manufacturer that produces blenders and mixers on separate production lines. The firm's marketing division is organized along territorial lines (East and West), and the products are sold by sales representatives through two marketing channels: (1) to wholesalers, who, in turn, distribute to small retailers, and (2) directly to large retailers. Order size is also important: channel costs are lower for orders of 100 units or more of either product.

If the Marketing Division Manager wanted to assess the profitability of his functional area, he might request an income statement. Under the full-cost approach to financial statements, costs would be separated according to function: cost of goods sold and operating expenses. A portion of the general expense of the company cost centers (accounting, corporate headquarters, etc.) would arbitrarily be allocated to the operating expense of the Marketing Division. (See Exhibit 1.)

This type of statement is, however, better suited to external reporting than to internal managerial planning and control, since it contains costs which do not directly affect decisions in the marketing area and which are not controllable by the Marketing Division Manager. Furthermore, in order to apply variance analysis to this kind of statement, comparing budgeted results with actual results for control

EXHIBIT 1. *Income statement models*

Full-cost approach	Contribution margin approach

Revenue
  Less: Cost of goods sold
	Revenue
	  Less: Variable manufacturing costs
	        Other variable costs directly traceable to the segment

Gross margin
  Less: Operating expenses
        (including the division's allocated
        share of company administrative
        and general expenses)
	Contribution margin
	  Less: Fixed costs directly traceable to products
	        Fixed costs directly traceable to the market segment

Net income	Segment net income

purposes, the costs would first have to be separated by activity before the analysis could distinguish between cost changes in the level of an activity and those due to other causes.

The main advantage of the modular contribution margin approach as a managerial tool for planning and control is that it separates costs, by behavior, into variable and fixed costs.[2]

Variable costs are those costs which vary predictably with some measure of activity during a given time period. For example, commissions on sales for D-W are set at 10% of sales revenue. Total commission expense varies as sales vary.

Fixed costs, on the other hand, are costs which do not change in the short run, e.g., the Marketing Division Manager's salary.

Cost Behavior and Controllability

The modular contribution margin model, which allows separation of costs by behavior, can be expanded to include separation of costs by controllability.

Controllable costs are those costs which originate in the particular organizational unit under consideration. Whether a cost is classified as controllable or uncontrollable obviously depends on the organizational segment under consideration. Territorial expenses in the statement for East Territory would be controllable costs for that territory and for the Marketing Division, but not for the West Territory.

As just suggested, controllability relates to the degree of influence over a cost by the relevant division manager. Labor costs that exceed standard costs for actual production in a particular department are a classic example of a cost for which the appropriate manager would be held accountable. However, even for this classification, a great deal of care must be exercised. Actual controllable labor costs may exceed standard because of many reasons beyond the manager's scope or control. For example, delivery time for shipments may be delayed by severe weather. Furthermore, controllability may be constrained by economic externalities. Selling costs would be a controllable variable cost of the Marketing Division, while the manager probably has little, if any, influence over a price decline precipitated by a competitor's action.

Controllable fixed costs are rarely controllable in the very short run. Once a fixed asset is acquired, there is virtually no control over the annual depreciation charges. One may select the depreciation method, but no differences will arise between actual and budgeted costs except in those situations where depreciation can be calculated on usage. There are, however, some intermediate-term fixed costs (often called discretionary or programmed costs because they are determined annually on

---

[2] Sophisticated methods for separating fixed and variable costs are shown in William J. Baumol and Charles H. Sevin, "Marketing Costs and Mathematical Programming," *New Decision-Making Tools for Managers,* Edward C. Bursk and John F. Chapman, eds. (New York: New American Library, Inc., 1963), pp. 247–65; and R. S. Gynther, "Improving Separation of Fixed and Variable Expenses," *Management Accounting,* June 1963, pp. 29–38.

a budgetary basis) which may be highly controllable; i.e., actual costs may exceed budgeted costs. Advertising and R & D costs fall into this category.

Uncontrollable variable costs are variable costs which are not incurred in the segment under consideration. Therefore, the costs should be expressed as standard costs so that a manager will not be held responsible for the inefficiencies of another department. Variable manufacturing costs of blenders and mixers would be indirect variable costs for the Marketing Division, and should be expressed in the budget as standard costs.

Controllable variable costs	Controllable fixed costs
Uncontrollable variable costs	Uncontrollable fixed costs

Uncontrollable fixed costs are not included in segmental income statements since any basis of allocation to the segment would necessarily be arbitrary. Uncontrollable costs are often called common costs and for the Marketing Division would include a portion of those costs of the corporate headquarters and those manufacturing costs which couldn't be directly allocated to blenders and mixers, such as the plant manager's salary.

Segmental Analysis

Contribution margin income statements by department are useful for budgeting, performance analysis, short-run decision-making, pricing, and decisions between alternatives—e.g., whether to close down a warehouse or relocate it; whether to lease a fleet of trucks or own them. Market segment income statements are also useful for such marketing decisions as whether to drop a product line and whether to alter the physical distribution system; and they aid in the redirection of effort to the company's more profitable markets. The usual market segmentation is by product line, territory, channel, order size, and customer, but any of the segmentation bases of the marketing matrix of the firm's target markets could be used.

A modular data base also facilitates statements focusing on functional areas, depending on management's judgment about what information is relevant for decision-making and control. For example, if transportation is judged to be a crucial function in the case of blenders, then the expense for shipping blenders would be coded by that function and by the relevant variables (territory, channel, product, order size, customer, date). Revenue, in turn, would be coded at the time of each transaction.

Unless the company's information system is somewhat sophisticated, there is usually some initial difficulty in constructing accounting statements of functional/ departmental areas. Costs for a specific department must be broken out of the natural accounts via estimation techniques. (Since costs are usually accumulated in natural accounts, such as salary expense, the salary expense for the Marketing Division would have to be calculated.)

Under the modular contribution margin approach not all costs are allocated to segments. Rather, only those costs are considered which would disappear if the company were to drop that department or segment. Note that this is acceptable only for purposes of internal decision-making, and *not* for differential cost justification under the Robinson-Patman Act (as demonstrated in the Borden case) or for general financial reporting purposes (audited reports to stockholders, IRS returns, and SEC reports).

Allocation of Costs

Other refinements can be added to the modular contribution margin model. The charge for the specific assets used by the department (depreciation) could be based on the decline in the market value of the resources during the period. Or an interest charge on the working capital used by the department (based on the firm's actual cost of capital) could be included to give a clear picture of the department's operations and actual contribution.

Allocation, however, cannot be made arbitrarily on the basis of sales volume since that focus might overlook other relevant information. For example, how do you attach distribution expense to blenders and mixers for a mixed shipment of both products, when blenders are bulkier, heavier, and require more handling? Or if mixers are easy to sell to large retailers, while blenders require extensive sales effort, the entry of salesmen's expenses to blenders and mixers should reflect this difference.

If costs are based on a factor such as weight or space occupied, this may allow an equitable basis of cost assignment. This does not always happen, though, and so assigning costs to departments on the basis of weight can be highly misleading for analytical purposes. Suffice it to say that wherever variable costs are predictable and vary with a given base, standard costs should be used in budgeting for the Marketing Division.

The value of a modular contribution margin statement is the ability to match costs with revenues for the smallest market segments desired and then to aggregate these modules into statements for larger segments. Essentially, the modular data base provides management with the capability of transforming accounting information into two systems: one based on departments within the firm, the other based on market segments.

Useful Information

The flexibility and responsiveness of the modular contribution margin approach for market segments can be shown by applying it to the D-W Appliance Company. The first step is for management to decide on the relevant factors for examination. In this example, *product line* was chosen as the basic unit of interest, and the market was further segmented by territory, channel, and order size. (The modular data base could just as easily have provided for primary segmentation by territory or channel, or whatever.) The accompanying exhibits show the possible modular income statements that can be constructed.

Exhibit 2 shows the hierarchy and linkages among the segmental contribution margin income statements illustrated here.

Basic data for the illustration is shown in Exhibit 3, the Master Cost Data Sheet. Unit sales and channel of distribution costs are broken down by territory, product, and channel in Exhibit 4.

Income for the entire firm is shown in Exhibit 5. It is the only statement containing $430,000 of costs (territory costs, joint manufacturing costs, and corporate head-quarters costs) which are joint to the product oriented segmental income statements shown in Exhibits 6–19.

Clues for Action

The loss at the corporate level (as shown in Exhibit 5) indicates that the firm should either strengthen, if possible, those segments which are weakest and/or reallocate more of its resources to those segments which are strongest.

In Exhibits 6 and 13, Total Income Statements for blenders and mixers, blenders are stronger than mixers in terms of Contribution Margin (32.7% versus 21.6%) although slightly less profitable after taking into account direct fixed costs (13.1% versus 14.8%). This may indicate that not enough programmed advertising costs are being budgeted to blenders. More advertising effort may be needed to effectively exploit the higher Contribution Margin of blenders.

At the same time, the further breakdowns indicate that the Segment Income of the West Territory is lagging behind that of the East Territory for both blenders and mixers (see Exhibits 7, 10, 14, and 17). The biggest reason for this poor performance is the very low Segment Income of the Wholesaler Channels in the West Territory (Exhibits 11 and 18).

Action to improve the situation is especially called for in the Wholesaler Channel for blenders in the West Territory. Not only is the Segment Income percentage (6.5%) the lowest for any segment in the whole analysis, but the corresponding Contribution Margin is relatively strong (27.9%). The problem is one of spreading

EXHIBIT 2. Segmental contribution income statements: D-W Appliance Company

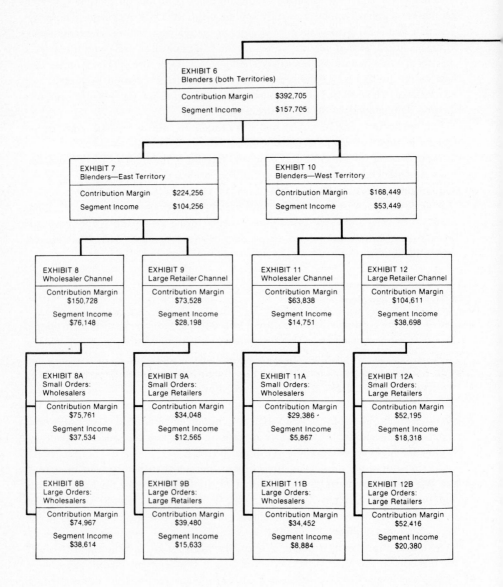

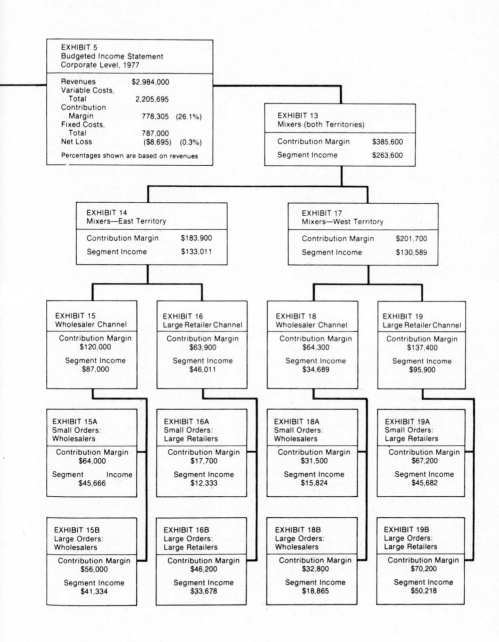

EXHIBIT 5
Budgeted Income Statement
Corporate Level, 1977

Revenues	$2,984,000	
Variable Costs,		
Total	2,205,695	
Contribution		
Margin	778,305	(26.1%)
Fixed Costs,		
Total	787,000	
Net Loss	($8,695)	(0.3%)

Percentages shown are based on revenues

EXHIBIT 13
Mixers (both Territories)

Contribution Margin	$385,600
Segment Income	$263,600

EXHIBIT 14
Mixers—East Territory

Contribution Margin	$183,900
Segment Income	$133,011

EXHIBIT 17
Mixers—West Territory

Contribution Margin	$201,700
Segment Income	$130,589

EXHIBIT 15
Wholesaler Channel

Contribution Margin
$120,000

Segment Income
$87,000

EXHIBIT 16
Large Retailer Channel

Contribution Margin
$63,900

Segment Income
$46,011

EXHIBIT 18
Wholesaler Channel

Contribution Margin
$64,300

Segment Income
$34,689

EXHIBIT 19
Large Retailer Channel

Contribution Margin
$137,400

Segment Income
$95,900

EXHIBIT 15A
Small Orders:
Wholesalers

Contribution Margin
$64,000

Segment Income
$45,666

EXHIBIT 16A
Small Orders:
Large Retailers

Contribution Margin
$17,700

Segment Income
$12,333

EXHIBIT 18A
Small Orders:
Wholesalers

Contribution Margin
$31,500

Segment Income
$15,824

EXHIBIT 19A
Small Orders:
Large Retailers

Contribution Margin
$67,200

Segment Income
$45,682

EXHIBIT 15B
Large Orders:
Wholesalers

Contribution Margin
$56,000

Segment Income
$41,334

EXHIBIT 16B
Large Orders:
Large Retailers

Contribution Margin
$46,200

Segment Income
$33,678

EXHIBIT 18B
Large Orders:
Wholesalers

Contribution Margin
$32,800

Segment Income
$18,865

EXHIBIT 19B
Large Orders:
Large Retailers

Contribution Margin
$70,200

Segment Income
$50,218

EXHIBIT 3. *D-W Appliance Company master cost data sheet for 1977*

	East		West	
	Blenders	Mixers	Blenders	Mixers
Revenue (per unit)	$ 42.00	$ 26.00	$ 38.00	24.00
Variable manufacturing costs	$ 20.00	$ 15.00	$ 20.00	$ 15.00
Variable selling costs (10% of revenue)	4.20	2.60	3.80	2.40
Total	$ 24.20	$ 17.60	$ 23.80	$ 17.40
Contribution margin per unit before channel costs	$ 17.80	$ 8.40	$ 14.20	$ 6.60
Programmed advertising costs[a]	$20,000	$12,000	$15,000	$10,000
Budgeted sales (units)	15,000	28,000	15,000	44,000

[a] Programmed advertising costs are fixed costs that are reviewed each year through the budget process. (Therefore, they are not in a direct relationship with sales revenue or units sold. This could result from having a particular ad aimed at only one channel member or group of channel members. An example would be a trade magazine ad in a conference program for a Wholesalers Convention. Such an ad would not reach the retailer.)

	Blenders	Mixers	East	West	Unallocated
Controllable direct manufacturing costs	$200,000	$100,000			
Territorial fixed costs (joint to products)			$50,000	$30,000	
Joint fixed manufacturing costs					$100,000
Corporate headquarters costs					$250,000

heavy fixed costs of manufacturing over more sales. The solution, again, would be to take advantage of the good contribution margin percentage through increased advertising effort or, perhaps in this case, by expanding the sales force.

As another indication of the revealing capability of this kind of analysis, consider the profitability of the two channels. If they had simply been compared in total (as a form of primary segmentation), the figures would have been:

Channel	Contribution margin %	Segment %	Income $
Wholesaler	26.3%	12.9%	$212,588
Large Retailer	27.8%	14.3%	$208,807

EXHIBIT 4. Budgeted channel of distribution costs

	Wholesaler small order	Channel large order	Large retailer small order	Channel large order
East				
Blenders:				
Budgeted sales (units)	5,119	4,868	2,381	2,632
Cost per unit	$3.00	$2.40	$3.50	$2.80
Total	$15,357	$11,683	$ 8,334	$ 7,370
Mixers:				
Budgeted sales (units)	10,000	8,000	3,000	7,000
Cost per unit	$2.00	$1.40	$2.50	$1.80
Total	$20,000	$11,200	$ 7,500	$12,600
West				
Blenders:				
Budgeted sales (units)	2,881	3,132	4,619	4,368
Cost per unit	$4.00	$3.20	$2.90	$2.20
Total	$11,524	$10,022	$13,395	$ 9,610
Mixers:				
Budgeted sales (units)	9,000	8,000	14,000	13,000
Cost per unit	$3.10	$2.50	$1.80	$1.20
Total	$27,900	$20,000	$25,200	$15,600

The two channels would have appeared to be very even in profitability. Yet recombining in various ways brings out still more information. Exhibit 20 shows that if the Wholesaler Channel in the West could have been improved to match the Wholesaler Channel in the East, the total Wholesaler Channel would have outperformed the Large Retailer Channel.

Within the Large Retailer Channel, blenders and mixers in the East are relatively more profitable in terms of both Contribution Margin and Segment Income percentages than their counterparts in the West. However, Segment Income in total dollars for blenders and mixers in the East ($74,209) is barely half of that for the corresponding products in the West for the Large Retailer Channel ($134,598). Maybe the East Territory for Large Retailers needs a greater dosage of advertising dollars to exploit its relative advantage. Perhaps the whole Large Retailer Channel needs some kind of revamping—a need that otherwise would never have been revealed except through segmental analysis.

EXHIBITS 5 and 6–12. Total income statements

Exhibit 5
Corporate Level, 1977

Revenues	**$2,984,000**	
Variable Costs:		
Manufacturing Marketing:	$1,680,000	
Selling	298,400	10.0%[1]
Channel Costs	227,295	7.6%
Total	**$2,205,695**	
Contribution Margin	**$ 778,305**	**26.1%**
Fixed Costs:		
Programmed Advertising	$ 57,000	1.9%
Direct (to product) Manu-		
facturing Costs	300,000	
Territory Costs	80,000	
Joint Manufacturing Costs	100,000	
Corporate Headquarters Costs	250,000	
Total	**$ 787,000**	
Net Loss	**($8,695)**	(.3%)

[1] Percentages shown are based upon revenues.

Exhibit 6
Blenders (Both Territories)

Revenues (30,000 units)	**$1,200,000**	
Variable Costs:		
Manufacturing Marketing:	$ 600,000	
Selling	120,000	10.0%
Channel Costs	87,295	7.3%
Total	**$ 807,295**	
Contribution Margin	**$ 392,705**	**32.7%**
Fixed Costs:		
Programmed Advertising	$ 35,000	2.9%
Direct (to product) Manu-		
facturing Costs	200,000	
Total	**$ 235,000**	
Segment Income	**$ 157,705**	**13.1%**

Exhibit 7
Blenders — East Territory

Revenues (15,000 units)	**$630,000**	
Variable Costs:		
Manufacturing Marketing:	$300,000	
Selling	63,000	10.0%
Channel Costs	42,744	6.8%
Total	**$405,744**	
Contribution Margin	**$224,256**	**35.6%**
Fixed Costs:		
Programmed Advertising	$ 20,000	3.2%
Direct (to product) Manu-		
facturing Costs	100,000	
Total	**$120,000**	
Segment Income	**$104,256**	**16.5%**

Exhibit 10
Blenders — West Territory

Revenues (15,000 units)	**$570,000**	
Variable Costs:		
Manufacturing Marketing:	$300,000	
Selling	57,000	10.0%
Channel Costs	44,551	7.8%
Total	**$401,551**	
Contribution Margin	**$168,449**	**29.6%**
Fixed Costs:		
Programmed Advertising	$ 15,000	2.6%
Direct (to product) Manufac-		
turing Costs	100,000	
Total	**$115,000**	
Segment Income	**$ 53,449**	**9.4%**

EXHIBIT 7
Blenders—East Territory

Exhibit 8
Wholesaler Channel

	Small Order (5119 units)		Large Order (4868 units)		Total	
Revenues	$214,998		$204,456		$419,454	
Variable Costs:						
Manufacturing Marketing:	$102,380		$ 97,360		$199,740	
Selling	21,500	10.0%	20,446	10.0%	41,946	10.0%
Channel Costs	15,357	7.1%	11,683	5.7%	27,040	6.4%
Total	$139,237		$129,489		$268,726	
Contribution Margin	$ 75,761	35.2%	$ 74,967	36.7%	$150,728	35.9%
Fixed Costs:						
Programmed Advertising[1]	$ 4,100	1.9%	$ 3,900	1.9%	$ 8,000	1.9%
Direct (to product) Manufacturing Costs[2]	34,127		32,453		66,580	
Total	$ 38,227		$ 36,353		$ 74,580	
Segment Income	$ 37,534	(17.5%)	$ 38,614	18.9%	$ 76,148	18.2%

[1] Direct to the Large Retailer Channel and allocated in accordance with revenues. The same procedure is used for channel analysis in later exhibits.

Exhibit 9
Large Retailer Channel

	Small Order (2381 units)		Large Order (2632 units)		Total	
Revenues	$100,002		$110,544		$210,546	
Variable Costs:						
Manufacturing Marketing:	$ 47,620		$ 52,640		$100,260	
Selling	10,000	10.0%	11,054	10.0%	21,054	10.0%
Channel Costs	8,334	8.3%	7,370	6.7%	15,704	7.5%
Total	$ 65,954		$ 71,064		$137,018	
Contribution Margin	$ 34,048	34.0%	$ 39,480	35.7%	$ 73,528	34.9%
Fixed Costs:						
Programmed Advertising[1]	$ 5,700	5.7%	$ 6,300	5.7%	$ 12,000	5.7%
Direct (to product) Manufacturing Costs[2]	15,783		17,547		33,330	
Total	$ 21,483		$ 23,847		$ 45,330	
Segment Income	$ 12,565	12.6%	$ 15,633	14.1%	$ 28,198	13.4%

[2] Allocated in proportion of number of units sold in each order size for this channel to total sales. The same procedure is used in later exhibits.

EXHIBIT 10
Blenders—West Territory

Exhibit 11
Wholesaler Channel

	Small Order (2881 units)		Large Order (3132 units)		Total	
Revenues	$109,478		$119,016		$228,494	
Variable Costs:						
Manufacturing						
Marketing:	$ 57,620		$ 62,640		$120,260	
Selling	10,948	10.0%	11,902	10.0%	22,850	10.0%
Channel Costs	11,524	10.5%	10,022	8.4%	21,546	9.4%
Total	$ 80,092		$ 84,564		$164,656	
Contribution Margin	$ 29,386	26.8%	$ 34,452	28.9%	$ 63,838	27.9%
Fixed Costs:						
Programmed Advertising	$ 4,312	3.9%	$ 4,688	3.9%	$ 9,000	3.9%
Direct (to product) Manufacturing Costs	19,207		20,880		40,087	
Total	$ 23,519		$ 25,568		$ 49,087	
Segment Income	$ 5,867	5.4%	$ 8,884	7.5%	$ 14,751	6.5%

Exhibit 12
Large Retailer Channel

	Small Order (4619 units)		Large Order (4368 units)		Total	
Revenues	$175,522		$165,984		$341,506	
Variable Costs:						
Manufacturing						
Marketing:	$ 92,380		$ 87,360		$179,740	
Selling	17,552	10.0%	16,598	10.0%	34,150	10.0%
Channel Costs	13,395	7.6%	9,610	5.8%	23,005	6.7%
Total	$123,327		$113,568		$236,895	
Contribution Margin	$ 52,195	29.7%	$ 52,416	31.6%	$104,611	30.6%
Fixed Costs:						
Programmed Advertising	$ 3,084	1.8%	$ 2,916	1.8%	$ 6,000	1.8%
Direct (to product) Manufacturing Costs	30,793		29,120		59,913	
Total	$ 33,877		$ 32,036		$ 65,913	
Segment Income	$ 18,318	10.4%	$ 20,380	12.3%	$ 38,698	11.3%

402

EXHIBITS 5 and 13–19. Total income statements

Exhibit 5
Corporate Level, 1977

Revenues	$2,984,000	
Variable Costs		
Manufacturing Marketing	$1,680,000	
Selling	298,400	10.0%[1]
Channel Costs	227,295	7.6%
Total	$2,205,695	
Contribution Margin	$ 778,305	26.1%
Fixed Costs		
Programmed Advertising	$ 57,000	1.9%
Direct (to product) Manu-		
facturing Costs	300,000	
Territory Costs	80,000	
Joint Manufacturing Costs	100,000	
Corporate Headquarters Costs	250,000	
Total	$ 787,000	
Net Loss	($8,695)	(.3%)

Exhibit 13
Mixers (Both Territories)

Revenues (72,000 units)	$1,784,000	
Variable Costs:		
Manufacturing Marketing:	$1,080,000	
Selling	178,400	10.0%
Channel Costs	140,000	7.8%
Total	$1,398,400	
Contribution Margin	$ 385,600	21.6%
Fixed Costs:		
Programmed Advertising	$ 22,000	1.2%
Direct (to product) Manufac-		
turing Costs	100,000	
Total	$ 122,000	
Segment Income	$ 263,600	14.8%

Exhibit 17
Mixers — West Territory

Revenues	$1,056,000	
Variable Costs:		
Manufacturing Marketing:	$ 660,000	
Selling	105,600	10.0%
Channel Costs	88,700	8.4%
Total	$ 854,300	
Contribution Margin	$ 201,700	19.1%
Fixed Costs:		
Programmed Advertising	$ 10,000	.9%
Direct (to product) Manufac-		
turing Costs	61,111	
Total	$ 71,111	
Segment Income	$ 130,589	12.4%

Exhibit 14
Mixers — East Territory

Revenues (28,000 units)	$728,000	
Variable Costs:		
Manufacturing Marketing:	$420,000	
Selling	72,800	10.0%
Channel Costs	51,300	7.0%
Total	$544,100	
Contribution Margin	$183,900	25.3%
Fixed Costs:		
Programmed Advertising	$ 12,000	1.6%
Direct (to product) Manufac-		
turing Costs	38,889	
Total	$ 50,889	
Segment Income	$133,011	18.3%

403

EXHIBIT 14
Mixers—East Territory

Exhibit 15
Wholesaler Channel

	Small Order (10,000 units)		Large Order (8,000 units)		Total	
Revenues	$260,000		$208,000		$468,000	
Variable Costs:						
Manufacturing						
Marketing:	$150,000		$120,000		$270,000	
Selling	26,000	10.0%	20,800	10.0%	46,800	10.0%
Channel Costs	20,000	7.7%	11,200	5.4%	31,200	6.7%
Total	$196,000		$152,000		$348,000	
Contribution Margin	$ 64,000	24.6%	$ 56,000	26.9%	$120,000	25.6%
Fixed Costs:						
Programmed Advertising	$ 4,445	1.7%	$ 3,555	1.7%	$ 8,000	1.7%
Direct (to product) Manufacturing Costs	13,889		11,111		25,000	
Total	$ 18,334		$ 14,666		$ 33,000	
Segment Income	$ 45,666	17.6%	$ 41,334	19.8%	$ 87,000	18.6%

Exhibit 16
Large Retailer Channel

	Small Order (3,000 units)		Large Order (7,000 units)		Total	
Revenues	$78,000		$182,000		$260,000	
Variable Costs:						
Manufacturing						
Marketing:	$45,000		$105,000		$150,000	
Selling	7,800	10.0%	18,200	10.0%	26,100	10.0%
Channel Costs	7,500	9.6%	12,600	6.9%	20,100	7.7%
Total	$60,300		$135,800		$196,100	
Contribution Margin	$17,700	22.7%	$ 46,200	25.4%	$ 63,900	24.6%
Fixed Costs:						
Programmed Advertising	$ 1,200	1.5%	$ 2,800	1.5%	$ 4,000	1.5%
Direct (to product) Manufacturing Costs	4,167		9,722		13,889	
Total	$ 5,367		$ 12,522		$ 17,889	
Segment Income	$12,333	15.8%	$ 33,678	18.5%	$ 46,011	17.7%

EXHIBIT 17
Mixers—West Territory

Exhibit 18
Wholesale Channel

	Small Order (9000 units)		Large Order (8000 units)		Total	
Revenues	$216,000		$192,000		$408,000	
Variable Costs:						
Manufacturing						
Marketing:	$135,000		$120,000		$255,000	
Selling	21,600	10.0%	29,200	10.0%	40,800	10.0%
Channel Costs	27,900	12.9%	20,000	10.4%	47,900	11.7%
Total	$184,500		$159,200		$343,700	
Contribution Margin	$ 31,500	14.6%	$ 32,800	17.1%	$ 64,300	15.8%
Fixed Costs:						
Programmed Advertising	$ 3,176	1.5%	$ 2,824	1.5%	$ 6,000	1.5%
Direct (to product) Manufacturing Costs	12,500		11,111		23,611	
Total	$ 15,676		$ 13,935		$ 29,611	
Segment Income	$ 15,824	7.3%	$ 18,865	9.8%	$ 34,689	8.5%

Exhibit 19
Large Retailer Channel

	Small Order (14,000 units)		Large Order (13,000 units)		Total	
Revenues	$336,000		$312,000		$648,000	
Variable Costs:						
Manufacturing						
Marketing:	$210,000		$195,000		$405,000	
Selling	33,600	10.0%	31,200	10.0%	64,800	10.0%
Channel Costs	25,200	7.5%	15,600	5.0%	40,800	6.3%
Total	$268,800		$241,800		$510,600	
Contribution Margin	$ 67,200	20.0%	$ 70,200	22.5%	$137,400	21.2%
Fixed Costs:						
Programmed Advertising	$ 2,074	.6%	$ 1,926	.6%	$ 4,000	.6%
Direct (to product) Manufacturing Costs	19,444		18,056		37,500	
Total	$ 21,518		$ 19,982		$ 41,500	
Segment Income	$ 45,682	13.6%	$ 50,218	16.1%	$ 95,900	14.8%

EXHIBIT 20. Aggregate comparison of wholesaler channel and large retailer channel

Channel	Contribution margin (%)	Segment %	Income $	Total
Wholesalers[a]	(26.3%)[c]	(12.9%)[c]		($212,588)[c]
West				
Blenders	27.9%	6.5%	$14,751	
Mixers	15.8%	8.5%	$34,689	
Subtotal				$ 49,440
East				
Blenders	35.9%	18.2%	$76,148	
Mixers	25.6%	18.6%	$87,000	
Subtotal				$163,148
Large retailers[b]	(27.8%)[c]	(14.3%)[c]		($208.807)[c]
West				
Blenders	30.6%	11.3%	$38,698	
Mixers	21.2%	14.8%	$95,900	
Subtotal				$134,598
East				
Blenders	34.9%	13.4%	$28,198	
Mixers	24.6%	17.7%	$46,011	
Subtotal				$ 74,209

[a] Exhibits 8, 11, 15, and 18.   [b] Exhibits 9, 12, 16, and 19.   [c] Aggregate totals.

EXHIBIT 21. Relative distribution costs by order size

Territory	Product	Large order[1]	Small order[1]	Relative cost excess[2]
Large Retailers				
West	Blenders	5.8%	7.6%	31.0%
West	Mixers	5.0%	7.5%	50.0%
East	Blenders	6.7%	8.3%	23.9%
East	Mixers	6.9%	9.6%	39.1%

Territory	Product	Large order[2]	Small order[3]	Relative cost excess[2]
Wholesalers				
West	Blenders	8.4%	10.5%	25%
West	Mixers	10.4%	12.9%	24%
East	Blenders	5.7%	7.1%	24.6%
East	Mixers	5.4%	7.7%	42.6

[1] Channel costs as a percentage of revenues from Exhibits 9, 12, 16, 19.
[2] Percentage is based on large order size; for example, 7.6%–5.8% = 1.8% and 1.8%/5.8% = 31%.
[3] Channel costs as a percentage of revenues from Exhibits 8. 11. 15. 18.

Another aspect of the problem lies in order size. Exhibit 21 reveals that this is most evident within the Large Retailer Channel in the West. Within that territory and channel, distribution costs for small order sizes of mixers are 50% greater per dollar of revenue than for large orders. Similarly, small orders of blenders in the West in the Large Retailer Channel are out of line relative to large orders (31% excess). Small order costs are also out of line relative to large orders for mixers in the East in both channels (39.1% and 42.6% for Large Retailers and Wholesalers). Efforts must be made to increase the size of Large Retailers' small orders, or the retailers responsible for these orders must be converted to buying from wholesalers.

Benefits of Segmentation

These are just a few of the possible areas where the use of the modular contribution margin income statement could improve management control and planning, for the sake of greater profitability. In addition, actual results can be compared against the projected budget for each segment to analyze managment's performance or the effect of uncontrollable factors on that performance.

If segmental analysis had not been done at all, or if the segmentation had been conducted just by product (or just by territory, just by channel, or just by order size), many ideas for corrective action or expanded effort might not have been generated.

While the benefits of segmental statements must exceed costs of preparation, the power of the computer should lessen costs enough to make segmental analysis beneficial to an increasing number of companies.

Exercises

25.1   Wollaton Company manufactures two consumer products in three processes. Both products go through process 1, although the operations are different. Product A is completed in process 2A, and product B is completed in process 2B. The production manager oversees the manufacturing operation, with a department head in charge of each process.

Marketing is under the direction of the vice-president of marketing. Products A and B are complementary and are marketed in two territories. A territorial sales manager is in charge of each territory. He is responsible for all advertising (television, newspaper, and radio) within his territory. Within each territory the products are distributed through two channels: a large retailer channel and a wholesaler channel.

Categorize each of the costs listed below in terms of its correct cell in the following grid for each of the organizational units, product lines, or channels listed.

Controllable variable AI	Controllable fixed AII
Uncontrollable variable BI	Uncontrollable fixed BII

1. Costs of a television ad in the East Territory for product A, reaching consumers who buy through both channels.
   a. Territorial sales manager of the East Territory
   b. The wholesale channel of the East Territory
   c. Product A
2. Cost of a television ad in the East Territory for both products, reaching consumers who buy through both channels.
   a. Territorial sales manager of the East Territory
   b. The wholesale channel in the East Territory
   c. Product A
3. A national ad for both product lines reaching all consumers.
   a. The territorial sales manager in the East Territory
   b. Product A
   c. The vice-president of marketing
4. Extra transportation costs resulting from a truck strike by a common carrier that affects only the wholesale channel in the East Territory.
   a. Product A
   b. The wholesale channel of the East Territory
   c. The territorial sales manager of the East Territory
5. Depreciation costs of a machine in process 2A.
   a. Product A
   b. Process 2A department head
   c. The production manager
6. Depreciation costs of a machine in process 1.
   a. Product A
   b. Process 1 department head
   c. The production manager
7. Costs resulting from the purchase of some raw materials that have a higher than normal breakage rate because the goods are slightly inferior.
   a. The department head in process 1
   b. The purchasing department head

25.2 Vostok Company manufactures two products which it markets in two territories. The two products are priced the same.

Sales for 1979

	Territory 1	Territory 2
Product A	$500,000	$300,000
Product B	250,000	200,000

Variable manufacturing costs are 40% for product A of selling price and 35% for product B. Selling commissions are 5% for each product line. Other information:

Direct fixed manufacturing costs for A	$100,000
Direct fixed manufacturing costs for B	75,000
Joint manufacturing costs	50,000

Programmed advertising costs

	Territory 1	Territory 2	Product A	Product B
Product A	$15,000	$10,000		
Product B	6,000	8,000		
Indirect to product	12,000	18,000		
Indirect to territory			$22,000	$19,000

Costs that cannot be easily allocated should not be allocated. Prepare:

1. Segmental statements by product line, with a secondary breakdown by territory using a contribution margin format.
2. Segmental statements by territory, with a secondary breakdown by product line using a contribution margin format.

New Approaches to Analyzing Marketing Profitability

26

Frank H. Mossman   Paul M. Fischer   W. J. E. Crissy

The name of the game in marketing is to maximize profit from the funds expended for the promotion and fulfillment of demand. The tools to do this are at hand. The purpose of this article is to present the basis for designing a marketing-accounting information system which facilitates the financial analysis of marketing performance. To assure that the system results in optimal actions within marketing segments, refinements of the model are also discussed.

Accounting for Marketing Costs

The desirability of using accounting information to measure marketing performance by segments has been advocated by several authors over the past 40 years. Recently, there has been a rejuvenation of interest in such analysis.[1] These articles differ from the earlier ones mainly in that they advocate the use of contribution analysis rather than traditional net income analysis. Contribution analysis deducts from the revenue of a segment only those costs specifically incurred for the segment. The excess of revenues over these costs contributes to the common costs and profits of the firm. By contrast, net income analysis allocates *all* of the firm's costs to marketing segments. Since costs common to multiple segments are allocated, the process is necessarily subjective and arbitrary.

Although the literature indicates a renewed interest in matching marketing revenues and costs by segments, a recent survey by the American Accounting Association Committee on Cost and Profitability Analyses for Marketing shows only limited use of such analyses by major corporations.[2]

The survey findings indicate that it is not unusual for a firm's accounting system

Reprinted with permission from *Journal of Marketing*, Vol. 38 (April 1974), pp. 43–48, published by the American Marketing Association.

[1] See W. J. E. Crissy, Paul M. Fischer, and Frank H. Mossman, "Segmental Analysis: Key to Marketing Profitability," *MSU Business Topics*, Vol. 21 (Spring 1973), pp. 42–49; and V. H. Kirpalani and Stanley J. Shapiro, "Financial Dimensions of Marketing Management," *Journal of Marketing*. Vol. 37 (July 1973), pp. 40–47.

[2] "Report of the Committee on Cost and Profitability Analyses for Marketing," *The Accounting Review*, Supplement to Vol. 47 (1972), pp. 575–615.

to be of little direct help to the decision-making and control process of marketing management. However, this does not mean that accounting is incapable of supplying relevant data. Rather, it indicates that most accounting systems are not currently designed to meet the specific needs of marketing management. Accounting systems were originally designed to report the aggregate effects of a firm's operations to its stockholders and creditors. In later years, accounting systems have been redesigned to meet the internal management needs within the production sector of the firm. The net result is an accounting system which is oriented towards both external reporting and production cost analysis.

Recently many firms have tried to extend the rigor of production cost analysis to marketing expenditures, including the costs of both promotion and distribution. To be successful, such an analysis must be two-pronged: it must analyze the propriety of expenditures by well-defined functions (such as selling, storing, and transporting), and it must determine whether the services of the functions are profitably employed within marketing segments. To date, the literature of accounting for marketing costs has dealt only rarely with the matter of controlling expenditures by function. The primary concern has been to analyze the profitability of marketing by areas of concern, such as product or customer segments.

Current accounting systems will typically record marketing costs in aggregated natural accounts (recorded by the nature of the expendure, such as sales, salaries, and delivery expense). Currently, popular methods of analysis accept this constraint and apply statistical analysis to these accounts. Seldom is an attempt made to attach the costs to functional responsibilities first. Costs are merely allocated directly to marketing segments according to some arbitrarily chosen measure of activity. It is not uncommon, for instance, to assign advertising to market segments in proportion to the sales revenue of each segment. Such analysis is an appendage by nature and is seldom timely. Vital information about the controllability, behavior, and relationship of the costs to segments is lost.

The Need for a Modular Data Base

To meet the needs of marketing management fully, an accounting system must be able to assemble costs by well-defined functions and then attach the functional costs to the sales segments relevant to analyzing marketing performance. A modular data base is needed to support such analyses. Such a data base may be viewed as a central storage system which contains revenue and cost information in a readily accessible form.

Essentially, the modular data base starts with a basic document such as a bill of lading or a commercial invoice. The transaction is then entered from this basic document and coded as to applicable segments. Other data may also be entered. The prime consideration is to enter all data which may require retrieval from the memory capacity of the computer. The central purpose of the system is to collect, monitor, and report information to management for decision-making and control purposes. Once the modular system is properly set up, one input into the system from source documents should be sufficient to accommodate all subsequent analyses. Specifically, a well-structured modular data base must take into account the following factors:

1. The information requirements of various levels of management
2. The meaning and use of the various information elements
3. Provision for estimating the effects of alternative courses of action prior to their implementation
4. Flexibility in updating and meeting changing information requirements

It is now appropriate to examine the general functioning of the data base for marketing costs and revenue. The data base must code each sale as to customer and product so that sales may later be aggregated by desired marketing segments. Marketing costs must be coded as to both function and the marketing segment for which the cost was specifically incurred. Figure 1 illustrates that cost and revenue data directly enter the data base from source documents. Revenue modules may be grouped for desired segmental analyses and be totaled for presentation in financial statements prepared for external reporting purposes. Cost modules are regrouped in three manners. First, the costs are consolidated into functions under common responsibility, allowing a comparison of estimated and actual costs by function. Second, cost modules are assigned to marketing segments. They are added to the

FIGURE 1. *Marketing cost and revenue flow*

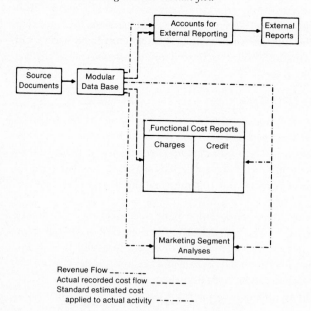

production cost of the products, and the total set of applicable costs is deducted from revenue to analyze the profitability of the segments. Last, cost modules are aggregated into the expense categories desired for external reporting purposes.

Refinements of the Data Base

Two refinements included in the data base are worthy of further discussion. The first is that cost modules are assigned only to the marketing segments for which they were specifically incurred. For example, the cost of advertising product A within sales territory X is first attachable to the sales of product A in territory X. The cost is not allocated to customers within the territory. The cost is, of course, included in any aggregation of sales which includes the segment defined as product A sales in territory X. Typically, as one proceeds to aggregate marketing segments, more costs will become specifically attachable. Conversely, the smaller the segment studied, the fewer the costs which will be specifically attached.

A second refinement pertains to the assignment of marketing costs where the level of cost incurred varies in a predictable manner with some measure of activity. Examples would be the tendency of delivery costs to vary with miles driven or storage costs to vary with cubic content and time stored. Where predictable cost behavior exists, the standard cost procedures of accounting for production costs are adapted to the data base. Figure 1 also presents a data base flow chart showing the flow of cost data where estimated standard costs are used. The functional cost reports become two-sided. The function is charged by the data base with actual costs incurred. The data base also credits the function with the estimated standard cost per unit of the function's service times the quantity of service provided in a given period. The estimated standard cost of the service provided to segments is also used to charge market segments. This procedure allows comparison of actual and estimated standard costs by function where the total estimated cost is adjusted automatically for actual service provided. Second, market segments are charged only for the reasonable estimated standard cost of services received. As a result, the analysis of segment profitability is not confounded with the operating efficiencies or inefficiencies of the various service functions.

Assessment of Data Needs

Current Use of Modular Costs

A 1972 survey of 75 firms from the *Fortune* list of 500 examined the methods currently being used to analyze the operating costs of marketing segments.[3] This recent survey showed that 50% of the 75 responding firms used estimated standard cost modules for budgeting physical distribution costs. In each case, costs per measure

---

[3] Same reference as footnote 2.

of activity, such as warehouse throughput for warehouse movement costs or distance traveled for delivery costs, were developed. These unit costs were then applied to the anticipated use of physical distribution services to build a budget. The survey indicated that 60% of the firms which developed estimated unit costs did so only for those costs which varied predictably with output. The remaining costs, termed fixed costs, did not vary predictably with output and were budgeted as lump sums. The other 40% of the firms which developed unit costs did so by adding to the variable cost of service an allocated portion of fixed costs. This practice resulted in the quotation of an average cost of service. It can be a misleading approach, since the fixed costs are given a false appearance of variability. Very likely the allocation of fixed costs over activity is a practice derived from procedures used in accounting for production costs. It should be noted that the calculation of average production costs is a practice which evolved primarily to meet external reporting requirements.

The reported use of unit cost modules for physical distribution costs extended beyond budget planning: 30% of the respondents used the same cost modules to design their physical distribution systems. The cost modules were used to make trade-off analyses between alternate levels and types of physical distribution services. Approximately 40% of the firms surveyed used the cost modules as a means of comparing the actual and planned costs of providing services. This type of variance analysis becomes a feedback mechanism designed to accomplish cost control. Finally, 20% of the respondents fully utilized the versatility of the cost modules by also using the costs to charge marketing segments for their use of services. These firms reported using cost modules as shown in Figure 1.

The significant use of cost modules to plan and control physical distribution costs has been confirmed by the A.A.A. survey. It is a need which must be fulfilled by an up-to-date accounting system. Unfortunately, the usefulness of the cost modules to analysis of the performance of marketing segments has not yet been developed fully in most firms.

The Need for Segmental Analyses

The accounting system proposed here uses the product sale to the customer as a basic informational input to which revenue and variable costs are attached. These modules are then aggregated for desired forms of segmental analyses. As the modules are aggregated, additional costs are added as they become applicable. The A.A.A. survey was used to determine the varieties of segmental analyses which might be required by a firm. Although analysis by product and customer was most popular, the particular segments used depended on the type of decision made. Table 1 indicates by type of decision the total number of requests for data reported by the responding firms. A firm typically made several requests for a given decision, since a single firm might require several reports for different levels of management, different segments, and to cover different time periods. The table also shows the rank choice of segments for each type of decision. Clearly, analysis by product and customer

TABLE 1. *Popularity and rank choice of segment type for use in marketing decisions*

Type of decision	Total requests	Product	Cus-tomer	Terri-tories	Chan-nels	Order size
Sales forecasting	611	1	2	3	5	4
Variance analysis	506	1	2	2	5	4
Budgeting	491	1	3	2	4	5
Planning the physical distribution mix	388	1	2	4	2	3
Planning the promotional mix	378	1	2	3	5	4

Source: Compiled from a survey conducted by the Committee on Cost and Profitability Analyses for Marketing of the American Accounting Association, 1971–1972.

is most popular. However, analysis by territory becomes popular for budgeting and variance analysis, and analysis by channels takes on importance in planning the mix of physical distribution services to be provided. While the basic product-customer sale module may easily be aggregated by any of these segments, careful coding of costs will be required to assure that only costs which are specifically applicable will be attached to a segment.

Further, the survey indicated that the frequency and timeliness of segmental analyses is important. The firms reported that analyses were needed monthly for the purposes of forecasting the dollar effect of projected sales and analyzing actual versus budgeted costs. There was also a significant demand for monthly analyses to budget marketing costs. Segmental analyses for planning the mix of both physical distribution services and promotional efforts were requested on a less frequent basis, such as quarterly or annually. Interestingly, several firms requested that the system have the ability to provide the projected costs of a specific order or product sale on a daily basis.

Assuring Optimal Decisions

The objective of a marketing–accounting information system is to facilitate decision making by market segments. The analytical methods used must assure not only that decisions made for a segment are optimal for the segment but also that they maximize the total profit of the firm. With such goal congruence in mind, an analytical format for measuring market segment performance has been designed. The approach is a refinement of Solomon's model for measuring divisional performance.[4] The format for measuring the profitability of marketing segments deter-

---

[4] For a discussion of Solomon's model for divisional performance, see David Solomon, *Divisional Performance: Measurement and Control* (New York: Financial Executives Research Foundation, 1965). For the detailed adaptation of the model to marketing segments, see reference in footnote 2. A summarized application can be found in the Crissy, Fischer, Mossman article referred to in footnote 1.

TABLE 2. *Market segment analysis*

Revenue	$500,000
Less: Production and marketing costs incurred specifically for the segment where such costs vary directly with a defined measure of activity	200,000
Segment contribution margin	$300,000
Less: Nonvariable costs (with respect to activity) which were incurred specifically for the segment during the current period	120,000
Segment controllable margin	$180,000
Less: A deduction for use of assets specific to the segment but benefiting multiple periods	50,000
Net segment margin	$130,000

mines the impact of the segment on the firm's profits in three steps. The approach is illustrated in Table 2.

Each of the three measures has a distinct meaning. The *segment contribution margin* reflects the interaction of revenues with those marketing and production costs which may vary with the activity. Such costs are to be minimized with respect to the volume of activity they support. They are thus controllable within the period analyzed. The *segment controllable margin* represents the net advantage (or disadvantage) to the firm of the segment's operation during the period. This is because revenues are reduced only by those out-of-pocket costs which would not have existed had the segment been discontinued. To assess the longer run impact of the segment on the firm's profits, a deduction is made for the expiration of multi-period assets used to produce the segment's revenue. The result is the *net segment margin*.

Since a cost incurred for several periods is being allocated to a single period, the deduction made must be somewhat arbitrary. Typically a portion of the original cost of the asset is allocated to subsequent periods using one of several accounting methods. Such a charge is not relevant for decision-making purposes. The real concern is the loss in the value of the assets due to their use within the segment for a given period. This is the real sacrifice to the firm of the continued use of the assets. To approximate this loss in value it is suggested that the charge made be an estimate of the fall in market value of the assets during the period. In this way consideration must be given to alternative uses for the assets employed.

Considering the Investment in a Segment

For the performance of a segment to be fully assessed, it must be related to the investment of the firm in the segment. The accounting literature offers two approaches. The first, return-on-investment analysis (ROI), expresses the *net segment margin* as a percentage of the value of the assets committed to the marketing segment. The second, residual income analysis, imputes an interest expense to the segment equal to the firm's overall cost of capital times the value of the segment's specific assets. The methods can best be understood through a simple example. Assume the following facts:

Operating results:		
Revenue		$100,000
Less: Variable costs	$ 35,000	
Incurred nonvariable costs	15,000	
Depreciation	20,000	70,000
Net segment margin		$ 30,000
Investment in segment:		
Receivables (less payables)	$ 10,000	
Inventory	40,000	
Plant and equipment	70,000	
Total	$120,000	
Cost of capital		15%

The ROI would be calculated as follows:

$$\text{ROI} = \frac{\text{net segment margin}}{\text{total specific assets}}$$

$$= \frac{\$ 30,000}{\$120,000}$$

$$= 25\%$$

The residual income would be calculated as follows:

Net segment margin	$ 30,000
Less: Cost of capital (15%) times $120,000 in total specific assets	18,000
Net segment margin, residual income approach	$ 12,000

It could be said that both methods yield the same results; that is, the segment is profitable if its ROI exceeds the cost of capital or if it has residual income.

In theory, then, the same conclusions should be reached under both methods. This is apparently why previous literature in this area offers the two methods as equally acceptable alternatives.

However, indifference in choosing between ROI and residual income approaches ignores the communicative and thus the motivational impact of the methods. ROI requires that a segment manager focus on two variables: maximization of net margin at a minimum level of investment. It is often easy to consider the effect of day-to-day decisions on costs without considering any possible accompanying change in the investment base. Simply speaking, the return (net segment margin) is managed but not the level of investment. Residual income analysis puts the costs of carrying an investment in assets on equal footing with all other out-of-pocket costs. The ramifications of a change in the investment base become as obvious as any change in out-of-pocket costs. A further advantage is that the behavior and controllability of the investment can be isolated. Table 3 is a detailed example of residual income analysis using the previous facts.

TABLE 3. Net segment margin under the residual income approach

Revenue		$100,000
Less: Variable production and marketing costs	35,000	
Imputed charge for investment in receivables and inventory (.15 × 50,000)	7,500	42,500
Segment contribution margin		$ 57,500
Less: Incurred nonvariable costs		15,000
Segment controllable margin		42,500
Less deduction for multi-period costs:		
Depreciation	20,000	
Imputed charge for investment in plant and equipment (.15 × 70,000)	10,500	30,500
Net segment margin, residual income approach		$12,000

Two major advantages accrue to segmental analysis using the residual income approach. First, that part of the investment base which is manageable in the short run is shown as a variable cost, such as investment in receivables and inventory. It, like any other variable cost, is to be minimized and is subject to trade-offs. For example, it may be desirable to reduce price to sell an item rather than to be charged interest on the item in subsequent periods.

Secondly, if both the depreciation and cost of capital charges for multi-period assets are based on their estimated market values, the total charge made will approximate a reasonable lease payment. This means that the charges made under the residual income approach are similar whether the assets are owned or leased. Contrast this with ROI, where a lease distorts performance, since any leased asset is omitted from the investment base.

To demonstrate, another look should be taken at Table 3. Suppose that the plant and equipment were leased at a cost equal to depreciation based on market value ($20,000) plus a 15% return on investment (.15 × $70,000 = $10,500). Residual income would remain unchanged; the lease expense would merely substitute for the former depreciation and cost of capital charge as follows:

Revenue	$100,000
Less: Variable costs (see Table 3)	42,500
Segment contribution margin	$ 57,500
Less: Incurred nonvariable costs	15,000
Segment controllable margin	$42,500
Less deduction for multi-period costs: lease expense	30,500
Net segment margin, residual income approach	$ 12,000

If, however, ROI were used, the $30,000 net segment margin from the operating data would become $19,500 ($30,000 + $20,000 depreciation − $30,500 lease expense = $19,500). Since the plant and equipment are now leased, the specific investment would be lowered to $50,000, the sum of the receivables and inventory. Thus, ROI would be calculated as follows:

$$\text{ROI} = \frac{\text{net segment margin}}{\text{total specific assets}}$$
$$= \frac{\$19,500}{\$50,000}$$
$$= 39\%$$

Consequently, it can be seen that accounting for the asset acquisition as a lease rather than a purchase leaves residual income unaffected while the same decision inflates ROI from 25% to 39%. The popularity of mingling leased and purchased assets together is certainly cause in itself to favor the residual income approach to performance measurement.

Summary

A unique type of two-pronged control is necessary to assure the profitable management of a firm's marketing activities. Marketing costs must first be analyzed within the functional units responsible for their incurrence. The costs of the function must then be attached to relevant marketing segments. This sophisticated control procedure requires the use of a modular data base.

The modular data base, once developed, must have the ability to marshal costs and revenues to a wide variety of marketing segments on a timely basis. Costs must be attached to segments in such a way as to make possible the calculation of the estimated economic impact of the marketing segment on the firm. This economic effect is best approximated by deducting from the revenue of the segment the specific costs incurred for that segment.

The full benefit of marketing segment analysis is achieved by using a residual income approach which isolates the behavior and controllability of the investment base for each segment.

Exercises

26.1. The Skyline Railroad hauls freight on three lines, between Pine Creek and Mountainview (50 miles), Pine Creek and Timberline (200 miles), and Timberline and Mountainview (500 miles).

In 1983, the Skyline Railroad lost $100,000 before taxes. (See Table 26.1.)

TABLE 26.1. *Skyline Railroad income statement, year ending December 31, 1983*

Total revenue	$1,600,000
Less: Specific attachable costs	(900,000)
Net segment margin	700,000
Common costs	(800,000)
Net income before tax	(100,000)
Income tax	52,000
Net income	(48,000)

The three products hauled by the Skyline Railroad are coal, food products, and transportation equipment. (See Table 26.2.)

TABLE 26.2

Products	% of total revenue
Coal	45%
Food products	20%
Transportation equipment	35%
	100%

There are three groups of attachable costs: *line-haul costs*, which include fuel and oil, parts and maintenance, engineer and other labor costs, taxes and fees, insurance, and depreciation on cars and equipment; *switching costs*; and *station or terminal costs*, including supervisory salaries, general labor, supplies and equipment, taxes, insurance, communications, utilities, depreciation on building, and clerical labor. Table 26.3 shows the percentage of costs that are attachable by product type.

Line-haul costs account for 70% of the railroad's specific attachable costs, switching costs account for 20%, and station costs account for the remaining 10%.

The Skyline Railroad was upset by its lack of profitability in 1983. Management collected additional information about the railroad operations of 1983, shown in Tables 26.4 and 26.5.

TABLE 26.3

Product	Line-haul cost	Switching cost	Station cost
Coal	55%	60%	10%
Food products	15%	15%	40%
Transportation equipment	30%	25%	50%
	100%	100%	100%

TABLE 26.4. Revenue by product by line

	% of coal revenue generated on each line	% of food products revenue generated on each line	% of transportation equipment revenue generated on each line
50-mile line	3	70	25
200-mile line	12	25	55
500-mile line	85	5	20
	100%	100%	100%

TABLE 26.5. Attachable costs by product by line

Coal incurred	15% of its attachable costs on the 50-mile line.
	25% of its attachable costs on the 200-mile line.
	60% of its attachable costs on the 500-mile line.
Food products incurred	40% of its attachable costs on the 50-mile line.
	45% of its attachable costs on the 200-mile line.
	15% of its attachable costs on the 500-mile line.
Transportation equipment incurred	55% of its attachable costs on the 50-mile line.
	35% of its attachable costs on the 200-mile line.
	10% of its attachable costs on the 500-mile line.

The Skyline Railroad has been given clearance by the Interstate Commerce Commission to do any of the following:

discontinue hauling over unprofitable lines;
discontinue hauling of unprofitable products; or
discontinue any combination of unprofitable product and line.

The railroad is prohibited from raising rates on any line or for any products.

The Skyline Railroad performance of productivity index is calculated as follows:

$$\text{productivity index} = \frac{\%\text{ contribution of segment/total contribution}}{\%\text{ revenue of the segment/total revenue}}$$

The demand forecast for 1984, in terms of percentage change from 1983 demand, is shown in Table 26.6.

TABLE 26.6

	50-mile	200-mile	500-mile
Coal	Same	−5%	+1%
Food	Same	+2%	Same
Transportation equipment	−4%	+4%	+5%

1. Calculate the net segment margin for each product segment.
2. Calculate the productivity index for each product. Which product is the most productive?
3. Calculate the net segment margin (per product per line).
4. What is the total contribution of each line to common costs?
5. Calculate the performance index for each line. Which is the most productive?
6. Rank the top five (product line) segments according to productivity index.
7. What should the railroad do to increase its profitability in 1984, given the forecast in Table 26.6.

26.2. Brown County recently opened two new medical clinics, one in the northern part of the county and the other in the southwest corner. Both clinics were opened with the intention of serving two broad areas of the public: children ages 2–10 and teenagers.

Each clinic offers two basic services to its patients: general preventive medical checkups and nonsurgical medical care for illnesses. Patients requiring surgery are referred to Brown County Hospital.

Attachable costs incurred by the clinic in giving medical checkups are X-ray, blood test, and doctor exam costs. Attachable costs incurred by the clinics in giving nonsurgical medical care to patients are infection treatment, broken-bone setting, and muscle treatment costs.

The head administrator of the two clinics must make a quarterly report to the Brown County Board of Supervisors. The Board of Supervisors is interested in knowing which customer-service mix is the most productive and which is the least productive in each clinic.

The head administrator has been too busy to build a good revenue and expense reporting system. She has, however, assigned an assistant to set up a system that will provide the information needed for the Board of Supervisors meeting.

The following bits of data have been given to the head administrator. Total revenue is $1,000,000, 60% of which is from Clinic 1 and 40% from Clinic 2. In Clinic 1, revenue is 40% from teens and 60% from children; in Clinic 2, it is 50%–50%. Table 26.7 breaks down revenue in terms of services; Table 26.8 breaks down costs in terms of services.

TABLE 26.7. Clinic revenue breakdown

	Clinic 1		Clinic 2	
	Teen	Children	Teen	Children
Preventive medical checkups	35%	40%	45%	40%
Nonsurgical medical care	65%	60%	55%	60%
	100%	100%	100%	100%

TABLE 26.8. Clinic cost breakdown

	Clinic 1		Clinic 2	
	Teen	Children	Teen	Children
X-ray costs	30	45	25	8
Infection treatment costs	40	40	10	50
Broken-bone setting costs	35	40	15	20
Blood test costs	10	30	25	20
Muscle treatment costs	35	50	50	10
Doctor exam costs	54	65	30	47

Answer the following questions:

1. For each clinic, which customer-service mix is the most productive:
   a. In terms of net segment margin?
   b. In terms of productivity index?
2. For each clinic, which customer-service mix is the least productive:
   a. In terms of net segment margin?
   b. In terms of productivity index?
3. For each clinic, in terms of net segment margin, which customer area is most productive? Which service?
4. Define the four types of market segments in this case. What factors influenced the use of these particular market segments?

Recommendations for Further Reading

Beik, Leland L., and Stephen L. Buzby, "Profitability Analysis by Market Segments," *Journal of Marketing*, 31 (July 1973), 48–53.

By tracing sales revenues to marketing segments and relating these revenues to marketing costs, the marketing manager can improve decision-making with respect to the firm's profit objective. Furthermore, the contribution approach to cost accounting serves to relate products, channels and/or other marketing components to the profitability of market segments. An example shows how segment profitability can be measured for items in a product line to the great benefit of product management decisions. Another example indicates how channel and other marketing management problems can be similarly gauged by a profit measure for a consumer product and for specific market segments.

Buzby, Stephen L., and Lester E. Heitger. "Profit Oriented Reporting for Marketing Decision Makers," *MSU Business Topics*, 24 (Summer 1976), 60–68.

Use of the concept of multidimensional market segmentation (simultaneously involving customers, territories and products) in tracing costs and revenues provides a valuable managerial tool. Most cost classification systems provide unidimensional data, indicating the contribution to profit of either a product, a customer or a territory. However, the necessary information must be available to determine contribution not only by a major category, i.e., product, but more specifically by product sales in each territory and even by product sales to each class of customer in each territory. The same data collection system will be useful in both identifying the costs associated with the various components of the marketing mix and estimating the likely impact of alternative mixes.

Crissy, W. J. E., Paul Fischer, and Frank H. Mossman. "Segmental Analysis: Key to Marketing Profitability," *MSU Business Topics*, 21 (Spring 1973), 42–49.

A three-step approach to bridging the communications gap between marketing and accounting is discussed, as well as identifying areas where marketing profitability can be improved. A contribution approach to segmental profitability is advocated despite industry's apparent preference for a full cost or net income approach. The importance of providing reliable, relevant and current information and of making allowance for the longer term effects of promotional expenditures

424

is stressed. Both the "residual income" and "return on assets committed" approaches to measuring segment contribution are outlined. Also presented is a form of break-even or cost-profit-volume analysis which indicates the volume at which the segment just covers its specific costs. The degree to which the contribution of the segment responds to changes in volume is also revealed. The same marketing cost system allows for flexible budgeting procedures. Comparing "actual" results with "budgeted-adjusted for volume changes" data is shown to make variance analysis a far more meaningful exercise.

Crissy, W. J. E., and Frank H. Mossman. "Matrix Models for Marketing Planning: An Update and Expansion," *MSU Business Topics*, 25 (Autumn 1977), 17–26.

An article written by the senior author in 1963 contributed in large part to the popularity of matrix approaches to marketing planning. After the essential elements of that approach are reviewed, the updating shows how new developments first in marketing information systems and then in segmental costing could be incorporated within such a matrix approach. How the contribution to profit of various levels of aggregation of the product-market matrix could be calculated receives particular attention, as does the subject of relative sequential performance indicators.

Kallimanis, William S. "Product Contribution Analysis for Multi-Product Pricing," *Management Accounting*, 49 (July 1968), 3–11.

Neither cost nor profit is really significant in a pricing decision, but rather the present value of the contribution that each product makes toward recovery of period (or fixed) costs and profit over its life cycle. A first step in the analysis of a multiproduct firm involves ranking each product in terms of not only its dollar sales but also its dollar contribution. The benefits of ranking salesmen, customers and territories by dollar contribution are also acknowledged. The essentials of a current value approach to evaluating three possible levels of price are then spelled out, with attention also being paid to the given product's stage in its life cycle and the firm's productive capacity. With knowledge of each product's current contribution picture and its state in the life cycle—and assuming reliable information on how price changes will affect sales—the contribution to profit and all other relevant dimensions of alternate pricing strategies can be determined.

Mullins, Peter L. "Integrating Marketing and Financial Concepts in Product Line Evaluation," *Financial Executive*, 40 (May 1972), 32–38.

Evaluation of different product lines based solely on their gross profit percentages can be misleading. Introducing inventory turnover concepts to develop a "turn and earn" (T&E) measure helps, but considerable margin for error still remains. Turn and earn calculations should at least be adjusted for the firm's trade credit balance—credit terms obtained from suppliers (accounts payable) and credit provided to customers (accounts receivable). It may also be possible to adjust for differences in operating costs (OE) associated with different product lines. The "fully adjusted" turn and earn figure for any product is generated by the following equation:

$$T\&E = \frac{CP - OE}{sales} \times \frac{sales}{advertising - AP/AR}$$

An example is then provided of how the inclusion of operating expenses and credit terms in the analysis can cause a complete reversal of the relative performance rankings suggested by "unadjusted" T&E calculations.

PART VIII

Planning and Control

Budgeting for Operational Planning and Control

27

Frank H. Mossman   W. J. E. Crissy   Paul M. Fischer

Marketing management has the responsibility to make sound and prudent use of the firm's financial resources in achieving marketing objectives. To facilitate this financial planning and control, budgets are constructed containing both revenues and expenditures. The marketing budget, once formulated, is a means of measuring and controlling the implementation of marketing plans.

General Marketing Budget Considerations

There are several criteria that need to be met in the preparation of a marketing budget:

1. The budget should be prepared in such a way that it is congruent with the firm's financial objectives, fiscal policies, available monetary resources, and likely marketing opportunities.
2. The necessary supportive data on projected costs and revenues should be included.
3. There should be provision for contribution centers by market segments.
4. Frequent checking and replanning needs to be done because of the numerous uncontrollable factors that can affect marketing. Sufficient flexibility must be allowed to permit tactical accommodation on the part of the firm to changing market factors.
5. The budget must be so planned and administered that cost/revenue information is easily deployed to the numerous action points within the organization.

The preparation of the budget normally starts with a constructively critical review of the firm's past budgeting experience. The projection of revenues into the forthcoming period rests on the firm's tactical view of the price and quantity of each item that will be sold in each of the firm's markets. This projection of revenue becomes the basis for projecting both functional and segmental costs that will be incurred to produce the forecasted revenues.

Checkpoints need to be established for reviewing actual performance against the projections. This integral part of budgeting assures that both control and replanning occur. Any variances in costs or revenues are noted and become the basis for management replanning at relevant decision and action points.

From *Financial Dimensions of Marketing Management* (New York: John Wiley & Sons), pp. 120–135. Copyright © 1978 by John Wiley & Sons, Inc. Reprinted by permission of John Wiley & Sons, Inc.

For a marketing-oriented firm, sales segments become the basic analytic units for profit optimization. They are the focal point for measuring the interaction of promotional efforts and contribution. A general analytic model will be developed, based on the residual contribution theory. The budget model will be used to analyze alternative plans and to quantify the final plan into the segment budget. The budget model will also become a control tool as it is used to measure actual segment performance. Stated properly, the budget is flexible and can be used to find allowable expenses for the actual sales volume resulting in a period.

Basic Budget Model

The basic budget model for sales segments is a multiple regression formulation incorporating product- and customer-related variables and constants representing attachable fixed costs. The model to be developed is expressed as:

$$\text{segment contribution} = c_1 x_1 + c_2 x_2 + c_3 x_3 - e_1 y_1 - e_2 y_2 - FC - PC$$

where

c_{1-3} is the contribution per unit of product. The contribution of a product unit is its revenue per unit less all product-related variable costs. These variable costs always include variable production costs but may also include inventory holding costs and transportation costs where such costs are a function of units sold.

x_{1-3} represents product unit sales. Where a particular product line segment is being analyzed, only one product unit variable may be needed. Where customer segments are being analyzed, the product unit variables may become extensive.

e_{1-2} represents variable expenses which behave as a function of a variable other than product units. Typically there will be physical-distribution costs that vary according to customer-related variabilities such as ton-miles shipped or invoices processed.

y_{1-2} are non-product-related factors of variability such as the ton-miles shipped or invoices processed. It is the measure of activity to which the non-product-related costs vary.

FC denotes specific fixed costs attachable to the segment being analyzed. This term excludes promotional costs but does include specific production and physical-distribution costs.

PC denotes promotional costs to be used to secure the segment contribution. These costs include advertising, general promotion, and direct selling costs. PC may be expanded to include a variable cost element where, for example, sales commissions are paid as a function of sales volume.

There are two features of the model that require additional comment. First, this is a residual income type model, which means that cost-of-capital charges are levied against the segment. Those cost-of-capital charges that are variable are included as variable costs. For example, inventory holding costs include a cost of capital charge; typically this cost is product-related and is deducted from the revenue of a unit to arrive at the contribution of a unit of product. Other variable cost-of-capital charges may be customer-related rather than product-related. For example, the cost of carrying receivables is a function of the customer's payment pattern. Remaining cost-of-capital charges, such as those resulting from the investment in fixed assets, are fixed in nature and are included in the fixed costs attached to the segment.

A second major concern of the model is the segregation of promotion costs. Since these costs are either variable or fixed in nature, it might appear that they could be included and commingled with the three other cost categories preceding them in the model. This is not desirable, however, from a planning perspective. Promotion costs should be considered the ammunition and at least partial cause of sales. Thus it is desirable to test the results of various levels of promotion costs. This means that promotion costs become a type of specified independent variable, while all other costs are dependent variables resulting from the sales volume estimated to correspond with a given level of promotional effort. Clearly, the planning use of the model would be impaired by not segregating the promotional cost component. In particular, it should be noted that sales commissions are often deducted from the revenue of a unit to arrive at its contribution. This is not desirable because it assumes that the commission is an inescapable product-related cost. This is not true since alternative promotion methods could be used and, in fact, should be considered. Thus, since salesmen's compensation is a relevant part of the promotion mix, it should be included in the ammunition, or PC, cost component.

Hierarchy of Segment Analysis

The general model developed above is applicable to any level of analysis ranging from the analysis of a single customer to the analysis of a sales territory, product line, or entire division. However, the includable components increase as one proceeds to more aggregated levels of analysis. The product unit contribution variable is applicable to all levels of analysis, since all segments reflect some aggregation of product unit sales. Generally speaking, remaining non-product-unit variable costs tend to be customer-related and are also calculable at all levels of analysis. An exception might include transportation costs incurred jointly for several customers such that the transportation cost could not be included in the analysis of a single customer but could be included in an analysis of the sales territory in which the given customer is located.

Fixed costs become increasingly attachable as one proceeds to higher levels of analysis. For example, there are probably no fixed costs that would attach exclusively to sales to a given customer. Likewise the fixed cost of maintaining a warehouse would not be specific to any one sales territory but would be specific to a sales district, made up of several territories which it serves. Similarly, the fixed cost of production machinery used exclusively for one product would not attach to any customer or product analysis that did not include all units sold of the product.

Special concern must be given to specific promotional costs. As is true with fixed costs, more promotional costs become attachable as one proceeds to higher levels of aggregation. However, as alternative levels of promotional efforts are considered for a given segment, the estimated results of the specific efforts must be considered in light of other promotional efforts which, though not specific to the segment, do affect its performance. For example, national advertising of a product is probably not attachable to the territory of a given salesman. Yet the results of specific efforts within the territory are due to the interactive and perhaps synergistic effects of the specific efforts and the national advertising.

Information Requirements

The model for segmental analysis achieves its full potential when it is linked to a modular data base which quickly and precisely supplies required contribution, variable cost, and specific fixed cost components. To use the modular data base, the alternative sales plan must specify, in addition to the level of promotional expenditure, the following information:

1. Sales projection in units; this allows the modular data base to project the contribution of the units sold by deducting product-related variable costs from the projected sales price of the units.
2. Estimate of the use of non–product-related factors of cost variability. This allows variable customer-related costs to be estimated. For example, the sales projection would specify what amount of sales would be made to given customers so that the accounts receivable, carrying cost, and transportation costs could be estimated. It is essential that estimates be made in units of measurement consistent with those used by the modular data base; the estimates should reflect the sensitivity of the segment's net margin to alternative usages of these variable costs.
3. A precise description of the segment being analyzed which is consistent with the fixed-cost attachment levels contained in the modular data base. This assures a simple attachment of relevant fixed costs to the segment.

The above information must also be supplied for actual sales results of a segment so that the budget may be applied to actual results to measure deviations in performance. The use of the budget model for variance analysis will be discussed in a subsequent section of this chapter.

Example of Applying the Model

Let us use a sales district as an example. Assume that three products are sold in the district and that the modular data base contains cost elements applicable to the district (Table 1).

TABLE 1. *Basic budget model*

Product unit related			
Product	x_1	x_2	x_3
Revenue per unit	$40.00	$50.00	$25.00
Standard variable production cost per unit	20.00	28.00	13.00
Inventory holding cost (3% of variable cost, 1 month holding period)	.60	.84	.39
Inventory handling	2.00	1.16	.61
Contribution per unit	$17.40	$20.00	$11.00

Other variable costs
  Transportation, $.80 per ton-mile
  Receivable holding cost, 1 month average payment period at a cost of capital charge of 18% annual rate or .015 revenue
  Order-processing cost, $1.20 per invoice equivalent

Specific fixed costs	
Fixed cost of district office:	
Short run, controllable	$18,000
Long run, noncontrollable	12,000
Total	$30,000

The data in Table 1 assume that the transportation cost is the same per ton-mile for all units shipped. The data also assume that the receivable holding costs and order-processing costs cannot be meaningfully isolated by product or customer attributes. The order-processing cost includes all paperwork resulting from customer sales defined in terms of the time taken to prepare an invoice. Thus the invoice equivalent becomes the measuring unit for paperwork costs caused by sales.

Analysis of a Market Plan

Marketing management wishes to test the likely financial results of the following promotional efforts: (1) advertising, $40,000; (2) promotions, $15,000; (3) salesmen's salary and travel, $60,000; and (4) sales commissions, 4 percent of sales. As a result of these efforts it is projected that:

1. Sales will be 10,000 units of x_1, 6,000 units of x_2, and 4,000 units of x_3.
2. 80,000 ton-miles of shipping costs will be required.
3. 1,800 invoice equivalents of paperwork will be required.

According to this projection, total sales revenue would be computed as follows:

$$10,000 x_1 \times \$40 = \$400,000$$
$$6,000 x_2 \times \ \ 50 = \ \ 300,000$$
$$4,000 x_3 \times \ \ 25 = \ \ 100,000$$
$$\text{Total} \quad \$800,000$$

The anticipated net segment contribution of the plan would be estimated using the general budget formula as follows:

$$\text{net segment contribution} = \$17.40x_1 + \$20.00x_2 + \$11.00x_3 - \$.80 \text{ ton-miles}$$
$$- \$1.20 \text{ invoice equiv.} - \$.015 \text{ revenue}$$
$$- \$30,000 \text{ fixed district cost}$$
$$- \$115,000 \text{ fixed promotion cost} - \$.04 \text{ revenue}$$

Inserting the values of the variables:

$$\text{segment contribution} = \$17.40 \times 10,000 + \$20.00 \times 6,000$$
$$+ \$11.00 \times 4,000 - \$.80 \times 80,000$$
$$- \$1.20 \times 1,800 - .015 \times \$800,000$$
$$- \$30,000 - \$115,000 - .04 \times \$800,000$$
$$= \$174,000 + \$120,000 + \$44,000$$
$$- \$64,000 - \$2,160 - \$12,000$$
$$- \$30,000 - \$115,000 - \$32,000$$
$$= \$82,840$$

Alternative sales projections may be tested by repeated applications of the general formula. The above projections are incorporated into the final segment budget shown in Table 2.

TABLE 2. Budgeted performance: District A (residual income approach)

Revenue		
$\quad$ 10,000$x_1 \times$ \$40	\$400,000	
$\quad$ 6,000$x_2 \times$ 50	300,000	
$\quad$ 4,000$x_3 \times$ 25	100,000	\$800,000
Less variable product related costs		
$\quad$ 10,000$x_1 \times$ \$22.60	\$226,000	
$\quad$ 6,000$x_2 \times$ 30.00	180,000	
$\quad$ 4,000$x_3 \times$ 14.00	56,000	462,000
Product contribution margin		338,000
Less variable physical distribution and promotional costs		
$\quad$ Transportation, 80,000 ton-miles $\times$ \$.80	\$64,000	
$\quad$ Invoice costs, 1,800 invoice equiv. $\times$ \$1.20	2,160	
$\quad$ Receivable carrying cost, .015 $\times$ \$800,000 revenue	12,000	
$\quad$ Sales commissions, .04 $\times$ \$800,000 revenue	32,000	110,160
District contribution margin		227,840
Less short-run controllable fixed costs		
$\quad$ District office	\$18,000	
$\quad$ Advertising	40,000	
$\quad$ Promotion	15,000	
$\quad$ Salesmen's salary and travel	60,000	133,000
Segment controllable margin		94,840
Less long-run noncontrollable costs		12,000
Net segment margin		\$82,840

Applying Basic Cost–Profit–Volume Analysis

Cost-profit-volume analysis is built on the premise of only one aggregated variable cost component which behaves as a function of revenue.

In order to convert the general segment model into the cost-profit-volume format, one must first express all variable costs in the segment as a function of revenue as follows:

Product x_1, 10,000 × $22.60	$226,000
Product x_2, 6,000 × $30.00	180,000
Product x_3, 4,000 × $14.00	56,000
Transportation $.80 × 80,000	64,000
Paperwork $1.20 × 1,800	2,160
Accounts receivable .015 × $800,000	12,000
Sales commissions .04 × $800,000	32,000
Total variable costs	$572,160
Total variable cost ÷ revenue of $800,000	.7152

Thus the cost-profit-volume equation would be stated:

$$\text{segment contribution} = \text{revenue} - .7152 \text{ revenue} - \$145,000 \text{ fixed costs}$$

Graphically it would appear as shown in Figure 1. The graph computes a break-even point of $509,129; stated another way, sales could fall 36 percent before the segment fails to justify its existence.

The simplification of the model into the traditional cost-profit-volume format is dangerous since by necessity a constant mix of products and a constant ratio of non-product-related variable costs is assumed to prevail at all volumes. Since this

FIGURE 1. *Cost-profit-volume analysis for a market segment*

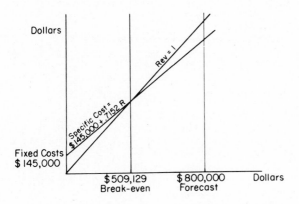

is not a realistic assumption, the simple cost-profit-volume model is limited in usefulness and should be used only to make a rough estimation of the effect on segment margin of an overall volume change where it may be reasoned that the product and service mix will not materially change.

Optimizing Segment Contributions

At each level of segment aggregation, it is the responsibility of management of that level to see that the underlying market segments make a sufficient contribution to cover the specific fixed costs of that level. In addition, there should be an adequate excess of the contribution over specific fixed costs to contribute to the remaining nonspecific fixed costs and to the firm's profit. For example, a district manager must attempt to see that the underlying sales territories bring forth sufficient contribution to cover the specific fixed costs of the district and to make a reasonable contribution to remaining corporate costs and profits. At the level of the firm, all costs become specific, and aggregated contributions will hopefully cover them and produce a profit. If, at any level, contributions of constituent segments are inadequate in terms of either profit goals or the segment's potential, the operating budget of the segment must be reformulated to more closely align with the firm's goals.

In reality, one cannot proceed to budget a firm's operations without recognizing the constraints upon the firm. Typically, the extent of promotional expenditures is limited by available funds and/or management time. If there were no contraints one would proceed to make promotional expenditures in each segment until the marginal contribution of the last dollar of expenditure equalled one. Where, however, funds are limited, the goal becomes one of equating the marginal contribution of the last dollar spent in each segment such that no shift of effort would increase total profit. However, it is not realistic to measure the marginal contribution of a dollar of promotional expenditure. Instead, one must settle for rough incremental measures of contribution versus expenditure. Insight into the effectiveness of promotional efforts across segments might be obtained by measuring incremental contribution versus incremental promotional expenditures by segment as follows:

	Sales territory		
	1	2	3
Increase in contribution, 1977 vs. 1976	$50,000	$30,000	$45,000
Increase in promotional expenses, 1977 vs. 1976	30,000	10,000	20,000
Incremental indicator	1.67	3	2.25

The above indicators should lead to a study as to the cause of the difference of the results and, unless the difference is caused by external intervening factors, would lead to a shift of efforts into territory 2. In order to encourage only the more potentially profitable increases in promotional efforts, corporate management might specify a minimum incremental indicator which must be met in order for a segment to receive added funding.

The incremental indicator may also be used to analyze adjustments to a segment's initial budget. For example, suppose that the segment having the previously developed budget formula saw the following opportunity: It is forecast that if $5,000 were spent on advertising the superior nature of product x_2, 2,000 added units would be sold; however, 1,000 fewer units of x_1 would be sold. The change in segment sales would add 2,000 more ton-miles of transportation and 100 added invoice equivalents. Without reworking the entire equation, the opportunity could be evaluated as follows:

Incremental contribution:	
2,000 units of x_2 × $20	$40,000
Less:	
1,000 units of x_1 × $17.40	(17,400)
2,000 ton-miles × $.80	(1,600)
100 invoice equivalents × $1.20	(120)
Accounts receivable $60,000 increase in	
revenue × .015	(900)
Increase in commissions, $60,000 increase	
in revenue × .04	(2,400)
Incremental contribution	$17,580
Incremental promotional cost	5,000
Incremental indicator, $17,580 ÷ $5,000 =	$3.52

A second type of constraint to be considered is the scarcity of capacity required to build or distribute the product. In theory such a problem is dealt with using linear-programming techniques at the corporate level. Strict adherence to linear-programming concepts will maximize the contribution of scarce resources but it also requires centralized decision-making. Several alternatives are available where decentralized decision-making is desired. A popular approach is to charge for the use of scarce resources at a value approximating their anticipated contribution to profits. In this way, what would otherwise be a fixed cost becomes a variable cost for planning purposes. No segment will use the capacity unless it can pay the cost, which means that the segment is earning more per unit of time of scarce resource than is required. Another alternative is to have segments compute their contribution per unit of use of the scarce resource and to allocate the resource to those segments producing the largest return.

Control through Variance Analysis

Variance analysis compares actual results of a segment to the original budget. The total variance in contribution is broken down into subvariances which explain the causes of a difference between actual and planned performance. This is done in order to spot a need for corrective action and/or to improve future planning. Prior to discussing means by which variances may be analyzed, two concepts must be emphasized. First, the analysis of sales performance by a segment should not be confused by cost variances resulting from the production of the units sold or the provision of physical-distribution services used. Such variances are the responsibility of the functional cost centers providing goods and services to sales segments. The managements of selling segments are given standard costs to use in decision-making, and thus standard costs must be used in measuring performance. Secondly, it must be realized that not all variances calculated for a segment are the responsibility of the segment's management. For example, a change in selling price will cause a variance for the segment even though it was ordered by a higher level of management. Thus the segment becomes an analytic unit for planning purposes and as such may reflect multiple responsibilities.

The analysis of actual versus budgeted performance may be broken down into three major components: an analysis of sales performance, analysis of nonproduction costs specific to the segment, and an analysis of incremental promotional productivity. Table 3 is an analysis of sales performance which focuses on the difference between the actual and budgeted product-contribution margin. The exhibit is based on total unit sales of 21,000, broken down as follows:

11,000 x_1 at $38		$418,000
4,500 x_2 at $50		225,000
5,500 x_3 at $23		126,500
Total		$769,500

Analysis begins by determining the deviation from budget caused by the actual sales price per unit. Actual versus budgeted price is analyzed at the actual level of sales for each product. The fact that products x_1 and x_3 were sold at a price below that budgeted reduced the district's contribution by $33,000. Attention is then directed to the product-mix composition of the 21,000 units actually sold. The change in district contribution caused by selling a larger proportion of x_1 and x_3 at the expense of x_2 reduces the district contribution by $13,000. The net mix variance is always zero as to units; the dollar discrepancy is caused by the trade-off of units with differing unit-contribution margins. The mix variance is easily calculated by comparing the actual sales of each unit with the unit sales that would have resulted had the total volume of 21,000 units been sold in the budgeted 50/30/20 mix. Since the sales price variance has already been isolated, the mix variance, in dollars, is computed using the budgeted sales price.

The final sales variance is a comparison of the actual versus budgeted total sales

TABLE 3. *Budgeted versus actual sales performance: District A*

Analysis of product contribution

| Actual product-contribution margin | | | | | | $308,900 |

Variance due to sales price:

Product	Actual price	Budget price	Variance	Units sold	Total	
x_1	$38	$40	$2 U*	11,000	$22,000 U	
x_2	50	50	—	4,500	—	
x_3	23	25	2 U	5,500	11,000 U	33,000 U

Variance due to mix:

Product	Actual units	Actual volume at budget mix	Variance	Standard contribution per unit	Total	
x_1	11,000	10,500 (50%)	500 F†	$17.40	$8,700 F	
x_2	4,500	6,300 (30%)	1,800 U	20.00	36,000 U	
x_3	5,500	4,200 (20%)	1,300 F	11.00	14,300 F	
Total	21,000	21,000	-0-			13,000 U

Variance due to volume:
21,000 units actual versus 20,000 budgeted equals 1,000 units favorable in standard mix:

Product	Contribution per unit	Unit	Total	
x_1	$17.40	500 (50%)	$8,700	
x_2	20.00	300 (30%)	6,000	
x_3	11.00	200 (20%)	2,200	16,900 F
Budgeted product-contribution margin				$338,000

*U: unfavorable.
†F: favorable.

volume. Table 3 shows that 1,000 units in excess of the budget were sold. Since variances due to sales price and mix have already been analyzed as they apply to actual volume, the contribution due to volume is quantified using the budgeted price and the budgeted 50/30/20 mix. The three sales variances explain the difference between actual and budgeted product contribution. It should be noted that all analyses are made using the standard product cost. Any variance between actual and standard product costs are isolated in the production cost center responsible for the variance, and the analysis of sales performance is not confused by their inclusion.

TABLE 4. *Analysis of District A performance at actual sales level*

	Actual results	Budget for actual sales level	Cost variances
Actual product contribution	$308,900	$308,900	
Less variable costs			
Transportation ($.80/ton-mile)	94,000/$75,200	91,000/$72,800	$2,400U*
Invoice cost ($1.20/ invoice equiv.)	1,820/ 2,184	1,850/ 2,220	36F†
Receivable cost (.015 × revenue)	13,000	$769,500/$11,543	1,457U
Sales commissions (.04 × revenue)	10,560	$769,500/$10,560	—
District contribution margin	207,956	211,777	3,821U
Less short-run controllable fixed costs			
District office	$18,780	$18,000	780U
Advertising	35,000	40,000	5,000F
Promotion	15,000	15,000	—
Salesmen's salary and travel	58,000	60,000	2,000F
Segment controllable margin	$81,176	$78,777	2,399F
Less long-run, noncontrollable fixed costs			
District office	12,000	12,000	—
Net segment margin	$69,176	$68,777	$2,399F

* U: unfavorable.
†F: favorable.

The next major component of performance analysis compared the costs incurred for and/or by the segment in order to produce and service the actual sales volume. In essence, the segment is studied to determine whether the nonproduction costs specific to the segment have been held under control. In the case of variable costs, a determination as to the allowable or budgeted use of the variable cost is made in view of the actual sales volume. For example, in Table 4 the actual product-customer sales mix would allow 91,000 ton-miles of transportation and 1,850 invoice equivalents of paperwork. The allowable use of variable costs is not that included in the original budget but rather reflects allowable use in view of the actual sales volume, mix, and price. Revenue-related variable costs are computed on the basis of actual revenue. Table 4 indicates that the district-contribution margin suffered by $3,821 due to a net unfavorable use of nonproduction variable-cost elements. The difference between the actual and budgeted use of these costs is based on only their standard costs, which is the cost used for planning by the segment. Finally, the actual versus budgeted level of specific fixed costs is compared. Since there is no behavior of fixed costs with respect to volume, the benchmark used is the original budgeted expenditure.

TABLE 5. *Analysis of promotional productivity*

	Actual, current	Budget current		Actual last period	
		Amount	Change	Amount	Change
District contribution margin	$308,900	$338,000	$ − 29,100	$290,400	$18,500
Specific promotional costs	108,000	115,000	− 7,000	103,000	5,000
Incremental indicator (change in margin ÷ change in promotional costs)			4.2		3.7

The last component of variance analysis is an attempt to again measure promotional productivity. Table 5 contains an incremental analysis of district sales performance relative to incremental fixed promotional expenditures. The analysis is based on a comparison of actual performance to both the budget and the performance of the previous period. The analysis indicates that each dollar of promotional effort over that of the previous year produced $3.70 of contribution margin (net of all variable costs). It is also suggested that each dollar of expenditure budgeted but not spent may have lost $4.20 in contribution margin. The implied cause-effect relationship is of course heavily influenced by unquantified intervening variables such as competitors' actions, the state of the economy, the weather, and others. The indicator does, however, provide some aid in attaining the optimal level of promotional expenditure.

Exercises

27.1. The Suds Brewing Company is proud of its Suds beer. Sales of this product have grown steadily since it was introduced thirty years ago. Currently, Suds ranks twenty-eighth in U.S. sales.

Three years ago, the Suds Brewing Company added two new beers. The first was named Light Suds and was light tasting, low in calories, and low priced. The second, named Suds Supreme, was rich tasting. It became the company's premium-priced beer. These three beers are the product line for Division 1 of the company.

The Suds Brewing Company has one other division, a snack foods division, whose product line consists of Suds Beer Nuts, Suds Spanish Peanuts, and Suds Pretzels.

The company's marketing manager is interested in budgeting the performance of his beer division for the Michigan sales district.

The following information is provided to the marketing manager from the company's modular data base:

1. Transport costs are $1.25 per ton-mile.
2. Depreciation on the storage facility used in Michigan is $16,000.
3. The price per six-pack is $1.85 for Suds, $1.60 for Light Suds, and $2.20 for Suds Supreme.
4. Processing of customer orders costs $0.30 per invoice equivalent.
5. District office building depreciation is $65,000.
6. The standard variable cost per six-pack is $1.00 for Suds, $.75 for Light Suds, and $1.00 for Suds Supreme.
7. Investment in fixed assets (district) costs $20,000.
8. Depreciation on district office equipment is $52,000.
9. Receivable holding cost is 2.5% of revenue.
10. District management salaries are $100,000.
11. Inventory holding costs are 4% of standard variable cost.

The marketing manager plans to promote Division 1 products in Michigan in the following way:

Salespeople's salaries, $80,000;
promotions, $25,000;
advertising, $110,000;
sales commissions, 2% of sales.

As a result of this promotional plan, the marketing manager forecasts the following figures for the Michigan sales district:

65,000 ton-miles of shipping will be required.

Sales of Suds will be 400,000 six-packs.
Sales of Light Suds will be 250,000 six-packs.
Sales of Suds Supreme will be 200,000 six-packs.
14,000 customer invoices will be processed.

1. Using the basic budget model, determine the District 1 net segment margin (residual income).
2. Create a final segment budget showing the projected product contribution margin, district contribution margin, segment controllable margin, and net segment margin.
3. Convert the basic budget model into the cost-profit-volume format. Calculate the break-even point ($ sales).
4. The marketing manager is contemplating changing the emphasis of the advertising budget in the Michigan district. If $15,000 of Suds beer advertising is shifted to Light Suds, the following is forecasted:

Suds sales would decrease 35,000 units.
Light Suds sales would increase 45,000 units.
The change in segment sales would add 1,800 more ton-miles of transportation and 800 more invoice equivalents.

If $15,000 of Suds beer advertising is shifted to Suds Supreme, the following is forecasted:

Suds sales would decrease 35,000 units.
Suds Supreme sales would increase 30,000 units.
The change in segment sales would add 1,500 more ton-miles of transportation and 440 more invoice equivalents.

What should the marketing manager do? Why?

27.2. The Perry Corporation has three divisions. Division 1 produces and sells three products. Recently, the budget director of Division 1 was handed the following list:

- The number of Division 1 customer orders processed is 10,000.
- Sales of product 2 are 4,000 units.
- Advertising for product 2 is $5,000.
- Revenue for product 3 minus variable production costs of product 3 is $30,000.
- Depreciation of the Division 1 plant is $15,000.
- Variable transportation costs per ton-mile are $50,000.
- Sales commissions on product 3 are 3% of sales.
- Revenue for product 1 minus variable product costs of product 1 is $25,000.
- Division management salaries are $200,000.
- Sales of product 1 are 2,500 units.

- The cost per customer order processed is $0.06 per order.
- Division 1 plant utilities cost $8,000.
- Revenue for product 1 minus variable product costs of product 1 is $14,000.
- The corporate publicity campaign costs $50,000.
- Depreciation on Division 2 equipment is $9,000.
- Investment in Division 1 assets is $4,000.
- Revenue for product 2 minus variable product costs of product 2 is $15,000.
- Sales of product 3 are 3,000 units.
- Ton-miles shipped by Division 1 products have reached 400,000.
- Sales salaries amount to $600,000 for Division 1.
- Common costs for the firm are $120,000.

As budget director for Division 1, identify each line in the above list in terms of the basic budget model components:

c_1	e_2
c_2	y_1
c_3	y_2
x_1	FC
x_2	PC
x_3	Is not a component of Division 1 model.
e_1	

How to Measure
Marketing Performance

28

Richard A. Feder

Given the size of advertising and sales promotion expenditures in the modern consumer products company, one would assume that management is supplied information which provides considerable insight into the effect of "marketing dollars" on profits. Such is not the case, with the result that the typical merchandising effort includes many spending inefficiencies which are considered unavoidable "costs of the marketing game." In this article I shall propose a method of identifying and correcting some of these wastes and inefficiencies.

Common Failures

Though estimates vary, many professional marketing men contend that the average consumer products company spends from 1% to 5% of its marketing funds at a loss, i.e., in areas where present and future profit potentials do not warrant investment spending. This is usually the result of many different factors, including the following:

- Attempts to achieve too high a share of an unusually competitive market, i.e., the profits generated by the sales responsible for the *last* share points added are less than the cost of the effort which produced them.
- Failure to adjust the level of marketing effort to compensate for local seasonal variations.
- Failure to adjust national spending strategies for local product preferences or for unique local competitive conditions.

Conversely, there are frequently areas which could profitably use more funds than they get. These include secondary markets in which the company and its competitors underspend in order to finance heavier efforts elsewhere. In these markets profits are often highly responsive to additional marketing activity.

Accounting's Answer

Failures such as those noted are all examples of the effect of employing an inappropriate level of marketing activity relative to the profit potential or profit responsiveness of a specific area. To be sure, attempts have been made by many companies to identify by area the responsiveness of profits to marketing effort. Typically, however, they use a breakdown of accounting figures, and the value of traditional financial data for this purpose is severely limited. For one thing, the conventions which underlie the accounting system were originally designed for auditing. Accordingly, "generally accepted accounting practices" dictate that marketing expenditures be written off when they are incurred—not when they produce sales. Within this framework certain advertising and promotional activities which create *retail* movement of goods are expensed against unrelated segments of *wholesale* movement.

In many companies market area reports are further distorted by the allocation of unidentified costs and bookkeeping adjustments which are irrelevant from the standpoint of profit responsiveness. Under full costing assumptions, many products in many markets normally show losses. In fact, some of these products are profitable from an incremental standpoint, but the profitable areas are not usually identifiable. Differences in product mix and complicated accounting practices produce a situation in which the amount of allocated fixed costs is not uniform or recognizable by market area. In an effort to avoid taking incorrect action in a profitable area, marketing management is normally reluctant to enact spending changes on the basis of these reports.

To these two complicating factors we must add still another. Traditional accounting periods do not necessarily correspond to the time span during which an advertising campaign produces its full increment of sales. An analysis performed on the basis of the results achieved in any one month would probably exclude a substantial portion of the sales generated by the marketing effort expensed in that period. On the other hand, considerably longer periods (say, a year) probably combine the results of many spending decisions, concealing both overspending and underspending. Here again traditional accounting conventions preclude the measurement of profit responsiveness.

Spending by Intuition

Lacking a tool which measures profit responsiveness by area and faced with the necessity of making a decision, marketing management usually apportions funds geographically on the basis of relative population, previous wholesale movement, and/or the relative size of each retail market. But a decision based purely on population does not take into account the facts that the kinds of people reached and the costs of reaching them are not constant from area to area. Allocations made on the basis of previous wholesale movement tend to perpetuate past mistakes. And spending in proportion to the relative size of each retail market ignores important differences among the competitive situations operative in each area.

Since each of these limiting factors has an effect on the rate at which a single company's marketing dollars produce profits, product management will not normally allocate funds on the basis of any *one* of the three standards. How does it relate them? Lacking a suitable alternative, it usually does so "intuitively," with the result that spending inefficiencies, as noted earlier, have come to be regarded as unavoidable "costs of the marketing game."

Proposed System

To improve marketing decisions, I propose that management have a list prepared (by the financial, market research, data processing, and product management functions) which shows optimum *past* marketing expenditures by market area.

When adjusted for the anticipated competitive and seasonal changes appropriate to each area, this list can function as a reasonable standard against which to compare and alter *future* marketing expenses. Of course, this tool is not perfect. However, preliminary testing indicates that it is a better method than those currently available to marketing management for controlling marketing spending.

Realistic Model

Of course, if the optimum levels of past expenditures are to be listed correctly, they must reflect the decision-making situation realistically; that is, they must reflect the goal of apportioning advertising and sales promotion funds to produce some ideal *combination* of short- and long-range profits. Reduced to the mechanics of a model, the marketing objective is to invest money in each market area up to the point where an additional dollar would produce greater *immediate* profits if spent elsewhere. The decision to spend beyond this point in an area requires the existence of an amount of *future* potential which justifies the sacrifice of immediate profits. (The future potential referred to could be either sales gains or the avoidance of sales losses.)

To the extent that our model is valid, measuring marketing effectiveness requires two elements: a financial tool which measures the *rate* at which the "last dollar" of marketing effort produced profits in each area, and market research data documenting the *variables* affecting these rates in terms of competitive changes and growth trends.

Controlling spending efficiency requires the early identification of potential problem areas. Naturally, any tool which attempts to report achievement rapidly will of necessity require a degree of compromise. The proposed approach assumes the existence of a discernible and consistent time lag between wholesale and retail movement in each market area. This system also analyzes profit responsiveness in a way which does not take into account every last sale produced by a unit of marketing effort. Because of these necessary expedients, the applied model is definitely *not* accurate enough to discern situations involving relatively small spending inefficiencies. It is designed, instead, to help marketing management anticipate and avoid the extreme spending errors.

By utilizing the necessary compromises described, we place certain limitations on the end use of this data. In particular, this system can be effective only when used by executives with extensive marketing experience. For instance, analysis of the profits achieved in each market area will disclose that many low-yield spending decisions which might appear to be mistakes to nonmarketing executives are, in fact, either unavoidable or instances of deliberate investment spending. Both the determination of appropriate past expenses and the adjustment of these expenses to compensate for anticipated competitive changes require a high degree of marketing insight. We should, therefore, regard this system as a tool to be used by marketing management, rather than on it.

Some executives, marketing and financial, might ask: "Can't we find these past spending inefficiencies by some kind of special analysis; do we need a whole system?" A system is needed because we require knowledge of where to look before we do look. Spot analysis guided even by the best marketing intuition will probably result in substantial oversights. In addition, it is doubtful that such analysis can be completed in time to make the kinds of spending changes to be discussed. When budgets are being drawn up or when advertising commitments are being reviewed, decisions usually have to be made right away on the basis of existing information.

Expenses & Revenues

Let us begin with the "nuts and bolts" of the new system—the mechanics of accounting for income and outgo. For concreteness, let us take a representative product line in a hypothetical but typical consumer products company, the ABC Corporation.

What would a traditional presentation of actual first-quarter performance of the product line look like? Such a presentation appears in Part A of Exhibit 1. This traditional style of profit and loss (P & L) statement tells little about marketing effectiveness.

As discussed earlier, a prerequisite of any meaningful financial information is the isolation of relevant incremental revenues and expenses. Accordingly, in Part B of Exhibit 1 the items listed in Part A have been reorganized to differentiate between those which have marketing significance (items listed above the "net marketing earnings" line) and those which do not. Within this framework, standard profit contribution (SPC) is the gross revenue produced by the marketing effort. We come now to two different groups of figures—one used by marketing executives for self-evaluation, the other used by corporate management for evaluating the marketing function:

1. Subtraction of the advertising and sales promotion expenses from the SPC gives us gross marketing earnings (GME). This earnings figure is the internal focal

EXHIBIT 1. *Varieties of profit and loss statement for a product of the ABC Corporation, January–March 1965 (in thousands of dollars)*

A. Traditional version

Sales		$15,000
Standard variable distribution costs	$ 760	
Standard variable manufacturing costs	6,030	
Budgeted fixed distribution expenses	100	
Budgeted fixed manufacturing expenses	870	
Distribution expense variances	14	
Manufacturing expense variances	(12)	
Inventory adjustments	(67)	7,695
Gross profits		$ 7,305
Administrative overhead expenses	$1,300	1,300
Profits before advertising		$ 6,005
Advertising	$2,007	
Sales promotion	1,568	
Commercial production	175	
Product management expenses	210	3,960
Net profits before taxes		$ 2,045

B. New version (unadjusted)

Sales		$15,000
Standard variable distribution costs	$ 760	
Standard variable manufacturing costs	6,030	6,790
Standard profit contribution		$ 8,210
Advertising	$2,007	
Sales promotion	1,568	3,575
Gross marketing earnings		$ 4,635
Commercial production	$ 175	
Product management expenses	210	385
Net marketing earnings		$ 4,250
Budgeted fixed distribution expenses	$ 100	
Budgeted fixed manufacturing expenses	870	
Distribution expense variances	14	
Manufacturing expense variances	(12)	
Inventory adjustments	(67)	
Administrative overhead expenses	1,300	2,205
Net profits before taxes		$ 2,045

EXHIBIT 1 (cont.)

C. New version (adjusted)		
Sales		$15,000
Standard variable distribution costs	$ 760	
Standard variable manufacturing costs	6,030	6,790
Standard profit contribution		$ 8,210
Advertising	$1,683	
Sales promotion	1,507	3,190
Gross marketing earnings		$ 5,020
Advertising and sales promotion accrual account: 3/31/65	$ 615	
(Advertising and sales promotion accrual account: 12/31/64)	(230)	
Commercial production	175	
Product management expenses	210	770
Net marketing earnings		$ 4,250
Nonmarketing expenses	$2,205	2,205
Net profits before taxes		$ 2,045

point of the marketing control system; that is, the responsiveness of profits to marketing effort is measured by marketing management in terms of the effect on GME of changes in the level of advertising and sales promotion expenditures.

2. Commercial production and product management expenses, on the other hand, are the incremental overhead costs of administering marketing funds. These expenses (sales promotion materials, advertising production, product management salaries, market research surveys, etc.) do not directly affect the SPC level in the same sense that media expenditures or trade allowances do. For this reason they are located below the GME line on the P & L sheet. Deduction of these overhead costs from the GME gives us net marketing earnings (NME). This amount, representing marketing management's contribution to corporate overhead and corporate profits, is the *external* focal point of the marketing control system; in other words, corporate management evaluates the marketing function on the basis of the size of the NME.

Other Expenses

We come now to the figures reported below the NME on the P & L statement. Because the levels of fixed distribution and fixed manufacturing expenses are independent of volume and outside the area of marketing management control, they have been separated from their variable counterparts and are included after the NME. (By contrast, the manufacturing and distribution cost figures used in the computation of the SPC are produced by the data-processing department. Computers multiply the appropriate standard rates for the *variable* portions of these two expenses by the actual sales volume.) Similarly, manufacturing and distribution variances are also reported after marketing profits. This is consistent with the fact that marketing management accepts as "givens"—and makes decisions on the basis of—standard manufacturing and distribution costs. Deviations from the budgeted amounts for either of these items are considered to be the contributions (deductions) of the respective departments to corporate profit.

Time Factors

Having isolated the relevant expenses, it is now necessary to adjust certain of these items in order to evolve financial results which correspond *in time* to the realities of the marketplace. This is the purpose of Part C of Exhibit 1. It will be noted that the advertising and sales promotion expenses under SPC differ from those in Part B. This is because these amounts have been adjusted to compensate for the fact that a major portion of the marketing effort is directed specifically toward retail, rather than wholesale, movement of goods. Retail sales deplete retail inventories, creating concomitant adjustments throughout the distribution chain. Eventually, manufacturer sales are increased.

On the adjusted P & L in Part C of Exhibit 1, marketing effort aimed at the retail level is matched with the subsequent wholesale movement generated by this inventory depletion. It is thus necessary to determine the approximate time lag between sales to the trade and sales to the consumer by correlating market research estimates of retail movement with factory sales. Let us suppose that, for our product line of the ABC Corporation, studies have shown this lag to be approximately 30 days in all market areas. The adjusted statement for the first quarter, therefore, reports sales and trade allowances for January, February, and March, but uses December, January, and February figures for media expenditures and coupon redemptions. Advertising and sales promotion accrual accounts are used to reconcile the level of marketing expenditure (and the NME) to the amounts reported in Part B. (These entries are mechanically the same as those used in traditional accounting for opening and closing inventories in the computation of cost of goods sold.)

Market Area Summaries

The upper portion of Exhibit 2 shows part of a series of reports which lists by market area all expenditures for advertising and sales promotion. The production of the full complement of market area summaries is a relatively straightforward programming assignment well within the data-processing capabilities of the average large consumer products company. Rather than show all of the individual areas in this exhibit, I have included only those which warrant special consideration. The basis on which these five were selected, and the significance of the financial analysis and market research data in these reports, will be discussed later.

Period of Analysis

As stated earlier, *the purpose of marketing-oriented financial data is to identify areas in which the company overspent or underspent relative to the immediate profit potential.* This requires the determination of the length of the period in which marketing effort generates immediate profits. For activities which produce trade sales indirectly, such

EXHIBIT 2. *Market area summaries, January–March 1965 (dollar figures in thousands except where noted)*

	Area A		Area B	
Standard profit contribution	$360		$770	
Advertising	42		203	
Sales promotion	58		172	
Gross marketing earnings	$180		$395	
Advertising and sales promotion				
accrual account: 3/31/65	28		115	
Financial analysis				
Average opportunity rate				
This period	2.60		1.05	
Last period	2.45		0.95	
Percent standard profit contribution	4.4%		9.4%	
Percent advertising and sales promotion	3.1%		11.5%	
Incremental standard profit contribution,				
this year vs. last year	($53)		($50)	
Incremental advertising and sales				
promotion, this year vs. last year	($20)		($85)	
Incremental gross marketing earnings	($33)		$35	
Incremental opportunity rate	(1.65)		0.40	

	This year	Last year	This year	Last year
Market research data				
Total dollar retail market	$1,790	$1,810	$6,150	$6,175
Percent share of retail market	50.2%	51.9%	35.6%	36.1%
Percent distribution	88.3%	88.2%	96.2%	96.2%
Media efficiencies: TV				
Cost per thousand homes*	$2.02	$2.11	$2.15	$2.12
Cost per thousand prime prospects*	$3.10	$3.26	$2.65	$2.70

* Dollar figures not in thousands.

as consumer advertising, this is a difficult matter to resolve logically. Past studies have indicated that a single unit of indirect marketing effort usually produces sales at a decreasing rate over an extended period of time. The type of analysis proposed here requires identification of the period within which such an effort produces the *greatest part* of its returns. Analysis which confines itself to the results achieved within this period, while not yielding precision, will allow the identification of *extreme instances* of overspending or underspending.

Now let us return to the ABC Corporation case. Suppose our inquiries disclose the following facts for the product line in question:

Area C		Area D		Area E	+ F + G … n	= U.S.Total	
$620		$850		$680		$8,210	
165		290		276		1,683	
130		191		124		1,507	
$325		$369		$280		$5,020	
110		138		150		615	
1.10		0.75		0.70		1.45	
1.45		1.00		1.20		1.70	
7.6%		10.4%		8.4%		100.00%	
9.2%		15.0%		12.4%		100.00%	
($75)		$115		$25		$744	
$10		$165		$100		$354	
($85)		($50)		($75)		$390	
(8.50)		(0.30)		(0.75)		1.10	
This year	Last year	This year	Last year	This year	Last year	This year	Last year
$2,590	$2,680	$7,525	$7,395	$5,900	$4,950	$54,650	$56,000
48.6%	50.3%	38.7%	32.4%	42.9%	46.1%	45.8%	44.6%
97.9%	98.1%	98.1%	97.9%	96.4%	96.6%	96.2%	96.2%
$3.95	$2.50	$1.75	$1.75	$1.95	$1.96	$1.95	$1.93
$4.67	$3.10	$1.92	$2.03	$2.15	$2.30	$2.30	$2.27

- Testing has indicated that the relevant variables respond consistently when analyzed *quarterly*, i.e., there seems to be a high degree of correlation between the behavior of sales, GME, marketing effort, market share, and market size *over a three-month period.* (Where good correlations have been absent, there have been obvious explanations.) For instance, given substantially increased competitive expenditures while the particular company's spending remains unchanged, marketing management should expect an increase in the size of the total market, a decreased market share for the company, and a smaller amount of gross profits (SPC) relative to the amount of marketing effort purchased by the company.
- Comparisons made between *shorter* periods do *not* evidence such behavior. And the use of longer periods does not seem to increase substantially the degree of observable consistency.

On the basis of these findings, indicating that a unit of marketing effort probably produces most of its sales within 90 days, it is decided that the adjusted P & L and the market area summaries (Exhibits 1-C and 2) should be issued at least quarterly, and preferably each month for the ensuing three-month period.

Financial Analysis

In the proposed system the capabilities of the modern computer are utilized to perform certain basic financial analyses of the market area results. The purpose of the analysis in Exhibit 2 is to focus marketing management attention on those areas which represent maximum profit improvement opportunities. These figures tell us:

1. *The rate at which the total marketing effort produced profits in each area*—Turning to the first line of control figures, for instance, we see that during the first quarter each dollar invested in advertising and sales promotion in Area D produced a rounded average of $0.75 GME ($369,000 GME ÷ $290,000 + $191,000 for advertising and sales promotion). Accordingly, 0.75 is referred to as the "average opportunity rate."
2. *The relative amount of marketing effort used in each area*—In the fourth line of control figures we see that Area E received 12.4% of total advertising and sales promotion funds yet produced only 8.4% of total SPC. This indicates that funds were diverted from other areas for use in Area E.
3. *The profits produced by changes in the level of marketing effort between comparable periods, and the rate at which these changes generated profits*—From the last four lines of control data we find, for instance, that in Area B SPC was $50,000 lower than during the first quarter last year; advertising and sales promotion were lower by $85,000 over the same period, resulting in a GME increase of $35,000; and additional profits were generated by this change at a per-dollar rate of 0.40, i.e.,

$35,000 \div \$85,000 = 0.40$. Since profits do not normally respond to increases or decreases of marketing effort at the "average opportunity rate" this "incremental opportunity rate" is of major interest to marketing management. (The incremental opportunity rate is assigned a positive or negative value depending on the basis of the direction of the GME change; i.e., spending changes which increase the GME always have positive signs, and vice versa.)

The choice of "this year versus last year" comparisons for deriving an incremental SPC rate is an effort to avoid the effect of seasonality; spending and market-size changes are generally smaller when computed on this basis than they are if calculated for consecutive periods. Of course, the incremental opportunity rate is not a "pure" figure. Since no two periods are identical from the standpoint of the level and mix of activity operative within the marketplace, one cannot assume that the spending changes on a product line are *solely* responsible for its profit differences. However, when considered in light of the changes in marketing conditions also to be documented in this analysis, the incremental opportunity rate can be a most useful tool.

Market Research

In Exhibit 2 most of the important marketing variables influencing the effectiveness or the desirability of past spending decisions are documented. These include:

1. *Market share*—Ideally, management would like a dossier on all competitive activity, but the practical difficulty of securing this information at a reasonable cost in time for decision making requires a compromise. Share-of-market estimates, easily available at moderate cost, are therefore included in this report. For instance, during the three-month period, ABC's share of the retail market was 38.7% in Area D, up from 32.4% a year ago, indicating a probable increased share of total effective marketing effort for the brand in this market area.

2. *Size and trend of the retail market*—During the retail period corresponding to the first quarter of wholesale business, the estimated total retail market for ABC's product was $54,650,000. Comparing this with $56,000,000 for the comparable period last year, we infer that the overall market is declining at a rate of about 2.4% per year.

3. *Retail distribution*—The report shows the percent of the total estimated retail grocery volume achieved by stores in which ABC had distribution. During the period under discussion, distribution in Area C was 97.9%, down from 98.1% during the comparable 1964 period. This is a relatively insignificant movement, indicating that distribution changes probably did not affect changes in the rate at which marketing effort produced profits in this area.

4. *Media efficiencies*—Since television is the primary advertising medium used by

the ABC Corporation, the market area summaries include the estimated cost per thousand households and the cost per thousand prime prospect households. (For the ABC product the latter figure represents a division of total TV expenditures by the estimated number of five-member households reached.) The sharp increase in both these indexes for Area C has no doubt affected the level of profits produced.

The fact that these media efficiency rates differ considerably from market area to market area is not necessarily significant, as all competitors using the same media within each area are normally subject to the same relative inefficiencies. Substantial changes within an area between comparable periods, however, would generally call for special attention.

Speed of Reporting

Traditionally the kinds of market research data included in Exhibit 2 are used in a way which does not have an immediate impact on profits. The function of the data on these reports, however, is to provide a basis on which marketing management can identify undesirable overspending or underspending *in time to take corrective action*. Since there is an obvious and direct relationship between the time it takes to identify spending inefficiencies and the cost in the marketplace of these inefficiencies, the value of the information proposed is directly proportional to the speed with which it can be delivered.

The mechanics of the financial data in Exhibit 2 are such that they can usually be performed by data processing within two weeks of the end of the accounting period. Since the required market research data document *retail* trends, and because we are relating wholesale profits to the activity of a *prior* retail period, the ABC Corporation has approximately six weeks in which to gather the desired market research data. Not all sources of this information report within six weeks. Data derived from a national consumer panel can be obtained in this time period; however, these data are thought by some to be less accurate than those developed on the basis of a retail store audit, which usually takes considerably longer. Whether or not this is so, the *direction* and *relative magnitude* of the significant *changes* reported by reputable research firms using *either* method are generally the same. Since it is the changes which are of primary importance for the kinds of decision making being discussed, the framework presented here assumes the use of the more rapidly developed information. The possible loss of marginal accuracy is accuracy is offset by the additional profit opportunities that are produced by the extra lead time.

Management by Exception

Having dealt with the mechanics of the system, we can now turn to its use. It will be recalled that the first thing which must be done is to isolate those areas in which past spending involved the sacrifice of immediate profits. While producing a P & L for each market area is not a difficult problem for the modern computer, the digestion of a great number of these statements can be a problem for the product manager. Here the rule of "management by exception" applies. Our desire is to reexamine those areas involving possible inefficiencies. Severe overspending or underspending will normally produce exceptionally high or low average opportunity rates.

Let us suppose that the marketing executives of the ABC Corporation apply the rule of "management by exception" and select five market areas for special attention. These are the areas detailed in Exhibit 2. How does the new system help ABC's executives learn from the past? And how can it help them plan better for the future?

Analysis of Past

Since additional marketing effort generally produces profits at a decreasing rate, the optimum level of spending (where marginal cost equals marginal revenue and gross marketing earnings are at a maximum) can be thought of as the point at which the incremental opportunity rate passes from a positive to a negative figure. (It must be kept in mind, however, that this assumes a degree of consistency between periods which does not in fact exist. Without the tempering influence of professional marketing judgment, the incremental opportunity rate can have only limited utility.)

Market Area A.   Here we have an instance of an underpromoted area. Management's review might be summarized as follows:

Facts.   This relatively small market received a smaller percentage of ABC's marketing effort than it earned. There have been decreases in market share, marketing effort, and GME; a high negative incremental opportunity rate is symptomatic.

Analysis.   The unusually acute responsiveness of profits to changes in the level of marketing effort indicates that this area is relatively "underpromoted" by all companies.

Judgment.   The past decision to decrease spending in this area was not the best one. It appears that the market might profitably have used an increase of the same magnitude or a spending level of $140,000 (actual first-quarter expenditures of $100,000, plus double the decrease of 20,000).

Market Area B.   In this territory the situation is quite different from that of Area A:

Facts.   ABC's market share in this area is lower than average. There is decreased marketing effort, an increased GME, and a low average opportunity rate but one that improved during the first quarter.

Analysis.   During the last quarter of 1964 management reviewed this market, and at that time the facts of low share and low average opportunity rate for a number of consecutive periods suggested that the presence of strong regional competitors made this an expensive market in which to "buy" sales. This led to the decision to seek a lower, more profitable share level in the first quarter.

Judgment.   Increased GME during the first quarter tends to confirm the desirability of this decision. However, a further reduction of effort might have been even more profitable. Before testing this hypothesis, management might decide to continue spending at the first-quarter level ($375,000) to determine whether there is any residual loss of share inherent in the past spending policy.

Market Area C.   Here ABC's managers find strong external influences at work:

Facts.   There are decreases in average opportunity rate, market share, and GME; there is an unusually high negative incremental opportunity rate; there are poor media efficiencies relative to the last period; and there is no significant change in the size of the total market.

Analysis.   Poor performance in this area is the result either of a sharp increase in competitive activity or of media inefficiencies. The latter is suggested by the fact that market size did not expand. Moreover, discussion with local sales personnel indicates that there was no noticeable change in the level of competitive effort during the period.

Judgment.   Media inefficiencies cost ABC $85,000; SPC was down $75,000, and advertising and sales promotion were up $10,000. In the opinion of management, this problem should be corrected within the framework of the first-quarter spending level of $295,000.

Market Area D.   Questions of investment spending arise here:

Facts.   Exhibit 2 shows an increased share (but low relative to the national average), a negative incremental opportunity rate, and a decreased average opportunity rate.

Analysis.   This is a highly competitive major market in which management has elected to pursue an investment-spending policy in order to expand the ABC franchise. The degree to which this investment is desirable is a function of its cost (in terms of the amount of immediate profits sacrificed) relative to the future profit potential of those additional customers who will try the ABC product during the investment spending period, be satisfied with it, and thus respond more readily to future ABC marketing efforts.

The immediate cost implicit in this policy is equal to the amount of funds diverted to the area times the rate at which they would have generated additional profits if spent elsewhere. During the first quarter, Area D received 4.6% more of total marketing effort than it earned (i.e., it got 15.0% of total advertising and sales promotion funds, and contributed 10.4% of total SPC). This represents additional funds of approximately $145,000 (i.e., 4.6% of total marketing expenses of $3,190,000). Had these funds been invested at the total U.S. incremental opportunity rate of 1.10, they would have produced about $160,000 additional GME. Instead, the use of these funds in Area D produced GME losses at the incremental rate of 0.30 or losses of $47,500. The cost of this investment spending decision can therefore be estimated roughly at about $207,000 (a ball-park estimate, not an exact figure).

Dividing ABC's annual SPC in Area D (not shown in this exhibit) by its average share of this market, we obtain an approximate annual gross revenue value of $80,000 for each share point. Since the repurchase rate after trial of ABC's product by users of competing products is estimated by the market research department to be 15%, the future annual value of each share point gained in the short run by investment spending in Area D is probably about $12,000. ABC corporate policy dictates a maximum payout period of three years for investment spending. It can, therefore, be inferred that each additional share point in this area justifies a maximum immediate loss of profits of $36,000. Since the share of market increase attributable to investment spending in this area during the first quarter was 6.3 points, management would regard this policy desirable if it cost no more than $225,000 (6.3 × $36,000).

Judgment. The cost of investment spending in this area during the first quarter was approximately $207,000 or less than its long-range value to the company. However, since marketing management deems it unlikely that further share gains above the 38.7 level can be made profitably during the second quarter, it is decided that the correct level of expenses to be adjusted for the ensuing period is the $316,000 spent in this area during the first quarter of 1963.

Market Area E.   Here we have a case where our market area summaries are less useful than in the other cases:

Facts.   Sharply increased market size and marketing spending; sharply decreased market share; a negative incremental opportunity rate—these are characteristics appearing in Exhibit 2.

Analysis.   There was a very heavy amount of competitive activity in this area during the first quarter. This effort, perhaps the result of a competitor adopting a strategy similar to the one used by ABC in Area D, created an environment in which projections made on the basis of the incremental opportunity rate would have no validity. The incremental rate relates changes of the SPC to spending changes. When additional major changes take place in the market (other than distribution or media efficiency changes), the incremental rate is not a realistic basis for analysis. In Area E it would be misleading to assume that the incremental expenditure of $100,000 produced only $25,000 more SPC. Had this additional spending not occurred, it is almost certain that the prior level of SPC would not have been achieved.

Judgment. While the market area summary does not lend itself to systematic analysis and decision making in cases such as this one, it can be a useful adjunct to the professional judgment of the marketing staff. Strategies which management believes will offset these competitive tactics can be evaluated in terms of the value of the "saved" share points as against the immediate profit sacrifice implicit in the diversion of effort. For example, on the basis of this kind of analysis and professional judgment at ABC Corporation, executives might well decide to employ a strategy in the following quarter involving a spending level equal to a seasonal adjustment of $450,000 in the first quarter.

Better Future Decisions

Having made the necessary judgments in the five areas in which spending resulted in an immediate profit sacrifice, the ABC management has developed a list of optimum past marketing expenditures for all its market areas. This list can now be adjusted for the seasonal changes appropriate to the next quarter on the basis of the normal monthly distribution of total retail sales in each area. While total retail sales data are not always a valid tool for apportioning effort between areas, these data are a satisfactory basis for allocating effort *within* an area. The reason for this is that competitive environments—in terms of competition and consumer attitudes toward alternative products—differ less when examined at two different times in the same area than when examined in two separate areas. Again, the basis for adjustment is not perfect, but it is better than available alternatives.

Once adjusted by the market research department for anticipated seasonal changes, these tentative spending levels must then be examined by product management to ascertain whether expected competitive activity necessitates any further alteration. The end product of this process of review and adjustment is a series of decisions on spending (not included here) against which planned and committed expenditures are compared. A list of planned marketing expenses is prepared by the data-processing departments of the firm and by its advertising agencies. Individual media commitments and sales promotion plans are supplied to these centers by product management shortly before the close of the preceding quarter. These plans are then broken down by machine and reported by media (or promotion) and by month for each market area.

Differences between planned and recommended expense levels will indicate where second-quarter spending inefficiencies are most likely to occur. The degree of change which marketing management can effect will be a function of many factors. While certain types of marketing effort are highly flexible, alteration of other types involves the payment of substantial production premiums and long lead times. It could therefore be assumed that at the time when ABC's managers receive the adjusted expenditure list (about the third week in April, for the first quarter), they would probably be considering changes of the local media expenditures for May. Alternatives such as buying or selling a "cut-in" on a network television show during May might also be arranged with other ABC lines.

With respect to June effort, management could consider altering certain national efforts. Given the extra lead time, it might possibly change network television lineups, buy regional editions of magazines, or exclude certain areas from previously scheduled (but unannounced) trade allowances. The specific changes actually selected will be a function of the adaptability of the product message to alternative marketing mixes and of management's ability to act creatively within these limitations.

Testing

An information system designed to influence a function as expensive and important as marketing must do more than make sense in the abstract. Only some form of projectable test can determine the value of this approach to a specific company.

An individual company can inexpensively approximate the impact on profits of the proposed system by a process of simulation. Market area summaries prepared manually from back data for eight quarters will usually provide an adequate basis for such a process. On the basis of each back report, marketing management can formulate spending decisions that it would have made for the following period if the new system had been used. The laws of coincidence are such that a certain number of the planned changes will actually have occurred. The frequency and amount of the incremental profits which these changes produced can be used as an indication of the profit potential of the information system had it been available to the company to guide spending decisions in all market areas.

Conclusion

In this article discussion has been confined to the use of the proposed information system as a guide for apportioning effort among market areas. The basis on which these decisions are made can also be used to apportion effort among lines of products and among varieties within the line. Similarly, this approach is also a valid framework within which to monitor media mix and product test markets. In all such cases the marketing objective is the same: to take funds from that area (or product, or strategy) where profits will decrease least and to use them in the area where profits will increase most.

To this end, I have proposed certain changes in the form and use of the financial data supplied to marketing management. The changes do not and cannot travel the total distance between imperfect and perfect information. More realistically, the financial data produced by this system are similar to the market research estimates with which they have been designed to coincide; both have a degree of error inherent in them. In spite of this limitation, both are of value as background for professional judgment in the making and monitoring of marketing decisions.

This is not a sophisticated system; it is a rough beginning—a place from which to move toward refinement. The nature of the ultimate refinement cannot be pre-determined. Perhaps marketing management will someday have information and techniques which will lead to an investment of marketing funds by area (and by product) such that the last dollar spent on each will return an equal amount. Ideally, this return would equal the company's cost of capital, adjusted for risk and discounted to compensate for investment spending against future profit potential, but that day is a long way off.

In the meantime, we can advance toward the ideal, allocating funds and effort ever more skillfully, if not perfectly. Any real progress we make will only come as the result of well-directed and well-coordinated effort on the part of the market research, product management, and financial functions. The proposed system provides this direction and allows more profitable decision making as gains are made.

Exercises

28.1. The regional quarterly meeting between Nancy Barker, the marketing director of Neptune Company, and the branch managers had ended on a less than amicable note.

The announcement of an increase in the current quarter's allotment of advertising and sales promotion dollars, which was well received by everyone, immediately became the subject of a heated discussion. Each of the managers wanted the extra money spent in his or her district. Barker, of course, wanted those promotional dollars spent in the areas where they would have the maximum impact. For example, if an extra dollar spent in area B produces $0.60 and the same dollar spent in area C produces only $0.50, the director is better off assigning it to area B.

A comparison of this particular quarter's figures and those of the same quarter a year ago (Table 28.1) was expected to yield several ratios that she hoped to use to straighten out the situation.

1. Based on the data provided by each manager, where would you assign any extra promotional dollars?
2. How would you explain your selection to the different managers?

28.2. At the close of the last district sales meeting, the regional sales manager, James Anderson, decided to increase promotional expenditures in all the districts under his portfolio for the next quarter, April–June. In line with overall corporate policy, the allocation of extra promotional dollars is to follow the rule of "management by exception"; i.e., if district A generates higher profits per extra promotional dollar than district B, the additional promotional dollar will be assigned to district A. Each district manager has furnished information on last quarter's sales figures as well as this quarter's. See Table 28.2.

TABLE 28.1. *Market area summaries (dollar figures in thousands)*

	District 1	+	District 2	+	District 3	+	District 4	+	District 5	+	6 ... n	=	Total
Fourth quarter this year:													
Standard profit contribution	$150		$275		$180		$400		$290				$2,575
Advertising and sales promotion	51		164		145		109		85				1,220
Fourth quarter last year:													
Standard profit contribution	155		255		200		435		275				2,800
Advertising and sales promotion	64		158		140		135		98				1,500

TABLE 28.2. *Market area summaries (dollar figures in thousands)*

	District A	+	District B	+	District C	+	District D	+	District E	+	F ... n	=	Total
April–June:													
Standard profit contribution	$200		$180		$240		$250		$480				$3,200
Advertising and sales promotion	79		100		196		165		255				1,250
January–March:													
Standard profit contribution	176		220		400		196		520				3,000
Advertising and sales promotion	82		165		300		145		248				1,200

1. For each district, calculate

   a. The average opportunity rate for this period and last period.
   b. The standard profit contribution percentage.
   c. The advertising and sales promotion percentage.
   d. The incremental opportunity rate.
2. Which districts would you recommend for additional promotional expenditures, and why?

A Strategic Framework for Marketing Control

29

James M. Hulbert   Norman E. Toy

The decade of the 1960's led many companies down the primrose path of un-controlled growth. The turbulence of the 1970's has drawn renewed attention to the need to pursue growth selectively, and many companies have been forced to divest themselves of businesses which looked glamorous in the 1960's, but faded in the 1970's. Simultaneously with this re-appraisal has come a much more serious focus on problems of control—a concern with careful monitoring and appraisal to receive early warning on businesses or ventures that are suspect.

Yet, despite the extent to which control is stressed by authors,[1] there does not exist a generally agreed upon strategic framework for marketing control, and there has been little successful integration of concepts in marketing strategy and planning with those of managerial accounting. In particular, the work of the Boston Consulting Group,[2] the results of the PIMS study,[3] and a variety of other sources[4] have stressed the importance of market share objectives in marketing strategy, coincidentally emphasizing the need to know market size and growth rate and thus the importance of good forecasts. Typically, however, procedures for marketing control have not been related to these key parameters. (Incredibly, market size is sometimes even omitted from marketing plans, according to one knowledgeable author.)[5]

In this article we seek to remedy that state of affairs by outlining a strategic framework for marketing control. Using the key strategic concepts discussed above,

Reprinted by permission from *Journal of Marketing*, vol. 41 (April 1977), pp. 12–21, published by the American Marketing Association.

[1] See, for example, V. H. Kirpalani and Stanley J. Shapiro, "Financial Dimensions of Marketing Management," *Journal of Marketing*, Vol. 37, No. 3 (July 1973), pp. 40–47; David J. Luck and Arthur E. Prell, *Marketing Strategy* (Englewood Cliffs, N.J.: Prentice-Hall Inc., 1968); Philip Kotler, *Marketing Management: Analysis, Planning and Control* (Englewood Cliffs, N.J.: Prentice-Hall Inc., 1972).

[2] Boston Consulting Group, *Perspectives on Experience* (Boston: Boston Consulting Group, 1968); see also Patrick Conley, "Experience Curves as a Planning Tool," in S. H. Britt and H. W. Boyd, eds., *Marketing Management and Administrative Action* (New York: McGraw-Hill, 1974), pp. 257–68; William E. Cox, "Product Portfolio Strategy: A Review of the Boston Consulting Group Approach to Marketing Strategy," in *Proceedings*, 1974 Marketing Educators' Conference (Chicago: American Marketing Association), pp. 465–70.

[3] Sidney Schoeffler, Robert D. Buzzell and Donald F. Heany, "Impact of Strategic Planning on Profit Performance," *Harvard Business Review*, Vol. 52 (March-April 1974), pp. 137–45; Robert D. Buzzell, Bradley T. Gale and Ralph G. M. Sultan, "Market Share—A Key to Profitability," *Harvard Business Review*, Vol. 53 (January-February 1975), pp. 97–106.

[4] See Bernard Catry and Michel Chevalier, "Market Share Strategy and the Product Life Cycle," *Journal of Marketing*, Vol. 38, No. 4 (October 1974), pp. 29–34; C. Davis Fogg, "Planning Gains in Market Share," *Journal of Marketing*, Vol. 38, No. 3 (July 1974), pp. 30–38.

[5] F. Beaven Ennis, *Effective Marketing Management* (New York: Association of National Advertisers, 1973), pg. 11.

we first present a framework for evaluating marketing performance versus plan, thus providing a means for more formally incorporating the marketing plan in the managerial control process.

The plan, however, may well provide inappropriate criteria for performance evaluation, especially if there have been a number of unanticipated events during the planning period. A second stage of this article, therefore, is to provide a means of taking these kinds of planning variances into account, so as to provide a more appropriate set of criteria for performance evaluation. Two conceptual developments are shown as Part 1 and Part 2 of the Appendix.

Performance vs. Plan

In Exhibit 1 we show the results of operations for a sample product, *Product Alpha*, during the preceding period. In the analysis which follows, we shall focus on analysis of variances in profit contribution. As we discussed elsewhere,[6] an analysis of revenue performance is sometimes required; the procedure here is analogous. Organizationally, one of the results we would like to achieve is to be able to assign responsibility, and give credit, where due.

A variety of organizational units were involved in the planning and execution summarized in Exhibit 1, and an important component of control activity is to evaluate their performance according to the standards or goals provided by the marketing plan. We should also note, however, that the type of analysis we shall discuss has limited potential for *diagnosing* the causes of problems. Rather, its major benefit is in the *identification* of areas where problems may exist. Determining the

EXHIBIT 1. Operating results for Product Alpha

Item	Planned	Actual	Variance
Revenues			
Sales (lbs.)	20,000,000	22,000,000	2,000,000
Price per lb. ($)	0.50	.4773	0.227
Revenues	10,000,000	10,500,000	500,000
Total market (lbs.)	40,000,000	50,000,000	10,000,000
Share of market	50%	44%	(6%)
Costs			
Variable cost per lb. ($)	.30	.30	—
Contribution			
Per lb. ($)	.20	.1773	.0227
Total ($)	4,000,000	3,900,000	(100,000)

[6] James M. Hulbert and Norman E. Toy, "Control and the Marketing Plan," paper presented to the 1975 Marketing Educators' Conference of the American Marketing Association.

factors which have actually caused favorable or unfavorable variances requires the skill and expertise of the manager.

The unfavorable variance in contribution of $100,000 for *Product Alpha* could arise from two main sources:[7]

1. Differences between planned and actual quantities (volumes).
2. Differences between planned and actual contribution per unit.

Differences between planned and actual quantities, however, may arise from differences between actual and planned total market size and actual and planned market share (penetration) of that total market. The potential sources of variation between planned and actual contribution, then, are:

1. Total market size.
2. Market share (penetration).
3. Price/cost per unit.

This format for variance decomposition permits assignment into categories which correspond to key strategy variables in market planning.[8] The analysis proceeds as follows.

Price-Quantity Decomposition

In order to measure volume variance with the standard yardstick of planned contribution per unit, actual quantity is used to calculate the price/cost variance. (This procedure is standard accounting practice.) To be more concise, we utilize the following symbols:

$$S\text{—share of total market}$$
$$M\text{—total market in units}$$
$$Q\text{—quantity sold in units}$$
$$C\text{—contribution margin per unit.}$$

We use the subscript "a" to denote *actual* values, and "p" to denote *planned* values. The subscript "v" denotes *variance*. Thus the price/cost variance is given by

$$(C_n - C_p) \times Q_a = (.1773 - .20) \times 22,000,000$$
$$= -\$500,000;$$

and the volume variance is given by

$$(Q_a - Q_p) \times C_p = (22,000,000 - 20,000,000) \times .20$$
$$= \$400,000.[9]$$

---

[7] To simplify this example, no variances in either variable costs or marketing program costs are included.

[8] For algebraic exposition, see Appendix, Part 1.

[9] Algebraically, we have:

$$(C_a - C_p)Q_a + (Q_a - Q_p)C_p = C_aQ_a - C_pQ_a + C_pQ_a - C_pQ_p$$
$$= C_aQ_a - C_pQ_p$$

The sum of these contribution variances therefore yields the overall unfavorable contribution variance of $-\$100,000$ shown in Exhibit 1.

Penetration—Market Size Decomposition

The second stage of the analysis is the further decomposition of the volume variance in contribution into the components due to penetration and total market size. Exhibit 2 is helpful in the exposition of the analysis.

As a first step, we should like to explain differences in quantities sold $(Q_a - Q_p)$, where actual and planned quantities are the product of the market size times share $(Q_a = S_a \times M_a,$ and $Q_p = S_p \times M_p)$. From Exhibit 2, rectangles I and II are clearly assignable to share and market size, respectively. Rectangle III, however, is conceptually more complex.

We argue that discrepancies in forecasting market size should be evaluated using the standard yardstick of planned share, just as the dollar value of the quantity variance is measured using the standard of planned contribution. Thus, actual market size is used to calculate share variance, while both share and forecast components (which together comprise the quantity variance) are measured using planned contribution. This procedure is also consistent with recommended accounting practice.[10]

EXHIBIT 2. *Variance of total market size vs. share*

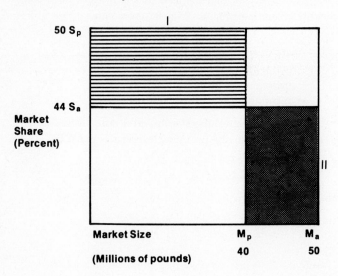

---

[10] "Report of the Committee on Cost and Profitability Analyses for Marketing," *Accounting Review*, Supplement to Vol. XLVII (1972), pp. 575–615.

Then the variance in contribution due to share is given by

$$(S_a - S_p) \times M_a \times C_p = (.44 - .50) \times 50,000,000 \times .2$$
$$= -\$600,000;$$

and the market size variance is given by

$$(M_a - M_p) \times S_p \times C_p = (50,000,000 - 40,000,000) \times .5 \times .2$$
$$= \$1,000,000.$$

The sum of the market size and share variances yields the overall favorable volume variance in contribution of \$400,000 derived in the previous section.

We may now summarize the variances which in total constitute the overall variance as follows (see Exhibit 3):

Planned profit contribution		\$4,000,000
Volume variance		
Share variance	(600,000)	
Market size variance	1,000,000	
		400,000
Price/cost variance		(500,000)
Actual profit contribution		\$3,900,000

Interpretation

Conceptually, variances may occur because of problems in forecasting, execution, or both. In using the results of the analysis for performance evaluation, however, responsibility will have to be assigned. Generally, variances in total market size, for example, will be viewed as the responsibility of the market forecasting group.

Share or penetration variances present a more difficult case. They may arise due to incorrect forecasts of what "expected performance" should be, or due to poor performance itself. Apportioning responsibility in this case clearly necessitates managerial judgment. However, where marketing and sales personnel participate in the development of market share objectives, or where share declines relative to previous performance, the burden of proof is more likely to fall on the operating unit than on a separate planning or forecasting group.

Responsibility for price variances may also be difficult to assign. For example, prices may be seriously affected by changes in market or general economic conditions beyond the control of the operating group but which should have been foreseen by forecasters or planners. On the other hand, prices are an integral part of the marketing mix, and variances may well indicate problems in marketing or selling tactics.

EXHIBIT 3. Ex post *performance evaluation: analysis of contribution*

Item	Composition	Type of variance		Variance totals	Reconciliation
		Planning variance	Performance variance		
Planned contribution					$4,000,000
Quantity variance share					
Planning variance	$(S_r - S_p) \cdot M_r \cdot C_p$				
	$= (.49 - .50) \times 49,000,000 \times .20$	(98,000)			
Performance variance	$(S_a - S_r) \cdot M_a \cdot C_r$				
	$= (.44 - .49) \times 50,000,000 \times .18$		(450,000)		
Total				(548,000)	
Market size					
Planning variance	$(M_r - M_p) \cdot S_p \cdot C_p$				
	$= (49,000,000 - 40,000,000) \times .5 \times .20$	900,000			
Performance variance	$(M_n - M_r) \cdot S_r \cdot C_r$				
	$= (50,000,000 - 49,000,000) \times .49 \times .18$		88,200		
Total				988,200	
Total quantity variance					440,200
Price variance					
Planning variance	$(C_r - C_p) \cdot Q_r = (.18 - .2) \times 24,010,000$	(480,200)			
Performance variance	$(C_a - C_r) \cdot Q_a = (.1773 - .18) \times 22,000,000$		(60,000)		
Total				(540,200)	
Total price variance		321,800			(540,200)
Total planning variance				(540,200)	
Total performance variance			(421,800)		
Total variance				(100,000)	
Actual contribution					$3,900,000

470

With these considerations in mind, we may now review the results of the variance analysis:

First, *the favorable volume variance of $400,000 was in fact caused by two larger variances cancelling each other out. And while one of these variances was positive, the other negative, both are undesirable! By not achieving planned share of market, we lost $600,000 in profit contribution.*

The loss of market share may be due to poor planning, poor execution, or both ... and managerial judgment is the key factor in diagnosing the causes of this discrepancy.

This unfavorable share variance was more than compensated for—or so it appears— by the $1,000,000 positive contribution variance due to the fact that the market turned out to be much larger than was forecast. This variance is unequivocally the responsibility of the forecasting group, though whether or not they should have been able to foresee the expansion is an issue which the manager must decide.

However, this nominally favorable variance is, in fact, a danger signal. *We seriously underestimated the size of the market, which was 25% greater, at 50 million pounds, than the forecast (40 million pounds).* As the dominant competitor, we have lost market share in what is apparently a fast-growing market, the kind of error which can soon lead to loss of competitive position.[11]

In this instance, then, the share/size decomposition of the volume variance serves to emphasize the importance of good planning—and good information for planning —in terms directly related to two crucial variables in strategy design. This form of decomposition, we submit, generates considerably more useful insight into issues of marketing control *than isolation of only the volume variance, which is much less clearly interpretable.*

The final variance component is the unfavorable price variance of $500,000. Again, interpretation is the job of the manager. However, we should note that the accounting procedures used here (and generally) treat price and volume variances as if they were separable. *Yet, for the vast majority of products and services, demand is price-elastic to some degree so that variances in total revenue are the combined result of the interaction, via the demand function, of unit prices and quantities.*

In this example, for instance, the lower levels of prices may well have been an important factor in expanding industry and company demand. Nonetheless, the fact remains that failure to attain planned price levels led to a $500,000 decrease in actual versus planned profit contribution. The reasons for this variance may lie with performance (e.g., poor tactics) or planning (e.g., inaccurate forecasts).

Diagnosis and responsibility assignment procedures will be explored in more detail in the following section.

---

[11] Boston Consulting Group, *Perspectives on Experience*, same as reference 2 above.

Monday Morning Quarterbacking

A crucial issue, which we have thus far skirted, is the appropriate criterion for performance evaluation. This is a basic yet nagging problem underlying the whole area of strategic control. In the foregoing analysis, for example, we assumed that the marketing plan provides an appropriate set of criteria. The objectives therein are usually derived after considerable participation, discussion, and negotiation between interested parties,[12] and may well represent the most appropriate set of criteria that are available, at least at the beginning of the planning period.

In many companies, however, performance during the previous planning period serves as an additional set of evaluation criteria. In fact, the search for more "objective" criteria for performance evaluation led to the origins, at General Electric, of the PIMS project and the subsequent "par" criterion.[13]

The facts are, of course, that the marketing plan—which we used as our criterion —is generally based upon the best information which is available on an *ex ante* basis. The conditions which are manifest during the planning period, however, may be vastly different from those envisaged at the time of plan development. In some company planning systems, some of these changes may be encompassed by contingency planning, while in others the plan is updated when major environmental changes occur.[14] In many other instances the plan is not updated—at least in any formal way.[15]

Nonetheless, irrespective of the comprehensiveness of systems to provide flexibility in plans, when the time arrives to review performance, most marketing managers use some *ex post* information. In other words, the criteria of evaluation—implicitly or explicitly—are generally "what performance should have been" under the circumstances which actually transpired. Nor is this "Monday morning quarterbacking" undesirable, for it is eminently more sensible than blind adherence to a plan which is clearly outdated by violation of planning assumptions.[16]

For example, supply may be affected unexpectedly; a major competitor may drop out of the market—or an aggressive new competitor may enter; or demand may have an unexpected change—e.g., because of weather. Either of these would likely change the appropriate par market share for the company. The purpose of this second stage of the analysis, therefore, is to provide a variance decomposition which permits comparison of performance versus the criterion of "what should have happened under the circumstances."

---

[12] John A. Howard, James M. Hulbert and John U. Farley, "Organizational Analysis and Information System Design: A Decision Process Perspective," *Journal of Business Research*, Vol. 3.

[13] Schoeffler, Buzzell and Heany, same as reference 3 above.

[14] Ennis, same as reference 5 above, pg. 57.

[15] Noel Capon and James M. Hulbert, "Decision Systems Analysis in Industrial Marketing," *Industrial Marketing Management*, Vol. 4, 1975, pp. 143–60.

[16] Joel S. Demski, "An Accounting System Structured on a Linear Programming Model," *The Accounting Review*, Vol. 42 (October 1967), pp. 701–12.

Naturally, there are inherent dangers in such a process. Re-opening the issue of what constitutes an appropriate criterion for performance evaluation may mean opening a Pandora's Box. Equally clearly, however, there are frequently occasions when unforeseen events can significantly affect what target performance should be. In such instances, it is surely preferable that any adjustment process be systematic and orderly, explicit and visible.

Using "Expert" Information

Continuing with our previous operating results, then, let us construct the scenario which occurred during the planning period, using the *ex post* information which would be available to the marketing manager at the time of performance review:

1. A new competitor—Consolidated Company—entered the market early in the year. The competitor was a large, well-financed conglomerate, which used an aggressive promotional campaign and a lower price to induce trial purchase.
2. A fire in the plant of a European manufacturer led to totally unforeseeable foreign demand for one million pounds of *Product Alpha*.

With a small amount of additional work by the manager, we may now develop an appropriate *ex post* performance analysis. For example, the fact that the new competitor was quite prepared to subsidize his entry into our market out of his other operations was an important cause of the price deterioration, and also guaranteed that he would "buy" a share of market sufficient for him to run his new plant at close to standard capacity. At the same time, this aggressive entry and the price competition which ensued was an important factor in further expanding total industry demand.

In quantitative terms Consolidated's effective mean selling price for the year was $0.465 per lb. We had forecast an industry mean of $0.495 and a price for our own product of $0.475, and we realized $0.4773 per lb. Competitive intelligence informed us that Consolidated's new plant had a capacity of only 1.33 million pounds so that its inability to supply more set a lower limit for market prices, above that of Consolidated's introductory price.

We now reconstruct the discrepancy between conditions forecast at the time of planning and the conditions which subsequently prevailed.

Market Share

As noted, our intelligence estimates indicated that Consolidated's capacity would be 1.33 million pounds. Our historical market share had hovered around 50% for some time, so that *everything being equal*, we might expect that 50% of Consolidated's sales would be at our expense. However, knowing that we were (a) the dominant competitor and (b) the premium-price competitor, we also knew that we were the most vulnerable to a price-oriented competitive entry. Consequently, we used as a planning assumption the supposition that 60% of Consolidated's sales would be at our expense. That is, we assumed that .6 × 1.33 million pounds, or 800 thousand pounds of sales volume which we would otherwise have obtained, would be lost to Consolidated. Thus, we had the following two conditions:

If no entry: forecast market share equal to $20.8 \div 40 = 52\%$
With entry: forecast market share equal to $20 \div 40 = 50\%$

Since we were certain that Consolidated would enter early in the year, we used the latter assumption. However, while our intelligence estimates on the size of Consolidated's plant were excellent, we did not glean the information that they would use three-shift operation rather than two shifts which have been standard practice for the industry. As a result Consolidated's effective standard capacity was raised from 1.33 to 2.0 million pounds. Under these conditions, then, assuming the 60% loss rate holds, we should have expected to lose .6 × 2.0 or 1.2 million pounds to Consolidated, rather than 800,000 lbs. Thus with perfect foresight we *should have* forecasted a market share of $19.6 \div 40$, or 49%.

Price

We had forecast an industry mean price of $0.495 per pound, and planned for a net price to us of $0.50 per pound. This $0.005 per pound premium had been traditional for us because of our leadership position in the industry, with slightly higher quality product and excellent levels of distribution and service.

The actual industry mean price was $0.475 per pound, and our net mean price was $0.4773, so that we only received a premium of $0.0023 per pound.[17] Here, then, we have some basis for separating the planning variance from the performance variance.

Although the basis for this distinction again involves managerial judgment, for present purposes we assume that the planning group should have foreseen that Consolidated's entry would be based on a low price strategy which would lead to an overall deterioration in market prices. On the other hand, our selling and marketing tactics were responsible for the deterioration in our price premium.

Market Size

Finally, there was no possibility that our planning group could have foreseen the European fire, and it would be demonstrably unfair to hold them responsible for this component of the variance.

On the other hand, the remainder of the market expansion should have been foreseen, and the responsibility should be assigned to them. Their failure in this regard was no doubt related to the oversight in the pricing area, for it seems entirely

---

[17] Some judgment is evidently involved here. Percentage differentials might well be used instead of absolute differentials.

plausible that demand was more price elastic than we had realized, and the price decrease brought a whole new set of potential customers into the market.

Variance Decomposition

The full *ex post* decomposition using this information is displayed in Exhibit 2.[18] To simplify the exposition, we employ a third subscript, "r," which indicates the standard which "should have been"—in other words, the plan as *revised* by *ex post* information. A number of useful insights are generated by the tableau.

The first issue is the nature of planning variances, which is somewhat counter-intuitive. Consider, for example, the planning variance in market share—a negative $98,000. What this is really telling us is that, considering only this factor in isolation, our planned market share was set unrealistically high, and that adjusting for this factor alone would have implied planning for a total contribution of $4,000,000 less the $98,000, or $3,902,000. Conversely, however, positive (or favorable) planning variances are in fact undesirable and represent, potentially, opportunity losses.

For example, the $900,000 favorable planning variance in market size, which is responsible for the fact that overall variance is favorable, represents lost profit contribution due to the fact that we had not correctly anticipated the market growth rate (given, of course, that there were no short-run capacity constraints). The $88,200 performance variance in market size is viewed as unassignable in this instance. We have decided that the planners could not have foreseen the foreign demand, and that we don't feel it should be assigned to sales.

Similar issues arise with the price variance. The planning group's failure to correctly predict market prices is responsible for the bulk of the price variance. However, there is no way that this component might have been recovered; it simply indicated the fact that our plan was subsequently shown by events to be unrealistic in its price expectations. In contrast, the failure of the marketing department to maintain our traditional price premium is reflected in the unfavorable performance variance in price of $60,000.

Again, however, we should point out that the most important element of the analysis is the market size/market growth rate issue. Picture the poor salesmen as they operate during the planning period. They know they are feeling some price pressure, to which, as we have seen, marketing responded. However, they also know that their quantity of sales is up—22 million pounds of product versus a planned amount of 20 million pounds.

Thus, it is entirely feasible that our salesmen were not pushing that hard, since they appeared to be having a banner year, handsomely exceeding their monthly volume quotas and prior periods' performance. In fact, during this period we were

---

[18] For algebraic exposition, see Appendix, Part 1.

frittering away our market position through our ignorance of the rate at which the market had expanded.

However, accurate and timely industry sales statistics, in combination with a flexible planning system which could readily incorporate these data in a revised plan and set of sales quotas, would preempt a problem which, by the time we recognized it, had developed into a fair-sized disaster. While market information is always important, it truly takes on new meaning for the company competing in a high-growth market.

Finally, we should note that the aggregate variances for quantity (including share and market size) and price/cost shown in Exhibit 3 do not agree with those developed in the first part of the article. The reason is, of course, that there are now two possible criteria or yardsticks against which to compare actual results: the original plan (subscripted "p") and the revised plan (subscripted "r").

Following the conceptual development of Part 2 of the Appendix, therefore, we have used what we believe to be the soundest analysis. Alternative decompositions which permit the retention of identical aggregate variances to the preliminary "versus plan" comparison are possible, but their conceptual framework is less defensible.

Summary

To be useful to the marketing manager, a framework for control should be related to strategic objectives and variables and, whenever possible, should permit assignment of responsibility for differences between planned and actual performance. The procedures described in this article utilize the key strategic variables of price, market share, and market size as a framework for marketing control.

The framework was first used to analyze marketing performance vs. plan, decomposing quantity variance into components due to under- or over-achievement of planned market share and over- or under-forecasting of market size. Then, recognizing that the plan may well not constitute an adequate criterion for evaluation, we extended the example to illustrate how *ex post* information might be utilized to develop more appropriate evaluative criteria, which permitted isolation of the planning and performance components of the variance.

While there is evidently a considerable amount of managerial judgment involved in the decomposition procedure, marketing planning and control has never been exectly bereft of managerial judgment. There is nothing radical about the procedure, which simply recognizes that it is not always possible to update and modify plans to reflect changing conditions, but that such changes may nonetheless be taken into account in appraisal and evaluation via *ex post* revision of the plan.

The example we worked with also indicates the dangers of not continuously monitoring markets and revising plans and objectives, particularly when market conditions are fluid. In such markets, good tracking procedures[19] and responsive

---

[19] John U. Farley and Melvin J. Hinich, "Tracking Marketing Parameters in Random Noise," in *Proceedings*, 1966 Marketing Educators' Conference.

tactics are essential for any company seeking to maintain or increase its market position. The importance of marketing control—so long a stepchild—will surely increase in the years ahead. The markets of the late 1970's will differ considerably from those of the 1960's, and pressures of costs and competition will force companies to be more effective in performance appraisal and evaluation.

APPENDIX PART 1. Variance decomposition—comparison with plan

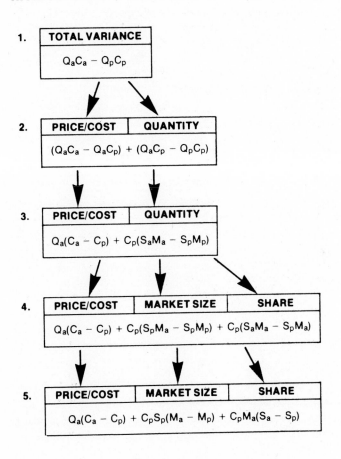

1. **TOTAL VARIANCE**

$$Q_a C_a - Q_p C_p$$

2. **PRICE/COST**   **QUANTITY**

$$(Q_a C_a - Q_a C_p) + (Q_a C_p - Q_p C_p)$$

3. **PRICE/COST**   **QUANTITY**

$$Q_a(C_a - C_p) + C_p(S_a M_a - S_p M_p)$$

4. **PRICE/COST**   **MARKET SIZE**   **SHARE**

$$Q_a(C_a - C_p) + C_p(S_p M_a - S_p M_p) + C_p(S_a M_a - S_p M_a)$$

5. **PRICE/COST**   **MARKET SIZE**   **SHARE**

$$Q_a(C_a - C_p) + C_p S_p(M_a - M_p) + C_p M_a(S_a - S_p)$$

LEGEND

Subscripts
a = actual
p = planned

Variables
Q = Quantity
C = Contribution Margin
S = Share
M = Market

APPENDIX PART 2. Variance decomposition—use of ex post information

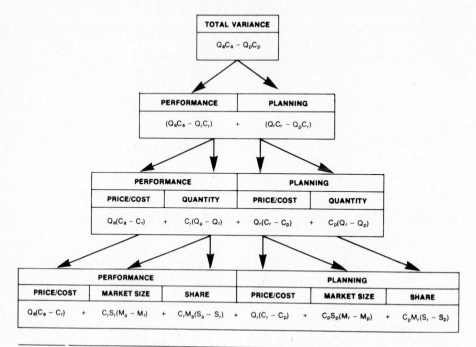

Legend

Subscripts	Variables
a = actual	Q = Quantity
p = planned	C = Contribution margins
r = revised	S = Share
	M = Market

Exercises

29.1.

1. The Putney-Wells Engineering Company is in the process of evaluating its fifth year's performance in the Brazilian market. Putney-Wells had planned for a sales revenue of $897,750 from sales of 1,050 of their irrigation pumps, at the standard price of $855. The total profit contribution which should have been achieved was $362,250.

In fact, Putney-Wells's actual performance was not up to planned standards. Actual variable cost per unit was $522, while the average manufacturer's selling price was only $817. The Brazilian marketing manager is now extremely worried, because even though selling prices were much below plan, she was able to sell only 924 of the pumps.

a. Calculate the total contribution variance.

b. Calculate the volume variance and the price/cost variance in contribution.

c. Interpret your answers to part b.

d. From a marketing perspective, what is the weakness of any variance decomposition involving the separation of price and volume components?

2. Putney-Wells had recently been involved in a program to upgrade the quality of its strategic planning. As a result, the company had developed explicit forecasts of the overall irrigation pump market, which it had forecast to be 3,500 for the year. The best information now available to Putney-Wells's marketing department suggests that actual industry sales were only 3,300 units.

a. What were the market share and market size variances in contribution?

b. Develop a schedule showing the complete breakdown of contribution variances computed in 1. and 2.

c. Interpret your answer to part b.

d. Based on this analysis, how would you summarize the problems faced by Putney-Wells's marketing department in Brazil?

29.2.

1. Mr. Donald Capley was recently appointed national sales manager (NSM) of Rywinton, a manufacturer of crackers and cookies, after spending five years in a senior planning position. During his time as planner, Mr. Capley had been involved in several long and sometimes vehement conversations with the previous NSM (since retired) over evaluating sales-force performance. Capley felt quite strongly that when planning assumptions were violated, the sales-force assessment procedure should be revised to take into account the fact that the situation had changed. His predecessor as NSM had disagreed strongly. Mr. Capley remembered one particularly long and heated discussion which the NSM had concluded by saying, "Give those bastards an inch and they'll take a mile. Why don't you leave me alone to run the sales force and get back to minding your own shop? That sales force had better understand that it's their job to produce results no matter what—or we're all in trouble!"

a. Based on the concepts presented in "A Strategic Framework for Marketing Control," how do you evaluate the arguments presented by the old NSM? What are the dangers of using an adjusted plan for performance evaluation (Monday morning quarterbacking)?

b. Suppose you, as Mr. Capley, decided to try to institute a formal system to enable sales-force assessment on the basis of a revised plan. What are the key issues with which you would be concerned in designing such a system?

2. As part of his quest for a better method of evaluating sales-force performance, Mr. Capley decided to review the previous year's performance in one of his key product lines. Using ideas presented in a paper he had read on strategic marketing control, he developed the schedule of information shown in Table 29.1.

TABLE 29.1

	Actual	Previously planned	Revised plan
Quantity sold (cases)	24,200	25,000	24,000
Case contribution	12.10	12.60	12.40
Market size (cases)	280,500	290,000	285,000

a. How would you analyze and interpret these results for control purposes, using only the information in the two left-hand columns? What would be the implications for evaluating the performance of the sales force?

b. Suppose you now take into account Mr. Capley's revised plan, which reflects what the plan would have been had the sales manager responsible for planning had perfect foresight about the events that were to take place during the year. What does your analysis now show? Is there any change in the implications for the sales force? For those responsible for planning?

A Marketing-Accounting Framework for Controlling Product Profitability

30

Robert F. Lusch   William F. Bentz

Throughout the 1970s, the environment of business in the U.S. and most industrialized economies became more turbulent. Rising levels of inflation, capital shortages and sporadic economic growth intensified competitive pressures and made marketing planning both more essential and more difficult. In turn the increasing turbulence made the monitoring of plans and the control of marketing efforts more important. In this era both marketing and financial executives began to place more emphasis on product profitability and cash flow. The purpose of this paper is to provide a product planning and control framework for the 1980s that merges concepts in managerial accounting and marketing.

The framework presented herein builds and expands upon a variance analysis approach to product planning and control developed by Hulbert and Toy (1977) in a recent article appearing in the *Journal of Marketing*. In short, the framework to be presented allows the marketing or product manager to partition the difference between planned and actual product performance into seventeen key control elements. Since a basic understanding of variance analysis is critical to the comprehension of this somewhat technical article, the interested reader may wish to refresh his or her knowledge of variance analysis by consulting several sources that do a good job of discussing variance analysis from a manager's perspective (Horngren, 1977, and Shank and Churchill, 1977).

Product Performance

In managing a product's performance, a product or marketing manager will be required to use financial criteria. One popular financial criterion is simply the product's profitability. However, managerial accountants and marketing managers often disagree, both with one another and among themselves, on how to best measure product profitability.

In theory and practice there exist two basic measures of product profitability—contribution margin and net profits (Kotler, 1976, pp. 461–62; Rayburn, 1973, pp. 985–91). The net profit approach involves subtracting from product revenues both

Technical portions of this article are similar to those presented in William F. Bentz and Robert F. Lusch, "Now You Can Control Your Product's Market Performance," *Management Accounting* (January, 1980), pp. 17–25. Reprinted by permission.

direct and indirect costs. This procedure axiomatically involves some arbitrary but useful allocations to ensure that all costs (either direct or indirect) can be attached to products. On the other hand, product contribution margin can be obtained by subtracting total direct costs from total product sales. The result is a measure of how much each product contributes to all other expenses and overall corporate profitability. Direct costs to be subtracted can be either variable and fixed *or* only variable. Subtraction of only variable costs is preferable for planning and control purposes, since it provides a measure of product profitability that should directly vary with unit sales. We adopt the approach of subtracting only variable costs for two reasons—one practical and one theoretical. On a practical basis it is easier for marketing managers to control product profitability within a framework that directly associates changes in volume with product profitability. On a theoretical basis, fixed costs, especially programmed fixed costs, require a unique control framework (Horngren, 1977).

Planning vs. Performance Factors

Control cannot be exercised unless a plan exists. Thus the product manager will need to forecast the economic, social, and competitive environments, over the planning horizon, to develop a planned contribution margin. At the end of the period for which the planning horizon extended, the product manager can compare the *actual* contribution margin obtained with the *planned* contribution margin. But to exercise control the product manager needs to be able to identify and isolate the factors that explain the gap between planned and actual contribution margin. We believe there are seventeen identifiable and measurable factors, which we portray in Exhibit 1.

Examination of the first branch in Exhibit 1 shows that actual contribution margins can be different from planned contribution margins because of errors in planning and/or performance-related factors. Product planning variances will occur when the actual environments experienced (i.e., social, economic, competitive, etc.) are different from those anticipated and/or forecast during the initial planning process. The increased level of uncertainty and turbulence in all the external environments of the firm make planning variances of some magnitude a contemporary fact of life for the marketing executive. The initial plan can never incorporate all events that may unfold in the external environments that could affect a product's performance. Or events may be foreseen but the product manager may be unable to pinpoint their timing or the severity of their impact upon product performance. Thus the product manager needs an *adaptive plan* which specifies achievable levels of performance for the environmental conditions actually experienced as opposed to the conditions which had been forecast prior to the planning period. Such a plan is adaptive in the sense that it is developed after the reporting period in order to incorporate information about the business conditions that existed during that period. Nevertheless, an adaptive plan is still a plan in the sense that it is based on anticipated

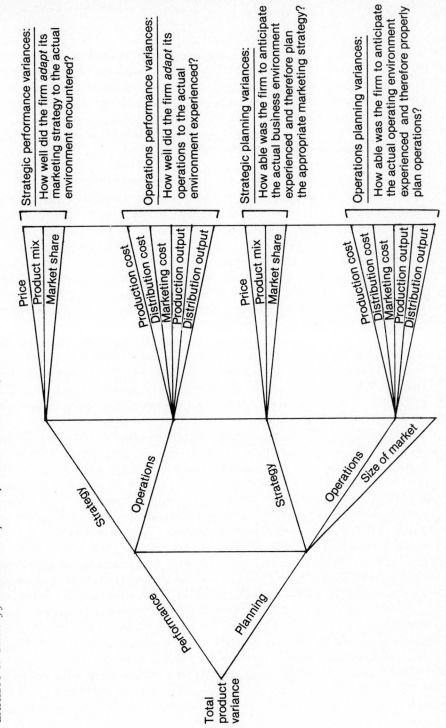

EXHIBIT 1. Causes of failure to achieve planned product contribution margin

Total product variance

Performance

Planning

Strategy

Operations

Strategy

Operations

Size of market

Strategic performance variances:

How well did the firm *adapt* its marketing strategy to the actual environment encountered?

Price
Product mix
Market share

Operations performance variances:

How well did the firm *adapt* its operations to the actual environment experienced?

Production cost
Distribution cost
Marketing cost
Production output
Distribution output

Strategic planning variances:

How able was the firm to anticipate the actual business environment experienced and therefore plan the appropriate marketing strategy?

Price
Product mix
Market share

Operations planning variances:

How able was the firm to anticipate the actual operating environment experienced and therefore properly plan operations?

Production cost
Distribution cost
Marketing cost
Production output
Distribution output

responses to changes in the business environment which evolved during the period, not on *ad hoc* rationalizations, based on hindsight, of what should have been done.

Product performance variances, on the other hand, are intended to portray how well a product performed in the environment actually experienced. Performance is thus assessed by comparing actual results with performance levels specified in the adaptive plan. Thus the performance variance summarizes how well the product manager was able to adapt to the actual environment.

Strategic vs. Operating Factors

Referring back to Exhibit 1 it can be seen that both performance and planning variances can be further subdivided into strategic and operating factors. We believe it will be useful for the product manager to recognize the difference between strategic and operating factors.

Typically a firm's marketing strategy involves some unique combination of product, price, promotion and place to attract identified target markets. Strategic failure or success in regard to planned contribution margins for a product can be related to pricing, product, mix, and market share factors. This is, if the firm's combination of the four P's is not proper, then the firm will not be able to obtain the *price* it should have, the *market share* it could have obtained, or the most profitable *product mix*. Now we certainly recognize that marketing strategy can be evaluated in terms of many other factors besides price, market share, and product mix; but, nonetheless, these factors are reasonable surrogates for most others and, as will be shown shortly, can be formally related to a framework for controlling product profitability.

Besides strategic factors, product profitability can be related to how well operations are managed. The firm may have a great strategy, properly executed; however, day-to-day operations may not be well managed. Operations management can be most directly tied to cost and output management. The major cost management areas for a product are (1) production costs, (2) distribution costs (order filling), and (3) marketing costs (order getting). The management of these costs will directly and immediately influence product profitability. Output management relates to production and distribution. Failure to adequately manage production facilities can result in the inability to produce the output that marketing is capable of selling. This production failure could be due to a variety of factors such as failure to obtain adequate raw materials, labor strikes, weather patterns, etc. At the same time distribution facilities may not be properly managed. The products may be produced; the customers may order them; however, distribution may fail to deliver them. A multitude of variables, such as a strike, poor fleet scheduling and routing, or failure of an automated warehouse, may cause this unfortunate circumstance.

The distinction between strategic and operating management has been made by Kollat et al. (1972). In terms of product planning and control this distinction is especially useful because distinct individuals tend to be responsible for strategic management vs. operations management. For example, in most firms the managers responsible for production costs and output or distribution costs are not those responsible for managing the optimal product mix, price or market share strategy. However, even if the same individual were responsible for strategic and operating functions, s/he would have a need for information which revealed how good a job s/he was doing in each area. In short, the partitioning of the difference between planned and actual performance, as presented in Exhibit 1, allows the manager to isolate problem areas in strategic and/or operating areas.

Four Types of Variances

With these general concepts in mind, we can examine the third branch of Exhibit 1 and see that there are four major types of variances that can be used to explain the difference between planned and actual product contribution margin. *Strategic performance variances* tell us how well the firm adapted its strategic factors of price, product mix and market share to the actual environment encountered. *Operating performance variances* capture how well the firm adapted its operating factors (as reflected in production, distribution and marketing costs and production and distribution output) to the actual environment experienced. *Strategic planning variances* reflect how well the firm was able to anticipate the actual business environment that unfolded and therefore plan the appropriate pricing, product mix and market share strategy. Finally, *operations planning variances* allow one to evaluate how well the firm anticipated the actual operating environment experienced and therefore properly planned production, distribution and marketing costs and production and distribution output.

Size of Market

In addition to the strategic and operating factors mentioned in Exhibit 1, another factor that could influence product profitability, but that is usually beyond management's control, is the overall size of the market. In Exhibit 1 the size of market variance is shown along the planning variance branch. The market may be larger or smaller than planned, and this uncontrollable factor should be taken into consideration when evaluating product profitability. Although size of market is usually beyond management's control in oligopolistic and monopolized industries, the size of market can be influenced by managerial and competitive actions. However, regardless of industry structure it is important to be able to isolate a "size of market" variance. In each application of our model the analyst needs to determine the extent of control, if any, which management has over the size of market.

With the preceding general concepts in mind, a formal framework will be presented for assessing planning, performance, strategic and operating variables and their quantitative impact on product profitability.

The General Framework

As an overview the general framework for analyzing the difference between planned and actual product contribution margin will parallel the seventeen variances outlined in Exhibit 1. The computational formulas will be presented in conjunction with an example. The illustration involves the tire industry. The tire industry can be divided into several meaningful components or markets. For purposes of this discussion we will be referring to the passenger car replacement tire market. Both the company (Hulbert and Toy Tire Company) and the data we refer to are hypothetical. But the types of products and industry setting are realistic and therefore allow us to make meaningful the types of things and/or events which can cause variances in distribution costs, pricing strategy, product mix, etc.

The illustration involves three product lines—bias ply, bias belt and radial tires. Industry trade sources (Modern Tire Dealer, 1979) identify these three product lines as comprising the passenger car replacement tire market. These three products are partial substitutes for each other; thus sales of the three tire types are interdependent. The example is for a single time period and uses the data contained in Exhibits 2(a), (b), (c).

Exhibit 2(a) provides the annual profit plan for passenger car replacement tires for the Hulbert and Toy Tire Company for the year ending December 31, 198X. This profit plan was based upon the firm's best estimate of developments in the

EXHIBIT 2(a). Hulbert and Toy Tire Company profit plan—passenger car replacement tires for the year ending December 31, 198X

Data	Tire type			
	Bias ply	Bias belt	Radial	Totals
Sales (000's of units)				
Market	55,000	37,000	68,000	160,000
H. T. Company	4,400	3,700	10,200	18,300
Market share (%)	8.00000	10.00000	15.00000	11.4375
Unit price	20.50	28.75	39.00	
Unit variable costs				
Production	8.20	10.90	12.10	
Distribution	1.00	1.00	1.00	
Marketing	.75	.80	1.20	
Unit contribution margin	10.55	16.05	24.70	
Loss in unit sales due to:				
Production malfunctions	2	1	1	
Distribution bottlenecks	0	0	800	
Product mix (%)	24.04372	20.21858	55.73770	

EXHIBIT 2(b). Hulbert and Toy Tire Company adaptive profit plan—passenger car replacement tires for the year ending December 31, 198X

	Tire type			
Data	Bias ply	Bias belt	Radial	Totals
Sales (000's of units)				
Market	50,000	39,000	74,000	163,000
H. T. Company	4,000	3,900	11,655	19,555
Market share (%)	8.00000	10.00000	15.75000	11.99693
Unit price	20.25	28.60	39.00	
Unit variable costs				
Production	8.36	10.90	12.35	
Distribution	1.05	1.05	1.12	
Marketing	.80	.84	1.22	
Unit contribution margin	10.04	15.81	24.31	
Loss in unit sales due to:				
Production malfunctions	1	1	150	
Distribution bottlenecks	0	0	800	
Product mix (%)	20.45513	19.94375	59.60112	

EXHIBIT 2(c). Hulbert and Toy Tire Company selected operating results—passenger car replacement tires for the year ending December 31, 198X

	Tire type			
Data	Bias ply	Bias belt	Radial	Totals
Sales (000's pf units)				
Market	50,000	39,000	74,000	163,000
H. T. Company	3,875	3,822	11,285	18,982
Market share (%)	7.75000	9.80000	15.25000	11.64540
Unit price	20.10	28.75	39.00	
Unit variable costs				
Production	8.40	10.90	12.35	
Distribution	1.05	1.05	1.15	
Marketing	.75	.80	1.20	
Unit contribution margin	9.90	16.00	24.30	
Loss in unit sales due to:				
Production malfunctions	1	1	200	
Distribution bottlenecks	0	0	800	
Product mix (%)	20.41408	20.13486	59.45106	

external and internal environments of the firm and how the firm would respond to those developments. It is not unusual for a company to develop an annual profit plan, by product line, similar to that shown in Exhibit 2(a).

In Exhibit 2(b) an adaptive profit plan is presented for each of the respective products. One of the most important concepts in the general framework is that of an adaptive plan. Adaptive plans are developed after the close of the reporting period for which the initial plan was developed. The adaptive plan lets management answer this question: If I had known at the beginning of the planning period what I knew at the end, what would have been my plan? A distinction between the original plan and the adaptive plan is crucial since it allows us to isolate planning variances. Although most companies develop initial plans, few develop a *formal* adaptive plan. Obviously a firm generally adapts its strategy and operations to changing business conditions. But few companies formally sit down at the end of the reporting period and go back and analyze unanticipated occurrences in the environment to assess how these occurrences should have affected strategy and operations as opposed to how they did affect strategy and operations. Credible adaptive plans, such as the one shown in Exhibit 2(b), are not easy to develop. In developing adaptive plans there is a tendency for executives to rationalize (*ex post facto*) that they properly adjusted their strategy and operations to the unanticipated environmental conditions that developed. If they did properly adjust, then all variances would be planning variances—an unlikely occurrence. In general it can be said that adaptive profit plans are currently not in use in many companies. Perhaps the framework developed herein will give companies a more justifiable reason for developing adaptive plans and/or will encourage researchers to investigate methods for developing valid adaptive plans.

Exhibit 2(c) presents data on selected operating results for the year ending December 31, 198X for passenger car replacement tires for the Hulbert and Toy Tire Company. The data in Exhibit 2(c) represents actual operating data and is the type of data many companies use to assess their performance in comparison to planned results. However, in the framework to be developed performance variances will be isolated by comparing actual results with the performance levels specified in the adaptive plan, not in the initial plan.

Total Product Variance

The analysis begins by examining the total product variance. For the case at hand only radial tires will be examined in detail; however, the results for bias ply and bias belt tires are presented in summary form in Exhibit 3.[1] The total profit variance for radial tires can be computed as follows:

---

[1] Due to rounding errors any of the computations in Exhibit 3 and the body of this paper may be off by as much as $1.

$$(Q_aC_a - Q_pC_p) = (11,285,000 \times \$24.30 - 10,200,000 \times \$24.70) \qquad (1)$$
$$= \$22,285,500 \text{ (favorable)}$$

where Q denotes quantity in units, C denotes contribution margin per unit, a denotes actual and p denotes planned. (Exhibit 4 provides a summary of the notation used in the formulas.) A positive total variance depicts a favorable situation (i.e., profits higher than planned) and a negative variance indicates an unfavorable result (i.e., profits lower than planned). Since the total profit variance for radial tires is favorable and quite large, one might conclude that management has done an excellent job. Our decomposition of this total variance will show that this conclusion is incorrect.

EXHIBIT 3. *Planning and performance variance for Hulbert and Toy Tire Company—passenger car replacement tires for the year ended December 31, 198X*

Item	Variance Performance	Variance Planning	Variance totals	Reconciliation
Total planned contri-bution margin				$357,745,000
Bias ply tires				
Strategic				
Price	−581,250	−1,000,000		
Product mix	1,206,979	3,599,564		
Market share	−2,461,979	19,549		
Total strategic	−1,836,250	2,619,113	782,863	
Operational costs				
Production	−155,000	−640,000		
Distribution	∅	−200,000		
Marketing	193,750	−200,000		
Total costs	38,750	−1,040,000		
Output				
Production	∅	−19,549		
Distribution	∅	∅		
Total output	∅	−19,549		
Total operational	38,750	−1,059,549	−1,020,799	
Market size	N/A	−7,819,564	−7,819,564	
TOTAL BIAS PLY TIRES	−1,797,500	−6,260,000		−8,057,500
Bias belt tires				
Strategic				
Price	573,300	−585,000		
Product mix	303,095	−699,782		
Market share	−1,536,275	∅		
Total strategic	−659,880	−1,284,782	−1,944,662	

EXHIBIT 3 (cont.)

Item	Variance		Variance totals	Reconciliation
	Performance	Planning		
Operational costs				
Production	∅	∅		
Distribution	∅	−195,000		
Marketing	152,880	−156,000		
Total costs	152,880	−351,000		
Output				
Production	∅	∅		
Distribution	∅	∅		
Total output	∅	∅		
Total operational	152,880	−351,000	−198,120	
Market size	N/A	3,909,782	3,909,782	
TOTAL BIAS BELT TIRES	−507,000	2,274,000		1,767,000
Radial tires				
Strategic				
Price	∅	∅		
Product mix	−1,707,243	7,494,836		
Market share	−6,302,666	7,936,858		
Total strategic	−8,009,909	15,431,694	7,421,785	
Operational costs				
Production	∅	−2,913,750		
Distribution	−338,550	−1,398,600		
Marketing	225,700	−233,100		
Total costs	−112,850	−4,545,450		
Output				
Production	−984,792	2,912,788		
Distribution	∅	∅		
Total output	−984,792	2,912,788		
Total operational	−1,097,642	−1,632,662	−2,730,304	
Market size	N/A	17,594,019	17,594,019	
TOTAL RADIAL TIRES	−9,107,551	31,393,051		22,285,500
Total variance	−11,412,051	27,407,051		
Actual contribution				$373,740,000

EXHIBIT 4. Variable definitions

Variable notation	Variable definition
Price	
P_a	Actual price per unit
P_r	Adaptive plan price per unit
P_p	Planned price per unit
Quantity	
Q_a	Actual quantity
Q_r	Adaptive plan quantity
Q_p	Planned quantity
Contribution margin	
C_a	Actual contribution margin per unit
C_r	Adaptive plan contribution margin per unit
C_p	Planned contribution margin per unit
Market share	
S_a	Actual market share
S_r	Adaptive plan market share
S_p	Planned market share
Market size	
M_a	Actual market size
M_r	Adaptive plan market size
M_p	Planned market size
Marketing costs	
V_{am}	Actual variable marketing cost per unit
V_{rm}	Adaptive plan variable marketing cost per unit
V_{pm}	Planned variable marketing cost per unit
Production costs	
V_{ap}	Actual variable production cost per unit
V_{rp}	Adaptive plan variable production cost per unit
V_{pp}	Planned variable production cost per unit
Distribution costs	
V_{ad}	Actual variable distribution cost per unit
V_{rd}	Adaptive plan variable distribution cost per unit
V_{pd}	Planned variable distribution cost per unit
Loss in production output	
Q_{lap}	Actual loss in output due to production
Q_{lrp}	Adaptive plan loss in output due to production
Q_{lpp}	Planned loss in output due to production
Loss in distribution output	
Q_{lad}	Actual loss in output due to distribution
Q_{lrd}	Adaptive plan loss in output due to distribution
Q_{lpd}	Planned loss in output due to distribution
Weighted contribution margin	
$\bar{C}_r$	Adaptive plan weighted contribution margin per unit
$\bar{C}_p$	Planned weighted contribution margin per unit

While of some interest, the total variance is of little value for product control purposes. The objective is to isolate the portions of the total variance that can be associated with the factors that caused the variance. For the illustration at hand, it will be demonstrated that the total product variance that has just been outlined can be traced to a combination of planning and performance factors. In particular, these planning and performance factors can be traced to strategic and operating factors, as was previously illustrated in Exhibit 1. The strategic and operating factors will be more completely dealt with once the planning versus performance distinction has been clarified.

Planning vs. Performance

The distinction between "planning" variances and "performance" variances is made possible by the development of an adaptive plan. If the environment were perfectly predictable then no adaptive plan would be necessary and any difference between planned and actual results would be due to performance factors. Unfortunately, future environments are not perfectly predictable and therefore management needs to adapt their original plan to the actual environment. In many cases the information required by an adaptive plan is readily available from trade-association and industry sources. In other cases, the adaptive plan may reflect a number of judgmental estimates in the absence of reliable statistics. The usefulness of an adaptive plan in marketing is further illustrated by Hulbert and Toy (1977).

Once an adaptive plan has been developed (as shown in Exhibit 2(b)), the total variance as shown in equation 1 can be partitioned to reflect planning and performance factors as follows:

Performance variance
$$(Q_a C_a - Q_r C_r) = (11,285,000 \times \$24.30 - 11,655,000 \times \$24.31) \qquad (2.1)$$
$$= -\$9,107,551 \quad \text{(unfavorable)}$$

Planning variance
$$(Q_r C_r \times Q_p C_p) = (11,655,000 \times \$24.31 - 10,200,000 \times \$24.70) \qquad (2.2)$$
$$= \$31,393,051$$

The subscript r denotes the adaptive plan.

Immediately the product or marketing manager for radial tires, even at this early stage of decomposing the total variance, is able to begin to see in an informative light how good or bad results actually were. For example, we saw overall that radial tires had a favorable variance of \$22,285,500 (equation 1). However, by isolating performance and planning factors it can be shown that, given the environment experienced, profits on radial tires could have been \$31,393,051 higher than initially planned; and therefore, since profits were only \$22,285,500 higher than planned, the company actually had poor performance in the radial tire market as measured by the unfavorable performance variance of \$9,107,551 (\$31,393,051–22,285,500).

That is, the Hulbert and Toy Tire Company failed to perform as well as it could have in the production, distribution and marketing of radial tires.

Let's reflect a moment on the interpretation of planning and performance variances at this macrolevel. The planning variance, whether positive or negative, can have an unfavorable impact. A positive planning variance may result in lost contribution margin due to an underestimation of the attractiveness of the business environment. A negative planning variance may result in unnecessary costs because of an over-estimation of the attractiveness of the environment. Thus, ideally, the planning variance should be close to zero. The net impact of planning (forecasting) errors depends on the ability of the firm to adapt to the changing conditions, which is reflected in the performance variance.

A positive performance variance, at this macrolevel, is favorable because it indicates that the company has achieved a higher total contribution margin for a product than the actual environment warranted. A negative variance, however, would be unfavorable since it depicts a situation in which the actual total contribution margin for a product is less than the firm should have achieved in the environment actually experienced.

Decomposition of Planning Variance

The prior analysis still does not provide the product manager with the maximal amount of information available. We know that the planning department should be held accountable for the $31,393,051 planning variance—however, where did they go wrong in their planning? A decomposition of the planning variance can allow us to answer this question.

Strategic Plannning Variances.   Errors in strategic planning that are directly tied to the contribution margin are centered around price, product mix and market share. The price planning variance is computed as follows:[2]

$$(P_r - P_p)Q_r = (\$39.00 - \$39.00)\ 11,655,000 \qquad (3.1)$$
$$= \$0$$

where P stands for price per unit. Since the price initially planned was identical to the best price, given the actual environment experienced, a zero price planning variance resulted.

A second strategic planning factor is product mix. The product mix planning variance is:

$$(Q_r - Q_p)(C_p - \bar{C}_p) = (11,655,000 - 10,200,000)(\$24.70 - \$19.54891) \quad (3.2)$$
$$= \$7,494,836$$

---

[2] From this point forward the reader will not lose the thrust of the article if s/he skips the computational formulas and only reads the narrative.

where $\bar{C}_p$ is the weighted average contribution margin based on the initial plan and can be computed as follows:

$$\bar{C}_p = C_{p1}\left(\frac{Q_{p1}}{Q_{p1} + Q_{p2} + Q_{p3}}\right) + C_{p2}\left(\frac{Q_{p2}}{Q_{p1} + Q_{p2} + Q_{p3}}\right)$$
$$+ C_{p3}\left(\frac{Q_{p3}}{Q_{p1} + Q_{p2} + Q_{p3}}\right) \qquad (3.2.1)$$

$$= \$10.55\ (.2404372) + \$16.05\ (.2021858) + \$24.70\ (.5573770)$$
$$= \$19.54891$$

where C_{p1}, C_{p2} and C_{p3} refer to the planned contribution margin per unit for bias ply, bias belt and radial tires respectively. The weighted average contribution margin $\bar{C}_p$ shows what the average contribution margin for the three types of tires would be if they were sold in the originally planned mix.

As shown in (3.2), more unit sales and production of radial tires should have been planned, *ex post facto*, than were initially planned. Since radial tires are more profitable than either bias ply or bias belt tires, the Hulbert and Toy Tire Company should have planned for an additional contribution margin of $7,494,836 (see equation 3.2). Therefore, because of errors in planning the product mix, the original plan was shy by $7,494,836 in contribution margin dollars of what it should have been. The individuals responsible for planning product mix should be informed of this. These individuals might be asked to identify the environmental factors that they had not anticipated and how these factors impacted upon the ideal product mix. For example, perhaps consumers shifted more to a preference for radial tires than the Hulbert and Toy Company had initially anticipated. But once this shift occurred, it was only natural that the firm place more emphasis on radial tires, given the company's historic leadership in this market.

Finally, a third strategic planning factor is market share. Market share is being increasingly monitored in today's contemporary environment and represents a major strategic goal of many firms (Buzzell et al., 1974; Catry and Chevalias, 1974; Fogg, 1974). The market share planning variance can be computed as follows:

$$[(S_r - S_p)M_r - (Q_{lrp} - Q_{lpp}) - (Q_{lrd} - Q_{lpd})]\bar{C}_p$$
$$= [(.1575 - .15)\ 74{,}000{,}000 - (150 - 1) - (800 - 800)]\ \$19.54891 \qquad (3.3)$$
$$= \$7{,}936{,}858$$

where S is market share, M is market size, Q_{lrp} is loss in quantity sold due to production problems based on the adaptive plan, Q_{lpp} is loss in quantity sold due to production problems based on the original plan, Q_{lrd} is loss in quantity sold due to distribution problems based on the adaptive plan, and Q_{lpd} is loss in quantity sold due to distribution problems based on the original plan. Formula (3.3) captures and isolates errors in planning market share and adjusts for any loss in market share that could be traced to production and/or distribution problems given the environment actually experienced. Thus the planned market share variance reflects only marketing factors since production and distribution bottlenecks have been washed out of (3.3). The variance of $7,936,858 tells the marketing controller that an additional contribution margin in the preceding amount should have been planned in view of the market share that the Hulbert and Toy Tire Company should have been able to attain in the radial tire market given the environment actually encountered. Those responsible for planning market share should be asked to analyze and explain the unanticipated developments that occurred in the business environment that called for the firm to aim for a higher market share in radial tires than initially planned. Perhaps as more households shifted to radials for replacement tires than anticipated, several companies in the industry were unable to immediately expand radial production. However, since the Hulbert and Toy Tire Company was one of the few firms in the industry able to expand radial production, they were in an opportune position to gain market share.

Operational Planning Variances. In addition to strategic planning factors, operations need also to be managed and controlled. The operating dimensions most directly tied to contribution margin are costs and output factors. The computational formulas for decomposing operational factors into cost and output will be presented next.

The variable costs of a product are related to three basic functions: (1) production, (2) distribution (order filling), and (3) marketing (order getting). Predictably, errors can arise in planning or budgeting these costs. The three respective planning variances for production, distribution and marketing costs for radial tires are:

Production costs

$$(V_{pp} - V_{rp})Q_r = (\$12.10 - \$12.35)11,655,000 \qquad (4.1.1)$$
$$= -\$2,913,750$$

Distribution costs

$$(V_{pd} - V_{rd})Q_r = (\$1.00 - \$1.12)11,655,000 \qquad (4.1.2)$$
$$= -\$1,398,600$$

Marketing costs

$$(V_{pm} - V_{rm})Q_r = (\$1.20 - \$1.22)11,655,000 \qquad (4.1.3)$$
$$= -\$233,100$$

where V stands for variable costs. The variable production cost per unit that the Hulbert and Toy Tire Company initially planned was $.25 lower than what the actual business environment warranted. As a consequence the company should have planned their total contribution margin on radial tires to be lower by $2,913,750. At the same time both distribution and marketing costs were too conservative for the environment actually experienced. As a result the Hulbert and Toy Tire Company should have planned the total contribution margin to be lower by $1,398,600 because of higher distribution costs and \$233,100 lower because of higher marketing costs.

Those individuals who plan production, distribution and marketing costs should be provided with the results of these variances and asked to explain the factors that unfolded in the business environment that caused them.

A second operating area relates to being able to deliver and produce the output that marketing is able to generate a demand for. Typically we would hope that production and distribution would be able to produce and deliver what marketing is able to sell; however, this is not always the case. Problems may arise because of the environment experienced. The planning variances related to production and distribution output for radial tires are as follows:

Production output

$$(Q_{lrp} - Q_{lpp})\bar{C}_p = (150,000 - 1,000)\$19.54891 \qquad (4.2.1)$$
$$= \$2,912,788$$

Distribution output

$$(Q_{lrd} - Q_{lpd})\bar{C}_p = (800,000 - 800,000)\$19.54891 \qquad (4.2.2)$$
$$= \$0$$

Note that the concept of the weighted average contribution margin is used in the output variances since the products are partial substitutes and because we desire to hold product mix constant since its effect was isolated in (3.2). Also notice that the production and distribution output planning variances are the two components that were washed out of the market share planning variance in (3.3). The individuals planning production and distribution, not those planning market share, should be held accountable for these variances. In short, those planning market share should be able to assume that production and distribution should be able to produce and deliver what marketing can sell (given sufficient lead time).

The \$2,912,788 production output planning variance for radial tires indicates how much contribution margins were overestimated because production planners were unable to anticipate 149,000 units of lost production output. What occurred in the operating environment to justify the production loss of an additional 149,000 radial tires? This is the question production planners must answer. In principle it could have been due to any number of unanticipated occurrences, such as a temporary power loss, abnormal machine malfunctions, or an unexpected shortage of raw materials.

Planning Market Size.   Changes in the size of the market, from that originally planned, are not generally due to performance factors but only to the firm's inability to precisely plan and correctly anticipate all environmental factors which might influence market size. There will of course be instances where collective action (such as the lowering of prices) by a group of firms in an industry will expand the total size of the market, but rarely will an individual firm be able to have a noticeable impact on the overall size of the market. Thus the market size variance was only considered under the planning dimension in Exhibit 1. The market size variance for radial tires for the Hulbert and Toy Tire Company is:

$$(M_r - M_p)S_p\bar{C}_p = (74,000,000 - 68,000,000)(.15)\$19.54891 \qquad (5)$$
$$= \$17,594,019$$

In this formula we use planned market share and planned average contribution margin since in other formulas (3.2 and 3.3) the impact of changes in market share and product mix were isolated. Formula (5) isolates the effect of changes in market size only, and in the case at hand it clearly reveals that because of an increase in the overall size of the radial tire market, from 68 million to 74 million tires, the total contribution margin from radial tires for the Hulbert and Toy Tire Company should have been planned at a $17,594,019 higher level.

A Recap of the Planning Variance.   In summary it has been shown that the Hulbert and Toy Tire Company should have planned an additional $31,393,051 contribution margin for radial tires. A useful summary of the planning variances for radial tires is presented in the second column of the bottom third of Exhibit 3. In terms of strategic planning, if the firm had been able to properly assess the environment and accordingly plan price, product mix and market share appropriately, an additional $15,431,694 in profit would have been planned. In regard to planning operations, if the correct environment had been forecast then better cost and output planning would have called for the total contribution margin for radial tires to be lower by $1,632,662. Finally, if the size of the radial tire market had been correctly anticipated then an added $17,594,019 in profit would have been planned. In recap form, the Hulbert and Toy Tire Company should have been able to earn an extra $31,393,051 (15,431,694 − 1,632,662 + 17,594,019) over their original plan—given the environment they experienced. Since they earned only $22,285,500 over their plan we know that performance wasn't what it should have been to the tune of $9,107,551 ($31,393,051 − $22,285,500). It is this $9,107,551 *unfavorable* performance variance that will now be analyzed in more detail.

Decomposition of Performance Variance

Overall we know that management has performed poorly in the environment experienced. Let's examine how strategic and operational performance can be assessed.

Strategic Performance Variances.   The firm's strategic performance for radial tires in terms of contribution margin can be formally tied to price, product mix and market share factors. The price performance variance can be computed as follows:

$$(P_a - P_r)Q_a = (\$39.00 - \$39.00)11,285,000 \qquad (6.1)$$
$$= \$0$$

where the subscript a denotes actual. The firm achieved the price they should have
and thus the price performance variance for radial tires was $0. In general, for
performance price variances, a negative variance is unfavorable and a positive
variance is favorable. If the variance is negative (unfavorable) then the price of the
product has been cut too much and thus contribution margins have suffered. On
the other hand, a positive (favorable) variance represents a situation where prices
charged were actually higher than the environment warranted. Importantly,
however, all strategic performance factors need to be viewed collectively since they
are not independent even though mathematically we have isolated their impact on
product profitability. For example, a favorable strategic performance price variance
may be more than offset by an unfavorable strategic performance market share
variance (possibly caused by charging prices higher than conditions warranted).

A second strategic performance factor is product mix. The variance formula for
evaluating this factor is:

$$(Q_a - Q_r)(C_r - \bar{C}_r) = (11,285,000 - 11,655,000)(\$24.31 - \$19.69583) \quad (6.2)$$
$$= -\$1,707,243 \quad \text{(unfavorable)}$$

For the example at hand we see that fewer radial tires were sold than should have
been, *and* since radials were the most profitable of the three product lines an
unfavorable variance in the magnitude of $1,707,243 arose. Positive performance
variances for product mix will be favorable and negative variances will be
unfavorable.

The last strategic performance factor that can be isolated is market share. This
variance shows the impact of not being able to achieve the market share that should
have been obtained in the environment experienced. This variance is computed as:

$$[(S_a - S_r)M_a + (Q_{lap} - Q_{lrp}) + (Q_{lad} - Q_{lrd})]\bar{C}_r$$
$$= [(.1525 - .1575)74,000,000 + (200,000 - 150,000)$$
$$+ (800,000 - 800,000)]\$19.69583$$
$$= -\$6,302,666 \quad \text{(unfavorable)}$$

The market share performance variance is adjusted for the change in market share
due to production and/or distribution output performance factors being more or
less of a problem than was recognized in the adaptive plan. This variance therefore
represents failure or success on the part of the marketing department in achieving
the market share the environment warranted. In the case at hand failure to achieve
a better market share in the radial tire market resulted in an unfavorable variance
of $6,302,666. Or put another way, if the firm had achieved a 15.75% vs. 15.25%
market share, their profits would have risen $6,302,666 *ceteris paribus*. The

marketing manager should be required to explain why a 15.75% share of the radial tire market was not achieved by the Hulbert and Toy Tire Company.

Operating Performance Variances. If costs and production and distribution output are not properly managed then total product contribution margins may also suffer. The major variable costs that must be controlled revolve around the functional areas of production, distribution and marketing. The measures that can be used to control these costs are:

Production costs

$$(V_{rp} - V_{ap})Q_a = (\$12.35 - \$12.35)11,285,000 \qquad (7.1.1)$$
$$= \$0$$

Distribution costs

$$(V_{rd} - V_{ad})Q_a = (\$1.12 - \$1.15)11,285,000 \qquad (7.1.2)$$
$$= -\$338,550 \quad \text{(unfavorable)}$$

Marketing costs

$$(V_{rm} - V_{am})Q_a = (\$1.22 - \$1.20)11,285,000 \qquad (7.1.3)$$
$$= \$225,700 \quad \text{(favorable)}$$

As formulated, all performance cost variances that are negative are unfavorable and all positive variances are favorable. An examination of the three preceding variances reveals that: (1) production costs were in control, which resulted in no loss of contribution margins; (2) distribution costs were out of control, which resulted in lost contribution margins of \$338,550; and (3) since marketing costs were lower than could have been expected, the result was favorable in the amount of \$225,700. The importance of separately analyzing costs in these three functional areas is dramatically revealed in this example. If we summed the three cost components (production, distribution and marketing) then costs would appear to be reasonably well in control. This, however, is misleading since, as has been illustrated, distribution costs were too high, marketing costs were favorably lower and production costs right on target. Aggregate results can be misleading!

Another area of operational control in the performance area is the management of production and distribution output. We attempt to answer the question—how well did production and distribution do in producing and delivering the output marketing was capable of selling? The two relevant variances are:

Production output

$$-(Q_{lap} - Q_{lrp})\bar{C}_r = -(200,000 - 150,000)\$19.69583 \qquad (7.2.1)$$
$$= -\$984,792 \quad \text{(unfavorable)}$$

Distribution output

$$-(Q_{lad} - Q_{lrd})\bar{C}_r = -(800{,}000 - 800{,}000)\$19.69583 \qquad (7.2.2)$$
$$= \$0$$

When these variances are negative they show that either production or distribution has caused more lost sales than it should have in the environment experienced. On the other hand, a positive variance would be favorable since it depicts a situation where either production or distribution caused fewer sales to be lost than could have been expected according to the adaptive plan. For radial tires the production output variance was unfavorable and for distribution output no variance existed.

A Recap of the Performance Variance. In summary, the unfavorable performance variance of \$9,107,551 was due in most part to poor strategic performance. Because of product mix not weighted heavily enough in favor of radial tires and a market share in the radial tire market below what could have been attained, the Hulbert and Toy Tire Company experienced an unfavorable strategic variance of \$8,009,909. On the operations side of the business production costs were in control, while distribution costs were too high and marketing costs were below what they could have been. Distribution bottlenecks were not in excess of what the environment warranted; however, there were more than the normal problems in managing production output and thus performance in this area was below standard. The net impact of poor operations management was an unfavorable variance of \$1,097,642. This unfavorable variance of \$1,097,642, due to operating problems, when combined with the unfavorable strategic variance of \$8,009,909, explains the total unfavorable performance variance of \$9,107,551. Exhibit 3 provides the summary data on the performance variances for radial tires. The variances for bias ply and bias belt tires are also included in Exhibit 3 for the interested reader.

Discussion and Conclusions

The preceding has not been just an interesting exercise in decomposing variances. On the contrary, we have attempted to illustrate that a wide array of product control information can be related to the comparison of planned versus actual product profitability. It is possible, as illustrated, to separately evaluate the planning and performance areas and to further evaluate strategic and operational factors. The approach highlights the importance of price, product mix and market share in controlling product profitability. At the same time the importance of controlling production, distribution and marketing costs is stressed. Further, the model isolates the problems that could be due to production or distribution bottlenecks. Finally, the impact of changes in market size from that initially planned is evaluated. In short, a general framework that requires reasonable data inputs is available to product managers, marketing executives and controllers for evaluating product profitability.

The model, although not completely comprehensive, does include in a systematic and quantitative fashion more variables than existing product evaluation frameworks. If the marketing executive combines insight and market intuition with the quantitative results of the model then product profitability should benefit in the long run.

Note: We are grateful to James M. Hulbert and Norman E. Toy for their article (Hulbert and Toy, 1977) which stimulated our thinking in this area and had a major impact on the framework we developed.

References

1. Buzzell, Robert D., Bradley T. Gale, and Ralph G. M. Sulton (1974), "Market Share—A Key to Profitability," *Harvard Business Review*, 53 (January-February), 97–106.
2. Catry, Bernard, and Michael Chevalias (1974), "Market Share Strategy and the Product Life Cycle," *Journal of Marketing*, 38 (October), 29–34.
3. Fogg, David C. (1974), "Planning Gains in Market Share," *Journal of Marketing*, 38 (July), 30–38.
4. Horngren, Charles T. (1977), *Introduction to Management Accounting* (Englewood Cliffs, New Jersey: Prentice-Hall, Inc.), 4th edition.
5. Hulbert, James M., and Norman E. Toy (1977), "A Strategic Framework for Marketing," *Journal of Marketing*, 41 (April), 12–20.
6. Kollat, David T., Roger D. Blackwell, and James F. Robeson (1972), *Strategic Marketing* (New York: Holt, Rinehart and Winston, Inc.).
7. Kotler, Philip (1976), *Marketing Management: Analysis, Planning and Control* (Englewood Cliffs, New Jersey: Prentice-Hall, Inc.) 3rd edition.
8. "Annual Facts/Directory Issue" (1979), *Modern Tire Dealer*, 7 (January 24).
9. Rayburn, Gayle L. (1973), "Analysis of Current Marketing Cost Methods," *The CPA Journal* (November), 985–91.
10. Shank, J. K., and N. C. Churchill (1977), "Variance Analysis: A Management-Oriented Approach," *Accounting Review*, 52 (October), 950–57.

Exercises

30.1.   The Fine Filament Company makes three grades of carpeting. A commercial grade (denoted C) is used primarily in hotels, motels, and offices. A high-quality grade (denoted RC) is used for both residential and selected commercial use. A medium-quality grade of carpeting (denoted R) is produced primarily for the residential market.

Fine Filament Company projects annual sales volume by forecasting the total market for carpeting and then multiplying this total by the proportion of the market that Fine Filament Co. expects to capture. The market share plan is based on the company's market share for the prior year, adjusted for projected market changes, and company plans for the following year. And finally, the company's share of the market is broken into projections of sales volumes for each carpet type. The result is a plan that specifies the total volume and the product mix for each planning period.

The *a priori* profit plan and the operating results for 19X9 are presented in Tables 30.1 and 30.2.

TABLE 30.1. Fine Filament Company profit plan for the year ending December 31, 19X9

| | Grade | | | |
	C	RC	R	Total
Sales (in rolls)	1,000	2,000	1,000	4,000
Per unit average:				
Sales price	$1,200	$1,800	$1,400	
Variable expense	800	900	850	
Contribution margin	$ 400	$ 900	$ 550	
Traceable fixed expenses	150	250	200	
Traceable margin	$ 250	$ 650	$ 200	

TABLE 30.2. Fine Filament Company operating results for the year ending December 31, 19X9

| | Grade | | | |
	C	RC	R	Total
Sales (in rolls)	800	2,100	1,100	4,000
Per unit amounts:				
Sales price	$1,150	$1,815	$1,425	
Variable expense	800	900	1,125	
Contribution margin	$ 350	$ 915	$ 300	
Traceable fixed expenses	150	250	220	
Traceable margin	$ 200	$ 665	$ 80	

Adaptive plan information:

- The original forecast was for a market of 100,000 rolls of carpet in the area served by Fine Filament Co.; but actual sales were 104,000 rolls, according to industry statistics.
- Because of the strong demand for carpeting during 19X9, along with inflationary pressures, carpet prices throughout the industry were 5% higher than originally forecast.

- Based on several developments during the year, Fine Filament believes it should have achieved a 4.2% share of the market, not the 4% used to develop the *a priori* profit plan.
- The relative mix should have been 22%, 50%, and 28% for grades C, RC, and R, respectively, based on the market conditions that developed during 19X9.

1. Determine the amount by which profits should have increased, based on the profit plan, as a result of the general increase in carpet prices.
2. What is the dollar impact on profits (using budgeted contribution margins) resulting from the difference between the planned product mix and the mix that should have been achieved during 19X9 according to the adaptive plan?
3. What is the dollar impact on profits (using contribution margins per the adaptive plan) resulting from the difference between the actual product mix and the mix that should have been achieved during 19X9?
4. What is the dollar impact on profits (based on planned contribution margins) of the increase in the size of the carpet market experienced during 19X9?

30.2. The Happyhour Tire Company produces bias ply, bias belted, and radial passenger car tires for both the original equipment and the replacement tire markets. The company develops an annual profit plan based on a forecast of the size of each of these markets. Once the total size of each market has been predicted, the relative sales mix of the three tire types is calculated for each market.

Next, Happyhour develops plans to achieve a specified share of the sales of each

TABLE 30.3. *Happyhour Tire Company* a priori *profit plan—passenger car replacement tires for the year ending December 31, 19X9*

	Tire type			
	Bias ply	Bias belt	Radial	Totals
Sales (000's of units):				
Market	55,500	36,500	66,000	158,000
H.T. Co.	5,550	18,250	20,600	44,400
Per tire averages ($):				
Sales price	18	26	35	29.1757
Variable expense	9	12	16	13.4809
Contribution margin	9	14	19	15.6948
Traceable fixed expenses	1	1	2	1.4640
Traceable margin	8	13	17	14.2308

TABLE 30.4. Happyhour Tire Company adaptive profit plan—passenger car replacement tires for the year ending December 31, 19X9

| | Tire type | | | |
	Bias ply	Bias belt	Radial	Totals
Sales (000's of units):				
Market	55,000	37,000	68,000	160,000
H.T. Company	5,000	18,500	23,120	46,620
Per tire averages ($):				
Sales price	17.50	26.00	37.00	30.5435
Variable expense	9.50	12.50	16.50	14.1619
Contribution margin	8.00	13.50	20.50	16.3816
Traceable fixed expenses	1.00	1.00	2.00	1.4959
Traceable margin	7.00	12.50	18.50	14.8857

Note: The adaptive plan includes an increase of $0.30/tire in variable production costs and an increase of $0.20/tire in variable distribution costs. No lost sales due to production or distribution problems are provided for in the 19X9 adaptive plan.

TABLE 30.5. Happyhour Tire Company selected operating results—passenger car replacement tires for the year ending December 31, 19X9

| | Tire type | | | |
	Bias ply	Bias belt	Radial	Totals
Sales (000's of units):				
Market	55,000	37,000	68,000	160,000
H.T. Co.	5,500	18,250	21,000	44,750
Per tire averages($):				
Sales price	17.50	25.50	36.00	
Variable expense	9.50	12.60	16.60	
Contribution margin	8.00	12.90	19.40	
Traceable fixed expenses	1.00	1.00	2.00	
Traceable margin	7.00	11.90	17.40	

Note: Production problems resulted in lost sales of 500,000 radial tires. No sales were lost on account of distribution problems.

TABLE 30.6. Planning and performance variances—Replacement market for bias ply, bias belted, and radial tires for the year ending December 31, 19X9 (in thousands of dollars)

Item	Variance Performance	Variance Planning	Variance totals	Reconciliation
Total planned contribution margin				
Bias ply tires:				
Total strategic				
Total operational				
Market size				
Total bias ply				
Bias belted tires:				
Total strategic				
Total operational				
Market size				
Total bias belted				
Radial tires:				
Strategic:				
Price				
Product mix				
Product share				
Total strategic				
Operational:				
Costs:				
Production				
Distribution				
Marketing				
Total costs				
Production output				
Total operational				
Market size				
Total radial tires				
Total variance[a]				
Total contribution margin earned				

[a] No basis exists to separate the variable cost performance variance into its production and distribution cost elements.

different tire type in the original equipment market and the replacement tire market. Because the original equipment and replacement tire markets are so different, separate market share plans must be developed for each of them. These market share plans are based on the shares achieved during the previous year, adjusted to reflect the expected effects of company plans and the market conditions forecast for the planning period.

The resulting sales volume forecasts are combined with pricing plans to develop revenue plans. These revenue plans, when merged with standard production and distribution costs, are used to complete the development of annual profit plans.

Tables 30.3, 30.4, and 30.5 present pertinent information from the *a priori* profit plan, the adaptive profit plan, and the operating results for 19X9. Both the plans and the operating results concern the production and sales of passenger car tires in the replacement tire market only.

1. Compute the total strategic, operational, and market size planning and performance variances for both bias play and bias belted tires.
2. Compute the planning and performance variances indicated in Table 30.6 for radial tires.
3. Use the format of Table 30.6 to reconcile the difference between the actual contribution margin earned in 19X9 and the amount called for in the *a priori* plan.

Recommendations for
Further Reading

Bursk, Edward C. "View Your Customers as Investments," *Harvard Business Review*, 44 (May-June 1966), 91–94.

Customers represent valuable investments of money, time, and effort. A company's investment in its customers is just as real as its investment in plant and equipment. A method of calculating the return on investment or worth of such customers is both outlined and illustrated. Examples are also provided of how different kinds of marketing action can be evaluated in terms of their effect on the net value of a company's customer-investment. That customer-investment can be a useful concept for analyzing marketing situations where the company depends on continuing patronage is clearly demonstrated.

Gane, Roger, and Nigel Spackman. "Costs and Pricing in Marketing Research," *Journal of the Market Research Society*, 14 (October 1972), 197–241.

Would widespread discrepancies in cost estimates be revealed if the results of asking a number of research firms to bid on standardized readership, product usage and group interview projects were published? If so, why would this be the case? The first paper in this special issue of the *Journal of the Market Research Society* reveals that in all three cases widespread differences in bids did exist. Representatives of "full service" and "specialized" research firms then comment on these findings and elaborate on the procedures issued in formulating their own bids. Finally, a large buyer of research discusses the appropriateness of competitive bidding both as a method of pricing research services and as a basis of choosing among suppliers.

Hogue, W. Dickerson. "What Should Market Planning Cost?" *Business Horizons*, 13 (April 1970), 61–69.

Since a marketing manager never possesses all the kinds of information that could possibly be relevant, he must decide which specific kinds of additional information and how much of that information should be collected. In making these decisions, the benefits of collecting such information must be weighed against the costs. A method of making this calculation that compares proposed expenditures with the value of improving either the estimates of the likelihood of success or failure or the payoffs associated with each outcome is first presented and then illustrated. The author also maintains that relatively successful marketers tend to overspend on planning and relatively unsuccessful ones tend to underspend. Strict adherence to costly formal planning procedures is criticized for encouraging the relative neglect of low-volume markets—either domestic or foreign—in which less spending on formal market planning would also prove profitable.

Kyle, P. W. "A Data Base for a Marketing Information System," *European Journal of Marketing*, 5 (Summer 1971), 22–29.

Problems and methods of providing firms with detailed information about their own sales and marketing costs is the author's principal concern. The traditional accounting approach, by the nature of the expenditure, has not provided sufficient information for intelligent marketing decisions.

The data base being proposed utilizes concepts familiar from marketing cost analysis. Such a system facilitates the generation of information on profitability by customer, product, or any market segment required. Anxieties about accuracy and the apparent failure to use a marginal cost approach are then discussed. Finally, it is shown that such a data base can easily be expanded into a complete marketing information system.

Myers, James H., and A. Coskun Samli. "Management Control of Marketing Research," *Journal of Marketing Research*, 6 (August 1969), 266–277.

Marketing research does not readily lend itself to control and evaluation in the traditional business management sense. Nevertheless, three areas where control or evaluation is possible are identified. First, procedures are reviewed for estimating the value of additional information to the decision maker in a manner that indicates whether marketing research is worthwhile. Considered next are methods of controlling individual research projects so that execution proceeds efficiently and costs are kept in line. Finally, means of systematically guiding and appraising the total marketing research activity are examined. Better control is necessarily related to the establishment of norms dealing with research inputs and processes.

PART IX

Organizational Barriers to
More Profitable Marketing
and Related Readings

Financially oriented tools of marketing analysis known to be in the public domain for many years are being less widely used than their potential contributions warrant. Why is this the case? Neither the data manipulation demands of the suggested techniques nor their analytical requirements pose major barriers. Computers can generate all the data conceivably required and then further process these data so as to provide any desired analytical output. The general educational level of corporate executives also continues to rise, and recent graduates of business schools should be capable of employing these new analytical tools.

Failure to consummate organizationally the corporate marriage of money and marketing may well be the most significant barrier to the increased use by marketers of financially based analytical techniques. This problem persists despite the fact that a rather substantial body of literature cries out for cooperation and/or chronicles existing shortcomings. Some of these specific appeals for meaningful interaction to deal with existing problems are reviewed in the next two sections. The many organizational barriers to more effective use by marketing of the firm's financial skills—whether such skills be housed in an accounting unit, a finance department, or the controller's office—are then examined. Attention is next shifted to the applicability of the marketing controller concept, one approach that has been recommended for bridging the chasm between marketing practitioners and financial methodology.

The Need for and the Benefits of Cooperation

There is no shortage of literature spelling out the benefits that would follow from closer cooperation between accounting/finance and marketing. Such literature has appeared with considerable frequency in publications serving both financial "types" and marketing executives. Following is a summary of a representative sampling of published material appearing in the United States in the 1960s and early 1970s which stressed both the need for and the benefits of cooperation. These few selections should be treated as illustrative rather than exhaustive; similar material was published both in the United States and in other industrial countries before, during, and after the 1961–1974 period. These specific contributions are being cited because of the importance of the publications in which they appeared and/or the thoroughness with which their authors dealt with the subject.

In a 1961 article appearing in *The Controller*, McGann insisted that the firm's controller very definitely belonged on its marketing team. More specifically, he argued that any controller who wishes to improve the marketing profits of his or her company should:

1. adopt the policy that all marketing operations must be profitable;
2. acquaint himself or herself with the basic tenets of sound marketing;
3. develop the confidence needed to discuss marketing issues with marketing management;
4. know the net profitability of each marketing segment;
5. analyze profitability statements to find the reasons behind strengths and weaknesses in marketing operations;
6. recommend how marketing weaknesses can be corrected and marketing strengths exploited; and
7. evalute the degree of progress made in reaching stated objectives.

What each of these steps involved was elaborated on, and useful illustrations were provided (McGann, 1961).

Two years later, Hudig's article in *Financial Executive* also stated a case for financial executives becoming more involved in efforts to control marketing costs. Among the specific contributions to be encouraged were the monitoring of field activities for profit leaks; calculation of the profitability of present and proposed orders; redesign of physical distribution systems; use of the product life cycle concept in profit planning and sales forecasting; efforts to improve the planning activities of salespeople; identification—through the use of either rule of thumb or more precise methods—of unprofitable accounts; and establishment of indices of relative regional performance. Effective pricing was presented as the most difficult aspect of profit planning, one where the decisions taken must be unique to the company, the product line, and competitive conditions. However, generally useful approaches to avoiding the underpricing of products and the needless sacrifice of profits through "head on" price competition were provided (Hudig, 1963).

In a July 1966 *Journal of Marketing* article, Kelley made a plea for timely and topical reports which focused primarily on variations from plans and on "below average" performance. Typical marketing requirements were defined as including prompt customer billing; sales activity reports; profit and loss reports by product line, territory, and customer; and information on stock availability and product cost. Kelley also correctly forecast the fact that computers would facilitate the preparation of flexible, tailor-made accounting systems (1966).

Three years later, an article by Kelso and Elliott appearing in *Management Accounting* took the position that traditional financial statements were practically useless to the sales and production managers expected to manage diverse, multi-product firms. Such managers, it was maintained, require information that pinpoints the nature and extent of all variances from profit plans. The authors then went on to outline a reporting format that highlighted any such variances between actual and budgeted gross profits. They illustrated how the contribution to such variances of differences between actual and planned price, volume, and production costs could be calculated. Appropriate reporting formats, Kelso and Elliott argued, were needed to bridge the communications gap between accountants and managers (1969).

In a July 1973 *Journal of Marketing* article, Kirpalani and Shapiro reviewed the assistance to managerial decision making and marketing control developed in the functional areas of accounting and finance. The various financial dimensions of marketing management were examined, and certain especially promising applications and techniques were reviewed.

Discussed at some length were the following:

1. the need for increased emphasis on the profit contribution of each relevant marketing segment;
2. the desirability of using a contribution-based decision-oriented approach in evaluating alternative courses of marketing action;
3. financial reporting approaches useful in disclosing segmental contributions;
4. what break-even analysis, despite its widely recognized faults, can contribute to marketing management;
5. the literature dealing with proposed ROI applications in marketing and the extent to which such techniques are actually being used;
6. guidelines to be followed in extending credit and modifying cash discount policies;
7. techniques that might lead to the more efficient allocation of marketing effort; and
8. how integrated marketing-financial information systems highlight the sources of variances from plan and report on profitability both by segment and by area of managerial responsibility (Kirpalani and Shapiro, 1973).

What kind of information does the marketing manager need? What are some of the ways the management accountant can meet these needs? To answer these questions, Spiegel's 1974 article in *Management Accounting* succinctly but nevertheless comprehensively discussed the typical role of both the marketing manager and the management accountant. Particular attention was paid to three broad areas where the management accountant can be of specific assistance to the marketing manager. The first such area is product costing and pricing, with considerable emphasis being placed on the importance of monitoring cost changes. The second is financial planning, with the plans in question taking a myriad of forms to meet a variety of objectives. Finally, the measurement of performance, with specific emphasis on the analysis of variances from plan and on contribution margin, was stressed (Spiegel, 1974).

Industry or Association Studies of Existing Practices

The aforementioned articles are essentially hortatory in nature. They discuss what it is that management accountants and other financially oriented executives could or should be doing for marketing executives. A remarkable contrast is to be found between these normative statements of what ought to be and what a number of important studies, conducted at various times over the same period, have revealed to be actual corporate practice. Harrison has summarized the nature, scope, and somewhat disturbing findings of two especially comprehensive studies (1978):

> Schiff and Mellman, under the auspices of the Financial Executives Research Foundation, examined the practices of a group of companies in the United States in respect of the analysis and control of their marketing costs (Schiff and Mellman, 1962). This was the first in-depth study of cost and profitability analysis for marketing during the marketing era, and, even though it was begun less than ten years after the inception of the marketing era, many companies studied showed acceptance of the general principles of the marketing concept (Ibid., p. 33). Evaluation of the reports being prepared by accounting for marketing in the companies studied revealed that while some useful reports were being utilized, they were inadequate in total and in concept when related to the professed informational requirements of marketing (Ibid., p. 145). Specifically, the following deficiencies were observed.
>
> 1. An overemphasis was noted on net-profit-based reporting (full-cost allocation approach) for product profitability analysis, with, in many cases, such reports being submitted to marketing management as the key reports to serve their varied control and decision-making needs.
> 2. Analyses of customers, channels of distribution, salesmen, and order sizes were not usually prepared.
> 3. Distinctions between fixed and variable costs, resulting in marginal earnings as the basis of specific management decisions, were rarely used.
> 4. Distinctions between controllable and non-controllable costs were, with few exceptions, not carefully developed.
> 5. The use of selling cost standards, which would have increased the utility of analysis in many instances, was observed in only one case.
> 6. The use of return on investment measure was observed in only one case. In that case, there was a discernible impact of the marketing executives in their perception of the significance of return on investment, and their use of the approach in decision making.
> 7. There was a lack of integration between the measures used by the field sales organization and the controller's reports relative to salesmen's activity. Such measures, which included cost per call, cost per customer, cost per order needed to break even, etc., were rarely provided.

The second major study carried out during this period was designed to examine the use of profitability analysis within the marketing function of selected North American consumer companies (Goodman, 1968). Goodman's study, although carried out twenty years after the advent of the marketing era, found similar deficiencies in the use of accounting and financial analyses, particularly in the areas of capital investment analysis, contribution techniques and the concepts for marketing segment analysis, and cost classification and behavior patterns for marketing costs. Goodman summed up the results of his research: "It would be an easy criticism to state that the accounting and control function is not a major problem in marketing, and that it is relatively well handled in most companies. The evidence at hand, including the earlier Financial Executives Institute study, currently indicates that such is not the case, and the results of my own research ... convince me that the problems and issues raised in that earlier study are still largely unsolved" (Goodman, p. 26).

A very important special report was published in 1972 by an American Accounting Association Committee on Cost and Profitability Analyses for Marketing. That report began by first reviewing and then evaluating current methods of accounting for marketing activities. The existing practices of many major corporations were shown to be deficient in a number of important respects.

Specific improvements that would enhance the usefulness of accounting data in allocating marketing effort and evaluating marketing performance were then recommended. A total cost systems approach for planning and efficiently controlling distribution costs was also presented. Use of a contribution approach and a common modular data base to measure both the past and the expected future performance of various marketing segments (customers, territories, products, channels, and salespeople) was advocated. The informational outputs required for segmental analysis were identified, and the use of variance analysis was then illustrated in some detail. This report was the source document upon which committee members drew in numerous subsequent publications (AAA Report, 1972).

Michael Schiff's important monograph, *Accounting and Control in Physical Distribution Management*, was also published in 1972. This study was based on a sample of fourteen large companies selected for their size, their representativeness, and the relatively advanced development of their physical distribution activities. Schiff reaches the following conclusions:

1. Financial profit reporting as it relates to physical distribution needs improvement;
2. Cost reporting within PD has been developed to a point in a number of companies where it permits effective control and makes available relevant information for decision making; and
3. The real gap is not in PD cost information, but in the evaluative systems currently used. The reward system in marketing does not focus on profit performance after the deduction of relevant PD costs (Schiff, 1972).

Finally, Lambert's published dissertation reported on a successful effort to develop a methodological framework that could be used by corporate management to determine the true costs of carrying inventory. The cost components that, in a nominal sense, "ought" to be included in calculation of inventory carrying costs were first identified. Six companies were then studied in depth to determine the availability of the necessary data. The analysis revealed that, for firms with a relatively sophisticated data base, the cost of determining inventory-carrying costs would be less than $300. Information on such costs was considered by management to be a necessary input in designing distribution systems, setting customer service objectives and/or levels, balancing production schedules, determining inventory levels, and analyzing product profitability. However, the inventory-carrying cost estimates actually being used by the companies studied were very different from those generated by the "optimal" methodology. In some cases, knowledge of "correct" inventory-carrying costs would have led to management's following very different courses of action (Lambert, 1976).

Why the Reluctant Dialogue?

The very fact that pleas for cooperation have been made so regularly for so long suggests that the desired degree of interaction has not been achieved. The short-comings that have been documented in existing practice are further evidence that a serious problem exists. A number of reasons can be advanced as to why organizational barriers persist and a meaningful two-way interchange between financial and marketing types does not routinely take place. These include organizational suboptimization, professional isolation, accounting's traditional mind set, possible differences in personality types, and even selective perception.

Finance (and accounting) and marketing are different units of the organization, with different values and different objectives. Indeed, the customary functional structure of corporations tends to encourage conflict by leaving marketing, finance, and production with overlapping and often conflicting interests (Fox, 1976). Also, representatives of accounting/finance and of marketing attend different conventions, read different business journals, and draw on different sets of academics.

One observer of the strained relationship between marketing and accounting attributed much of the problem to the unfamiliarity of accountants with the marketing concept and the problems of marketing management. "We don't think the accounting departments have fully comprehended the marketing task and they have the ancient notion that marketing is nothing but selling. They don't understand the marketing concept. Their orientation is manufacturing and since they have done so well for manufacturing—developing systems and controlling costs to the point where they can almost force a decision and predict results—they feel marketing has the same attribute as does manufacturing" (Schiff and Schiff, 1965).

The history and the intellectual framework of accounting are other barriers to more effective communication. "Accounting places its emphasis on reporting not decision-making. As a result of training and experience, accountants, when entering a room, walk backwards. All of the generally accepted accounting principles are oriented to the reporting requirements of the profession. These reporting requirements, regretfully, may have no relevance to a decision today that will affect an outcome tomorrow" (Goodman, 1972).

Feder has also commented on the inadequacy for marketing purposes of "generally accepted accounting principles." He took particular exception to the accounting profession's full costing propensities and their reluctance to treat promotional outlays as investments to be amortized over time rather than as expenses to be charged in their entirety against current income (Feder, 1965).

Another partial explanation may lie in the different characteristics and interests of those who gravitate to financial functions as opposed to marketing, and especially to sales. "Financial types" could be, on the average and with many exceptions, different kinds of individuals from "marketing types." Once associated with a financial or marketing unit, these two types of executives may then grow further apart in outlook and even in manner as they accept the norms and values of their entrenched colleagues.

Selective perception or tunnel vision also contributes to the problem. One recent survey in which divisional advertising executives and either divisional or corporate financial directors employed by the same corporations were separately interviewed suggests considerable difference even in what the two groups consider to be presently occurring at the interface between marketing and finance:

> Financial executives and advertising executives within the same company disagreed in many ways on issues of reported fact and opinion. They differed on how they perceived their ad budgeting practices and methods; they differed on (reported) usage of computers; they differed on who within their companies drafts and finally approves the budgets (San Augustine and Folley, 1975).

Empirical Studies of Organizational Relationships

The problems affecting the organizational interface between marketing and accounting/finance have been examined in some detail by researchers in the United States, Canada, and Australia. In late 1967 and early 1968, Goodman conducted separate interviews of two to three hours' duration with the senior marketing and financial personnel of twenty major East Coast consumer goods firms. He concluded that the following were the major areas of professional concern between accounting (or finance) and marketing:

- accounting's reluctance to place a person within marketing to offer quantitative advice and assistance;
- an accounting preoccupation with financial reporting that has inhibited acceptance of such decision techniques as relevant costing;
- rigidities in accounting statements that inhibit marketing flexibility and, more generally, accounting's lack of a marketing orientation;

- imprecision in marketing's definitions and the fact that responsibilities under the marketing concept are not clearly delineated;
- failure to define the corporate controller's role in decision making;
- senior management's frequent inability to understand, and therefore its reluctance to sanction, the best use of profitability concepts;
- insufficient opportunity for both marketing and finance to speak out at formal strategy sessions.

Goodman's recommended solutions included greater emphasis within accounting on managerial problems in general and marketing considerations in particular; greater corporate familiarity with the potential contribution of EDP and management science, and a reexamination of the relevance of traditional departmental boundaries in a quantitative era (Goodman, 1972).

The extent to which major Canadian corporations were then utilizing financial and/or accounting oriented techniques to improve the quality of their marketing decisions was investigated in early 1976. In-depth interviews were conducted with the ranking marketing executives of ten Montreal-based corporations (or divisions thereof) with annual sales of at least $30,000,000, and with another ten of their financial counterparts. The results of this qualitative investigation can be summarized easily enough:

- The financial executives of these large firms (or divisions) all recognized a responsibility to provide relevant information to marketing decision makers, though only half of the firms had individuals in the finance department who specifically "worked for" marketing.
- Many of the individuals within the finance function working for marketing had only limited operational exposure to marketing, and in turn most marketing executives receiving financial evaluations of marketing's performance had not been extensively trained in the financial dimensions of marketing management.
- Respondents were divided in their opinions as to whether formal, as opposed to "on the job," training in the opposite discipline was necessary for financial specialists servicing marketing or for marketing practitioners.
- Half of the ten responding organizations reported that improved communication between marketing and finance would have improved the quality of past marketing decisions.
- A wide variety of financially based techniques, many specifically geared to a given corporation or division's principal line of business, were being employed to improve decision making and control in the marketing area. In addition, the contribution approach and various return on investment techniques were being employed by most of the organizations surveyed.
- A number of the responding organizations were attempting to develop new financially based techniques, usually computer based, that could be used by marketing decision makers. "Lack of time" was repeatedly identified as the

factor limiting progress in the development of these new techniques.

- Of the ten companies interviewed, only three had employed the computer as a problem-solving or decision-making tool to facilitate the allocation of marketing effort. The remaining organizations still used computers primarily as an aid in data manipulation.
- There was fairly general agreement that, in order for marketing to be provided with better information, existing corporate accounting systems would have to be either thoroughly revised or, at least, considerably improved in areas of obvious relevance to marketing.

While these Canadian results are easily summarized, drawing conclusions is a more difficult task. This admittedly qualitative study suggests that, circa early 1976, large Canadian-based organizations had recognized the importance of the financial/marketing interface but were having difficulty developing the institutional arrangements to facilitate the communication that such an interface necessitates. One is also left with the uncomfortable feeling that the literature on the financial dimensions of marketing management had considerably outstripped Canadian corporate practice. With the possible exception of the Boston Consulting Group's now famous learning curve, none of the proposed financial applications found in the literature were revealed as having been abandoned because they were proven deficient. The problem, rather, was a relatively slow rate of acceptance of techniques of unquestioned value. The financially based techniques then being employed by marketing executives were not generally the most advanced, while frequent references to lack of time revealed that although progress in operationalizing new applications may have been considered, it was apparently not a "top priority" issue (Shapiro and Scheuer, 1976).

Harrison studied the extent and effectiveness of the interface between the accounting and marketing disciplines in a number of large Australian consumer goods companies. A number of factors were revealed as limiting the realization of the management accountant's potential role in marketing. Interestingly enough, the similarities between this study, conducted in 1977, and Goodman's investigation a decade earlier were far more pronounced than the differences.

> The Australian study identified several groups of factors which were operating to impede development of an effective interface between the accounting and marketing functions in the companies studied. The most important of these groups were cognitive, attitudinal, and organizational factors. Cognitive factors reflected a lack of knowledge and understanding, on the part of accountants, of the nature and problems of marketing generally, and of the marketing practices and policies of the individual companies in particular. Attitudinal factors classified that group of events and actions which suggested that many accounting personnel did not accept marketing as a separate and distinct managerial function. The final group of factors included those aspects of organizational and departmental design which were seen to be impeding communication between the accounting and marketing functions.
> Analysis of these factors revealed constant and consistent reference to the emphasis

of the accountant towards his role in management as it had been established more than twenty-five years earlier: displaying a concentration on cost control, and a predisposition towards the production function. Numerous examples of a tendency to regard the accounting function as having a priority of servicing the manufacturing section were found in the organizational and political structures of the companies. In a majority of companies studied, for example, the accounting and manufacturing functions were physically juxtaposed, with the marketing section geographically separate from both. The consequences of a physical separation between the disciplines were adverse to an effective accounting-marketing interface in several ways. First, the problems of a lack of interpretation of accounting information, which were uncovered in the study, were exacerbated by the failure of the formal communication system to be complemented by an effective informal system. Second, the accounting function, located with manufacturing, tended to devote more time to the more accessible and immediate problems of production; and third, accounting staff tended not to consult directly with marketing personnel at equivalent hierarchical levels.

Other major factors identified in this study pointed to a perceived lack of acceptance on the part of many accountants of the importance of marketing as a business discipline in its own right. This attitude manifested itself in several ways; particularly in a reluctance on the part of some accountants and accounting sections to provide timely financial information to marketing management to assist the evaluation of alternative marketing strategies. In many cases, these strategies were apparently viewed by the accounting sections as hypothetical, with little prospect of eventual action being taken. Consequently, they were accorded low priority in relation to the demands of production and of central reporting (Harrison, 1978).

Is the Marketing Controller the Answer?

Goodman has championed the concept of the marketing controller as one possible solution to existing organizational barriers. In his aforementioned 1968 study, he found that "all twenty [major consumer goods] companies endorsed the concept with an enthusiasm that ran the gamut from moderate to strong." Three of these firms were, over a decade ago, already moving toward establishing such posts. Since that time, marketing controller positions have been created with increasing frequency. Consequently it seems appropriate to review the proposed responsibilities and reporting relationships of the marketing controller, the skills and technical training required by such controllers, and the organizational context in which marketing controllers have proved most effective.

What, specifically, does a marketing controller do? What are his or her actual responsibilities? A recent investigation identified the following as core responsibilities common to most position guides or marketing controller job descriptions:

- to perform financial evaluations of strategies, plans and programs, before implementation, so as to identify their impact on profitability and other corporate objectives;
- to assist marketing management in the development of sound short- and long-range profit plans;

- to provide financial reporting that is actionable, timely, and accurate, and that meets the needs of marketing management;
- to monitor and evaluate overall departmental performance as well as that of significant strategies and programs;
- to develop and maintain a control system and to recommend actions required for adhering to budget limitations;
- to identify regularly areas of opportunity for profit improvement or possible declining profitability;
- to coordinate preparation of the marketing budget (Trebuss, 1976).

To whom should the marketing controller be responsible? Goodman considered it essential that such a controller be positioned within the marketing department and report to the corporation's (or division's) ranking marketing executive. Otherwise, the controller would be viewed not as a colleague but rather as a potentially hostile outsider all too likely to be critical of the marketing effort. Goodman did not consider it unduly difficult for such a divisional or corporate marketing controller to maintain a "broken" line consultative relationship with the firm's ranking financial officers (1972).

Goodman credited Michael Schiff with being among the first to recognize the importance of locating this financial capability within the marketing department. Schiff maintained as early as 1965 that marketing departments required their own in-house accountants. Such individuals would retain their ties with the accounting profession and their firm's accounting department, but they would be on the staff of the marketing operation and provide financial services to the marketing vice-president (Schiff and Schiff, 1965).

H. D. Fuld, like Goodman, once a marketing controller at Nestlé's, has taken issue with Goodman's view that the primary reporting relationship of the marketing controller must be to marketing, with only technical guidance being received from accounting or finance. It was of no great importance, Fuld maintained, whether the marketing controller reported directly to the marketing function (and only indirectly to finance) or vice versa, as long as such a controller has immediate access to all pertinent information; the financial impact of all major marketing decisions was considered before their implementation; and both marketing and finance took part in the marketing controller's performance appraisal (Fuld, 1974). However, a recent Canadian study revealed no examples of a marketing controller reporting to the corporate controller or the vice-president in finance. Indeed, such an arrangement was criticized, for reasons Goodman had correctly anticipated almost a decade earlier, by both marketing and financial executives in all of the firms that either had appointed a marketing controller or anticipated doing so in the near future (Trebuss, 1978).

The same Canadian study identified a number of professional qualifications and personal characteristics generally possessed by effective marketing controllers and those occupying other interface positions. These included a business degree and/or a professional accounting designation, expertise in accounting and finance, and, ideally, some background in marketing. Several years of experience with the company also seemed essential. Normally expected personal qualities included excellent communication skills, identification with the requirements of marketing, tact, persuasiveness, sufficient strength to exercise control, a mind open to new ideas, and some degree of creativity. Interpersonal skills of the highest order are essential, since the marketing controller must demonstrate loyalty to both marketing and finance without compromising the requirements of either. Such controllers are usually "high potential" managers from finance for whom this position is a training ground. The career path of the typical Canadian marketing controller is generally within finance, although such controllers have occasionally moved into marketing management for some time (Trebuss, 1978).

Research by Trebuss in Canada also suggests that the marketing controller concept, rather than guaranteeing a reasonably good relationship between marketing and finance, presupposes the existence of such a relationship. More specifically, the necessary organizational prerequisites were considered to be an already satisfactory marketing-finance interface, an adequate marketing information system, and the support of all key personnel. The same author also suggested that the marketing controller concept might fruitfully be examined as one of the most advanced stages, although in some cases an unduly complex and expensive one, in a gradually evolving organizational relationship between marketing and finance.

> The development of an effective marketing/finance relationship must begin with the establishment of an environment conducive to cooperation. Four organizational factors are key to the development of this environment.
>
> - top management which clearly expects and actively encourages cooperation between marketing and finance;
> - clearly defined corporate objectives to which both marketing and finance executives are committed;
> - roles and authority for marketing and finance which are clearly defined and accepted by both; and
> - personnel who are compatible with a cooperative style of management.
>
> Companies in which an effective marketing/finance relationship exists display common characteristics in their functioning and in the attitudes of their personnel. These traits, which indicate the nature and influence of such relationships, are
>
> - a positive outlook among executives and a feeling that they are in control of corporate performance;
> - an orientation among executives, such that their view is toward the welfare of the company rather than the attainments of their individual functions;
> - a management role for marketing and a service role for finance, with a shared view among marketing and finance personnel that these are the appropriate roles;
> - the resolution of conflicts through discussion at the functional level;
> - marketing access to the financial information system;
> - programs to expose marketing and finance personnel to each other's functions; and
> - in some instances, an interface position which provides an effective contribution.
>
> Once a reasonably cooperative environment has been developed, many, though not

all, companies find that a formal mechanism is required to adequately mesh the more specific activities of marketing and finance. It is at this time that the introduction of an interface position may be advantageous. The types of interface positions, ordered in a natural progression of their responsibilities and involvement with marketing, are

- a financial analyst in finance, assigned to marketing;
- a financial analyst in marketing;
- a financial manager in marketing; and
- a full financial service in marketing.

The introduction of an interface position is often a difficult stage in developing an effective marketing/finance relationship because it has direct impact on the activities of lower and middle level managers and their acceptance and support must be secured. A number of issues which have significant influence on the position's potential contribution require consideration:

- A generally cooperative environment is a prerequisite to the position's successful establishment.
- The purpose in establishing the position should be only to provide a medium for integration between marketing and finance.
- The implementation of interface positions should be viewed as an evolutionary process, with successive positions geared to the development of acceptance, appropriate information, and expertise in personnel.
- The need for an interface position and the optimal position toward which evolution is to be directed should be determined on a cost-benefit basis.
- The person selected for the position is critical to the realization of its full potential. Good technical and interpersonal skills are required.
- The interface position will become effective more rapidly if its role is clearly and realistically defined from the outset, and if it is introduced in a manner which does not raise resentments.

Executives in those companies which have successfully established interface positions summarize the advantages as improved corporate performance through more efficient marketing and more effective coordination of the functions' activities (Trebuss, 1978).

In summary, the organizational barriers to a more effective functional interface appear to be real, frequently encountered, and neither quickly nor easily overcome. The potential benefits of a corporate marriage of money and marketing will not be fully realized until each firm resolves in a manner appropriate to its own nature and structure the people problems encountered in any marriage. Appointment of a marketing controller may not always prove to be the most appropriate course of action. Rather, the marketing controller is but one of a number of organizational options that deserve serious consideration if the potential benefits of closer liaison between marketing and accounting/finance are to materialize.

References

American Accounting Association (1972). "Report of the Committee on Cost and Profitability Analyses for Marketing," *The Accounting Review*, Supplement to Vol. 47, pp. 1–13.
Feder, R. A. (1965). "How to Measure Marketing Performance," *Harvard Business Review*, Vol. 43, No. 3, May-June, pp. 132–142.

Feld, H. D. (1974). "The Marketing Controller," (Mimeographed paper presented at IMEDE, July 11), p. 1.

Fox, Harold W. (Spring 1976). "Production Efficiency and Customer Satisfaction," *Business and Public Affairs*, pp. 33–39.

Goodman, S. R. (1968). "The Marketing Controller," New York University, Graduate School of Business, Ph.D. dissertation.

Goodman, S. R. (1972). "The Marketing Controller" (New York: A.M.R. International).

Harrison, G. L. (1978). "Factors Affecting the Accounting/Marketing Interface," Educational and Organizational Research Paper No. 156, School of Economic and Financial Studies, Macquarie University, February.

Hudig, J. (1963). "Marketing Costs and Their Control," *Financial Executive*, Vol. 31, No. 7, July, pp. 16–20.

Kelley, T. C. Jr. (1966). "The Marketing-Accounting Partnership in Business," *Journal of Marketing*, Vol. 30, No. 3, July, pp. 9–11.

Kelso, R. L., and R. A. Elliott (1969). "Bridging Communications Gap Between Accountants and Managers," *Management Accounting* (U.S.A.), Vol. 51, No. 3, November, pp. 41–43.

Kirpalani, V. H., and S. J. Shapiro (1973). "Financial Dimensions of Marketing Management," *Journal of Marketing*, Vol. 37, No. 3, July, pp. 40–47.

Lambert, D. M. (1976). "The Development of an Inventory Costing Methodology: A Study of Costs Associated with Holding Inventory" (Chicago: National Council for Physical Distribution Management).

McGann, T. J. (1961). "Yes! The Controller Belongs on the Marketing Team," *The Controller*, Vol. 29, No. 8, August, pp. 377–382.

San Augustine, A. J., and W. F. Folley (1975). "How Large Advertisers Set Budgets," *Journal of Advertising Research*, 15, October, pp. 11–16.

Schiff, Jack, and Michael Schiff (1965). "The Role of Accounting in Marketing," *Sales Management*, December 3, pp. 36–45.

Schiff, Michael (1972). *Accounting and Control in Physical Distribution Management* (Chicago: National Council of Physical Distribution Management), 217 pp.

Schiff, Michael, and Martin Mellman (1962). *Financial Management of the Marketing Function* (New York: Financial Executives Research Foundation), 262 pp.

Shapiro, S. J., and P. Scheuer (1976). "The Financial/Marketing Interface in Ten Major Quebec Corporations," *Proceedings of the Fourth Annual Meeting of the CAAS*, Laval University.

Spiegel, R. S. (1974). "Accountant, the Marketing Manager and Profit," *Management Accounting* (U.S.A.), Vol. 5, No. 5, January, pp. 18–20, 36.

Trebuss, S. (1976). "The Marketing Controller: Financial Support to the Marketing Function," *Canadian Business Review*, Vol. 3, Autumn, pp. 30–33.

Trebuss, S. (1978). "Improving Corporate Effectiveness: Managing the Marketing/Finance Interface," a report from the Research in Marketing Division of the Conference Board in Canada.

Improving Corporate Effectiveness: Managing the Marketing/Finance Interface 31

A. Susanna Trebuss

The economic environment of the 1970s has raised the relationship between marketing and finance as an increasingly important management issue in many companies. As top managements have become more conscious of the profitability achieved in each component of their business, increasing attention has been turned to the financial efficiency of marketing plans and expenditures. This involves a significant change in many companies, as marketing has often operated with minimal financial input and has largely escaped the constraints of financial objectives normally applied to other functions and to the company as a whole.

The perception of marketing as properly subject to financial considerations carries with it a need for an increased application of financial skills to marketing and for a new level of co-operative effort between the functions. Means of providing financial information and analyses which are specifically oriented to marketing decisions and activities, and also monitoring and control systems which are effective but which allow the flexibility required in marketing, must be developed. Further, personnel in each function must acquire a better appreciation of the objectives and requirements of the other, and marketing personnel must become more aware of the financial implications of their actions.

Counter to these requirements, however, a traditional lack of co-operation and understanding between marketing and finance continues to exist in many companies. It has also become evident that in many instances traditional functional organizations cannot accommodate the desired supportive relationship between these functions. It has, therefore, become necessary to give specific attention to the problems of establishing a satisfactory relationship.

1. About This Study

The noted concern among Canadian executives as to how a satisfactory integration of marketing and finance can be achieved, and the limited attention this topic has received in business research and literature, suggested that it warranted study in some depth. This report presents the results of such a study.

The research explored the following areas:

Reprinted with permission from A. Susanna Trebuss, *Improving Corporate Effectiveness: Managing the Marketing/Finance Interface*, Canadian Study No. 52 (Ottawa: The Conference Board in Canada, 1978).

525

- the types of relationships existing between marketing and finance and the reasons for these;
- the organizational arrangements, or interface positions, by which companies have attempted to enhance the effectiveness of the relationship; and
- the role and influence that these various arrangements have in the relationship.

Although the position of Marketing Controller is the best known of those used for integration, several companies have developed other positions for the same purpose. Therefore, attention was paid to several alternatives, ranging from an analyst in finance assigned to marketing to a full financial service in marketing.

This study is based on interviews with the chief marketing and financial executives in 21 companies. Where an interface position was known to exist, the person holding it was also interviewed. In all but two cases, these interviews were conducted separately so as to ensure that perceptions of one another's roles, how they were filled, and the adequacy of the relationship between the two functions could be fully explored. Confidentiality was promised to all participants.

The companies involved were selected on specific criteria. All those that could be identified as having an interface position at the time of the study were included. To the extent possible, each of these was matched with another company of the same industry and size, not known to have such a position. So as to provide greater balance in the industries represented, these matched pairs were supplemented with a few companies from additional industries.

The sample includes companies from consumer packaged goods, resource, transportation, retail, wholesale, transportation equipment, electronic, chemical, and mineral processing industries. These companies range in size from $20 million to over $1 billion in sales.

2. The Meaning of a Financial Orientation in Marketing

A financial orientation in marketing has one specific purpose: to enhance corporate performance in the short and long term by optimizing the financial performance of marketing. It entails the recognition of financial measures as primary among objectives and performance measures, and the acceptance of financial tools as key in marketing operations and decision-making. Major indicators of a financial orientation in any marketing operation would be:

- the use of financial criteria (e.g., profitability, return on investment) throughout marketing as the primary objectives and measures of performance;
- the use of financial techniques in marketing decision-making, with alternatives judged by their financial impact on the firm;
- the use and acceptance of financial monitoring and control systems in marketing as tools toward attaining optimal performance;

- the existence of an information system upon which the use of financial objectives, performance measures, and techniques can be based; and
- an attitude among marketing personnel that financial responsibility in marketing is appropriate.

The meaning of a financial orientation in marketing was summarized by one executive as:

> Profitability and return on capital employed, or the financial contribution to the firm, supersede volume as critical measures. This means a shift of focus in marketing operations and decisions, from sales to the financial impact of achieving those sales. This obviously involves an emphasis on financial considerations and, thus, a much greater use of financial information and techniques.

3. The Importance of the Marketing/Finance Relationship

The increased attention to a financial orientation in marketing derives largely from the external pressures brought by the economic environment of the 1970s. The following factors were identified by the executives interviewed:

- the long-term pressure exerted on profits by inflation and recession, resulting in greater corporate emphasis on marketing profitability;
- the difficulty in increasing prices, requiring that attention be paid to internal efficiency and thus, the efficiency of marketing expenditures;
- the slower growth rate in many markets, making necessary greater discipline in planning and more attention to the productivity of each marketing dollar spent;
- the high rate of interest on short-term borrowing to meet cash flow requirements, resulting in greater attention to inefficiencies caused by marketing activities; and
- the poor investment climate, requiring strong profit performance both to provide retained earnings for reinvestment and to attract the available investment.

Some also noted that acceptance of a financial orientation in marketing was a natural step in the evolution of marketing, from a sales to a management function. The need for volume in a capital intensive industry and the importance of market share in a market of limited size are arguments used by a few executives against a financial orientation in marketing

4. Organizational Factors Required for an Effective Relationship

Marketing and finance are generally required by their responsibilities to be in frequent contact. Such required interactions do not, however, signify an effective relationship. Poor co-operation and a lack of respect for each other often characterize these interactions and, also, may be heightened by the dependence of the performance of each on the quality of input from the other.

The unity of purpose necessary for an effective relationship is difficult to achieve because the managers in each function develop different concerns, attitudes and behaviour from their experiences in their own function. As each of these orientations is valid and necessary to the effective operation of the company, the functions must be brought together in some manner which allows full expression of the differing orientations, but also encourages their integration into a cohesive effort.

Thus, the development of an effective relationship requires the creation of an environment conducive to co-operation and productive conflict resolution. Four organizational factors are essential to creating this environment.

Leadership

The demonstrated commitment of the president to an effective marketing/finance relationship is the most important factor. Not only is he responsible for the establishment of the other organizational factors, but also his behaviour toward the functions has a strong influence on the nature of the relationship.

With regard to his influence, the president must clearly state his expectation for cohesive effort and must confirm this expectation by his behaviour. This confirmation has three major aspects:

- He must involve both vice presidents in decisions affecting both functions.
- He must accomplish an appropriate integration of the different orientations himself and demonstrate this balanced orientation in his actions and decisions.
- He must promote conflict resolution at the functional level by urging discussion and refusing the role of arbitrator whenever possible.

Common Objectives

Commitment by both functions to clearly defined corporate objectives creates a common resolve, fostering co-operation and communication. In companies where there are no defined objectives or only functional objectives, continuing conflict is most probable as each function attempts to maximize its performance in its own area of responsibility.

Once corporate objectives have been defined, commitment to them must be secured. A cohesive effort to the firm's best advantage becomes important to the executives when their performance is assessed on the basis of the corporate objectives.

In some companies, joint objectives are used at lower management levels to commit these managers to a similar co-operative effort.

Clear Definition and Acceptance of Authority

The role and authority of each function must be clearly defined and accepted by both. This further implies relative levels of authority which are mutually accepted and appropriate to an effective relationship.

Where role and authority have not been defined, each function will attempt to fill a role and exercise authority that it has defined for itself. A struggle for predominance is almost inevitable.

The more common problem, however, is dissatisfaction with the power structure as it exists. This does not necessarily lead to open conflict, but does deny the possibility of an effective relationship. The necessary mutual trust, respect and support cannot be expected as the dissatisfied function will not provide consistent support to those whose relative power it wishes to reduce, and the satisfied function will wish to hinder the efforts of those who attempt to increase their relative stature.

Acceptance of one another's authority does not, however, necessarily lead to effective integration. If one function is very strong and the other subservient to it, the orientation and expertise of the weaker function may not receive the necessary consideration. Thus, the harmony achieved could be unhealthy for the company.

Compatible Personnel

Personnel must be compatible with the organization structure and style of management desired. They must be willing to commit themselves to the development and maintenance of an effective relationship.

The compatibility of personalities with one another is seen as a major issue only in companies with a poor marketing/finance relationship. In these cases, however, it must be remembered that the individuals considered to be incompatible are interacting in an environment where other factors foster friction or open conflict.

The presence of these four organizational factors creates an environment in which it is highly desirable for individuals, and thus their functions, to commit themselves to an effective integration of their activities. In all companies where marketing and finance have a good understanding of each other's orientations and achieve a high level of co-operation, each of these factors is well developed.

5. Characteristics Associated with Effective Relationships

An effective marketing/finance relationship is achieved when the integration between marketing and finance is such that they provide an optimal contribution to the firm's performance. Integration is the quality of the union of the functions' effort and expertise and is dependent on the level of co-operative effort, the amount of relevant input to each other's activities, and the degree to which conflict is productively resolved in the interactions of the functions.

Companies in which an effective marketing/finance relationship exists display common characteristics in attitude and functioning, while those without this type of relationship share different traits. These characteristics are described in this chapter to portray the nature and influence of effective relationships.

General Outlook

In companies with an effective relationship, the executives consider the performance of the company to be superior due to greater efficiency both in marketing operations and in the co-ordination of the functions' activities. They also have a positive outlook and a sense of control regarding the company's future performance. Where the relationship is less effective, the outlook of executives is significantly less confident and they do not exhibit an attitude of control with regard to corporate results.

Orientation

Executives in companies with an effective relationship display a strong corporate orientation: their focus is on corporate welfare rather than the position and attainments of their own function. They consider each function to be an integral part of the corporate body and view corporate performance as the result of a collective effort. Where an effective relationship does not exist, the vice-presidents do not see corporate welfare as their first responsibility and focus primarily on the achievements of their own functions.

Perceptions of Roles

Marketing may be defined as having a sales or a management role, while finance may be seen as having a custodial or a service role. Of the four role combinations possible, the one offering the greatest potential for integration is management-service. This is the only pair of roles in which the objectives and responsibilities of the functions are fully consistent with the concept of integration. In companies with an effective relationship, the executives have a common perception of the appropriate role for each function and these accepted roles are management for marketing and service for finance.

Conflict Resolution

The existence of an effective relationship does not signify complete agreement between marketing and finance. These functions have different but equally valid orientations which, if fully exploited to the company's benefit, must bring them into conflict. Companies with an effective relationship are unique, however, in that conflict is resolved by the functions themselves through full and open discussion. Also, conflict is seen as an opportunity to forge better solutions to problems by bringing the orientations of both functions into full consideration. Where the relationship is less effective, conflict is often handled by an agreement to disagree or by a presidential ruling. In extreme cases, any form of resolution may be evaded to the extent possible.

Access to the Information System

In companies with an effective relationship, marketing has access to the information system in that it can obtain the information it requires in a relevant form through co-operation with finance. Such access is usually limited or non-existent when marketing and finance have a less effective relationship.

Cross Functional Exposure

Many companies where there is an effective relationship have programs to introduce marketing and finance personnel to each other's functions with the purpose of promoting better understanding between them. Some methods of providing this cross functional exposure are:

- an assignment in finance for product management trainees;
- business teams to which a product manager and financial analyst are assigned;
- company courses with a functional mix of personnel in attendance; and
- assignment of personnel to positions in the other functions.

In companies without an effective relationship, cross functional exposure is often viewed as unnecessary or wasteful.

Formal Medium for Integration

A formal medium for integration is not always necessary for, and does not guarantee, an effective relationship. However, in those companies with an effective relationship an interface position is able to mesh the capabilities and requirements of the functions so as to provide an optimal contribution. The position is less successful where marketing and finance are involved in a less satisfactory relationship.

6. The Relationship Between Characteristics and Organizational Factors

The characteristics developed in companies with effective relationships are directly related to the fulfilment of the four organizational factors. These factors and characteristics are summarized in Table 1, and various aspects of their interdependence are noted below.

- The attitude of control over corporate performance and positive outlook are based on the existence of a corporate orientation and a co-operative relationship.
- A corporate orientation evolves from a commitment to common corporate objectives. It is made possible by an accepted power structure and personnel who are compatible with the defined style of management.
- A common perception of roles is highly dependent on the clear definition of roles and authority. Common objectives and the resulting corporate orientation

TABLE 1. *Characteristics and organizational factors in effective marketing/finance relationships*

Characteristics of companies with an effective relationship	Organizational factors required for an effective relationship

1. A positive outlook and an attitude of control over corporate performance among executives
2. A corporate orientation among executives
3. Role perceptions which are:
  a) common, and
  b) appropriate to effective integration (i.e., management-service)
4. Conflict resolution through discussion at the functional level
5. Marketing access to the information system
6. Programs to provide cross functional exposure
7. An effective medium for integration, where required
	1. Leadership which clearly expects and encourages co-operation
	2. Common objectives to which both functions are committed
	3. Roles and authority which are clearly defined and accepted in both functions
	4. Personnel who are compatible with a co-operative style of management

dictate a pair of roles in which mutual support to the best advantage of the firm is possible (usually management–service).

- Conflict resolution through discussion follows from the expectations and encouragement of appropriate leadership. It is made possible by an accepted power structure, common concern for corporate welfare, and personalities compatible with this style of management. Further, discussions are guided by the common objectives.

- The provision of marketing access to the information system becomes advantageous to finance when there is a commitment to common objectives and, thus, a desire to enhance corporate performance through support to marketing.

- The provision of cross functional exposure results from commitment to an effective integration of the activities of the functions. It arises from the realization that personnel must be introduced to each other's functions to promote an understanding of the differing orientations, and that such understanding is necessary throughout the management structure to sustain the relationship of mutual support.

- An interface position is established when a formal mechanism is required for integrating the needs of the functions. It is effective when all factors are fulfilled, as it requires commitment to integration from both functions to provide its full contribution.

7. The Types of Interface Positions

Once a reasonably co-operative marketing/finance relationship has been developed, many companies find that a formal medium for integration is required to adequately mesh the more specific activities of marketing and finance and to reinforce the expectation for cohesive effort at lower levels of management. This chapter describes five types of organization that may be used to achieve an effective integration of marketing and finance.

No Organized Financial Support to Marketing

This is the preliminary case in that no formal interface mechanism exists. It has the advantage of simplicity and is adequate in companies where informal procedures can satisfy the requirements for integration. The potential disadvantages center on the fact that the functions have no formal access to one another and therefore may encounter difficulties in meshing their requirements and capabilities.

Financial Analyst in Finance, Assigned to Marketing

With this type of interface position, responsibility for servicing marketing requirements is assigned to an analyst in finance. The responsibilities are financial analysis of marketing proposals, servicing of information requirements and possibly monitoring of performance, and co-ordination of planning and budgeting. This formal link between marketing and finance allows the requirements and capabilities of the functions to be better meshed. Potential problems arise from the position's junior status and location within finance.

Financial Analyst in Marketing

This position varies from the previous one primarily in that it reports within the function it serves. Its advantages result from the greater involvement of the analyst with marketing operations and personnel. The junior status of the position, and the limited experience of the person normally holding it, present potential disadvantages.

Financial Manager in Marketing

The critical difference between this position, most commonly known as the marketing controller, and that of the financial analyst in marketing is that the analyst provides a link between marketing and financial management, while the marketing controller provides financial management to marketing. The responsibilities include financial input to marketing planning, provision of an appropriate information system, monitoring and analysis of performance, control, and co-ordination in planning and budgeting. The marketing controller's background as an experienced financial manager, his more senior status, and his location within marketing provide numerous advantages. There are, however, potential problems in the position's responsibility to two functions, and with the staff required. Also, this is a more costly alternative and requires a high degree of acceptance in both functions, as well as the availability of fairly sophisticated information and analytical tools.

Full Financial Service in Marketing

This form of interface organization occurs only in companies where marketing is an autonomous profit centre. The position has full responsibility for all financial functions of direct relevance to marketing. The primary advantage is that marketing can be held fully responsible for its financial performance as it has full control of its own financial management. However, this alternative involves a relatively high investment in staff and an independent information system, and is viable only in companies where marketing is an autonomous profit centre.

8. Issues in Establishing an Interface Position

The introduction of an interface position is often a difficult stage in achieving an effective integration between marketing and finance. It has direct impact on the activities of lower and middle level managers and their acceptance and support must be secured.

A number of organizational issues influence the contribution achieved from an interface position.

- A reasonably good marketing/finance relationship must exist prior to the establishment of an interface position. The position itself cannot forge such a relationship, nor can it fulfil its responsibilities without it.
- An interface position has only one appropriate goal: to provide a medium through which the activities of marketing and finance can be better integrated, thereby improving the financial support available to marketing. In companies where integration can be adequately achieved through informal relationships, an interface position is unnecessary.
- The implementation of interface positions should be viewed as an evolutionary process geared to the development of acceptance among personnel, an appropriate information system, and expertise in both functions. Establishing a more advanced form of interface at the outset usually creates problems in that the position is unlikely to be accepted or to provide an effective contribution.
- The optimal position toward which evolution is directed should be determined on a cost/benefit basis. Two major determinants are the size of the company and the impact of marketing activities and expenditures on company performance. As these change, the optimal position may change.
- The characteristics of the person assuming the position will strongly influence its degree of success. Strong technical and interpersonal skills and a balanced orientation are particularly important.
- Attention to appeasing the probable reactions of staff prevents the development

of additional resentments against the position and thus promotes acceptance. A clear and realistic description of the position's responsibilities, as well as the visible support of key personnel in both marketing and finance, are particularly important to the position's successful establishment.

In companies where interface positions have been successfully established, the executives summarize the benefits attained as more effective planning, improved communication and co-ordination between marketing and finance, and, consequently, better corporate performance. They also feel that these positions will become increasingly prevalent due to their positive impact on corporate performance.

9. Selecting the Appropriate Person

The selection of the individual to hold an interface position is critical to its success: the position can be only as effective as the person occupying it. One vice president stated the concern as follows:

> One of the most critical factors is the individual chosen for the position. Inadequate performance or inappropriate behaviour on his part will cause other latent problems to surface, particularly in terms of acceptance and co-operation. Also, the quality of the financial input can be no better than his abilities.

Because the development of acceptance and informal authority are vital to the position's contribution, the incumbent must exhibit skills and behavioural patterns which will foster these. To achieve acceptance in both functions, he must have a balance in his orientation such that his views and attitudes are not judged as foreign by either and can be accepted by both. This further implies an ability to empathize with the views and behaviour in each function and to communicate effectively with each in its own language.

He also requires strong technical skills, with the ability to apply these to marketing issues in a relevant manner, as this will determine, to a large extent, the competence ascribed to him. An appropriate balance in orientation and perceived competence will lead to a level of informal authority which encourages personnel to seek and accept advice from the position and greatly enhances its input to the management process.

As the skills and characteristics of the individual chosen have such influence on the position's success, they require serious consideration in advance of the selection process. The qualifications and personal qualities deemed important by those companies employing some form of interface position are described below. In general, the importance and the required degree of each of these increase as the responsibilities and involvement with marketing of the position increase.

A business degree and/or a professional accounting designation is normally required. It is essential that the person have expertise in accounting and finance. A basic understanding of marketing is necessary, with some experience often preferred. Several years of experience within the company becomes a requirement when the position is that of a financial manager or director of a full financial service.

In addition, the following personal qualities are normally expected:

- A sound appreciation of business: As well as a general understanding of business operations, this entails an ability to recognize business opportunities and challenges, whether suggested by marketing personnel or the person's own analyses. It also includes, as noted by one executive, "the ability to separate wishful thinking from reality."
- Integrity: This requires that the person be capable of allegiance to both marketing and finance without compromising the requirements of either. He must, therefore, be inclined to deal objectively and honestly with each. He further requires the strength of character to support his position in a dispute with either function while also being able to recognize and admit error on his part.
- Tact and persuasiveness: Because there is a staff relationship with both marketing and finance, the ability to sell the position and its services to personnel in both functions and to establish and maintain goodwill is important. This requirement further includes the ability to negotiate solutions when the functions' needs or activities are conflicting.
- Communication skills: In addition to the communication skills implied above, the ability to communicate with each function in the language it understands is essential. Also required is the skill to draw people out in discussions, so as to ensure that all relevant factors in a problem are known.
- Initiative and creativity: Because the degree of involvement with marketing will be dependent on the initiatives taken, the person must be inclined to seek out opportunities for the use of his skills. A degree of creativity is often required in applying financial techniques to marketing problems; it becomes essential when the responsibilities include recommendations and information development.
- Commitment: Commitment to the concept of integrating the activities of marketing and finance, of enough depth to withstand the resentments and pressures that may be faced in either function, is essential. In essence, the person must want to prove the value of the position.

As a final note, the selection of the individual to hold an interface position, as well as reviews of his performance, should normally involve both marketing and finance. This is only appropriate as the position deals extensively with, and has responsibilities toward, both.

Index